THE PRINCETON REVIEW

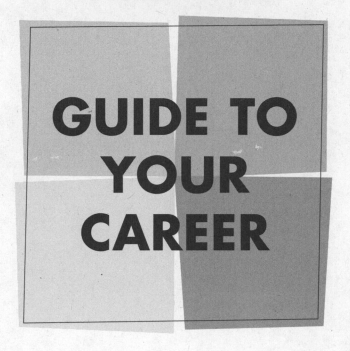

GUIDE TO YOUR CAREER

THE
PRINCETON REVIEW

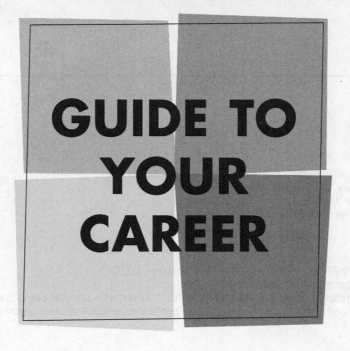

GUIDE TO YOUR CAREER

BY ALAN B. BERNSTEIN, C.S.W., P.C.,
AND NICHOLAS R. SCHAFFZIN

Random House, Inc. New York 1997

http://www.randomhouse.com

DEDICATION

To my mother and father, who gave me just enough rope not to hang myself.

—*Alan Bernstein*

Princeton Review Publishing, L.L.C.
2315 Broadway, 2nd Floor
New York, NY 10024
e-mail: info@review.com

ISBN 0-679-77869-1

Designed by Meher Khambata
Illustrations by John Bergdahl

Manufactured in the United States of America on partially recycled paper.

9 8 7 6 5 4 3 2 1

1997-98 Edition

ACKNOWLEDGMENTS

First, family without whose support this would never be imaginable: my dear wife, Anne; my daughter and son in-law, Rachel and Brad Heitman; my brother and sister in-law, Carl and Harriette, and niece Elizabeth; all the "cousins" in the cousins club, especially Robert and Joan, Dan and Lesley, Paula and Judy and Richard; and Lesches *tout*, Peter and Nanschi, Rose and Lynn, Lisa and Derek.

Then, an abbreviated list of the friends who supported me in this project in uncountable ways: the Gewirtz family, George and Janice, Evan and especially Scott, whose voice remains; Jay Kriegel; Michael Sand; Richard Friedman; Jim Behrman; John and Astrid Trauth, readers and boosters all.

My professional colleagues, mentors, friends and above all, benignly critical thinkers: Dick Bolles, Louis Ormont, Larry Epstein, George Weinberg, Daniel Porot, Roger Birkman, Claire and Perry Carrison, Jim Green, Tim Sadler, Connie Charles.

The Princeton Review associates, who recognized the value of this approach and constantly reflected that back to me: John Katzman, Andy Lutz, Elizabeth Barrekette, and my prized editor, Celeste Sollod.

My indefatigable editorial assistant, Jennifer Pass.

Consultants whose creativity and vision buoy my own: Ana Maria McGinnis, Bruce Crowley, Scott Kalish, Steve Kornblau, Craig Meisner, Ruth Shuman. And for this 2nd Edition to Melanie (the magician) Sponholz, who pulled this out of her hat.

—Alan Bernstein

I would like to thank all the people who made this book possible: the researchers—Kristen Azzara, Kaura Gale, Lila Kal, David Potak, Jessica Radin, Angela Saldanha and Anita Saldanha; the writing staff—Brenda Campbell, Nancy Chinchar, Andy Dunn, and James Worthington, the editorial staff—Linda Reiman, Maria Russo, and Celeste Sollod; the copyediting staff—Bruno Blumenfeld, Kristin Fayne-Mulroy, and PJ Waters; the production group—John Bergdahl, Greta Englert, Adam Hurwitz, Richard Infield, Sara Kane, Meher Khambata, Jefferson Nichols, Glen Pannell, Irina Tabachnik, and Chris Thomas. Particular thanks go to Celeste Sollod, the lead editor on this gargantuan project, for her patience and insight. A loud thank you goes to Jane Lacher and Jeannie Yoon for their help and guidance before, during, and after the project. Thanks to my family for their belief and support, and thank you Beth Young, for your unquestionable endurance, faith, and love.

—Nick Schaffzin

A SPECIAL ACKNOWLEDGMENT

To Richard Bolles, author of *What Color is Your Parachute*, who has been a vast creative force in live/work planning. This book (and I) owe a great debt to your ideas and mentorship.

—*Alan Bernstein*

TABLE OF CONTENTS

INTRODUCTION

You hold in your hands a book dedicated to *action*. Most of us have moments of clarity during which we see vivid images of what our future careers will be like but lack a method to make these ideas reality. *Guide to Your Career* is designed to build on years of thought and experience, to move you from impulse to deed, thought to action, anxious planning to specific goal setting. We have laid out a plan to help you implement your goals, while anticipating some of the places where you may get stuck or let down in your efforts. Our method focuses on two types of information gathering—intuitive and objective—as we lead you toward assembling the information you need to make a creative and informed decision about your life.

We believe in the creative style of career search. This means getting to know *thoroughly* what *interests* you have, the *style* in which you enjoy pursuing them, and the personal *needs* that should be met for you to operate at your highest potential. After developing a strong and precise vocabulary to describe yourself to potential employers (you will be practicing extensively with friends and fellow enthusiasts first), you will develop a thorough working knowledge of the potential fields, careers, or professions that interest you. What do people do every day? How did they reach their positions? How do they think? How do they dress? Our goal at The Princeton Review is to help you present yourself as a resource to the industry or profession you have chosen. Not in an empty, self-aggrandizing manner, but as someone who demonstrates a working knowledge of challenges and opportunities in that field. We will help you make yourself indispensable to an employer's future. This metamorphosis from career-seeker to industry resource requires extensive preparatory interviewing, professional or trade journal reading, and persistent information gathering.

To help develop your E.Q.[1], we have included a custom-designed, self-scoring version of the Birkman Personality Profile, which will give you a way to understand and describe your interests and style. In addition, we have developed a second method for heightening self-awareness through selected memories. We call this "poetry for engineers" because intuitive ideas are explored through reasoned analysis. You can be guided to gain insight through our suggested questions and techniques. As a psychotherapist, I have been trained to appreciate how people can develop an awareness of their *needs*, the parts of themselves that must feel appreciated and understood to function at their most creative. And I can help you do the same!*

---

[1] From Daniel Goleman's evocative book *Emotional Intelligence.* E.Q. is a derivative equivalent of the intellect's I.Q. It refers to a person's ability to perceive emotions and establish intimacy.

* All first-person references, here and subsequently, refer to Alan Bernstein.

PART I

CAREER CREATION

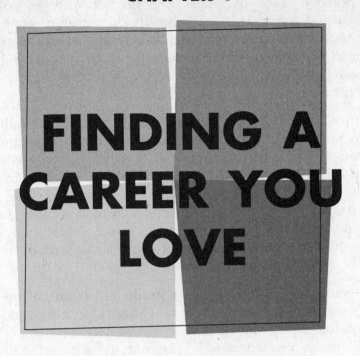

## CHAPTER 1

FINDING A CAREER YOU LOVE

WHAT DO YOU LIKE TO DO?
HOW DO YOU LIKE TO DO IT?

I remember to this day the panic I felt when graduating college over thirty years ago, realizing I didn't have a clue about how to make my way in the world. I did what many of you have done or might do—I took a year off from my prescribed education to wander the world and try to discover what I needed by poking about in "life." Although I had a great year, this approach prepared me for only one option—more school. While this isn't so bad on its own, I ended up simply returning to the subjects in which I got the best grades. The truth is, I was afraid to lose the structure in which I knew how to negotiate: pleasing teachers and getting good (enough) grades. In effect, I was condemned to perpetuate the system, enrolling in a Ph.D. program at Rutgers. I stayed there long enough to be sure that I did not want to teach English literature as a career. But, like many of the people I now work with as a counselor—lawyers who do not want to practice law, physicians who do not want to participate in managed care—I had to face the frustrating prospect of giving up time I had invested in my career, and the money and status it afforded me. Worse, I had to enter another program for more schooling. I had never really researched any careers outside school, where I was safe, where I had mastered the rules.

I fell into my first profession, college teaching, by default. Realizing after a few years that I preferred a profession that brought me into more intense emotional contact with people, I discovered psychotherapy, a profession I hadn't even known existed. By then I was nearly thirty, married, with a child, and I had to take a new degree in a different graduate program. Believe it or not, I consider myself lucky. I was able to complete my education (those were the days of National Institute of Mental Health Fellowships) and I entered my career with only a decade of lost time.

A generation later, my daughter graduated from college and went through exactly the same process I had. Nothing had changed. Preparation for graduating from college is as necessary as any science or economics course. Society needs a program to help graduating students determine what their interests are, evaluate their options, and research these options thoroughly enough to make intelligent career choices. Unfortunately, few colleges offer any such guidance. That's why we wrote this book.

You might think of *Guide to Your Career* as an entry to a job. That is only one of its potential uses. It's something else as well, a way to fill in parts of your education that school—high school, college, or graduate education—may never have addressed. We'll help you answer the following questions:

- Who am I? What makes me tick?

- What do I really enjoy? What gives me genuine satisfaction?

- Is there a way to convert what I most enjoy doing, my skills, my personal needs, and the ways in which I like doing things into a money-making career?

Guide to Your Career has been developed to give you the opportunity and methods for answering these questions.

The first part of the book will help you figure out *how you like to do things*. You'll learn not only what interests you, which you probably know already, but also the personal style in which you like to pursue your interests. You'll learn to work with preconscious[2] as well as conscious knowledge to interpret yourself and to understand your own needs and interests the same way you would an interesting work of art or poetry. We'll show you how to recognize aspects of yourself, frequently your greatest gifts, which you take for granted because they are so natural.

WHAT CAN WE PROVIDE?

The most frequently asked question in my office is "How do I know what I *really* love compared to what I've been told I *should* do?" It is useful to have interest inventories, such as the Birkman Career Style Summary™, to help us select and narrow down our interests, or even just to corroborate what we've always known. We'll help you hone your sense of personal style and clarify the unique ways in which you enjoy pursuing your interests. The Birkman Method™, from which the Career Style Summary is derived, is a program used by major corporations to assess the strengths of individuals. The Birkman Career Style Summary™ allows you to gain access to *broad* information about yourself. The questions use the Birkman Method™ research material to clarify both your interests and your style. This will be a major asset in defining not only *what* you are drawn to, but *how* you like to achieve. They have created The Princeton Review's self-scoring test specifically for *Guide to Your Career* to enable you to develop a sense of the style in which you like to pursue your interests. For example, if you were to say, "I love working out at the gym," you would be establishing your interest. But some people might mean they love the team effort of a pick-up basketball game, or working with a group in an organized aerobics class, while others might be referring to the solitude and concentration of weight lifting or a rowing machine. The interest (working out) is the same, but the style determines the ways in which a person feels happiest and most productive.

Next, we'll show you how to use selected memories to learn more about which types of professions would satisfy you the most. As a psychotherapist, my interests include not only conscious life but, as I mentioned, the vast territory we call the preconscious. I would like to show you how to use your memory to activate important material from your preconscious that we can explore to establish what might satisfy you in the future. Reading your memory complements the research studies and information we will be sharing with you in the career profiles. I call this technique "poetry for engineers" because we combine intuitive skills with precise methods for understanding and applying our history. By utilizing this method, we can help you confirm

- your chief interests

- how you enjoy using these interests

- what environment, both physical and emotional, produces the greatest satisfaction for you

> Recognizing and understanding intuitive and precognitive needs will largely determine how satisfied you will feel in your career.

Using your memories and the Birkman Career Style Summary™ together, we will be balancing intuitive and subjective information with objective data based on 1.5 million people who have taken the full Birkman Method™.[3]

CREATING YOUR CAREER

Next, we'll show you how to create your new career. We encourage you to undertake the *career creation* process with at least one other person, preferably a group such as the ones we put together at The Princeton Review. The feedback and support of your peers is essential to evaluating the results of tasks involved in career creation. *Guide to Your Career* will help you set up a schedule for your career search and take you step-by-step through the process. After you define your goals, we'll show you how to pursue your new career interests through interviews and original research in the field you have chosen so that you can comfortably converse with prospective employers. You'll become a creative researcher, developing the skills to find the best uses for your interests and abilities.

---

[2] Preconscious ideas are available to the conscious mind with disciplined attention; subconscious material requires skilled interpretation and is frequently coded as symbolic language.

Addresses accompanying each career profile will give you starting points for your exploration. We'll tell you how long you should expect to spend at each stage of your career search. Finding the right job may take longer than you'd like it to, but methodical, steady application will eventually land you where you want to go.

And that's only the beginning.

BROADENING YOUR HORIZONS

Princeton Review researchers have surveyed and interviewed hundreds of professionals in 166 careers so you can get some idea of where your skills and methods of working would be best applied. We'll answer your questions about scores of professions, some of which you might never have heard of. What does a social worker, carpenter, or actuary do all day? What do you have to do to become an artist, astronomer, chef, or editor? What personal qualities are necessary to thrive in each profession? We have isolated key issues that may affect your sense of success or failure in your chosen field based on how well they serve your needs as an individual. We've also provided ways in which your personality can be specifically utilized to your advantage in your job, provided that you understand yourself and recognize what situations you thrive in.

How did each profession come into being, and what does the future hold for it? We've outlined the issues facing significant professions and industries so you'll know how your life might change in a particular field. We've surveyed professionals to find out what a day is like in their careers, at the beginning, after five years, and after ten years. *Guide to Your Career* will help you select a career option that taps your creative resources.

Good luck on your career creation journey, and bon voyage!

---

[3] The Princeton Review Seminar uses the computer-scored, extended version of the Birkman Method, but this version must be interpreted by a certified Birkman provider.

CHAPTER 2

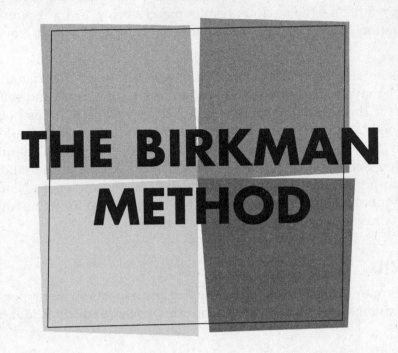

THE BIRKMAN METHOD

WHAT IS THE BIRKMAN METHOD?

The Birkman Method™ is an effective instrument for personal and organizational development. It is not a psychological clinical assessment but instead profiles behavior of normal, functioning people. Many other professional aptitude assessment instruments in the marketplace today began as psychological assessment tools for use in diagnosing problems (MMPI, 16PF). Others rephrase your answers in their terminologies (Strong Campbell, DISC) or label you in off-the-shelf-categories (Myers-Briggs). No other assessment instrument offers the depth of the Birkman Method™.

The Birkman Method™, endowed by the National Foundation for Science, has been in existence for over forty years. The database used for generating the results of the Method, featuring individuals from almost every walk of life and nationality, is one of the most comprehensive ever created. The Birkman is nonjudgmental. No one person's style is better than any other's—the various results merely bring to light your unique combination of interests and behavior that will help you in your career choice.

This version of the Birkman Profile is a simple way to visualize your overall behavior. The following questions are a condensed and self-scored version of the Birkman Method™ created especially for this book. As I mentioned in chapter 1, The Birkman Career Style Summary™ allows you to gain access to broad information about yourself. The questions presented here use the Birkman Method™ research material and enable you to apply it to clarify both your interests (symbolized by *) and your style (symbolized by S). This will be a major asset in defining not only *what* you are drawn to, but *how* you like to achieve.

THE GRID

The Birkman Career Style Summary™ plots aspects of your personality and behavior on a grid with four quadrants; each quadrant is identified by a color.

The Lifestyle Grid is based on a model of how people behave in general, and this particular model has been used for thousands of years. The first person to use it was probably Hippocrates, the "father of medicine." Hippocrates claimed that he could take all the people in the world, divide them into four categories, and accurately describe how they would act or behave. Sometimes the Grid is called the "Hippocratic Model." According to Hippocrates, there are four basic temperaments. He describes people as Implementors, Communicators, Planners, and Administrators, and bases his model on this idea. Models or pictures are not perfect; they are only generalizations. This one, however, is a very good generalization of how most people behave most of the time.

The Lifestyle Grid

Outgoing
Exerts Direct Authority

RED	GREEN
IMPLEMENTORS	**COMMUNICATORS**
Task oriented	People oriented
Organizer	Director
Delegates to get results	Works *with* people to
Acts direct	get results
Feels direct	Acts direct
	Feels sensitive

Factual
Objective

Feelings
Subjective

YELLOW	BLUE
ADMINISTRATORS	**PLANNERS**
System oriented	Idea oriented
Controller	Planner
Uses system to get results	Uses ideas to get results
Acts sensitive	Acts sensitive
Feels direct	Feels sensitive

Reserved
Exerts Indirect Authority

The Grid Symbols

There are two aspects of your personality and behavior that appear on this Grid:

(*) An asterisk indicates your interests, <u>what you want to do</u>—that is, your work preferences, as indicated by your interest patterns; the type of results you want and the kind of activities that will give you the most satisfaction. *This does not measure skill or ability around those interests*, only preference. The color location of your asterisk suggests <u>what you like to do</u>.

(S) An S indicates <u>how you like to do things</u>, or what your usual behavior is. The S describes your style, or active behavior, for pursuing your interests. This is your preferred mode for achieving your personal goals and is descriptive of the way in which you like to operate when all your needs are met. It is how other people see you acting most of the time. It is *how you do things* when everything is going your way. If your style color results feel antithetical to your real-life style, consider whether you are operating under stress on a day-to-day basis, and remember that when considering your score.

The way someone behaves—style—does NOT necessarily relate to the way someone wants to be treated—needs. Thus, your style does not indicate that you need others to exhibit a similar style.

Now, please take the Birkman Career Style Summary™. After the Summary you will want to put your interest symbol (*) and your style symbol (S) in your Lifestyle Grid.

Your Lifestyle Grid

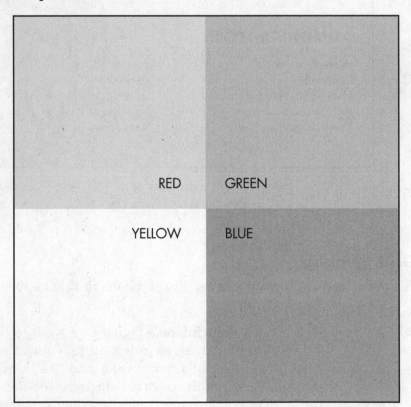

BIRKMAN CAREER STYLE SUMMARY™

Instructions:

In order to develop an estimate of your "Birkman Colors" for your Interest and Style, you will need to complete and self-score the items below. To do this, read each pair of phrases and decide which side of the pair is most descriptive of you, then put a check mark by that phrase. As you make your choices, assume that all jobs are of equal pay and prestige.

	Column A	Column B
1.	❏ I would rather be a wildlife expert.	❏ I would rather be a public relations professional.
2.	❏ I would rather be a company controller.	❏ I would rather be a TV news anchor.
3.	❏ I would rather be a tax lawyer.	❏ I would rather be a newspaper editor.
4.	❏ I would rather be an auditor.	❏ I would rather be a musician.
5.	❏ I would rather be a production manager.	❏ I would rather be an advertising manager.
6.	❏ I would rather be an accounting manager.	❏ I would rather be a history professor.
7.	❏ I would rather be a bookkeeper.	❏ I would rather be an electrician.
8.	❏ I would rather be a writer.	❏ I would rather be an elected official.
9.	❏ I would rather be a clerical worker.	❏ I would rather be a carpenter.
10.	❏ I would rather be a payroll manager.	❏ I would rather be a manager of engineering.
11.	❏ I would rather be an audit manager.	❏ I would rather be a safety manager.
12.	❏ I would rather be an artist.	❏ I would rather be a salesperson.
13.	❏ I am usually patient when I have to wait on an appointment.	❏ I get restless when I have to wait on an appointment.
14.	❏ It is easy to laugh at one's little social errors or "faux pas."	❏ It is hard to laugh at one's little social errors or "faux pas."
15.	❏ It is wise to make it known if someone is doing something that bothers you.	❏ It is wise to remain silent if someone is doing something that bothers you.
16.	❏ It's not really OK to argue with others even when you know you are right.	❏ It's OK to argue with others when you know you are right.

17. ❏ I like to bargain to get a good price.

❏ I don't like to have to bargain to get a good price.

18. ❏ It is easy to be outgoing and sociable at a party with strangers.

❏ It is hard to be outgoing and sociable at a party with strangers.

19. ❏ I would read the instructions first when putting a new toy together for a child.

❏ I would just "jump in" and start putting a new toy together for a child.

20. ❏ It is usually best to be pleasant and let others decide if your ideas are worth accepting.

❏ It is usually best to be forceful and "sell" your ideas to others.

21. ❏ I usually like to work cautiously.

❏ I usually like to work fast.

22. ❏ Generally I prefer to work quietly with a minimum of wasted movement.

❏ Generally I prefer to move around and burn some energy while I work.

23. ❏ I don't like to have to persuade others to accept my ideas when there is strong forceful opposition or argument from others.

❏ I like to sell and promote my ideas with others even when it takes some argument.

24. ❏ It is better to listen carefully and be sure you understand when topics are being discussed.

❏ It is better to speak up quickly and be heard when topics are being discussed.

Scoring Your Answers:

Now that you have made your choices, you can score them to determine the "color" of your Interest and Style. To accomplish this, you will need to count the number of items you marked in **Column B** and enter these counts in the four spaces below.

- First, count the number of items checked in **Column B** for the first six (1-6) items and place that count in this space: _____ (Interest H)

- Second, count the number of items checked in **Column B** for the second six (7-12) items and place that count in this space: _____ (Interest V)

- Third, count the number of items checked in **Column B** for the third six (13-18) items and place that count in this space: _____ (Style H)

- Fourth, count the number of items checked in **Column B** for the last six (19-24) items and place that count in this space: _____ (Style V)

Your Interest Color:

Now that you have these four counts, *estimate* your Interest and Style Colors. To do this for Interest, simply read the four statements below and see which one describes your counts for Interest. The color associated with the statement that is correct for your counts is the best *estimate* of your Interest Color you can make from this exercise.

- **BLUE**—Your Interest Color is probably BLUE if your **Interest H** count is 4 or more (4, 5, or 6) and your **Interest V** count is 3 or less (1, 2, or 3). You like creative, humanistic, thoughtful, quiet types of job responsibilities and professions.

- **GREEN**—Your Interest Color is probably GREEN if your **Interest H** count is 4 or more (4, 5, or 6) and your **Interest V** count is 4 or more (4, 5, or 6). You like persuasive, selling, promotional, and group-contact types of job responsibilities and professions.

- **RED**—Your Interest Color is probably RED if your **Interest H** count is 3 or less (1, 2, or 3) and your **Interest V** count is 4 or more (4, 5, or 6). You like practical, technical, objective, and hands-on, problem-solving types of job responsibilities and professions.

- **YELLOW**—Your Interest Color is probably YELLOW if your **Interest H** count is 3 or less (1, 2, or 3) and your **Interest V** count is 3 or less (1, 2, or 3). You like organized, detail-oriented, predictable and objective types of job responsibilities and professions.

Now place an asterisk, indicating your Interests, in the appropriate color square of the blank grid earlier in the chapter.

Your Style Color:

To *estimate* your Style Color, simply read the four statements below and see which one describes your counts for Style. The color associated with the statement that is correct for your counts is the best *estimate* of your Style Color that you can make from this exercise.

- **BLUE**—Your Style Color is probably BLUE if your **Style H** count is 4 or more (4, 5, or 6) and your **Style V** count is 3 or less (1, 2, or 3). You prefer to perform your job responsibilities in a manner that is supportive and helpful to others with a minimum of confrontation. You prefer to work where you and others have time to think things through before acting.

- **GREEN**—Your Style Color is probably GREEN if your **Style H** count is 4 or more (4, 5 or 6) and your **Style V** count is 4 or more (4, 5 or 6). You prefer to perform your job responsibilities in a manner that is outgoing and even forceful. You prefer to work where things get done with a minimum of thought and where persuasion is well received by others.

- **RED**—Your Style Color is probably RED if your **Style H** count is 3 or less (1, 2 or 3) and your **Style V** count is 4 or more (4, 5 or 6). You prefer to perform your job responsibilities in a manner that is action-oriented and practical. You prefer to work where things happen quickly and results are seen immediately.

- **YELLOW**—Your Style Color is probably YELLOW if your **Style H** count is 3 or less (1, 2 or 3) and your **Style V** count is 3 or less (1, 2 or 3). You prefer to perform your job responsibilities in a manner that is orderly and planned to meet a known schedule. You prefer to work where things get done with a minimum of interpretation and unexpected change.

Now place an "S," indicating your Style Color, in the appropriate quadrant of the grid that appears earlier in the chapter.

APPLYING YOUR SYMBOLS

Now that you have a color for Interest and a color for Style, what do they mean?

Your Interest Color:

If your Interest Color suggests the same activities as the other techniques, then you will want to pay special attention to exploring the career options from this book that are described as consistent with your Interest Color.

Birkman organizes the * symbol, occupational interests, as:

OCCUPATIONAL INTERESTS

Red likes to:
- Build
- Organize
- See a finished product
- Solve a practical problem
- Work through people

Green likes to:
- Sell and promote
- Persuade
- Motivate people
- Counsel or teach
- Work with people

Yellow likes to:
- Schedule activities
- Do detailed work
- Keep close control
- Work with numbers
- Work with systems

Blue likes to:
- Plan activities
- Deal with abstraction
- Think of new approaches
- Innovate
- Work with ideas

As you begin to reflect on the career or profession you are drawn to, you will want to consider whether it contains aspects of the *interests* you are likely to wish to use. If your occupational interest is green, for example, you will likely feel natural in an environment that calls for promotion or persuasion.

Your Style Color:

Your style symbol (S) describes how others might describe you. It shows how you like to act, indicating your active behavior. Knowing the *style* in which you tend to pursue your interests is the first step toward *describing the way in which you would like to pursue your interests*. Your Style Color adds extra insight for possible career choices. It is not uncommon for a person's Interest and Style colors to be different. A person may like the types of job responsibilities associated with her Interest, but prefer to practice these responsibilities in a manner and within an environment that is consistent with her Style. For example, a GREEN Interest and BLUE Style combination suggest a career option that involves persuasive interest performed in a humanistic, creative, and supportive manner. This is a person who likes selling, promoting, persuading, and group contact responsibilities but will still be most comfortable with a cause or product in which he holds conviction. A RED Interest would likely be drawn to an active career or profession, say a visible leadership role in a company. If her Style is BLUE, however, she will likely need some downtime to withdraw and reflect on the *meaning* of proposals, while a RED Interest, RED Style might maintain an entirely proactive work style. A RED Interest with a YELLOW Style may be drawn to a leadership role, but is likely to operate conservatively with a close eye on the bottom line.

Birkman divides the style or active behavior as follows:

ACTIVE BEHAVIOR

Red appears:	*Green appears:*
Objective about people	Personable
Commanding	Directive
Competitive	Outspoken
Practical	Independent
Forceful	Enthusiastic about new things
Yellow appears:	*Blue appears:*
Sociable	Perceptive
Orderly	Agreeable
Cooperative	Conscientious
Consistent	Reflective and creative
Cautious	Cautious

When we use the Birkman model in the career seminars at The Princeton Review, we separate the colors, and then divide a page into two columns as follows. On the lefthand column, we define some characteristics that people associate with a specific color, for example Red Interests, and on the right, we list the tasks and fields which these interests might correspond with in a work environment.

Red Interests:	Red Fields:
doing	manufacturing
building	managing
implementing	directing
organizing	small-business owning
producing	surgery
delegating	
leading	

Similarly, we might list adjectives describing Red Style in the left hand column and translate them on the right.

Red Style tends toward being:	Which might thrive in an environment that is:
straightforward	self-structured
assertive	high-pressured
logical	hierarchical
personable	production-oriented
authoritative	competitive
friendly	
direct	
resourceful	

Green Interests:	Green Fields:
motivating	marketing
mediating	advertising
selling	training
influencing	therapy
consensus-building	consulting
persuading	teaching
debating	counseling
delegating authority	public relations
	law
	entertainment
	lobbying

Green Style tends toward being:

spontaneous
talkative
personal
enthusiastic
convincing
risk-taking

Which might thrive in an environment that is:

team-oriented
adventurous
informal
innovative
big picture-oriented
varied
competitive

Yellow Interests:

ordering
numbering
scheduling
systematizing
preserving
maintaining
measuring
specifying details

Yellow Fields:

research
banking
accounting
systems analysis
tax law
finance
government work
engineering
archives
office management

Yellow Style tends toward being:

cautious
structured
loyal
systematic
solitary
methodical
organized

Which might thrive in an environment that is:

predictable
established
controlled
measurable
orderly

Blue Interests:

abstracting
theorizing
designing
writing
reflecting
originating

Blue Fields:

editing
teaching
composing
inventing
mediating
clergy
writing

Blue Style tends toward being:	**Which might thrive in an environment that is:**
insightful	cutting-edge
reflective	informally paced
selectively sociable	organized in private offices
creative	low-key
thoughtful	future-oriented
emotional	
imaginative	
sensitive	

These lists come directly from the students at a Princeton Review Seminar and demonstrate the way brainstorming works to enlarge these concepts. For application, it is best for you to do your own associations.

Characteristics of Your Interest Color

Describe your interests.

_____

_____

_____

How would these apply on a day-to-day basis in a career setting?

_____

_____

_____

Potential Occupations?

_____

_____

_____

Characteristics of Your Style Group

How do you act and what style do you exhibit when things are going well?

_____

_____

_____

How would this apply on a day-to-day basis on the job?

_____

_____

_____

Potential Occupations?

_____

_____

_____

As you isolate your interests and style and reflect on how they may be translated into *specific on-the-job applications*, you might want to ask yourself the following questions:

What constructive action should I take?

_____

_____

_____

What strengths would I like to develop, based on my Interest and my Style?

_____

_____

_____

How will I seek opportunities to do this?

_____

_____

_____

You are now developing a vocabulary to describe yourself to a potential employer: what interests you and how you have applied these interests; what your style is at its best; and how you might apply it. As you isolate your major interests and style, what further developmental work may be required?

USING YOUR INTEREST COLOR AND STYLE COLOR ESTIMATES

Now that you have an *estimate* of your Interest and Style colors, you are ready to use them to begin exploring possible career options. As you use your Interest and Style colors, please remember that they are just estimates and, as such, you should not make significant life choices based solely on them. These estimates are to be used as guides to help you explore possibilities. You will want to compare and work in conjunction with the other methods in *Guide to Your Career*, the "memories" you will recall in chapter 3 and your informational interviewing (chapter 4) to develop a full picture of your *interests*, *style*, and *needs*.

You are now prepared for chapter 3, associating your *interests* and *style* with your *needs*, and analyzing how in your life to date these have come together to encourage your most creative activity.

CHAPTER 3

APPLYING YOUR MEMORIES

REMEMBRANCE OF THINGS PAST

This is for me the most tantalizing part of your career creation process. You can train yourself to be an educated reader of your own preconscious mind through close observation and careful thought. This will require intense concentration, the kind you needed when you first analyzed a poem or when you put together your first stereo system. It's strange and unfamiliar, but not difficult. This kind of scrutiny helps you to interpret what you *really* want. We assign you a simple task with complex meanings: asking you to remember "stories" from your past. We define stories as isolated snapshots of incidents from your past that had the following characteristic:

You were asked, or asked yourself, to accomplish a task, something you were not sure you could do. In doing this project you found not only that you could complete it, but that time had slipped away. You were in a state of "flow" and ordinary linear time disappeared.

In connection with the Birkman Career Style Summary™, these snapshots give us information about what conditions are necessary for you to do your most creative work.

We find at The Princeton Review that it is best to work either with a friend or a group of people who are also trying to establish their career goals. Fresh insights help to solidify your sense of your interests and style. As you write your memories, reading them aloud to objective and interested listeners will help you free your preformed associations and enhance creative understanding of yourself and others. As mentioned in chapter 1, one of your goals is to expand your E.Q., your capacity to empathize with and express interest in others. Later on, in chapter 4, you will find this a significant skill when you begin your informational interviewing.

Try to remember those environments in which you've been most creative. They can be school, work, Boy Scouts or Girl Scouts, camp—wherever you've felt that you were completely satisfied to be doing what you were doing in the way you were doing it. See if you can isolate some common themes.

What I Was Doing When I Felt Happiest

1. _____

2. _____

3. _____

4. _____

5. _____

For some of you critical thinkers, this may be a rough task, so we've developed a reverse twist to jog your memories:

Places Where I've Felt My Worst

1. _____

2. _____

3. _____

4. _____

5. _____

The purpose of this second list is to work by default, examining what absences created the bad feeling, whether physical or psychological. You may then be able to work backwards to create your list of what conditions encourage your feeling happy and creative.

After you've finished your lists, select at least five specific memories in which *timelessness* was a key ingredient, when you were so involved in a project, accomplishing some task or solving a problem, that you can recall the sense of ordinary linear time slipping away so that you couldn't tell how long you'd been working. Choose memories in which there was a challenge and that in facing that challenge, at some point you were so caught up that you felt, as the ancient Greeks distinguished, not Chronos, or clock time, but Kairos, or timeless time.[1] When you recall these specific occasions, jot them down, because they will be core events about which you will construct key stories.

---

[1] I am indebted to the group analyst Dr. Malcolm Pines for pointing out to me this verbal distinction in the original Greek.

Selected Memories

1. _____

2. _____

3. _____

4. _____

5. _____

Following this, I would like you to order these memories subjectively, placing the ones you remember with most pride or pleasure at the top. Select one memory and write a 250- to 350-word story telling your reader (your friend or group) what happened. Be specific; appeal to our senses. What did it feel like to be there; were there colors, odors, textures? Really bring your audience in. What were you doing? What were you trying to accomplish? Did you expect to be able to do it? Who were you with? Was it necessary that they were there? How long did you expect it to take? How good did you think it would be when you were done? Your memory-story should answer these questions in detail. Imagine yourself reading the story to a group of your peers, say, at a Princeton Review Seminar. They want to know what happened next. What were the results?

In going through your remembered stories, we will take you through a checklist of questions you can ask yourself to determine the most *needed* motivators, the ones that make you ask, "Why this memory?" What qualities make it seem so highlighted, so clearly remembered by you? What elements of your personality were heightened by the experience of the memory?

MEMORY AS LANGUAGE

It may be useful at this point to go over my first "story," the first memory that I selected out of a group of memory options that occurred to me.

> When I first bought a car, a used Peugeot 403, I was totally intimidated by the task of having to care for it. In my high school years I had secretly borrowed the family car one night and blown its engine as, unknown to me, it had an oil leak. Needless to say, the idea of caring for a foreign car (this was 1964) seemed both overwhelming and exotic. I had a friend who was an engineer and a creative type, a rare combination in those days, and he agreed to help me rebuild the head of the engine, as the valves had to be ground. One late afternoon we started the project, continuing well into the evening by the glow of flashlight and oil lamp. I was exhilarated to be actually working on a technical, mechanical project and not ruining or breaking it, but fixing it. I was the only one in my immediate family with any interest in or inclination toward mechanics, and I felt I had transcended some inherited, even genetic, barrier by loosening screws in an orderly manner, and uncoupling things from one another in such a way that they could be healed.

Now you might imagine, upon first hearing this story, that I wanted to be a mechanic. Well, you'd be partially right. It might help you to know that I worked in a bicycle shop during my junior and senior years of college, but my passion isn't really for being a mechanic.

What were my *interests* here? What kinds of things was I drawn to? Well, clearly there was a car, there was the support of friendship; and there was the negotiating and purchasing of items, and the organizing of the project.

What did I learn from this memory? One of the ways that we find meaning in this is by orienting ourselves to see what *active behaviors* we're actually drawn to, and what *style* we have when we are working at our best. In this case, what were the actions that made the experience so meaningful to me? I enjoyed:

- Working with my hands

- Creating a solution to a problem

- Sharing the experience

- Completing the project

- Being my own boss

- Taking a risk, knowing that the project could fail, but that I could make it succeed

Finally, and in some ways the most subtle and yet most important elements of the story, what *needs* of mine were being met? It seems to me, in retrospect, that I was making up for my high school failure to understand how an engine worked and that it needed oil. Secondly, I needed to take on a project that was bigger than I was comfortable with and complete it. Thirdly, I wanted to explore an area with which I was totally unfamiliar. My family lived in a rented apartment in New York City; we called the handyman to change the lightbulb. So, to me, the notion of mechanically caring for something as complex as an automobile was tremendously exciting and almost frightening. Additionally, and perhaps more subtly, I was beginning a career in which I would take things apart and try to put them back together so that they came out better than when I started. Now, this may seem to be an inflated reading of a story about fixing an engine, but bear in mind that I have selected this story out of perhaps thousands, even millions, of incidents that have taken place over the course of my life. So I have to assume that it has more than ordinary significance for me, that some special ideas, some germs of real passion, made this moment especially exciting to me.

When I told this story to my career group they isolated the following skills:

- Negotiating to buy the car

- Learning to maintain the car

- Selecting a mentor

- Persisting in figuring out how to care for the car

- Dedicating myself to a project

- Researching the project

- Organizing the project

- Taking risks

- Developing physical dexterity to use the tools

- Venturing outside my comfort zone

- Freeing myself from preconceived notions

- Not being discouraged by my previous error

- Presuming that I could do better than I feared

Reading Memories

Now we have the basics of how preconscious memories function, how a special moment contains information for us about what our favorite interests are, in what environment or style we enjoy doing them, and what inner experiences or needs are being met. And yet we can go even further as we become more comfortable in our self-analysis, if we choose. For example, it may interest you to know that my father was a surgeon and that I considered medicine as a career. However, I found myself far more comfortable with literary and psychological ideas than with science courses and so became an English major. But, an intuitive reader may speculate, was I not in some controlled way introducing myself to surgery, finding a unique and personal integration of entering a closed body (a car engine), opening it, and replacing bad parts with good ones? Can you imagine my beginning search for a form of work in which I too could heal people in a way that met my needs? Can you see me motivating others to use their unique strengths in an environment of intellectual curiosity and emotional readiness? I certainly can. When you reconsider my initial story in which two friends worked on a car, you may see how such a memory can be understood or explored in this way.

You will want to think about and apply the results of your Birkman Grid from chapter 2 to what you learn from your story. In my Birkman Career Style Summary™, my Interests are green and my Style is blue. My Green Interests were totally fulfilled; I had promoted a project that grabbed my friend's attention. This project required concentrated time and energy and some creative planning, characteristically appealing to my Blue Style. My needs are more subtle. Partly I was relieved at not failing, not making anything worse. But even more deeply I enjoyed creating solutions to problems, whether mechanical or human. The environment was one in which I felt like an explorer and my friend felt like an expert, so that together we had defined exciting roles. Furthermore, we were working on a mechanical project, something with a beginning and an end, yet in an atmosphere where we could take as long as we needed.

SETTING OUT ON YOUR INNER JOURNEY

How can *you* isolate the motivators, the needs, the key intangibles that gave you a feeling of deep satisfaction? Look over your selected memories and ask yourself: Are there related links between them? What is different at the end of each story from the beginning? What has changed? When you think of movies you have loved, or plays, or even sporting events that thrilled you, can you see similarities that link them? Do you like reversals, come-from-behind situations? Or consistent smooth teamwork? In movies or plays, what is the quality of change that grips you? Do you prefer dramas where good triumphs over evil? Or where people are ennobled and enlightened by internal changes?

You have by now selected five memories in which you were attempting to accomplish something, and you've written about one of them; ideally, over the course of this task, you felt a loss of ordinary time, a sense of excitement or urgency which altered your sense of time. If you have not selected your memories and written your story yet, do it *now*!

Interpreting Your Story

Now read your story to your group or friend. First, note what you did—what you are drawn to, what the action or subject is, in short, your *interests*. In my story, for example, it was fixing a car. Then observe your *style*, in what manner you were operating in this memory. Were you alone, with one other person, or in a group? If you were in a group, were you leading or following?

We might ask you to consider, for your *style*, which of the following are the most important:

- Having plenty to do
- Having to make clear-cut decisions
- Having others be direct and logical
- Having objective supervision
- Knowing exactly what to do
- Being able to work without interruption
- Low-key direction
- Being trusted
- Having others be democratic
- Utilizing a variety of skills
- Having others encourage competition
- Novelty and variety of work
- Having others encourage expression of feelings
- Freedom from unnecessary rules or guidelines
- Having personal respect
- Freedom from constant social demands
- A self-determined schedule
- Individualized rewards
- Knowing who is in charge

Now make your own "style" notes of what modes of activity are important to you. Refer to my story about the car if you wish.

_____

_____

_____

_____

Next, we might ask what *needs* were being met. In these memories you are operating with all your needs being met, so if we find similar styles of activity in your memories, we may surmise that operating in this manner is important to your success and sense of well-being. Sometimes asking backwards is a useful entry point. For example, what parts of the story, if changed, would have taken away the feeling of achievement in your memory?

What *needs* did you find gratified or satisfied from your memory?

- Did you demonstrate independence?
- Did you contribute to a feeling of community?
- Were you working alone?
    - With one other person?
    - With a group?
- Were you working for self-gain?
- Were you working to be important to others?
- Were you working for philosophical or altruistic purposes?
- Were you working for yourself?
    - For someone else?
    - For an organization?
- Were you directing and controlling the situation?
- Were you playing an indispensable role?
- Were you carrying out orders?
- Were you directing others?
- Were you helping others?
- Were you learning something new?
- Were you utilizing creativity?
- Were you influencing others?

Now make your own "needs" notes about what conditions are present when you feel fulfilled.

_____

_____

_____

_____

Stress Reactions

For those who work best critically or negatively, you may find that operating from *stress*, the absence of needs being met, is easier.

How do you behave when many of your needs are *not* being met?

_____

In which environment (people, place, stress levels) are you least productive?

• People I work worst with:

_____

• Places I can't stand:

_____

• Stress Level: I do my worst work when I am:

_____

Summarize: I work *best* in the following circumstances:

_____

_____

_____

After you have defined your favorite interests, the style in which you prefer to pursue them, and the needs that you must meet to operate at your most creative level, we ask you to isolate the skills you used over the course of your story. Are they consistent with the level you would need to operate in your style? For example, had I wished to become a car mechanic, I would have had to go to school or apprentice myself at a garage. Assess the compatibility of your skills to your *interests, needs, and style*. You will have to consider, both by using the careers section of the book and in your informational interviewing (see chapter 4), whether you can upgrade your skills, and if so, whether you can do so on the job, at school, or in some other way such as mentoring or an internship.

Terminology

Analyzing Your Story

Let's review some of the terminology that we've been throwing around. This way, you will be able to incorporate some of the information from your Birkman Life Style Grid.

Interests

These are things you are drawn to, what you like to do. They also tell you what your goals are, or what you are trying to achieve. They are <u>not</u> an indication of your ability or skill.

Style

This is how you like to behave or act when you are doing the things you like to do. Your usual style of behavior assumes that all your personal and psychological needs are being met. Your story is about a time when you were working at your best, and you were charged because all your needs were being met. How you behaved during that time is an indication of your preferred behavioral style. Your style is very important because it will be one of your greatest selling points when interviewing for a job. Your skills emerge in your behavioral style. Your *actions* are ways of reading your style, what other people would see if they described what you were actually doing.

Needs

Environment is critical to our operating at our best. For the same sense of satisfaction that you had in your story, your needs should be met. When they are met, you feel a sense of self-approval. You like yourself as you are doing what you're doing; it's the right thing at the right time. Ideally, your bosses and colleagues give you the same sense of approval.

Skills

These are the abilities and resources that you would bring to an employment situation. There is something to the old adage that "people enjoy doing what they are good at," but in this specialized age it is becoming more and more important to know exactly what those skills are instead of assuming that we will succeed in whatever occupation we choose.

Story Analysis

1. What interests were revealed in your story?

_____

_____

_____

2. What was your style? How did you carry out the actions in your story?

_____

_____

_____

3. Why was the situation satisfying? What needs were being met?

_____

_____

_____

4. What skills were revealed?

_____

_____

_____

5. Why did you choose this story?

_____

_____

_____

APPLYING MEMORIES

Now I would like to take you through another story, this one written by a woman in a Career Creation group in 1994.

AMELIA'S COAT

1992 was not a good year for George and me, and at this moment—August—I did not realize how bad it would get. We had started the year with the news that Amelia would need open-heart surgery, then a second pregnancy that we had not planned, and finally George not making partner at Coopers. At this moment, George had left for a three-week life planning course. In his admirable way, he had marshaled unbelievable energy and organizational skills in his job search. It was hot and muggy and I was lonely. I should have gone away to visit my family but George's departure was last minute and I was gripped in a torpid moment. Amelia was one and a half, and typically in August I began to lust for cooler, autumnal weather. I decided to make Amelia a plaid car coat and took out a lovely plaid woolen fabric I had been saving since my days at Pemberton Woolens. I settled on a hooded double-breasted style and decided to make the coat reversible in a matching navy blue wool I also had. Years ago I had made a plaid coat for myself which I thought came out well, though not perfect because the lining did not sit well in the lower hem and I never could bring myself to add buttons and buttonholes. So I'd had some practice but still went slowly, carefully following instructions as I have now learned to do in sewing and not cutting corners to save time. (Basting and ironing are the two most important aspects of sewing!) I purposely made the coat big so it would last several years and also made a matching skirt. It is my finest work to date with perfect matching at all the seams. When Amelia wears it, it makes her look unique—which she is—and I feel so proud to say I made it. I took this picture and sent it to my mother, who had taught me to sew, so she could enjoy my success also. Even George has told others that I made it.

The group started by exploring her *interests*—what drew her to this project?

- a sense of fashion ("I settled on a hooded double-breasted...")

- her enjoyment in self-education ("carefully following instructions and not cutting corners to save time")

- her desire to complete unfinished projects ("years ago I had made...came out well, though not perfect...")

These are their observations about her *style*:

- She enjoyed converting feelings into artistry.

- She liked working with her hands.

- She tended towards meticulousness.

- She showed perseverance.

- She demonstrated an ability to express and transmit her experience.

As you read the story and think about the person in it, ask yourself, "What changes came about for her in the course of this memory; what could be the source of this memory?"

What can we say about the writer of this story and what does she want to express about herself? We have outlined her general style but have not covered the elements that make her and her story unique. Let us go over other kinds of observations from her story that may help you create working material:

- Challenged, she eventually becomes active ("in a torpid moment...I decided to make").

- Though her feelings impel her toward paralyzing responses ("I should have gone away...I was gripped"), her aesthetic and pragmatic responses are her deeper needs ("I decided to make...carefully following instructions...and not cutting corners").

- She generates self-respect through her achievements ("It is my finest work...I feel so proud...").

How could you use this in-depth information about yourself? At our Princeton Review seminar we would ask what actions we noted. We would note her:

- hand/eye skills (sewing, ironing etc.)

- ability to learn ("...carefully following instructions...")

And then we would examine more subtle but nevertheless significant parts of her memory, such as:

- her capacity to file and remember details ("a lovely plaid woolen fabric I had been saving...")

We might ask, in what ways did she feel rewarded? What needs of hers were met?

- her self-esteem ("I feel so proud to say I made it...")

- others' praise and appreciation ("my mother...could enjoy my success...even George has told others...")

Are there other aspects of the story we note that we can develop as we imagine a career that responds to the needs of this creative person?

- She found an active way to feel close to her mother, her daughter, and her husband, through an achievement.

- She is able to transform strong feeling into an aesthetic shape ("I was gripped," "I began to lust for," became the creative wellspring for "I decided," "I had been saving," "I settled on," and are eventually transformed into "a reversible coat" with "perfect matching at all the seams").

We might then further ask, "How do you think someone who was present might have described the writer's *actions*, in other words, what style of activity does she use?" We have already noted how methodical and skilled in using resources she is, following instructions and saving fabric. Have we noted, though, her response to her "bad…year" (her daughter's surgery, an unplanned pregnancy, and George's three-week absence and uncertain professional future)? We might note that this is a person who in an uncertain and depressing period becomes focused, decisive, resourceful, and self-challenging. The form of her challenge is aesthetic and filled with meticulous and daunting detail; she reminds us that earlier, "the lining did not sit well…and I never could bring myself to add buttons…."

We could then compare the writer's memory to her Birkman Career Style Summary™ and see what correspondences there might be:

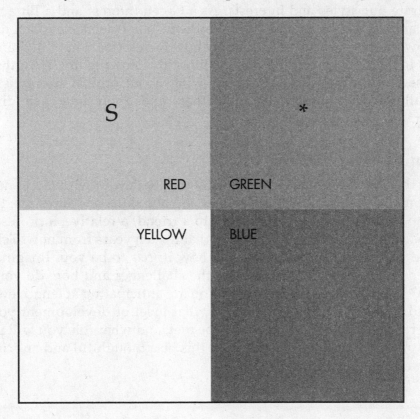

Her occupational interests are green, suggesting the promotional elements found in the photo she sent to her mother, "so she could enjoy my success." Her style is red, suggesting a strong need to convert her experiences into tasks and her desire to manage in such a way that she brings operations to completion. What doesn't show on the grid, and what emerged through her memory and discussion with her group, was her need for aesthetic expression. Trained as a technical marketer of home products, and highly rewarded and accomplished in that field, she wanted to be more challenged in creative and aesthetic ways. She has since been hired as president of an international company renowned for aesthetic taste and quality workmanship. Predictable? Perhaps, but only after clear focusing on her part.

Now that you have focused on your interests, style, and needs, you can explore different careers with a stronger sense of what you are trying to achieve and in what manner or style you prefer to function. The stories help us access our depository of treasured memories and the intensely valuable information they can reveal. The Birkman Career Summary™ corroborates the memories' links to personality and suggests how to best integrate our styles and interests. As a Green Interest and a Blue Style, I regularly create ideas and promote them, but I need companions with Yellow Interests to make sure I know how to describe what I'm doing, and Reds to help my dreams become realities. By knowing my strengths, I get to use them regularly. And by knowing about others' strengths, I can (usually) work comfortably with others and appreciate their different input.

Visualize Your Future

Now that you have a nodding acquaintance with your wishes and needs in life, and a sense of how they connect to your skills and interests, I'd like you to write a letter about yourself to a friend, a relative, a professor, or anyone else you choose, pretending that it's ten years from now. Tell your friend what you do every day and how it *feels* to be you. Imagine your career. What do you do? What are the challenges and how do you meet them? This is a memory in reverse. You are anticipating at length how you would like to be using your skills, what level of development you will have reached, how your needs will be met, and what role you will play in your profession or organization. Let this be a thoughtful and anticipatory roadmap to your future.

## CHAPTER 4

INTERVIEWING AS AN ART FORM

CAREER CREATION

Now that you have a working vocabulary to describe your favorite interests, the style, or manner in which you prefer to pursue them, and some of your needs which should be met to give you a feeling of satisfaction and creativity, how will you go about putting your new knowledge, and yourself, to work? *Guide to Your Career* provides original research into 171 professions which you can use as a starting point for your own exploration. Now that you've researched yourself using memories and The Birkman Career Style Summary™, it's time to research careers.

If you don't already have a group with whom you discussed your memories, ask a friend or group of friends to form a career creation group now. Even if everybody you know has a job, many of them may be wondering how to develop a career they love. Your friends can give you objective feedback about your skills; you can help each other stay on schedule, and you can boost one another's morale when the searching seems fruitless. Not all parts of looking for a job will be easy; disappointment, frustration, canceled interviews, and other unknowns will surely show up along the way. In The Princeton Review Seminars we work in small groups to provide an environment of multiple points of view all oriented toward a similar goal. Setting up a support system will help you complete each task in your career search.

Of course career creation recognizes traditional "job hunt" needs, and there are several good books that tell you how to go about searching, including The Princeton Review's *How to Survive Without Your Parents' Money* and *Trashproof Resumes*. However, *Guide to Your Career* has a different orientation; you will concentrate on defining benefits mutual to both you and your potential employer. In-depth research is required. Rather than thinking, "Please, anyone, offer me a job; I'll take anything," you'll be thinking, "Here's what I have to offer an employer and I *know* he needs these skills." And believe it or not, the employer prefers to fulfill your interests and needs. The better utilized you are, the more creatively you will work. We'll show you how to develop your research techniques so that you feel like a naturally inquisitive person, not like a hustler, when looking for a career.

Keeping Yourself on Track

Your career creation group or friend will be there to support you in this sometimes difficult search, but the following exercise will help you keep yourself on track as well.

Before you get too far into the career creation process, list how you're likely to get yourself to fail. Tax those old brain cells; given your unique style, how might you falter? Answers that have come up in other groups I have led include some tried-and-true beauties, such as:

- Forgetting to do assignments
- Blaming others (mother/father/teacher) for not having prepared you for these assignments
- Trivializing the work
- Quitting
- Taking the first job offered
- Not setting objectives

- Rationalizing that the current job is really not that bad

- Becoming overwhelmed by too many ideas

You get the idea; become familiar with the ways you're likely to undermine yourself. Then, when obstacles come up, you'll know how you might trip yourself up and you can avoid doing any of the things that are likely to make you quit. Do your list *now*, based on how you've managed to short-circuit in the past.

My Favorite Ways to Fail

1. _____

2. _____

3. _____

4. _____

5. _____

6. _____

7. _____

8. _____

9. _____

10. _____

Now, knowing how you're likely to fail is a big help in starting out. You'll be able to go back to this list along the way. I'd like you to develop a second list now. You can be as funny as you want, but remember, this list may save your behind when you don't feel like making a call one day and you recognize that you've anticipated that problem.

What to Do When I Feel Like Failing

1. _____

2. _____

3. _____

4. _____

5. _____

6. _____

7. _____

8. _____

9. _____

10. _____

Now that you've got your failure prevention lists, let's get down to the business of career creation.

PIE INTERVIEWING

In Career Creation, we follow the PIE (Pleasure/Practice, Information, Employment) interview formula first developed by Daniel Porot, a career expert in Europe. In PIE development, each interview develops skills needed in the following stage. For example, the practice interviews develop skills in establishing emotional contact with a stranger. At best, this becomes second nature during the information-gathering phase, so that you establish contact automatically while gaining information. In doing so, you are cueing your interviewer, silently encouraging him to be interested in your well-being. This can elicit important help, such as making calls to help set up other informational contacts for you. Finally, by the time you feel prepared for employment, speaking the language of a new field should feel as comfortable as if you had mastered the subject matter at school. You will also be adept at attuning yourself to the emotional flow of the interview environment, so that you minimize the feelings of being a novice and potential liability to this person. Be persistent. The worst that can happen is that you'll feel like a pest. But people are often hired for their persistence. Employers believe that if they want the position so much, they will do a great job.

The following chart outlines the PIE process.

	P Pleasure/Practice	I Information	E Employment
Kind of Interview	Practice field survey	Informational interviewing or researching	Employment or hiring interview
Purpose	To get used to and learn to enjoy talking with people: to penetrate networks	To find out if you'd like a particular field before you try to get into it	To get hired for the work you have decided you would most like to do
How You Go to the Interview	You can take somebody with you	By yourself or you can take somebody with you	By yourself
Who You Talk To	Anyone who shares your enthusiasm about a (for you) non-job-related subject	A worker who has a job similar to what you are thinking about doing	An employer who has the power to hire you for the job you have decided you would most like to do
How Much Time You Ask For	10 Minutes (and DON'T run over—making an 11:50 appointment may help, since most employers have lunch at noon)		Not your option as an interviewee

What You Discuss	Any questions about your shared interest or enthusiasm
	Suggested questions:
	1. How did you start, with this hobby, interest, etc.?
	2. What excites or interests you the most about it?
	3. What do you find is the thing you like the least about it?
	4. Who else do you know of who shares this interest, hobby or enthusiasm, or could tell me more about my curiosity?
	  a. Can I go and see them?
	  b. May I mention that it was you who suggested I see them?
	  c. May I say that you recommended them?
	Get interviewer's name and address
		Any questions you have about this job or this kind of work
		Suggested questions:
		1. How did you get interested in this work and how did you get hired?
		2. What excites or interests you the most about it?
		3. What do you find is the thing you like the least about it?
		4. What kinds of challenges or problems do you have to deal with in this job?
		5. What skills do you need in order to meet those challenges or problems?
		6. Who else do you know of who does this kind of work but with this difference: _____
		Get interviewer's name and address
			Tell them what it is you like about their organization and what kind of work you are looking for.
			Discuss:
			1. The kinds of challenges you like to deal with.
			2. What skills you have to deal with those challenges.
			3. What experience you have had in dealing with those challenges in the past.

Afterward: The Same Day	Send a thank you note	Send a thank you note	Send a thank you note

Pleasure

The "P" stands for pleasure or practice. Get used to talking with people you don't know (strangers!) about a subject about which you are knowledgeable and enthusiastic. Practice conversations will help you learn how to talk to people who are older or more successful; and enable you to feel comfortable talking to people even if you are shy, or feel you have nothing to contribute. Spend ten minutes with someone you haven't talked to before discussing a subject you know they enjoy or have a vested interest in (shop owners are perfect for this). Send a thank you note; they'll appreciate your thoughtfulness. You want your conversation to have a shared enthusiasm, much as you would if you were speaking to an interviewer about a career you both liked. You are training yourself to be as unself-conscious as you can. This may take a few interviews, but DON'T SKIP IT. You want shared enthusiasm to be your second nature. You'll find that you make mental notes as you're talking together—is the other person speaking enough? Am I giving signs of encouragement? These are significant parts of the interview process. For many of you, this will be a rare foray outside your generational boundary, where you encounter an older person in order to share a pleasurable interest, rather than as an authority. Make sure you're comfortable with this! To start this exercise, fill out the following:

"P" Exercise

Please list up to ten subjects that you thoroughly enjoy talking about.

1. _____

2. _____

3. _____

4. _____

5. _____

6. _____

7. _____

8. _____

9. _____

10. _____

Choose one of these subjects for your first interview.

Your Goal

Establish a connection with the person you are "interviewing" while discussing:

1. How he or she became interested or involved in this subject

2. What they like most about it

3. What, if anything, frustrates them about the subject

4. Who else they know who shares your interest

(Write the questions on a card and take it to the interview if you want.)

What did it feel like to "interview" someone about a subject in which you both shared an interest?

1. Did you both enjoy it?

2. Did it feel like you were juggling time, attention, and interest?

3. Were you both alert and involved?

_____

_____

_____

Information-Gathering

The "I" or information-gathering phase of career creation is when you start to learn more about the fields that interest you. In this phase, you want to have enthusiastic conversations with people in the industry(ies) that interests you, called informational interviews. The person will not have a job to offer, but she can give you information about her field, her job, and how she became a successful professional. Informational interviewing is perhaps the most critical phase of this process. You will be gathering the knowledge which separates you from the "job beggars," people who take what's available whether it suits them or not, and the resource person you aspire to be. Having clarified your interests and the style in which you like to pursue them, you are now ready to attach these interests to fields in which you might like to use them. Remember Amelia's mother? With interests (sewing and designing) and her style (meticulousness), she needed to find a field in which the language spoken appealed to her. With her group, she decided that a field in which high aesthetic standards were paramount would be the field or daily environment in which she would thrive. As you narrow your search to include your interests, style, and needs, you may wish to consider the fields in which you might like to pursue them. Look through the careers corresponding to your interest color to get a sense of where you may wish to begin your own informational interviewing.

What do you hope to accomplish in the "I" interview stage of PIE? Remember that in addition to being a fact-finding mission, an "I" interview is a sales event. An informational interview is a two-way process. You want to learn as much about the industry as you want the interviewer to learn about you. You wish to:

- Enlist the person as an ally in your job search
- Find out:
  1. How to enter the industry
  2. The future of the industry
  3. How the person recommends you proceed in your search
  4. If the person were starting out again, would he enter this industry? If not, why?
  5. If you match up well with this industry
  6. What skills are used in the field
  7. What challenges are present in the industry
- Try to obtain three new names

Preparation for Your Informational Interviews

Let's revisit my story from chapter 3. Taking into account some of the information we extracted from my story, I would want to answer the following questions in an informational interview that I would conduct:

- Do I make my own schedule?

- Can I work with others or am I always on my own?

- Is there recognition for individual achievement?

- Can I be innovative or is there a procedure manual?

- Are there learning opportunities on the job?

- Is advancement based on merit or seniority?

What are the key questions for you in a work environment?

_____

_____

_____

What interests do you want to see present in the career area you are interviewing for?

_____

_____

_____

What kinds of career satisfactions in this industry or profession are you noting as you gather information in the interview?

_____

_____

_____

No matter how comfortable you become with the social side of interviewing, it is important that you get specific information when conducting your interviews. The following seven questions, which can be phrased in a variety of ways, tend to elicit the essentials:

- How did you get started in your profession?

- What do you like most about your profession?

- What frustrates you most?

- What skills do you make use of?

- What challenges or obstacles are facing you now and in the future?

- Could you refer me to anyone else in your field that would be as excellent a source of information as you have been?

- May I stay in touch with you as I continue in this process?

The "Thank You" Note

Immediately following your interview you will want to write the thank you note we noted in the chart above. You might be thinking "What a pain," but this note is more important than you can believe. It should:

- At best be handwritten

- Have the individual's name and title spelled correctly

- Make specific reference to subjects discussed

- Make reference to any personal knowledge you came by in the course of the interview

- Ask the question: "May I stay in touch with you?"

The information you discover will help you plan your transformation into a resource person for the industry or profession you are exploring. At this point, you might want to start using a binder to store your (growing) list of interviewees. Here is an example of a contact sheet from a career creation group:

CONTACT SHEET

Date _____   Name _____
                             Title _____

Phone _____   Company _____
FAX _____   Address _____
                             _____

Referred by _____

Recap of Meeting _____

_____

_____

_____

_____

_____

_____

_____

_____

_____

_____

Personal Information _____

_____

_____

_____

Next Step _____

_____

_____

Follow-Up _____

_____

_____

Additional Contacts
1. _____
2. _____
3. _____

❏ Follow-Up Letter Sent

Employment

Finally (and none too soon), the "E", or employment phase. Where and for whom do you wish to work? How can you help them? How can your skills help meet the challenges in their industry? How have you used your skills in similar situations (not necessarily money-making) to help solve similar challenges to the ones in their field? Your critical task in this phase is to develop your "pitch," a clear and concise representation of how your research has demonstrated the way in which your skills can be a resource to this company. You must clearly articulate beforehand what you see as a challenge, and how your background and experience would make you a resource in helping to meet this challenge. You must be familiar with the language and thinking in the industry and have done your informational research. If you do not have paid experience, use examples from other areas, either as an intern, volunteer, or member of a community. Develop a history of experience whether you have worked or not. Why do you wish to work for this person? By now, you can convincingly state this. If you must, would you work for free for two months to show them what you can do? Wilder offers have been made and accepted. This is your pitch, and you should practice, practice, practice.

Assuming that you have spent some quality time in the "I" phase, you

- Are extremely comfortable with interview situations

- Have built a network of contacts through which you have located the industries/jobs in which you are likely to succeed

- Know how to enter the industry

- Have identified a potential career or job that matches your ideal work environment

- Know the challenges facing the industry

- Can present yourself and your achievements in a manner that addresses these challenges

By the way, it's the last one that gets you the job!

"E" Checklist

Here are some suggestions to follow as you begin setting up your employment interviews:

- Avoid personnel offices in scheduling employment interviews.

- Hold back your resume for as long as possible so you can tailor it to a specific position.

- Meet with the person with the power to hire you as early as possible.

- When asked about salary, be prepared to answer with a range.

- If possible, have the employer mention salary numbers first.

Don't forget to send a thank you note as you did in the information-gathering phase, and keep using the contact sheets to keep your career creation process organized.

SCHEDULING GUIDELINES

You and your friend/group should complete the first stories within a week. You will want to have your list of prioritized favorite interests and skills within a month of starting, including a working knowledge of the style in which you like to use them and the needs that are vital to your sense of creativity and well being. You can then begin the practice interviews. Schedule at least three in the following week. They shouldn't be anything elaborate, just ten minute conversations. Do these until you actually enjoy them, or at least aren't staring at your feet most of the time. The next step, informational interviewing, may take a good deal of time, at least three or four months, but schedule informational interviews regularly—three a week if possible. This is where you develop knowledge, confidence, and the opportunity to decide if this is a good field for you. Do it! Don't walk through this phase and take the first job offered to you (unless it's exactly what you want).

GETTING YOUR SHOW ON THE ROAD

The following pages on careers can help you select areas of interest or specific careers. Keep your interests and needs in mind as you do your research. The descriptions we've provided will leverage your career creation process. The purpose of our research is to cut down the grunt work in yours. Take advantage of it.

Good luck (which, as we all know, favors the prepared mind!).

---

*If you're stuck and want career advice we recommend the list found in the 1997 edition of *What Color is Your Parachute*, in the section, "What Color Reference Guide." You should certainly consider this if you've gone a month without an interview.

PART II

CAREER OPTIONS

CHAPTER 5

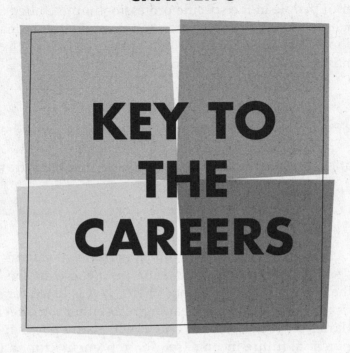

KEY TO THE CAREERS

NOTE ON SIDEBAR STATISTICS

The statistical information in this book came from a variety of sources, including government publications, published reports, broadcast news reports, industry self-reporting statistics, telephone interviews, and internet resources. No reported statistics for any industry are from before 1992. They should all be used as guidelines; individual statistics vary within each industry. A summary of how to interpret each statistic is included below.

People in Profession

The number of people in the specific profession in the United States. This does not include cross-career statistics, for example, the human resource manager who is also an accountant will appear as one or the other, not both, depending on how they choose to self-report.

Hours

The number of hours a professional in this field works each week. Individual reports vary based on company need, additional responsibilities, personal initiative, and projects involving travel.

Salary

Salary One

Entry-level salary. For industries in which entry-level salaries vary with experience, salary one is comparable for the people in the bottom 25 percent of the entry-level salary pool. Where N/A is listed for salary one, this indicates that salaries are not meaningful as either the career is not one in which salaries *per se* are paid, or one in which any pay is insignificant relative to potential future income (see "entrepreneur" for an example).

Salary Two

This statistic is the two- to five-year salary as reported for each profession. For industries in which two- to five-year salaries vary with pace of promotion, experience, and starting salary, salary two is comparable for the people in the middle 50 percent of the two- to five-year salary pool. Where N/A is listed for salary two, this should indicate for this career, salaries are not meaningful as either the career is not one in which salaries *per se* are paid, or one in which any pay is insignificant relative to potential future income (see "entrepreneur" for an example).

Salary Three

This statistic is the five- to ten-year salary as reported for each profession. For industries in which the five- to ten-year salaries vary with pace of promotion, bonus levels, experience, competitive bidding, starting salary and rising industry salary base, salary three is comparable for the people in the top 25 percent of the five- to ten-year salary pool. Where N/A is listed for salary three, this should indicate for this career, salaries are not meaningful as either the career is not one in which salaries *per se* are paid, or in which any pay is insignificant relative to potential future income (see "entrepreneur" for an example).

Major Associations

These are major associations recommended by government sources, professionals in their industry, and major employers in the field. They are not intended to be comprehensive listings of associations. Candidates are encouraged to use them as springboards for further research.

Major Employers

These are large employers of professionals in their associated career. Where possible, we have tried to list employers that would provide professionals with a range of work, style, geographic choices, and schedules. In some cases, we have indicated that professionals in the industry are primarily employed as single practitioners, in partnerships, or at small companies. Listing these companies does not constitute an endorsement of them or their practices. They are provided for informational purposes only.

Any insight you have into careers would be appreciated for future volumes of this book. Our challenge is to keep it relevant to the people who are searching for the right place for themselves in the workforce. Through your comments and your suggestions, we can continue to make this book a valuable resource to professionals like yourself.

Please send any comments to:

Guide to Your Career
The Princeton Review
2315 Broadway, Third Floor
New York, NY 10024

INTERPRETING THE ICONS

Salary

Average salary level in the industry as it relates to other fields:

 Generally low salary

 Generally middle salary

 Generally high salary

Hours

Average number of hours worked weekly compared with other fields:

 Generally low hours

 Generally medium hours

 Generally high hours

Male/Female

This describes the breakdown in the profession between men and women. Statistics are self-reported for each industry.

 More than 60 percent men

 Between 40 and 60 percent men; between 40 and 60 percent women

 More than 60 percent women

Education

The level of academic education generally needed to enter the profession:

 High school diploma

 College undergraduate degree

 Graduate or professional degree

Lifestyle

Subjective view of the lifestyle the average professional in the field can expect to have:

 Basic lifestyle

 Comfortable lifestyle

 Luxurious lifestyle

Social value

Subjective view of the social benefit of each profession:

 Small benefit to society

 Medium benefit to society

 Large benefit to society

TOP TEN LISTS

The Top Ten Jobs For People Who Like to Keep Learning

1. Software Developer
2. Physicist
3. Diplomat
4. Journalist
5. Architect
6. Benefits Administrator
7. Physician
8. Computer Programmer
9. Teacher
10. Writer

The Top Ten Jobs for People Who Need to Pay Off Student Loans RIGHT AWAY

1. Investment Banker
2. Financial Analyst
3. Management Consultant
4. Construction Manager
5. Banker
6. Service Sales Representative (potentially)
7. Stockbroker
8. Court Reporter
9. Carpenter
10. Marketing Executive

The Top Ten Jobs for People Who Can't Stand Ties or Pantyhose

1. Computer Programmer
2. Artist
3. Writer
4. Actor
5. Petroleum Engineer
6. Coach
7. Philosopher
8. Zoologist
9. Anthropologist
10. Child Care Worker

The Top Ten Jobs for Type-A Personalities

1. Attorney
2. Investment Banker
3. Management Consultant
4. Pilot
5. Military Officer
6. Architect
7. Baseball Player
8. Coach
9. Astronaut
10. Stockbroker

The Top Ten Jobs for People Who Long For Unpredictable Days

1. Detective/Private Investigator
2. FBI Agent
3. Police Officer
4. Restaurateur
5. Firefighter
6. Musician
7. Advertising Executive
8. Petroleum Engineer
9. Promoter
10. Agent

The Top Ten Jobs for People People

1. Teacher
2. Human Resources Manager
3. Guidance Counselor
4. Career Counselor
5. Psychologist
6. Social Worker
7. Child Care Worker
8. Physical Therapist
9. Fundraiser
10. Hotel Manager

The Top Ten Jobs for People Who Like to Work With their Hands

1. Carpenter
2. Mechanic
3. Dentist
4. Machinist
5. Zoologist

6. Printer
7. Robotics Engineer
8. Avionics Technician
9. Physician
10. Chef

CHAPTER 6

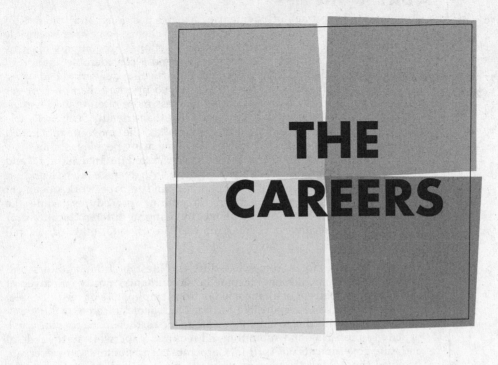

THE CAREERS

ACCOUNTANT/AUDITOR

A DAY IN THE LIFE

Accountants keep track of payments, financial positions, and transfers of capital or income for individual or institutional clients. Some are responsible for examining the tax implications of those actions. Accountants must be comfortable with numbers, but must also spend a considerable amount of time reviewing other people's work and, in particular, delivering bad news. As a "financial physician" (a term that cropped up more than once in our surveys), you'll be the bearer of unpleasantness more often than blessings, and can expect to be greeted, at times, in a less-than-friendly fashion. People who enter accounting mention this stigma as the most unanticipated downside of the profession. "I didn't know how many people just don't pay attention to their own numbers," wrote one frustrated internal auditor, "and how defensive people are when they're wrong." An average internal auditor spends a surprisingly small 35 percent of her time on paperwork, document review, and (usually computerized) accounting procedures, while the remainder is spent either on the phone, traveling to different locations, or meeting with executives, clients, representatives, and other divisional auditors.

Tax accountants face a somewhat different lifestyle from auditors and general accountants. Personal income tax accountants, mostly employed at small firms (80 percent of all income tax firms employ five or fewer people) or self-employed, are responsible for tracking clients' income, making any quarterly payments due to federal or state agencies, then managing the crush of activity preparing and submitting all required paperwork to the federal and state governments on April 15. Corporate tax accountants, however, are involved throughout the year in corporate decision-making, analyzing the tax effects of corporate investment policy, and advising other company managers on tax-planning issues. Corporate tax accountants face a seasonal surge in April similar to the one personal tax accountants face, although to a significantly lesser degree.

The level of satisfaction in the profession is high. Since the bulk of what a professional accountant does is well-covered in school, those who don't find accounting enjoyable in school tend not to enter the professional accounting world.

PAYING YOUR DUES

Most in the industry enjoy the straightforward path to becoming an accountant. Nearly all firms require at least a bachelor's degree in accounting, finance, or a related discipline. Many employers look favorably on students with significant computer proficiency or work experience in number-intensive jobs, and some job candidates enhance their profiles by earning a master's degree in business, accounting, or finance. The most common certification accountants are asked to complete soon after hire is the state-licensed Certified Public Accountant (CPA) exam. This rigorous four-part exam is rapidly replacing the Public Accountant (PA), Registered Public Accountant (RPA), and the Accounting Practitioner's (AP) exams as the working degree of choice. Different states have different licensing requirements, so write to the National Association of State Boards of Accountancy to find out the requirements for your state. Many boards are currently considering requiring an additional thirty hours of post-graduate accounting coursework for state accreditation.

ASSOCIATED CAREERS

Accounting degrees are often paired with law, marketing or advertising degrees as a means of specialization, but by no means are these the only careers associated with auditing and accounting. Accountants move to positions in bank operations, budgeting offices, financial analysis, management consulting, the FBI (where accountants track, analyze, and report on illegal interstate money transfers and hidden asset recovery—FBI accountants even brought down Al Capone), and full-service brokerage firms. It is not unusual to see an accountant become an entrepreneur and use her expertise to begin, manage, and nurture a start-up company as its financial officer.

PAST AND FUTURE

Financial records certifying transactions and recording inventory levels have been found at the sites of ancient Greek and Roman towns, but accounting didn't become a "science" until 1494 with the publication of a book by mathematician Luca Pacioli describing the principles of accounting, including the double-entry bookkeeping system still in use today. In the United States, accounting grew significantly as a profession with the passage of federal legislation mandating income tax in 1913 and the excess profits tax in 1917.

The future of accounting looks great for some types of accountants while potentially bleak for others. Corporate tax advising, tax planning, internal auditing, and small business consulting are expected to grow at a steady pace. Internal auditing, in particular, should grow in popularity as small businesses learn the value of managing their capital soundly. Personal tax accounting, however, could change significantly if any of the "flat tax" proposals are voted into law (an unlikely but possible event). When the tax laws change, accounting professionals must reeducate themselves as they did when the 1986 tax law reforms were passed.

QUALITY OF LIFE

Two Years

Most entry-level accountants and auditors are highly supervised, basically apprenticed to more experienced professionals in the field as cost-accountants or junior internal auditors. During the first two years, many people study for their CPA exam, which only 25 percent of test-takers pass at any given administration. Nearly half of the 15 percent who leave the profession in the first two years do so to gain further schooling in a related field.

Five Years

Mobility becomes the most significant feature of the profession after five years. Professionals begin to specialize in private or public accounting, and reach levels of greater responsibility, such as budget director or accounting manager. Some start their own firms; others become internal auditors in client firms. Accountants also enter related fields such as banking, financial analysis, and asset management. The 10 to 20 percent who leave the field are dissatisfied by the unpredictability of hours and the unflattering public perception of the industry. For those who remain, both hours and salary increase.

Ten Years

Private practitioners have established their own firms or, if unsuccessful, re-entered the corporate environment. Those who followed a corporate track all along are now not only involved in tax-planning issues and accounting procedures, but business decisions and actual corporate strategy. Salary increases significantly at this point for the independent practitioner who has built a considerable client base. A variety of management positions unrelated to accounting, previously unavailable, open up, such as strategic planning, operations development, and budget oversight. Some accountants become independent consultants and begin to work shortened hours, deciding to place more emphasis on family life and free time. A significant few enter government service and/or academia.

THE BIRKMAN LIFESTYLE GRID

Red Green
Yellow Blue

This career is suitable for people with Red interests.

You'll Have Contact With

Attorneys
Bankers
Bookkeepers
Record Keepers

Major Associations

American Institute of Certified Public Accountants
P.O. Box 2213
Jersey City, NJ 07303-9956
Tel: 201-938-3100

Foundation for Accounting Education
530 5th Avenue
5th Fl.
New York, NY 10036
Tel: 212-719-8300
Fax: 212-719-3364
Contact: Danielle D'Angelo

National Association of State Boards of Accountancy
380 Lexington Avenue
Suite 200
New York, NY 10168-0002
Tel: 212-490-3867

ACTOR

A DAY IN THE LIFE

One actor we interviewed referred to his life as a modified version of the song "Do the Hustle," where he ran from audition to audition, checking his answering machine for messages every two hours for news of a possible call-back. An actor's satisfaction with the profession seems to vacillate with whether he is working or not. Many working actors would agree with the one who wrote that he found the occupation "challenging, thrilling, exciting, and wonderful." Some non-working actors might agree with the one who wrote that acting can be "a dead end to nowhere." In various ways, most actors described their choice of career as not a choice at all; "There was nothing else I wanted to do," wrote one woman, "I guess I'm just demented." The community of similarly demented professionals is the most supportive aspect of this otherwise cutthroat career. Why else would they stay in a profession where 80 percent of SAG members earned less than $5,000 from acting annually, and fewer than 5 percent earned more than $35,000 from their chosen profession?

In general, actors lead grueling, difficult, financially unrewarding lifestyles, working on their craft and hoping to land significant roles. The indignities the profession offers are endless: long hours, uncertain work, self-doubt, financial hardship, lack of institutional health care, and many others. Most aspiring actors find employment as temporary workers, waiters, bartenders and freelance writers—any position that allows them flexible hours to continue to audition for roles. One unusual feature of this profession is that a rise to stardom, although enormously unlikely, can happen in the blink of an eye. One good audition, one good role, or one good review can change the life of an actor forever. Successful actors, however, sometimes find the fame they discover a little too intrusive. All aspects of their personal lives become common knowledge, and many complain that they got exactly what they wanted: Recognition by everyone.

PAYING YOUR DUES

No formal training is required to become an actor, but the number of "natural talents" who spring fully groomed into a successful professional career is very small. Most actors study acting, appear in low-budget and local productions, learn from those appearances, and then begin the cycle again. Some study acting in college; others find it helpful to study further and receive a Master of Fine Arts in acting. Working actors are constantly going on casting calls, finding agents, and getting reviewed (favorably, if possible); all of these are arduous and time-consuming tasks, more often than not meeting with rejection rather than success. Many actors choose to move to major cities (in particular New York for theater and Los Angeles for film and television) because more opportunities exist in those places. Regional theaters can be excellent but provide only limited exposure. Generally, actors who have been hired for a union production can apply to the Screen Actor's Guild (SAG) and/or Actor's Equity for membership, two unions which demand higher wages for their performers.

ASSOCIATED CAREERS

Actors become many things during and after their careers—directors, producers, designers, choreographers, composers, writers and, in one notable case, president of the United States. Others use their experience to teach acting and related disciplines; still others use their acting talents in careers involving personal interaction, such as marketing or sales. While many careers have a direct line of progression to a pinnacle, acting is an end in itself; many professionals are extremely satisfied to have the chance to work as actors their entire lives.

PAST AND FUTURE

Acting might trace its roots to the campfires of prehistoric man, where hunters would reenact the story of the hunt and praise their deeds in a communal ceremony. It is truly a phenomenon of humankind rather than any specific country—the Greeks defined the art form with their theological and political plays; Japanese Kabuki theater portrayed historical events intended to illuminate the human condition. Acting is a storied and respected profession that rewards its stars with fame, fortune, and adulation.

Over half of all acting revenues in the United States last year were from commercials, and this trend is expected to continue. The remainder of revenue is derived primarily from films. As production costs for feature films and theater productions decline while those for independent filmmakers and producers grow, the available non commercial acting parts for working actors should increase. Please note, however, that the likelihood of becoming a star remains slim.

QUALITY OF LIFE

Two Years

As at all levels in the profession, the attrition rate is high—over 30 percent. Actors go to open casting calls which may attract hundreds of people auditioning for a single part, audition for everything from commercials to dramatic roles, and juggle paying jobs and (usually) non paying acting careers. Most people continue to study acting by attending workshops, enlisting private instructors, and reading. New actors practice their craft by acting in productions at smaller theaters and assisting other productions in unpaid (or low-paying) jobs.

Five Years

Those who survive for five years as actors have an improved quality of life. By this point, they are likely to have agents, who send them on auditions for suitable parts; they've received some reviews, have made some connections in the casting community, and have supplemented money-earning jobs with paying acting jobs. Many actors have become members of the SAG or Actor's Equity unions, which command higher wages for their members, as well as offering discounted rates on health-benefits. While they may audition for parts more selectively, the level of acceptance remains low. Many turn to teaching acting.

Ten Years

Unlike other professions where, if you have survived for ten years, you've achieved a reputation or some level of financial security, in acting it just means you've been working for ten years. Some members of the profession will have achieved this and more, including international fame; for most, however, the struggle continues with improving their skills and getting work. While actors span a variety of ages, nearly 60 percent of all roles are scripted for people in the 20- to 40-year-old range. This is not to say that there are no parts for younger or older actors; the competition just gets fiercer the longer you manage to survive in the profession.

THE BIRKMAN LIFESTYLE GRID

This career is suitable for people with Green interests.

You'll Have Contact With

Agents
Directors
Publicists
Producers

Major Associations

Screen Actors Guild
5757 Wilshire Boulevard
Los Angeles, CA 90036
Tel: 213-954-1600
Fax: 213-549-6656
Contact: Public Relations

Actor's Equity Association
165 West 46th Street
New York, NY 10036
Tel: 212-869-8530

ACTUARY

A DAY IN THE LIFE

An actuary assembles and analyzes facts and estimates risks and returns to make financial planning decisions in a specific area of expertise. As an actuary, you'll spend a lot of time working with numbers. You'll also spend up to 65 percent of your time working with people, establishing goals, reviewing work, and researching figures. "It's a real learning experience at first—not at all like school," one actuary wrote, referring to the interpersonal and communication skills that were required in her job.

A significant portion of the aspiring actuary's time is spent studying for the multifaceted, information-specific exams that every actuary must pass. Initial examinations test basic mathematical skills, such as probability, calculus, and linear algebra, and are used as "litmus tests" to eliminate those unsuited to the actuarial life. Surprisingly, we found little mention of the long hours spent outside of work studying for the exams and the lack of a social life this hard study encourages. Actuaries seem to enjoy the constant education the profession requires, regardless of the personal cost. These exams provide good indicators of progress as an actuary; full passage of the exams takes between five and ten years.

Pension actuaries and actuaries who work with the federal government lead a different life from those employed by the private sector. They must learn and follow very specific regulations and accounting procedures that clearly define the role of the actuary and adopt prescribed formulas and methodologies. In the private sector, a premium is placed not only on adherence to standard models, but also on creative thinking and creative problem solving. Actuaries who work in the private sector agree that their profession provides them with a high level of satisfaction and challenge.

As actuaries progress in their careers, they find the specific skills learned in each department to be less and less transferable to other areas. For example, it is unusual for an actuary specializing in pensions to transfer to being a casualty actuary. It would be like a brain surgeon transferring to become a heart surgeon; they're skilled in very different and very specific areas. Because of this, the question of specialization is critical to the level of satisfaction felt by most actuaries. Those who like to analyze behavior and are comfortable with creating new models do better in the field of casualty analysis; those who like to analyze effects and are good at finding patterns in existing statistical groupings of people do better in the pension arena.

PAYING YOUR DUES

Becoming an actuary requires some of the skills of a gambler and some of the skills of a marathoner. You need a gambler's understanding of statistics, probability, and risk-analysis. Most actuaries graduate college with a degree in mathematics or a business-related field, although the industry trend of late is to hire more liberal-arts students who can demonstrate a high mathematical aptitude. The endurance of a marathoner is required not for the hours, which are fairly acceptable, but to make it through the actuarial examinations, which can take as long as ten years to pass. These tests are administered biannually by three associations: The Society of Actuaries, the Casualty Actuarial Society (for casualty actuaries), and the American Society of Pension Actuaries. While each agency provides certification for a certain specialization, the first few tests are general enough that they may be taken without regard to any specific career path.

ASSOCIATED CAREERS

As you advance as an actuary, your career path will depend mainly on the complementary skills you bring to the profession. While some move to administrative and executive positions in underwriting, accounting, or information departments, others with more of a business background may move into supervisory positions in such diverse fields as marketing, planning or corporate strategy.

PAST AND FUTURE

With the rise of the science of probability, described mathematically by Blase Pascal and Pierre de Fermat, came the ability to create probability tables for any given event—death, accidents, even loan defaults. In 1792, the Equitable Society of London (an insurer) decided to use these tables to determine their premiums, and thus was born the role of the actuary. Edmund Halley—after whom Halley's Comet is named—developed the first table of mortality, thereby giving birth to the life-insurance industry.

The need for actuaries should rise over the next decade as insurance companies, pension plans, and large corporations recognize the need for accurate statistical analysis and cash-flow-management. Computer skills are crucial at the cutting edge of actuarial development, particularly in the field of liability analysis. Another emerging field is actuarial health care science; with unpredictable changes in medical technology and the emergence of epidemic viral strains, life expectancy is becoming more difficult to predict and more variable-dependent. Some actuaries believe these probabilities are describable and are working with complicated mathematics to find a way to explain them.

QUALITY OF LIFE

Two Years

In the beginning, actuaries, referred to by professional societies as "associates," are rotated among different jobs within the company to learn the variety of processes that an insurance or pension company follows. Entry-level actuaries spend much of their time researching and preparing data. Many people enjoy the lack of professional responsibility these early years offer, mainly because it allows plenty of free time to study for the exams that mark the first few years. Attrition is low; satisfaction is average.

Five Years

"Fast-trackers" diverge from others at this point, and those who have trouble with the exams or find producing analyses on other people's demands unsatisfying leave (18-22 percent). Salaries rise, and some attain the professional title of "fellow." Hours increase and specialization becomes critical—those who leave the profession beyond this point do so primarily because of a dissatisfaction with their area of specialization. Job performance is the distinguishing characteristic during these years; actuaries tend to view their jobs and colleagues as "very competitive."

Ten Years

Actuaries who have had success start their own actuarial consulting firms. Many leave the pure actuarial side and enter management and corporate strategy development. Some continue up the actuarial ladder, moving to "chief" or "head" of actuarial science. Others are recruited by the government or independent research panels for their statistical skill and their experience in a specific area of expertise.

THE BIRKMAN LIFESTYLE GRID

Red   Green
Yellow Blue

This career is suitable for people with Red interests.

You'll Have Contact With

Accountants
Bankers
Computer Programmers
Statisticians

Major Associations

American Academy of Actuaries
1100 17th Street, NW
7th Floor
Washington, DC 20036
Tel: 202-223-8196
Fax: 202-872-1948
Contact: Elizabeth Hartsfield

Society of Actuaries
475 North Martingale Road
Suite 800
Schaumburg, IL 60173-2226
Tel: 708-706-3500
Fax: 847-706-3599
Contact: Pat Holmberg

Casualty Actuarial Society
1100 North Glebe Road
Suite 600
Arlington, VA 22201
Tel: 703-276-3100

ADVERTISING EXECUTIVE

A DAY IN THE LIFE

Advertising professionals combine creativity with sound business sense to market products with the aid of financial, demographic, and psychological research. To ensure this complicated process works smoothly (and many we surveyed mentioned that you have to be prepared for it not to happen smoothly), you'll spend a lot of time in the office (a six-day week is not unusual). The majority of time is spent brainstorming and sifting through research data; a significant amount of time is also spent meeting with clients or pitching advertising campaigns. Fluidity of daily activity marks the life of the advertising executive who jumps from project to project, but attention to detail is crucial. It takes a very disciplined person to handle both the creative end and the detail-oriented administrative side. Advertising executives work in teams on projects, so working with others is crucial; those who are successful have the ability to add to other people's ideas and help them grow. "It doesn't help to have a huge ego in this business," mentioned one executive, "but everybody seems to have one."

In most agencies, there are four major areas of employment—creative (art and writing), media (analyzing markets and buying advertising space), research (market demographics, consumer preferences, etc.), and account management (representing the agency to clients). The two most likely paths to success are in creative and client management; but while it is the rare creative executive who devotes himself seriously to client management, client service people tend to be well "trained" in the creative process. Most account executives arrive with MBAs in hand—it's almost a must today, since the client contact will most likely have one too. The bigger agencies have their own account management training programs in research and media.

Like most project-oriented careers, you can expect periods of intense activity during which you have little, if any, free time. At other times, the work load can be light, and maybe a bit mundane. A number of people interviewed said what they liked best about the profession is that "you get recognized when you have a good idea." They also mentioned that failure is always recognized. The ability to work with specialists such as designers and copywriters is one of the most important skills an advertising executive can have; however, camaraderie is not the typical reason people enter advertising. Aggressive selling is at the heart of the matter, and you have to be willing to "swim with the sharks" in order to make it in advertising.

PAYING YOUR DUES

In general, an outgoing, well-spoken, well-informed person with confidence and common sense is a typical advertising candidate. A degree in communications, graphic design, English, psychology or any medium of expression does not hurt in the competition for advertising jobs. It helps to be a "media junkie" with a tolerance for high volumes of television and magazines, since it's essential to be current in these media. The requirements differ depending on whether you work for an advertising firm or within a large manufacturing company. If you are working for a manufacturer, you should have a degree or previous work experience that relates to their product line and/or their demographic profile. Professional connections (gained through extensive "networking") are the quickest way to power in the notoriously schmoozy biz.

ASSOCIATED CAREERS

The skills you obtain in the advertising industry may be transferable to other media-oriented settings, such as marketing and consulting. Specialization in a particular area sometimes leads to a move in-house at a particular company to direct marketing efforts or review which advertising firms to hire.

PAST AND FUTURE

Ancient Romans advertised by placing large painted signs on walls. Advertising as a profession has come into its own in the 20th Century, particularly in the wake of World War II and the prosperity that brought consumerism to new heights. Commercial progress, both individually and collectively, has been encouraged by advertising. It is not unusual for products you use in your home to have had significant advertising budgets and for your tastes or interests to have been unconsciously influenced by modern advertising.

The need to be flexible can not be emphasized enough. Smaller, more focused "shops" (as agencies are known in the industry) are reemerging after the era of gargantuan players in the 1970s and 1980s (although the latter remain dominant). As a number of large players in the industry move toward "computer-based brainstorming"—a way in which creative ideas are kept in a fluid database without regard to account—specificity-computer skills will become more valuable. Advertising is expanding into new media, particularly electronic media. Advertising on the World Wide Web offers unprecedented opportunities for marketers to tailor advertisements according to the tastes of individual shoppers. Moreover, the manually drafted layout is now a thing of the past; high-powered computer graphics software now generate presentations. In advertising as in business in general, the future is coming to a terminal near you.

QUALITY OF LIFE

It is important to note that this career has a significant rate of burnout at all levels; nearly 35 percent of people who leave the profession have reached the level of Executive Vice President or higher. Also, advertising is an industry of booms and busts, and an executive's success can be as fickle as the clients whom they serve.

Two Years

Entry-level positions, mostly assistantships, can mean answering mail, entering computer data, returning phone calls and proofreading copy text. Getting ahead requires the right combination of persistence, luck, and the help of someone currently in a position of authority. The first years are best spent observing, following, and listening to experienced advertising executives. There is heavy attrition—around 20 percent in the first couple of years.

Five Years

Rising young account representatives take on responsibility for coordinating the variety of parts involved in a campaign, but there is still little client contact. Salaries rise steeply after the first couple of years, but the hours become deadly, and many young professionals (some 25 percent), frustrated with the small amount of creative input allowed, leave the profession. The few who have the opportunity to make creative input to a campaign see the results of their input and feel the ramifications of that responsibility.

Ten Years

After ten years, the average industry professional has changed jobs three times, and seen at least half of her contemporaries leave the profession for other industries. With mastery of some specialty in an industry, demographic, or advertising medium (TV, print, radio, Internet), an advertising executive's pay can skyrocket—but it can also plummet to zero when experience is sacrificed for "freshness."

THE BIRKMAN LIFESTYLE GRID

This career is suitable for people with Green interests.

You'll Have Contact With
Graphic Designers
Media Specialists
Market Researchers
Art Directors

Major Associations
American Advertising Federation
1101 Vermont Avenue, NW
Suite 500
Washington, DC 20005
Tel: 202-898-0089
Fax: 202-898-0159
Contact: Education Department

American Association of Advertising Agencies
405 Lexington Avenue
18th Floor
New York, NY 10174
Tel: 212-682-2500
Fax: 212-682-8391
Contact: Publications Department

Association of National Advertisers
155 East 44th Street
New York, NY 10017
Tel: 212-697-5950
Fax: 212-661-8057

Aerospace Engineer

A DAY IN THE LIFE

"I'm a rocket scientist," one of our survey respondents wrote in a sentiment echoed by many others; "who wants anything more?" Aerospace engineers examine, analyze, design, produce, and occasionally install components that make up aircraft, spacecraft, high-altitude vehicles, and high-altitude delivery systems (missiles). Satisfaction with the romantic image of rocket-building can buoy many engineers through the highly anonymous work environments that many of them face. Individuals don't assemble rockets; teams do, dozens of teams working in highly supervised coordination. An aerospace engineer plays some part on one of the teams, spending more of her time (roughly 70 percent) in a lab, at a computer, and assembling reports than doing anything else. Not being able to see the "big picture" frustrates some professionals. "What do I do? I don't know," wrote one engineer, who later claimed himself a victim of this moonshot myopia. Due to the complexity of the final product, an intricate and rigid organizational structure for production has to be maintained, severely curtailing any single engineer's ability to understand his role as it relates to the final project. It is not unusual to be pulled off one project without explanation and thrown into the midst of another already in progress. As one person explained it: "This is not referred to as disorganization; it carries the name prioritization."

Others dismissed the "hive mentality" as a mere annoyance rather than a problem with the profession and waxed eloquently about the dual practical and theoretical nature of aerospace engineering: "People's lives are in our hands, and that's tough to remember in the lab all the time." The curiosity to explore and create a safe and powerful place to study larger questions of the universe accounts for a strong attraction to the engineering life. Another attraction is the intellectual environment and the joy of being with similarly big-brained people. The combination, however, can lead to some clashes of egos: "When you have something important to say," mentioned one engineer, "be ready to shout. No one listens unless you shout." You have to have a strong sense of self and a strong sense of purpose in this occupation; those who do have a solid level of satisfaction.

PAYING YOUR DUES

The path to becoming an aerospace engineer is a rigorous one, but those who manage to survive the difficult lift-off emerge with an above-average degree of career satisfaction. Academic requirements are strict and wide-ranging: Physics, chemistry, computer science, mathematics, materials science, statistics and engineering courses provide the base for any aspiring rocket scientist. Some colleges offer a degree in aerospace engineering; others offer a more generalized engineering degree with some coursework in aerospace engineering. These courses might include aerospace guidance systems, extreme-altitude material science, and the physics of high-altitude radiation. Internships, summer jobs, and any experience in the field are helpful, as entry into this industry is highly competitive. Many aspirants may need to relocate to California, Washington State, or Texas, where the majority of defense industry aerospace work is done.

ASSOCIATED CAREERS

Aerospace engineers end up teaching far more frequently than do members of most other professions. This isn't surprising due to the dual nature of the discipline; professionals love what they do in exploring concepts and building them, and in academia, they avoid the anonymity the profession fosters. Most people who leave the profession do so because of lack of work, lack of responsibility, or lack of control. Jobs are highly responsive to defense industry spending and anticipated aerospace orders. Those who leave tend to find themselves satisfied in other scientific or manufacturing positions.

PAST AND FUTURE

Flying has been a dream of man's since he was capable of watching birds swoop through the air and navigate the highest reaches with ease. The first plane flight, in 1903, by Charles and Orville Wright at Kitty Hawk, North Carolina, was the first major step in making that dream a reality.

In the present and future, the dream extends into space and beyond. Aerospace engineers who currently design shuttles, military aircraft, rockets, and missiles will design craft that can land on and take off from the surfaces of other planets. The occupation would have a potentially limitless future but for its dependence on military funding; as budget issues come more and more to the forefront, uncertainties in funding and issues of cutbacks and layoffs make the potentially crucial and exotic future of aerospace engineers uncertain indeed.

QUALITY OF LIFE
Two Years

Junior members of research staff are swamped with work, both in the lab and in offices, crunching data and organizing research. More like "lab assistants," their early years are marked by relatively menial tasks (testing of equipment, tracking results) with little input into the testing or recommendation process. Average hours and pay characterize these environments, but education continues apace. Few people leave the profession during these years; the hours already devoted in school make it easier to tolerate these few extra workplace indignities.

Five Years

Five-year veterans lead research teams and turn into people managers as well as project managers. This is an unanticipated turn of events for some, as it removes them from the challenging, intellectually rarefied environment they enjoy and places them in a more administrative role. Most significant design and production work is done in these years. Over 25 percent leave, frustrated with the anonymity of the profession and limited opportunity to pursue what they believe to be promising and interesting ideas.

Ten Years

About 5 percent start their own aerospace research and development firms, based on patents, contacts, and access to adequate financing. Those who become project and personnel managers have significant input on the direction of research, but little contact with the actual day-to-day functioning of these research and development teams. Budgeting, oversight, and intra-company contacts all become important parts of the ten-year survivor's life. Hours remain about the same and satisfaction tends to level off; salary increases occur, but after this point, without equity interest in smaller, private companies, administrators can only expect cost-of-living salary increases. The attrition rate has slowed, but those who leave from this point go back into academia, training programs, or private consulting.

THE BIRKMAN LIFESTYLE GRID

This career is suitable for people with Red interests.

You'll Have Contact With
Avionics Technicians
Computer Programmers
Electrical Engineers
Government Officials

Major Associations
Air Force Association
1501 Lee Highway
Arlington, VA 22209
Tel: 703-247-5800
Fax: 703-247-5853
Contact: Kathy Snodgrass

American Institute of Aeronautics and Astronautics
1801 Alexander Bell Drive
Suite 500
Boston, WV 22091
Tel: 703-264-7500
Fax: 703-264-7551
Contact: Patrick Gouhin

Junior Engineering Technical Society
1420 King Street
Alexandria, VA 22314
Tel: 703-548-5387
Fax: 703-548-0769
Contact: Cathy McGowen

AGENT

A DAY IN THE LIFE

The worst part is listening to the stories agents told us. And told us. Everyone seems to have an "I got screwed by an agent" story; the hostility that agents face is not trivial. In reality, an agent has very little power to make or break any deal. An agent is a representative who advises her client in a certain area of expertise. Agents represent athletes, writers, models, actors, producers, performers, and other celebrities. They help make their clients' successes happen. If the client doesn't do well, the agent doesn't survive. But there's a significant paycheck for those whose clients strike it rich; Deion Sanders, for example, recently signed a $35 million contract to play football for the Dallas Cowboys. His agent (assuming a standard 15 percent commission) stands to make $5.2 million dollars from that one deal. These kinds of paydays can make that uncertainty of income palatable.

An agent spends most of the day on the telephone arranging meetings, discussing prospects, networking connections, and keeping in touch with the industry trends and deals. Nearly one-third of all phone time is spent with clients, explaining what the agent is doing on their behalf and strategizing. Face-to-face meetings are also important. Negotiating skills are the agent's bread and butter. Some believe that "You never get killed in a negotiation—you only get a little less than you want." An agent has to be willing to find creative compromises and live with them. Those who are successful must have tenacity, the willingness to fight for their clients, and the ability to sell ideas effectively and communicate clearly. Agents must have access to those able to make deals to be effective for their clients, so cocktail conversational skills and power-lunch political savvy are important as well.

It is important to know that other agents will not necessarily welcome prospective agents with open arms. Other agents will acknowledge you; they will even discuss their work with you, but they will not offer you their contacts and they will not tell you any of their secrets. Much of the difficulty of being a successful agent is developing your own contacts, your own strategies, and your own techniques. Despite this arms-length relationship, agents record high levels of respect for each other.

PAYING YOUR DUES

No specific academic requirements exist to become an agent, although most agencies say that a college degree is "preferred." College major is unimportant (although marketing and statistical analysis are looked upon favorably), but the candidate must show a knowledge of the field, an ability to work under pressured and difficult circumstances, and an ability to relate to her clients. Specialization happens early on, as representation in different areas (film, literature, sports) requires a different set of contacts and skills. Often beginning in smaller, more hands-on firms provides many agents with their first jobs and exposure to the duties associated with agents. Jobs are marked by low wages (often with incentives), long hours, and significant "face time," when agents must entertain clients, reassure them of their advocacy, and keep in touch with their clients' needs.

ASSOCIATED CAREERS

The connections agents make in their careers come in handy if they decide to leave. Many enter the field their clients are in, such as producing, editing, publishing, and in rare cases, writing and directing.

PAST AND FUTURE

Representation and negotiation by a third party has existed ever since people began to communicate with each other. In merry old England the official "facilitator" would, for a fee, match up people who wanted audiences with important officials or royalty. In the United States, the profit-centric efforts of large, monopolistic movie studios in the early 1930s and 1940s demanded the rise of agents to protect the interests of stars. For example, in 1937 and 1938, Mickey Rooney's films outsold those of Clark Gable and any other Hollywood icon; he was paid (through a non-agent-negotiated deal) $2,000 a week. While good money at the time, the studios made nearly $240,000 a week from his films.

While the Michael Ovitzes of this industry are still powerful players, they no longer control the flow of talent as they once did. Some think the migration of established stars will expand the market to allow smaller agencies who are hungrier and more attentive to their clients' needs to thrive. Others feel that these small agencies will rise initially, and then fall as they become large enough for the major agencies to notice, then crush them. In either case, the role of the agent is secure.

QUALITY OF LIFE

Two Years

Administrative duties fill the first two years of aspiring agents' lives as they learn the stock-and-trade of the agenting business. New agents familiarize themselves with contracts, the pace of negotiations, client interaction, and the means of pursuing new clients. Many new agents aggressively pursue unknown talent, taking risks that later would be unthinkable. A large number of agents (30 percent by some measures) leave the profession because of dissatisfaction with the lack of glamour, the pace of progress, and the menial responsibilities the job offers. Hours are long, and pay is low.

Five Years

Client contact has increased considerably, and those who began at large firms either become "senior agents" or leave to start their own firms (a solid 18 percent). Most agents who found their own firms do so within four to nine years after beginning in the profession. Satisfaction at this stage in the career depends on the person's suitability to their chosen field and their success in their chosen area of specialization. Fifteen percent leave, lured by promotional, publicity, or public relations departments, and their siren song of consistent and solid paychecks. Hours have increased, but pay has as well.

Ten Years

Many agents go independent by this point (35 percent); those who remain at larger firms guide less experienced agents. Mentoring was cited by a majority of ten-year survivors as important to the sense of satisfaction. Agents now have scads of direct client contact, and head up campaigns to recruit new clients. Interpersonal skills are supplanted by financial and directional decision-making abilities as the primary concern of ten-year-vets.

THE BIRKMAN LIFESTYLE GRID

Red Green
Yellow Blue

This career is suitable for people with Green interests.

You'll Have Contact With

Attorneys
Producers
Publicists
Publishers

Major Associations

Professional Arts Management Institute
110 Riverside Drive
Suite 4E
New York, NY 10024
Tel: 212-245-3850

Association of Authors' Representatives
10 Astor Place
3rd Floor
New York, NY 10003
Tel: 212-353-3709

Association of Talent Agents
9255 Sunset Boulevard
Suite 318
Los Angeles, CA 90069
Tel: 310-274-0628
Fax: 310-274-5063

ANIMATOR

A DAY IN THE LIFE

Nearly everyone has seen some animated sequences in their life, whether it was in a science-class filmstrip or a Saturday morning cartoon. Animators create sequences of motion-based art that tell a story or communicate a message. Some animators are graphic artists who draw "cells," which are individual pictures that are strung together to create the illusion of motion. The majority are computer or "technical" animators, whose jobs require less graphic design expertise but more familiarity with animation programs such as Macromedia's Director and other, less commercial ones.

Nearly all animators work as part of a team and have a specific area of specialization. The low wages and the struggle to emerge as individually talented are difficult obstacles to overcome. Another more formidable one is having to constantly produce work to someone else's specifications and rely on their approval or disapproval. For creative people (a common trait of those who are attracted to the profession), this is the intellectual equivalent of a straightjacket. An animator can work on certain characters, scenes, or sequences, but others have the job of assembling these pieces into a coherent whole. Scripting and planning are critical to success for the large-picture animator. Most animation jobs are in commercials (of which over 20 percent have animated sequences) and cartoons.

Many people spend their own money (between $5,000 and $125,000) producing short, animated movies that showcase their talents, and then enter these in animation competitions, hoping to receive exposure and financial reward. These festivals have grown in reputation and importance over the past ten years, and it is considered a significant feather in one's cap to have received an award at one of them. Some animators begin their own production companies, and recruit funds to develop their own animated products, usually for either foreign markets, sample shorts, or animation festivals.

PAYING YOUR DUES

As in most fine arts fields, no formal education or training is required; if you are talented and are able to get your work viewed, you stand a reasonable chance of finding a job. But it is extremely difficult to achieve the level of professionalism expected in this industry without study. A bachelor's or graduate degree in graphic design with an emphasis on computer skills is extremely helpful in getting interviews or portfolio reviews. Certain universities offer specific one-semester courses in computer animation on Oxberry Animation Cameras (the kind that filmed *Fantasia*), or using Silicon Graphics computer work stations with 2- and 3-D software (the kind used in *Jurassic Park* and *The Mask*). The most important thing for an aspiring animator is that your work be of exceptional quality, and to that end, many would-be animators intern or work for little pay to learn the craft at the side of established animators, game designers, and programmers. As with most creative fine arts fields, the supply of people wanting to become animators exceeds the demand; therefore, positions are competitive. The rate of success in the field is low, but those who do achieve it are extremely satisfied.

ASSOCIATED CAREERS

Producing animated sequences is like producing any complicated art-and-technology product, so many people who leave the profession go on to software development and design. Some continue on to work on mainstream movies, cartoons, commercials, illustration, or any area that emphasizes their strongest animation skill.

PAST AND FUTURE

It is impossible to mention the history of animation without mentioning Walt Disney. His popularization of the animated form, through such groundbreaking strips as the "Steamboat Willie" character (which later became Mickey Mouse), and the classic features *Snow White* and *Cinderella*, defined the form and intertwined a sense of magic with the American entertainment experience. Disney Studios still produce what are regarded in the industry as the top-quality commercial animation products.

The marketplace success of *Aladdin* and *Toy Story* have spurred other companies to produce more animated features, and the trend in that direction should continue through the end of the decade. The majority of work in the industry, however, is in commercial work, animating small sequences in limited portions of 30-second spots. Animated commercial sequences have been entering the marketplace at a substantial and increasing pace; the future of animation will be determined by how far the technology can progress and how receptive audiences are to the influx of more well-produced animation.

QUALITY OF LIFE

Two Years

Many animators learn the necessary skills traveling from job to job. Exposure to the various sides of animation—sketches, drawings, computer skills, voice-dubbing technology—lead the young professional to a greater understanding of how the whole film is developed. The skills critical to success in this business—understanding the technology, working with computers, and film production—are learned while assisting with responsibilities such as production coordination, background design and progress tracking. The pay is low and the hours are long, but this period of "dues-paying" is critical to learning the process.

Five Years

Animators begin to get real and complete areas of responsibility. Full animation, individual client responsibility, and concept design are all part of the job. Animators hone their filmmaking skills—story development, directing, cinematography, and editing—as they apply to the task of animation. Many are in charge of location-scouting for the pre-production work that marks many of the larger-scale projects, such as *Pocahontas* and *Beauty and the Beast*. Hours skyrocket; pay increases and can rise significantly for those with a strong record of achievement.

Ten Years

Those who have survived ten years in this occupation (around 20 percent of those who began in it) run projects and have complete responsibility for final products. Many find their advancement moves them from the nuts-and-bolts of animating to more of an oversight and administrative position, where responsibilities include budgeting and scheduling. Industry reputations and networking are the lifeblood of smaller, more commercial houses that produce small animated sequences for commercials in about three months; large houses produce feature films, which may take two to three years before release. Pay increases significantly, but tends to level off after this. Satisfaction in the profession, at this level, is high.

THE BIRKMAN LIFESTYLE GRID

This career is suitable for people with Blue interests.

You'll Have Contact With
Artists
Computer Programmers
Producers
Voice Actors

Major Associations
The American Institute of Graphic Arts
164 5th Avenue
New York, NY 10010
Tel: 212-807-1990
Fax: 212-807-1799
Contact: Human Resources

Women in Animation/NY
330 West 45th Street
New York, NY 10036
Tel: 212-765-3030
Fax: 212-765-2727
Contact: Human Resources

Society of Illustrators
128 East 63rd Street
New York, NY 10021
Tel: 212-838-2560
Fax: 212-838-2560

ANTHROPOLOGIST

A DAY IN THE LIFE

Anthropologists examine, analyze, report on, and compare different cultures and how they grow, develop and interact. How people live and what their cultures are and were like offer insights into modern life and how significantly (or, more often, how little) we have changed as a people and how similar we are in our basic systems of interaction. Anthropologists can travel to exotic lands and spend time in primitive conditions or work in developed countries, such as the United States, comparing regional concerns. Cultural anthropologists might compare the culture of the medical world to that of the world of finance, or the culture of professional athletes to that of the legal profession. Some anthropologists take a cross-disciplinary approach to the field, studying linguistics, chemistry, nutrition, or behavioral science, and applying those disciplines' methodologies to their study of culture. Qualities that encourage success in this field include a nonjudgmental, inquisitive mind, patience, and the ability to make inferences from incomplete information. An individual can make discoveries working alone, unlike in other sciences where significant funding and sizable research teams are usually necessary.

Most anthropologists are employed by universities; they teach and review other's work to earn their daily bread. It is rare for an anthropologist to spend more than 15 percent of his career outside the university setting. An anthropologist spends a lot of time writing, editing, doing field work, teaching, consulting with other professionals, and producing papers for professional journals.

Anthropological research relies on the funding decisions of the federal government, universities, and foundations, the three major and nearly exclusive employers in the field. "Don't go into this profession unless you've got the stomach to play politics," said one professor; "It never gets any easier and it never gets any better." The immediate return on an investment in anthropology is impossible to quantify, and therefore hard to justify as a spending item. Anthropology is a competitive field, and those who wish to rise must find creative ways of getting their skills recognized. Successful anthropologists quickly learn successful grant-writing skills, find areas of unexplored anthropological concern, and publish articles, essays, and books as early and as often as they can. The ability to network and self-promote are important for those serious about pursuing a long-term career.

PAYING YOUR DUES

Many aspiring anthropologists work as assistants doing ground-level research and writing surveys before they have advanced degrees. College coursework should include anthropology, cultural linguistics, sociology, biology, and language (for those considering anthropology in foreign locations). Specialization happens very early on. Anthropologists must have Ph.Ds. Graduate students choose between linguistics, sociocultural anthropology, biological-physical anthropology, or archaeological anthropology. Many associate themselves with an undergraduate or graduate professor for their first field job, while others work with museums, research groups, or government programs in order to begin their careers. Candidates must bring an open mind, an ability to put others at ease, and strong communication skills.

ASSOCIATED CAREERS

Anthropology is associated with archaeology, writing, sociology, history and even geology. Many ex-anthropologists choose to specialize in one of these other scientific fields. Linguistics and ethnology (reviewing methods of communication and cultural histories) are major fields of choice for the anthropologist who finds physical anthropology less exciting. In the end, few anthropologists leave the profession because of the amount of time, resources, and intellectual energy invested in becoming an anthropologist—usually, those dissatisfied with their choice of career leave during graduate school, before their careers have truly started.

PAST AND FUTURE

Anthropology has existed since Greek times, although it only began to flourish with the rise of mercantilism and the age of exploration. Contact with other cultures and histories led to the growth of archaeology and social sciences. The growth of anthropology has also been linked to its attendant sciences such as geology, biology and sociology, as each tends to inform the others.

Anthropology is becoming smaller and more specialized. Those with strong ethnic studies and science backgrounds are being asked to gain language skills; those with language and cultural skills are asked to learn scientific and statistical skills; these additional responsibilities, while at first seeming like a broadening of one's area of responsibility, actually create small sub-specializations. Subcategories of study, particularly those with applications in current issues of the day, such as race relations or economic structure, often follow current trends and gain popularity for brief periods of overexposure, then wane. Funding uncertainties make any venture into this field a calculated risk—but one whose reward can be personally significant.

QUALITY OF LIFE

Two Years

Many aspiring anthropologists make initial connections with professors in college or graduate school to work as administrative assistants on research projects. Typical duties include reading and digesting publications for the anthropologist's review, handing out surveys and coordinating the assimilation of data, transcribing tapes, and proofreading papers. The experience beginning anthropologists get in learning how to study, review and value data becomes invaluable in the next five years. Over 20 percent leave the profession in the first two years, frustrated by these severely proscribed duties; however, the community is said to be "intensely understanding and supportive."

Five Years

Five-year survivors focus on getting published in academic journals or writing successful grant proposals. Many move to secondary collaboration positions with more established, higher profile anthropologists. Duties include interviewing, writing, reviewing and analyzing data. Many serve as mentors to entry-level assistants, giving them daily direction on duties. The majority of field work is done in these beginning years, where hours are dawn-to-dusk. Salaries rise. The life gets more trying, but the potential rewards and interest level are sky-high.

Ten Years

A select few remain in the field, their anthropological achievements well-documented and well-publicized. The majority return to university settings, teaching anthropology, working through government research grants, or working as adjunct professors under foundation grants. Many publish regularly and review the work of their peers; a notable few are named to editorial boards on industry-prestigious magazines. Some ten-year veterans act as consultants to government outreach programs and international industrial concerns. Under 3 percent leave the profession after ten years; this career satisfies those who can see through the long hours, the academic-level pay, and the initial indignities to the fulfilling interaction beyond.

THE BIRKMAN LIFESTYLE GRID

This career is suitable for people with Yellow interests.

You'll Have Contact With
Editors
Lab Technicians
Linguists
Professors

Major Associations
American Anthropological Association
4350 North Fairfax Drive, Suite 640
Arlington, VA 22203
Tel: 703-528-1902
Contact: David Givens

Wenner-Gren Foundation for
Anthropological Research
220 Fifth Avenue, 16th Floor
New York, NY 10001-7708
Tel: 212-683-5000
Fax: 212-683-9151
Contact: Dr. Sydel Silverman

The American Anthropological Association
4350 N. Fairfax Drive
Suite 640
Arlington, VA 22203
Tel: 703-528-1902

ANTIQUES DEALER

PROFESSIONAL PROFILE

# of people in profession	124,200
% male	70
% female	30
avg. hours per week	40
avg. starting salary	$18,500
avg. salary after 5 years	$27,000
avg. salary 10 to 15 years	$49,000

Professionals Read

Antiques Magazine
American Antiques
Art and Antiques

Books, Films and TV Shows Featuring the Profession

Dead Again
The Old Shoppe
Masquette

Major Employers

Christie's
502 Park Avenue
New York, NY 10022
Tel: 212-546-1000

Sotheby's
1334 York Avenue
New York, NY 10021
Tel: 212-606-7000
Fax: 212-606-7028
Contact: VP Personnel, Daryl Krimsky

Discovery Emporium
448 Amsterdam
New York, NY 10024
Tel: 212-595-4410
Fax: 212-595-4384

A DAY IN THE LIFE

An antiques dealer buys and sells antiques: art, furniture, jewelry, books, rugs, clothing, or any other item that can survive the ravages of time. While some dealers earn specific titles specializing in one type of relic, many are generalists who examine pieces of any type with historic, aesthetic, and financial value. "It is difficult to describe the life of an antiques dealer," wrote one of our respondents, "because it involves so many things. An antiques dealer must know the pieces they sell . . . the clients they sell to . . . [and how to] manage their offices [and] . . . their finances." It is difficult to become and remain an antiques dealer. Few professions require participants to exhibit such a diverse range of skills. The profession provides high levels of satisfaction at all levels for those people who are interested in history, business, psychology, and aesthetic concerns. The joys of being surrounded daily with items of financial and historical value seem to buoy many people through the long hours, the paucity of compensation, and the difficulty of achieving independence from established dealers. Many respondents had nothing but high praise for their co-workers. One referred to them as "a good resource, both intellectually and emotionally."

Antiques dealers invest substantial capital in inventory. The high level of investment means a high degree of risk and great pressure on the dealer to assess carefully the value of items before purchase and to sell items purchased aggressively. The pressure for value on both ends can translate into pressure for those working in the industry; those who are unaware of this "results-based" operation of many antique houses are surprised at the importance of the bottom line in the business. The job of an antiques dealer requires a person to trust her own understanding of a piece's value and put herself on the line every time she makes a decision. It is natural that betting on your own skills would create worry. People mentioned that if you make a mistake in overpaying for a piece, you can often "sell your way out of it," if you have the customer skills. Successful dealers rarely try to take advantage of long-term customers, however. Those relationships are based on trust.

PAYING YOUR DUES

A variety of undergraduate degrees lend themselves to becoming an antiques dealer, but no specific major is required. Art history majors enjoy the interaction with beautiful works; business students appreciate the investment and dealing aspects of the profession; history majors love the continuous education the job represents. Becoming an antiques dealer requires spending long hours inspecting pieces, visiting other antiques dealers, reviewing documentation, and researching histories. Most aspiring antiques dealers begin as interns at auction houses or at the side of established professionals and learn as assistants, take care of correspondence, make research trips to the library, and schedule appointments. An attention to detail serves the prospective antiques dealer well, as deciding the value of a piece—the most difficult aspect of being a dealer—can hinge upon a slight detail. Graduate work is less important than practical experience, and specialization can begin either midway through or late in a dealer's career.

ASSOCIATED CAREERS

Antiques dealers work with restorers, financiers, and auction houses regularly, and when they leave the profession of antique dealing (as many do) they enter these three fields more than any others. Some become professional valuation specialists, working with auction houses and other antiques dealers as appraisers. A small number of ex-antiques dealers become teachers and lecturers in graduate fine arts programs.

PAST AND FUTURE

Antiques dealers before the seventeenth century were more closely associated with archaeology, as craftsmanship of prior pieces was less interesting compared with the artisanship, patterning, and construction of artifacts from different and ancient civilizations. Beginning in the seventeenth century, though, craftsmanship emerged as the favorite means of wealthy home beautification, and this demand spurred the production of high-quality, aesthetically pleasing pieces of furniture. Within seventy years, these pieces were being sold as antiques or "specialty items."

Antique sales are one of the recession-insensitive industries, proving even more active during years of financial lassitude. Those who aspire to become part of this industry should understand that most successful antiques dealers have to have a "critical mass" of audience (client base) to make the profession self-supporting. As a result, urban or suburban antiques dealers do better than rural ones, and that trend is expected to continue.

QUALITY OF LIFE

Two Years

Two years into the profession, antiques dealers are usually working alongside an established professional, learning inventory systems, bookkeeping methodology, and payment schedules. Many assist with client contact and valuation decisions, learning the less quantifiable aspects of the profession. The hours are long and the pay is low, but the responsibility levels—in terms of inventory management and presentations—is high. A number of new dealers take art history, history, and appraisal courses.

Five Years

The majority of five-year antiques dealers have switched positions at least once during these middle years, either to learn different specialties, gain greater responsibilities, or work in a larger client community. Eight percent return to school to receive their MBAs. Most antiques dealers network with other professionals and seek out areas of opportunity during this time. Few open their own shops at this juncture; good connections are difficult to establish.

Ten Years

Ten-year veterans begin to assemble the pieces they will need to open their own shops. In many cases, that means making a bid to their current employer. One respondent mentioned that "over 90 percent of dealers think about opening their own shop, but only about 40 percent do it." This yen for independence is expected at this stage in a career. Contacts have been established, experience is strong, and dealers have matured, learning the tangible and intangible aspects of the industry. Salaries do not rise beyond this point unless people open their own shops, which encourages the mass exodus to self-employment. Of the new dealers, only around 25 percent are around after eighteen months.

THE BIRKMAN LIFESTYLE GRID

Red Green
Yellow Blue

This career is suitable for people with Green interests.

You'll Have Contact With

Appraisers
Art Historians
Auctioneers
Restorers

Major Associations

Art Dealers Association of America
575 Madison Ave.
New York, NY 10022
Tel: 212-940-8590

National Antique and Art Dealers
   Association of America
12 E. 56th St.
New York, NY 10022
Tel: 212-826-9707

ARCHAEOLOGIST

A DAY IN THE LIFE

Archaeologists excavate, preserve, study, and classify artifacts of the near and distant past in order to develop a picture of how people lived in earlier cultures and societies. The profession combines a broad understanding of history with sophisticated digging procedures and plain old hard work, making it one of the most demanding and competitive branches of the social sciences.

An archaeologist's natural curiosity about the past and the secrets it holds make the profession a fascinating one. However, the work is slow and exacting. Archaeologists may carefully dust a fragment of a Mayan temple with a toothbrush or measure and examine thousands of tiny, nearly identical chipped stone axes. Since most of the world's great archaeological sites are located in the Earth's temperate zone, archaeologists often spend long hours working in the hot sun.

Some archaeologists work under the aegis of a major research institution, such as a university or a museum. A handful are employed by major corporations whose work may lead to the destruction or displacement of rare historical artifacts. Most archaeologists are at major universities, teaching in the history, anthropology, or archaeology departments, as this is how they earn a living between research grants and excavations. When they are not teaching, many archaeologists are working on digs far from home.

PAYING YOUR DUES

The average archaeologist has a master's degree, and most archaeologists have a doctorate. Coursework valuable to a career as an archaeologist includes ancient history, anthropology, ancient languages, German, geology, geography, English composition, and human physiology. Sign up to work on your professors' archaeological digs during your vacations. Expect to perform menial tasks on these digs. With a master's degree, you may be offered an instructor's position or work on a university-sponsored dig. You'll be expected to pursue a doctorate before you can be considered for an assistant professor's job. Only the most distinguished (or lucky) archaeologists become prominent in the field, and there are fewer full professorships available than there are archaeologists to fill them. One way to draw attention to your work is by publishing articles in academic journals.

ASSOCIATED CAREERS

Archaeology is often paired with anthropology. Archaeology is the study of entire cultures and societies while anthropology is the study of the development of people within societies. In drawing their conclusions, anthropologists rely heavily on the work of archaeologists. Individuals who no longer wish to be archaeologists may join any of the various disciplines that the archaeologist must be familiar with; they may, for example, become historians, linguists, or surveyors. Corporate archaeologists may find work writing environmental impact statements.

PAST AND FUTURE

Since the eighteenth century, with the chance rediscovery of Pompei's well-preserved ruins, the systematic study of lost communities has gripped our imaginations. Napoleon's invasion of Egypt was inspired in part by a desire to explore the remnants of the remarkable culture that once thrived there, and it led directly to the discovery of the Rosetta stone. In the nineteenth century, Heinrich Schliemann fixed the location of Troy's ancient ruins as well as the ruins of Mycenae. Although it has come to light that many of Schliemann's "discoveries" had been made by others and that his excavations often destroyed as much as they unearthed, his work reminded historians that the mythology of the distant past had more than a grain of truth to it.

Hoping to avoid Schliemann's errors, Howard Carter approached his work with a careful eye for procedure and detail. Not only did his discovery of King Tut's Tomb cause a worldwide sensation, but it also involved one of the first uses of modern archaeological techniques. Later in the twentieth century, discoveries made in Mexico led to a complete reappraisal of ancient Mayan culture, dispelling many long-standing myths. Today's broad interest in the history of disparate and distant regions has opened up new avenues of opportunity for archaeologists everywhere. Contemporary archaeologists pursue these avenues eagerly, in an effort to outpace the encroachment of modern industrial society and prevent the secrets of the past from being lost forever.

QUALITY OF LIFE

Two Years

Halfway through your undergraduate years, be prepared to plunge into the study of archaeology. Because of the profession's numerous requirements, it will take at least two years of specific and related courses to generate a transcript that will get you into the archaeology department of a well-known graduate school. Since entry into the field is very competitive, your graduate school's reputation and its involvement in current archaeological exploration are important. Obtain as much field experience as you can.

Five Years

Master's and doctoral candidates in archaeology pursue their studies and work for their graduate school department. Museums, excavations, and classrooms are all places where graduate students work to gain experience. Hours are long because students must complete their studies and work at the same time. Remuneration is slight, and graduate students rely on grants and other financial aid.

Ten Years

Archaeologists add the role of manager to their many duties. Full professors must publish regularly and make discoveries that justify the expenses that their excavations incur. In addition, archaeologists staff and operate their excavations, which often involves coping with the business practices of distant countries, where customs may be quite different. Respected archaeologists have greater opportunity to select and develop their own projects and follow their own curiosity.

THE BIRKMAN LIFESTYLE GRID

This career is suitable for people with Yellow interests.

You'll Have Contact With
Anthropologists
Researchers
Sociologists
Translators

Major Associations
Archaeological Institute of America
656 Beacon Street
Boston, MA 02215-2010
Tel: 617-353-9361
Fax: 617-353-6550
Contact: Elise Ramsey

Society of American Archaeology
900 2nd Street NE
Suite 12
Washington, DC 20002-3557
Tel: 202-789-8200
Fax: 202-789-0284
Contact: Brighid Brady-de Lambert

Center for American Archaeology
P.O. Box 22
Kampsville, IL 62053
Tel: 618-653-4316
Fax: 618-653-4232
Contact: Jodie O'Gorman

ARCHITECT

A DAY IN THE LIFE

Most people enter architecture with a vision, a desire to build, and a pre-discovered engineering ability; unfortunately, most architects don't get to exercise any of these skills until many years after entering the profession. Beginning architects research zoning, building codes, and legal filings, draft plans from others' designs, and build models at the side of a more experienced architect. The accomplished architect doesn't spend as much time as he would like designing, either; he spends it on the phone, in meetings, and consulting closely with his clients. Of the people we surveyed, each was surprised by the amount of time they had to spend "selling" or "explaining" their ideas. The most financially successful architects seemed to be the ones best at communicating their unique vision.

Becoming an architect is a long process; spending years as a draftsman or researcher leads those without patience to grow frustrated and dissatisfied with their choice of career. Even after the grueling "weeding out" period, surviving as a working architect is difficult. Most architecture firms employ five or fewer people, and the work firms do is mostly commercial or pre-planned residential housing with strict budget and practical limitations. Only a select few architects get to "design" in the way that most budding architects imagine they will. Perpetual revision of plans based on client needs, contractor inefficiency, and budget strictures are daily features of the architect's life. Plans and priorities have to be re-evaluated daily and revised accordingly. One architect said, "Practically every plan you draft will look something like what you build, but don't count on it." A successful architect needs talent, practical, interpersonal, and organizational skills, and most of all, patience.

PAYING YOUR DUES

The requirements for becoming an architect are stringent because, like an attorney or a physician, an architect must take all legal responsibility for his work. A prospective architect must complete an academic degree specifically focused on architecture. This can be a five-year Bachelor of Architecture program, an affiliated two-year Master of Architecture program, or, for those whose undergraduate degrees were in a field unassociated with architecture, a three- to four-year Master of Architecture program (one architect we surveyed received a bachelor's degree in Animal Behavior). Nearly all states require three years of practice in the field as a junior associate, draftsman, or researcher before you are eligible for accreditation. Aspiring architects must also have an accredited sponsor. Last, each candidate must pass all sections of the Architect Registration Exam (ARE), a rigorous multi-part test. Greater emphasis is now placed by employers on those applicants who have mastered computer assisted design (CAD) programs, which promise to become required knowledge for any architect as technology continues to develop.

ASSOCIATED CAREERS

Architects move into a variety of careers and often delve into different careers simultaneously with their architectural duties. Once architects have reached a level of professional achievement, some go on to teach at universities, lecture, and write books. Many get involved in public design debates and discussions. Some move to private design firms, including furniture, housewares, and product design. Architects frequently work as consultants to projects already underway, advising on such details as materials, construction, and scheduling.

PAST AND FUTURE

Architecture reflects the times and people the architect emerges from; the cultural signature of man has been found on every structure built by humans. Greek societies focused on aesthetic and mathematical harmonies, as displayed in their architecture, such as the Parthenon. Renaissance Italy created ornate public buildings and palaces reflecting the country's wealth.

Modern architecture as a profession seems to be heading in two directions at once. First, advancements in the technology of computer aids should improve the productivity and creative capabilities of architects. Some believe this computerized "evening" of the tables (small and large firms alike will use the same software) will lead to a great democratization of architecture, with many more architects being able to handle and coordinate massive construction projects. Others believe that since job prospects are driven by local construction cycles, the future of architecture is tied to the future of local economies. In the future, architects must be willing to relocate for periods of time to find work, must become involved in electronic communications where design and theory meet, and will work under less generous conditions than currently enjoyed by the profession.

QUALITY OF LIFE

Two Years

In the first two years, prospective architects work as interns or research assistants to established architects, with salaries in the low twenty-thousand-dollar range. Duties include researching zoning regulations, working with subcontractors (electricians, plumbers, etc.), and drafting plans, either manually or with computer assistance. Long hours and little responsibility characterize these first few years, when many study for the ARE. Nearly 25 percent leave the profession.

Five Years

Responsibility and areas of control have increased. Finally, candidates get a chance to design parts of a building (a bathroom, a closet). Others are given areas of responsibility (lighting, heating, air conditioning), and work with partners or senior associates learning the practical end of turning plans into production. These five-year survivors get their first taste of client contact and, in many cases, become the primary contacts on smaller jobs. Most work with contractors and inspect work to make sure it matches up with plans. Some are involved in planning and pitching new contracts, depending on their interpersonal skills. Hours increase with responsibility, and another 20 percent decide to leave the occupation, based on either frustration with the slow degree of advancement or difficulty with the ARE. Those who remain become accredited between years three and seven.

Ten Years

Those who last ten years in this profession are competent designers and coordinators, able to recruit business, successfully communicate with clients, and distinguish themselves professionally. Architects at this stage of their careers are more involved in designing and creative planning, and less involved in implementation, construction, and detail work. They've become supervisors and teachers to newer entrants to the profession. Some re–enter academia either to pursue graduate work or teach basic architectural studies. But self-employed architects always remember that they have only as much work as their clients give them: Recruiting business and self-promotion are an integral part of the successful ten-year-surviving architect's life.

THE BIRKMAN LIFESTYLE GRID

This career is suitable for people with Red interests.

You'll Have Contact With

Construction Managers
Civil Engineers
Draftsmen
Structural Engineers

Major Associations

American Institute of Architects,
New York Chapter
200 Lexington Avenue
New York, NY 10016
Tel: 212-683-0023

Associated Landscape
Contractors of America
12200 Sunrise Valley Drive
Suite 150
Reston, VA 22091
Tel: 703-620-6363
Fax: 703-620-6365
Contact: Roy Saunders

National Architectural Accrediting Board
1735 New York Avenue, NW
Washington, DC 20006
Tel: 202-783-2007

ART DEALER

PROFESSIONAL PROFILE

# of people in profession	6,000
% male	50
% female	50
avg. hours per week	50
avg. starting salary	$30,000
avg. salary after 5 years	$70,000
avg. salary 10 to 15 years	$175,000

Professionals Read

Art Direction
Journal of Contemporary Art
American Art Review
Art Forum

Books, Films and TV Shows Featuring the Profession

Legal·Eagles
Missing Monet
9 1/2 Weeks

Major Employers

Christie's
502 Park Avenue
New York, NY 10022
Tel: 212-546-1000
Contact: Kitty Ijams

Sotheby's
1334 York Avenue
New York, NY 10021
Tel: 212-606-7000
Fax: 212-606-7028
Contact: Daryl Krimsky

Leo Castelli Gallery
420 West Broadway
New York, NY 10013
Tel: 212-431-5160
Contact: Representation Department

A DAY IN THE LIFE

In general, a person becomes an art dealer because he has a passion for art. The pleasure that comes with making a living combined with the freedom of owning one's own business can make this an extremely gratifying career. Successful art dealers have the ability to cultivate a network of artists and simultaneously establish connections with collectors and museums who are interested in the work of their artists. The very best dealers develop reputations for anticipating swings in taste and value. Some seem to be able to create demand for an artist by simply agreeing to represent her. Most dealers specialize in a period, style, or type of art, such as Eighteenth-century painting, works of the New York School, or contemporary sculpture. All dealers must keep up with developments in the art world, particularly in their areas of specialty, so their careers depend upon maintaining a wide range of contacts among critics, curators, auction houses, artists, and collectors. This is a career for the social-minded person, since much of the business is conducted at openings and in sales proposals made to collectors and museum curators. Most successful art dealers enjoy spending time with people in the art world and cultivating contacts with people who are interested in art.

Art markets are notoriously volatile, and the fortunes of gallery owners rise and fall with the markets. In the most recent crash, which occurred in 1990, art prices fell 30 to 50 percent and seventy out of New York City's 500 art galleries were forced to close. Galleries that develop reputations for representing specific styles see their fortunes rise and fall as tastes change, and anticipating these changes is difficult, even for the most experienced professionals. The pleasures and possibilities for huge profits in the profession seem to offer rewards that balance the risks in art dealing, however. Many dealers have long and successful careers, and there is a steady supply of those whose taste and talent in the art world leads them to establish galleries.

PAYING YOUR DUES

There are many paths to becoming an art dealer; almost all involve some participation in the art world. Many dealers begin with degrees in art history and work their ways up as assistants in other galleries, developing the contacts with clients and artists to enable them to strike out on their own. Others are former museum and auction house curators who decide to establish galleries specializing in the areas of art in which they have worked. Some artists discover that they have the business and social skills necessary to sell art, and they use their contacts with other artists to develop a body of work to represent.

As with any entrepreneurial venture, strong business and sales skills are a must. Most of the revenue earned by a typical gallery is generated by personal sales pitches to prospective buyers; this demands sales and social skills different from those that would be required to run a corner hardware store. Access to capital is also vital; gallery cash flow is variable. To survive in the long run, a gallery must be able to withstand dry spells. Frequently, galleries are partnerships in which one partner contributes capital and the other contributes the connections and knowledge to successfully operate the business.

ASSOCIATED CAREERS

Gallery owners whose galleries don't succeed often remain in the art world. Some go to work for other, more successful galleries, while others pursue careers as museum or auction curators, art critics, academics, or practicing artists. Some who are hit by downturns in the art market use one or more of these options to weather the storm and then reestablish their galleries when times improve.

PAST AND FUTURE

For as long as there have been artists and buyers of art, there have been dealers, providing access to and information about the art world to those who wish to invest in or acquire art. The profession has existed in Europe since the Middle Ages, though galleries, providing a place for the public to come and view a dealer's stock, are a more recent innovation. Many of the best known and longest lasting art galleries in the United States were originally founded in the 1920s, as American wealth in the world and greater post-war exposure to Europe created a wave of interest in art investment that caused the auction and gallery markets to grow significantly. Like all art booms, this one passed and was followed by other rises and falls. It is unlikely that the future will be any different, but galleries will persist as long as there is a demand for art.

QUALITY OF LIFE

Two Years

The art dealer develops connections with the artists, collectors, and curators who will be crucial to her gallery's success. Much depends upon decisions made at this point; the most successful dealers are those who can anticipate tidal swings in the world of artistic taste. Signing up artists who will be hot a decade hence is a sure-fire recipe for success. Of course, knowing which artists will be successful a decade hence is what distinguishes the talented and lucky dealers from the rest.

Five Years

By now, the dealer who has stayed in business has a network of buyers and artists. She has survived at least one swing in the art market and can start to look forward to the luxury of developing long-term dealer-buyer relationships. Her gallery is by no means mature, however, and the search for new talent that fits her buyers' tastes continues.

Ten Years

A gallery that lasts for ten years has staying power, the ability to establish values that can weather the storms of the art market. In other words, the dealer who makes it this long has begun to establish a reputation, perhaps the most valuable commodity in the art world. The dealer's challenge is to maintain his network of buyers, which often includes museum curators by now, and to continue to anticipate the vagaries of the art market.

THE BIRKMAN LIFESTYLE GRID

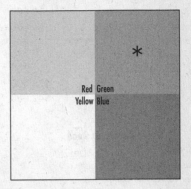

This career is suitable for people with Green interests.

You'll Have Contact With

Artists
Bankers
Event Planners
Publicists

Major Associations

Art Dealers Association of America
575 Madison Ave.
New York, NY 10022
Tel: 212-940-8590

National Antique and Art Dealers
Association of America
12 E. 56 St.
New York, NY 10022
Tel: 212-826-9707

ARTIST

A DAY IN THE LIFE

"If you're lucky, you'll spend most of your time alone and working," wrote one twenty-year veteran painter. Trying to express a specific and unique vision through painting, sculpture, drawing, or mixed media characterizes the artist's life. While many spend time in workshops, attending other artists' shows and seminars, and doing research, the heart of the matter—the reason why people choose to join the unremunerative and very selective fine arts—is because they love what they do. As a purely self-expressing career, 90 percent of artists make, on average, under $1,000 per annum on their art. The financial rewards come to few, and generally later in life. The work itself and the supportive community make this financially uncertain lifestyle worthwhile.

The frustration that can accompany this profession is significant. Unscrupulous gallery owners and untrustworthy agents can make an artist's life difficult, to say the least. Most artists use their specific set of marketable tools as freelance commercial artists, producing work on consignment to another's specifications, to pay the rent. Some note that this "selling" of their skills at times affects their ability to produce their own work. "It's hard to paint my own pictures when I'm sketching a box of oats all day," said one. But a commercial artist can earn as much as $40,000 per year in part-time work. Many artists return to school to learn the possibilities of computer and computer-enhanced art. This is only one of the ways in which artists engage themselves with the frontiers of their world. It is this openness to the world at large, the many changes that take place in it, and the multiple possibilities that it offers that, in the end, is the hallmark of the profession of artist.

PAYING YOUR DUES

History is rife with examples of self-schooled artists with no formal educational training who are both brilliant and innovative; unfortunately, history is also rife with examples of starving artists, dying in obscurity. Formal educational training in this field is becoming the norm, with most earning BFAs in graphic design, painting, or art history. Some find it helpful to continue their education and earn graduate degrees (primarily MFAs), particularly if they desire to teach painting at the secondary level or above. Many academic programs provide at least an introduction to computer-assisted art. Artists tend to congregate around major urban centers, such as New York and San Francisco, where the multiplicity of galleries and artists makes it easier to form working connections and for an unproven artist to get shown.

ASSOCIATED CAREERS

Artists have a number of opportunities available to them, both during their careers as artists and after they've decided to hang up their brushes. Many work as commercial artists, computer artists, and electronic layout consultants using their aesthetic and representational skills in higher-paying professions. Some become art directors for magazines, on-line services, software companies, publishing houses and manufacturers. Others move into advertising, promotion and product design.

PAST AND FUTURE

Art has been practiced for ages, as evidenced, for instance, by the animal drawings discovered in caves in Lascaux, France, which date back to 30,000 B.C. Portraiture has a long European history as an honored profession, and one of the greatest supporters of the arts through the ages has been the Catholic Church (also, at times, one of the most strident critics). Commercial art, as a separate industry, arose with the advent of the modern advertising industry, and produces over 75 percent of all art available for view in the United States in every year.

The methods and mediums of art may change, but the intention has remained the same: To reinvent, to communicate in a new and fascinating way. In the future, the role that art plays will not change drastically, but painting, photography, sketching, sculpting, metalworking, and many other historically used mediums will be joined by computer art, mixed-media art and other emerging forms that will reflect the ages from which they emerge. The real danger to the prospective artist lies in the future of funding for the arts, both individually and societal. The National Endowment for the Arts faces drastic slashing of funds; tax proposals may eliminate the tax advantages of private contributions; universities are reducing art staffs. Patrons, dealers and collectors may exert an even greater influence over the life of the artist. Some degree of support for the arts will always continue—the level, however, is uncertain.

QUALITY OF LIFE

Two Years

Most artists spend their first few years learning their craft and making connections. Many seek other employment, as these early years are marked by little or no income from their own art. Hours are long, but many say that in these early years, the long hour is more spent on examining other people's art, making introductions to dealers and critics, and networking through the art community rather than producing their own work. Many take classes, join workshops, and use this time to explore their craft.

Five Years

Many five-year survivors have had their art shown and reviewed and made significant connections in the art world. A number of those who have received some good reviews are now sponsored by dealers, galleries or agents. They continue to work at their craft and concentrate on producing art. Most artists at this point have found consistent ways to pay the rent.

Ten Years

For those who have lasted ten years and received little praise, remember that there is no fixed timeline for progression as an artist. The sense of frustration, however, is significant for those who haven't received much positive encouragement. Those who remain may experience "second life blues," where initial success has been tempered by the difficulty of following up and reinventing. Those with good connections and excellent reputations may find themselves gaining academic, teaching, or colony credentials. A number of artists at this age apply for and receive grants from the NEA and other funding sources. While ten years is a significant milestone in a number of professions, as an artist, timing is nothing; continuing and evolving is everything.

THE BIRKMAN LIFESTYLE GRID

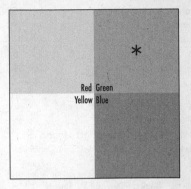

This career is suitable for people with Green interests.

You'll Have Contact With

Art Dealers
Agents
Advertising Executives
Product Designers
Curators

Major Associations

American Design and Drafting Association
PO Box 799
Rockville, MD 20848-0799
Tel: 301-460-6875
Contact: Rachel Howard

American Institute of Graphic Arts
1059 Third Avenue
New York, NY 10021
Tel: 212-807-1990
Fax: 212-807-1799
Contact: Publication Department

New York Artists Equity Association
498 Broome Street
New York, NY 10013
Tel: 212-941-0130

ASTRONAUT

A DAY IN THE LIFE

Astronauts command spacecraft and high-altitude vehicles that venture into space. Astronauts come from a variety of fields, train for a year or two on the chance of being chosen as a member of a shuttle crew, and then return to their original jobs. They rise early and work late into the night, training for potential space missions during which as many hours as possible will be utilized for intensive experimentation. This stamina comes in handy. Most astronauts only sleep for five hours at a time on their missions. Astronauts-in-training participate in scenarios that simulate weightlessness, heavy gravity (excessive G-forces) and navigate nature's call in an unbroachable interstellar suit. Intensive psychological screening, required of all applicants, is supposed to weed out those with claustrophobia, but one or two are discovered annually in the program and dismissed. Other unusual skills astronauts learn include eating and drinking through straws, washing their entire bodies with a hand cloth, and sleeping in a noisy environment, buckled to a bed so they don't float around the craft uncontrollably. Nearly every basic task taken for granted on earth offers unusual difficulties in space and must be relearned. This retraining of basic skills is a difficult coming-down for those scientists—many of whom are Ph.D.s—who are used to navigating more intellectual and more ostensibly difficult tasks. Roughly ten candidates per year are asked to leave because they cannot master these basic maneuvers.

The ability to focus is the most important feature of the successful astronaut, but the ability to make choices under pressured and limited-option situations is also important. In only rare circumstances does an Apollo 13-type crisis situation come to pass; more often, the most difficult decision an astronaut faces is how to juggle a variety of experiments in limited time. Members of shuttle launches (the only space missions of the 1990s) overschedule their time in the event that their mission is delayed; since this is often the case, every potential free moment is scheduled.

The ability to work as part of a team is enormously important, and much of the training associated with becoming an astronaut focuses on developing this team mentality and working together in a cramped environment. The rigorous training fosters a strong sense of camaraderie. While only a few make the final cut to be members of a space-bound crew (the constituency is based on the needs of the mission), over one hundred people train at any given time at the Johnson Space Center, in Houston, Texas. They live, train, eat and exercise together, many of them working in concert on research projects that have components that can only be completed in space. The environment is said to be supportive and mutually encouraging, partly because each astronaut has no idea who will be picked to be a crew member on the next mission, and who they might be paired with.

PAYING YOUR DUES

Nearly every child dreams, at one time or another, of becoming an astronaut, but few carry this dream through to adulthood, and for a good reason: It's damn tough to become an astronaut. Requirements include an excellent academic record (undergraduate and graduate) in any of a number of scientific fields, including aerospace engineering, medicine, biology, chemistry, physics, astronomy, optics, and computer science. Candidates are usually very accomplished in another field before they apply to become astronauts. They must be in excellent shape physically and mentally, between 5'4" and 6'4" tall, and be willing to spend a full year training for a space mission. They must also be willing to brave the odds, because in any given year, the greatest number of NASA astronauts that has been assigned to a flight was sixteen. Their year of rigorous training offers no guarantee of being assigned as a crew member on a mission. Most importantly, applicants must pass the NASA standards for astronauts, which includes jet-pilot qualifications and flight experience, a rigorous security check and an in-depth personality profile. The average shuttle launch costs one billion—that's right, BILLION—dollars. Since NASA is footing the bill, they tend to be quite selective about who they offer seats to. Of the eleven to twelve thousand people each year who apply to become astronauts, only between one and two hundred make it through the difficult screening.

ASSOCIATED CAREERS

Most return to research, teaching, flying, or the military, whatever their occupations were prior to becoming an astronaut; a few, like Senator John Glenn, enter politics. The major difference between becoming an astronaut and going into other professions is that the former is an end in and of itself. One does not progress or advance from being an astronaut; one returns to normal life. Astronauts occasionally become celebrities due to their unusual status, and a few parlay their fame into media-supported careers.

PAST AND FUTURE

The career of astronaut began in fiction in the 1800s and as an intellectual exercise in 1923, with the publication of the book *The Rocket into Interplanetary Space*, which described the potential problems with space travel. In October of 1957, the cold war between the U.S. and the U.S.S.R. heated up with the Russian launch of *Sputnik I*, the first orbiting satellite. Just twelve years later, American Neil Armstrong became the first human to set foot on the moon. Beginning in 1981, the space shuttle became the vehicle of choice for cross-atmosphere travel.

The duties of an astronaut should change with increasing technology, but since future opportunities for the improvement of existing systems depend on more flights, and because these flights are extremely expensive, any anticipated increase in the number of astronauts would be optimistic. Budget restrictions tend to cut back on the most immediately nonprofitable segments first. NASA has never shown a direct profit, but their unique ability to place satellites into orbit and do unusual zero-gravity scientific experiments mean that some level of funding will continue.

QUALITY OF LIFE

As astronauts are only astronauts for a year or two of training, quality of life issues as the career progresses are inapplicable.

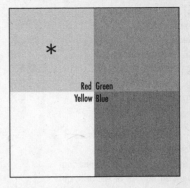

ASTRONOMER

A DAY IN THE LIFE

One would think that staring at the stars and pondering the interactions of large bodies of matter would involve a life of quiet contemplation, removed from the petty day-to-day distractions of the working world. But if one were to voice that opinion at a convention of astronomers, one would be ridden out on a rail. Astronomers track, study and review data of energy emitted from stars, movements of planetary bodies, and the interactions between these two phenomena. This highly cerebral environment requires a person attentive to detail, willing to work with others, and able to play political academic games.

Large telescopes (usually radio telescopes) track interstellar phenomena, collect light from distant starts, sense radioactive emissions, and locate and identify new stellar bodies. Astronomers collect and analyze this data and work with astrophysicists and mathematicians to find better ways of describing the interaction between various bodies of stellar matter and energy. Much work is done using computers to examine how received data matches against expected data; those who have computer skills have a significant edge in the early years of this profession. One professor described the life this way: "We search for all the wonder the universe has to offer by examining every corner and every edge the universe presents us, and yet we are surprised, because in truth, some of the universe we do not understand." Most astronomy jobs are with observatories and universities with large computing departments. Observatory jobs usually involve some communication and/or operation with the academic community. It is not unusual for an astronomer to do research at an observatory while also employed as an instructor in an astronomy department. Those who are not associated with universities are employed by research institutions, planetariums, or as consultants for other areas of scientific inquiry, such as electronic communication technology.

PAYING YOUR DUES

Only around 175 American universities offer astronomy as a degree on the undergraduate level, and around sixty offer study on the graduate level, so as each university reaps a new crop of graduates, competition increases for the few faculty and research positions available. A Ph.D. is generally required to work in the field. Only those students with strong undergraduate backgrounds in physics, math and computer science find the graduate work manageable. Close associations with professors during undergraduate and graduate work account for many of the initial positions people attain in the field. Working under close supervision, aspiring astronomers can anticipate long hours, extensive number crunching, and some teaching assistantship work—the latter may entail grading undergraduate papers and tests. Once they receive their doctorates, competition among Ph.D.s for positions is intense. For those astronomers who wish to rise in the profession, publishing academic articles is important; being assigned to government research panels is another significant achievement. Satisfaction among those employed in this field is, on the average, strong.

ASSOCIATED CAREERS

Astronomers who leave go into a variety of professions where their science training can be put to use. Refugees from astronomy enter physics, astrophysics, computer science, high-altitude physics research programs, and space exploration programs.

PAST AND FUTURE

The Mayans, the Babylonians, and the Egyptians all used calendar systems based on the stars. The heliocentric theory of the universe, proposed by Nicolaus Copernicus in 1543, gave birth to modern astronomy, allowing experimental data to match cleanly with expected results. Twentieth-century technology, such as radio telescopes, spectroscopy measurements of background radiation shifts, and neutrino detection devices, has added to the basic work of Newton, Kepler, Galileo, and Edwin Hubbell.

Most agree that the future of astronomy lies in the marriage of technological advances, which can probe further into the unknown, and breakthroughs in theoretical modeling. Astronomers have untold numbers of questions about the universe, and only with more refined and farther-reaching experimental data will they be able to begin to address them. Funding, however, defines how much and how positive the future direction of astronomy will be.

QUALITY OF LIFE

Two Years

Most two-year astronomers still have not completed graduate school and work as research assistants, teaching assistants, and graders. Many came to the attention of their professors as undergraduates who excelled in their classes. Daily duties divide the time of the beginning astronomer between the observatory and the classroom. Beginning astronomers often spend three to six nights per week at the observatory, mapping the night sky and being "on call" for any unusual events in the sky. Those who work for the government spend these early years as "assistants" on large-scale long-term government astronomy projects, usually dealing with phenomena in our own solar system. Hours are long; pay is limited or in the form of academic credits.

Five Years

The five-year survivor becomes involved in the planning and development stages of research projects (although full professors and more experienced astronomers still have final say). "Assistants" become "associates." Many who have had success are moved into more project-manager type jobs rather than the research and number crunching they were doing in the first two years. Teaching assistantships have either evolved into teaching positions or been offered to other more promising candidates. The two most accurate bellwethers of success in this field at the five-year stage are the number of articles published in quality astronomy journals and the number of research projects that are approved for funding. Between years two and seven the greatest migration from this profession takes place—around thirty percent. Hours increase, as does pay, but the most significant aspect of these years is that hands-on responsibility increases.

Ten Years

Ten-year survivors fall into two categories: the shooting stars, who become tenured professors, research institution heads, and observatory managers because of their professional reputations and their record of performance, and the workhorses, who have strong records of being team players at research institutions and observatories. The workhorses usually have areas of specialty, such as in exotic phenomena, or spectroscopy analysis. Many shooting stars publish books, lecture, and lead conferences on their area of expertise. Others remain as tenured professors at universities. Duties include setting research agendas, approving grant proposals, acting as consultants to NASA, participating in international astronomy organizations, and serving on government panels in the sciences. Ten-year veterans may find themselves in the unusual position of dealing less with the science of astronomy and more with the politics of academic and governmental funding.

THE BIRKMAN LIFESTYLE GRID

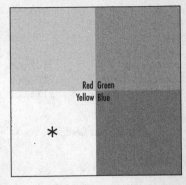

Red Green
Yellow Blue

*

This career is suitable for people with Yellow interests.

You'll Have Contact With

Computer Programmers
Mathematicians
Physicists
Researchers

Major Associations

American Physical Society, American Center for Physics
1 Physics Ellipse
College Park, MD 20740-3844
Tel: 301-209-3100
Fax: 301-209-0847
Contact: Theresa Braun

American Astronomical Society,
University of Texas
RLM 15.308, University of Texas
Austin, TX 78712
Tel: 512-471-3000
Fax: 512-471-6016

PROFESSIONAL PROFILE

# of people in profession	626,000
% male	70
% female	30
avg. hours per week	50
avg. starting salary	$42,000
avg. salary after 5 years	$79,000
avg. salary 10 to 15 years	$134,000

Professionals Read

Various Law Reviews
ABA Journal
National Law Journal

Books, Films and TV Shows Featuring the Profession

To Kill a Mockingbird
The Firm
The Verdict
Inherit the Wind

Major Employers

Weil Gotshal & Manges
767 5th Avenue
New York, NY 10153
Tel: 212-310-8000
Fax: 212-310-8007
Contact: Stephen Reiss

Sidley & Austin
One First Street National Plaza
Chicago, IL 60603
Tel: 312-853-7000
Fax: 312-853-7036
Contact: Sally Wilcock

Simpson, Thatcher & Bartlett
425 Lexington Avenue
New York, NY 10017
Tel: 212-455-2000
Fax: 212-455-2502
Contact: Dee Pefer

A DAY IN THE LIFE

Lawyers counsel their clients on matters pertaining to the law. Law can be intellectually fascinating, and many take great satisfaction in the daily challenges. Detail mavens and big-picture thinkers alike find a friendly home in the loose definition of attorney. But not all were as gushing as this respondent: "You are paid to provide expert counsel to someone in a specific area of expertise, where usually the answers aren't black-and-white. This pushes you and makes you think harder than you ever have before. It's the last job you'll ever want." The last is an overstatement; over 30percent of those who receive law degrees are not practicing law (regularly) ten years after graduation.

It is impossible to mention attorneys without mentioning the public perception of attorneys. One attorney reminds us of the joke: "What's the difference between a run-over snake and a run-over attorney? There are skid marks in front of the snake." Attorneys are blamed for a variety of social ills, from the litigious nature of our society, to hindering new inventions from reaching the marketplace, to getting guilty people set free due to technicalities or sloppy police work. While these labels speak to the excesses within the profession, many people apply them to the profession as a whole. "It's hard to work fourteen-hour days researching a case when you know that even your client thinks you're a bloodsucker," wrote a New York attorney.

The work is hard. Attorneys can work eighteen-hour days and spend up to 3,000 hours per year on cases. "On some level you have to like what you do, because you're doing it all day long," mentioned one attorney. Many lawyers are subordinate to senior associates and partners for the majority of their careers. Attorneys usually work at a number of firms before finding a position perfectly suited to them. Many spend their first few years finding out if they want to focus on transactional work (corporate law or real estate law) or litigation (criminal or civil cases). Some specialized lawyers have restricted areas of responsibility. For example, district attorneys prosecute accused criminals and probate lawyers plan and settle estates. The quality of life is low during the early-to-mid-years, but many find the financial rewards too enticing to abandon. Those considering entering this field should have solid work habits, a curious mind, and the ability to work with, and for, others.

PAYING YOUR DUES

Attorneys must have a law degree from an institution accredited by the American Bar Association. Many find that undergraduate majors with heavy reading and writing loads, such as history, English, philosophy, and logic, prepare them well for law school. In addition, students must take the Law School Admissions Test. Application to the 175 accredited U.S. law schools is competitive. In law school, students first take general courses, which include such classes as torts, contracts, constitutional law, property, and trusts and estates. They then move on to specialized study in an area of expertise. Law students spend their summers working for potential employers, finding out what the working attorney's life is like and discovering whether or not they want to work in a particular area. Before an attorney can practice in a given state, he must pass a state bar exam, a two-day written examination that tests the prospective attorney's knowledge of the specific laws of that state. Following passage of the written part of the test, many states require "character and fitness" oral examinations to test the ability of a person to practice law in a given state.

ASSOCIATED CAREERS

Many people become attorneys with the understanding that the career is an excellent springboard to other professions. Lawyers enter business, accounting, finance, entrepreneurship, and academia after being in the profession a number of years. Some become judges. Many enter politics, and a number have become presidents.

PAST AND FUTURE

The field of law has a long and storied history. The Sumerians wrote Hammurabi's Code, the first written laws of mankind. Ancient Greek civilization trained youths in logical thinking and rhetorical skills, a key part of legal training. The English under Henry II developed a system of common law, matching offenses with standard penalties. America operates under the general guidelines of statutory law, in which elected lawmakers enact statutes which can be reviewed by the judiciary. The number of lawyers grew exponentially in the 1980s when commercial activity was at a peak. When the economy slowed down, so did the need for attorneys. But people will always need attorneys to represent them, and the profession should remain the stable, lucrative field it is today.

QUALITY OF LIFE

Two Years

Second-year attorneys work grueling hours, but they use their paychecks to buoy their spirits. Those who work in the field of public interest law and those who clerk for judges often find they work as hard, but they don't get the paycheck to show for it. However, their positions are prestigious and the experience they gain makes them all the more valuable if they choose to re-enter the job market.

Five Years

Many find it difficult to switch specializations beyond this point. Career paths diverge for those pursuing partner-track opportunities at large firms and those who choose to dedicate time to other aspects of their life. Partner-track associates can work thousands of hours a year, spending most of their time in the office. A number of attorneys pursue work at smaller firms or as in-house counsel at corporations, where the chances of advancement are greater and the hours are more palatable. Salary, however, declines for those who choose this work.

Ten Years

Those who have survived ten years as attorneys have accrued valuable knowledge in their area of specialization and have established reputations. Attorneys pursuing partnership at a sizable firm try to recruit new business to prove that they can be valuable assets not just as attorneys, but as "rainmakers," who bring in business. Those who are passed up for partnership either migrate to smaller firms or take positions with corporate firms that need in-house counsel. Hours may have declined somewhat.

THE BIRKMAN LIFESTYLE GRID

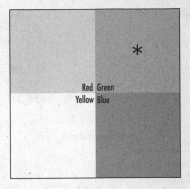

Red Green
Yellow Blue

This career is suitable for people with Green interests.

You'll Have Contact With

Accountants
Judges
Paralegals
Secretaries

Major Associations

American Bar Association
740 15th Street, NW
9th Floor
Washington, DC 60005
Tel: 202-662-1000
Fax: 202-662-1032

American Bar Foundation
750 North Lake Shore Drive
4th Floor
Chicago, IL 60611
Tel: 312-988-6500
Fax: 312-988-6579

National Lawyers Guild
126 University Place
New York, NY 10003
Tel: 212-627-2656
Fax: 212-627-2404

AUCTIONEER

PROFESSIONAL PROFILE

# of people in profession	9,500
% male	95
% female	5
avg. hours per week	35
avg. starting salary	$16,500
avg. salary after 5 years	$23,000
avg. salary 10 to 15 years	$36,000

Professionals Read
The Auctioneer
American Antiques
Art and Auction

Books, Films and TV Shows Featuring the Profession
The Flanders Panel
Secrets of Fast Talkers
Without Reserve
East/West

Major Employers
ADT Services
435 Metroplex Drive
Nashville, TN 37211
Tel: 615-833-6984
Contact: Human Resources

Christie's
502 Park Avenue
New York, NY 10022
Tel: 212-546-1000
Fax: 212-606-7028
Contact: Daryl Krimsky

Sotheby's
1334 York Avenue
New York, NY 10021
Tel: 212-606-7000
Fax: 212-606-7107
Contact: Kitty Ijams

A DAY IN THE LIFE

Auctioneers manage public sales where property or merchandise are sold to the highest bidder. These items can be anything from real estate or farm equipment to jewelry or exotic animals. Because knowledge of the value of such goods is important to the successful auctioneer, many choose to specialize in three or four types of auctions. Auctioneers represent sellers but should also be able to work with buyers One should have a strong voice, a good sense of humor, and an agile mind. Auctioneering is a fast-paced, unpredictable career that can bring financial rewards to those who show ability in all these areas.

Auctions can take place in large convention centers, barns, yards, and parking lots. Travel is often required. An auctioneer faces the crowd (usually between fifty and ten thousand people), introduces items, and calls out bids with the help of assistants or "ringmen." While many use public address systems, bid calling for four to six hours per day still puts considerable strain on the voice. Over 75 percent of auctioneers are independent contractors who work for a daily fee or a percentage of sales. As independent contractors, marketing and drumming up business are the auctioneer's responsibilities, so business skills are important. Auctioneers also render appraisal values in two realms; on the value of the asset itself and the price the asset is likely to command. Successful auctioneers have some understanding of the psychology of the auction as well as a blanket appraised value. The range of value of sales at auctions can run from $2,000 all the way to $300 million, so financial acumen is critical.

The community of auctioneers is fairly supportive, and the majority of auctioneers belong to one of the major professional associations. Many entrants to the field work for (or with) more established members of the community. The old vision of the auctioneer as slick bid-chanter has changed with the scale of auctions in America; one auctioneer mentioned "There...has been an improvement in the area of ethics in the auction industry," and was very positive about the future of auctioneering. Many auctions take place under the auspices of the federal government, so an understanding of federal regulations and the ability to work with federal agencies is important.

PAYING YOUR DUES

An auctioneer must have at least a high-school education, and more and more auctioneers are going to four-year colleges, agricultural colleges, or two-year specialty colleges. Coursework should include finance, accounting, management, psychology, and public speaking. Many auctioneers have experience in marketing and a few cited acting as a helpful course of study. Many spend a year or two learning about valuation in their intended area of specialization; others work as assistants or ringmen in the industry first, then choose an area of specialization. An auctioneer should have a quick mind, an ability to speak clearly and honestly with prospective buyers and sellers, and strong organizational skills. Many states require licensing (particularly for those auctioneers who intend to preside over real-estate auctions), and others require passage of an examination and some apprenticeship, so check with local authorities to find out the restrictions in your area.

ASSOCIATED CAREERS

Auctioneers' strong valuation skills and excellent communication skills transfer well into marketing and sales fields. Auctioneers become brokers, merchants, professional buyers, entrepreneurs, and salesmen. Those whose specialties focused on the psychological and financial aspects of auctioneering find employ in financial institutions, marketing, and public relations. A few go into public speaking and negotiation-skills teaching for private firms.

PAST AND FUTURE

The profession of auctioneer was first established so that rural families could sell their goods when no established store or market existed in their region. These families would hire an auctioneer who presided over the sale of all the items to eliminate any semblance of unfair play and dispensed of them quickly. Auctions spread rapidly to urban centers. Now auctioneers work at auction houses, charitable events and large-scale liquidation of assets, providing a means of sale that can be both fun and profitable.

In terms of demand, the future of auctioneering looks very much like the present. Continuous turnover of estates, farm equipment changing hands, and charities' increased reliance on donations of goods and services to raise money as opposed to receiving straight capital—all provide a steady market for auctioneers. A new breed of auctioneer is developing on the Internet: a cyber-auctioneer, who sends out announcements of times and places for bidders to meet, then manages a forum based on people bidding for goods.

QUALITY OF LIFE

Two Years

Many auctioneers begin as ringmen, assistants who take bids and tend to the details at auction. New auctioneers learn the protocol and procedures for different auctions; the larger the scale of the auction, the more specific skills are required. Many learn about the computer software associated with auctions, as well as the intangible and people-oriented skills. Professional reviews are brutally honest in these first years, which may account for the 30 percent attrition rate.

Five Years

Auctioneering skills improve; but many auctioneers move from ringmen positions to others, particularly in the marketing department, and learn how to publicize, run auctioneering ventures, and make them profitable. Pay doesn't necessarily increase, but the attrition rate shrinks to 10 percent—below average for professions during this period. People split into two groups; those who work for national auctioneering services for a salary, and those who start their own businesses. The majority start their own businesses between years four and six. People begin to develop specialties and regional reputations. Satisfaction is high, as many enjoy the freedom their profession brings.

Ten Years

Ten-year auctioneers are, for the most part, independent practitioners with established reputations. Many have regular clients, often including local law enforcement agencies and large banking establishments who hold foreclosure auctions regularly. Nearly all auctioneers have established specialty areas, such as livestock, restaurant equipment, aircraft, art, or firearms. Industry associations are significant in networking and finding new business. Salaries rise, but because private practitioners can only preside over as many auctions as days they are available, increases beyond this point are not considerable.

THE BIRKMAN LIFESTYLE GRID

Red Green
Yellow Blue

This career is suitable for people with Green interests.

You'll Have Contact With

Antiques Dealers
Art Dealers
Attorneys
Ringmen

Major Associations

California State Auctioneers Association
3016 S. Valley View Boulevard
Las Vegas, NV 89102
Tel: 702-363-1616
Fax: 702-248-0888

National Auctioneers Association
8880 Ballentine
Overland Park, KS 66214
Tel: 913-541-8084
Fax: 913-894-5281
Contact: Exec. VP - Jill Keefhazer

New York State Auctioneers Association Inc.
PO Box 496
Whitney Point, NY 13862
Tel: 607-692-3516

Auto Mechanic

PROFESSIONAL PROFILE

# of people in profession	739,000
% male	95
% female	5
avg. hours per week	45
avg. starting salary	$17,000
avg. salary after 5 years	$31,000
avg. salary 10 to 15 years	$46,000

Professionals Read

Engineers Digest
Car and Driver
Buy 'n Sell

Books, Films and TV Shows Featuring the Profession

Repo Man
IQ
Some Kind of Wonderful
Heart Like A Wheel

Major Employers

Automobile Association of America
1415 Kellum Place
Garden City, NY 11530
Tel: 212-586-1166
Contact: Personnel Department

Midas Muffler
Tel: 312-670-2505
Contact: To apply for a position with Midas, call the main office for the location of the franchise nearest you.

Jiffy Lube
Tel: 713-568-6718
Contact: Call main office to find franchise nearest you.

A DAY IN THE LIFE

Auto mechanics repair and maintain cars. Some mechanics work on all parts of any car, while others specialize in one area or on one type of car. The most challenging aspect of car repair is often the mechanic's favorite part: diagnosing the problem. Speed and accuracy in diagnosis and quoting prices to the customer are crucial if the mechanic intends to keep long-term clients. The mechanic examines the engine while it is running (if possible) to see if his initial assumptions are correct. Electronic diagnostic equipment is useful but the good mechanic can tell a lot by using eyes, ears—even nose—as he searches for problems and potential hazards. Sometimes he repairs parts, but if the part is worn or damaged, he replaces it. Some mechanics compare their field to that of the physician, because most people come in only when their car is in dire straits, not when regular preventive maintenance could have avoided the problems altogether. When people come in for an automotive check-up, mechanics often replace worn parts before they become hazardous to the driver, even though drivers can be suspicious of mechanics who recommend the replacement of parts that haven't stopped functioning.

The best mechanics have mastery of a wide variety of integrated skills: electrical systems (a car's wiring is more complicated than an average home's); computerized electronics (a television set seems simple by comparison); fuel systems and refrigeration (a car's "plumbing" is a Byzantine maze of tubes). Auto mechanics proudly compare themselves to doctors (though not, unfortunately, in salary range), since they mainly see people with complaints; but whereas the human body and its problems have remained essentially unchanged for millennia, the designs of cars change every year. As a result, the job requires more preparation than ever before.

More and more, cars are controlled by electronic instruments, so mechanics are using computers constantly. "Computers have become as much a part of the tool box as wrenches," said one mechanic. Most auto mechanics intern while still in automotive repair school, then work full time at the same dealerships. They read trade papers daily to keep abreast of changes and trends in their industry. As they gain experience they can move into higher-paying, specialized positions. They can also rise to the ranks of supervisor or manager, particularly if they have strong interpersonal skills to calm cranky customers who are displeased by high service bills and inconvenience.

PAYING YOUR DUES

The days of the uneducated grease monkey are over. Aspiring auto mechanics must have increasingly sophisticated vocational skills and must constantly adapt to continually changing technology. The integration of computers in automobiles means mechanics must be familiar with complicated new systems. While this emphasis on ongoing training intimidates some, most soon find that motivation and an enthusiastic instructor can help. Students begin their training by studying car processes in manuals and then work on older cars. Most mechanics find themselves in technical educational programs after graduating high school, but a few high schools offer four-year automotive programs that culminate in certification. All auto mechanics are required to be certified (not by law, but by employers—few will hire uncertified personnel). To obtain certification, students spend over 1,000 hours working on cars and must pass a written exam. There are test preparation guides for all certifying exams. Community college programs encourage students to complete an applied science degree and then acquire an automotive technology certificate. A number of training programs work with local shops to place students in internships with car dealerships or service centers during their studies. Most mechanics are responsible for obtaining their own sets of tools, but employers are responsible for supplying large power tools and electronic testing equipment. Some shops require union membership.

ASSOCIATED CAREERS

Teaching auto repair is a growing field. Many older instructors do not possess the sophisticated computer knowledge required to teach today's aspiring auto mechanics. Those who do can easily obtain employment. If you enjoy cars but don't want to get your hands dirty, perhaps auto body repair is for you. These men do cosmetic repairs on cars or custom paint them. Salespeople in dealerships also need sophisticated knowledge of cars. The glamorous world of professional racing is another option for the exceptionally gifted mechanic. Being a part of a pit crew involves anticipating problems and making repairs with perfect accuracy under pressure. Pit crew positions, however, are extremely difficult to come by.

PAST AND FUTURE

Automobiles were first produced in the 1890s, when they were little more than novelties for the very rich. As cars entered mass production and the manufacturing process grew more complex, owners came to rely increasingly on specialized auto mechanics. By the 1980s the computer had become an integral part of automotive design and troubleshooting. Just five years ago, fewer than 20 percent of the parts of a car were computerized, whereas now over 80 percent are, a situation that has forced mechanics to update their skills. One community college instructor said that every one of his students who completes his program gets a job. Currently, there is a shortage of approximately 60,000 auto mechanics. The field is anticipated to grow since the trends are for people to keep their cars longer and replace them with increasingly complex models. The profession is relatively immune to fluctuations in the economy as a car is a necessity, not a luxury, for many people.

QUALITY OF LIFE

Two Years

Mechanics generally enter the field after a lifetime fascination with cars, so it is rare that they jump ship to another profession in the first two years. Many enjoy the challenge of making cars safer and more useful. This coupled with the fact that auto mechanics have extremely low levels of unemployment leads to high levels of satisfaction for the novice. The money is good, but hours can be long.

Five Years

Mechanics are earning their reputations and exposing themselves to a variety of automotive problems. Many of them have gained enough experience to become specialists. Those who are dissatisfied with the long hours go into non-automotive repair jobs. Well-trained technicians are more efficient even using fewer expensive gadgets than their untrained counterparts—so proper and continuous training is an imperative.

Ten Years

Experienced and ambitious mechanics often open their own shops eventually and hire other mechanics. Those working for big dealerships and shops should by now have risen to supervisory positions. Others who have not updated their skills may be forced into lesser-paying jobs. The majority remain automotive mechanics for the rest of their careers.

THE BIRKMAN LIFESTYLE GRID

This career is suitable for people with Red interests.

You'll Have Contact With
Auto Manufacturers
Car Dealers
Insurance Agents
Parts Suppliers

Major Associations
American Automobile Manufacturers Association
7430 Second Avenue
Suite 300
Detroit, MI 48202
Tel: 313-872-4311

Automotive Service Association, Inc.
520 Central Parkway East
Suite 114
Plato, TX 75074
Tel: 214-578-0307

AUTO SALESPERSON

A DAY IN THE LIFE

Car salespeople like the challenge of learning about autos and the unique features of each model and brand, and finding the appropriate match for a customer. "I don't know of another profession," mentioned one salesman, "where there's so much excitement and uncertainty. Everyone who walks into your business wants to buy a car. You've got to find a way to make them want to buy your car. You've got to understand what they need." This psychological aspect to the profession cannot be minimized. People buy cars for a variety of reasons, and the automobile salesman's job is to discover what those are. Successful salesmen are combinations of businessmen, advisors, and friends.

The average automobile salesman sells between 200 and 1,000 cars per year. Most average over one per day. Although many salesmen work partially for salary, many include "commission on sales" as a significant part of their compensation, placing them under some pressure to sell cars. Professional turnover, based primarily on production, is high. Those who can't sell cars aren't given a long chance to prove themselves; dealers are under pressure to sell cars themselves. Automobile dealers follow their clients from the moment they walk into the dealership through their signing of the final paperwork. Successful salespeople exude honesty and interest. Integrity is respected. Car sales requires someone who thrives on the excitement of the deal and has a strong degree of self-confidence. Other important qualities are the ability to listen, a thorough knowledge of product line, and an understanding of financing options.

The most significant schism in the industry is between those who work for initial dealerships, and those who work for used car dealerships. Not only must the used-car salesman be aware of the features associated with a variety of models, she must also be familiar with mileage, modifications, rebuilds, and the quirks of each car on the lot. As well, the used-car salesman works against a stereotype as a slick, oily con-artist looking to make a quick buck. Part of this may be due to the larger commissions used-car salesman make on each sale, thus encouraging them to complete as many sales as possible.

PAYING YOUR DUES

A high-school education is required mainly by the large employers. College coursework in such fields as marketing, finance, sales, psychology and public speaking is becoming more common. Large employers have their own sales-training methods, and many new salesmen spend three or four weeks at a national training center, where they learn about the manufacturing process, each model's features, all available options, general negotiating strategies and the culture of the company they work for. Others are trained by other salesmen and have an initial probationary period where all deals must be overseen and approved by more experienced colleague. Voluntary certification through the National Automobile Dealers Association (NADA) and the Society of Automotive Sales Professionals (SASP) is gaining popularity, but is not required.

ASSOCIATED CAREERS

Automobile salesmen use their personal finesse and their deftness with numbers in a variety of professions as salesmen. Some move into real-estate sales, where the same abilities are important. A few become supply-house salesmen, and negotiate large scale contracts and long-term relationships between retail salesmen and suppliers. Others who are successful and can get financing start their own car dealerships where they hire other car salesmen. Most automobile salesman continue to work at least part-time as automobile salesmen with increasing commissions, finding the excitement of the deal and the challenge of selling such a high-ticket item addictive.

PAST AND FUTURE

Automobile salesman have been around since the time cars were first mass-produced in the 1870s. Though marked by years of stereotyping as oily, pressure-bearing, and vaguely misogynistic misinformants, car salesmen have become a different breed in the modern era. Competition between dealerships, well-advertised financing terms, and a populace with computer and published resources all have forced the car salesman to be a better listener, more honest, and more informative.

The general responsibilities of car salesmen are not expected to change in the near future, but the resources available to car buyers are expected to further expand. Car buyers can now research their purchases via books, the Internet, software, and comparative consumer studies on various makes of cars, so salesmen have to find new and creative ways to make their products seem more attractive. No longer can they rely completely on impulse-shopping consumers who choose cars based on their color or a television commercial jingle. Well-informed salespeople with a sound product should find this profession inviting in the future.

QUALITY OF LIFE

Two Years

The training period lasts between two and six weeks. The first three months may be considered a "probationary" period. By the end of the second year, salespeople have reasonable salaries, regular hours, and a professional ease in conducting sales. The majority of those unsuited to the profession leave within the first six months (40 percent).

Five Years

At the five-year mark, automobile salesmen have managed to produce and sell at regular levels. Many have achieved bonus-triggering sales levels and some have renegotiated the amount of commission they receive. Fluidity of employer marks these years, as successful producers look for the best commissions deals they can cut and the most appropriate shop for their talents. A number find themselves surprised by the difficulty of moving from one realm of car sales—for example, the $9,000–$14,000 range—to another, such as the $20,000–$40,000 luxury car range. Those trying to increase sales work more hours; a few top salesmen sell near 1,000 cars per year.

Ten Years

Ten-year veterans are senior sales associates at large dealerships, and have found the level of consumer they are good at selling cars to. Many supervise newer employees and administer dealership responsibilities. A few who truly enjoy the world of sales continue their dealership-floor or used-lot responsibilities, usually with good success. Around half of ten-year veterans stay in sales part-time and take on other dealership duties. Salaries settle down, but quality of life improves with this choice. Satisfaction is average, as are hours.

THE BIRKMAN LIFESTYLE GRID

This career is suitable for people with Green interests.

You'll Have Contact With
Auto Manufacturers
Auto Mechanics
Bankers
Insurers

Major Associations
Automotive Service Industry Association
8400 West Park Drive
Mclean, VA 22102
Tel: 703-821-7000
Fax: 703-821-7025
Contact: Ted Orme

National Automobile Dealers Association
99 Canal Center Plaza
Suite 500
Alexandria, VA 22314-1538
Tel: 703-519-7800
Fax: 703-519-7810
Contact: Human Resources

American International Automotive Dealers
Association
5999 Stevenson Avenue
Alexandria, VA 22304
Tel: 703-823-4599
Contact: Virginia Moore

AVIONICS TECHNICIAN

A DAY IN THE LIFE

Without avionics technicians, most military and high-tech planes would be unsafe at any speed. Avionics technicians test, maintain, and produce aviation electronics, including missile-guidance systems, jet engines, and flight-control circuitry. Much of an avionics job is preventative. Technicians work unusual hours, providing maintenance and support to private research concerns, aerospace companies, the military, and other government agencies. Levels of satisfaction in the industry are high, mainly because it provides intellectual curiosity with a very close attention to detail. The installation of electronics devices, their calibration, and their testing are all critical to the success of any aviation endeavor.

Many avionics technicians specialize in one area of expertise, such as microcircuit television microscopy, oscilloscope review, or computerized guidance systems. Since the field is evolving, many people's specialties change over time. Because of rapid changes in technology, continuing education through professional reading, and attending company-sponsored seminars, industry events, and conferences is the norm in this field. Most technicians are also educated through interaction with their colleagues; while each member has an assigned responsibility, the majority of technicians work as part of a team. Communication skills and the ability to write comprehensive and complete reports are as important as technical skills.

Two discrete professional categories exists for those in the industry. The first are those involved in the research and development (design and testing stages) of new electronic equipment. These technicians must have curious minds that can imagine potential problems that might occur, including atmospheric conditions, magnetic field interference, and weight limitations. The second category are those involved in the direct installation and maintenance. These people must be extremely attentive to detail, organized, and interested in high degrees of responsibility and long hours. The two fields do cross over at a variety of points, but in general, the fields are separate.

PAYING YOUR DUES

Most people attend a specialty school or community college that specializes in electronics engineering for one to three years. Major aerospace employers run their own schools and training centers; but corporate-run schools teach only about each company's own product line. General coursework at these schools includes electronics, the physics of electricity, circuit design, and computer science. Familiarity with math (calculus-level studies are preferred) and a degree of manual dexterity are both helpful. If communications equipment is part of your job, you also will need an Federal Communications Commission (FCC) license as a restricted radio-telephone operator. Most specific skills, such as use of an oscilloscope, or a circuit analyzer, are part of on-the-job training.

ASSOCIATED CAREERS

Some avionics technicians continue their education and become aviation engineers, electrical engineers (specializing in circuit design and testing), or communications engineers. Others become repair consultants, in-house electronics designers, or join research groups that test and rate developed products. But few avionics technicians leave the field, due to the interesting work and competitive salaries the profession offers.

PAST AND FUTURE

Avionics developed with the rise of modern warfare. The number of electronic devices used in navigation, control, maintenance and flight multiplied by a factor of 100 between the World War II B-29 bomber and the current B-58 supersonic bomber. Missile technology, including the development of SCUDS, ICBMs and other "smart" missiles, has also matured. The current demand for aviation technicians is significant.

While strong demand exists for technicians now, much of the direction of avionics technicians relies on defense spending, and with budget slashing looming on the horizon, this career faces an uncertain financial future. Aerospace work will continue to be done at some level, but to what degree and by how many people is the question. Research project support and government funding sway from supporting laser-based missile defense systems, to backing propulsion-based systems, from encouraging the development of stealth weapons and high-altitude aircraft, to supporting nothing at all.

QUALITY OF LIFE

Two Years

Avionics technicians make the transition from school to the practical work environment during these early, busy years. Many participate in one- to two-month on-the-job training programs sponsored by their aerospace employers. Beginners join research teams as "junior" members and their work is carefully scrutinized by more experienced members. Duties include calibration and installation of communication and other, less complicated, electronics systems. Salaries are reasonable, as are hours, but many entering the field mentioned that the technical journal-reading burden, a feature of most evolving professions, is one unexpected time-stealer.

Five Years

Five-year survivors are now the senior members of research teams, and, in rare cases, are leading them. Those involved in the design and research stages of products now have significant input into the testing protocols and installation procedures. Those involved in maintenance have regular schedules and may have some oversight responsibility for newer entrants to the field. The majority of avionics technicians—over 70 percent—remain with their original employer through their first five years, possibly due to the paucity of aerospace companies.

Ten Years

Ten-year avionics technicians spend their time running research projects, working with designers and producers, and managing less-senior avionics technicians. Those who have advanced not only understand the technical specifications and the electronic requirements of what they do, but the spirit of cooperation that must take place for teams in this industry to function efficiently. The majority of ten-year veterans are employed by the major aerospace companies, with the government employing the second-largest number. Satisfaction is high and hours increase.

THE BIRKMAN LIFESTYLE GRID

Red Green
Yellow Blue

This career is suitable for people with Red interests.

You'll Have Contact With

Aerospace Engineers
Electrical Engineers
Pilots
Safety Inspectors

Major Associations

American Institute of Aeronautics & Astronautics
85 John Street
4th Floor
New York, NY 10038
Tel: 212-349-1120
Fax: 703-264-7551
Contact: Public Affairs

Professional Aviation Maintenance Association
1200 18th Street, NW
Washington, DC 20036
Tel: 202-296-0545
Fax: 202-296-0618

Future Aviation Professionals of America
4971 Massachusetts Boulevard
Atlanta, GA 30337
Tel: 770-997-8097
Fax: 770-997-8111
Contact: Human Resources

BANK OFFICER

A DAY IN THE LIFE

Bank officers are in charge of every aspect of retail banking (as distinguished from investment banking—see separate listing on page 242), from making certain that accounting procedures are followed, to approving loans, to marketing the bank to potential customers. Bank trust officers act as trust and estate managers; loan officers manage, evaluate, and distribute loans; operations officers handle the interface between banking institutions and technology, such as computer systems; and marketing officers identify customer needs and evaluate service. They all work together to ensure the proper functioning of the bank on a day-to-day basis. The intricate networks of responsibility are internally reviewed and subject to the supervision of the U.S. government. Interaction is marked by a sense of professionalism; while few bank officers cited "closeness" as a way of describing their relationships with their co-workers, many said that they could and did rely on them every day.

Each type of officership requires a different set of strengths. For example, those who become trust and estate managers must have a strong understanding of tax implications, an ability to anticipate future problems, and excellent communication skills as they will work closely with clients. Loan officers, on the other hand, must have an understanding of statistics and strong judgment skills, anticipating a potential borrower's future ability to repay a loan. Our respondents emphasized the enormous responsibility most banking officers face. "You have to make real decisions that have real responsibilities attached, and you've got to be smart [about them]" mentioned one. Beginning employees aren't thrown into the industry without training or supervision, but they are given a surprising amount of power for people with little work experience. Banking requires an agility with numbers, good organizational skills, sound interpersonal skills, and a strong fundamental work ethic. Those in the banking industry ranked the intensity of their day-to-day jobs in the top 10 percent of all professions; this career isn't for someone who pines for long vacations and sinecures.

PAYING YOUR DUES

While tellers and occasionally bank managers can find work with as little as a high-school education, most senior bank officers have at least a bachelor's degree (most large employers look favorably on finance, banking, economics, accounting, and marketing majors), if not an MBA. International banks may request proof of language skills. Many request work experience that demonstrates a facility with numbers or the ability to handle a wide area of responsibility. Bank officers come in contact with confidential information every day, so new hires may be required to sign nondisclosure agreements. Upon hire, many bank officers spend three weeks to six months training for their positions. Officers must have a solid understanding of financial rules and regulations, and many firms require that new employees pass an in-house test which assesses their knowledge before they are allowed to begin their positions.

ASSOCIATED CAREERS

Retail bankers who yearn for higher risk and challenges (and higher rewards with success) become investment bankers. The more risk-averse move to accounting fields where responsibilities are limited and tasks more discrete. A number of former bank officers enter the securities industry and become brokers, traders, and salesmen. A few operations officers move into the computer industry and become programmers, operations specialists, or hardware specialists.

PAST AND FUTURE

Banking in the U.S. began immediately following the American Revolution, but that bank failed, so the federal government formed a second bank of the United States, and that failed too. States then took up the slack and formed large and powerful state banks, which issued their own currencies and proved very successful. The Federal Reserve was then formed, with twelve branches, and given the job of coordinating these large state banks. As banks grew and became less centralized, a bank officer position was developed for each area of responsibility.

Currently there are around 10,000 banks in operation, but most analysts believe that the industry will undergo a wave of consolidation and acquisition over the next ten years, settling at somewhere between the 4,000 and 6,000 bank range. A natural result of this consolidation is the reduction of jobs with overlapping functions, which means that many bank officers will face layoffs. The ascendancy of automatic teller machines (ATMs) has further contributed to displacement as workers are shunted from customer service to back-office functions (if they are lucky enough to stay employed at all). The banks that survive consolidation will be stronger, larger, and more efficient, with excellent prospects for growth. Bank officers who survive the next several years should thrive in well-positioned companies looking to expand in the years to come.

QUALITY OF LIFE

Two Years

Bank officers spend the first two years at hectic on-the-job training sessions, learning their professions at the side of more experienced employees. Hours are long, and time spent doing professional reading or attending industry seminars can be significant. Responsibility levels are high for trust officers and marketing officers, but loan officers have significant departmental oversight. Duties include budgeting, scheduling, administrative work, and report writing. Communication skills are important during these early years, more to ensure that the education process progresses smoothly than to ensure the duties of the job are managed.

Five Years

Five-year officers are termed "senior" officers of the bank and many head up staffs composed of less-experienced colleagues. Relocation is a major issue during these years, as is fluidity of employer. Well-considered officers are important strengths in any bank; those with creative and effective strategies are in strong demand. Hours become even longer for those looking to rise to V.P. status or beyond: the ambitious take additional coursework (many take time off to pursue MBAs after garnering a couple of years' on-the-job experience, which most business schools expect from candidates) and a few try to achieve either industry accreditation or assume significant roles within professional associations ("networking" is as important in banking as any industry). Those who enjoy their current level of success work on honing managerial skills. Salaries and responsibilities increase; job satisfaction is average. Twenty percent will leave the field during these years, mainly to enter the related areas of corporate finance, investment banking, and accounting.

Ten Years

Ten-year survivors either have established areas of responsibility or are aggressively pursuing the title of vice president. Salaries have risen and satisfaction is high; those who remain in the profession after ten years are most likely to remain in it for life. The low attrition rate after this point—under 5 percent—is notable.

THE BIRKMAN LIFESTYLE GRID

Red Green
Yellow Blue

This career is suitable for people with Green interests.

You'll Have Contact With

Accountants
Attorneys
Auditors
Software Engineers

Major Associations

American Bankers Association
1120 Connecticut Avenue, NW
Washington, DC 20036
Tel: 202-663-5000
Fax: 202-828-4547
Contact: Human Resources

Bank Administration Institute
1 North Franklyn
Suite 200
Chicago, IL 60606
Tel: 312-553-4600
Fax: 312-683-2426
Contact: Human Resources

Institute of Financial Education
111 East Wacker Drive
Suite 900
Chicago, IL 60601-4389
Tel: 312-946-8800
Fax: 312-946-8802
Contact: Lynn Murray

Bar/Club Manager

PROFESSIONAL PROFILE

# of people in profession	15,000
% male	65
% female	35
avg. hours per week	50
avg. starting salary	$15,600
avg. salary after 5 years	$21,000
avg. salary 10 to 15 years	$30,000

Professionals Read

Hype
Bar Supply Monthly Report

Books, Films and TV Shows Featuring the Profession

Cocktail
Road House
Pug Trencher's House of Dreams
Cheers

Major Employers

Palladium
126 East 14th Street
New York, NY 10003
Tel: 212-473-7171
Fax: 212-473-9469
Contact: Monica Michaels

Limelight
47 West 20th Street
New York, NY 10003
Tel: 212-807-7850

DV8
540 Howard Street
San Francisco, CA 94105
Tel: 415-957-1730

A DAY IN THE LIFE

Managing a bar or club is a high-profile job, but don't let anyone tell you it is glamorous. "When you have to, you do everything from carrying kegs of beer up flights of stairs to mopping up spills," mentioned one bar manager. At the end of the night, the responsibility for the smooth functioning, and on some levels, the profitability, of the bar or club rests with the manager. The manager has a significant degree of input on the attitude and operation the club, and can impress her sensibility on the patrons' experiences. "You can give them the night you always wanted," said one, "and that feels great." The most enjoyable aspect about being a club or bar manager is the creativity the profession entails. Most work closely with owners on developing marketing strategies based around theme nights, entertainment, advertising, and special events. Financial analysis skills—basic cost benefit analysis, for the most part—are important for club and bar managers to propose interesting yet fiscally sound marketing schemes. Such events as "Open Mike Nights," "Happy Hours," and "Couples Night" all are examples of themes that many clubs and bars find successful in attracting new patrons. The bar and club manager must be creative in these ways without sacrificing the attention to detail that is the day-to-day nature of the profession.

Bar or club managers must be comfortable with people—from the professionals they work with—accountants, wait staff, suppliers, and government regulators (including representatives from the liquor, fire, sanitation, and health departments)—to the patrons they entertain. Managers must understand local regulations and accounting procedures to ensure the establishment functions legally and smoothly. According to our survey, most people thought the job would be fun—which many say it is—but they didn't understand the degree of responsibility it required. "You have so much to keep track of. Everything is important," said one club manager. Managers must be comfortable claiming and enforcing authority as the liaison between the owners of the establishment and the employees.

PAYING YOUR DUES

There is no specific educational requirement to become a bar or a club manager, but most have a high-school education and many have some college accounting, finance, or management coursework. Work experience is more important than educational requirements. Employers seek those who have experience managing others and keeping track of large budgets and inventories, and who have generally demonstrated a strong sense of responsibility. The workday usually extends from late afternoon to late into the night, and weekends are regularly part of established shift schedules. Those who leave the profession often cite "schedule" as a significant reason for their departure.

ASSOCIATED CAREERS

The organizational aspects of bar and club managing equip ex-managers for inventory control positions, staff management positions, human resource departments, and employment companies. Others use their patron-relations skills as party planners, caterers, public relations professionals, and salesmen. Note that many of these related occupations require a different level of educational achievement than bar and club manager. Only a limited percentage of those employed as bar and club managers see it as a career profession, mainly because only certain establishments offer positions with any benefits whatsoever.

PAST AND FUTURE

Bars and clubs used to be managed by their owners, but as owners opened second and third clubs, they had to find people whom they could trust to run them. The position of manager evolved as one close to ownership and has become, frequently due to corporate ownership, that of intermediary between owners and staff.

Bars and clubs will consistently need creative managers who can ensure that the public has a fresh and exciting perception of the establishment and it runs as smoothly as possible. Management software is becoming more important for those who are looking to enter this profession, and many three-week courses provide instruction in these systems.

QUALITY OF LIFE

Two Years

Bar and club managers usually rise from staff positions such as bartenders, waiters, and (less often) bar backs. They usually manage their establishment under strict supervision for two to three nights unpaid, in order to learn the ropes. There are three months of a probationary period when loose supervision and limited responsibilities are offered. Two-year managers are responsible for assembling, managing, and paying staff, as well as opening and closing the club or restaurant. Duties include ordering supplies and managing inventory. Hours are long, 4 p.m. to 2 a.m., for example, as the new managers learn their job; pay is reasonable and many are satisfied.

Five Years

Five-year managers have significant input into promotional efforts to make the public aware of the club or bar. Many are given complete latitude to determine and advertise events, with responsibility for the bottom line. Duties remain the same, but managers usually have developed good relationships with vendors and have established systems of employee scheduling. At the five-year mark, managers have honed employee evaluation skills, and are given reasonable latitude to offer holiday bonuses to exceptional employees. The position becomes one of culture and policy; the five-year manager determines the tone and attitude of the establishment and the way it functions on a day-to-day basis.

Ten Years

A mere 20 percent of managers remain with their initial clubs or bars for ten years, and the majority leave between years five and nine. Why this massive exodus? Some claim that it is difficult to remain fresh and innovative at the same location. Others claim that bar and club popularity levels are cyclical, and when owners see any dip in profits, the first person who carries the blame is the manager. A third group claims that there is little challenge to the job once managers have smoothed operations and reinvented locations. Many of those who choose to remain at their original locations attempt to buy some sort of stake in the bar or club; this new role of ownership seems to provide the spark many need to reinvent themselves.

THE BIRKMAN LIFESTYLE GRID

This career is suitable for people with Green interests.

You'll Have Contact With

Bartenders
Bookkeepers
Suppliers
Waiters
Entertainers

Major Associations

Educational Foundation of the National Restaurant Association
250 South Wacker Drive
Suite 1400
Chicago, IL 60606
Tel: 312-715-1010
Fax: 312-715-0807
Contact: Customer Service

National Restaurant Association
1200 17th Street, NW
Washington, DC 20036
Tel: 202-331-5900
Fax: 202-331-2429
Contact: Membership Deptartment

Club Managers Association of America
1733 King Street
Alexandria, VA 22314
Tel: 703-739-9500
Fax: 703-739-0124

BASEBALL PLAYER

A DAY IN THE LIFE

A baseball player plays baseball. Bet you could have guessed that. Although very few people actually get to do this for a living, we've included it in this book because it is a dream job for so many. This internationally played sport attracts millions of viewers worldwide who admire, trust and respect the men who play the game.

A baseball player's career has two distinct and very different stages: the minor leagues and the major leagues. At the beginning of the overwhelming majority of players' careers, they are ushered into the three-tier system of minor-league professional baseball: Single-A baseball (the lowest minor league level), double-A baseball (the middle minor league level) and triple-A baseball (the highest minor league level). Working in such exotic locations as Toledo, Norwalk, and Columbus, baseball players follow the instructions of their coaches and work on specific baseball skills, general conditioning, and emotional maturity. The last is the most underrated portion of the profession, but it is a significant factor in making it to the major leagues. Hours are long. Players pack and carry their own luggage for long bus trips to games. Many hold additional jobs in the off-season to make ends meet, which can be hard to do on a salary of about $180/week. Satisfaction is low in the minors, but players enjoy a strong sense of camaraderie with other aspiring major leaguers. Many remain late after practices and games to work on skills, weight training, and conditioning.

Major league players have the advantage of a strong union, and the minimum salary for entry-level players is $109,000 per season, which lasts roughly eight months, from March through October. They do not carry their own luggage. Practices are plentiful in the spring, but do not take place during the season. Players are required to show up at least one hour before game time prepared to play, to be in reasonable condition, and to obey the direction of the manager and coaches. Baseball players are under a great deal of pressure to perform during games. They lack job security; one significant injury, such as a torn ligament or an eye disorder, that prevents a player from playing at his best level could mean the end of a career. On an even less dramatic level, playing inconsistently and losing the trust of your manager can lead to the same result.

PAYING YOUR DUES

It takes skill, luck, and hard work to have a shot at becoming a baseball player, and even then, your chances are slim. No academic requirements exist for baseball players; in fact, many are drafted immediately out of high school. First, you need talent—excellent hand-eye coordination, the right body-type, and specific baseball skills. Then, you need good coaching and training, so that you stand out from the other millions of young people who play baseball. This can be accomplished through hard work and dedication, in addition to your incredible skill. Then you need luck to play in a game where a scout or a college recruiter can observe you, and you need to play well on that day. If you make it to the minor leagues, you find that everyone else is as young, talented, and highly thought of as you are. Around 700 players participate in the major leagues each year. Once there, the average career lasts 2.7 years.

ASSOCIATED CAREERS

Many players enter businesses where their high level of dedication and performance is appreciated. Those who are very successful need not have another career after baseball, but many become entrepreneurs, commentators, or coaches. A significant few make solid livings from memorabilia shows, autographs, and product endorsements.

PAST AND FUTURE

Baseball, an American version of the English game of cricket, was invented by Alexander Cartwright (not Abner Doubleday, as many think) in 1845. The world championship (first known as the American League championship) has been played since 1903. Baseball has seen the most significant global fan base growth of any major sport (although basketball is fast approaching baseball's popularity) and is particularly popular in the Caribbean. Baseball has also been the sport with the most work stoppages in its history.

Baseball is in crisis. The most recent work stoppage (caused in 1994 by stalemated negotiations between the Players' Association and the owners of all major league teams) fostered significant resentment between fans and the game they grew up loving. The remainder of the 1994 season was played with no agreement in place. The size and dedication of the fan base determines the demand for the sport, the demand for the sport determines the revenues the sport receives, and the revenues the sport receives determines the salaries major league baseball players earn.

QUALITY OF LIFE

Two Years

Players are in the minor leagues, learning skills and training along with other hopefuls. Superstars and career minor-leaguers are treated alike at this point, encouraging camaraderie. Promotion is based on performance, and many need to mature emotionally and physically. They also need to improve their skills. If one fails and is dropped from a single-A roster, it is very difficult to reenter baseball.

Five Years

Five-year veterans have progressed at least to double-A minor league baseball and specialize in one position. They work with strength coaches, flexibility coaches, hitting instructors, fielding instructors, and pitching coaches to learn their skill on a professional level. The majority of prospects who have exceptional talent are promoted to the major leagues by this point, but few have extensive major league experience. Salaries skyrocket. Most do not make it this far.

Ten Years

Ten-year veterans have led a storybook life, survived in the major leagues, played before hundreds of thousands of people, and acquired at least modest television and tabloid fame. The majority of successful players are on the downside of their careers with their best years behind them. Those with five years of major-league playing time become eligible for Players' Association pension funds, which can support a marginal major league player for the rest of his life.

THE BIRKMAN LIFESTYLE GRID

Red Green
Yellow Blue

This career is suitable for people with Red interests.

You'll Have Contact With

Agents
Coaches
Managers
Reporters

Major Associations

Major League Players' Association
12 East 49th Street
New York, NY 10017
Tel: 212-826-0808
Fax: 212-752-3649
Contact: Human Resources

BENEFITS ADMINISTRATOR

Professionals Read
Employee Benefits News
Best's Review of Business Insurance
Benefits Administrator
Pension Performance

Books, Films and TV Shows Featuring the Profession
Long-Term Care
The Crisis of Care

Major Employers
Farmer's Insurance Group
6901 South Yosemite Street
Suite 107
Englewood, CO 80112
Tel: 303-770-4449
Fax: 303-796-8719

Aetna
151 Farmington Avenue
Hartford, CT 06156-3400
Tel: 860-273-0123
Fax: 203-273-1757
Contact: Recruiting

Cigna Corporate
1601 Chestnut Street
46th Floor P.O. Box 7728
Philadelphia, PA 19101-9463
Tel: 215-761-2244
Contact: Human Resources

A DAY IN THE LIFE

"I like to think about myself as a teacher," said one benefits administrator, and her job description seemed to match up with her perspective. Benefit administrators explain, summarize, and publish material that describes to employees their rights and obligations under their benefit plans. Benefit administrators handle grievances, take suggestions, and act as intermediaries between benefits providers and employees. Administrators with strong communication skills, sharp minds, and the instinct to explain, to teach, find their choice of occupation gives them a high degree of satisfaction. Over 40 percent of the benefits administrator's day is spent on the telephone, either with providers or clients, explaining procedures and getting information. Another 40 percent of the day is spent writing, reading, and researching reports.

Benefits administration is one outcropping of the corporate culture it supports; many who enter the industry with the belief that employee benefits should help the employee at any cost are rudely awakened. Decisions on benefits are made in the context of this corporate culture, particularly with an eye to the bottom line. Benefits administration is a way of providing employees with support, a safety net, and advice on investments, but any decisions that help the employees should help the company as well.

Administrators must have a strong sense of self and an ability to explain benefits plans clearly. "Expect to be blamed for everything from the client not filling out their forms properly to a rude pharmacist," said one seven-year veteran. Balanced delicately between the clients and the providers, benefits administrators prove good targets for dissatisfied members of either side. This was cited as the largest downside of the profession, and may contribute to the number of administrators who leave the field between years three and six (nearly 35 percent). But this frustration is frequently offset by the general sense of helpfulness that benefits administrators feel in offering people options, educating them about their plans, and helping them through a confusing and intimidating healthcare system.

PAYING YOUR DUES

Candidates should have at least a bachelor's degree. Favorably viewed majors include English, communications, psychology, history, business, and economics. While benefits administrators work for large and small firms alike, most entry-level opportunities exist in larger firms with entire benefits administration departments. Smaller companies usually combine benefits administration duties with other responsibilities. No professional accreditation programs are required in this profession, but a familiarity with issues in the field, an understanding of the areas of responsibility for benefits administrators, and a willingness to work hard and learn are all critical.

ASSOCIATED CAREERS

Benefits administrators make business decisions and help others, and the two fields that people enter from benefits administration most often satisfy these two needs. Business-oriented benefits administrators go into a variety of banking and financial positions, such as management consulting and securities analysis, while people-oriented administrators go into human resources, career counseling, and job training programs. A few administrators enter the insurance industry.

PAST AND FUTURE

As corporations grew in size and personnel issues and benefits programs became a significant portion of employee compensation beginning in the 1960s, benefits administrators came into being. Initially employed only by the largest companies to handle questions and respond to unusual situations, benefits administrators, or at least their responsibilities, have become part of the human resources department in most companies.

Health care, once an afterthought for most companies, has taken center stage in the discussions of employee benefits. Most benefits programs are moving toward managed care (HMOs) as a part of cost-cutting measures, and this means that benefits administrators have a large job to do in terms of coordination and education. As benefits plans and insurance procedures become more complex, the number of administrators is expected to grow through the year 2000. Benefits administrator training programs and professional societies are likely to become more significant, but they will not affect the daily job or create licensing pressure for people entering the field. Today, benefits administrators are the fastest-growing level of vice-president at U.S. companies that employ thirty people or more.

QUALITY OF LIFE

Two Years

Two years into the profession, the benefits administrator has been exposed to the major areas of responsibility—insurance, compensation, and bonus structure—and has significant responsibility in each. Duties include co-authoring (with more senior personnel) summary description plans of benefits services, managing the distribution of materials to clients of the system, and meeting with members of the insurance industry who explain their products and services. Most attain the title "analyst" and begin to specialize in one specific area.

Five Years

Five-year veterans separate into two categories: those who have taken one area of specialization, and those who have chosen to move to a number of areas. The latter role isn't necessarily chosen—many people are plucked out of the mix and asked to make themselves experts in a variety of fields. This "star-selecting" is based primarily on performance and capabilities; many mentioned that the political process of networking, while existent, was not the primary means of advancement. Those who have chosen to specialize have mostly attained the title "senior analyst" in their area of expertise, and are managing less senior employees. Input is accepted on a variety of high-level issues, such as performance of plans and potential modifications to these arrangements. Hours are average; salaries rise significantly.

Ten Years

Ten-year veterans' lifestyles differ based on the size of the company they are associated with. Those in smaller firms head up departments, negotiate directly with vendors, work with top executives on benefits packages, and set corporate policy. Those in larger firms have areas of responsibility such as "domestic packages of compensation" or "dental plans for North America." While this requires a degree of specialization, the head or vice president assumes all responsibility for planning, implementation, and education. Decisions are still overseen by generalists who have risen faster or who have greater experience, but are rarely countermanded. For those in small firms, salary increases are limited beyond this point; for those in larger firms, salary increases can still be significant.

THE BIRKMAN LIFESTYLE GRID

This career is suitable for people with Green interests.

You'll Have Contact With

Actuaries
Compensation Analysts
Human Resource Personnel
Pension Consultants

Major Associations

American Compensation Association
14040 Northsight Boulevard
Scottsdale, AZ 85260
Tel: 602-951-9191

American Society for Training and Development
1640 King Street
Box 1443
Alexandria, VA 22313-2043
Tel: 703-683-8100
Fax: 703-683-1523
Contact: Customer Service

BIOLOGIST

A DAY IN THE LIFE

Biologists study humans, plants, animals, and the environments in which they live. They may conduct their studies—human medical research, plant research, animal research, environmental system research—at the cellular level or the ecosystem level or anywhere in between. Biologists are students of the world, interested in learning from every facet of life. Although this scope may seem overwhelming, in practice, biologists specialize in discrete areas that they feel drawn to.

Biologists' daily activities are driven by their area of specialization. Marine biologists study marine populations and physiology, working off boats, at oceanography centers, at aquariums, and at a variety of coastal sites. Biochemists spend most of their day in a laboratory analyzing tissue samples and designing and carrying out research projects to test new hypotheses. Agricultural scientists analyze crop yields produced from different soils, fertilizers, or chemicals. Biologists study life to uncover its secrets and to find ways to solve problems, such as finding a cure for a disease. Much research is done in ecologically diverse areas such as the Brazilian Rain Forest, where nature—the world's largest laboratory—has produced biological compounds scientists cannot yet create on their own.

Biologists generally love what they do. Many put in long hours, compelled by their dedication to work beyond the requirements of their job. Significant time at the lab, in the field, and at lectures and conferences all contribute to many biologists' lack of a personal life outside the discipline. Within the field, colleagues are aware of and sensitive to others' research progress and philosophical approach. Relationships with colleagues can be intense and often are substitutes for average social interaction. The rarefied knowledge and dedication required to analyze the basic stuff of life may be one reason why biologists choose to spend even more time with other biologists: They understand each other's devotion to their work. From botany to zoology, biologists are engaged in a demanding and creative scientific endeavor. One biologist described it as "assembling the pieces of nature's puzzle."

PAYING YOUR DUES

Academic requirements are strict in this discipline. Most individuals in positions of authority have extensive post-graduate degrees, but entry-level positions are available for people with only a bachelor's degree in a biological science. Most researchers have a master's degree; they direct research and perform out-of-lab functions, such as on-site sampling and interviewing about medication side effects. Those who wish to direct the research functions must obtain a Ph.D. in a biological science. The largest employer of biologists is the federal government, particularly the Environmental Protection Agency (EPA), the National Institutes of Health (NIH), the Centers for Disease Control (CDC), and the Department of Agriculture. Biologists at these organizations conduct practical research on existing biological compounds. Pharmaceutical companies employ the next-largest block of biologists in their research labs. Certification is available from certain professional organizations, but it is not required.

ASSOCIATED CAREERS

Biologists who leave the field generally look for a career that will satisfy both their scientific and social interests. They become doctors, veterinarians, laboratory managers, statisticians, and even dentists at a higher salary than do those who leave most other professions.

PAST AND FUTURE

Biological research traces its foundations to the physicians of antiquity and to the Catholic Church. Research on biological systems and their relationships began in ancient Greece, but little of this work was recorded. Early physicians explored the microbiological elements, looking for the causes and effects of disease, malnutrition, and deformity. In the fourteenth century, the Catholic Church began keeping comprehensive records of public activities and health. The data provided by the Catholic Church began with the study of large systems and their methods of interaction. A combination of the Church data and the data of the early physicians forms the foundation of the biological sciences.

The prospects for biologists depend not on the demand for their services—the demand for biologists will probably increase in the coming years—but on funding. Pharmaceutical companies will continue to fund potentially lucrative pharmaceutical projects. The U.S. government will continue to fund the testing of health products to release to the public; but universities, private research concerns, and foundations will all face strict budgetary limitations. Therefore, it's uncertain how biologists will fare in the next ten years. Those who succeed will be strong academically in a specific area of specialization and will have excellent technical skills.

QUALITY OF LIFE

Two Years

Biologists are primarily technicians, operating equipment, conducting tests, and recording data for more senior researchers. They spend significant time performing routine tasks regardless of their experience prior to hire. The hours can be long, and most time is spent in the lab. Although others may scoff at this "internship" of sorts, technicians generally expect to pay these dues in their first few years, and satisfaction remains high. A number of aspiring researchers ally themselves with more experienced and well-known researchers in order to put themselves in a position to become future researchers in their field of interest.

Five Years

Field work arrives and satisfaction generally increases. Those who are not promoted to research positions either gravitate to other fields or return to school to get additional credentials that will make them more attractive candidates in their chosen field. The hours can be long and the work environment unpredictable, but responsibilities and salary increase. Some seek to publish their research and theories to make their ideas known and to distinguish themselves from their contemporaries.

Ten Years

Many researchers have assumed positions as assistant directors of research or with limited control of disbursement of funds and distribution of personnel. Some are still finishing their Ph.D.s and are having a difficult time juggling work and school life. Some researchers join professional organizations or advisory committees in order to add another feather to their cap. A number enter academia. Hours flatten out, ambitions remain high.

THE BIRKMAN LIFESTYLE GRID

This career is suitable for people with Green interests.

You'll Have Contact With

Chemists
Ecologists
Researchers
Statisticians

Major Associations

American Institute of Biological Sciences
1444 I Street, NW
Suite 200
Washington, DC 20005
Tel: 202-628-1500

American Society for Microbiology
1325 Massachusetts Avenue, NW
Washington, DC 20005
Tel: 202-737-3600
Fax: 202-942-9329
Contact: Amy Chang

Botanical Society of America
1735 Neil Avenue
Columbus, OH 43210-1293
Tel: 614-292-3519
Contact: Kimberly Hiser

BOOK PUBLISHING PROFESSIONAL

PROFESSIONAL PROFILE

# of people in profession	175,000
% male	75
% female	25
avg. hours per week	45
avg. starting salary	$16,000
avg. salary after 5 years	$25,500
avg. salary 10 to 15 years	$44,000

Professionals Read
Publisher's Weekly
Kirkus Reviews
New York Review of Books
Editor & Publisher

Books, Films and TV Shows Featuring the Profession
Bright Lights Big City
A Biography of Max Perkins
Dream On

Major Employers

HarperCollins
10 East 53rd Street
New York, NY 10022
Tel: 212-207-7000
Contact: Personnel

Farrar, Straus & Giroux
19 Union Square
New York, NY 10003
Tel: 212-741-6900
Contact: Human Resources

Random House
201 East 50th Street
New York, NY 10022
Tel: 212-751-2600
Contact: Personnel

A DAY IN THE LIFE

Book publishing is an extraordinarily large business, and those who enter the profession have no illusions that what they do is just artistic in nature. "You've got to keep things on schedule. You've got to make them pay for themselves, or you're out of business," said one publishing professional, adding that "publishing" is a term that can encompass many positions within a publishing house. The most high-profile job is that of editor (see entry on Editor in this book), who works with authors to produce a quality product, but many other positions are available for those interested in the industry, including managing editors, who control production flow, publicity managers, promotions specialists, subsidiary rights managers, production managers, and salespeople. These occupations are all critical to the successful functioning of a publishing house, and those who want to pursue a career in this industry should examine their own skills in the light of the variety of opportunities available for ambitious and creative personnel who find the idea of working with books exciting.

Managing editors are the traffic-controllers of the publishing industry. They track production schedules and budgets, allocate personnel, and control the flow of material between departments. A large publishing house can have hundreds of projects running simultaneously, and the managing editor needs to be attentive to detail and be able to anticipate problems before they occur. Publicity, promotions, and sales positions reward the creative and outgoing personality who can use her interpersonal skills to drum up consumer interest or encourage sales by bookstores. Salespeople spend significant time on the road, meeting with bookstore buyers and managers. Subsidiary rights departments are usually broken into two arms: Domestic and international. "Subrights" people negotiate international publishing deals with foreign houses or contract for copyrighted work to appear in another medium. The most lucrative rights for works of fiction, movie rights, are usually negotiated only by senior personnel experienced in negotiating with production companies. It requires putting in long hours to rise from assistant and administrative positions to ones of responsibility. For all but the highest up, salaries remain relatively low in this profession.

People in the publishing industry were quick to note that contacts are crucial. Those who want to advance pursue opportunities zealously, and any advantage one can gain over other candidates is important. Few described the profession as cutthroat, however, instead praising their associates and co-workers. The intense lifestyle and the need to remain friendly with people in case they are promoted could contribute to this sentiment. Publishing is a financially tough life, but it's ideal for those who are dedicated to books and want to spend their days with like-minded people.

PAYING YOUR DUES

Publishing has no formal educational requirements, but most professionals have college degrees in fields such as English, literature, or journalism. Degrees that indicate specialized knowledge, such as chemistry or biology, can be useful to those who wish to go into textbook publishing or academic publishing positions. Many people return to school for master's degrees in English, writing, or literature, but additional credentials are not necessary to rise in the field. Employers have a paucity of positions available for a large number of candidates, so be persistent and willing to take anything to get a foot in the door. Editorial or publishing work on college literary magazines, newspapers, or journals are advantageous for applicants. Those who wish to advance in this profession should understand that work may occasionally take up all of their free time.

ASSOCIATED CAREERS

Book publishers have experience in putting together projects, either production, promotion, or sales. Many move into advertising positions, magazine publishing jobs, project management, and writing. Some return to graduate school in law or business, and make the transition to financial careers.

PAST AND FUTURE

Publishing as an industry widened its horizons with the invention of moveable type by Johannes Guttenberg and his publication of the Bible in the mid-1400s. Paper milling and printing technologies advanced, and small publishing houses in many countries were established. The most recent advance in the industry is the development of desktop publishing, which allows publishers with limited capital to produce quality works.

Publishing is stable in some respects, and moving downward in others. Sales positions, promotions, and publicity seem to all be areas of future growth opportunities for those entering the industry. The internationalization of product, also, should lead to a greater demand for subsidiary rights personnel. Publishing houses, however, are receiving a record number of applications for limited positions. Also, publishing is an industry very responsive to the bottom line: Houses are not afraid to fire personnel they cannot afford.

QUALITY OF LIFE

Two Years

These first two years are marked by menial tasks, limited responsibility, long hours, and "slave wages," as one respondent put it. Many change jobs several times during these first few years, jockeying for the positions most likely to lead to advancement. Many publishing professionals have close relationships with colleagues that prove important in later years.

Five Years

Many have changed publishing houses, and made the decision whether to work for a small or a large house (a difference in both attitude and type of work). Hours have flattened out and responsibilities have increased. Those involved in sales are on the road for significant periods of time, making contact with book dealers in a variety of regional markets. Promotions and publicity personnel are running projects of reasonable size but find that they must be creative in using their small budgets wisely. Contact with writers is common at this point, particularly for those in editorial and promotions positions.

Ten Years

Ten-year veterans have made significant choices concerning where they want to work, which department, and at what level of responsibility. Those who wish to become senior managing editors or chiefs of promotion increase their schedules at this point to demonstrate their abilities. Those who are comfortable at the levels they have attained try to improve their production methods and develop a life outside the profession. Satisfaction is high.

THE BIRKMAN LIFESTYLE GRID

This career is suitable for people with Red interests.

You'll Have Contact With

Bookstore Owners
Agents
Reviewers
Writers

Major Associations

Association of American Publishers
71 Fifth Avenue
New York, NY 10003
Tel: 212-255-0200
Fax: 212-255-7007

BOOKKEEPER

A DAY IN THE LIFE

Bookkeepers track all cash flows, billing, and lines of credit that affect their companies. They must be detail-oriented and tenacious; they have to track down and rectify any discrepancies, however small, in the company accounts. Most bookkeepers work as internal accountants for small firms that do not have an accountant on staff. They have a large amount of responsibility to the company, and sometimes (particularly at the end of the year and around tax-preparation time) have to work long hours in order to do their job properly. The majority of bookkeepers work for smaller firms. Many become involved in financial tangles mid-stream—they find themselves deciphering records from up to a year before they were hired. Bookkeepers must be flexible and able to adjust to unusual circumstances.

Many bookkeepers we talked with mentioned that the most difficult part of their jobs was not maintenance of financial records, which accounted for a good 50 percent of their time, but communication with the other members of the same company. "You have to keep track of everyone's activities, and nobody thinks it is important to keep the bookkeeper apprised every day of what they're doing." This lack of smooth transfer of information has led many companies to buy bookkeeping software so that each employee can keep track of her daily activities and a bookkeeper can then assemble all the information and verify its accuracy. Computer skills are growing in importance in the industry, and even those who are already familiar with the double-entry system of bookkeeping mentioned that knowing how to use this software is considered a strong point by employers. Many small firms aren't used to being run as businesses and many find keeping track of all interaction difficult at first. Bookkeepers must communicate their needs clearly and follow up with consistent requests for similar information. Those who enter the field with an open mind find that being a good bookkeeper "makes all the difference in the world when the boss looks at what direction he wants to take the company." The statistics and data bookkeepers compile are "snapshots" of the daily activities of the company that make up its history.

PAYING YOUR DUES

Bookkeepers are financial recordkeepers, much like accountants, but they are not required to be accredited by any organization or institution. As a positive, they have less of a fiduciary obligation than an accountant and therefore less liability; however, they are paid commensurably less. They usually maintain the records of a single company rather than having many companies as clients. No specific educational requirement is required to become a bookkeeper, but prospective employers favor applicants with finance, record-keeping, or business majors. Basic coursework in accounting is very helpful for those entering the field, but on-the-job training is neither unusual nor discouraged. With the increasing simplicity of accounting software in the workplace, less and less formal accounting training is required for these positions. The work requires attention to detail and a good method of keeping track of constantly fluctuating items, which leads most bookkeepers to adopt the double-entry method of accounting. Much of a bookkeeper's work involves not only the entering of information, but the review of information and the reconciling of accounts. While some people remain career bookkeepers at one company, most rotate between companies or leave the field altogether for supervisory or managerial positions.

ASSOCIATED CAREERS

Bookkeepers become accountants and inventory control experts at a higher rate than any other profession. Those who leave the record-keeping industry altogether use their bookkeeping skills to understand various tasks within an industry, then move to positions of managerial control. The people who take this route, however, usually supplement their bookkeeping skills with courses, seminars, or second positions where they can demonstrate their management ability.

PAST AND FUTURE

About 3000 B.C., the Egyptians employed an inventory system to keep track of grain shipments and warehouse storage; this system formed the basis of modern day bookkeeping. From one of the most active trading centers in the modern world, Venice, came the Italian Luca Pacioli, who developed double-entry bookkeeping. Over the years, this became the world-wide standard method of keeping track of income and outlay, profits and losses. As technology has developed, many bookkeeping systems have become computerized.

Bookkeepers face a strong demand for services over the next decade, but must be aware of the trend of computerization in the industry, as that will grow faster than job opportunities. Those who study accounting and current accounting software packages should be in a good position for entry-level opportunities. More positions are expected to become available in the Southeast and Southwest, and in urban centers more than rural sectors.

QUALITY OF LIFE

Two Years

A two-year bookkeeper designs or implements systems of inventory and accounting control, and works with each department of a company and with accountants on year-end financial statements. Daily responsibilities include entering account activity and reviewing revenue and expenditure streams. Bookkeepers also cut all checks the company issues. Salaries are reasonable and hours are long because new bookkeeepers are still learning. Satisfaction is average, but those who have more input into the bookkeeping systems used seem happier than others.

Five Years

Five-year veterans offer significant input to bookkeeping systems and methodologies adopted by companies. Bookkeepers work closely with accountants and management to plan expenditures and revenue streams over the course of a year. Many people move from job to job during these middle years, looking for a position that fits their ideal match in terms of size, challenge, and manageability. Hours become more regular; satisfaction is average.

Ten Years

Ten-year veterans head up bookkeeping departments. Many have significant influence on accounting procedures and internal financial controls. Salaries rise, hours remain average, and satisfaction increases.

THE BIRKMAN LIFESTYLE GRID

This career is suitable for people with Yellow interests.

You'll Have Contact With

Accountants
Bankers
Office Managers
Product Vendors

Major Associations

New York Society of Independent Public Accountants
509 Westchester Avenue
Rye Brook, NY 10573
Tel: 212-719-8300
Contact: Susan Beckett

National Society of Public Accountants
1010 North Fairfax Street
Alexandria, VA 22314-1574
Tel: 703-549-6400
Contact: Ryan Reynolds

American Institute of Certified Public Accountants
1455 Pennsylvania Avenue NW
Washington, DC
Tel: 202-737-6600

BUYER

A DAY IN THE LIFE

Being a professional buyer is a glamorous, powerful job in many respects. But the glitter and glitz cloud the hard work and keen intellect required to make it in this competitive field. Professional buyers examine goods and work within reasonable budgets to make competitive bids for products to resell. Don't underestimate the amount and the scale of negotiations necessary. "People eat you alive if they think they can get away with it," wrote one buyer. Those comfortable with negotiating reported a higher-than-average satisfaction with their job. The decisions a buyer makes—color, size, quantity and price—are some of the most important in determining whether a company makes a profit in a given year. The power to influence sales, beat competition, and earn high profits through your own action gives many buyers satisfaction in a high-pressure position. The bottom line in this job is "how am I selling and what is my margin." "It's the closest thing to gambling, including picking stocks. You don't really have a lot of research—you have to go with your taste and your gut feeling," mentioned one long-term buyer, "It's addictive." Some buyers said that it is important to stick with what you know and not think about commercial profitability, because "you're just as likely to pick a winner or a dog either way. Consumer taste is fickle." A buyer must have confidence in his choices, and be able to assert his preferences and defend his selections.

Buyers work long and sometimes unusual hours, traveling to fashion shows, industry conferences, seminars, and trade-shows. They investigate producers' lines, then place orders, usually with a limited amount of discussion. Professional buyers work with retail sales people to get feedback on how choices they have made responded to the market. This back-and-forth dialogue is important to a buyer's understanding of any problems the sales force has moving the product. A significant number of respondents mentioned the support the other members of the field provided. While many times buyers will come into conflict over purchases and sales, the profession is so grueling that many find themselves sympathetic with one another in spite of that conflict.

PAYING YOUR DUES

Almost any major can prepare you to become a buyer; it depends on what you want to buy. A book buyer might have been an English major; someone who buys hospital supplies might have majored in biology. Any college major with a business or managerial skills background will prepare you for the career. All employers require new employees to learn the specifics of their own business. Large companies usually have internal buyer training programs lasting from one to five years that expose the new employee to all aspects of the business. Many trainees begin as salespeople and learn about inventory policy, stock maintenance, and shipment checking. Aspiring buyers receive extensive training on proprietary computer and inventory tracking systems. The abilities to plan ahead, predict consumer habits and make difficult decisions mark those who emerge successfully from training programs. Those who continue in the profession find it helpful to achieve the professional designations recognized in each state, such as Certified Purchasing Manager (CMP) and Certified Purchasing Professional (CPE). To become an official purchasing agent for the government, applicants must pass a two- or three-part exam to attain federal certification.

ASSOCIATED CAREERS

Professional buyers are usually in touch with a taste or a sensibility in a given field, and many use their knowledge in other careers. Some become fashion consultants for celebrities, others become internal managers for production firms, a third group moves into retail and opens their own stores. A significant number enter advertising, where their guesses as to consumer preference and experience working with salespeople prove invaluable.

PAST AND FUTURE

Professional buyers were part of the growth of large retail concerns, where stores would stock the same merchandise in the same region. Professional buyer was a position created to centralize these responsibilities and standardize inventory.

Buyers face a shrinking market for their services. The industry trend among major retail stores has been consolidation and/or bankruptcy. In 1995, eleven major retail chains filed for Chapter 11 (bankruptcy protection). Industry consolidation means shrinkage of redundant positions and further standardization of inventory, so buyers have fewer opportunities to buy. This shrinkage of jobs at large retail stores may be offset by the growth of chains, but not enough evidence exists yet to decide how likely this is.

QUALITY OF LIFE

Two Years

Professional buyers have begun, and in some cases completed, buyer training programs. Lessons include budgeting, accounting, retail sales, computer systems, inventory control, company protocol, an overview of the industry they are involved in, and some basic financial skills. Many have begun "externship" parts of their program where part of the time is spent in classrooms and the rest is spent working in retail sales departments. Many cite working in retail as invaluable to their development as professional buyers. Salaries and responsibilities are low, but many enjoy these years for the education and quality of life (free time) they offer.

Five Years

Those involved in long training programs have finished them and become assistant buyers with discrete accounts and responsibilities. Many pursue additional education through coursework, industry publications, and professional seminars. Those with good reputations for hard work and shrewd bargaining can advance to full buyer status with accountability to the head of the department. Numerous opportunities arise for aggressive buyers to distinguish themselves; the price for this risky behavior can be significant—over 20 percent of the workforce is let go by year five, primarily for lack of "aptitude" at the profession.

Ten Years

Hours increase, responsibilities increase, salary increases. Years seven to eleven are when most professional buyers settle into the roles they will assume for most of their careers. Those who've wanted to move into management have by this point, and those who wish to remain buyers have carved out comfortable territory for themselves. Work changes from directly negotiating deals to overseeing other buyers and assistant buyers. Many have established relationships with producers. Over 30 percent of ten-year members of the industry are still with the companies they began their careers with.

THE BIRKMAN LIFESTYLE GRID

Red Green
Yellow Blue

This career is suitable for people with Green interests.

You'll Have Contact With
Inventory Managers
Manufacturing Executives
Market Researchers
Retail Salespeople

Major Associations
National Contract Management Association
1912 Woodford Road
Vienna, VA 22182
Tel: 703-448-9231

National Institute of Governmental Purchasing
11800 Sunrise Valley Drive
Suite 1050
Reston, VA 22091
Tel: 703-715-9400
Contact: James E. Brinkman

CAREER COUNSELOR

A DAY IN THE LIFE

A career counselor is a teacher, confidant, and advisor to his clients. He helps people examine their interests, their styles, and their abilities to find and enter the profession that best suits them. They can be helpful both to those who have yet to choose a career and those who are unhappy with their choice.

A career counselor spends most of his day meeting with clients. The early sessions explore the history and behavior of the client to help the clients understand their own motivations and desires more thoroughly. This process can be hard work. "People expect to come out a week later with a perfect understanding of what job they should do for the rest of their life," said one career counselor. "It's not that simple, and it's not that quick." Most career counselors have degrees in psychology or are licensed therapists. Therapists and counselors alike are facilitators—the client must be an active part of the process.

After conducting a thorough evaluation of the client's personality traits, the counselor must use his expertise to help the client assess her skill base and direct her to a career wherein those skills might be most profitably employed, both financially and in terms of job satisfaction. Counselors are responsible for knowing what skills are needed in a broad variety of professions, how much they pay, and what a hiring authority will want to see in a successful applicant. They then coach the client through the process of researching fields that match their interests, setting up informational interviews with people to supplement their research, and finally targeting or creating specific job positions that meet their needs. Counselors try to empower the client to become as active as possible in their search. "A lot of people come in and want to sit back passively and have you get them a job," complained one counselor. "We can teach them the skills they need—how to write effective letters, highlight their skills in an interview, negotiate a salary, and make people remember them—but in the end, they have to get out there and do it."

PAYING YOUR DUES

Most career counselors have some degree of higher education, often a master's in a field such as mental health counseling, psychological counseling, or community counseling. At the moment though, career counseling is an unregulated field, so people can come to the profession through a variety of paths. Some come from social work or human resources management. Others come to career counseling from a discipline such as law or medicine and then use their industry expertise to counsel people in their former field.

Familiarity with basic personality, interest, and skills tests, such as the Holland Code, the Myers-Briggs Analogy Test, and the Birkman Personality Assessment (a customized version of which appears in this book) are invaluable aids in assessing clients' occupational aptitudes. Usually, a successful career counselor works as an independent counselor but gets references from other services, therapists, or agencies. This entails long hours, intense listening and assessment skills, and the ability to think objectively without being swayed by emotion.

ASSOCIATED CAREERS

Career counselors have skills that involve helping other people understand themselves better and take proactive steps to improve the quality of their work lives. Many career counselors are able to transfer these skills to the realms of teaching, vocational counseling in school, and social work; others

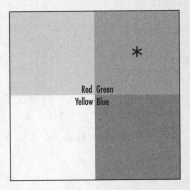

go on to get advanced degrees and become therapists. Those who are more interested in the business applications of their craft go into outplacement, corporate recruitment and professional head-hunting.

PAST AND FUTURE

Many occupations, such as high school vocational counselors, job retrainers, and psychotherapists, used to have career counseling as one part of their overall job description. But in recent decades career counseling has come into its own as a discrete profession.

Indeed, career counseling is a rapidly growing field. It's now estimated that the average person will have as many as half a dozen distinct jobs in the course of his career, and the need for this service is likely to increase. Many therapists whose clients have included people with career issues are crossing into the field, and still there is adequate demand to support nearly twice the number of career counselors. The recent wave of corporate downsizing has generated a steady supply of mid-level executives, and there is much focus in career counseling on outplacing and retraining these new clients. On the flip side, a number of people have done very well in professions that have nonetheless left them bored or unhappy, and these people may now have the luxury to ask "What do I really want to do?"

QUALITY OF LIFE

Two Years

Typically, career counselors start out by working with established professionals who have an existing client base. Many are still moving through training programs associated with established testing authorities, and spend significant time attending professional seminars and keeping up with professional reading. A number of career counselors come into the profession as psychotherapists, and many make the transition to career counseling gradually. Expect few dramatic success stories in these early years—the training can be a lengthy process.

Five Years

By now, most counselors have begun to see progress among their clients—many of whom have successfully shifted careers in these first five years. Recommendations are a key component of a successful career counseling practice, especially in the early years. Among the more successful counselors, client bases have broadened through word-of-mouth. Salaries have gone up, hours are significant, and satisfaction is strong. Those who began with more established counselors break off between years four and seven to establish independent practices. Marketing skills become important. Many career counselors become involved in professional education seminars, conferences, and other professional establishments to train in cutting-edge counseling techniques.

Ten Years

Those who've survived ten years in the profession have earned solid reputations and have shepherded many clients to new occupations. Education continues throughout this profession. Many established professionals begin scaling back hours and professional commitments during these later years, in order to increase their quality of life or perhaps to devote more time to writing and research; many ten-year veterans of this profession are prolific contributors to professional journals and mainstream publications. Salaries level off as professionals work fewer hours at higher hourly rates.

THE BIRKMAN LIFESTYLE GRID

This career is suitable for people with Green interests.

You'll Have Contact With

Clients
Occupational Therapists
Psychologists
Vocational Testing Consultants

Major Associations

American School Counseling Association
5999 Stevenson Avenue
Alexandria, VA 22304
Tel: 703-823-9800

National Board for Certified Counselors
3 Terrace Way
Suite D
Greensboro, NC 27403
Tel: 910-547-0607

American College and Career
Counseling Center (ACACCC)
2401 Pennsylvania Avenue, Suite 10-6-51
Philadelphia, PA 19130
Tel: 215-232-5225

CARPENTER

A DAY IN THE LIFE

Carpenters are craftsmen who build things. The occupation rewards those who can combine precise detail work with strenuous manual labor. Carpenters construct two categories of items: those used in the erection, maintenance, and aesthetic mix of structures, and those used as furniture, art, or framing. Similar skills are important in each category: The abilities to turn blueprints and plans into finished objects, to pick good wood, and to use all woodworking tools. But structural carpenters enjoy a larger market for their services and a more consistent demand than piecework carpenters do. The satisfaction levels in both fields are high, but the lifestyle in each is quite different. "The best thing about building things is that you know you can do a good job that will last for years. It's great to walk by a place ten years after you built it and say 'you know, I put up those walls and put in those floors.'" This sense of pride came through in the majority of structural carpenter surveys we received. Structural carpenters work with supervisors and construction managers on the production of multimaterial products. They work with fiberglass, drywall, and plastic as well as wood, and they use saws, tape measures, drills, and sanders in their jobs. They shape and join material to the specifications of blueprints or at the direction of their contractor. This can entail long hours of physical labor, sometimes in unpleasant circumstances. "Putting up a house in November isn't fun at all," said one carpenter from the Northeast. Structural carpenters also spend significant time checking their work with plumb bobs, rules, and levels. The injury rate among structural carpenters is above average.

Detail carpenters usually work indoors, some involved in maintenance and refinishing, others involved in creation. The majority work as furniture restorers and repairmen. They fix, sand, even, and stain used furniture. Detail work requires a good eye for prior construction methods, an understanding of restoration techniques, and patience. Other detail carpenters fashion and create their own pieces of furniture, choosing the wood, designing the final product, then shaping and assembling the parts. Many then sell these pieces to retail houses and private buyers. Detail carpenters work directly with clients more than structural carpenters, so interpersonal skills are much more significant.

PAYING YOUR DUES

Carpenters learn their trade on the job and through apprenticeships. Many of the apprentice programs are administered by the Associate Builders and Contractors and the Associated General Contractors, Inc., as well as by such unions as the United Brotherhood of Carpenters and Joiners of America and the National Association of Home Builders. You have to be at least seventeen years old and show a capacity to learn, the ability to do sustained, difficult, physical work, manual dexterity, some mathematical aptitude, and a willingness to take direction. Most apprenticeships last three to four years. The market for carpenters is tied to local construction markets, and while the education gained by being a carpenter is invaluable for someone who wants to be involved in the construction industry, the unpredictability of the work is something applicants should be familiar with before entering this profession. Applicants may also need to relocate at times in order to find work.

ASSOCIATED CAREERS

Structural carpenters have a large exposure to the different areas of construction, so it is not surprising that many who leave the profession go into plumbing, electrical wiring, or contracting. Detail carpenters go into graphic design, sculpture, and glasswork. Those who leave usually do so because of lack of opportunity rather than dissatisfaction with the profession.

PAST AND FUTURE

Carpentry has been around since human beings built structures, but methodologies and powerful construction tools have developed through the ages. In particular, the development of the flexible nail made construction of objects that could survive shipping, stress, and settling possible.

Carpenters will be in strong demand for the next ten years, subject to normal considerations of real-estate construction cycles and local economies. In general, the field has a high turnover rate, due to retirement and injury. The potential increased use of prefabricated components in the construction industry means fewer carpenters will be needed to build the same number of structures, but even this will not be enough to dam the growth of job prospects through the end of the century. Carpenters unions have taken creative steps to ensure occupations for many of their members; one New York-based union made a bid to buy a convention center to ensure year-round employment for its members.

QUALITY OF LIFE

Two Years

Many carpenters are in training programs or are assistants to established carpenters. Long hours working in the field on construction sites are complemented by extra hours in the classroom learning blueprint reading skills, techniques of construction, and instruction in safety and first-aid. Minor injuries during these first two years are common, mainly from overexertion and lack of experience. Pay is low, but many find these years pass quickly, as each day brings new experiences.

Five Years

Five year carpenters have chosen an area of specialty, completed their training programs, joined a union, and established their reputations among regular employers. The hours are long and the work plentiful, and many get involved in their unions, which provide powerful contacts. Satisfaction is high during these years, and many of our respondents went out of their way to say they socialized with their co-workers and felt they were "supportive."

Ten Years

Ten-year carpenters are subject to injury much less than their younger and older counterparts, having found that safe balance between expediency and experience. Those who go into contracting use their union connections to employ efficient, hardworking carpentry crews. Those who remain often head up carpentry teams and work as managers under general contractors. Ten-year detail carpenters have established reputations with retailers, taken work on contract, and even work closely with architects in the design and aesthetic configuration of houses and their furniture. Salaries rise, but beyond this, only true stars earn extraordinary incomes.

THE BIRKMAN LIFESTYLE GRID

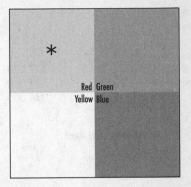

Red Green
Yellow Blue

This career is suitable for people with Red interests.

You'll Have Contact With

Architects
Construction Managers
Interior Designers
Restorers

Major Associations

American Furniture Manufacturers Association
PO Box HP-7
High Point, NC 27261
Tel: 910-884-5000

Associated General Contractors of America, Inc.
1957 E Street NW
Washington, DC 20006
Tel: 202-393-2040

CATERER

A DAY IN THE LIFE

A caterer works closely with clients to design, prepare, and serve menus for events, including wedding dinners, charity balls, holiday brunches, office lunches, and any other occasion where people gather and consume food. A caterer must understand how certain dishes work together, have strong interpersonal, particularly listening, skills, and the ability to manage a cooking and serving staff. Over 70 percent of all catering services are owner-run, so many caterers must also have sharp business acumen. Most people are drawn to the industry because of their love of cooking or preparing elegant meals for special events. In their first few years in catering many find that talent only gets you so far. "You can have dozens of clients, great reviews, and the best products—and you can still lose money hand over fist," said one ten-year veteran. Management and organizational skills are critical for those who wish to keep their catering concerns solvent. Caterers spend considerable time developing menus, a unique style, and a business plan.

"You have to oversee everything," one caterer mentioned to us, "that's why catering services never get too large." While some catering services do employ hundreds of full- and part-time staff, the large majority have fewer than six full-time employees, and hire temporary staff for the rest. Business is driven by season. A caterer may have three to five meetings with prospective clients to work out details of the event. The caterer provides menus and the clients choose their favorite dishes and work with the caterer to assemble a meal where each dish compliments the others. Successful caterers are able to gently guide people to decisions that will benefit the event.

PAYING YOUR DUES

There are no educational requirements for becoming a caterer, though many choose to attend a culinary academy to learn the basics of certain schools of cooking. Others attend restaurant management school, or at least take coursework in schools that reflect some of the concerns of the business, such as finance, management, and organization. Those who do not attend any special schools should have some type of professional food preparation experience; cooking food for large numbers of people in a limited time-frame is a skill to be learned. Caterers have to be certified for sanitary cooking conditions and safe equipment, so contact the local board of health in your area. Most offer two- or three-day courses in health laws for prospective caterers and restaurants.

ASSOCIATED CAREERS

Caterers are chefs of a sort, and many become chefs when catering concerns fold (and they do at a significant rate). Others become involved in the service end of the industry, and become event coordinators, party planners, and waiting staff managers. A small number go into the mass-produced food industry, but many view that life as "selling out." Most frequently, caterers who leave the industry take some time away, review their situations, then enter the field again with a little more knowledge and a little more experience.

PAST AND FUTURE

Catering used to be the prerogative of wealthy, manored families who would have their in-house cooks or chefs prepare meals for large events or parties. In the late-1800s, as the tap-room gave way to the fine restaurant, these families began to expect the same quality and service they received at restaurants at their private events. Deals were initially struck with those restaurants to provide service, and restaurateurs began to see a market. In the mid-twentieth century catering concerns blossomed, and they continue to do so today.

Caterers will still face the roller-coaster of success that has marked the industry for the past twenty-five years. Greater specialization seems to be taking place, with caterers choosing their territory more carefully in terms of cuisine and products.

QUALITY OF LIFE

Two Years

In the early years, caterers develop their identities, define menus, learn to manage events successfully, and network. Many introduce their services to local restaurant owners who do not cater themselves, to persuade the owners to recommend them to clients who need catering services. Earnings are generally low; hours are long and strenuous. Fewer than half of those who start out as caterers last two years in the profession. The majority go out of business in under eighteen months, due to failure to manage costs, market successfully, or establish a positive reputation.

Five Years

Caterers who have lasted five years have local reputations, established specialties, and records of performance. Many caterers attempt to expand during these years, but overexposure, lack of centralized quality control, and rising costs, all can make expansion a mixed blessing at best. Hours are long, but many have established areas of responsibility for each of their full-time employees and learned how to delegate. Satisfaction is high, and earnings have become livable.

Ten Years

Caterers who last ten years have experience running a business, an established expertise in an area of cuisine, and a repeat client base. Efforts at reinvention, though numerous during this period, are generally not well received by the client base. Reputations for service have also brought with them an expectation of menu selections, but many caterers find that their satisfaction wanes after ten years of preparing the same dishes. Earnings are consistent and strong. Many pass their businesses to newer entrants in the field over the next ten years, teaching them the skills and responsibilities of the job while gradually passing on greater and greater client responsibility. When most people sell their catering concerns, it is usually to a long-term partner.

THE BIRKMAN LIFESTYLE GRID

This career is suitable for people with Red interests.

You'll Have Contact With

Event Planners
Restauranteurs
Suppliers
Waiters

Major Associations

National Restaurant Association
1200 17th Street, NW
Washington, DC 20036-3097
Tel: 202-331-5900
Contact: Public Affairs

Educational Foundation of the
National Restaurant Association
250 South Wacker Drive
Suite 1400
Chicago, IL 60606
Tel: 312-715-1010
Contact: Customer Serice

Mobile Industrial Caterers Association
1240 North Jefferson Street
Suite G
Anaheim, CA 92807
Tel: 714-632-6800
Contact: Kelly Ramirez

CHEF

PROFESSIONAL PROFILE

# of people in profession	134,000
% male	75
% female	25
avg. hours per week	50
avg. starting salary	$19,000
avg. salary after 5 years	$31,000
avg. salary 10 to 15 years	$47,000

Professionals Read
Restaurant Business
Restaurant News
Food and Wine
Gourmet

Books, Films and TV Shows Featuring the Profession
Eat, Drink, Man, Woman
The Cook, The Thief, His Wife and Her Lover
Who is Killing the Great Chefs of Europe?
Kitchen Lies

Major Employers
Tavern on the Green
Central Park West and 67th Street
New York, NY 10023
Tel: 212-873-3200
Contact: Bob Logan/Patrick Clark

Four Seasons Hotel
57 East 57th Street
New York, NY 10022
Tel: 212-758-5700
Contact: Human Resources

Le Dome
8220 Sunset Boulevard
Los Angeles, CA 90069
Tel: 310-359-6919
Fax: 310-659-5429

A DAY IN THE LIFE

Chef is among those professions that people dream about, imagining leading a crack platoon of sous chefs in a glamorous, stainless steel kitchen and presenting fabulous meals to hundreds of people. Parts of this description are true, and those who become chefs have very high levels of satisfaction with their profession. One chef said his career "is only for the very crazy. It is hard work, it is grueling work, it is important work, and still, I would do nothing else." Many mentioned the long hours, the painstaking attention to detail, and being constantly surrounded by food as parts of a job they love. The profession rewards the talented and the daring who can see opportunity and grab it.

The best thing in urban centers, chefs were quick to mention, was the support of the community of chefs. "You start out knowing absolutely nothing and these experienced, exciting chefs you've idolized all your life will show you how to run your kitchen. It's like having a living library at your disposal." Rural chefs said the sense of isolation can be discouraging. Chefs work long and unusual hours, making it difficult for them to socialize outside of working hours. One mentioned that "only doctors and truck drivers work the 4:00 p.m. to 2:00 a.m. shift." This leaves limited opportunity for meeting others, particularly if they are in a part of the country with few chefs.

The first few years are an education. Few chefs survive cooking school who don't understand the physical requirements of the profession: lifting heavy pots, being on your feet for eight hours, stirring vats of sauces, rolling pounds of dough. Many chefs specialize in a certain type of cuisine. It is difficult for new chefs to have their skills recognized without an established history of success in a variety of workplaces. Those who leave the profession do so with heavy hearts; they genuinely enjoy the companionship of fellow chefs, the creativity involved in working with food, and the aesthetic beauty of sound presentation. But they leave anyway due to the lack of opportunity, the daily pressures (which can be considerable), and the low wages for those who do not advance immediately to positions of authority.

PAYING YOUR DUES

While the profession used to offer a direct progression for new entrants—begin as a preparation chef, move on to assistant chef, then get a chance at becoming your own chef—it is becoming more difficult to become a head chef unless you demonstrate exceptional talent and an extremely creative mind and can inspire financing. There are over 550 cooking schools in the country, and employers are beginning to impose higher culinary academic standards on their prospective employees. Some are even turning to organizations such as the American Culinary Federation, which has certified a mere 70 of these 550 schools, for recommendations. Most training programs are practical; cooking, preparation, working as part of a team, instrument maintenance, and personal hygiene (yes, that is a course) are all taught by example and as part of basic cooking principles. Programs last up to four years. Specialization is important in this industry for those looking to work at swankier restaurants, those interested in entree preparation (the most sought-after work), aspiring pastry chefs, and those specializing in a geographically distinctive type of cuisine.

ASSOCIATED CAREERS

While most chefs view their profession as a job for life, many become restaurateurs or enter some related food-industry position. A few chefs move into catering.

PAST AND FUTURE

Chefs were once under the sole command of nobility because they were the only people who could afford to pay professionals to prepare their food. The rise of commercial eating establishments in Europe allowed others to benefit from chefs' skills. Restaurants trained young chefs, often under the supervision of head chefs. Head chefs who achieved international fame, such as Auguste Escoffier, began their own cooking schools.

Opportunities for chefs are expected to rise by more than 20 percent over the next ten years due to the restaurant industry's experiencing sizable growth.

QUALITY OF LIFE

Two Years

Many start out as cooks, assistant chefs, preparatory chefs, and unpaid interns, sacrificing long hours for low wages to gain the practical experience necessary in a number of fields before they can assume positions of responsibility in a professional kitchen. Some gain these positions while finishing up their second, third, or fourth years at culinary academies. Those who are successful cite being able to listen carefully, work hard, and grab any opportunity to demonstrate skills as factors in their advancement.

Five Years

Five years into the profession, many chefs have moved from cook to assistant chef, or from assistant chef to chef with a special area of responsibility, such as vegetable chef or saucier. Years four to nine are the most active portion of prospective chefs' careers, both in terms of amount of work and job-movement. Many manage staffs of assistant chefs and preparatory chefs. Salaries, responsibilities, and hours all increase. Many find their fates tied to those at the head of the kitchen; if the head chef is fired from his job, entire staffs may go too.

Ten Years

Ten-year professionals who have attained the position of chef have had experience in a number of different areas and have held a variety of positions managing and overseeing sub-chefs and prep workers. Many have found positions that offer them significant satisfaction, although the majority attempt to open their own establishments during years ten through fifteen. A chef must have a unique and clearly explainable vision of what her restaurant should be to work well with a financial restaurateur. Networking with both chefs and patrons is at its peak, and a significant number of professionals spend free time away from their chef duties researching other restaurants' menus, prices and service. For most, wages rise.

THE BIRKMAN LIFESTYLE GRID

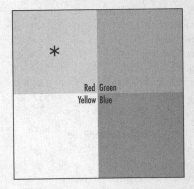

This career is suitable for people with Red interests.

You'll Have Contact With

Assistant Chefs
Restauranteurs
Sommeliers
Suppliers

Major Associations

National Restaurant Association
1200 17th Street NW
Washington, DC 20036-3097
Tel: 202-331-5900
Contact: Public Affairs

Educational Foundation of the
National Restaurant Association
250 South Wacker Drive
Suite 1400
Chicago, IL 60606
Tel: 312-715-1010
Contact: Customer Service

Chefs de Cuisine Association of America
155 E. 55th St.
#302B
New York, NY 10022
Tel: 212-832-4939
Fax: 212-832-4939

CHEMICAL ENGINEER

PROFESSIONAL PROFILE

# of people in profession	52,000
% male	80
% female	20
avg. hours per week	43
avg. starting salary	$39,200
avg. salary after 5 years	$44,800
avg. salary 10 to 15 years	$52,500

Professionals Read
Chemical Engineering
Chemicals Weekly
Chemical and Engineering News
Chemical Engineering Progress

Books, Films and TV Shows Featuring the Profession
Production Principles

Major Employers
Advance International
1200 Zerego Avenue
Bronx, NY 10462
Tel: 718-892-3460
Contact: Anthony D. Iannuzzzo

Air Products and Chemicals Inc.
17330 Brookhurst Street
Suite 260
Fountain Valley, CA 92708
Tel: 714-968-5648
Fax: 714-964-4054
Contact: Max Monestime

Allied Signal
665 Lybrand St.
Postville, IA 56162
Tel: 319-864-7321
Fax: 319-864-4231
Contact: Personnel Director

A DAY IN THE LIFE

The headline of the brochure for the American Institute of Chemical Engineers states that chemical engineers are responsible for the production of items, "from microchips to potato chips." Chemical engineers work in the chemical, fuel, aerospace, environmental, food, and pulp and paper industries, among many others. Responsibilities range from research and design to development, production, technical sales, and, for those with good communication skills, management. Chemical engineering is a problem-solving profession with a practical bias; expect to answer the question "how" more than any other. Chemical engineers translate the discoveries chemists make into real-world products. If a chemist invents a better fertilizer, for example, a chemical engineer might design the method to make mass production of that fertilizer possible. Much of this work is planning: theoretical "modeling" of production processes and analysis that takes place on computer or in preliminary reports. Chemical engineers work with chemists, accountants, human resource personnel, and regulators to create efficient, safe and cost-effective methods of reproducing valuable items. Chemical engineers work in teams, mostly for large corporations. Engineers thrive on the intellectual challenge they get from their work. Good chemical engineers are always trying to refine their systems, improve them, and make them safer and more efficient.

PAYING YOUR DUES

Like all engineers, the would-be chemical engineer must pass a rigorous set of academic requirements. Coursework must include a full spectrum of chemistry courses, some physics, electrical engineering, mathematics, computer science, and biology, as well as some applied materials science courses for those who want to go into manufacturing industries. English courses are extremely helpful, as many chemical engineers must write and review reports. Over 140 colleges and universities offer accredited chemical engineering curricula. Master's and doctoral degrees are preferred for those who hope to achieve any supervisory or directed research positions.

The most difficult thing about becoming a chemical engineer is adapting theoretical knowledge to a practical discipline. Many engineers find it helpful to attend professional seminars and subscribe to publications, such as Chemical Engineering, which explore their area of responsibility in the light of industry breakthroughs. Others enjoy the support of professional organizations, such as the American Institute of Chemical Engineers (AIChE). Employers, for the most part, view chemical engineering as a practical discipline and look for experience in production, manufacturing, or management to verify these traits in potential employees. Each state has its own written exam for chemical engineers who wish to work in the public sector.

ASSOCIATED CAREERS

Chemical engineers use their skills to become entrepreneurs and managers in a number of fields, ranging from patent law to microbrewing. A notable few become astronauts. The majority of chemical engineers rotate within the profession rather than leave it.

PAST AND FUTURE

Chemical engineers have been around since the first distilling process took place. Chemical engineering became a science beginning in the Renaissance, with the codification of experiments and results. This organization was coupled with achievements in pure (not applied) chemistry. Chemical engineering began to be taught as a discipline in 1888 at the Massachusetts Institute of Technology.

Currently, 40 percent of chemical engineers are employed by the chemicals industry, followed distantly by environmental organizations, the food industry, biotechnology companies, and electronics. The level of employment is expected to remain static, with the notable exception that many employed in the chemicals industry, which includes the petroleum industry, will migrate to the emerging bio- and electronic-technology fields. While the number of jobs is expected to remain stable for the next ten years, fewer applicants are expected to vie for these jobs, leading to a potentially bright future for the aspiring chemical engineer.

QUALITY OF LIFE

Two Years

Chemical engineers work in teams as data collectors and computer modelers. Many have limited input and low levels of responsibility during these early years. Hours are unremarkable, but professional associations, professional reading and additional research may eat up the time of the ambitious chemical engineer. Those who leave get the yearnings to do so in these early years, but few follow through until later. Satisfaction is average.

Five Years

Five years into the profession, many chemical engineers have specialized in research, design, production, development or technical sales. Responsibility has increased, and many get their first taste of managerial status. Significant input is expected from the five-year engineer. People skills become more important. Five-year veterans are judged on the success of their track record. Those who leave to start their own companies most often do so between years seven and nine.

Ten Years

Ten-year chemical engineers are "senior" engineers and many have been promoted to levels of personnel and project management. Many are involved in the coordination and development phase of projects (the initial planning stages) and offer experienced direction without having to do any of the more mundane modeling that more junior chemical engineers undertake. Private firm employees earn larger wages than those in the public sector, but many choose to work for the EPA or the Department of Agriculture, citing more regular hours and less corporate politics.

THE BIRKMAN LIFESTYLE GRID

Red Green
Yellow Blue

This career is suitable for people with Red interests.

You'll Have Contact With

Chemists
Lab Technicians
Production Managers
Researchers

Major Associations

American Chemical Society
1155 16th Street NW
Washington, DC 20036
Tel: 202-872-4600

Water Environment Federation
601 Wythe Street
Alexandria, VA 22314
Tel: 703-684-2400
Contact: Nancy Blatt

Industrial Chemical Research Association
1811 Monroe Street
Dearborn, MI 48124
Tel: 313-563-0360

CHEMIST

Professionals Read

The Chemist
Science
Chemical Engineering Progress
Chemicals Weekly

Books, Films and TV Shows Featuring the Profession

Dr. Jekyll and Mr. Hyde
The Biography of Linus Pauling
The Elixer
Lorenzo's Oil

Major Employers

Advance International
1200 Zerego Avenue
Bronx, NY 10462
Tel: 718-892-3460
Contact: Anthony D. Iannuzzzo

Air Products and Chemicals Inc.
17330 Brookhurst Street
Suite 260
Fountain Valley, CA 92708
Tel: 714-968-5648
Fax: 714-964-4054
Contact: Max Monestime

Alliedsignal
665 Lybrand Street
Postville, IA 10462
Tel: 319-864-7321
Fax: 319-864-4231
Contact: Personnel Director

A DAY IN THE LIFE

Chemists "are paid to be creative, careful, and productive" said one of our survey respondents, and the rest agreed. "It's a career for people who think about the future," mentioned another. Chemists analyze the basic properties of matter. In the commercial sector, they find new uses and applications for it. In the academic sector, they study the implications of newly discovered chemical properties. Chemists spend over 60 percent of their time in the lab or in front of their computers analyzing data. Most work is done in teams, and more than one respondent pointed out that teamwork skills are "essential" to success in this field. Specific duties may include modeling, analysis, synthesis, research, limited fieldwork, or even sales and information management. There are as many specialties, such as quality control chemists or organic chemists, as there are areas of application of chemical principles. A chemist's specialty would depend on his style of working, but the desire to search for the ability to manipulate matter and make more useful materials is common to all chemists.

Chemists work closely with other experts, including chemical engineers, who plan the production and development of discoveries made by chemists; sales forces, who explain their products; and academic chemists, who share information at cutting-edge levels. This requires good interpersonal skills and an ability to always keep end goals in mind. "You don't spend a lot of time hanging out with other chemists, but you do spend a lot of time reading about them." Professional reading can be significant in this profession, as discoveries can change the understanding of the physical systems that are critical to this profession. Chemists are challenged, excited and satisfied with the profession in which the majority spend their entire careers.

PAYING YOUR DUES

About 600 colleges offer undergraduate degrees in chemistry, and 300 offer graduate degrees. Quality control, assistant, and production chemists generally need only an undergraduate degree in chemistry, but many employers look for cross-disciplinary studies including biology, physics, materials science, English, and communications courses. The commercial sector hires chemists most often in the petroleum, chemicals, medical, food, and production industries, while the academic sector hiring of chemists is dominated by universities and research institutions. As most chemists work in teams, a growing number of employers look for strong interpersonal skills: "The ability to play well in the sandbox," as one of our survey respondents put it. This means that intelligence, for a long time the single factor in determining job opportunities in the field of chemistry, is no longer the only consideration. Later in their careers, many find it helpful to join a professional organization such as the American Chemical Society (ACS).

ASSOCIATED CAREERS

Chemists become chemical engineers more often than anything else, but their analytic skills recommend them to many professions. They become entrepreneurs, research managers, and hazardous waste managers, as well as software and sales engineers. Any field that rewards a curious, organized mind is open to an emigrant from the field of chemistry.

PAST AND FUTURE

Chemistry has been around as a learned discipline since people started to rely on the medicinal value of herbs and plants. While an understanding of the reasons behind the curative effects of these plants was lacking, the original cause-and-effect study of them laid the foundation for modern chemistry. Notable luminaries in the development of chemistry include Mendeleyev and Meyer, who developed the periodic table of elements in the nineteenth century, and Niels Bohr, who correctly postulated the structure of the atom early in the twentieth century.

Chemistry as a profession is downsizing. The mid-1990s saw chemical, petroleum, and food companies all tighten their operations in the name of efficiency and profits. As these are the three major employers of chemists, hiring came almost to a standstill. While many believe that the market for chemists will rebound and that this cutting back was only one step in a strengthening process, the job market has yet to reflect a bounce back. Those with the brightest futures are those who combine their chemistry degrees with a mastery of other subjects such as biochemistry or mathematics (for theoretical chemists).

QUALITY OF LIFE

Two Years

Chemists work as general assistants, performing experiments and recording data under the direction of more experienced, more senior chemists. Many are shunted to areas that they did not anticipate, such as quality control or information management. These early years are marked by average hours and reasonable levels of satisfaction. Few chemists have any illusions about the mundane duties that will be their responsibilities.

Five Years

Five-year veterans have chosen an area of specialization that matches their style, and many have been put in charge of research, production, or development teams. Tasks include the assembling and analysis of data based on computer models. Many have managerial duties as well as hands-on tasks to complete. Those who wish to rise above this project-managing level should note that personnel management skills are important beyond this point.

Ten Years

Ten-year chemists have found their responsibilities extend more in terms of direction, budgeting and planning than actual research and development. Many use management skills more than research abilities. Significant connections help those who start their own research companies. Hours rise; salaries increase; satisfaction remains level.

THE BIRKMAN LIFESTYLE GRID

Red Green
Yellow Blue

This career is suitable for people with Red interests.

You'll Have Contact With
Chemical Engineers
Lab Technicians
Pharmaceutical Executives
Researchers

Major Associations
American Chemical Society, Career Services
1155 16th Street NW
Washington, DC 20036
Tel: 202-872-4600

Chemical Manufacturers Association
1300 Wilson Boulevard
Arlington, VA 22209
Tel: 703-741-5000

American Pharmaceutical Association
2215 Constitution Avenue NW
Washington, DC 20037-2985
Tel: 202-628-4410
Fax: 202-783-2351

CHILDCARE WORKER

A DAY IN THE LIFE

Child care workers live with the reality that there is no perfect substitute for a family in raising a child; but while parents are at work, away, or otherwise unavailable, responsibility for the care and supervision of their children is a serious concern, and there are great possibilities for personal fulfillment in any career of service to young people. "Rewarding" is how most child care workers describe their jobs, and the joy of helping children grow is one of its most appealing features.

A number of child care workers are hired by government agencies and large corporations to run in-house daycare centers. These centers allow parents to work and still be close to their children, receiving a valuable benefit for little or no charge. More and more firms are recognizing that having an on-site day care center provides them with significant advantages, notably reduced absenteeism, higher productivity, and better morale among workers, for relatively few dollars.

Other child care workers are employed by individual families; responsibilities in these positions may be more comprehensive, from live-in twenty-four-hour assistance to cooking duties. Arrangements are made individually between parents and the child care provider. Recent events have brought the widespread lack of Social Security payments for child care workers to national attention. Employers are responsible for these payments by law; many employers do not realize this until it is brought to their attention.

A child care worker manages a child's day, most often attending to the child from early morning through early afternoon—keeping the child engaged with games, exercise, meals, and study. "If you're not organized, you're going to have lots of problems," said one ten-year child care worker. But professionals must be flexible within a framework. With young children, "anything can happen and anything will," wrote another. Children need to trust and feel "at home" with the people around them, and the successful caregiver deals with situations as they arise, from health-care emergencies to calming a very active child. The ability to provide a solid framework of activity, a flexible outlook, and a sense of caring, fun, and energy, are all important facets of being a good child care worker.

PAYING YOUR DUES

Perhaps the most important characteristic of the child care worker is a delicate balance of maturity and wonder. Child care providers work long hours under trying circumstances with children who are grasping to understand their world. A professional must be mature enough to act responsibly with and around the child but be filled with enough wonder to share in the child's excitement at learning. No specific educational requirements exist for the profession, but since child care workers have responsibility for the care of children, courses in basic first aid, childhood development, early childhood education, and nutrition are helpful. The better day care centers require bachelor's or master's degrees in early education. Extensive personal screening is routine in this field, particularly for candidates who work through an agency. Recommendations are more important in this field than in just about any other, and so the worker with excellent references will have a great advantage through word of mouth.

One of the most difficult aspects of being a child care worker is maintaining seemingly infinite patience in the handling of young and excitable children. Another great challenge is the lack of adult human contact. Most who are dissatisfied with the profession claim it is due not to lack of enjoyment of teaching and nurturing children, but more to the desire for peer contact and communication. Wages rise inconsistently for both the day care center worker and the family nanny alike, and without assuming further responsibilities, there is not much of a "ladder" to climb.

ASSOCIATED CAREERS

Child care workers enjoy working with children, and many translate this interest into teaching. Many become teachers, learning specialists, and guidance counselors. Many people work as child care professionals while young and then go on to a variety of wholly independent careers.

PAST AND FUTURE

During the Middle Ages, branches of the Catholic Church managed orphanages and "public houses" for abandoned children. Royal and wealthy families always employed a staff of specialists who were responsible for raising and educating the children, with each staff member holding a discrete responsibility, such as nurse, tutor, or physical fitness instructor. Now, when both parents work, it is common to hire part-time nannies or send children to day care centers.

Child care positions are expected to become more and more available with rapid job growth of around 18 percent over the next five years. Many jobs will become available through religious, private, and community-based organizations that recognize the need for more child care options and the value of economies of scale in this profession (i.e., it doesn't cost that much more to have one person look after three children instead of two). Private companies will also contribute significantly to this job growth, which should take place evenly across the United States.

QUALITY OF LIFE

Two Years

Two years is a relatively long period for child care workers to be employed at a single location. Many work part-time to supplement another, less remunerative occupation. Those who excel at their job are likely to receive raises and supervisional responsibilities within two years. Family child care workers can expect salaries to rise and duties to change, based on the growth and needs of the child. Turnover is significant during these years-around 20 percent of part-time child care workers leave the profession in the first two years.

Five Years

Five-year veterans generally fall into two categories: those who are running daycare centers and child care programs, and those who work as individual practitioners for families. At this point, the former have supervisory, staffing, and budget responsibilities. The latter have significant relationships with families—especially those workers with "live-in" positions; a long-term child care worker has likely bonded with the child and has become a very important person in that child's life. Many caregivers are forced to shift from one family to another when the children begin attending school. Many find it difficult to sever their ties, as the relationships can become intense.

Ten Years

Child care workers who have lasted ten years in the profession gain strong satisfaction from their choice of occupation. Nearly all have worked a number of jobs and have good reputations and strong opportunities for employment. Many ten-year day care center veterans open their own day care centers, but, they may find that while they gain greater control over their work environment, they wind up spending more time running the business than actually caring for children.

THE BIRKMAN LIFESTYLE GRID

This career is suitable for people with Blue interests.

You'll Have Contact With
Nutritionists
Psychologists
Teachers
Social Workers

Major Associations
Association for the Care of Children's Health
7910 Woodmont Avenue, Suite 300
Bethesda, MD 20814
Tel: 301-654-6549
Fax: 301-986-4553

Child Life Council
11820 Park Lawn Drive, Suite 202
Rockville, MD 20852-2529
Tel: 301-881-7092
Fax: 301-881-7092

National Association of Social Workers
750 First Street NE
Washington, DC 20002
Tel: 202-408-8600
Fax: 202-336-8310
Contact: Karen Kaplan

Council for Early Childhood
Professional Recognition
2460 16th St. NW
Washington, DC 20009
Tel: 202-265-9090
Tel: 800-424-4310

National Association of Childcare
Resource and Referral Agencies
1319 F Street NW, Suite 606
Washington, DC 20004
Tel: 202-393-5501

CHIROPRACTOR

A DAY IN THE LIFE

Chiropractic is a holistic health care discipline which focuses on promoting correct physical alignment to maintain health. Chiropractors believe that structural problems can cause dysfunction in the nervous system leading to a host of aches, pains, and other conditions. Their goal is to realign the body in a way that restores and preserves health, and to accomplish this without drugs or surgery.

Much of the day in the life of a chiropractor is spent seeing patients, and doing the paperwork that accompanies them. Doctors check the functioning of the neuromuscularskelatal system and analyze the spine using the unique system of chiropractic diagnosis. Chiropractors use "manipulations" to correct the spinal alignment and do treatments with massage, heat therapy, and ultrasound to restore balance to the system. They may prescribe changes in diet, exercises or supports to aid the process. "Compassion is the greatest asset a chiropractor can have," said one pracitioner. Good listening skills help chiropractors detect hidden factors that contribute to their patients maladies. Good communication skills also help establish rapport with patients, which in turn helps build the practice. Chiropractors need to continue educating people about the field as the public becomes more interested in holistic health.

PAYING YOUR DUES

To be admitted to pursue a Doctor of Chiropractic (D.C.) applicants must have at least two years of college with courses in organic and inorganic chemistry, biology, and physics as well as a grounding in the social sciences and humanities. There are twenty-one chiropractic colleges accredited by the Council on Chiropractic Education (CCE). A handful of these grant baccalaureate degrees in conjunction with liberal arts colleges. This reciprocal agreement allows candidates to combine their courses of study and achieve the D.C. degree a year earlier than usual. The last year of school is spent seeing patients under the supervision of a clinic director. The D.C. hopeful must see a certain number of patients to graduate.

New graduates must pass the National Board exams. There are also board exams required to practice in some states. In addition, most states require a certain amount of continuing education per year to maintain a chiropractic license.

ASSOCIATED CAREERS

Chiropractors work with nutritionists, exercise physiologists, physical therapists, accupuncturists, neurologists, podiatrists and other specialists, such as people who specialize in ergonomics. A chiropractor might cross-over into one of these fields if their interests changed, but the majority of people with a doctor of chiropractic practice, or teach.

PAST AND FUTURE

The profession of chiropractic was founded in 1895 by D.D. Palmer, a magnetic healer. The janitor in his employ, Harvey Lillard, was deaf. Palmer was convinced it was due to the strange lump on his shoulder. After one manipulation, Palmer enabled Harvey to hear and began to study the relationship between the musculoskelatal system and other body functions. But it was his son, B.J. Palmer, who really developed the discipline. He lectured on the science of chiropractic a great deal and eventually founded The Palmer College of Chiropractic in Davenport, Iowa.

Chiropractic is gaining much greater acceptance as American society becomes interested in alternative medicine. Chiropractic is now covered by almost every HMO and PPO in the country, and in the past five years hospitals have started admitting chiropractors on their staff. As a result, the field is becoming increasingly competitive. Though officially only two years of college are required to apply to study for a doctor of chiropractic, most candidates nowadays have a bachelors degree. Colleges report that their applicant pool is getting better every year. The Council on Chiropractic Education is in the process of developing the CCAT, a standardized test for admission to chiropractic college. Fortunately, the growing interest in chiropractic means an increased demand for chiropractors and good job prospects.

High technology has also had a dramatic impact on the field of chiropractic. Chiropractors now regularly use CAT scans, MRI, and thermography as diagnostic tools. Treatment too, has changed with technological advancements: ultrasound, and electromuscular stimulation are commonplace now. These new practices use expensive machinery, however, which significantly increases the cost of setting up a practice. As a result, there will probably be a trend toward larger practices in the future.

QUALITY OF LIFE
Two Years
In the beginning of their career, chiropractors generally work for someone else. They could become an associate in a small or mid-sized practice or assist at a large clinic. Either way, this gives them the mentorship of experienced professionals and helps them begin to build a client base.

Five Years
At this stage of their career chiropractors often decide whether they will buy into the practice in which they work and become a partner, or open their own practice as a sole proprietor. Many also go back to school at this point to train in advanced techniques and develop a specialty. Some pursue a Ph.D. in their specialty, which will allow them to teach.

Ten Years
By this time a chiropractor has built his practice to the point of it becoming self-generating; some may be considering opening a second office. After a decade of practice many chiropractors teach part-time and have become active in the politics of the profession. They may be involved with groups that want to educate the public about the field of chiropractic such as their school alumni, or other regional or national organizations.

THE BIRKMAN LIFESTYLE GRID

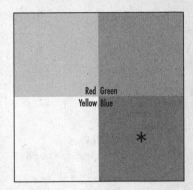

This career is suitable for people with Blue interests.

You'll Have Contact With
Nutritionists
Physical Therapists
Occupational Therapists
X-Ray Technicians

Major Associations
American Chiropractic Association
1701 Clarendon Blvd.
Arlington, VA 22209
Tel: 703-276-8800

International Chiropractors Association
1110 North Glebe Road
Suite 1000
Arlington, VA 22201
Tel: 703-528-5000

World Chiropractic Alliance
2950 Dobson Rd.
Suite 1
Chandler, AZ 85224-1802
Tel: 602-786-9235

CITY PLANNER

PROFESSIONAL PROFILE

# of people in profession	10,000
% male	70
% female	30
avg. hours per week	45
avg. starting salary	$21,000
avg. salary after 5 years	$33,000
avg. salary 10 to 15 years	$47,000

Professionals Read

Journal of the American Planning Association
Planning
Transportation Journal

Books, Films and TV Shows Featuring the Profession

City Hall
The Power Broker: Robert Moses and the Fall of New York
Atlas Shrugged
Olmstead
The Fountainhead
The Park and the City

Major Employers

Contact local government infrastructure committees for more information.

NYC Transit Authority
370 Jay Street
Room 611
Brooklyn, NY 11201
Tel: 718-834-7075

U.S. Army Corps of Engineers
20 Massachusetts Avenue, NW
Washington, DC 20314
Tel: 202-272-0365
Contact: Headquarters Support Office

A DAY IN THE LIFE

City planners help design cities, determine such things as the height of buildings, the width of streets, the number of street signs, and the design and location of "street furniture" (everything from bus stops and lamp posts to newsstands and wastebaskets). Deciding how a city is set up involves creativity, and a career in city planning demands a knowledge of basic engineering principles, the ability to compromise, political diplomacy, and financial acumen. Strong analytic skills and sheer force of will are required to be a successful urban planner.

Every building or structure must be designed with an understanding of its relationship to other elements of the city, such as coordinating the construction of water and power facilities while still allowing people access to light, heat, and fresh water, or designing housing complexes that will be close to public transportation. Aesthetic design, another feature that the planner must consider, can be the subject of hot debate. The urban planner has to design with an understanding of the policies of the city and create economically viable plans. This last can be difficult—urban planning projects nearly always run over budget and past deadline, and even the most frugal design can be expected to run into opposition from some quarter.

The planner begins by surveying sites and performing demographic, economic, and environmental studies to assess the needs of the community and encourage public participation in the process. If the planner is redeveloping an area (as opposed to groundbreaking or landfilling it), he must evaluate existing buildings and neighborhoods before determining what can be done to change the standing structures. During these phases, planners work closely with economic consultants to formulate a plan that makes sense for both the economy of the region and the residents. The next step is to create maps and designs. When the architects draft plans for the construction of bridges, radio and telephone towers, and other large pieces of infrastructure, the urban planner works closely with them. The planner does substantial research regarding zoning and landscaping laws. Occasionally, urban planners must also design or refurbish the town's zoning regulations on building usage, in the manner that is best for the region. He meets with community groups to obtain information on transportation and land usage. Financing is a delicate aspect of the profession which requires that the planner unite social, budgetary, and developmental concerns to respond to the community's need for progress while still presenting a fiscally sound proposal to governments and private investors.

Urban developers are employed by many different agencies, and many travel throughout the country to find continuous employment. Recent graduates should look to their state's Department of Transportation or look into civil engineering courses sponsored by the U.S. Army Corps of Engineers. Experienced engineers often work in private firms or with general contractors, where the planner enjoys far more independence.

PAYING YOUR DUES

Urban planners should have an undergraduate degree in an area such as civil engineering, architecture, or public administration. Most schools do not offer undergraduate degrees in structural engineering, but many employers look favorably on candidates who have studied SE at the master's level. A master's degree in city or regional planning or structural engineering is the highest laurel, respected by all employers. One thirty-year structural engineer noticed that many recent graduates handle textbook problems wonderfully, but are less apt at identifying and coping with real-life problems. While studying for a master's degree, students often do internships to acquire as much practical experience as possible to alleviate this problem. Internships can convert to paid positions upon graduation.

After four years of working full time, urban planners are eligible to take a step-one licensing test. There are two of these tests (step one and step two); which one a planner takes depends on his interests and area of expertise. After getting this license and working for four additional years, serious candidates take another test to obtain the title Professional Engineer. These certifications are not required, but they are respected within the profession. Generally, acquiring these licenses leads to a promotion and an increase in salary.

ASSOCIATED CAREERS

Geotechnical engineers explore subsurface areas to determine if the soil and rock will hold up the structure. Architects and draftsmen design the structures. Housing specialists relay the community's needs to the planner. Transport planners design plans for public transportation systems and roads. Any of these professions provides a solid home to the migrating ex-urban planner.

PAST AND FUTURE

Urban planning began in the U.S. in the early twentieth century as a response to the rapid development of suburban towns and the renovations of historical cities. Laws placing the control and regulation of building in the government's hands were passed in New York in 1916. Now, every city and many towns have offices for urban planning and development.

QUALITY OF LIFE

Two Years

While, at any given time, two-thirds of urban planners work for the government, neophyte planners find themselves in their employ in even larger percentages. The novice planner is working under the supervision and guidance of other planners. Many work as interns for part of these initial years. Hours can be long.

Five Years

The urban planner's responsibilities increase and he develops a specialty, such as housing, land use, or zoning. Many planners are becoming quite adept at pitching ideas, working within constrained budgets, and political maneuvering. The majority of planners who leave the profession migrate about this time, fed up by lack of professional progress or failure to pass licensing exams.

Ten Years

As urban planners they now lead projects and create policy. Many have become directors or senior planners. A number have mentor roles where they train and educate newer members of the profession.

THE BIRKMAN LIFESTYLE GRID

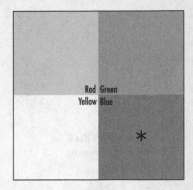

Red Green
Yellow Blue

This career is suitable for people with Blue interests.

You'll Have Contact With
Bankers
Civil Engineers
Government Officials
Sociologists
Lawyers
Real Estate Developers

Major Associations
American Planning Association
1776 Massachusetts Ave. NW, Suite 400
Washington, DC 20036
Tel: 202-872-0611
Fax: 202-876-0643

Urban Land Foundation
625 Indiana Avenue, NW, Suite400
Washington, DC 20004-2930
Tel: 202-624-7062
Tel: 800-321-5011

National Urban Affairs Council
2330 Shawnee Mission Parkway
Westwood, KS 66205
Tel: 908-561-6989

American Society of Landscape Architects
4401 Connecticut Avenue NW, Fifth Floor
Washington, DC 20008-2369
Tel: 800-787-2752

National Trust for Historic Preservation
1785 Massachusetts Avenue NW
Washington, DC 20036
Tel: 800-944-6847
Net: http://www.nthp.org

CIVIL ENGINEER

A DAY IN THE LIFE

"If you're the type of kid who built whole cities out of blocks in his bedroom, look into civil engineering." Civil engineers build real cities, from roads and bridges to tunnels, public buildings, and sewer systems. Projects have three phases: preconstruction planning, implementation, and infrastructure maintenance. The preconstruction phase involves surveying land, reviewing plans, assessing funding and needs, then making decisions about schedule, materials, and staffing. Most work is done indoors during this phase. Implementation is when construction begins, and many civil engineers spend considerable time on-site reviewing progress and coordinating all construction. One engineer said, "Sometimes you live out there for two or three days at a time." Problems must be solved on the spot, and civil engineers are the only ones with the knowledge and responsibility to do so. Infrastructure maintenance, which includes stress-tests, evaluations, and ongoing support, takes place after construction is finished. Civil engineers move back to their offices to wrap up all paperwork and make all final adjustments to the project. Then it is time to start the process again.

Civil engineers work hard. Hours can be long, government funding cuts can destroy a project, deadlines are firm, and weather can throw projects off schedule. If the timetable degenerates, an engineer has to overcome scheduling obstacles with ingenuity. Nearly all our surveys mentioned creativity as the first or second-most important trait a civil engineer can have. About half of all civil engineers are employed by federal, state, or local governments, which means they must be ready for bureaucratic delays, political stalls, and lots and lots of paperwork. Though civil engineers don't know where or when their next project will be, this doesn't seem to faze them. "Projects can last up to ten years, so it's not exactly like you're moving every week," said one engineer we spoke with. Satisfaction is strong; most wouldn't trade their occupation for any other.

PAYING YOUR DUES

Civil engineers must have an engineering degree from a school accredited by the Accreditation Board for Engineering and Technology and three to four years of work experience. They also must pass a state-sponsored Professional Engineer examination. Many civil engineers find it helpful to join a professional association, such as the American Society of Civil Engineers (ASCE).

ASSOCIATED CAREERS

Civil engineers are planners by nature, and many pursue managerial jobs that allow them to use this skill. They are particularly good at estimating labor and materials needs, and many become professional staffers and materials buyers. Some become materials researchers, while others become inspectors, checking the work of other civil engineers and receiving more regular hours for less pay.

PAST AND FUTURE

Civil engineers in Egypt at the time of the Pharoahs built pyramids; civil engineers in classical Greece and Rome built temples, aqueducts, and great public buildings; civil engineers in China built the Forbidden City. Cities could not have been built without civil engineers; they designed every major infrastructure system in the United States today.

Civil engineering work over the next decade will be rebuilding, as opposed to constructing, America's crumbling infrastructure. Most of this will take place in urban areas where budgets are tight and only projects that are in a state of crisis are funded. Civil engineers will also be building water-treatment plants and hazardous waste processing sites. Demand for civil engineers is expected to be strong, but applicants should be willing to relocate to areas of need in order to pursue these opportunities.

QUALITY OF LIFE

Two Years

Two years into the profession, civil engineers are still cutting their teeth, earning the work experience that will allow them to take the state-sponsored engineering exam. Many do routine construction or administrative assistant work. Many are "junior" engineers directed by more experienced, licensed professionals. Hours are long, but satisfaction is high.

Five Years

Those who have lasted five years have achieved "assistant" or "grade one" -level civil engineering status. Many put in their hardest work in years three through eight, trying to distinguish themselves from other applicants. Fifteen-hour days are not unusual for those on-site. Valuable experience is gained. Many must relocate to find positions of responsibility, and few leave. Satisfaction remains high; hours increase.

Ten Years

Civil engineers who've lasted ten years are in supervisory or management roles. Many are heavily involved in the preconstruction stages of development, but spend less time at the site during the construction phase than they did in earlier years. Some become research engineers, using their practical experience to explore new materials, methods, and ways of building infrastructures. Satisfaction remains high; hours decrease; salary rises.

THE BIRKMAN LIFESTYLE GRID

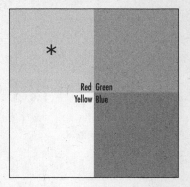

Red Green
Yellow Blue

This career is suitable for people with Red interests.

You'll Have Contact With

Architects
Construction Managers
Structural Engineers
Urban Planners

Major Associations

American Society of Civil Engineers
345 East 47th Street
New York, NY 10017
Tel: 800-548-2723
Contact: Claude Crudo

Institute of Transportation Engineers
525 School Street, SW
Suite 410
Washington, DC 20024
Tel: 202-554-8050
Contact: Louisa Ward

Junior Engineering Technical Society
1420 King Street
Suite 405
Alexandria, VA 22314
Tel: 703-548-5387
Contact: Cathy McGowen

CLERGY—PRIEST, RABBI, AND MINISTER

A DAY IN THE LIFE

Clergy are responsible for the religious education, spiritual guidance, and moral counseling of the members of their faith. Many seem uncomfortable calling their jobs "careers" or a "profession;" they frequently said in surveys and interviews that they became members of the clergy in response to an internal sense of being "called" to the occupation. This sense of "divine request" supports the clergy member through long hours, low pay, hierarchical politics, and at times, weak congregational support for their own ministries. "You have to be very confident that you are doing the right thing, because when you're preaching to one or two people in the whole church, there's not a lot of positive feedback," wrote one Protestant minister. While many mentioned the demoralizing aspect of sporadic attendance in church or synagogue, all agreed with the one who said, "We are not the focus of what we do. Our community is the focus, and how they are doing is how we judge ourselves."

This is not a job for those whose only desire is to help others; clergy often run large organizations and need the willingness and skills to do so. Office and administrative responsibilities, fundraising, and sermonizing are important parts of the job. Clergy must be able to get along with all factions of their congregation. Frequently, clergy members will specialize in one aspect of the profession, such as one who has a reputation as a powerful sermonizer or an exceptional fundraiser, and delegate other aspects of the job to more junior professionals. Being organized and attentive to detail helps in managing administrative tasks while keeping "doctor's hours: We're always on call." In most cases, the rigorous coursework involved in becoming a member of the clergy aids in the acquisition of these traits. Additionally, strong communication skills, patience, intellect and dedication are required.

Perhaps the most compelling thing our surveys conveyed about the field was a sense of excitement and extreme satisfaction. The religious community is a growing, vibrant arena where the free exchange of opinions and ideas and the chance to make real, spiritual insight become possible. "The feeling I get every day," wrote one Presbyterian minister, "is that I'm a witness to everything wonderful about people." Many wrote about the unique perspective and the unusual opportunity they had to contribute positively to the human experience.

PAYING YOUR DUES

The education of a clergy member depends on religious and denominational affiliation. Many Protestant churches require their ministers to complete a three-year graduate degree; rabbis complete a course of study lasting four to five years in a Jewish theological seminary; training for the Catholic priesthood usually entails eight years of study beyond high school at a Catholic seminary. The curricula studied at each religion's seminary is, surprisingly, quite similar. All training includes some form of study in homiletics (preaching), history, religious laws, counseling, and the practical aspects of ministering to a congregation. A significant number of denominations are requesting that their prospective clergy have practical experience in running a business, social counseling, or teaching before they are sponsored to assist their congregations. Each denomination has specific restrictions on who can become a member of the clergy—for example, women cannot become priests, Orthodox Jewish rabbis, or ministers in certain Protestant denominations. Many clergy-in-training are apprenticed to a clergymember responsible for an established congregation, and spend two to six years after school studying the practice of ministering to a congregation and assuming certain areas of responsibility, such as running Sunday school courses or managing holiday festivals.

ASSOCIATED CAREERS

Those who leave the clergy do so for a variety of reasons: dissatisfaction with their advancement, a loss of the sense of "calling," or the general difficulty of dealing with the downside of the human condition. When they leave, many continue to apply their ministering skills and become social workers, vocational guidance counselors, psychologists, teachers, and substance-abuse counselors. Some return to school for advanced degrees in fields such as psychology, philosophy, comparative religion, and medicine.

PAST AND FUTURE

Judaism has been around for roughly 4,000 years, and Christianity for around 2,000. While keeping a core set of beliefs intact, these two religions have been in a continuous state of revision and evolution. In general terms, Christians (including Catholics and Protestants) and Jews both believe in the sanctity of the Old Testament. Christians believe that Jesus the Messiah was the son of God, and follow the teachings presented in the New Testament. Jews do not. Catholics and Protestants split during the Reformation when Martin Luther put up his ninety-five theses in protest (hence the PROTESTants) against the abuses of the Catholic Church.

Judaism and Christianity face the same challenges today that they have always faced: providing each of their believers with moral guidance, and educating their adherents. Now, religions must also prove themselves relevant in a chaotic and demanding world. But religion has been around for a very long time, and the demand for new clergy members should remain steady.

QUALITY OF LIFE

Two Years

Two years into the profession, many members of the clergy continue in their studies and assist an assigned local congregation under the direct supervision of experienced clergy members. Duties are mainly administrative and assistant-level, and many new members are merely observers for up to one year on the job. Hours are long in study, but light in pressure.

Five Years

Five-year clergy members have assumed additional responsibilities, most notably counseling members of the congregation on faith, worship, the teachings of the sect, and issues of family, marriage, and childrearing. A clergy member's success is often based on the depth of his personal involvement. Other duties may involve teaching, sermonizing, inviting speakers, and working with members of other congregations on joint charitable projects. Satisfaction is high, but hours can be excruciatingly long.

Ten Years

Ten-year clergy members have established strong links to their community and are leaders in both civic and religious matters. Many oversee the more junior members of the clergy and supervise religious education. Moves between congregations, which occur with relative frequency in years one through seven, drop as clergy find their professional matches. Satisfaction is high; hours continue to be long.

THE BIRKMAN LIFESTYLE GRID

This career is suitable for people with Green interests.

You'll Have Contact With

Fundraisers
Parishioners
Psychologists
Social Services Workers

Major Associations

American Association of Rabbis
350 Fifth Avenue
Suite 3304
New York, NY 10118
Tel: 212-244-3350

National Conference of Diocesan
Vocation Directors
P.O. Box 1570
Littleriver, SC 29566
Tel: 803-280-7191

National Organization for Continuing
Education of Roman Catholic Clergy
1337 Ohio Street
Chicago, ILL 60622
Tel: 312-226-1840

Clergy and Latin Concerned
340 Mead Road
Decatur, GA 30030
Tel: 404-377-1983

Pontifical Missionary Union of
Priests and Religious
366 Fifth Avenue, 12th Floor
New York, New York 10011
Tel: 800-431-2222
Tel: 212-563-8700
Fax: 212-563-8725

CLOTHING/JEWELRY/COSMETICS GENERALIST

A DAY IN THE LIFE

People in jewelry, clothing, cosmetics production and sales all need a similar set of day-to-day skills. Each industry employs designers, buyers, production personnel, retail salespeople, and inventory control personnel, but with the exception of designers, most initial entrants are hired as "generalists" who rotate from department to department until a match is found between their skills and a department's needs. A generalist must be flexible and able to switch from task to task on a moment's notice. The skills this occupation requires are best cultivated in someone who has the desire to learn, the ability to take direction, and strong decision-making abilities. Professionals spend their days attending meetings, planning production and shipping, and working with different departments. About 25 percent of their time is spent on paperwork and over 20 percent is spent on the phone. Working with others is a large part of this profession: Wrote one cosmetics executive, "If you don't listen to people in your division, expect to lose their respect." Over 80 percent of our respondents rated communication skills as either the first or second most important ability to have.

Strong decision-making abilities and aesthetic skills are valued in generalists. Since specialization occurs later in this career than most—after ten years or more—in manufacturing, inventory management, distribution networks, retail sales or advertising, one has a chance to explore the field thoroughly. It is not unusual to be transferred to five, six, even seven different areas during the first three years before spending any significant time at one. This rapid and broad exposure to the full range of career options within the industry is both praised and denounced. "Knowing the whole production process helps me in sales," mentioned one high-end jewelry salesman, referring to an earlier five-month stint abroad at his company's South African manufacturing facilities. Another advertising buyer in the clothing industry countered, "working on the manufacturing floor in Columbus was the biggest waste of two months. Ever."

Satisfaction recorded is below average in this profession, and this discontent is linked to the short-term reliability and the lack of continuity of jobs. Forty percent of people in the industry change jobs either between companies or within the same company every single year. Also, because the work environment is so fluid and fast-paced, the camaraderie between workers seems to suffer: "For the first two years, I'd look over my shoulder and see a new face every month," said one manager. The competitiveness within these industries and the challenge of achieving success are high, so for those who like a difficult test of their abilities, a career in clothing, jewelry or cosmetics seems a perfect fit.

PAYING YOUR DUES

No specific bachelor's degree is required for someone to enter the clothing, jewelry or cosmetics fields, but applicants with finance or inventory backgrounds, communications skills, or computer skills have an advantage. Candidates go through extensive cutthroat training programs which involve them in all aspects of clothing, jewelry and cosmetics manufacturing and sales. Trainees are educated in the entire process, from product conception and development, through raw material purchasing, product manufacturing, marketing, sales, and customer service. The bulk of the cost of becoming a professional in these fields is front-loaded into the early years, with their retail-sales-like rotational structures, low pay, fierce competition, and long hours. Some members spend hours outside work socializing with colleagues, attending seminars, and taking additional courses to enhance their profile.

ASSOCIATED CAREERS

People in cosmetics, jewelry, and the clothing industry exit to a number of managerial and sales fields. Many go into industrial management and commercial goods production, corporate strategy, and professional buying. Others use their retail skills and enter other retail or direct-marketing industries. A few gravitate to publishing, advertising, or professional-event planning. The ability to rapidly adjust to changing circumstances and different projects makes the transition from these professions to others less jarring.

PAST AND FUTURE

Clothing, cosmetics, and jewelry have been around for centuries. Significant inventions in the clothing industry were the spinning jenny (spinning wheel) in 1764 by James Hargreaves and the invention of the cotton gin, which allowed the mass milling of cotton from plant to usable fiber by Eli Whitney in 1793.

All of these industries are extremely sensitive to imports, and with the dropping of North American tariffs as per the recently signed NAFTA agreement, they may face additional competition. Moreover, since over 70 percent of the companies in these industries employ fewer than fifty workers, sensitivity to one bad season or one bad market cycle may prove disastrous to smaller, less well-capitalized companies. Despite these vulnerabilities, the market for these products is strong, and should remain unchanging throughout the end of the decade.

QUALITY OF LIFE

Two Years

Two-year generalists rotate among a variety of departments. Duties may include warehouse inventory control, production assisting, buyers assisting, retail sales agenting, and client complaint department work. These early years provide the generalist with a broad range of experience and determine a solid match between the generalist's temperament and skills and available positions. Satisfaction and wages are low during the first two years, when over 25 percent of new hires leave the occupation.

Five Years

Generalists with specific skills who have found a good match begin the process of specialization. Most, however, rotate on an annual basis between different positions. Many are promoted and earn different titles, such as "inventory manager" or "quality control supervisor." Salaries and responsibilities increase, and hours can become very long. Many generalists switch firms to gain higher salaries and greater responsibility.

Ten Years

Ten-year veterans have found their specialties and earn such titles as "executive materials buyer," or "senior management generalist." They set large-scale policies, manage professionals in charge of day-to-day functioning of each department, and do long-term strategic planning. Salaries rise (beyond cost-of-living increases) only for those who move onto senior executive management. Hours decrease and quality of life improves.

THE BIRKMAN LIFESTYLE GRID

This career is suitable for people with Green interests.

You'll Have Contact With

Buyers
Inventory Control Managers
Market Researchers
Textile Manufacturers

Major Associations

American Apparel Manufacturers Association
2500 Wilson Boulevard
Suite 301
Arlington, VA 22201
Tel: 703-524-1864
Contact: Ralph Reinecke

International Association of
Clothing Designers
475 Park Avenue South
17th Floor
New York, NY 10016
Tel: 212-685-6602
Contact: Norman Karr

National Association of
Purchasing Management, Inc
P.O. Box 22160
Tempe, AZ 85285-2160
Tel: 602-752-6276

COACH

A DAY IN THE LIFE

Coaches teach athletic skills, provide generalized fitness training, and train athletes to perform in physical and competitive environments. "I'm a teacher, a leader, a friend, and I hate it when we lose," wrote one high-school varsity football coach, "but not as much as the kids or their parents do." Being a coach requires the successful juggling of these various caps. The athletes and the coach each motivate the other to perform at a higher level; this relationship demands commitment, awareness, and dedication. People who find themselves satisfied in this profession have strong teaching skills, an abundance of motivation to work additional hours, and excellent communication skills. "Leadership skills are essential," wrote one college volleyball coach, "otherwise your good athletes won't respect you enough to listen to you."

What sport and age-level you wish to coach will have a substantial impact on what preparation is needed beyond knowing your chosen sport very well. The skills required to coach high-school tennis, for example, are quite different from the skills required to coach professional baseball. Competition is significant for entry-level positions; on more advanced levels, special skills such as weight-training expertise, stretching, and psychological training become more highly valued. Progression is difficult within and between coaching levels. One person articulated the dilemma clearly: "You want to work for the best coaches to learn your job, but the best coaches never get fired or leave, so you've got to jump into another system somewhere else and start all over again." Many coaches enjoy going to conferences to meet other professionals and to learn new methods of fitness training and injury prevention.

PAYING YOUR DUES

Coaching different age levels requires different sets of skills. If you want to coach high-school sports, you should have comprehensive knowledge of your sport, knowledge of physical-fitness training, and some basic training in injury prevention, first aid, and childhood development. Many employers look for a history of athletics in the sport—being on a high-school, college, or professional team will stand you in good stead. Having worked for a youth league or summer camp as a coach works to your advantage.

On the college level, you should have an understanding of a specialty within a sport—for example, in football, you might be a defensive line coach, or a quarterback coach—and the ability to translate that knowledge into terms college athletes can understand and envision. Applicants should have at least three semesters worth of physical training and a history of success coaching at the high school level or above. Many college coaches are hired in part because of personal relationships with the coaching staff, so cultivate contacts. Professional seminars, successful interviewing skills, and recommendations from former coached pupils can help. Many coaches work with "high talent" stars, thereby associating the athlete's fame and prowess with their own skills.

All of the above-mentioned criteria are required for coaching professional teams. Strong candidates have had successes at the college level, attained national exposure, and most likely, have refined a specialty, such as "special teams coach" (a football term for kicking teams or kick-returning teams) or "shooting coach."

ASSOCIATED CAREERS

Many coaches return to teaching if they leave coaching. Over 25 percent return to school to get graduate degrees in physical therapy, nutrition, exercise physiology, or medical training. A number use their leadership skills to run team-oriented projects in business settings. Around 10 percent migrate to occupations which allow them to be outdoors and active, such as policemen, firemen, park rangers, personal trainers, and semi-professional athletes.

PAST AND FUTURE

With the advent of professional sports, coaches gained power, money, and additional responsibilities, such as media communication commitments and negotiation involvement. A professional football coach today is as much a recruiter, public-relations specialist, and budget director as he is a teacher.

While the number of amateur and professional coaching positions is expected to increase on all levels, competition for these positions is expected to increase as well. But coaches who can find the right opportunity and situation should continue to achieve high levels of satisfaction.

QUALITY OF LIFE

Two Years

Coaches are "jacks of all trades" who work with athletes in a particular sport on issues of general fitness, flexibility (stretching), strength (weight training), skills, teamwork, and attitude. Many are assistant coaches under more experienced professionals. Many hone their abilities by expanding their knowledge of strategy, coaching, and training during their free time. Hours are long; pay is low. Around 35 percent leave due to frustration with advancement, wage dissatisfaction, or emotional burnout. This is the largest exodus from the profession; over the course of a career, only half the entrants quit by the ten-year mark.

Five Years

Five-year veterans are usually assistant coaches at large schools or head coaches at smaller ones. Those who have designed their own programs begin to see results around the second or third year of implementation. Few leave the profession between years two and five, as many have found positions which suit their level of abilities. Coaches begin to cement professional and personal relationships which are invaluable later in their careers. Satisfaction is high; pay has become respectable

Ten Years

Ten-year veterans can go into head coaching, higher level coaching, or specialization. Head coaches are involved with every aspect of the day-to-day job, from overseeing training to making decisions that affect the play of the team. Those who wish to rise to a higher level of coaching (such as national team or professional coaching) concentrate on building winning programs and recruiting high-profile athletes. Self-promotion becomes an important part of the career for those who wish to enter the professional coaching ranks. Specializing in one area of coaching and excelling at it makes it easier for professional teams to envision the role you would play with them. Satisfaction is high; few leave the profession beyond this point.

THE BIRKMAN LIFESTYLE GRID

This career is suitable for people with Green interests.

You'll Have Contact With
Athletes
Nutritionists
Physical Therapists
Sports Psychologists

Major Associations
American Alliance for Health,
Physical Education
1900 Association Drive
Reston, VA 20091
Tel: 703-476-3410
Contact: Starla King

American Federation of Teachers
555 New Jersey Avenue, NW
Washington, DC 20001
Tel: 202-879-4400
Contact: Associate Members Department

National Federation Interscholastic
Coaches Association
P.O. Box 20626
11724 NW Plaza Circle
Kansas City, MO 64195
Tel: 816-464-5400
Fax: 816-464-5571

Nationa High School Athletic
Coaches Association
P.O. Box 5020
Winter Park, FL 32793-5020
Tel: 407-679-1414

COLLEGE ADMINISTRATOR

A DAY IN THE LIFE

College administrators make recommendations on admissions, oversee the dissemination of university materials, plan curriculum, oversee all budgets from payroll to maintenance of the physical plant, supervise personnel, keep track of university records (everything from student transcripts to library archives), and generally help students navigate the university bureaucracy for financial aid, housing, job placement, alumni development, and all the other services a college provides. Many eventually specialize in one field, such as financial aid, in which responsibilities include the preparation and maintenance of financial records and student counseling on financial aid. Another specialization is information management, where the university official is responsible for coordinating and producing the majority of university publications. Most of the people in the field had positive experiences in college and entered the profession because they wanted to help students in their academic lives and personal growth. From the responses we received, a more nurturing intellectual and emotional environment among colleagues at the entry level would be difficult to find.

As professionals climb the ladder, they can focus on admissions, financial issues, or information management. Competition begins with the onset of specialization. At upper levels, a graduate degree in education, business, or information management is required. Hours increase, and administrators spend even more time away from the office at university events or at other schools. Also, since vertical movement is difficult, as established admissions and administrative directors are firmly entrenched in their positions, many administrators have to be prepared for lateral movements. Those who are willing to relocate to pursue opportunities have a significant advantage.

PAYING YOUR DUES

There are stringent academic requirements for positions as college administrators. While entry-level positions in financial aid offices, registrar's offices, and admissions and academic offices often require only a bachelor's degree, a Ph.D. or an Ed.D. is standard for those who hold influential positions in college administrations. Many administrators pursue advanced degrees while working at entry-level administrative positions because learning is complementary to their occupations and they often receive educational stipends, making it either inexpensive or free to study at their school. Candidates for administrative positions should have good managerial instincts, strong interpersonal skills, and the ability to work with faculty and students. Those involved in the financial aspects of administration, including administering financial aid, should have significant statistics backgrounds and mathematical skills. Computer proficiency is necessary at all levels.

Universities are just that: miniature universes. Most operate all functions of a big corporation, even a small city, within the larger community in which they are located. A person can work for the same university for twenty years and have twenty different jobs during that time! And employees who move laterally can enjoy the benefits of variety without sacrificing the security of a single employer.

ASSOCIATED CAREERS

Forty percent of college administrators never change fields. Those who do leave often become professors, teachers, corporate managers, financial aid officers, or human resource coordinators in a variety of settings. One ex-college administrator interviewed had entered the ASPCA as a national administrator and mentioned that even there, unfortunately, paperwork remains a large part of her job.

PAST AND FUTURE

In 1865, the average-sized university in the United States employed approximately four administrators for all its students. After World War II, with the passage of the GI Bill, which allowed veterans to return to college for little or no cost, thousands of new applicants entered universities and administrative staffs blossomed. By 1965, the average administrative staff at a United States university was over 225. Today that number is closer to 500.

The number of administrators at a university depends on funding, except for admissions offices, which exist nearly independently of funding decisions. The number of universities in the United States is expected to remain static through the end of the decade, and the number of administrative positions at each seems to have leveled off as well. If universities continue to be funded at their present levels, the number of positions available each year should roughly equal the number of applicants for those positions.

QUALITY OF LIFE

Colleges and universities tend to be intellectually stimulating environments. Interaction between administrators, faculty, and students can contribute to higher-than-average job satisfaction. University employees also enjoy perquisites including liberal vacation time and discounts on concerts, lectures, and sporting events, offsetting the slightly lower wages that middle managers earn compared to those in private-sector jobs. Retirement plans tend to be liberal–and tax-exempt–unlike corporate 401(K) plans.

Two Years

These are the most hectic and difficult years for college administrators. Most train on the job and are assigned responsibilities immediately upon hire. Duties include tracking students' financial aid obligations, counseling students on course of study, and assisting in the resolution of student bureaucratic difficulties. Responsibility levels are high and pay is average. Hours can be long as most inherit student caseloads from previous employees, and files must be reviewed.

Entry-level professionals spend over 40 percent of their time writing reports, reviewing documentation and doing research; and another quarter of their time on the road, promoting the school. Contact with students can diminish to almost negligible levels during the first year, but rebounds in years two through six. Combating this sense of frustration is the community of dedicated professionals who enter the industry. "The people are what makes this job worthwhile—they always want to learn, to discuss, and to help out," noted one.

Five Years

University administrators break into two tracks at the five-year point. Those who are happy with their positions frequently begin taking classes at the university which employs them; some enter graduate programs, others supplement the skills they use on the job every day, including financial and communication skills. Those who enjoy the profession but dislike their positions aggressively pursue other university administration positions. The majority of position switching among university administrators happens in years three to seven. Geographical mobility is frequently a factor in gaining the best opportunities.

Ten Years

Ten-year veterans have supervisory authority and administrative responsibility. Nearly every ten-year veteran has specialized in admissions, financial aid, or information management. Many have complete responsibility for the administration of substantial budgets and become more personnel managers than student advocates, a trend that may explain the sag that occurs between years seven and eleven in terms of satisfaction. Pay increases; hours remain static.

THE BIRKMAN LIFESTYLE GRID

Red Green
Yellow Blue

*

This career is suitable for people with Yellow interests.

You'll Have Contact With
Financial Aid Officers
Fundraisers
Professors
Students

Major Associations
American Association of Collegiate Registrars & Administration Officers
One Dupont Circle, NW
Suite 330
Washington, DC 20036
Tel: 202-293-9161
Contact: Wayne Becraft

National Association of Student Financial Aid Administrators
1920 L Street, NW
Suite 200
Washington, DC 20036
Tel: 202-785-0453

Association of American Colleges and Universities (AAC&U)
1818 R Street, NW
Washington, DC 20001
Tel: 202-387-3760
Fax: 202-265-9532

National Education Association
1201 16th St., NW
Washington, DC 20036-3290
Tel: 202-822-7642
Contact: Employment Manager

COMEDIAN

PROFESSIONAL PROFILE

# of people in profession	10,750
% male	90
% female	10
avg. hours per week	50

Professionals Read

Spy
Harvard Lampoon
National Lampoon
Comedy Magazine

Books, Films and TV Shows
Featuring the Profession

Seinfeld
Punchline
The Life of Jack Benny
Mr. Saturday Night

Major Employers

Center Theater Ensemble
1346 W. Devon
Chicago, IL 60660
Tel: 312-508-0200
Fax: 312-508-9584
Contact: Casting Department

Second City Comedy
1616 North Wells
Chicago, IL 60614
Tel: 312-642-8189
Fax: 312-664-9837
Contact: Kelly Leonard

Caroline's
1626 Broadway
New York, NY 10019
Tel: 212-956-0101
Fax: 212-956-0197
Contact: Lewis Faranda

A DAY IN THE LIFE

Comedians get a thrill out of making people laugh. A comedian develops a unique style, skill, and body of work as an entertainer. Most non-comedians are only familiar with comic superstars, such as Steve Martin, Jim Carrey, Robin Williams, Whoopi Goldberg and Roseanne, to name a few. Most of the comedians we surveyed mentioned these visible successes as partially responsible for their staying in the profession, however unlikely a similar meteoric rise might be. Most of the surveys received from comedians were distinctly unfunny in their responses to our questions about how they live day-to-day. "Everybody in the world thinks they're funny. It's just that I'm crazy enough to bet on [my prospects as a comedian]," wrote one professional comedian from Denver who quit his job as a salesman to pursue a career in comedy full–time. A comedian works long hours for little (if any) pay, and endures enormous uncertainty, never knowing where the next paycheck will be coming from. The average stand-up comedian earns around $50 for two twenty-minute sets at a comedy club. While this translates into a solid hourly wage, a new comedian may do four sets per week, with the rest of the time spent writing material, watching other comedians, and keeping an additional job to pay the rent. A successful comedian must be quick-witted, able to think on his feet, dedicated, and lucky. A great deal of self-confidence is required if one is to last over two years in this profession (and over half don't), since failure, disappointment, and rejection are standard.

Comedy troupes develop, perform, and publicize their own material. Most of the members maintain freelance or day jobs that allow them to pursue this career. They usually schedule a weekly show, bracketed around rehearsal and workshops where they critique each other's sketches and performances. Because attendees will not return to see the same material, it is a highly pressured large-output environment. A troupe comedian must adapt to peers' comments and take criticism well. The ability to work with others is critical to success in comedy groups. The troupes are often formed in major urban centers where actors and comedians congregate due to the larger opportunity for work.

Solo comedians perform on club circuits around the country, usually one after another on a given night, creating a very competitive atmosphere. Being a solo comedian can be an "if-you-win-I-lose" type of career. "There are only so many laughs on any given night, and if possible, you want to get all of them," wrote one regular at a comedy club in New York. Solo stand-up comics face a significant level of backstabbing and isolation. At the same time, studying performers' material, style, delivery, and presence are all facets of the successful comedian's life.

PAYING YOUR DUES

Playing in dingy nightclubs before an audience of one and unpaid stand-up sets are all part of the aspiring comedian's dues. No academic requirements exist, but many get their start in college acting or comedy troupes, thereby gaining some exposure to large audiences. Stand-up comedians have a more uncertain road than troupe comedians, going from club to club, writing material, practicing and refining it, and hoping for a break. It is not unusual for an aspiring stand-up comic to log over 200 days per year away from home.

ASSOCIATED CAREERS

Over 30 percent of exiting comedians slide smoothly into acting, where they face much the same odds against success. Others find homes in advertising, teaching, writing and one mentioned that he ended up in law enforcement. The skills associated with comedy—the ability to make others laugh, to defuse tense situations with a well-timed remark, and to think on one's feet—are invaluable assets in any other career.

PAST AND FUTURE

Comedy has historically been the mirror of every age, from the Greek playwright Aristophanes to the sarcastic drollery of Dennis Miller. Every known culture has its own form of comedy and the smile and the laugh seem hardwired as responses in the human brain.

Comedians have been in entertainment ascendancy of late, with Jim Carrey receiving over $20 million for *The Cable Guy*, and the network success of Roseanne's television show. But, in general, comedians should expect to face the same odds in the career tomorrow that they face today.

QUALITY OF LIFE

Two Years

Progression in this profession is unpredictable, but for the majority of comedians it follows the scenario outlined below. A two-year comic is just developing her comic persona and getting her feet wet on the comedy circuit. She has just started writing her material and experimenting with different styles. She goes to open mike nights to try new material, to get to know the clubs and let them get to know her, and to make contacts with other comics. The new comic is lucky to get a few bookings. Persistence and confidence are key to working at all.

Five Years

Comedians are skilled self-publicists by this point and some even have agents. After five years in the profession, a comic knows clubs around town and around the country and has, hopefully, performed at many of them. He could be a regular at one or two. Club managers know him and his style, and he knows where his material will be welcomed and where it's not appropriate. Other comedians have seen his work, and he has probably auditioned for a few comedy troupes and maybe even started working with one.

Ten Years

A comedian who has lasted ten years in the profession has attained a measure of success in her field and probably has a strong regional following. She has had many opportunities to show her work, possibly including TV specials and performing for specific groups, such as political associations or college clubs, depending on her material. She's probably worked for a comedy troupe, at least for a while. The comedian keeps seeking out new venues for her performances, writing and developing new material, and hoping for a big break.

THE BIRKMAN LIFESTYLE GRID

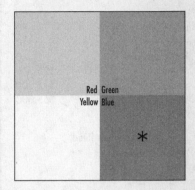

Red Green
Yellow Blue

*

This career is suitable for people with Blue interests.

You'll Have Contact With

Agents
Club Managers
Producers
Publicists

Major Associations

Theatre Communications Group
355 Lexington Avenue
New York, NY 10017
Tel: 212-697-5230

American Guild of Variety Artists
184 5th Avenue
6th Floor
New York, NY 10010
Tel: 212-675-1003
Contact: Membership Deptment

American Federation of
Television & Radio Artists
260 Madison Avenue
New York, NY 10016
Tel: 212-532-0800

Computer Engineer/Systems Analyst

A DAY IN THE LIFE

"Expect the unexpected," said one computer engineer about her profession, and this statement was reflected on all the surveys we received. Computer engineers coordinate the construction, maintenance, and future growth of a company's computer systems. They work with all departments, discovering each one's computer needs, then make suggestions about what technical direction the company should proceed in. While this occupation sounds quite organized and logical, most computer engineers enter the profession at companies who have already made uncertain steps into the technical world. Faced with uncertain budget restrictions, presented with old or misapplied systems, and expected to know the nuances of each department's needs, systems analysts must rapidly become experts in the company's and each department's functions and learn how to use second-best systems to satisfy their needs. "Getting people to tell you up front all the things they want to do is like pulling teeth," wrote one engineer. Flexibility, strong interpersonal skills, and a friendly disposition are highly valued traits in this industry.

The bottom line is performance, and those without strong technical skills find themselves quickly outpaced by the expertise their job demands. Over 30 percent of systems analysts did not intend to become full-time systems analysts: In most smaller companies, the position develops as an ancillary responsibility for the most technically savvy of the current employees. As the company realizes the benefits of a full-time computer representative, that position becomes permanent and exclusive. "I was hired as a researcher," noted one analyst, "and now all I use is my screwdriver." Many who have fallen into the profession point to continuing education as an attractive part of the job. Others find themselves hamstrung by decisions others have made before them and the technical limitations of the systems they inherit.

The high level of satisfaction these high-tech tinkerers feel might be related to the creative thinking and problem solving aspects of their job. "It's like having the most expensive Tinkertoy set in the world—I love it!" said one systems analyst. Few occupations allow the physical construction of an object and the intellectual challenge offered by computer engineering. For those who can make the most of limited resources and listen carefully for the distinction between what people want and what people need from their computer systems, computer engineering is an excellent profession.

PAYING YOUR DUES

Computer engineers come from all walks of life and all professional fields: accountaunts, researchers, inventor-managers, programmers and others who found the technology they worked with fascinating, who assumed responsibility for those systems, and who continued their education in the field. All computer engineers must be good with details and know how to approach structural problems logically. But practical experience is the most important credential. Nearly all the surveys returned to us from computer engineers stressed that experience is significantly more important than education in this field. "I don't even look at the education portion of the resume," one candid senior analyst mentioned, "just tell me what problems you've encountered and what you've done about them." Technology changes rapidly in this field, so continuous study and learning are part of a professional's life. Certain certifications are gaining credence in the field, such as the Certified Systems Professional (CSP) credential and the Certified Quality Analyst (CQA) designation, but none are required.

ASSOCIATED CAREERS

For those who enjoy their profession and who want to pursue it on a more structured and ground-up level, the position of systems architect is responsible for the same structural decision making and maintenance, but for systems not yet in place. Around 60 percent of computer engineers leave after ten years to pursue other opportunities. Ten percent of those who leave follow their more technical leanings by becoming computer repair personnel. Another 35 percent become programmers, librarians, information managers, on-line service producers or specialists, and around 15 percent enter the world of Local Area Network (LAN) companies.

PAST AND FUTURE

A relatively new field, computer engineers have been around since the early 1970s, when computers became more widespread in the business sector. Many companies purchased computers individually without considering how they could work together. Out of incompatibility rose LAN systems, which promised to link individual users in each office to a central software, database, and routing computer.

The profession of computer engineering is likely to grow very fast and become a significant position within many large and small corporations. The most interesting aspect of computer engineering is that for the first time, it is becoming a unique and distinct occupation that people study in school and look for work in. Certain firms have arisen that act as solely systems analyst "hired guns" who handle all computer issues at a company. Computer consulting businesses are expected to grow much faster than other types of consulting firms.

QUALITY OF LIFE

Two Years

These first years are marked by a hectic pace, limited input, and a high degree of personal accountability. Computer engineers find these first years frustrating, as many have inherited awkwardly created systems and are asked to make them run smoothly. Pay is average; hours are long.

Five Years

Five-year engineers maintain and upgrade existing information systems, and have significant input on future purchases and system architecture. Responsibilities and salaries increase. Professional connections become more important as over 20 percent of five-year engineers change jobs. Satisfaction is high; hours are long. Many who have been attending professional courses officially enroll in degree programs.

Ten Years

Many ten-year computer engineers open their own consulting firms which examine and analyze systems, then propose methods of information flow. Veteran engineers are very valuable assets to any company, and their salaries reflect this. Hours remain static, and many are put in charge of managing two or three other engineers instead of doing installations and maintenance themselves. Those who remain at the ten-year mark are likely to remain computer engineers for life.

THE BIRKMAN LIFESTYLE GRID

Red Green
Yellow Blue

This career is suitable for people with Red interests.

You'll Have Contact With

Computer Programmers
Information Managers
Office Managers
Telecommunication Specialists

Major Associations

IEEE Computer Society
1730 Massachusetts Avenue, NW
Washington, DC 20036-1992
Tel: 202-371-0101

Computer-Aided Manufacturing International
1250 East Copeland Road
Suite 500
Arlington, TX 76011
Tel: 817-860-1654

Semiconductor Industry Association
181 Metro Drive
San Jose, CA 95129
Tel: 408-436-6600

COMPUTER OPERATOR/PROGRAMMER

A DAY IN THE LIFE

Programmers write the code that tells computers what to do. System code tells a computer how to interact with its hardware; applications code tells a computer how to accomplish a specific task, such as word processing or spreadsheet calculating. Systems programmers must be familiar with hardware specifications, design, memory management, and structure, while applications programmers must know standard user interface protocols, data structure, program architecture, and response speed. Most programmers specialize in one of the two areas.

At the start of projects, applications programmers meet with the designers, artists, and financiers in order to understand the expected scope and capabilities of the intended final product. Next, they map out a strategy for the program, finding the most potentially difficult features and working out ways to avoid troublesome patches. Programmers present different methods to the producer of the project, who chooses one direction. Then the programmer writes the code. The final stages of the project are marked by intense, isolated coding and extensive error-checking and testing for quality control. The programmer is expected to address all issues that arise during this testing. Systems programmers may be hired on a Monday, handed the technical specifications to a piece of hardware, then told to write an interface, or a patch, or some small, discrete project that takes only a few hours. Then on Tuesday, they might be moved to a different project, working on code inherited from previous projects. Systems programmers must prove themselves technically fluent: "If you can't code, get off the keyboard and make room for someone who can," wrote one. Both arenas accommodate a wide range of work styles, but communication skills, technical expertise and the ability to work with others are important in general.

Programmers work together respectfully; they help each other when they want to. But there are no significant professional organizations which might turn this group of people into a community. The best features of this profession are the creative outlet it provides for curious and technical minds, the pay, which can skyrocket if a product you coded is a major success, and the continuing education. A few programmers we surveyed indicated that an aesthetic sensibility emerges at the highest levels of the profession, saying that "Reading good code is like reading a well-written book. You're left with wonder and admiration for the person who wrote it."

PAYING YOUR DUES

Academic requirements are gaining in importance for entry-level positions in the field of programming. Coursework should include basic and advanced programming, some technical computer science courses, and some logic or systems architecture classes. The complexity of what first-time programmers are asked to code is growing, as is the variety of applications, such as compatibility to the Internet and the ability to translate into a marketable CD-ROM. Long hours and a variety of programming languages—PERL, FORTRAN, COBOL, C, C++—can make the initial programmer's life a whirlwind of numbers, terms and variables, so those who are not comfortable working in many modes at once may find it difficult to complete tasks. The programmer must remain detail-oriented in this maelstrom of acronyms. For mobility within the field, programmers should concentrate on developing a portfolio of working programs that show competence, style, and ability.

ASSOCIATED CAREERS

A number of programmers take on additional duties to become systems architects, software producers, or technical writers. Others take their programming expertise to a related profession, such as graphic designer or animator. Those who go into government work can become computer security consultants, encryption specialists, or federal agents specializing in computer science. A few who enter the business world become Management Information Systems Specialists (MISSs) who analyze, improve, and maintain corporate information systems for (usually) large, multinational corporations.

PAST AND FUTURE

Originally, in the 1960s, all software was known as "freeware," and was distributed among the few technical eggheads who built their own computers. During this period, one young Harvard student sent a letter to his fellow programmers saying that he thought freeware was a destructive concept, that people should trademark and copyright all their programs in order to receive the value of what these programs would eventually be worth. Most scoffed at this young impudent for his arrogant vision of the future of the personal computer and his denial of the 1960s sentiment of sharing and community. Young Bill Gates decided to stick to his opinions, and, $12 billion later, it is hard to argue with his success.

Programming right now is understaffed and the field will continue to grow for the next five years at a fast pace. Many industries are just now realizing the benefit of having tailored and modular code written to address their specific needs. Staffing levels at many major programming corporations are expected to increase, and individual freelance "hackers for hire" are expected to become valuable out-sourcing resources for these companies.

QUALITY OF LIFE

Two Years

Two-year professionals work under the supervision of established programmers, handling sections of code or modular pieces of programs. Little responsibility is offered to new hires in terms of defining program architecture and creating new methods of handling data or graphics. They are, however, given reasonable autonomy on their own section of code. Satisfaction is high. Pay is average. Many work for between one and two years at a given firm, then move to another with greater challenges.

Five Years

Salaries rise, and hours increase significantly. Duties include defining programming architecture, coding, and debugging more junior programmers' codes. Many have contact with executives and clients. Those who progress possess strong communication skills and understand what the client wants and needs. Travel may be a feature of the five-year programmer's life, going on-site to address client needs. A few begin their own businesses.

Ten Years

Ten-year professionals have either begun their own businesses as independent programmers, or consolidated their positions as experienced programmers at large concerns. Hours increase, but the position becomes one more of defining program architecture, working with staffs of programmers, and managing a variety of projects. Few ten-year professionals do basic coding; a number of those who love it do some, but delegate the detail work to less-experienced junior programmers. Satisfaction is high; salaries can become significant.

THE BIRKMAN LIFESTYLE GRID

This career is suitable for people with Red interests.

You'll Have Contact With

Computer Engineers
Network Administrators
Software Developers
Telecommunications Specialists

Major Associations

Institute for the Certification of Computer Professionals
2200 East Devon Avenue
Suite 247
Des Plaines, IL 60018
Tel: 708-299-4227

Data Processing Management Association
505 Busse Highway
Park Ridge, IL 60068
Tel: 708-825-8124

The Association for Computing Machinery
1818 R Street, NW
Washington, DC 20001
Tel: 202-387-3760
Fax: 202-265-9532
Contact: Heretini Kanthou

CONSTRUCTION MANAGER

A DAY IN THE LIFE

Coordinating one aspect of a construction is a difficult task. But coordinating the entire process, from initial planning and foundation work, through the final coat of paint in the last room, takes someone with the managerial skills of Lee Iacocca, the force of will of General Patton, and the patience of Job. Being a construction manager demands organization, attention to detail, an ability to see the "big picture", and an understanding of all facets of the construction process, usually acquired through experience. A construction manager is the intermediary between his clients and his workers, between the architect and his subcontractors, and between the project and any regulatory personnel.

"It's exciting" and "It's hard" were the two comments that cropped up most often in our surveys. The wide range of responsibilities that the construction manager faces means that he should have a wide variety of skills and knowledge, including plumbing, basic electrician training, standard construction techniques, blueprint reading, budgeting, and purchasing. The most underrated skill a construction manager needs is the ability to convince and persuade. He may have to convince a client that a last minute change suggested by the architect will mean innumerable delays or cost increases, or convince an unmotivated subcontractor to complete his job as required by a previous agreement. "You can always do your job better if you can make other people do their jobs better," said one manager. The ability to motivate and exact good work has to be tempered with understanding the limits of your workers, and knowing when a change in plans already underway is worth fighting and when it is not.

It helps if a construction manager has experience in obtaining permits and certifications for work; "expediters" who promise to obtain permits faster can charge up to $25,000 for their services, so construction managers familiar with the process who can trek through local bureaucracies can save their clients a considerable amount of money. "Take the time to learn your local building codes," mentioned one construction manager: "Do it at the beginning so that you don't get surprised in the middle of the job."

Aside from the high level of stress the day-to-day occupation fosters, the sense of satisfaction among people in the industry is high. Many point to the intimate relationships between builder and buyer, between architect and construction crew, and between construction workers and their contractors as positive experiences. People in this profession work hard, but they are rewarded for the large burdens they assume.

PAYING YOUR DUES

"Practical study," said many of our respondents about requirements in the field. For the most part, construction managers enter the career as construction workers after high school (either as a plumber's assistant, carpenter, concrete, or steel structure worker), and decide later on to manage construction sites. A number follow their dreams through apprenticeship programs, two-year junior college programs, or classes at accredited universities in mathematics, building codes, and blueprint reading. All point to on-the-job experience as the best instructor, recommending that anyone interested in this field should get as broad an experience as possible in the construction industry before going back for further education. Roughly 80 percent of all construction inspectors (another avenue of work for construction managers) worked for the government at the Federal and State levels, often for the U.S. Army Corps of Engineers, the Department of Housing and Urban Development, or the Tennessee Valley Authority.

ASSOCIATED CAREERS

Construction managers who leave the field revert to areas of expertise, specializing in plumbing or foundation work, or return to educational programs to become electricians or, occasionally, architects. Most people come to be construction managers later in life as a result of working in related sub-professions, so the departure rate due to reasons other than retirement or bankruptcy is under 15 percent.

PAST AND FUTURE

Construction managers have been part of all large-scale building projects throughout history, although under various titles. While at one time the profession required a harsh hand forcing slave labor to work under deathly conditions, current managers require a much more savvy, rather than brutal, set of skills.

The future of construction managers will likely stay on its present course. Because construction in any region of the country is tied to local economies and residential preferences, construction markets are difficult to predict on longer than an eighteen-month basis (the length of time in which people apply for financing to start new projects). The role of construction manager, however, is secure. No technical innovations, labor restructuring, or consumer advocacy can replace the need for a person who can coordinate all the elements of raising a building.

QUALITY OF LIFE

Two Years

Most aspiring construction managers are in training programs, which combine academic rigor with physical labor. Most work on-site as assistants to established construction managers, and act as the contact between construction workers and the manager on that feature. The majority of the two-year's time is spent learning the trade, local building codes, construction methodology, and how to communicate effectively with subcontractors. This experience, while financially unrewarding, is invaluable. Responsibilities are few; hours are long.

Five Years

"Busy" is an understatement for the working five-year manager. Construction managers supervise all stages of construction and manage all filings with local authorities. Stress is significant; over 60 percent of respondents cited it as a major factor. Client-communication skills are learned in years four through eight, and construction managers can find themselves spending what they believe to be too much time in meetings and too little time supervising on site.

Ten Years

Ten-year veterans have established reputations. They spend long hours at the construction site, but have learned how to delegate, so professional life is less hectic. Client contact is critical at this stage. Many construction managers find work through connections and word of mouth. Ten-year managers manage people on a daily basis less frequently, but they oversee all work and sign off on it before crews are moved to different areas of responsibility. Satisfaction is high at this stage, but so is stress; the incidence of heart attacks among contractors rises by 50 percent after ten years in the profession.

THE BIRKMAN LIFESTYLE GRID

Red   Green
Yellow Blue

This career is suitable for people with Red interests.

You'll Have Contact With

Architects
Carpenters
Construction Workers
Suppliers

Major Associations

American Institute of Constructors
466 94th Avenue North
St. Petersburg, FL 33702
Tel: 813-578-0317

Associated Landscape
Contractors of America
12200 Sunrise Valley Drive
Suite 150
Reston, VA 22091
Tel: 703-620-6363
Contact: Lori Saunders

Associated General Contractors of America
1300 North 17th Street
Rosslyn, VA 22209-3883
Tel: 703-812-2000

CORPORATE LAWYER

A DAY IN THE LIFE

Corporate lawyers ensure the legality of commercial transactions. They must have a knowledge of statutory law and regulations passed by government agencies to help their clients achieve their goals within the bounds of the law. To structure a business transaction legally, a corporate lawyer may need to research aspects of contract law, tax law, accounting, securities law, bankruptcy, intellectual property rights, licensing, zoning laws, and other regulations relating to a specific area of business. The lawyer must ensure that a transaction does not conflict with local, state, or federal laws.

In contrast to the adversarial nature of trial law, corporate law is team-oriented. The corporate counsel for both sides of a transaction are not strict competitors; together they seek a common ground for their clients. They are, in the words of one lawyer, "the handmaidens of the deal." Facilitating the business process requires insight into the clients needs, selective expertise, flexibility and most of all, a service mentality.

Corporate law requires an incisive mind and excellent communication skills, both written and oral. Through the negotiation process, lawyers constantly write and revise the legal documents which will bind the parties to certain terms for the transaction. This process is lengthy and typically corporate lawyers work extremely long hours. As a deal moves towards its closing, it becomes an exercise in stamina as much as skillful negotiation. As one person observed, "The most important trait a lawyer can have is a leather-ass. You've got to be able to put your butt in a chair and do the work."

The upside to this profession is the compensation is good and you usually work with smart people. One corporate lawyer remarked that she liked this side of the law precisely because the transactions take place among peers: There is no wronged party, no underdog, and usually no inequity in the financial means of the participants.

PAYING YOUR DUES

In law, the pressure starts early. Law school admission is extremely competitive—the top twenty-five schools have an admission rate of about 10%. You can get tracked early: The kind of school you attend affects what kind of summer job opportunities you may have, which in turn affects the kind of permanent job you secure.

The starting salary and kind of experience you have as a corporate lawyer can vary greatly depending on the size of the firm and geographic location. In a smaller firm, you will have more responsibility and more client contact early on, but the salaries can be tens of thousands of dollars lower than in a large firm. The content of your practice will be different too: A small town lawyer may take care of a house closing, drafting a will and a divorce settlement in a day; big city lawyers can spend months negotiating one commercial transaction.

ASSOCIATED CAREERS

If they decide not to pursue partnership in their firms, corporate lawyers often make use of their expertise as an in-house counsel for a corporation. Others go into a related business such as investment banking, and a few teach.

PAST AND FUTURE

Thomas Jefferson introduced the first academic law program to the United States when he created a professorship in law at William and Mary in 1779. George Wythe, a Virginia judge at the time and, later, a signer of the Declaration of Independence, was the first to fill the post. Harvard was not far behind, and was already producing lawyers of repute in the mid-1700s.

The number of corporate lawyers grew exponentially in the 1980s when commercial activity was at its peak. When the economy slowed down, so did the need for attorneys. The practice of corporate law is less cushy now; the days of the endless expense account are gone. The state of the economy always shapes the nature of corporate law; changes in the interest rates, the tax code, and other regulations affect the kind of transactions being done and how they are structured.

QUALITY OF LIFE

Two Years

New associates spend their days reviewing documents and doing legal research. They gather information on statutes that affect their clients' transaction to insure that it can be done legally and keep track of the paperwork needed for the closing. The work is hard. Expect to put in long hours and work weekends.

Five Years

By five years, lawyers are negotiating and drafting the major operative documents for their deals. Senior associates are the primary client contact, and run deals and closings by themselves. They have increased responsibility and are trying to develop a reputation in their specialty. Often they supervise the training of new associates. At the five-year mark associates decide if they want to be on a partner track. Those who do put in very long hours before their review (which usually takes place around seven years). Others leave for a related position in business or become an in-house counsel at a corporation.

Ten Years

At ten years, corporate lawyers are structuring their own transactions. They have developed keen judgment and create "big picture" strategies. They know what issues will likely arise for a particular case and which experts to call to resolve them. As one lawyer said, "I'm a highly experienced generalist who knows all the right specialists." Usually, associates have made partner by this time. With partnership comes management responsibilities. Partners must recruit and train new associates of the firm, manage the workflow on client transactions, and oversee the internal affairs of the firm. All this work is on top of their normal billable hours. In addition, partners must put in time cultivating clients and selling the business. Firm partners are usually involved in bar association activities, write for professional journals, and speak at national conferences. The compensation at this level is quite good.

THE BIRKMAN LIFESTYLE GRID

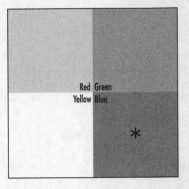

This career is suitable for people with Blue interests.

You'll Have Contact With

Paralegals
Bankers
Accountants
Business Executives

Major Associations

American Corporation Counsel Association
1225 Connecticut Avenue, NW
Suite 302
Washington, DC 20036
Tel: 202-296-4522
Fax: 202-331-7454

American Bar Association
740 15th Street, NW 9th Floor
Washington, DC 60005
Tel: 202-662-1000
Fax: 202-662-1032

National Lawyers Guild
126 University Place
New York, NY 10003
Tel: 212-627-2656
Fax: 212-627-2404

COSMETOLOGIST

A DAY IN THE LIFE

Do you know who gave Bill Clinton a haircut on the tarmac of an airport runway in 1991? A cosmetologist. Cosmetologists are the fairy godmothers of style and change. A cosmetologist can create a more beautiful you. Cosmetologists help their clients improve on or acquire a certain look with the right hairstyle and hair coloring, manicured nails, and either a properly trimmed beard or carefully chosen makeup, depending on your testosterone and estrogen levels. Cosmetologists also shampoo, cut, color, and style hair and advise clients on proper hair care. They add permanent waves or straighten hair in addition to giving manicures, facials, and scalp treatments, and caring and styling for wigs.

This is a profession that requires considerable tact and diplomacy in dealing with patrons. Cosmetologists are intensely people-oriented and must be able to inspire the confidence of those they service. With an emphasis on personalized care and services, cosmetologists must understand the individual characteristics of their clients to be able to chose the hair styles and makeup colors and tones that are uniquely suited to them. One New York City stylist remarked: "It's simply important to get to know and understand your clients . . . their likes and dislikes . . . and you work with that, finding styles that enhance aspects of their personality." The move toward more personalized care and services means that cosmetologists with charm, good communication skills, and the ability to inspire trust in their clients will be very successful. Constantly updated skills in new hair treatments and techniques give the ambitious cosmetologist the edge.

Cosmetologists must keep on top of the latest styles and trends in hair fashion and beauty techniques. For example, if, in 1996, you didn't know the hair style that all the women on the television show "Friends" were wearing, you'd be sunk. If you knew next year's hot hairstyle, you'd be a hit. If you created next year's hot hairstyle, you'd be a star. Because evenings and weekends are the busiest times for salons, cosmetologists must be willing to give up or minimize their social life if success is their goal. Long and irregular hours spent on their feet are the norm for cosmetologists. They are exposed to hair and nail chemicals that could possibly affect their health. But true beauty is worth a little suffering.

PAYING YOUR DUES

Cosmetologists face varying licensing requirements in different states, but essentially a high school diploma, formal training at cosmetology or vocational schools, and in some states, completion of an apprenticeship, will make you a cosmetologist. The recently certified stylist can expect to perform duties that amount to sheer drudgery. Newcomers are left to washing, blowdrying and setting customers hair, occasionally being given the task of a simple hairstyle pattern. New workers should perform these tasks with glee, knowing full well that practice makes perfect and soon enough they'll develop followings of their own, make better wages, and collect bigger tips. New cosmetologists should be especially careful in following the instructions of patrons and seeking help and direction if unsure of a particular procedure. Remember: This is an industry which relies on the proper use and application of chemicals. Hair and nail disasters can make the cosmetologist and the management of the establishment vulnerable to law suits.

ASSOCIATED CAREERS

Cosmetologists can virtually step into any area of the beauty business. Hair-color stylists, manicurists, makeup artists, and aestheticians are in constant demand to service the fashion conscious and the whimsical. Sales, marketing, and distribution of hair care products and supplies is another option for the cosmetologist looking for a change of pace.

PAST AND FUTURE

Wilma Flintstone's cosmetologist apparently advised her that a bone in her hair would be attractive. But we've come a long way, Baby. For many years in America, women let their hair grow long and put it up during the day. A woman's tresses were considered her crowning glory. Then, in the 1920s, the age of the flapper began, and bobbed hair arrived on the scene. Cosmetologists have been steadily employed ever since.

Now they are busily snipping, dying, and polishing so that customers can follow every fad that emerges. Cosmetologists are expected to ride the current boom right into the year 2000 and at least several years beyond that. Once patronized largely by the leisure class, cosmetologists now see clients from every walk of life who are bound together by their sense of fashion and its ever-changing styles and trends.

QUALITY OF LIFE

Two Years

At this stage the licensed cosmetologist is taking on more and varied responsibilities, including fairly simple cuts and styles. Drudge work is still very much a part of the workday routine, but now the cosmetologist is able to see more scope and possibilities.

If he is an exceptionally talented stylist, then he has already begun to acquire a list of satisfied clients. At the two-year level, the cosmetologist is still attempting to create his signature style.

Five Years

With five years experience comes an unmistakable style and with it, hopefully, a faithful clientele, those who will move thousands of miles away, but come for a visit because they must get their hair cut by you, and only you. If the cosmetologist is not yet managing his own studio or salon, this is the ideal juncture at which to consider such a move. He should be on the very cutting edge of the latest techniques in styling and coloring.

Ten Years

The cosmetologist should, after ten years in the business, be a veritable artist directing his own salon with faithful and ever-flocking patrons. With such vast experience, the cosmetologist can offer his establishment as a possible training ground for prospective students, start a cosmetology school or become an instructor. Other options include opening a business as a beauty or fashion consultant or becoming a sales representative for a beauty products company. Also, at this point, the enterprising cosmetologist could expand his line of service to include other areas of beauty care.

THE BIRKMAN LIFESTYLE GRID

Red Green
Yellow Blue

This career is suitable for people with Blue interests.

You'll Have Contact With

Beauty Consultants
Clients
Cosmetics Executives
Fashion Consultants

Major Associations

National Cosmetology Association
3510 Olive Street
St. Louis, MO 63103
Tel: 314-534-7980

American Association of
Cosmetology Schools
901 North Washington Street
#206
Alexandria, VA 22203

Association of Cosmetologists and
Hairdressers (ACH)
1811 Monroe Street
Dearborn, MI 48124
Tel: 313-563-0360

COURT REPORTER

Professionals Read

Journal of Court Reporting
Court Reporting
Court Technology Bulletin

Books, Films and TV Shows Featuring the Profession

The Court Reporter
The Transcript

Major Employers

Court reporters are needed in most municipalities across the U.S. Contact your local state or federal court system for further information.

A DAY IN THE LIFE

The O.J. Simpson trial recorded over 12,000 pages of transcripts that reporters waited by the courtroom door for each night. None of the information would have been recorded without the court reporter. A court reporter's responsibility is to accurately record who says what and when at trials, during depositions, and any time someone feels words being spoken are important enough to hire an accurate transcriber. In a career that requires little emotional commitment for good pay, court reporters find their lives divide into two non-interlocking segments: work and other. "It is a good career to be able to do other things," mentioned one court reporter/actor. Most professionals work through agencies that act as clearinghouses for able, certified court reporters.

Court reporting is a learnable skill requiring coordination, concentration, and study. Court reporters need strong grammatical skills and lots of patience. "Awareness is the most important thing about this career," a fifteen-year court-reporting veteran told us. Frequently, the exact words you type in are crucial to the decision rendered in a given case. A court reporter is responsible for certifying that what has been entered, is, to the best of his abilities, an accurate representation of what took place before him. Unqualified court reporters usually lose all referrals with the first or second incident that arises from carelessness. Because of this high standard of performance and the natural isolation (only one court reporter is in the court room at any given time), significant pressures are placed on court reporters. Of the 25 percent who leave the profession between the first and second years, most cite "stress" as a major factor in their decision.

At its best, a reporter told us, "You go into a zone where you're not concentrating anymore and the words are going straight from your ears through your fingers and onto your disk." This near Zen-like experience was mentioned by several of our respondents as the most pleasant and rewarding of job features. At its worst, the career places not only mental demands but physical ones on people in the field. The incidence of repetitive motion disorders, such as carpal tunnel syndrome, in this career is second only to those found in word-processing departments. For a court reporter, the inability to use her hands or fingers translates into an inability to work. Since most court reporters work as agents of a larger service, they are responsible for their own health care costs and bear the full burden of any work-precluding injuries. "I can't even play touch football," lamented one reporter new to the field, "I'm scared I'll break a finger." Since there is no true hierarchy in this profession, and therefore advancement is not an issue, little if any politics enter the daily routine.

PAYING YOUR DUES

Only about a third of the 300 schools and colleges that offer court reporting programs (either two or four years) are accredited by the National Court Reporters Association, one of whose requirements is to teach computer-aided transcription, so be careful which school you attend. If you can study on your own and pass the rigorous Court Reporting Exams, then a degree from one of these institutions is helpful, but not required. Some states demand that court reporters be notary publics, and others demand that they pass additional state-specific certification tests, such as the Certified Court Reporter (CCR) test or the Registered Professional Reporter (RPR) two-part exam. Specialization for such designations as medical transcriber and court transcriber may require additional training and sphere-specific certification. The requirements for employ by the federal government stipulate that court reporters transcribe at least 175 words per minute; private firms often require a minimum of 225 words per minute.

ASSOCIATED CAREERS

Court reporters often become medical transcribers after a further period of training. Many have word-processing backgrounds and return to word-processing pools, secretarial jobs, or assistant jobs after they leave. Nearly 70 percent remain in the field, however, choosing to pursue this lifestyle as either a well-paying profession requiring little weekend or evening work, or as a part-time position that pays well enough to pursue other career options, usually in the arts.

PAST AND FUTURE

Accurate transcription of historical events has taken place since the first formalized "trials" of ancient Greece. These historiographies were originally written after the completion of the trial at the request of the ruler who wanted history to record the verdict (just or unjust), as proof of his enlightened wisdom. With the modern advocacy system in the United States which required trials open to the public, a more formal means of record keeping was established with the use of court reporters.

Court reporters have become part of the technical revolution that is sweeping America's courtrooms. Once punched into tape, then typed into common 8-1/2- by 11-inch form in a back room (delaying the receipt of transcripts by up to two days), court transcripts are now recorded on computer disks used to store input text, thus allowing them to become available within hours. Real-time transcripts are expected to become more common as courtrooms are wired for simultaneous data transfer. The occupation will remain stable and constant (with significant opportunities available for those in entry-level positions) until voice-recognition software has become more refined—most likely not for another forty to fifty years, by current estimates.

QUALITY OF LIFE

Two Years

The court reporter is just getting up to speed for the first few years, continuing with on-the-job training and learning the trade, the different agencies, and the style of each judge or court.

Five Years

While the career doesn't change much from one year to the next, the reporter's increasing knowledge of the different courtroom styles gets him more frequent assignments.

Ten Years

Employment is fairly secure at this stage, and wages are high due to demand for experienced personnel. Aside from frequent complaints of repetitive strain disorders, job satisfaction is generally high.

THE BIRKMAN LIFESTYLE GRID

This career is suitable for people with Yellow interests.

You'll Have Contact With

Attorneys
Judges
Transcribers
Translators

Major Associations

National Court Reporters Association (NCRA)—
Contact local chapters for more information.
8224 Old Courthouse Road
Vienna, VA 22182
Tel: 703-556-6272
Fax: 703-556-6291

CRIMINOLOGIST

A DAY IN THE LIFE

"Being a criminologist is exciting," wrote one respondent. "It's interesting," said another. "It's unpredictable," ventured a third. The number of adjectives that describe the world of the criminologist would fill more than a page, but one thing is certain: Few occupations require that people be as skilled on both a detail level and a large-picture level as that of criminologist. A criminologist studies normal social behaviors and how certain factors influence deviation from that norm. They work with and often for law enforcement offices (both local and federal), analyzing the behavior and methods of criminals for a variety of reasons: to increase the chances of criminals being apprehended; to predict patterns and motives for behaviors in certain demographic groups; and to assess the responsiveness of crime to various methods of law enforcement. These duties border on the territory of the statistician, and many of the same skills are required of the criminologist, but the additional analytic component of psychological insight and sociological patterns of behavior make this profession unique.

Criminologists' duties can be as distant from police work as reviewing a pattern of behavior among a certain demographic group and writing a profile of the pressures which increase that behavior. Or they may involve going to crime scenes, attending autopsies, and questioning potential suspects to see if they fall into the general psychological profile constructed of the suspect for that crime. One criminologist said the work can be "gruesome," but the type of personality that likes the intellectual task of understanding patterns and deviations from patterns is well challenged in this profession; a number of respondents included the word "fascinating" in their description.

Many cited the intellectual challenge and their fellow law-enforcement officers as the two most positive features of their profession. It is important to note that the opportunity for advancement in this career is limited to the sphere of employment; in other words, if you are hired by a state law enforcement agency, you can rise within that agency, but few move from state agencies to federal agencies, or vice versa. Some members of the profession feel that criminologists are at a distant remove from the actual process of law enforcement. "Sometimes it feels that I write reports that no one ever reads," mentioned one frustrated three-year criminologist, but for the most part, enthusiasm for the profession is high and most enjoy the hard and varied work this profession can bring.

PAYING YOUR DUES

There are comprehensive and rigorous academic requirements to become a criminologist because the job is academic in nature, as much of criminology rests on evaluating and predicting the foundations of behavior based on incomplete information. The overwhelming majority of criminologists are sociology and psychology majors. Coursework should include statistics, writing, computer science, and logic. While many enter the profession with only a bachelor's degree, a significant number continue for graduate work in the behavioral sciences, and those who wish to teach are expected to pursue a doctorate in psychology or sociology. Since most criminologists are employed by law-enforcement agencies, background and security checks are standard. Employers look for candidates who have demonstrated responsibility, creativity, and logical thinking. Criminologists must know how to design and construct sound research projects. Written examinations are required in a number of states to license criminologists, so check with your local law-enforcement agency for requirements in your state and county.

ASSOCIATED CAREERS

Criminologists work closely with many law-enforcement officers, and the few who leave often pursue a variety of law-enforcement careers. Criminologists become police officers, FBI agents, and state medical examiners more often than any other careers. A number use their psychological training as springboards to careers as therapists, psychologists and counselors.

PAST AND FUTURE

Criminology is a relatively modern science, and emerged on two levels simultaneously. National interest in the cause and effects of criminal behavior sparked the FBI to commission a number of studies of federal crimes and criminals in the late 1960s and early 1970s. At the same time, economic and political pressure led urban police departments to commission studies on a much smaller level. The successes of these two endeavors in preventing crime became evident immediately.

Criminologists face much the same demand as sociologists in general. Police departments are loathe to lay off street officers compared with easily replaceable criminologists. Currently, applicants face a competitive market. This bottleneck of qualified candidates for limited positions is expected to continue into the foreseeable future.

QUALITY OF LIFE

Two Years

"Junior" or "assistant" criminologists are in charge of data collection, report proofing, and computer work. These years are marked by low responsibility, average hours, and average levels of pay. Much of the time is spent learning the specific methods, protocols and procedures involved in law enforcement.

Five Years

Five-year veterans may have earned the title "criminologist," depending on the size of the department and the opportunities for advancement. Most work as part of a team, assembling the data collected by more junior members and providing analysis. Their work is overseen by head or chief criminologists, but responsibilities (compared with the first two years) have skyrocketed. Satisfaction levels have increased, but so have hours. Field work is more common than in the early years, and many criminologists now are involved in discussions of policy and procedure, though few have any direct influence. Pay increases. Most of those who were going to leave the profession—a mere 15 percent—have left by this point, frustrated by the nature of the work in the first two years.

Ten Years

Professionals have, for the most part, become chief or head of criminology at their agencies. Many are project developers and manage staffs of junior criminologists, overseeing their research and directing projects through final report status. This position, while more financially rewarding, removes criminologists from one of the most attractive features of their profession: analysis. Many merely review what associates have written and offer advice and guidance. Satisfaction levels dip, but as members of law enforcement agencies, many criminologists benefit from liberal retirement policies.

THE BIRKMAN LIFESTYLE GRID

This career is suitable for people with Red interests.

You'll Have Contact With

Attorneys
FBI Agents
Police Officers
Pathologists

Major Associations

American Society of Criminology
1314 Kinnear
Suite 214
Columbus, OH 43212
Tel: 614-292-9207
Contact: Sarah Hall

American Sociological Association
1722 N Street, NW
Washington, DC 20036-2981
Tel: 202-833-3410

Sellin Center for Studies in Criminology and Criminal Law, U of Pennsylvania
3733 Spruce St.
#437
Philadelphia, PA 19104
Tel: 215-898-7411

CURATOR

A DAY IN THE LIFE

Curators (sometimes referred to as archivists in libraries) collect, maintain, and protect objects of historical and aesthetic importance primarily in museums, libraries, and private collections. Curators are responsible for the safety and proper presentation of the works. "It's all so fascinating and beautiful, that you can find yourself touching history," wrote one respondent. This sense of connection to the motion and beauty of history as expressed through objects is something nearly all the curators who responded mentioned. Almost none of them entered college with the expectation of becoming curators. The profession seemed to "just appear out of thin air." Satisfaction and responsibility are high in this profession at all levels.

Curators' duties include labeling exhibits, keeping track of inventory accurately and carefully, making sure that climate and pest-control issues are seen to, and at times, overseeing research on collection pieces to make certain the integrity of the piece is maintained (such as dating tests for fossils or x-ray analysis of paintings to determine origin). "I've got a Ph.D. and I'm trying to find a good way to deal with termites," said one curator. These varied and wide-ranging duties require someone with a mind attuned to details. Another facet of the curator's job is educating the public about the objects and publicizing their existence. Most literature one receives at a museum, or audiotracks one listens to there, were written by a curator. Grant writing is the third area of responsibility for most curators; much of this is done in consultation with collection managers and curatorial assistants. Curators should have excellent written communication skills. Managing a large staff, including interns and volunteers, is the most unexpected side of the profession. Many find the classification and preservation skills they know useless in coordinating the tasks of a full, dedicated staff. "You have to learn to delegate to peoples' levels of competence," mentioned one veteran curator, and others agreed. "Although you're in charge," said another, "you can't do it alone." Curators who can manage a staff and the details of their job are, for the most part, successful in and excited by their choice of career.

PAYING YOUR DUES

Both graduate education and practical experience are required for those who wish to become curators. Aside from an extensive knowledge of history and art, it is useful to have a basic understanding of chemistry, restoration techniques, museum studies, and even physics and public relations. Curators must have basic skills in aesthetic design, organizational behavior, business, fundraising, and publicity. Many employers look favorably on foreign language skills as well. To become a collection manager or a curatorial assistant, a master's degree is required. To become a curator at a national museum, a Ph.D. is required along with around five years of field experience. The market is competitive, and academic standards are very high. Useful graduate degrees include restoration science, curatorship, art history, history, chemistry, and business administration. Nearly all curators find it helpful to engage in continuing education. Research and publication in academic journals are important for advancement in the field.

ASSOCIATED CAREERS

Curators become art historians, college professors, museum vicepresidents, and museum presidents. A notable few become independent consultants and independent researchers, but significant achievement in the field is required before these opportunities become available.

PAST AND FUTURE

Curatorship arose from the needs of museums, libraries, and societies to maintain and preserve their collections while at the same time publicize them, encourage donations, and expose the public to their artifacts. Curatorship existed as early as 1750 in the United States but without any specific label until the early 1900s. The years 1950 to 1984 were strong years for museum growth and funding, but beginning in 1985 and continuing into the present, museums have been under severe financial pressure due to lack of government funding and general economic trends.

Those who are interested in becoming curators should note that during lean-funding years, the position involves much more grant writing, publicity, and fundraising than collection maintenance and acquisition. Extra time spent at social functions to raise money can be significant. Funding decisions, however, are cyclical; what is true for the industry today may change within a very short period of time.

QUALITY OF LIFE

Two Years

Most curators are still in graduate school. Many take curatorial assistant positions, as well as collection manager jobs (which are more task-oriented) in order to gain experience and begin making connections which will prove invaluable later in their careers. Duties of assistant curators include cataloging existing items and research. Some with good writing skills may be assigned to grant-writing positions. A significant number get jobs through the recommendations of their professors. The hours are long; the pay is low, if any pay is forthcoming at all.

Five Years

Five-year veterans have completed at least a master's degree, and many continue along the Ph.D. track. A number of curatorial assistants have become curatorial associates with expanded responsibilities and hours. Many who are not in school may be asked to travel during these periods; others who are in school may be asked to work odd hours, when there is no museum traffic. Duties include overseeing interns, volunteers, and researchers, along with coordinating access to artifacts with scholars and academics who need access for research projects. A few begin to write copy for educational and promotional literature. Salaries appear during this stage of the career.

Ten Years

A number of professionals have achieved the status of curator or senior curator. These people are involved in staffing, budgeting, trading items with other museums, and piecing collections together for display. Responsibilities are extraordinarily high; salaries become commensurate with the work. Curators direct any internal museum research on pieces and invite academics to join in the study. The newest responsibility that curators have is working with the president and chairman of the museum to direct all fundraising efforts. Political skills are crucial for this position. Many teach at local schools, publish research, and review academic articles for publication. Hours are long, but satisfaction has never been higher. Ten-year curators face a strong future in this competitive and demanding field.

THE BIRKMAN LIFESTYLE GRID

This career is suitable for people with Yellow interests.

You'll Have Contact With

Art Historians
Fundraisers
Professors
Researchers

Major Associations

American Association of Museums
1225 I Street, NW
Suite 200
Washington, DC 20005
Tel: 202-289-1818

Independent Curators Incorporated
799 Broadway
Suite 205
New York, NY 10003
Tel: 212-254-8200
Fax: 212-477-4781

International Council of
the Museum of Modern Art
11 West 53rd Street
New York, NY 10019
Tel: 212-708-9470
Fax: 212-708-9740

DENTAL LAB TECHNICIAN

A DAY IN THE LIFE

Dental technicians provide back-office support to dentists. After the dentist has taken a mold of the patient's teeth, the dental technician uses the mold to produce a wax replica of the teeth, from which he constructs any needed crowns, bridges, or false teeth, and later makes any adjustments to these appliances as directed by the dentist. Dental technicians work closely with dentists and orthodontists.

Our survey respondents pointed out that DTs are often confused with dental hygienists, who work with the dentist and mostly "clean" teeth and treat periodontal (gum) disease. Dental lab technicians insist that they "don't scrape plaque or put our fingers in anybody's mouth!" In fact they have patient contact only in unusual situations that require a visual inspection of the patient's teeth. Though many labs are large, some technicians are sole practitioners in their studios and can work under contract with a dentist. The painstaking detail work is largely solitary. "If you're afraid of being alone, don't sign up," said one DT.

Successful DTs say it's important to be able to make adjustments on the fly. They create facsimiles of people's teeth, and, while impressions can be perfect, they often need minor adjustments, and the DT must work from information provided by the dentist to adjust molds to imitate the patient's mouth. "You can get through grinding and shaping three or four times and the dentist still isn't satisfied," wrote one. Another added that "it's not personal, but it can be very frustrating." They share certain skills with sculptors and don't mind working hard on making their molds accurate and useful; after all, without a precise fit, these casts are useless. A good eye and a good ear serve candidates well in this exacting profession.

PAYING YOUR DUES

No formal college major is required to become a dental technician. Most candidates learn, on the job, how to shape, mold, and grind their materials. Many train on the job for two to three years before becoming sole practitioners. About forty-five dental colleges in the country offer dental technician programs accredited by the American Dental Association. In their final years at those colleges, students choose one area of specialization, such as orthodontics or crowns and bridges, then take licensing exams (such as the one offered by the National Board of Certification), although these licensing exams are not always required.

ASSOCIATED CAREERS

Construction of medical devices requires attention to detail and knowledge of anatomy; people with these skills become prosthetics manufacturers, lens grinders for optometrists, and oral hygienists.

PAST AND FUTURE

There used to be only a handful of dental technicians who provided highly technical assistance for patients in oral crisis (e.g., massive tooth decay, full bridge replacements, or jaw deformity). With the rapid growth of orthodontics in the 1970s, work for dental technicians expanded and people began to enter the profession in significant numbers. Over the years many have had to return to school to keep up with new technology and new methods of construction, but the most pressing force behind change in the industry has been the use of new materials in making impressions and molds.

Demographic trends suggest there will be a continuing demand for specialists as America's population ages. For people who work in gerontological dentistry in particular, the future looks more promising. Because the bulk of DT work consists of standard procedures (such as brace making and tooth spacing), economies of scale have come into play, favoring larger firms that can process these requests quickly and efficiently. But every set of teeth is slightly different, and specialists must create solutions in unpredictable situations.

QUALITY OF LIFE

Two Years
Most of those who work in supervised environments have just completed their on-the-job training programs and are working as assistant dental technicians, grinding molds to specifications, creating wax castings of teeth for crown construction, and shaping jawline impressions. Other relatively new professionals are now full dental technicians and continue to work with their initial employers. Most work in offices of five people or fewer, so these early years are marked by close relationships and tight working conditions. Hours are long; satisfaction is average.

Five Years
Job mobility becomes significant; over one-third of dental technicians go into private practice at this point, either buying an existing shop or working as an independent contractor affiliated with a number of dentists or HMOs. The remainder move between dental offices, finding temporary matches between themselves and their employers. Satisfaction increases and so do hours.

Ten Years
Ten-year professionals have chosen areas of specialization such as ceramics, partial and complete dentures, orthodontic appliances, or crown and bridge replacements. Salaries increase, and many sole practitioners hire less experienced technicians to help them in their work. Satisfaction is at its highest as ten-year veterans are experienced technicians with a reliable client base and good business-recruiting skills. Those who lack any of these elements of a successful technician seek an associated career that satisfies them in the same way.

THE BIRKMAN LIFESTYLE GRID

Red Green
Yellow Blue

*

This career is suitable for people with Yellow interests.

You'll Have Contact With
Dentists
Oral Surgeons
Orthodontists
X-Ray Technicians

Major Associations
American Dental Association
211 East Chicago Avenue
Chicago, IL 60611
Tel: 800-621-8099
Fax: 312-440-7494

American Association for Dental Research
1619 Duke Street
Alexandria, VA 22314
Tel: 708-548-0066
Fax: 703-548-1883

American Society of Master
Dental Technologies
P.O. Box 248
Oakland Gardens, NY 11364
Tel: 718-428-0075

DENTIST

A DAY IN THE LIFE

A dentist is an accredited medical professional who specializes in the care of teeth, gums, and mouths. As with most medical professions, a keen eye for detail, comprehensive medical understanding, manual dexterity, and strong interpersonal skills are important. Dentists deal with procedures that involve actual manipulation of the teeth or gums. Problems dealing with the jaw or any invasive oral procedure are usually undertaken by an oral surgeon, and dental hygienists and dental assistants do much of the routine work-cleanings, maintenance, and X-rays. A significant part of a dentist's job involves educating patients about ways to preserve a healthy mouth, and the best dentists are skillful communicators. Gum disease starts out painless but ultimately attacks over 87 percent of the population. Cavities can develop and worsen for a long time undetected by a patient, and sometimes the only remedy is root canal therapy (less painful than in the early days but still expensive) or extraction of the tooth. Dentists are the preventative doctors par excellence, ever alert for early signs of swollen or bleeding gums, tooth decay, etc., but often they simply step in and correct the results of their patients' less-than-stellar personal hygiene.

Dentists work seven- to ten-hour days, except when emergencies arise, which can occasionally lengthen the workday. The life of a dentist is very similar to that of any other doctor, except that dentists keep regular office hours—one notable attraction of the profession. Many of the dentists we surveyed responded that although the hours are long, one is able to lead a fairly predictable life, take standard vacations around major holidays, and enjoy weekends with family. Reasonable hours were cited on over 90 percent of our surveys as one of the most important features that led people to dentistry as opposed to any other medical specialty.

Dentists pay enormous premiums for liability insurance, large sums for fixed costs such as rent and equipment, and significant overhead for qualified personnel and quality products. Since each patient treated corresponds to additional revenue received, dentists often try to see as many patients as they can on a given day. A dentist usually spends one afternoon a week managing paperwork and insurance claims. The amount of time required to process this paperwork is likely to increase as changes in health care management force doctors to spend more time filing and defending claims of even routine prevention for their insured patients.

PAYING YOUR DUES

Prospective dentists must complete a set of rigorous academic and professional requirements. Academic coursework on the undergraduate level should include anatomy, chemistry, physics and biology. All prospective dentists must complete four years of an American Dental Association accredited school and pass the individual exams administered by each state. Passage of the National Dental Board Exam (administered twice a year), however, can exempt the candidate from the written portion of the state exams. If you wish to teach, do dental research or engage in a dental specialty, an additional two to five years of study is required.

After passing the exams and receiving a Doctor of Dental Surgery (DDS) or Doctor of Dental Medicine (DD.M) degree, a new dentist may choose to "apprentice" under an established practitioner for several years after which time junior associates may either buy a larger share of the partnership or leave to start their own practices. Nearly a quarter of all graduates buy into or purchase outright an existing practice immediately upon graduation. Securing financing is rarely a problem, as most dental practices are considered good investments by banks, as long as the practice's internal cash-flow is properly managed.

ASSOCIATED CAREERS

Including retirement, health problems, death, migration to other fields, and return to school for further education, only 9 percent leave the industry each year. A few decide to specialize in reconstruction, orthodontics, periodontics, oral surgery, or a related medical field. Few leave the medical field altogether.

PAST AND FUTURE

Records of dental exams have been found among artifacts from ancient Egypt, when dentists doubled as surgeons. Long an independent branch of medicine with its own subspecialties, dentistry will continue to be a growing industry for the coming years. But as with all medical professions, the future of tax—and health-care reform will significantly affect the financial attractiveness of the career. The field is also changing in other respects. More destists are entering group practices instead of private. This cuts back on insurance and overhead expenses. The focus of dentistry is shifting towards preventative care and cosmetic procedures.

QUALITY OF LIFE

Two Years

Hours can be long initially, as new dentists must take time to familiarize themselves with their patients' histories, needs, and personalities. It is crucial for new dentists to earn their patients' trust. Job satisfaction increases as dentists begin to hone their "chairside manner" and develop a daily routine that suits them. It should be noted that some dentists find themselves disillusioned with their chosen career. Many are frustrated to find that, although they are similarly educated to physicans, they do not receive the same respect in the public eye. It can also be depressing to repeatedly hear people say, "No offense, but I hate dentists."

Five Years

Five-year veterans have established reputations and built up a client base. Take-home pay rises as they pay off the initial charge of buying into an existing practice. Many work long hours during years three to eight to build their practice with the expectation of future rewards. The downsides are high partnership failure and the ongoing crisis in private vs. group practice.

Ten Years

Dentists who have practiced for ten years earn reasonable satisfaction from what they do. They have established a consistent and loyal client base, have a range of experience and a degree of expertise, and earn significant income. Many become involved in professional associations and professional philanthropy (where businesses donate services to people in need), and write scholarly articles. Hours are still long, but drop off over the next ten years. Most dentists are still working full-time even at the thirty-year mark, and a significant number continue for as long as four decades before retiring.

THE BIRKMAN LIFESTYLE GRID

Red Green
Yellow Blue

This career is suitable for people with Red interests.

You'll Have Contact With

Dental Hygienists
Dental Lab Technicians
Oral Surgeons
Medical Supply Salesmen

Major Associations

American Dental Association
211 East Chicago Avenue
Chicago, IL 60611
Tel: 800-621-8099
Fax: 312-440-7494

American Association for Dental Research
1619 Duke Street
Alexandria, VA 22314
Tel: 708-548-0066
Fax: 703-548-1883

American Association of Women Dentists
401 North Michigan Avenue
Chicago, IL 60611
Tel: 312-644-6610
Fax: 312-321-6869

American Academy of Dentistry
211 East Chicago Avenue
Chicago, IL 60611

DETECTIVE/PRIVATE INVESTIGATOR

A DAY IN THE LIFE

The Raymond Chandler–spawned image of the hard-boiled detective, sipping scotch, fighting in dark alleys and being pursued by rich, beautiful women gave way on the entertainment circuit twenty years ago to those more like James Garner as Jim Rockford. On *The Rockford Files*, a scrappy street-smart ex-con eschewed violence and ducked moral stands in favor of maintaining personal safety. For the first time, detectives were portrayed doing what they really do: "Mostly it's just background checks and finding lost people," said one detective from Dallas; "usually it's between family members." Detectives fulfill client requests for research and surveillance; over 40 percent of their work has to do with divorces. Most detectives spend a lot of time using computer searching resources. Familiarity with credit checks, Lexis/Nexis/Dow Jones searches, and Internet-searching facilities is crucial. Detectives frequently search credit reports, birth and death records, marriage licenses, tax filings, news reports, and legal filings. Involvement with legal issues and lawyers is cited as one of the most prominent features of daily life. Usually, only the final stages of searches for lost or missing people involve significant travel.

Detective work for smaller agencies involves a high quotient of solitude and isolation. A solo practitioner must have solid budgeting and client-relations skills, a strong work ethic, and an independent style. Most detectives are paid per project; there are usually limitations on the time that any fee will cover. Those who join larger agencies must be skilled at prioritizing, writing reports, using a variety of institutionalized resources, and working with teams of other detectives. Large firms sometimes have annual contracts with corporations to investigate internal problems and provide security. Maintaining contacts and personal recommendations is critical.

PAYING YOUR DUES

The skills acquired during an academic career aren't the skills that a detective uses, so degrees are relatively unimportant. At larger firms a degree in criminal behavior, psychology, or law enforcement may be a plus on a resume, but the primary traits employers look for are experience in related fields and an appropriate temperament. Over 75 percent of all private detectives learn the investigative skills required for the profession and make contacts with other future private detectives in the military, local law enforcement, federal law enforcement, or private security firms. Others attend private detective schools, which teach students how to fingerprint, take samples, write reports and use firearms. Over 25 percent have experience as bodyguards and over 80 percent have licenses for firearms. Few use them, however: "If you want to be a gunslinger, rent a movie. Private detectives investigate and report. That's all," said one. Specific computer search skills are usually taught by any hiring firm.

An investigator should be able to work alone, think logically, react quickly to changing circumstances, use sound judgment, and keep a professional distance from her work. Maturity is a must. Some states require private detectives to pass certain exams and post a bond to ensure their compliance with state regulations; check with local authorities for the laws in your area.

ASSOCIATED CAREERS

Investigators who leave the profession often return to the law-enforcement, security work, or military setting from which they came. The uncertainty of detective work seems the most significant reason people leave; a few cite burnout as the hours are long and the pay is uneven. Detectives also often go to law school when they want to switch careers.

PAST AND FUTURE

Most law enforcement between the Revolutionary and Civil Wars was primarily work for hire by bounty hunters and so-called "thief takers." They walked on the border of the law to achieve their goals. The Pinkerton Detective Agency, founded in the 1850s by Allan Pinkerton, was the first private detective firm to promise integrity and trustworthiness for a daily wage (as opposed to bounty-based pay).

Private detective agencies are expected to grow rapidly and increase in size over the next ten to fifteen years. Private detective firms are more in demand than ever; as more and more local governments downsize their police forces, communities, companies and individuals need to hire private detectives. Economies of scale make it likely that larger, more technologically advanced firms will begin to consolidate many of the smaller firms.

QUALITY OF LIFE

Two Years

Private investigators in large firms work with more experienced mentors and learn the methods and protocols the firm employs. Many spend significant amounts of time doing library, courthouse, and city hall based research and reviewing reports written by their colleagues. Most work purely behind the scenes. Those who wish to advance aggressively pursue additional duties and responsibilities, such as late night and weekend projects. Small firm or solo investigators have all the same problems small business owners face: client recruitment, instability of income, and unpredictable staffing needs. Satisfaction is average; hours can be long.

Five Years

Five-year survivors are experienced private investigators. Many have learned valuable computer searching skills, have established contacts in a variety of record-keeping industries (such as credit-reporting companies, city hall, and the police department), and have seen a number of cases from inception to completion. Members of large firms have contact with clients. Many have supervisory roles. Small firm practitioners add bodyguard and security duties to their investigative roles in order to attract more clients and to ensure a more steady stream of income. Satisfaction is, again, average; hours are still long.

Ten Years

Private investigators who have lasted ten years in the profession have strong reputations and valuable experience. The majority who leave the profession do so between years four and eight, dissatisfied with the limited range of responsibilities. Those who are going to begin their own firms have done so by this point, and many supervise instead of doing field investigative work. A number of ten-year veterans find this transition jarring, as the skills that make one a good investigator do not necessarily translate into making one a good supervisor. Salaries increase, hours decrease, and satisfaction goes up for those who like the new job role, and down for those who dislike it.

THE BIRKMAN LIFESTYLE GRID

This career is suitable for people with Red interests.

You'll Have Contact With
Credit Agents
Government Record Clerks
Police Officers
Researchers

Major Associations
World Association of Detectives
P.O. Box 1049
Severna Park, MD 21146
Tel: 800-962-0516

National Association of Investigative Specialists
P.O. Box 33244
Austin, TX 78764
Tel: 512-719-3595
Fax: 512-719-3594

DEVELOPER

PROFESSIONAL PROFILE

# of people in profession	14,250
% male	95
% female	5
avg. hours per week	60
avg. starting salary	$21,000
avg. salary after 5 years	$24,100
avg. salary 10 to 15 years	$29,900

Professionals Read
New York Foreclosures
Land Sales
Real Estate Monthly

Books, Films and TV Shows Featuring the Profession
The Art of the Deal
Real Profit Estate
Superman
Gremlins 2

Major Employers
Grubb-Ellis
55 E. 59th St.
New York, NY 10022
Tel: 212-759-9700
Fax: 212-326-4802
Contact: Human Resources

Trump Organization
725 5th Ave.
New York, NY 10022
Tel: 212-715-7200
Fax: 212-935-0141
Contact: Human Resources

Tramal Pro-Reality
2001 Ross Ave.
Suite 3500
Dallas, TX 75201
Tel: 214-979-5100
Fax: 214-979-6005
Contact: Personnel

A DAY IN THE LIFE

Developers find undeveloped property, or what they believe to be incorrectly developed property, and build on it or convert it to its optimal use. The day moves at a frenzied stride. Successful developers love the pace and feel that without it, the job would be "just another paper shuffle." To get a deal together, developers need to quickly coordinate the financial side, the production side, and the end-sales side. Few properties are developed these days without tenants already lined up for post-construction, placing an added burden on the developer, who must give the tenants a date they can move in.

Developers' responsibilities depend on which of three areas they specialize in: finance, construction or recruitment. Those involved in the finance end are busiest at the initial stages of projects, when they research, explore and negotiate the terms of new deals. They work with banks, government agencies, and financial consultants calculating the feasibility of projects, reviewing sites, and planning for contingencies. Deals are very risky—they seem to earn either a continuing 18 to 22 percent return or a 35 to 44 percent loss. Financial developers oversee all payments, rates of production, and negotiations with banks during and after the development of a site.

Construction liaisons work with construction managers and local agencies to ensure that the structure is up to local building codes, that all necessary permits are obtained, and that production moves along on schedule. An understanding of basic engineering and construction principles is helpful, as are strong communication skills. Within development, professionals in this area seemed least satisfied with their positions. Eighty percent of respondents cited the role of "policeman" on the job as the least enjoyable, and several said they felt isolated. Developers who supervise construction can be caught between financial oversights of the financial developer and the mistrust of the general contractor. However, this position records the highest intellectual satisfaction among the three.

A recruiter puts together statistics, models, and plans for the site and then sells rental space to tenants. Recruiters must have strong selling skills, excellent negotiating instincts, and a grasp of construction scheduling. They must be comfortable working with numbers. Construction delays, labor hold-ups, or permit problems are not considered valid excuses for delays of occupancy, so many clients insist on penalties for missing the date of completion. Successful recruiters trade to a large extent on their expertise in construction scheduling.

While some thrive on the pace, the pressure gets to others. A staggering 18 percent of developers in their first five years in the profession leave each year. Most aspiring developers have to travel to be able to work on a variety of projects or risk long periods of time when their expertise is of little or no use. The ultimate goal for most people in development is working on their own projects. To do this one must have expertise, access to capital, and a strong stomach for high-risk stakes against unfavorable odds.

PAYING YOUR DUES

The aspiring developer needs an academic background emphasizing real estate, finance, managerial skills, psychology, or accounting. Many developers work for a few years and then return to school for an MBA, the degree of choice. Work experience in real estate or finance is important, too. Some employers require new employees to have real estate licenses or accounting accreditations prior to starting work. As specialization occurs within the industry, such accreditations as CPA and CFA become significant.

Unlike many other fields where applicants are exposed to the entire process then slotted to their specific skill set, employees are hired for a specialization within a development company and immersed in the details of the occupation right away. Many spend extra hours and free time learning about the other parts of the process.

ASSOCIATED CAREERS

Developers who leave the field often move on to banking, investment banking, construction financing and real estate sales, all less potentially lucrative professions, but ones that carry much less potential downside and more regular income.

PAST AND FUTURE

The United States Pre-Emption Act of 1841 encouraged people to go west and settle unused government land, then claim it as their own (so successful was this program the act was abolished in 1891). Speculation ran high during these years, and many fortunes were made. This speculative instinct continues on an institutional level for the modern developer.

Developers are subject to the caprice of many different independent variables, among them interest rates, general economic optimism, urban-rural migration rates, cost of equipment, new construction projects, and local permit restrictions. In general, the market for developers should remain at its current level for the next few years, and many believe that a balanced budget will help long-term interest rates, encouraging large-scale development projects which will not be sensitive to short-term interest rate fluctuation. Even without a balanced budget, though, the developer's role is secure for the foreseeable future.

QUALITY OF LIFE

Two Years

Two-year developers are assistants who do anything and everything senior developers need, including preparing reports, researching topics, and coordinating meetings between parties. A number are on-site representatives monitoring construction progress, double-checking figures, and keeping track of files for prospective clients. Aggressive opportunity seeking and long hours of careful work mark those who advance beyond this stage. Many, dissatisfied with the low levels of responsibility and recognition, leave between years two and three.

Five Years

Developers attain "associate" status and have responsibility for more junior members of the profession. Positions are marked by long hours, average pay, and hard work. Client and contractor contact and sales responsibility are significant. Developers dream of working on their own projects, and spend free time socializing with financial, construction, and property managing contacts to further the possibility of that dream coming true.

Ten Years

Ten-year developers have worked on many projects (perhaps a number of them simultaneously) and have seen the best and worst the industry has to offer. Many consult on running one specific area of development: The construction end, the financing end, or the sales end. Hours increase, but financial reward does as well. Most try to get some percentage of a deal in exchange for a low base pay. Experience is valuable, and most employers recognize this fact.

THE BIRKMAN LIFESTYLE GRID

This career is suitable for people with Red interests.

You'll Have Contact With

Attorneys
Bankers
Construction Managers
Real Estate Brokers

Major Associations

Building Owners and Managers
Institute International
1521 Ritchie Highway
Arnold, MD 21012
Tel: 410-974-1410
Contact: Student Development Department

Institute of Real Estate Management
430 North Michigan Avenue
Chicago, IL 60611
Tel: 312-329-6000

DIPLOMAT/ATTACHE/FOREIGN SERVICE OFFICER

A DAY IN THE LIFE

The Foreign Service represents the U.S. around the world. Members interact with local governments as emissaries of the United States, staff U.S. embassies and consulates, and provide resources for Americans traveling abroad. Over 60 percent of a foreign service officer's working hours are spent handling reports—assembling facts, writing, proofreading, and reading. "Reading is fundamental," wrote one member of the diplomatic corps, "and if your writing isn't up to snuff, you'll be selected out—fired, that is." Strong communication skills are a must for anyone thinking about entering the profession. Diplomats are posted to positions abroad for terms of two, three or four years with nine-month stateside stints every two to four years, but they can be recalled at the discretion of the State Department at any time.

The foreign service handles all problems of Americans abroad including: negotiating with local governments for individual United States companies who wish to manufacture, produce, or do business abroad; providing information about the host country; and issuing replacements for lost documentation. Foreign consulates also issue visitation and residency visas to foreigners wishing to enter the United States. These tasks consume a minimum of thirty hours of the workweek; "My hourly wage in 1992 was $3.45. I calculated it, adding in all the unpaid overtime I put in," said one diplomat. Since additional internal duties (including writing reports) and social functions (which are an important part of the job) can take up another forty hours per week, those who are looking for a sinecure are ill-advised to enter the foreign service. Members who are most satisfied with their profession enjoy the responsibility: the ability to look at a host country from the inside, write a considered opinion of the state of that country, and have it seriously regarded by officials making decisions about international relations.

PAYING YOUR DUES

To enter the foreign service, you must be an American citizen between the ages of twenty and fifty-four, and have a bachelor's degree. Helpful college or graduate school courses include English, any foreign language, government, geography, international history, economics, public speaking and commerce. Applicants must pass the competitive foreign service exam, offered every December in most major urban centers and at consulates abroad. Those who pass take a secondary exam, which includes a day-long assessment, a physical, a rigorous background exam and a final review of all the candidates strengths and weaknesses. Candidates are expected to be familiar with another language, but fluency can be acquired after posting.

Those who pass all the tests are given a ranking and put on a list of eligible candidates for future posting. As positions become available, candidates are offered suitable postings. Note that at most, a few hundred slots open up each year. While many start their tenure with a nine-month stint in Washington DC to learn the protocols of being a diplomat (termed the "pregnancy period" by one of our respondents), others begin in the field and learn and are trained on the fly. Please be aware that if you are listed on the sheet of eligibles, and no position opens up for you within eighteen months, you will have to begin the procedure again. All names are removed from the list at that point.

ASSOCIATED CAREERS

Over half the foreign service officers find life-time careers in the foreign service, particularly with the understanding that retirement is mandatory at age sixty and one is eligible at age fifty after serving for twenty years. Those who leave use their unique perspective and their skills to work for other branches of the government, such as the department of defense, the CIA, the INS, the commerce department or teach at the university level.

PAST AND FUTURE

The Constitution provided that a foreign service be developed, but one did not exist in practice in any reasonably funded form until the mid-1800s. Until 1924, the foreign service was the plumb of patronage and supportable only by those in the upper class. The wages were so scandalously low that no one else could afford to take a position. The Rogers Act in 1924 provided reasonable wages and democratized the process of entering the foreign service. The process has become even more egalitarian with current application methods.

The foreign service is and will continue to be a vital service of the United States. As with any government office, it is subject to budget whims, but as it is currently thinly staffed and highly competitive, future funding cuts should not come in this area. Expect competition for limited positions to remain high—strong preparation for the foreign service exam is your best ally.

QUALITY OF LIFE

Two Years

Halfway through their probationary period, which lasts roughly four years, new diplomats are expected to have made significant headway in learning a foreign language. Many are called staff specialists; the majority of candidates for positions do not receive officer status upon hire. Duties include filing reports, assembling data, and providing any research or coordination under the direction of foreign service officers or ambassadors.

Five Years

Five year veterans have established themselves as officers, information specialists, or staff specialists. Each year, appointees receive ratings from their supervisors and are advanced in the profession through six grades of classification, with grade six being lowest. Around 30 percent of those who began in the foreign service have left, due to low ratings, lack of progress in language skills, or lack of opportunity in their area of expertise.

Ten Years

Those who have survived ten years in the diplomatic corps have been rotated back to Washington for at least two periods of "re-education" in the American experience, have been consistently rated well by superiors, and have at least earned a classification of grade three: Those who aspire to "career minister" (a high-level foreign service office position) continue to accrue additional responsibilities and hours. A few who have shown great promise are sponsored to go to the Foreign Service Institute for high-level additional education—a true feather in the cap of the career diplomat. Those who are not advancing find their abroad status in jeopardy, and may be asked to return to back-office work in Washington. A few may become ambassadors, but this position is usually a political appointment.

THE BIRKMAN LIFESTYLE GRID

Red Green
Yellow Blue

This career is suitable for people with Green interests.

You'll Have Contact With

Analysts
Government Officials
Tourists
Translators

Major Associations

Executive Council on Foreign Diplomacy
818 Connecticut Avenue, NW
12th Floor
Washington, DC 20006
Tel: 202-466-5199
Fax: 202-872-8696

DISC JOCKEY

A DAY IN THE LIFE

Whether you're a disc jockey for a radio station or a nightclub, the best aspect of the job is the creativity it allows. Radio disc jockeys play music, chat, deliver news, weather, or sports, or hold conversations with celebrities or call-in listeners. Club DJ's mix music, sound effects, and special effects and occasionally provide time-filling chatter between songs. Each must be in command of their specialty—genre of music or demographic of audience—and sensitive to listener responses.

A radio disc jockey must be able to spin off on an item in the news or a hot new song. "I think about how things connect," said one. Being extremely organized and synchronized is critical to the radio station. Songs must fill a certain span of time; commercials have to be aired during specific blocks. Disc jockeys must be able to coordinate what plays when within time and audience constraints while on the air. A radio DJ must build an audience. Most specialize in a specific musical genre, have a consistent approach, and field calls and requests from interested listeners to develop a consistent, loyal listening public. Since only one person is usually on the air at a given time, the DJs get lonely. Over 75 percent of our surveys mentioned "isolation" as one of the biggest drawbacks.

A club disc jockey keeps regular hours, usually working from 8:00 p.m. to 4:00 a.m. Most DJs don't socialize regularly with those who do not keep the same unusual hours. Isolation, again, creeps in. A club DJ must keep the crowd interested in dancing, so she must know a wide variety of styles and songs which appeal to different groups. Record promoters and agents try to flood high-profile DJs with new albums, hoping to provide exposure for their acts. Over 40 percent of all DJs work part-time and find it difficult to land regular, reasonably-paying gigs. Many club DJs move to large urban centers to find a market which will support their services, but it's still difficult to get hired initially without a following that you can be expected to draw to the club.

PAYING YOUR DUES

No specific educational requirements exist to become a disc jockey, but most radio disc jockeys have experience at college radio stations or in small markets; others intern while in school to learn the equipment used in the industry and to get a taste of the style of successful radio personalities. Many create tapes of their shows and save clippings to use as introductions to professional radio stations. A radio jockey must be familiar with current or specialty (subgenre) musical trends and how specific songs fit together. He must be able to fill empty space with information and have a clear, clean speaking voice and a certain amount of technical skill. A club or nightclub disc jockey must know how to mix beats so music progresses smoothly, how to design a night of music around a specific theme or requested type of music, and how to use lighting and special effects to best advantage. As first introductions, many DJs must work for free at established clubs on off nights. Close contact with record promoters is important in getting unreleased demos or other songs which can distinguish you from other DJs. A DJ trades on his reputation, so staying current with musical trends and responding to listener feedback is critical to success.

ASSOCIATED CAREERS

Over 60 percent of DJs rotate from one position within the radio industry to another; moving to news anchoring, call-in shows, specialty shows, and sports shows. Another 7 percent write copy for radio broadcasts, television broadcasts, and newspapers. Club disc jockeys move to careers in the record industry, primarily as liaisons between other DJs and the company itself.

PAST AND FUTURE

The first commercial radio station started in 1920 as station KDKA, broadcasting from Pittsburgh, PA. During the "golden years" of radio (the 1940s), radio personalities were paid as much as movie stars and treated with the same celebrity. Club disc jockeys reached their apex in the mid-1970s/early-1980s, when disco was the craze and nightclubbing was de rigueur for those in social circuits.

More and more radio stations are finding it cheaper to buy nationally syndicated shows rather than produce their own, so opportunities for radio DJs could shrink in the coming decade. Successful club DJs will always have followings, but opportunities for success could be limited by an uncertain market for clubs.

QUALITY OF LIFE

Two Years

Opportunities are difficult to come by. Aspiring DJs pursue auditions, running from club to club or radio station to radio station, actively self-promoting. They bring clippings, taped samples of their work, and recommendations to prospective employers. Many take "test nights" at clubs, where return engagements are determined by the size and activity of the crowd that shows up that night. Radio DJs often take internships or menial jobs at radio stations in order to get themselves introduced to those who decide on-air talent. The hours are long and often unrewarding.

Five Years

If a disc jockey is making a living at her profession, she's doing well. The majority have regular stints at a number of clubs or functions, or have earned at least secondary on-air responsibilities, and are very busy between promotion, work, and keeping current on musical trends. A number have made connections in the record industry by this point, and spend a significant amount of time scouting emerging bands for signs of talent.

Ten Years

DJs who have survived the club circuit for ten years are on the back end of their careers, because the life is rigorous and it's rarely forever. The connections a ten-year DJ has provide him with ample opportunity to enter the record industry, the promotion industry, or the club-managing scene. Radio disc jockeys who have lasted ten years in the profession have solid followings, an established taste and attitude, and a regular stint on a local radio station. Those who wish for national syndication must make their shows unique, exciting, and creative. Hours increase for those pursuing fame; salaries become significant between years seven and fifteen.

THE BIRKMAN LIFESTYLE GRID

This career is suitable for people with Green interests.

You'll Have Contact With

Advertising Executives
Music Executives
Musicians
Promoters

Major Associations

National Association of Broadcasters
1771 N Street, NW
Washington, DC 20036
Tel: 202-429-5300
Fax: 202-429-3931

Radio-Television News Directors Association
1000 Connecticut Avenue, NW
Suite 615
Washington, DC 20036
Tel: 202-659-6510
Fax: 202-223-4007

ECOLOGIST

Professionals Read

Nature
Natural History
Ecoverse

Books, Films and TV Shows Featuring the Profession

Arctic Wolves
Losing Ground
Ecoconservatism

Major Employers

EPA
401 M Street, SW
Washington, DC 20460
Tel: 202-260-2090
Contact: Personnel Officer

Natural Resources Defense Council
40 West 20th Street
New York, NY 10011
Tel: 212-727-4400
Fax: 212-727-1773
Contact: Human Resources

Texas A&M University
809 East University Street
Suite 101A
College Station, TX 77843
Tel: 409-845-5154
Fax: 409-847-8877
Contact: Human Resources

A DAY IN THE LIFE

Ecologists examine the relationship between the environment and actions that affect it, including rainfall, pollution, temperature shifts, and industrialization. The vision of an ecologist as a bearded, outdoorsy, mountain-man standing on a pile of litter is based on about 1 out of 100 of all ecologists. "We're not all Grizzly Adams!" wrote one ecological scientist, and she is right; the most accurate picture of an ecologist would be in a lab coat or poring through volumes of collected data. Some ecologists work for not-for-profit environmental groups; others work for large corporations or the government. Ecologists work with scientific and mathematical models to analyze and interpret correlations between actions and effects on the environment, which translates into significant time looking at data. "You've got be able to find the assumptions which underlie every study or you're history," mentioned one ecologist. Over 40 percent of those we surveyed used the phrase "keen analytic mind" to describe a trait of the most successful members of their profession. Some fieldwork is required—at the most, three to six months per year, but more often two to four weeks per year.

Those who enter the profession with strong academic training in the issues presented have no difficulty; over 80 percent of environmental science majors who enter the field stay ecologists for at least five years. For those who come to the career through other routes, the path is less certain: Only 55 percent remain in the profession after five years. People with strong essay writing and report-writing skills last longer than those without them. "I had to learn to think all over again, and once I had done that, I had to learn how to write all over again," said one professional. A solid majority of respondents ranked writing the second- or third-most important skill in this profession. An ecologist can make a difference in how the general population treats the environment with rigorous scientific research and presentation of their ideas in well-written reports and articles which educate others.

One ecologist described her colleagues as "smart people who love looking at big systems and, if possible, saving them." Many researchers review others' articles and papers before they are sent out to publishers. The sense of community often sustains ecologists in their careers when little, if anything, is done with their recommendations. Aspiring ecologists should be aware of the institutional difficulties in making any headway against environmental degradation: This sense of frustration can be significant for those entering this profession.

PAYING YOUR DUES

Most ecologists are scientists with backgrounds in chemistry, environmental science, geology, biology, climatology, statistics and, in many cases, economics. The depth of knowledge in each field determines the specialty area each candidate works in; a master's degree in a science or ecology itself is becoming more and more common as the minimum requirement. Nearly all aspiring ecologists are expected to have some field experience.

ASSOCIATED CAREERS

Ecologists, because of their exposure to the growing mountain of numbers which indicate that we are ravaging our own planet, often become environmentalists, using their scientific and statistics-based background as a resource for their educational and lobbying efforts. They also often become teachers, addressing the problem of environmental degradation that way.

PAST AND FUTURE

Ecological issues came to the forefront during the industrialization of Europe. Coal, the main fuel, had blackened the sky of many heretofore pristine countries, contributing to public health problems. Unsafe mining practices led to the contamination of otherwise arable land. In the U.S., ecology became a public issue in the early 1970s. In the early 90s, recycling bins appeared in almost every home and office.

Ecology is one of the fastest growing professions surveyed in this book. Ecological concerns across the globe are becoming more widespread, giving rise to the need for more experts. The number of impact studies made by private employers, governments, and developers who need global ecological information is expected to double over the next twenty years. Opportunities are emerging which will make the profession more visible, significant, and rewarding.

QUALITY OF LIFE

Two Years

Ecologists have done field research, collected and assembled data, and produced reports. All of their work is supervised, and many are assigned to specific tasks by senior ecologists. Nonscience majors spend these early years learning about ecological science topics, while science majors brush up on their writing skills. Hours are average but satisfaction (particularly among science-friendly personnel) is high. Wages are low.

Five Years

Ecologists are promoted from assistants to associate ecologists, a position which has greater responsibility for data collection, report presentation, and supervising junior ecologists in their daily tasks. Many pursue advanced degrees in materials science, chemistry, ecology, and economics. Satisfaction is average; those unsuited to the lifestyle leave between years four and nine.

Ten Years

Ten-year ecologists direct research, allocate funds, and manage personnel. They are involved in independent research and publishing and lecturing. Those who teach classes begin to do so during these years. Fieldwork drops significantly after year six in the profession. Many professionals become involved in high-profile debates on the effect of certain behaviors on the environment.

THE BIRKMAN LIFESTYLE GRID

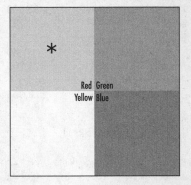

Red Green
Yellow Blue

This career is suitable for people with Red interests.

You'll Have Contact With

Biologists
Environmentalists
Researchers
Waste Managers

Major Associations

American Institute of Biological Scientists
1444 Eye Street, NW
Suite 200
Washington, DC 20005
Tel: 202-628-1500

Ecological Society of America
2010 Massachusetts Avenue, NW
Suite 400
Washington, DC 20036
Tel: 202-833-8773
Contact: Malcolm Tyson

Student Conservation Association
P.O. Box 550
Charlestown, NH 03603
Tel: 603-543-1700
Contact: Sally Miske

The Nature Conservancy
1815 North Lynn Street
Arlington, VA 22209
Tel: 703-841-5300

Association for the Study of
Man-Enviroment Relations
P.O. Box 57
Orangeburg, NY 10962
Tel: 914-634-8221

ECONOMIST

A DAY IN THE LIFE

The field of economics rewards creative and curious thinkers. Economists study data and statistics in order to spot trends in economic activity, economic confidence levels, and consumer attitudes. They assess this information using advanced methods in statistical analysis, mathematics, computer programming; finally they make recommendations about ways to improve the efficiency of a system or take advantage of trends as they begin. While economists were previously relegated to the academic and government communities, they are now finding employment in significant numbers throughout the private sector. The number of privately owned economic consulting firms has grown by about 150 percent over the last six years, to reach about 5,000 as of this writing. These firms offer advice to and predict economic scenarios for individuals and large corporations, and occasionally act as consultants to branches of the government. However, universities and research groups remain the largest employers of economists, followed by the government.

"I love being an economist. I get a glimpse of the future, or what we think it's going to be," raved one economist we surveyed. High levels of satisfaction are found throughout this field, which encourages discussion, detailed examination, and lively disagreement. Economists work closely with each other and share ideas fairly easily, which leads to a strong sense of community within the profession. Perhaps the most challenging aspect of the profession is its highly theoretical nature. One ex-partner of a private advertising and economics firm wrote, "It's all numbers which assume perfect market behavior. People don't work that way. The don't buy according to their optimal strategyóthey buy because they feel like it." The lack of a clear-cut relationship between theoretical modeling and reality eats away at some economists' belief in what they do.

The daily routine of each economist is determined by the specialty chosen. Financial economists meet with members of Wall Street firms and government officials to predict the movement and pace of global financial markets. International economists may spend as much as 30 percent of their time traveling and 40 percent of the time on the phone researching current trends in foreign economic systems (for this subgroup, language skills are important). Other fields include agricultural economics, labor economics, and law and economics.

PAYING YOUR DUES

Graduates with bachelor's degrees in economics find entry-level positions in which their primary responsibilities are the collection, assimilation and preparation of data. For positions with greater responsibility, such as those in teaching or government, a master's degree or Ph.D. is required. The more quantitative course requirements of the economics major include statistics, regression analysis, and econometrics. These form the core of business life, but at the same time, those who are comfortable with the written or spoken word have a significantly higher rate of advancement and overall job satisfaction than those who are not. Applicants should be comfortable with computers, numbers, and long academic papers. Many women who start in academia find they are more successful in the private sector.

The ability to distinguish yourself from other economists is key, but can be difficult, especially within a particular company's or industry's accepted economic assumptions. Creative thinkers and those who have taken cross-discipline course loads, such as philosophy or marketing, seem to find it easier to break from the pack and propose new, interesting additions to the economic canon. Technological breakthroughs bring countless new possibilities to economic analysis for economists to explore and present.

ASSOCIATED CAREERS

Economists who leave the profession find a wide range of careers open to them. Their statistical and mathematical skills make them well-suited for careers as statisticians, bankers, stockbrokers, options traders, equity research analysts, and any other profession that requires systems modeling. Their research and writing skills allow them to become financial journalists, research analysts, academics in other fields, and administrative managers.

PAST AND FUTURE

Adam Smith, the father of economics, came up with "laissez-faire" and the so-called law of supply and demand. John Maynard Keynes, with his theories on unemployment and the system of economic sponsorship, was one of the first modern economists to garner international fame. In post W.W.II economies, the role of economists has been recognized as valuable by all governments and numerous industries in the financial sector.

In the future, computer modeling will help economists formulate their economic visions for a wide variety of clients, including third-world countries and multinational corporations. Private industries should hire approximately 30 percent more economists over the next five to ten years, mostly in urban centers, particularly Washington, New York, and Los Angeles (for economists specializing in the analysis of Pacific Rim economies).

QUALITY OF LIFE

Two Years

Economists who pursue graduate degrees often work while still in school, so these first few years pass at a frenzied pace. For the first few months in the working world, economists learn the assumptions and models used by the hiring company. Tasks focus on computer modeling, report writing, and working as part of larger, highly supervised research teams. Salaries are low. Projects usually have strict deadlines, so expect some weekend work. Economists in academia start out as assistant professors, lecturing, grading papers, and teaching sections.

Five Years

Nearly 30 percent of those who began five years ago have either returned to school to pursue higher degrees in economics or to get out of the field altogether (in many cases, to become bankers). Since most private consulting firms employ fewer than fifty people, those who stay can rise rapidly. Successful economists are team leaders, managing large research projects, working with clients, and reviewing materials prepared by junior associates. Academics, now teaching their own seminars, are likely to have shifted among universities to those with strong opportunities for advancement and are publishing papers and articles other than thesis material.

Ten Years

By this point, economists have significant client experience, strong managerial skills, and an ability to deliver promised services. Over 25 percent of ten-year veterans start their own consulting firms. Others become in-house employees at banks, brokerage houses, or other types of financial consulting firms (usually at the vice-presidential level or higher). Academics are now professors, publishing articles, working with graduate students, and angling for the extra-university awards and consulting agreements that can provide a significant boost to income and prestige within the profession.

THE BIRKMAN LIFESTYLE GRID

Red Green
Yellow Blue

This career is suitable for people with Green interests.

You'll Have Contact With

Bankers
Government Officials
Researchers
Statisticians

Major Associations

National Association of Business Economists
1233 20th Street, NW
Suite 505
Washington, DC 20036
Tel: 202-463-6223

American Economic Association
2014 Broadway
Suite 305
Nashville, TN 37203
Tel: 615-322-2595

EDITOR

PROFESSIONAL PROFILE

# of people in profession	283,000
% male	70
% female	30
avg. hours per week	40
avg. starting salary	$21,500
avg. salary after 5 years	$26,000
avg. salary 10 to 15 years	$45,000

Professionals Read
Editor and Publisher
Publishers Weekly
Kirkus Reviews

Books, Films and TV Shows Featuring the Profession
The Novel
The Paper
Lou Grant
A Biography of Max Perkins

Major Employers
Edit Ink
5907 Main Street
Williamsville, NY 14221
Tel: 716-626-4431
Fax: 716-6264388
Contact: Denise Sterrs, President

Conde Nast Publications
350 Madison Avenue
New York, NY 10017
Tel: 212-880-8800
Fax: 212-880-8086
Contact: Human Resources

John Wiley & Sons
605 Third Avenue
New York, NY 10158-0012
Tel: 212-850-6000
Fax: 212-850-6049
Contact: Beth Nabi

A DAY IN THE LIFE

For people who love the written word and know they have the ability to plan, organize, and see printed material through its several stages of production, editing may be the ideal job. A critical link between authors and the reading public, editors control the quality and nature of printed material, working with authors on rewrites, correcting grammar, and smoothing out inconsistencies. Editors have significant input on turning out quality material, analyzing work for quality of content, grammatical correctness, and stylistic consistency. The work requires patience, thoroughness, and an ability to see both small details and the big picture simultaneously. Editors must be able to work closely with writers, diagnosing problems and offering advice on how to avoid them in the future. This takes a keen, analytical mind and a gentle touch.

An editor meets frequently with others working on publication, including artists, typesetters, layout personnel, marketing directors, and production managers. In most areas of publishing, the success or failure of a product relies on continuous and open communication between different departments; a snag in any one may throw off the scheduling of another. As links between different departments, editors must be able to handle personality issues diplomatically, be comfortable with the rigorous scheduling and economics of publishing, and must coordinate and communicate their requirements clearly and effectively.

Editorial positions are available in many types of companies, from established publishing house to on-line service companies. A magazine editor has a different schedule and handles different matters than an acquisitions editor or a newspaper editor. Interests, opportunities, and luck lead editors to an area of specialization. People who wish to progress in this field nearly always read manuscripts in their spare time or stay late to do extra work. Competency is rewarded, and lateral and upward mobility within large houses is common. Over 40 percent of our respondents registered discontent with their current jobs, but over 80 percent recorded pleasure with the choice of career and lifestyle. The 15 percent a year who leave the profession do so because their expectations of immediate impact and recognition remain unmet by this competitive and underpaid occupation.

PAYING YOUR DUES

No specific academic degree is required, but most editors were English, communications, or journalism majors in college. A history of editorial positions on college newspapers or literary magazines and a body of work to show is important. Most employers require potential editors to take word-processing and proofreading tests before hire, so it's a good idea to be familiar with standard word-processing programs and proofreading symbols. Familiarity with publishing software and graphics systems is extremely helpful. Some find it beneficial to take a six-week publishing seminar to enhance their resumes, but no employers require it. Because of the relative paucity of entry-level editorial positions, many people enter publishing firms, magazines, and newspapers in advertising, marketing, or promotion departments and use these positions to network into editorial departments.

ASSOCIATED CAREERS

Those who leave editing usually do so because of lack of mobility and low pay. Editors can translate their skills into business, human resources, and governmental administrative careers. Others go into non-editorial aspects of publishing, such as subsidiary rights or production.

PAST AND FUTURE

With Johannes Gutenberg's invention of the printing press in the fifteenth century, publishing became an industry. Authors would work with printers and sell their work to booksellers, who soon realized that they needed someone in-between to assure the quality of the product. Thus editors were born.

Technology has affected and will continue to affect the field. More written work is produced each day in the United States than was produced in the world before 1700. Since technological advancement and a lowering of fixed publishing costs now make it easier for smaller houses, magazines, and newsletters to produce quality products, the future of publishing may lie in smaller houses where a variety of skills are required by each editor, including layout and graphic skills. The lowering of fixed costs, however, may also mean that larger, well-funded houses that can attract established authors will be in a better position to drive smaller, less organized companies out of existence. Material online will still need editing as well. The position of editor should remain, but the auxiliary skills needed will change.

QUALITY OF LIFE

Two Years

Expect to work hard and earn little as an "editorial assistant" or "assistant editor." Starting positions include some menial tasks—proofreading, correspondence, assisting senior editors, and copying. Over 60 percent of our respondents mentioned that they worked late, worked on weekends, or took work home with them. Many new editors have responsibility for smaller, easily managed projects to learn the ropes. While new editors sometimes work directly with authors, contact is limited and the responsibility level is low. People are constantly networking to find positions with greater responsibility and better remuneration.

Five Years

Often a full-blown editor by now, the five-year veteran starts to gravitate to a specialty. Skills have improved both technically and interpersonally and responsibilities have increased. Earnings have gone up to the point of self-sufficiency (you can go out to dinner occasionally). On average, a five-year editor has held at least two jobs—a significant turnover rate.

Ten Years

At the ten-year mark, an editor has significant editing experience, has been through every major snafu possible, and has a steady stream of responsibility. Those with strong managerial and organizational skills become publishers. A notable few begin their own magazines or imprints. Most editors remain editors for as long as their stomachs and hearts hold out. Most of the lure of editing comes from a love of good writing; that sensibility supports most editors for a long time.

THE BIRKMAN LIFESTYLE GRID

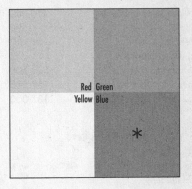

This career is suitable for people with Blue interests.

You'll Have Contact With

Printers
Promotion Specialists
Proofreaders
Writers

Major Associations

American Society of Magazine Editors
919 3rd Avenue
New York, NY 10022
Tel: 212-872-3700
Fax: 212-888-4217
Contact: Information Center

National Conference of Editorial Writers
6223 Executive Boulevard
Rockville, MD 20852
Tel: 301-984-3015
Contact: Cora Everett

ELECTRICAL ENGINEER

A DAY IN THE LIFE

From radar to motors, electrical engineers design, implement, maintain, and improve all the electronics everyone uses everyday. "Most EEs love to talk about technology," mentioned one, "and that is a wonderful thing." Many engineers enter the profession for the intellectual stimulation and are generally driven people who aim to strike a balance between competition and mutual support. Over 85 percent of the EEs we surveyed cited interaction with their peers as the most positive aspect of the profession.

Daily activities include studying technical manuals, articles, and other publications; designing, testing, and assembling devices; and writing reports and keeping track of various assignments. Computer skills are a must. Over 40 percent of the time is spent attending meetings, working on strategic planning, and tracking projects. The amount of interpersonal communication can be disconcerting to many project-oriented engineers; over 15 percent of newly hired EEs take in-house management organization or writing skills courses. Contact between professionals and clients is infrequent. This sense of "project vs. product" isolation actually seems to be valuable.

Beyond designing and creating new circuits for televisions, VCRs, slot machines, or stereo equipment, engineers with creative instincts usually flock to more esoteric, unproved areas such as cutting-edge medical technology and HDTV. Specialization is important and happens quickly, with engineers moving into such areas as quantum electronics, acoustics, signal processing, and ferroelectrics. EEs must have patience; the average span of time from the design of a product to placement on a shelf is two years.

PAYING YOUR DUES

An undergraduate degree in electrical engineering will suffice for most entry-level positions, such as tester and data collector, but an MS or Ph.D. will be necessary for those who intend to progress further. Coursework includes physics, chemistry, some biology, heavy mathematics and statistics. The defense industry provides a large portion of the job market for aspiring electrical engineers, so passing a security check may be required. The aviation industry provides another sizable segment of jobs. Candidates should be familiar with production, testing, and assembly of electronics components, the general methods and means of power transference, and, if possible, computer electronic modeling. Aspiring EEs who want to work for large corporations should be willing to follow already established procedures and protocols. Some of the most exciting and revolutionary innovations come out of smaller companies.

ASSOCIATED CAREERS

Those who choose to become electrical engineers usually do so for life. The fewer than 5 percent who leave mostly become physicists, electricians, aviation engineers, or computer scientists. A number of former electrical engineers head to Wall Street, where intellectual acuity can be rewarded on a higher salary scale.

PAST AND FUTURE

The twentieth century is the information age—made possible in large part by electrical engineers. The science as we now think of it essentially began with the invention of the microchip in the 1960s, giving rise to the modern personal computer. Through the 1970s, most major EE advances emerged out of defense industry-sponsored research, but in more recent years that trend seems to have reversed, with the most significant advances coming from the consumer electronics industry, particularly the computer sector.

Product development is becoming more and more closely tied to the use of the microchip. It is estimated that of the $17 billion annually spent in the U.S. on research and development, over $7 billion in some way involves work done by electrical engineers.

QUALITY OF LIFE

Two Years

"Out of the frying pan and into the fire," said two of our respondents about their initial years in electrical engineering. The pay is reasonable, but recent graduates—used to flexible deadlines and accommodating professors—find the transition jarring. Some 20 percent change jobs in their first three years, trying to find the match for their own personal working style. Work is highly supervised and highly compartmentalized; expect to be unable to distinguish yourself for the first two years, since you will be buried in the details of modeling, computer analysis, and drafting.

Five Years

Specialization takes place between years three and five. Many move from "assistant" to "designer" or "quality control" areas. Pay and responsibility increase. Playing the corporate game is crucial for those at large firms. Contacts made early on are very important for those wishing to form start-up companies on their own. Just ten percent change occupations within the industry if there exists even a remote chance at advancement in the current firm.

Ten Years

Almost 35 percent of electrical engineers control equity stakes in their firms, have filed for their own patents, or have started their own companies. A significant number of ten-year veterans become upper management and direction guiders within their own company. Electrical engineers spend more time forming budgets, allocating resources, and overseeing production than designing, drafting, modeling and testing. Ten years is regarded by some as an enormously significant time-frame in this profession; at this point, your academic education has been exploited to its fullest and the rapidly changing electronics industry requires that you change with it or be left behind.

THE BIRKMAN LIFESTYLE GRID

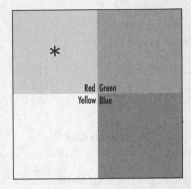

This career is suitable for people with Red interests.

You'll Have Contact With

Computer Programmers
Electricians
Production Managers
Technicians

Major Associations

American Electronics Association
5201 Great America Parkway
Suite 520
Santa Clara, CA 95054
Tel: 408-987-4200
Contact: Customer Service Department

Electronic Industries Association
2500 Wilson Boulevard
Arlington, VA 22201
Tel: 703-907-7500
Fax: 703-907-7501
Contact: Carol Benda

Institute of Electrical and
Electronics Engineers
1828 L Street, NW
Suite 1202
Washington, DC 20036-5104
Tel: 202-785-0017
Contact: Bill Anderson

ELECTRICIAN

A DAY IN THE LIFE

Many of our survey respondents said that they had been fascinated by electricity ever since they were small, and few were disappointed with their choice of careers. There are two general types of electrical work: Construction work, which includes reading blueprints, wiring, installing, and testing electrical systems; and maintenance work, which involves troubleshooting, testing, and fixing already installed, improperly functioning, electrical systems. Most construction electricians are employed by contractors during the secondary phases of building. Maintenance electricians work as freelancers or for large factories, office buildings, or hospitals.

"If you make it through the training, and spend a little time with someone good, you'll be all right," commented one electrician. Almost all electricians go through an academically rigorous apprenticeship program. Only people with a careful eye for details, responsible work habits, and sound on-the-spot judgment should consider becoming electricians. Electricians must know how to read blueprints and specifications and install, connect, and test electrical devices and power sources. They must be familiar with local and federal electrical codes and regulations. Those who succeed have a sound theoretical understanding of electrical systems and good manual dexterity and patience. While on-the-job injuries are not uncommon, electricians are seriously injured by electricity at half the rate of the general population, while taking ten times the amount of risk. Most of these injuries occur at the end of long hours, when being rushed to complete a task, or when blueprints have been incorrectly drawn. An important part of becoming a good electrician is knowing when it would be dangerous to proceed.

Electricians are finding that their profession is becoming linked with those who do computer and telecommunications wiring. These systems are installed at the same time, and more often than not, new structures are wired for networks and telecommunications immediately. Over 15 percent of electricians take additional classes on telecommunications systems, wiring, and the electrical interfaces to do this work themselves.

PAYING YOUR DUES

Electricians work indoors and out, under both difficult and ordinary pressures, and are subjected to daily tests of mental acuity and physical dexterity. One of the few careers in this book that requires only a high school degree, electricians enjoy one of the higher-paid specialty-industry fields with a solid future, as America becomes more dependent on consistent and well-maintained supplies of electricity. Most people become electricians by entering an apprenticeship program through the sponsorship of an existing electrician. These programs are run by such unions as the International Brotherhood of Electrical Workers or the National Electrical Contractors Association. Most programs take four to five years to complete. Candidates must attend nearly 160 hours of classroom instruction per year, but the emphasis is on practical experience. Over 800 hours of practical training are provided annually. Aspiring electricians should be mature and responsible, and have strong mathematical skills and good physical dexterity and stamina. Most states have their own licensing exams that test knowledge of local regulations as well as information contained in the National Electrical Code, the national register of electrical regulations. Please note that color-blind people cannot become electricians, as all wiring is color-coded to avoid mistakes and injuries.

ASSOCIATED CAREERS

Few electricians leave the field, unless work in a particular region becomes unavailable. Some of the 10 percent who do leave the profession each year are retirees. Some become electrical inspectors, enter teaching programs, or work as construction consultants specializing in secondary building systems. A few enter training programs to become contractors.

PAST AND FUTURE

In the 1900s, when electricity was developed, electricians were responsible for the wiring, testing, and constructing of every electrical system, groundline, and socket in the U.S. Electricians are in high demand these days, primarily for maintenance rather than construction. Outdated electrical systems need upgrading. As sources of electricity change over time, methods of delivery and capacity differentiation will require that the electrician engage in continuing education. With the population growing and the power usage rising, the demand for electricians should be steady for the next ten years. Current population-shift trends indicate that more work should be available in the South and Southwest than in the North and Northeast.

QUALITY OF LIFE

Two Years

Most training programs have progressed nearly halfway, and those who couldn't hack the academic rigor of these programs have been weeded out. At the two-year mark, the emphasis switches from classroom-based learning to practical considerations. Work is still highly supervised and tasks are limited to basic installation, testing, and maintenance. Blueprint-reading skills are developing. Wages are low for the industry, but many say this is not a problem "as you are learning a career."

Five Years

Nearly everyone has finished the training program and is a certified electrician. Those who haven't yet passed state and federal requirements work as "electrician's assistants" while they study for them. Those who have passed these tests pursue work through local sponsoring guilds and unions; already employed electricians or general contractors who are hiring sub-contractors, a process which also goes through the local guild or union; or on-site maintenance contractors that may or may not go through the union. Local electrician unions are powerful forces in the electrician's working life; it is suggested that one join the local union as soon as possible after certification. Many electricians work odd but not exceptionally long hours.

Ten Years

At ten years, an electrician has established himself as a valuable and capable player in the industry. Skills are excellent; a variety of unusual situations, such as remodeling entire buildings with outdated wiring, or meeting the demands of companies with unusual power needs, have been encountered and handled. Most have formed relationships in the industry, which, in the end, often replace formalized partnerships. While in many other industries a significant number of ten-year veterans form their own consulting companies, only around 20 percent of ten-year electricians do this. The hassles for private electrical contractors are many—insurance, liability, unhappy clients—and the pay as a freelance electrician working for individual contractors is good. A few of the teaching-inclined have gone back to the apprenticeship programs as instructors who work for slightly less pay but with more consistent and less taxing hours.

THE BIRKMAN LIFESTYLE GRID

Red Green
Yellow Blue

This career is suitable for people with Red interests.

You'll Have Contact With

Construction Managers
Electrical Engineers
Property Managers
Telecommunication Specialists

Major Associations

Associated Builders and Contractors
1300 North 17th Street
Rosslyn, VA 22209
Tel: 703-812-2000

Independent Electrical Contractors, Inc.
507 Wythe Street
Alexandria, VA 22314
Tel: 703-549-7351
Contact: Ike Casey

National Electrical Contractors Association (NECA)
3 Bethesda Metro Center
Suite 1100
Bethesda, MD 20814
Tel: 301-657-3110
Contact: John Grav

ENTREPRENEUR

A DAY IN THE LIFE

An entrepreneur risks his own capital, services, and skills to start a company (or several companies). Entrepreneurs exemplify the American dream—using their own two hands to build a livelihood. Successful entrepreneurs seem to have a number of similar qualities. First, they are extremely motivated. Second, they know and like the business world. And they had better, because the average successful entrepreneur works seventy hours a week while his company is getting going. Third, successful entrepreneurs become obsessed with—or at least fascinated by—all parts of their chosen area of expertise. No aspect of the business is too large or too small to consider.

What entrepreneurs like best about running a company is that they control their own destinies to a greater extent than if they were working for someone else. No one judges their work and assigns a value to their services, and everything they do goes toward their betterment. This puts immense pressure on the entrepreneurs (they pay for their mistakes, too), but it can also be the source of immense pleasure.

If everything goes well, this can be pretty rewarding (think Microsoft). However, over three-fifths of new businesses and franchises *fail within eighteen months* of opening their doors. Most fail because they're undercapitalized. The entrepreneur must be on top of issues of cash flow, expansion (or consolidation), liquidity, and corporate governance. Other factors are uncontrollable by the entrepreneur; if she's trying to sell widgets, and a widgets superstore opens down the street, she may be sunk. Being an entrepreneur means thinking about the business all the time, accepting its responsibilities and its failures. But being one's own boss, owning a business, and reaping all the rewards are powerful enough forces to attract people in droves.

PAYING YOUR DUES

If you feel capable of running a business, and you have the capital, initiative, money, creativity, and nerves of steel, you may want to become an entrepreneur. A background in finance helps; those who don't should find an advisor who does. Entrepreneurs should know their product, their market, and their competitors. Research in the field is a must, as is access to capital. Some people can go to a bank and use their knowledge of the field with a solid business plan to request a loan. Certain loan programs are available through the federal government for small businesses. Municipalities, small business associations, and private organizations also offer financial assistance and planning. Contact your local chamber of commerce for information.

ASSOCIATED CAREERS

Although most entrepreneurs run into difficulty, few people think to arrange a back-up plan in case of failure. Many return to the industries they came from. Others venture into new companies again and again. Take heart—many great industrialists failed four, five, six times before they succeeded in their speculative ventures. The most important thing is to learn from mistakes and address them when planning a new entrepreneurial venture.

PAST AND FUTURE

Private ownership and personal control is more than just an American phenomenon, but American history has been linked closely with this ideal. The notion that the U.S. has no entrenched class system but operates purely on a merit-based system is the foundation for the Horatio Alger story, in which anyone can move from ôrags to riches,ö and the idea that opportunity is available to all. Any observer of American life knows that this American dream is largely a myth, but successful entrepreneurs prove that the myth is not entirely groundless.

Entrepreneurs make their own opportunities, and they will continue to do so. The franchising trendùpeople purchasing the exclusive rights to one of a nationally recognized chain of storesùpeaked in the late 1980s and early 1990s. Franchises are in decline, and more and more people are choosing to undertake only one part of an entrepreneurial venture: Providing expertise, financing, or managing. With three or more individuals involved in the same project, issues of corporate governance are more complicated, but areas of responsibility become more clearly delineated.

QUALITY OF LIFE

Two Years

Entrepreneurs are most likely to fail during the first two years, but their failure generally doesnÆt come about from lack of effort. Many spend the majority of their waking hours working, trying to promote support. Still, there is no substitute for experience and reputation. Those whoÆve lasted two years have learned an enormous amount about how to run a business. Even many of the successful ones earn just enough to support themselves.

Five Years

Five-year entrepreneurial survivors have established business plans, expanded when necessary, and restructured according to common sense. Many engage in long-term financing relationships at this point as they have established a track record of being able to maintain a financially viable company. Many are earning significant incomes from their business, and they must make a key decision. Do they remain in the profession, or do they sell out and cease to be an entrepreneur? Perhaps they should seek out new businesses for profit? Most entrepreneurs begin their businesses to sell a chosen product, so they usually chose to remain.

Ten Years

Those whoÆve remained in the same business for ten years cannot really be considered entrepreneurs anymore; they are truly businessmen of their chosen field. Many still apply the mind-set of expansion, growth, and profit to their corporations or partnerships, but this in no way distinguishes them from the CEOs of hundreds of other non-entrepreneurial companies. Hours remain high, but survivors have gained immeasurable financial, managerial, and interpersonal expertise.

THE BIRKMAN LIFESTYLE GRID

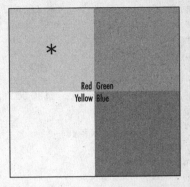

Red Green
Yellow Blue

This career is suitable for people with Red interests.

You'll Have Contact With
Accountants
Attorneys
Bankers
Suppliers

Major Associations
Committee of 200
625 North Michigan Avenue
Suite 500
Chicago, IL 60611
Tel: 312-751-3477
Fax: 312-943-9401

Center for International Private Enterprise
1615 H Street, NW
Washington, DC 20062-2000
Tel: 202-463-5901
Fax: 202-887-3447

Center For Entrepreneurial Management
180 Varick St.
Penthouse Suite
New York, NY 10014
Tel: 212-633-0060
Fax: 212-633-0063

ENVIRONMENTALIST/ENVIRONMENTAL SCIENTIST

A DAY IN THE LIFE

"I became an environmentalist because I wanted a profession that would let me sleep well at night," wrote one respondent. Nearly all our respondents said their desire to better the world was key in their becoming environmentalists, and many said that even if their jobs didn't pay, they would still do environmental work. Environmentalists help the public make informed decisions about the use of limited natural resources. They do research, produce reports, write articles, lecture, issue press releases, lobby congress, fundraise, and campaign. The daily routine depends on the specialty. Environmental researchers measure decay and its pace and patterns, including the depletion of the ozone layer in space or contaminated groundwater in suburban communities. Policy-determining environmentalists determine how behavior can be modified in the future to avoid these problems. Other environmental positions involve office work, policy analysis, lab work, or computer analysis.

Some companies sell "environmentally friendly" goods and services such as recyclable products or products with recycled content. Not-for-profit environmentalist companies, account for 70 percent of the industry, engage in more aggressive campaigns to educate the public about environmental causes and often work in education campaigns on college campuses, where much of the scientific work is done. In the private sector, at least 80 percent of the not-for-profit companies have ten or fewer employees. Over 50 percent of the companies in this field rely on non-guaranteed sources of income such as federal grants, private donations or corporate sponsorship.

The occupation can entail long hours, difficult and sometimes severely under-funded work situations, and a sense of frustration that "no one listens, and even if they listen, no one does anything." But environmentalists are drawn to their work by a sense of satisfaction in doing something they really believe in—even if the warm feelings about their work rarely translates into a strong financial rewards.

PAYING YOUR DUES

Understanding the issues involved in environmentalism—degradation, conservation, recycling, and replenishment—is central to finding work in the environmental care and maintenance industry. An academic background is recommended but not required (some colleges now offer degrees in environmental science). Many entry-level positions are highly competitive and require a rigorous set of interviews. By letting representatives from a range of areas meet and talk with prospective candidates who have majored in anything from psychology to natural science to economics, these companies ensure they get people who can fill a number of roles and who are dedicated to hard work. Entry-level employees use many skills, from interviewing and writing, to organizing events or mailings to raising funds, to scientific testing in a laboratory environment. Continuing education is the norm, since the work deals with a physical, changing system.

ASSOCIATED CAREERS

Those who leave the profession are most likely to do so out of frustration with the slow pace of progress rather than a repudiation of the environmentalist agenda. They become high school teachers at a faster rate than any other profession we have statistics on. Others become ecological scientists, policy analysts, lobbyists, campaign organizers, advertising executives (the art of persuasion is crucial in both industries), or graphic designers. Most continue environmental policy debates on a local, official or personal level by encouraging recycling and promoting "green"— environmentally friendly—products.

PAST AND FUTURE

Environmental concerns arose with the land use changes brought by urbanization and increasing population density. As early as 1300, London was thick with smoke from excessive coal use. Today, Los Angeles is one of many cities with a substantial smog problem. While the 1970s were a time of growing environmental awareness, the 1980s saw a loosening of environmental regulations and a surge in the use of fossil fuels and other natural resources. The 1990s are a time of environmental reconsideration.

Air pollution control alone is now a $45 billion industry; hazardous waste management (see separate listing) is also a fast growing industry. The biggest question is whether environmentalists' concerns will be addressed through legislation in the next few years. More regulation for a cleaner, environment could dramatically increase the demand for people in the environmental sciences. Deregulation and a return to the "laissez-faire" attitude of the 1960s will result in a weakening of these prospects. But environmental crises are ongoing; one-shot disasters such as the Exxon Valdez oil spill in Prince William Sound in Alaska or continuous ones such as the steady deforestation of the Brazilian rain forest will continue to pose challenges—and opportunities—for environmentalists for years to come.

QUALITY OF LIFE

Two Years

At the beginning, this profession involves a lot of paperwork and phone calls. New environmentalists learn the specific concerns of their companies, acquire contacts needed to get information quickly and accurately, and assist in the ongoing educational process. Specialization happens right away; your company's concerns become yours immediately. Client contact, responsibility, and pay are limited. Hours are not bad. The burnout rate is a very high 35 percent, perhaps due to unfulfilled expectations for immediate change in environmental attitudes.

Five Years

Responsibilities increase; environmentalists oversee projects and write articles, reports, and press releases. Many organize conferences on specific topics, using contacts within the industry to bring together notable speakers and players. Salaries go up, but so do the hours. Some earn the title of "senior environmentalist" between years four and seven. The attrition rate levels off at seven percent for the five-year veterans.

Ten Years

Most remaining environmentalists have attained the title of vice-president or its equivalent at small companies or moved on to other industries, most often the private sector. Fifteen percent become freelance consultants to other industries, advising ways of improving their environmental education and environmental friendliness. Many environmentalists begin their own businesses. While over 20 percent of these companies fail within the first year, ten-year survivors can trade on their reputations and experience to find other companies and begin again.

THE BIRKMAN LIFESTYLE GRID

Red Green
Yellow Blue

This career is suitable for people with Red interests.

You'll Have Contact With

Ecologists
Lobbyists
Publicists
Researchers

Major Associations

National Association of Environmental Professionals
5165 MacArthur Boulevard, NW
Washington, DC 20016
Tel: 202-966-1500

National Resources Defense Council
40 West 20th Street
New York, NY 10011
Tel: 212-727-4400

FARMER

PROFESSIONAL PROFILE

# of people in profession	1,313,000
% male	85
% female	15
avg. hours per week	65
avg. starting salary	$21,000
avg. salary after 5 years	$28,500
avg. salary 10 to 15 years	$40,000

Professionals Read

Farm Forum
Progressive Farmer
Successful Farming
North American Seeds

Books, Films and TV Shows
Featuring the Profession

Witness
Country
The Milagro Bean Field War
The Grapes of Wrath

Major Employers

Borden Inc.
180 E. Broad Street
Personnel, 22th Floor
Columbus, OH 43215
Tel: 614-225-4000
Contact: Senior Recruiter, Celena
Catanzarite

Cargill, Inc.
PO Box 5697
Minneapolis, MN 55440-5697
Tel: 612-742-7575
Fax: 612-742-7022
Contact: Human Resources

DOW Elanco
9330 Zionsville Road
Indianapolis, IN 46268-1054
Tel: 317-337-3000
Contact: Human Resources

Archer Daniels Midland Company
4606 East Faries Parkway
Decatur, ILL 62526-5666
Tel: 217-424-5230
Fax: 217-424-2688
Contact: Recruting Coordinator's Office

A DAY IN THE LIFE

Few other occupations provide the variety of physical work, productivity, and intangible rewards associated with farming. Part of the high return rate of family members to the profession of farming is due to an emotional attachment to the lifestyle; those who choose it often wouldn't choose to do anything else. Most farms employ fewer than thirty workers, and a sense of family pervades many of these communities: "When you spend fifteen hours a day with people working to exhaustion, you get to know each other really well." Even with modern advances in farming technology, it's hard, grueling work requiring critical decision-making skills, and long, thankless hours. Long-term planning of crop yields and profits is extremely difficult, as production and income are determined by a combination of weather, disease, price fluctuation, and domestic and foreign subsidy and tariff policy. Farmers have a higher-than-average level of daily anxiety, but in general enjoy what they do and certainly enjoy what they produce. "I've never been more tired," said one farmer, "but I wouldn't trade it for the world."

Farmers tend to specialize in one or a limited number of crops. The producer chooses his crop based on the climate, the land, the market and the history of growing in the region. Each crop utilizes different types of equipment and each requires different maintenance and personnel decisions. Farmers make difficult decisions about how to allocate resources and deal with unanticipated problems, such as insect infestation, drought, and fire. Over the course of any year, regular equipment and land maintenance requirements must be made. Self-motivation is a must, because those who don't take advantage of downtime to take care of long-term projects can find themselves relying on unreliable machinery or storage facilities. Farmers also arrange for the storage, transportation, purchase, and sale of produced items, and negotiate and coordinate all agreements relating to them. Note that during the 1970s and 1980s, prices for goods fell to a level where farming provided lower-than-subsistence income. Sizable federal subsidies installed during this period remain in place today, but are scheduled to be phased out by the year 2002.

PAYING YOUR DUES

For some people, owning or running a farm is a childhood dream, fostered in their high school Future Farmers of America (FFA) organizations or their neighborhood 4-H youth educational programs. For many, farming is the family business (nearly 35 percent of all farms are family owned or employ multi-generational workers). Operating larger, less centralized farms, however, requires more study. It is recommended (and sometimes required) that people who want to run their own farms attend a two- or four-year agricultural college located in the state where they want to work. All states have land-grant colleges with agricultural programs whose course catalogs include dairy science, farm economics, horticulture, crop science and animal science. Some people choose to gain certification as an Accredited Farm Manager (AFM) through the American Society of Farm Managers and Rural Appraisers, although these certifications are more encouraged than required. Work is rigorous and challenging and requires a variety of managerial, scientific and practical skills.

ASSOCIATED CAREERS

Farmers usually choose the profession for life, and those who leave are more hamstrung by the paucity of viable opportunities rather than dissatisfied with the lifestyle. A number of farming refugees become ranchers; others become businessmen in the agricultural field (fertilizer supplier, seed supplier, equipment maintenance programs); a smaller number become commodities traders for goods such as cotton, soybeans, and frozen orange juice, where people with experience as producers have insight about how external events influence production.

PAST AND FUTURE

Over 90 percent of America's first settlers were farmers, and agriculture will always be a vital profession. The future of farming is tied to the future of agricultural science. As methods of crop-breeding, land rotation, soil enrichment, and shortening growing periods develop, the farmer's job can be expected to get both more specialized and busier. Currently, farmers face difficult decisions; prices for produce and farm goods have been effectively flat, while mortgage rates, lines of credit, cost of machinery and cost of labor have risen. Farming is consolidating, and the old family farm is rapidly giving way to large agribusiness, who trade their goods on the commodities exchange to ensure the best price for their goods.

QUALITY OF LIFE

Two Years

Duties of the beginning farmer include crop tilling, fertilizing, composting, and harvesting. The new farmer rotates among different jobs, all integral to the practical running of a farm; he may also supplement his income with nonfarm employment. Many take night classes at local agricultural colleges or rural community colleges with agricultural programs, or take courses sponsored by large farming concerns. The variety of tasks undertaken in the first two years is the best part of the job; the physical hazards is the worst-farming ranks among the most dangerous professions, with some 40 percent of all workers losing at least one week during the first two years to injury. Pay is low; the work is taxing, especially during the spring (planting) and fall (harvesting) seasons.

Five Years

Five years into the profession, those who have taken the requisite courses, shown ability in managing other workers, and shown ambition and energy move to positions of management. Those who have found areas of specialization—such as harvesting, storage management, or soil analysis—continue their education through practical conferences and conventions. Pay rises to reasonable levels, but continues to be influenced by meteorological and legislative whimsy.

Ten Years

A ten-year survivor of the agricultural production industry has faced growing, business, and distribution challenges. By now, many have purchased or soon will purchase their own land, using their successful experience as an asset to secure financing. On average, ten-year veterans will remain farmers for another thirty-five years.

THE BIRKMAN LIFESTYLE GRID

This career is suitable for people with Red interests.

You'll Have Contact With
Commodities Dealers
Government Inspectors
Ranchers
Shipping Agents
Salesmen

Major Associations
American Dairy Science Association
11 North Dunlap Avenue
Savoy, IL 61874
Tel: 217-356-3182
Fax: 217-398-4119
Contact: Public Relations Dept.

Agronomy Crop and Soils
677 South Segoe Road
Madison, WI 53711
Tel: 608-273-8080
Contact: Cleo Tindall

American Farm Bureau
225 Toughy Avenue
Park Ridge, IL 60068
Tel: 312-399-5200
Contact: Dick Keshner, President

FASHION DESIGNER

PROFESSIONAL PROFILE

# of people in profession	87,000
% male	50
% female	50
avg. hours per week	55
avg. starting salary	$13,500
avg. salary after 5 years	$21,500
avg. salary 10 to 15 years	$49,525

Professionals Read

Vogue
Women's Wear Daily
Fashion Daily

Books, Films and TV Shows Featuring the Profession

Pret a Porter
Unzipped
Absolutely Fabulous
The Catwalk

Major Employers

Donna Karan
240 West 40th Street
New York, NY 10018
Tel: 212-869-3569
Contact: Human Resources

Liz Claiborne
1441 Broadway
New York, NY 10018
Tel: 212-354-4900
Fax: 212-626-1800
Contact: Janet Hamlin

Giorgio Armani
114 5th Avenue
New York, NY 10011
Tel: 212-366-9720
Fax: 212-366-1685
Contact: Human Resources

A DAY IN THE LIFE

Ever wonder what Giorgio Armani, Betsey Johnson, Donna Karan, and Ralph Lauren do all the time? Work! Few other professions depend so much on keeping on top of fickle popular opinion and watching what competitors produce. The life of a designer is intimately linked to tastes and sensibilities that change at a moment's notice, and she must be able to capitalize on, or— even better—influence those opinions. Designers reflect society's sensibilities through clothing design. "You have to know just about everything that's been done before, so that you can recognize it when it becomes popular again," wrote one respondent. Fashion designers are involved in every phase of designing, showing, and producing all types of clothing, from bathing suits to evening gowns. Those with talent, vision, determination, and ambition can succeed in this difficult, demanding, and highly competitive industry.

Fashion design can be more glamorous than a 1940s Hollywood musical or drearier than a bank statement, but it's always taxing. A designer's day includes reading current fashion magazines, newspapers, and other media that reflect current trends and tastes. She looks at materials, attends fashion shows, and works with other designers on projects. A designer should be able to communicate her philosophy, vision, and capabilities clearly and comprehensively through sketches, discussions, and, occasionally, samples. No matter what her personal style is, a designer must produce a creative, exciting, and profitable product line.

As in most professions that produce superstars, it is easy for a competent but otherwise unremarkable designer to wallow in obscurity, designing small pieces of collections, generic lines (the plain white boxer short, for example), or specialties (cuffs, ruffles, etc.). The personality that raises itself above this level must be as large as the vision of the designer; perhaps that's why the word "crazy" showed up in over 75 percent of our surveys as a plus in fashion design.

PAYING YOUR DUES

The most difficult thing about being a fashion designer is becoming a fashion designer. Those entering the field should have a good eye for color, style, and shape, an ability to sketch, and some formal preparation in design. An excellent portfolio is a must for the job search. A two- or four-year degree in fashion design is helpful, as is knowledge of textiles and a familiarity with the quirks of a variety of fabrics, but no formal certification is required. Candidates should have a working knowledge of business and marketing. Hours are long for a fashion designer and the initial pay is very limited. This is one of those hit-or-miss occupations where beginners work as someone's assistant until, when they can muster up enough confidence in their abilities and sell that confidence to their superiors, they design a few pieces themselves. The superstar rise is an unlikely event, but it happens. Based on the number of "international star designers" in the last ten years and the number of people who have entered the profession, the estimated odds of becoming an internationally famous designer is roughly 160,000:1.

ASSOCIATED CAREERS

Fashion designers who become unhappy with the lifestyle (low pay, long hours, hard work, low chance of advancement) leave to do a variety of things. Some use their color and design skills to become interior designers, graphic designers, or fashion consultants. Over one quarter of those who leave remain in the clothing industry, either on the production end or on the institutional buying end. Another 10 percent enter the advertising or promotions industry.

PAST AND FUTURE

With the invention of the sewing machine by Elias Howe in 1846, cheap reproducible garments became available to the public. Individuals could rapidly design and commission their own wardrobes. Fashion opened up to the public. At its highest levels, called "couture," fashion is available only to the wealthy—couture dresses and gowns can sell for over $15,000 each. But the concept of fashion, applied to the world at large, has become a democratic principle.

As the fashion market expands, some predictors hold that pockets of smaller, more unique brands of clothing will be marketed over television, the internet, and the mail. The ability to reach large numbers of people for little cost will determine if this future is real or merely a pipe dream dangled in front of young, aspiring fashion designers.

QUALITY OF LIFE

Two Years

Surprisingly few people (under 8 percent) leave the profession in these rough early years, perhaps because they are prepared for the rigorous, unremunerative entry-level jobs. Hours are long, duties are ill-defined—one day it might be tracking down magazine articles on the resurgence of 1970s style, another it may be finding the phone numbers of five dance clubs and finding out which night is most popular with the nineteeen- to twenty-seven-year-old crowd. Connections and networking are important during these early years; most designers learn as much about the business as they can. Some take part-time jobs in other fields in order to pay the rent.

Five Years

Frustration with the slow pace of progression, a leveling of responsibilities for those who have failed to rise, and increased competition for the few available jobs are cited as the main reasons for a massive professional exodus; nearly 50 percent leave the profession at this point. Those who remain are actually designing partial lines and simple pieces. Designers gain valuable experience around this time working with production people and advertising people.

Ten Years

As competent and proven "senior designers," ten-year veterans have specialized areas of responsibility. One may be in charge of shepherding all designs through the production process. Another may be in charge of scheduling lines based on season and available fabrics. A third may be in charge of overseeing the young designers and their partial lines, scouting for talent. They become both producers and educators, as newer designers look to them for advice and guidance. Wages are solid, hours are long but manageable, and connections are extensive. The constant challenge ten-year designers face is in reinventing themselves and proving themselves relevant in the fast-changing world of fashion design.

THE BIRKMAN LIFESTYLE GRID

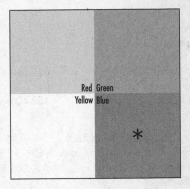

Red Green
Yellow Blue

This career is suitable for people with Blue interests.

You'll Have Contact With

Advertising Executives
Production Managers
Publicists
Textile Manufacturers
Models

Major Associations

Council of Fashion Designers of America
1412 Broadway
Suite 2006
New York, NY 10018
Tel: 212-302-1821

Fashion Jewelry Association of American
3 Daval Square
#135
Providence, RI 02903
Tel: 401-273-1515

FBI Agent

A DAY IN THE LIFE

Do you see yourself as Clarice Starling (Jodie Foster) tracking Hannibal Lecter (Anthony Hopkins) in *Silence of the Lambs*? Do you want to fight for truth, justice, and the American way on American soil? FBI agents investigate people suspected of violating federal law, including serial killers, kidnappers, bank robbers, bombers, and perpetrators of mail fraud. Strong deductive skills, flexibility, and irreproachable moral character are key traits for those who want to succeed in the FBI. The sensitive nature of the work requires a person with sound judgment and discretion. The application process is one of the most rigorous and selective in the nation.

Agents research and gather evidence on suspected criminals. Duties include surveillance, transcription, research, coordination with local authorities, and report-writing. Those in the scientific division work in labs and in the field collecting and analyzing evidence and working with private labs. Many in the profession feel that the variety of tasks keeps the job fresh and exciting. By themselves, FBI agents have limited power to arrest and no power to punish those suspected of violating federal law. An FBI agent investigates and reports, and when other government agencies make the arrest, they often invite the FBI agent or agents who were involved with the case, but merely as a courtesy. It is common for the agent to move on to another case before any arrests are actually made.

The most difficult part of being an FBI agent is the sense of isolation it can foster. Most agents work by themselves or, if necessary, in pairs. They often travel for long periods. The project-based nature of this career may keep it exciting, but the uncertainty of it can lead to frustration. Wrote one agent from New York, "My wife and I were married on May 25 of last year. I was assigned to a case two days later and couldn't tell her where I was or when I would be back or what was going on. I next saw her July 14." Even with all the pressures the work entails and the lifestyle limitations it demands, only 4 percent of agents leave each year (not including retirees). There must be something really great about being an FBI agent, but of course it's a secret.

PAYING YOUR DUES

To become a member of the FBI, you must be a United States citizen between twenty-three and thirty-seven years of age, meet stringent physical requirements, and hold at least a bachelor's degree and in many cases more than that. The FBI has five entry programs: Law, Accounting, Science, Language, and Diversified, and each program has its own specific academic requirements. The application process is renowned for its rigor and thoroughness. In addition to giving each applicant difficult written tests and interviews, the FBI conducts intensive background checks including criminal record checks; credit checks; interviews with associates, roommates and landlords; professional references; and academic verifications. Each candidate takes a drug test, physical exam and, at the discretion of the FBI, a polygraph (lie detector) test. After making it through this microscopic examination, new agents spend four months at the FBI Academy in Quantico, Virginia, studying investigative techniques, personal defense, and firearms. The FBI will disqualify any candidate who has physical or emotional handicaps that will not allow him to perform important and dangerous duties within acceptable parameters.

ASSOCIATED CAREERS

Since there is mandatory retirement of field agents after twenty years or at age fifty-five, older ex-FBI agents are scattered throughout a number of fields in the United States. They usually find a career in their areas of expertise when they leave the FBI. Local law enforcement and other federal agencies—

the CIA, the Bureau of Alcohol, Tobacco and Firearms, the Federal Marshals, the NSA—hire many ex-agents. Others move into consulting at private laboratories, go into teaching, or become practicing attorneys, and a few become private investigators.

PAST AND FUTURE

Founded in 1908 under the U.S. Department of Justice, the Federal Bureau of Investigation (FBI) was meant to be the active investigative arm of federal law enforcement. The FBI wasn't that significant until J. Edgar Hoover took over in 1924 and increased its responsibilities, its scientific methods, and its efficacy. The modern FBI has one of the world's most advanced crime laboratories; their fingerprint division contains the largest database of fingerprints in the world.

Like all government agencies, the future direction of the FBI is highly dependent on changing political climates and federal budget restrictions. The need for the FBI, however, has never been more apparent. Domestic federal crimes have been rising at an annual rate of 6 percent and there is no sign of this trend abating.

QUALITY OF LIFE

Two Years

New FBI agents, as "special agents," are usually paired with experienced agents in a specific division. Usually the work involves travel, investigation, surveillance, and report-writing. Techniques discussed in the classroom are used in real-life situations, and those who expected glamour are disappointed by the generally unexciting nature of the work. Satisfaction levels are low, but rebound in the next few years as agents are rotated among a number of cases and gain valuable and varied experience.

Five Years

Five-year veterans have worked with a number of other government agencies on cases, and their skill levels have risen dramatically. Hours decrease, pay increases, and satisfaction levels are high. Field agents who wish to combine a more predictable lifestyle with a career in the FBI can apply for more desk-bound coordination positions. Those who show talent become senior agents and take charge of investigations. Communication and analysis skills are at a premium in these years, when agents are involved in investigations in a hands-on fashion while also reporting to assistant directors.

Ten Years

Halfway to a pension, most agents are still driven by the same motivations that encouraged them to enter the profession. Pay and responsibilities have increased, and satisfaction levels are solid. Those who show talent in organization and management move into assistant directorship positions on a local level and, while emergencies still rule the day, can control their hours to some degree. Those who enjoy the life of a field agent remain on cases, liaise with other government departments, and work with newer employees. A very successful few return to Quantico at this point as instructors, trainers, and educators for the FBI training program.

THE BIRKMAN LIFESTYLE GRID

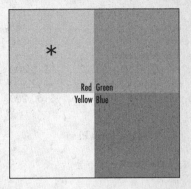

This career is suitable for people with Red interests.

You'll Have Contact With

Attorneys
Criminologists
Customs Agents
Police Officers

Major Associations

FBI agents have strict loyalty and confidentiality obligations which make participation in general professional associations difficult.

National Association of Investigative Specialists (NAIS)
P.O. Box 33244
Austin, TX 78764
Tel: 512-719-3595

FILM DIRECTOR

Professionals Read

Variety
On Location
Hollywood Reporter
Movieline

Books, Films and TV Shows Featuring the Profession

The Player
Heart of Darkness
Day For Night
The Final Cut

Major Employers

Walt Disney Studios
500 South Buena Vista Street
Department JOBL
Burbank, CA 91521-737
Tel: 818-558-2222
Fax: 818-558-2868
Contact: Staffing Services

Warner Brothers
4000 Warner Boulevard
Burbank, CA 91522
Tel: 818-954-6000
Contact: Personnel

Columbia Studios
3 West 51st Street
New York, NY 10019
Tel: 212-245-8058

A DAY IN THE LIFE

"What I really want to do is direct." If this applies to you, read on. A director turns a script into a movie; he is responsible for the quality of the final product and its success. In most cases, directors work on films far longer than any actor, technician or editor, from the first day of brainstorming to the final release; it is no wonder that directing is physically, mentally, and emotionally draining. Directors work with actors, makeup artists, cinematographers, writers, and film, sound and lighting technicians. They determine all the particulars of how scenes are to be shot: From visual requirements to the placement of the actors and the appropriateness of the script.

Directors cast actors who can bring their vision to the screen. Sound judgment and an open mind are important during these initial phases. A director guides actors to a greater understanding of their characters' motivations and encourages them to perform at a high level. Sometimes a director gently cajoles; sometimes she yells. Anything to get the job done. His unique vision of the final product and ability to communicate that vision effectively and immediately are critical. After the film has been shot, editorial skills are important. Directors must have a good feel for pacing and structure, and must know how to integrate and cut scenes so they work effectively.

Issues of finance are important in this industry—making films is expensive. First-time directors find it difficult to get work with any large-budget house, so many start with small-budget directing, using existing sites and sets creatively, convincing technical assistants to work for little (or more often, convincing friends to work for free), and using editing and cutting rooms during off hours to save money. One director funded his first film entirely on his credit cards.

PAYING YOUR DUES

Nearly all film directors are film school graduates. Film school students must complete their own short films by graduation; you should be prepared to work under difficult conditions, share space, and convince actors to work for little or no money. Aspiring film directors prove themselves by directing stage productions, doing film lighting design, or establishing a history of assistant or associate directorships. This last is the most common route, as professional experience and networking contacts can be combined in a brief but rigorous period of time. There is no specific ladder to climb. Many aspiring directors develop clips of work to recommend them to industrial or television or commercial directing jobs, which pay well and serve as working credentials. Those entering this career should be warned that twenty-hour days are not unusual.

ASSOCIATED CAREERS

For the most part, directors who leave enter another area of the entertainment industry. A number use their financing experience to move into the producing end of film development. Others move into script development or teaching. Some become critics, reviewers, or reporters for film-related magazines. Others become movie or television writers. A few become actors. Those who go into business enter a wide variety of fields including costume supply, lighting rentals, casting agencies, site location, and acting schools.

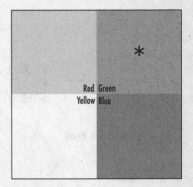

PAST AND FUTURE

Film directors sprang into being with the birth of the industry in the early 1900s. Some important directors who have brought their visions to light include D.W. Griffith (*Birth of a Nation*) Orson Welles (*Citizen Kane*), Alfred Hitchcock (*Rope*), and Martin Scorsese (*Raging Bull*).

Directing will either become larger and more megalithic as a profession, as suggested by the consolidation of such film companies as Warner Communications and Time-Life Affiliates, and Turner Communications, Disney, and ABC/Capital Cities, or it will tend toward small and independent projects, as the popularity of such independent film festivals as Sundance heralds. In the first event, directing possibilities will be limited and difficult—extremely difficult—to obtain. In the second event, directing positions will be more available but much less remunerative. In either case, the road to becoming a director is long and the odds are slim, but the rewards for those who succeed are great.

QUALITY OF LIFE

Two Years

Hopeful directors start out doing production work, learning how to piece a film together. Academic lessons from film school are supplemented with practical experience in the different facets of making a movie, from choosing locations and getting proper permits to budgeting, scheduling, and arranging transportation. Early years are marked by low responsibility, long hours, little pay and an enormous amount of learning.

Five Years

Five years into the profession, young directors have had a chance to produce at least a short film to enter in competitions or to use as an audition reel. Areas of strengths and weaknesses have been identified; those willing to pay the hard wages of growing as filmmakers will work on their weaknesses. They might become sub-directors with discrete areas of authority. Opportunities exist for those who have made strong networking connections and those who have distinguished themselves through good work and aggressive self-promotion. Those who are less vocal about their accomplishments either remain in assistant positions or leave the profession altogether. As a matter of fact, even those who have good reputations begin to leave the profession due to long hours and competing offers in specialty industries for much more certain pay.

Ten Years

A mere 35 percent who began with the intention of becoming a director are still around, and many of them leave over the next five years. Those who remain have significant opportunities available to them, if they have managed to refine their craft, communicate their vision clearly, match up a script with a production company—and land the job of directing it. If it seems like the success stories at the ten-year mark are qualified by a number of "ifs," that's because they are. The success rate in this field is abysmal. But those who manage to fight their way to the top reap financial and emotional rewards.

THE BIRKMAN LIFESTYLE GRID

Red   Green
Yellow   Blue

This career is suitable for people with Green interests.

You'll Have Contact With

Actors
Cinematographers
Film Editors
Producers

Major Associations

Association of Independent
Video & Filmmakers
304 Hudson Street
6th Floor
New York, NY 10013
Tel: 212-807-1400
Fax: 212-463-8519
Contact: Membership Services

American Film Institute
New Hampshire Avenue at Rock Creek
Parkway
Washington, DC 20566
Tel: 202-785-4601

Motion Picture Association of America
1600 Eye Street, NW
Washington, DC 20006
Tel: 202-293-1966
Fax: 202-293-1299

FILM EDITOR

PROFESSIONAL PROFILE

# of people in profession	12,418
% male	90
% female	10
avg. hours per week	60
avg. starting salary	$20,000
avg. salary after 5 years	$50,000
avg. salary 10 to 15 years	$70,000

Professionals Read

The Independent
Variety
Hollywood Reporter

Books, Films and TV Shows Featuring the Profession

The Player
The Stuntman
Day For Night
The Final Cut

Major Employers

Walt Disney Studios
500 South Buena Vista Street
Burbank, CA 91521-737
Tel: 818-558-2222
Fax: 818-558-2868

Warner Brothers
4000 Warner Boulevard
Burbank, CA 91522
Tel: 818-954-6000
Contact: Personnel

Columbia Studios
3 West 51st Street
New York, NY 10019
Tel: 212-245-8058

A DAY IN THE LIFE

Film editors assemble footage of films, shows, strips, and industrial videos into a seamless end product. They manipulate plot, score, sound and graphics to make the parts into a continuous and enjoyable whole. On most films, the film editor is chosen before cast members and script doctors; people in Hollywood recognize that the skills of a good film editor can save a middling film. In the same way directors use certain actors they appreciate over and over again, they also use film editors they know and are comfortable with. These relationships give stability to a film editor's life; otherwise, be prepared to submit video resume after video resume, trying to get work. Editors can express themselves through their unique styles; Spike Lee's editor, for example, is well known for his.

The hours are long, and the few editors who had the time to write comments to us tended to abbreviate their thoughts. "Dawn/Dusk. Rush jobs. After test audiences, do it again. Lots of frustration. Lots of control, though," wrote one. Film editors spend a long time perfecting and honing their craft, just as directors do. They work with computers, eight-plate Steenbecks with twin picture heads, Movieola Flatbeds and Revis Splicers for sound. Beginners work on four- or six-plate Steenbecks as they learn their craft. Many editors stay removed from the project during the film itself so as not to steer the director away from his concept of the film. Film editors work closely with sound editors and musical directors, as anything an editor does affects the overlay of those two parts of the film. Interpersonal skills and endurance are key to success in the career. Long hours and significant isolation while actually editing can make even the most positive-minded film editor question his career choice.

Many film editors begin as technical or production assistants, watching directors in action, seeing how film editors try to work within the director's vision, then learning the appropriate skills. Others work as assistant editors at the side of an experienced editor who has existing relationships with directors. While this is a popular route, many complain that "if [you] don't know [a director] to hire you solo, then you're [expletive deleted]." It becomes difficult for an assistant to disentangle herself from an established and in-demand film editor. Film editors undertake a long internship before they become their own bosses—up to eight years as an assistant or working solely on industrial and commercial videos is about average.

PAYING YOUR DUES

Film editors need extensive academic and professional experience. Standard coursework should include filmographies, basic editing, and commercial editing. Some aspiring editors may take directorial courses and direct plays or films, knowing this training will be helpful in the working world. It costs a lot to borrow film-editing equipment from the university and graduate school film programs that have it. Most aspiring film editors work as interns, production assistants, or animation-editing assistants while in graduate school. Once out of school, editors usually work in the production field or for an established film editor for little money. Those who really want to pay their dues and become independent, self-supporting film editors take note: Four to ten years of on-the-job training before making enough connections, building up a significant body of work, and being able to start your own editing service is more than common. It's the only way.

ASSOCIATED CAREERS

Film editors sometimes become directors and sound editors, but more often it is the other way around. Those who leave film editing go into video promotion and sales, film-equipment sales, and editing-equipment sales and development. A few enter animation companies, where editing is not an issue (because footage is created with the final script in mind and no excess footage or outtakes exist) but creative direction—editing the script with an understanding of how these pieces will seam together—is.

PAST AND FUTURE

In 1980, the average feature film had one film editor assigned to it, and that person, for all intents and purposes, exerted as much influence over the final product as the director of the film did. Now, with the increasing complexity of film editing, graphic overlays, computer animation sequences, and rising budgets, feature films have an average of nine editors attached to each.

Editors will continue to enjoy strong demand for qualified professionals who produce quality service. Those who demonstrate good ability and willingness to work with others will be rewarded with good jobs. The industry seems to be moving toward "non-linear" film-editing technology, such as digital processing. Work should continue to concentrate in New York and Los Angeles, and although large production houses do well, smaller independent houses (such as the one that edited *Pulp Fiction*) are expected to be popular in the years to come.

QUALITY OF LIFE

Two Years

Beginning film editors learn technical skills in editing, cutting, splicing, and seamlessly integrating different scenes. Long hours and low pay are mitigated by a rapid learning curve. Beginners gain valuable experience in working with sound and music editors, a must for those who wish to continue in the profession. What little responsibility you do get is important; those who don't show maturity and quickness are encouraged to leave the profession.

Five Years

Five-year veterans have gained an increase in responsibility, a growing network of contacts, and enough editing work to begin a solo career, join an existing editing company as a partner, or go under contract to a large production house. By now, editors specialize in the type of work done (commercial, industrial, or software/Internet) or in the genre of film done (drama, comedy, thriller). Close relationships with directors and producers are significant. Pay, responsibility and hours rise.

Ten Years

A film editor now has a solid reputation, a healthy paycheck, and reasonable hours. Most work as independent contractors, editing films and video releases of films. Others are permanent specialists and act as consultants to other editors. Contact with other editors becomes important at this stage, and duties become much more general. Creative possibilities increase.

THE BIRKMAN LIFESTYLE GRID

Red Green
Yellow Blue

*

This career is suitable for people with Yellow interests.

You'll Have Contact With

Film Directors
Producers
Production Assistants
Technicians

Major Associations

American Cinema Editors
1041 N. Formosa Avenue
West Hollywood, CA 90046
Tel: 213-850-2900
Fax: 213-850-2922

FINANCIAL AID OFFICER

A DAY IN THE LIFE

Anyone who has requested financial aid knows that the process takes you into the land of bureaucratic paperwork nightmares. Getting aid can be confusing and complex; an educational institution's financial aid officers ferry applicants across this river of confusion safely and comfortably. FAOs assess students' needs, determine eligibility, help complete paperwork, and work with loan-takers to make certain they pay the money back. Our respondents cited interpersonal skills and organizational abilities as the first- and second-most important strengths needed to succeed as a financial aid officer. People in the field express a strong degree of satisfaction in their choice of occupation. Many are former (or current) clients of the national financial aid system, and view their roles as student financial advocates. "It's great to be the one helping people get money; it's tougher when things don't work out and there's nothing you can do."

Entry-level positions usually involve managing large paperwork caseloads, following current students through their changes in status and informing people of their obligations and options. Candidates should be comfortable with numbers and able to learn a complicated paperwork organization structure quickly. Those who enter the career should expect occasional brusqueness from clients of the system who are frustrated with the bureaucratic channels and invasive questioning that these loan programs require. Our surveys mentioned that the attitude of students who don't receive all the financial aid they want is demoralizing; in many cases, they blame the messenger and lash out at the aid counselor. This can be frustrating, especially when one financial aid officer can be expected to handle up to 2,000 cases per year. The public's often negative impressions of financial aid officers is another potential drawback.

A good financial aid counselor has to be familiar with the changing restrictions and obligations that face borrowers. The ability to elicit a fair assessment of the student's current loan obligations, work situation, and prospective income is critical to the FAO, who must recommend an amount of money the student should request and determine what programs are available to help the student. Continuing education is very important in this field, and many financial aid officers go to conferences, seminars and lectures to keep abreast of current trends in financial aid.

PAYING YOUR DUES

No specific bachelor's degree is required to become a financial aid officer, but coursework should include mathematics, statistics, or some financial topics; psychology and English are also helpful. A financial aid officer writes reports, recommendations, and memos, so strong writing skills are significant. Most important, however, a financial aid officer should be a good communicator, able to explain confusing and difficult concepts to people who may be at the end of their ropes. Listening skills were cited as the largest difference between a good and a bad financial aid officer. No official certification is required, but familiarity with Pell Grants, Stafford Loans, Plus Loans, Newman Grants, Federal Nursing Scholarships and Perkins Loans is important.

ASSOCIATED CAREERS

Financial aid officers, while having a reasonable understanding of complex financial constructs, are statistically more likely to end up in human resources, career guidance, or individual counseling jobs than financial ones. The instinct that leads someone to become a financial aid officer lies somewhere between the desire to help others and the ability to manage a large bureaucracy. This mix is best suited to high-volume environments that involve a lot of contact with people, such as loan departments at banks or the vocational counseling departments of private companies.

PAST AND FUTURE

Educational financial aid began with the influx of post World War II GIs returning to school on the GI bill. The federal government decided to encourage the rapid growth of enrollment by providing guarantees on low-interest loans for those who wished to return to college. In the initial years of these programs, students had a phenomenally high rate of repayment of loans—so much so that the private sector clamored to become involved. With the astronomical rise of the cost of education in the 1980s, many banks began to move away from this position, fearing that the burden of educational debt might be too great for many to bear.

Financial aid officers' roles are growing in number and importance; even moderately well-off families need to borrow some amount to send a single child to college. The big question surrounding this profession is: What role will the government play during times of economic budget slashing? As large cuts loom on the horizon, institutional educational support seems to be waning, and the declining statistics of student loan repayments may be the final nail in subsidized education's coffin. But then financial aid officers may need to be all the more creative in finding ways to help students pay for college.

QUALITY OF LIFE

Two Years

Junior financial aid officers are thrown into the mix headfirst: Assigned cases on their first day. A "sink-or-swim" attitude is part of the entry-level trial that faces the beginning FAO, although coworkers are cited as extremely helpful in making sure that new employees don't flounder too much. At times, difficult cases are routed away or reassigned from new personnel. By the end of the first two years, FAOs have received two educations: one on how to network through financial aid systems, another on how to work as part of a supportive team.

Five Years

Pay rises, though not enough according to many. Responsibility and hours increase, and the level of difficulty of the casework assigned rises. Those who have achieved senior status in the office have some supervisory responsibility, and may work with the budget and financial offices of the university to reconcile accounts and ensure the smooth progression of money from promise to actual payment. Exit interviews, in which borrower's obligations are explained to them in stark terms, are part of the daily routine. Those interested in progressing within university administrations take courses in other areas such as management and policy to supplement their skills.

Ten Years

Many ten-year veterans are running financial aid offices by this point, and a significant number of them have switched universities to pursue opportunities. Those who remain "caseworkers" have decided that the managerial life is not for them and that they prefer client contact and student interaction. Those who leave after ten years only do so because of unique opportunities, burnout from exhaustion, or retirement.

THE BIRKMAN LIFESTYLE GRID

This career is suitable for people with Yellow interests.

You'll Have Contact With

Bankers
Government Officials
School Administrators
Students

Major Associations

National Association of Student Financial Aid Administrators
1920 L Street, NW
Suite 200
Washington, DC 20036
Tel: 202-785-0453

FINANCIAL ANALYST

A DAY IN THE LIFE

Financial analysts gather information, assemble spreadsheets, write reports, and review all non-legal pertinent information about prospective deals. They examine the feasibility of a deal and prepare a plan of action based on financial analysis. Being an analyst requires a vigilant awareness of financial trends. Analysts have a heavy reading load, keeping abreast of news stories, market movements, and industry profiles in financial newspapers, magazines, and books. Most analyst jobs are in banking houses or for financial-advising firms, which means following corporate culture and wearing corporate dress. If a deal demands it, they must be prepared to travel anywhere for indeterminate lengths of time. Those who wish to rise in the industry should note the necessity of significant "face time," attending social events and conferences and spending down time with people in the profession, which can be expensive; this social circle tends to gravitate to high-priced attire and costly hobbies, habits, and diversions.

Analysts sacrifice a lot of control over their personal lives during their first few years, but few other entry-level positions provide the possibility of such a large payoff come year's end. Many employers use bonuses, which can be equal to or double the beginning analyst's salary, to attract and hold intelligent personnel. Successful financial analysts become senior financial analysts or associates after three to four years of hard work at some firm. Those with strong client contacts and immaculate reputations start their own financial consulting firms. Many work as analysts for about three years and then return to school or move on to other positions in banking.

Financial analysts work long hours, and deadlines are strict. "When you have to get the job done, you get the job done. Period," emphasized one. The occasional fifteen-hour day and night spent sleeping in the office is mitigated by the high degree of responsibility these analysts are given. The long hours breed a close kinship. Over 65 percent called their co-analysts extremely supportive, and many labeled them a "major reason" they were able to put up with the demanding work schedule. Most people become financial analysts because they feel it is the best way to immerse themselves in the world of finance and a great way to earn a lot of money. They're right on both counts, but be aware that the immersion is complete and somewhat exclusive, and although people earn a lot of money, few have the free time to spend it all how they'd like to.

PAYING YOUR DUES

Entry-level positions are highly competitive. A bachelor's degree in any discipline is acceptable, so long as the potential analyst's course of study demonstrates an ability to understand and work with numbers. Those with computer science, physical science, or biological science backgrounds may find the field more welcoming than do liberal arts majors. Business majors don't necessarily have an advantage; each company trains the incoming class of financial analysts before they begin the job. To become a financial analyst you need to have a strong sense of purpose—it is not a job for those who are uncertain that their future lies in the financial world. Candidates must be able to meet and interact with clients, handle a heavy workload, prioritize and complete work under strict deadlines, work as part of a team, and work with computer spreadsheet and valuation programs. Many find the travel stimulating initially, but "after your third week in Jopbsug, Tennessee at the ball-bearing plant, it gets old."

ASSOCIATED CAREERS

Those who progress along corporate financial-analyst tracks can expect to eventually find different jobs in the financial community, perhaps as investment bankers, investment advisors, or financial consultants. Those who enjoy the more interpersonal side of finance move into management consultant positions, where they can use their people skills as well as their financial skills. Over 45 percent head to business school within five years and another ten percent go to law school. A few become in-house financial advisors or officers in the industries they covered as financial analysts.

PAST AND FUTURE

The obligations of today's financial analyst were covered by more experienced individuals as late as the 1970s, but with rapid deregulation of ownership in industries in the early 1980s and the rapid growth of the financial sector during those same years, the need arose for a structured and continuing stream of intensively trained professionals familiar with the financial industry. Larger firms, which consolidated their programs in the early 1990s, are cautiously beginning to expand them again, finding opportunities in such new and developing industries as software development, biotechnology, and aerospace technologies.

QUALITY OF LIFE

Two Years

Long hours, low base pay, and a fair amount of responsibility characterize the early years. Analysts travel, pore through documents, meet with clients (on a highly supervised basis) and prepare valuation analyses. They work together on teams that are rotated quickly when needed. Lack of control over hours and personal life are common in the first two years. The burnout rate is surprisingly low in the beginning—around eight percent—because most who enter the industry have few illusions about the demands the job will place on them.

Five Years

At the five-year mark, those who remain have achieved the rank of "associate" or "senior financial analyst." Responsibilities shift from producing to pitching, and client contact increases. Many study for professional degrees during these years. Over 70 percent of those who began in the field have either changed firms, returned to school, or changed jobs within the industry. While loyalty is tangible between analysts, the same sense of fidelity doesn't seem to apply to the companies that employ them. Salaries remain relatively stable but bonuses, which once were merely large, can become astronomical; hours, for those who are successful, can actually increase.

Ten Years

Successful financial analysts have moved on to vice-presidential positions in the investment banking, financial analysis, or valuation departments of the company. While bonuses still account for the bulk of income, salaries are significant as well. Hours can decrease but responsibility increases and pressure develops to solicit new business. Responsibilities also include personnel decisions and hiring.

THE BIRKMAN LIFESTYLE GRID

This career is suitable for people with Green interests.

You'll Have Contact With

Accountants
Bankers
Investment Bankers
Researchers

Major Associations

Association for Investment
Management and Research
P.O. Box 3668
Charlottesville, VA 22903-0668
Tel: 804-977-6600
Contact: Information Central Dept.

American Financial Services Association
919 18th Street, NW
3rd Floor
Washington, DC 20006
Tel: 202-296-5544
Fax: 202-223-0321

Financial Executives Institute
10 Madison Avenue; P.O. Box 1938
Morristown, NJ 07962-1938
Tel: 201-898-4600

FIREFIGHTER

A DAY IN THE LIFE

"We try to save things and protect people," is how one New York City firefighter describes one of society's nobler professions. A firefighter protects people, their property, and their goods against destruction or damage due to fire. The successful firefighter is an approachable, good communicator with the ability to take decisive action under trying circumstances. Firefighters must be able to perform strenuous physical tasks, such as carrying unconscious people down flights of stairs, directing the flow of a hose that carries 2,000 gallons of water per minute, or breaking down doors locked from the inside. The profession is very dangerous—over one in four firefighters have to take time off for work-related injuries, ranging from slipped disks to disfiguring burns—and requires a strong sense of commitment to public service.

Firehouses are manned around the clock. Firefighters must be able to deal with brief bursts of intense activity, then long periods of "crushing boredom." "Get good at solitaire," wrote one, alluding to the amount of downtime he faces. The firemen who responded to our survey were unanimous in their estimation of their colleagues: "The best people I've ever known," said one ten-year veteran, "I count on them to guard my life every day." This reliance on each other encourages close companionship among members of any firehouse, who can boast the unique professional bond of having "been through hell" together. Most firefighters are deeply proud of what they do.

Aside from taking on extra responsibilities, such as becoming a company leader or training other firefighters, firefighters don't have any kind of "corporate ladder" to climb. They keep abreast of technological or technique-oriented changes in firefighting through seminars, conferences, and conventions. Retirement is usually available at half-pay at age fifty for twenty-year veterans. Most firefighters enjoy structured raises based on seniority and job performance. The largest fire departments have many battalions and divisions, with lieutenants, captains, battalion chiefs, division chiefs, fire marshals, and investigators, with substantial pay hikes for those making it into senior positions.

PAYING YOUR DUES

While many colleges offer courses in fire science, these are usually taken by firefighting professionals after they've been in the field for a while. To become a firefighter you need to be between eighteen and thirty-one years of age, you need a high school diploma, you must have corrected 20/20 vision, and you must pass the firefighters' examination, offered annually by local governments throughout the country. Applicants who have good scores on the written portion of the test and demonstrate physical dexterity, strength, and mental alertness, should be able to find employment. Many departments now require an Emergency Medical Technician (EMT) certificate as a condition of employment. The hours are long, and you should check with the firefighter's association in your area for details (some have 24 hours on, 48 hours off; most cities average between 48 and 56 hours a week). Firefighters can become members of the firefighters' union (affiliated with the AFL-CIO) and some become members of the International Association of Firefighters.

ASSOCIATED CAREERS

Firefighters who leave the profession (14 percent annually, including those who are put on disability retirement) generally continue in public service. A number apply to become police officers, frustrated with the "reactive" nature of firefighting. Roughly five percent return to school to be trained in paramedic or medical duties. Others go into teaching or fire safety consulting. Those who wish to rise to positions of advice and influence, particularly on a national level, become private consultants or authors, or take high-profile political jobs elsewhere. Firefighters are in general very satisfied with their choice of career, and the majority of those who leave do so in the first few years. Those who remain firefighters for the first six years tend to stay for twenty.

PAST AND FUTURE

Fire departments began as locally organized groups of residents and merchants who would come to each other's aid in times of crisis. They formed unofficial "bucket brigades" that would make a human chain from the nearest water supply, passing buckets to each other to the mouth of the fire. At the turn of the century municipalities formed professional fire departments of their own. Many smaller communities still rely on volunteers who keep their ears open for the alarm whistle or carry beepers to alert them to a fire emergency.

Although technology has improved considerably and safety records are set each year for the protection of firefighters, unforeseen circumstances and unique developments all require competent and experienced professionals to make snap decisions and take decisive action. The number of firefighters hired each year corresponds roughly to population increases, so an awareness of shifting demographics can help the aspiring firefighter find a location that needs him.

QUALITY OF LIFE

Two Years

At the beginning of their careers, firefighters are put through a rigorous three- to sixteen-week training program to learn firefighting techniques. Attrition rate is highest in these initial years—almost 25 percent. Many find the lifestyle too uneven (extremely pressured or overly dull), and rookies are generally stuck with the late-night "graveyard" shift, making it hard to have any kind of personal life at the beginning.

Five Years

During these years, attrition declines to between three and five percent for those who leave the profession due to dissatisfaction. Over 20 percent of firefighters receive on-the-job injuries in years four through seven, as those who have survived five years have battled a number of different types of fires and may become a touch overconfident in their abilities. Most of these injuries only result in three to twelve weeks of missed time. Those who wish to move up take additional courses during these years and begin to teach at local training academies or give fire-prevention lectures at schools. Some get promoted to "chief" or "manager" of the firehouse.

Ten Years

Ten-year veterans have more control over their hours and higher pay, but do basically the same job they were initially hired to do: Fight fires. Halfway to their pension, most firefighters who've lasted this long have enough experience in action to avoid disabling injuries. A curious note: Of those who have the option to retire at 50, only about half accept. People who see themselves as firefighters enjoy the profession for as long as they can.

THE BIRKMAN LIFESTYLE GRID

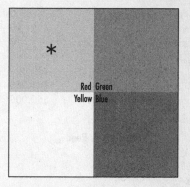

This career is suitable for people with Red interests.

You'll Have Contact With
Paramedics
Police Officers
Safety Inspectors
Teachers

Major Associations
International Association of Fire Chiefs
4025 Fair Ridge Drive
Fairfax, VA 22033-2868
Tel: 703-273-0911
Contact: George Kerr

International Association of Fire Fighters
1750 New York Avenue, NW
3rd Floor
Washington, DC 20006
Tel: 202-737-8484
Contact: Vincent Bollon

National Fire Protection Association
1 Batterymarch Park
Quincy, MA 02269
Tel: 617-770-3000
Contact: Public Affairs

California Forestry Association
1311 "1" Street, Suite 100
Sacramento, CA 95814
Tel: 916-444-6592

FOREIGN EXCHANGE TRADER

A DAY IN THE LIFE

A foreign exchange trader looks at the various factors that influence local economies and rates of exchange, then takes advantage of any misvaluations of currencies by buying and selling in different foreign exchange markets. Those with the most information, the best contacts, and strongest decision-making skills come out ahead. "It's the wild west of trading," wrote one foreign exchange (FX) trader, "and remember: A lot of people died in the wild west." Those who are comfortable with a high degree of risk and uncertainty should look into this exciting career.

A foreign exchange trader manages an account, looks at reports, reads the press from various countries, and most importantly, spends time on the phone. He may spend up to 80 percent of the day on the telephone and working at his computer. Traders must act fast to exploit valuation differences: "You've got seconds to decide how millions of dollars should be spent," said one trader, "so you have to have confidence." Confidence ranked second right after "guts" in qualities important in new traders. A sharp analytic mind is also crucial; while a variety of degrees are helpful, those with technical or scientific analysis backgrounds tend to find the job more manageable. Accounting strengths are helpful in keeping track of positions and profit and losses throughout hectic days.

FX traders specialize early in their careers, following one currency and the underlying economy of its country. Many traders specialize in groups of geographically related countries, such as those who trade Central American currencies or Pacific Rim currencies. Since foreign exchange trading is international, it can take place at any time of day. Many managers run twenty-four-hour shops and do business around the clock; most employees do have regular shifts, but world events may demand being summoned from bed late at night. Eighty percent of the traders we surveyed were satisfied with their choice of profession, but over 40 percent responded that they were exhausted at every day's end.

PAYING YOUR DUES

Economics, mathematics, and statistics majors have a distinct advantage in applying for positions in this field, as do history majors whose coursework included economics. A bachelor's degree is required. Any experience in a trading environment is valued, as is any work that demonstrates the ability to work hard, make fast and accurate decisions, and manipulate numbers. Many employers appreciate study abroad, international work experience or fluency in a foreign language. As a number of entry-level positions are account representatives as opposed to trading positions, candidates who have good interpersonal skills and access to capital may have an advantage. While on the job, keeping abreast of changes in the industry is important; continuing education is the norm. Few people leave to get advanced degrees in this field—there is a reverse snobbery associated with most trading floors that holds that traders are born, not made, and that no advanced degree will ever make anyone a more competent trader.

ASSOCIATED CAREERS

FX traders are good at strong and immediate decision making, and many apply this skill to other trading environments, such as stock trading, sales, or institutional buying. Their mathematical and financial skills recommend them to Wall Street firms in a number of positions, from back-office account settlement to options valuation analysis. In general, though, FX traders seek the adrenaline rush of trading and enjoy the open unregulated market—the number who leave (a small 20 percent over the course of a career) actually provide the largest single industry donation of manpower to the world of professional gambling.

PAST AND FUTURE

Foreign exchange was originally the province of multinational corporations that would collect revenue in one country and need to return the funds to the parent corporation in another. This left the companies extremely vulnerable to interest rate shifts over short periods of time and made valuation of foreign assets difficult if not impossible. The in-house foreign exchange manager determined areas of exposure and maintained financial equilibrium among corporations and their foreign outposts. As these divisions proved profitable on their own, a market developed in speculating risk in the 1940s and 1950s in countries with exchangeable currency. To date, these companies control the flow of over $74 billion around the globe each year.

The market for foreign exchange is growing steadily, and opportunities for those interested in the business should grow. However, legislative changes should shape the way that foreign exchange markets do business over the next ten years, whether through the establishment of a clearinghouse system, conversion to a different form altogether, or the protection of the status quo.

QUALITY OF LIFE

Two Years

After a general training program in which trading skills, valuation methods, and company protocols are taught, many young professionals become account executives who work with clients, offer advice and act as liaison between the trader and the client, before becoming traders. Those who do work in the trading arena can expect long hours, little pay, a frantic work environment, and an education in the process of foreign exchange trading.

Five Years

Those who have not become actual traders by year five often leave. Client contact increases across the board and salary, bonus, and account reviews happen every six to twelve months. The level of satisfaction is highest at this point and actually declines later on; perhaps that is because those who are good at trading tend to move between firms (much of years five to ten are spent looking for the perfect position) and those who are bad tend to see their responsibilities decline and their pay stagnate. Hours increase, but personal styles and the wealth of experience each person has accrued makes the job more enjoyable and less frantic.

Ten Years

Ten-year veterans either head up trading floors and manage other traders or are major producers with significant responsibilities in their firms. Some are in-house consultants for major international firms while others have become independent traders, capitalizing on past success. Many who do not go independent only spend another five years in the profession before retiring or finding another position; the pace and pressure eventually exhaust even the most passionate of traders.

THE BIRKMAN LIFESTYLE GRID

Red Green
Yellow Blue

This career is suitable for people with Green interests.

You'll Have Contact With

Bankers
Economists
Statisticians
Translators

Major Associations

Foreign Exchange and Money Brokers Association
Contact: Contact local chapters for more information.

FUNDRAISER/INSTITUTIONAL SOLICITOR

A DAY IN THE LIFE

People who are successful at fundraising develop large plans and execute the tiniest details in them, identify a target audience and tailor a unique appeal to that demographic, have excellent writing skills, a good understanding of how and when to approach people, and an unbelievable sense of organization. Fundraising on a large scale may entail up to seven different appeals to over 20,000 potential donors; fundraisers without organizational skills quickly get dragged under by the tide of material that passes through their hands. Planning and attending meetings takes up the majority of the professional fundraiser's day. Fundraisers must remain abreast of the concerns of potential donors, be responsive to the changing needs of their institution, and build up a successful system of reaching donors. Fundraisers spend ample creative energy recreating campaigns to ensure success year after year.

While broadbased fundraising (letter campaigns, high-profile events, and programs) are all important for the visibility, publicity, and support, the real work high-level fundraisers do comes through presentations, education, and targeted solicitation. Meeting skills, educational skills, and a touch of finesse are all critical to the successful fundraiser. Meetings with patrons, employees, and executives can take place after hours or late in the day. "It takes a lot of your free time and great social ability to pull it off, too," mentioned one director of fundraising for a private school. "You have to have the courage to sell what you believe, and to not blink when you ask for an enormous sum of money," wrote another respondent. The ability to communicate the value and the need of your employer to others is required in this occupation, and makes the difference between those who succeed and those who fail.

PAYING YOUR DUES

No specific bachelor's degree is required, but communication, English, finance and psychology majors all are considered good preparation for entry-level positions. Aspiring fundraisers need a gentle yet firm touch to communicate a platform and a position in writing and convince people to donate goods, services and money. Entry-level applicants should be good with numbers, graphics, and design and have an excellent sense of timing, since fundraising on an ongoing basis requires knowing when not to ask for donations as much as knowing when to ask. One other requirement for this job is the ability to withstand significant rejection. A fundraiser should be able to bring together disparate elements within a community to work toward a goal. Fundraisers sometimes earn advanced degrees in finance, marketing, or public relations.

ASSOCIATED CAREERS

Those who leave fundraising find plentiful work in public relations (twenty percent), advertising (ten percent), teaching (five percent), and administration (ten percent). Many return to school for advanced degrees in business, education, administration, and law. Fundraising rewards communication, persistence, and creativity, traits that are valued in any people-related industry.

PAST AND FUTURE

Fundraisers have existed since there have been causes that required funding. English private schools long relied on charitable donations from their alumni to support them in times of low enrollment. Orphanages and foodhouses in early America solicited donations of food and services from local merchants and wealthy patrons. Those who first became professional fundraisers were the wealthy in America who were connected with other wealthy patrons, and who could encourage them to donate to specific causes. These used to be called "benefactor" positions. As annual, regular fundraising became significant, they became known as "fundraising" positions.

Job opportunities in fundraising should increase through the end of the decade, and very likely beyond. With dramatic cuts in federal and state funding for many not-for-profit organizations, private donation solicitation will become increasingly widespread and important. Specialization will be the wave of the future; those who have unique skills in mail solicitations, phone solicitations, organizing fundraising events, or campaign tracking will be hired for discrete fundraising tasks under the umbrella of a generalized fundraising coordinator.

QUALITY OF LIFE

Two Years

Long hours, hard work, little free time, and an entire fundraising system to learn make the first few years difficult. Responsibilities are limited; tasks might include proofreading, tracking mail, entering computer data, making phone calls and arranging meetings with donors. Do not expect to attend these meetings or have any impact on policy. Input can be offered and accepted, but those who expect to make an immediate splash in the fundraising pool should be aware of the limited role these first few years offer.

Five Years

Lifestyles for five-year survivors are significantly different for those fundraising for smaller, more specific organizations than those fundraising for large, extremely hierarchical organizations. Those in small companies become associate fundraisers or head fundraiser, depending on their success and available opportunities. Many remain with their original organizations if advancement opportunities exist. Five-year fundraisers meet with large, individual donors, propose new audiences to appeal to, devise and organize seasonal campaigns, and make presentations on goals to executives at their company. Those in larger firms have less responsibility but more defined areas of control. A typical five-year at a large firm may be in charge of Northeast solicitations for the twenty-two-to-twenty-eight-year-old age range for those who graduated college with liberal arts degrees. Duties might include purchasing of mailing lists, coordinating production of solicitation materials, and tracking responses. Salaries and hours increase. Many fundraisers work as fundraisers for fewer than three years or more than ten; roughly half leave between years three and six.

Ten Years

By this point, fundraisers have most likely held a number of positions at two or more companies, led and directed successful fund drives or annual campaigns, and reinvented themselves with the times. Experienced fundraisers often take on challenges of a different scale, such as moving to a much larger organization or heading a department. If you've lasted ten years in this profession you are statistically likely to last another fifteen to twenty-five years in this challenging, exciting, and difficult job.

THE BIRKMAN LIFESTYLE GRID

This career is suitable for people with Green interests.

You'll Have Contact With
Direct Mail Consultants
Event Planners
Market Researchers
Curators
Promoters

Major Associations
American Association of
Fund-Raising Counsel
25 West 43rd Street
New York, NY 10036
Tel: 212-354-5799
Fax: 212-768-1795

Association of Fundraisers and Direct Sellers
5775 Peachtree-Dunwoody Road
Suite 500-G
Atlanta, GA 30342
Tel: 404-252-3663
Fax: 404-252-0774

Direct Mail Fundraisers Association
445 West 45th Street
New York, NY 10036
Tel: 212-489-4929
Fax: 212-489-7155

GEOLOGIST

A DAY IN THE LIFE

One geologist said she owns a bumper sticker which reads "I've got rocks in my head." A little levity may be appreciated in between analyzing rock formations, interpreting data, and fieldwork studying rocks. Geologists who are reviewing land in the field or consulting on environmental issues can expect to spend five to fifteen hours a day outdoors, usually during the more pleasant months of the year. They take samples and measurements and explore underneath the initial layers of the earth. Once they've completed their field work, most return to the lab and test their samples for content and composition. One geologist said, "You'll be asked simple questions, and you've got to come up with ways of answering them when no one method is foolproof. Is there oil under here? If so how much? How long will it take to get it out? Those questions can only be answered with probabilities, not certainties." It takes a person not only good at approaching problems but also good at dealing with people to satisfy all requirements of this occupation.

Many geologists do prospective development for the potential value of land sites for the oil and gas industry. They write reports recommending whether or not to purchase a particular plot of land. A good geologist can be worth millions to a venture–capital based oil company. "Don't count on seeing any of the money you make for them," wrote one semi-disgruntled geologist. Pay is low in this academic industry. Many who enter it cite the intellectual challenge and the ability to work both in a lab and outdoors as the most positive features of the profession. Geologists appreciate the supportive and very involved community of geological scientists: "You learn every day from your peers and the world around you. It's a perfect combination." A geologist may find herself in the field for somewhere between three and seven months per year. Those long periods abroad can make life not so predictable for those who value family life and a stable work environment. Those who don't work in the private sector may find work under the auspices of the largest hirer of geologists, the federal government. Many are employed by the Department of Agriculture, the Department of the Interior, and the Department of Defense.

PAYING YOUR DUES

A geologist must have at least a bachelor's degree in geology or geophysics. Those who wish to advance should consider a Master's degree and, in certain cases, a Ph.D. Coursework includes such scientific staples as math, physics, chemistry, and statistics, but should also include mineralogy, stratigraphy, and structural geology. Entry-level positions, characterized by a lack of responsibility and paltry remuneration, include field research assistant and lab assistant. Most people work in teams. "I've never heard of an occupation that depends more on how well you work with others," wrote one geologist, "and you'll never hear more jokes about rocks." Someone interested in this career should be good with numbers and people, be interested in sciences and natural formations, and should be comfortable working both alone and in groups. This person should also be willing to work long hours under uncertain working conditions (indoors and out) and be happy with a smaller-than-average paycheck.

ASSOCIATED CAREERS

Few geologists—about ten percent—leave the profession, and when they do, they tend to migrate to other, related sciences. Some of these, such as geophysics and statistics, have direct correlations to geology. Others, such as oceanography and petroleum engineering, are applied versions of geological knowledge in specific areas. Some move to the EPA in their enforcement division, or the National Parks Service as land surveyors. Others return to school to receive advanced degrees in related or geological sciences.

PAST AND FUTURE

At the end of the eighteenth century, literature on the beginning and history of rock formations first began to be published in England by A. Werner and J. Hutton. The field grew with explorations in Europe and the New World.

In the near future, geological jobs opportunities should remain about the same but over the next twenty years, the nature and the process of the job should change dramatically. Technological innovations will be important in changing methods of ground exploration and analysis, and the number of undiscovered sites will diminish, shrinking the available job pool. Geologists may find their role more related to environmental questions than resting on issues of venture capital.

QUALITY OF LIFE

Two Years

Most geologists do field exploration and lab testing in their first two years. Usually paired with a "mentor" or "senior geologist," entry-level employees visit sites and learn how to take samples, label and store them. Back at the office, duties turn to proofreading, summarizing professional articles and learning specific lab techniques. While not glamorous, the education is important, and those who rise in the profession cite those initial training years as important to their continued success.

Five Years

Most who've decided to leave the profession have left by this point, although a few more will leave between years six and eight. Many in the field are promoted to "senior geologist" positions which involve the supervision of newer geologists and have more supervisory and oversight responsibilities, moving away from those as tester or field agent. Hours become more predictable and schedules become more flexible to allow for greater family and personal life. Many write articles on their own experiences or projects which act as an introduction to the community of geologists. A number of respondents cite the discovery of this community as significant to their satisfaction.

Ten Years

The majority (over 60 percent) of ten-year geological survivors are employed by large companies, universities, or the federal government. The remaining 40 percent are private consultants or work for small firms with fewer than six employees. Salaries have increased, but from here on out, geologists can only expect cost-of-living adjustments. Many Ph.D.s who once worked in the private sector have returned to academia, relying on their experience to help them as teachers. Government geologists have settled in administrative and oversight positions, and more direct issues of policy and administration rather than individual testing and report writing. Those who leave the profession at this point do so for reasons of health or retirement.

THE BIRKMAN LIFESTYLE GRID

Red Green
Yellow Blue

This career is suitable for people with Red interests.

You'll Have Contact With

Developers
Geophysicists
Petroleum Engineers
Surveyors

Major Associations

American Association of
Petroleum Geologists
P.O. Box 979
Tulsa, OK 74101
Tel: 918-584-2555
Fax: 918-560-2665
Contact: Communications Dept.

American Geological Institute
4220 King Street
Alexandria, VA 22302-1502
Tel: 703-379-2480
Fax: 703-379-7563
Contact: Marilyn Suiter

Geological Society of America
P.O. Box 9140, 3300 Penrose Place
Boulder, CO 80301
Tel: 303-447-2020
Fax: 303-447-1133
Contact: Terry Morland

GEOPHYSICIST

A DAY IN THE LIFE

A geophysicist must have a strong science background, a curious mind, and a fascination with natural phenomena to succeed. Geophysicists measure, examine, and explore the physical properties of earth, from below the ground to the atmosphere, from the depths of the ocean to the tops of volcanoes. Daily duties include studying readouts of measurement equipment, examining natural phenomena (such as tidal waves and electromagnetic fields), and writing reports which correlate the two. Geophysics is an academic field which crosses over into the practical arena in a number of areas.

Specialization is significant early on—when applying for jobs—in geophysics. For example, the work a seismologist does—studying seismic readings and trying to predict earthquakes—is like that of the tectnophysicist, who studies the movement of tectonic plates, but very unlike what a volcanologist does, measuring underearth temperatures and examining other readings which might predict the formation or eruption of volcanoes. Some geophysicists work with gravity, others with electronic fields. Most of the work of each of the specialties is done primarily in the lab, with some field work. Geophysicists often have to rush to a spot on the globe to examine an immediate phenomenon; unlike geologists, they do less steady on-site work. Geologists also analyze fairly static systems; geophysicists usually examine systems in flux. Those who succeed in geophysics seem to have the ability to be flexible and the willingness to challenge previously held assumptions if their data proves those assumptions untrue. Successful geophysicists generally have wide-ranging minds to encompass the complexities of their profession.

Many geophysicists move through a number of areas of specialization in five-year blocks. Initial specialization is important because it leads to five years of learning that particular aspect of the field. Professionals tend to enjoy learning how geological systems interrelate, and they are interested in learning about the systems which interact with the ones they already know. Learning about new specialties often happens gradually and unconsciously. Geophysicists take home the most amount of out-of-work reading of any profession in this book, with the possible exception of editor. The continuous challenge and the perpetual education this occupation encourages seem to be two of the major reasons geophysicists are so satisfied with their work.

PAYING YOUR DUES

Geophysicists study geology and physics; a bachelor's degree is required in the field, although more and more employers are requesting either a Master's degree, a Ph.D, or three years' experience. Coursework should include a basic geological core curriculum—stratigraphy, structural geography, and mineralogy—and basic physics curriculum—quantum mechanics, classical physics, electromagnetism, and gravity. It should also include logic, mathematics, and ecological science, a recent addition which is becoming more important to employers. Many companies which use geophysicists, such as hydroelectric power plants and research institutions, put new hirees through an intense, two-day-to-two-week training course in mission, internal protocols, and responsibilities. A mature outlook and sense of professional obligation are helpful in this career. Much of the work that geophysicists do is unsupervised, and the only line of defense against sloppy research is the withering academic stare of the geophysics' community.

ASSOCIATED CAREERS

Geophysicists leave the profession only when they retire, die, or find a scientific challenge more interesting, which happens about five percent of the time. Some venture into more obscure branches of physics, led by their initial interaction with geophysics. The most common reason people leave the profession? They go into teaching at university settings. What do they teach? Geophysics.

PAST AND FUTURE

Amalgam professions, such as biochemistry and geophysics, are new entrants to the sciences as discrete areas of study. Geophysics grew out of geology and the recognition of geologists that it is a different concern to study a living, moving system than the results of a historical system. It is like comparing the study of history to the study of current events; both are valuable, but they require different intellectual processes.

Geophysicists are limited by what they are able to see and examine; this means that new opportunities aren't created, they just happen when the earth shows some activity. The job market should remain stable, with positions opening up and research duties still available, but to expect an explosion of geophysicist jobs would be an aggressive posture indeed.

QUALITY OF LIFE

Two Years

A geophysicist's first years offer two distinct challenges: One, the transition from the shelter of the academic community to the working world seems to strike geophysicists more roughly than most professionals. While the sense of encouragement continues in the community of geophysicists, the daily tasks of taking readings, assembling large bodies of data, and finding patterns in that data is more monotonous and less challenging than the work students face in college. Two, more often than not, the candidate has to relocate for work, often to remote places where readings can be taken without significant man-made equipment interfering. Hours are reasonable and pay is low to average.

Five Years

Most geophysicists reach the limits of their current specialization (not the limits of knowledge in the profession, just their area's professional limits), and begin to branch out into new areas of study. Many begin to write articles and circulate them among colleagues. Those who have been successful as field researchers and lab analysts are given supervisory responsibilities over newer entrants to the profession; many teach elective courses at local universities. Geophysicists gain some control over the direction of their research, and many move into government service. Those who leave the profession do so at critical junctures when they cease to be challenged by their activities for a time.

Ten Years

A large number of geophysicists return to academic circles as they reach the limits of their specialties, both in terms of responsibility and independence. Teaching, particularly at research institutions, allows greater leeway in investigation. Geophysicists can expect only cost-of-living adjustments to their salaries from here on.

THE BIRKMAN LIFESTYLE GRID

Red Green
Yellow Blue

This career is suitable for people with Red interests.

You'll Have Contact With

Civil Engineers
Geologists
Lab Technicians
Petroleum Engineers

Major Associations

American Association of
Petroleum Geologists
Communication Dept., P.O. Box 979
Tulsa, OK 74101
Tel: 918-584-2555
Contact: Communications Dept.

American Geological Institute
4200 King Street
Alexandria, VA 22302-1507
Tel: 703-379-2480
Contact: Marilyn Suiter

Geological Society of America
PO Box 9140, 3300 Penrose Place
Boulder, CO 80301
Tel: 303-447-2020
Contact: Terry Morland

U.S. Antartic Research Program (USARP)
National Science Foundation
4201 Wilson Boulevard, Room 755
Arlington, VA 22230
Tel: 703-306-1031

GRAPHIC DESIGNER

PROFESSIONAL PROFILE

# of people in profession	339,000
% male	65
% female	35
avg. hours per week	40
avg. starting salary	$16,700
avg. salary after 5 years	$26,000
avg. salary 10 to 15 years	$40,000

Professionals Read
Computer Graphics and Applications
Adobe Magazine
Design

Books, Films and TV Shows Featuring the Profession
Clean Lines
The Color Perfect
The End of Print

Major Employers
Microsoft
One Microsoft Way FTE 303
Redmond, VA 98052-8303
Tel: 800-892-3181
Fax: 206-882-8080
Contact: Personnel

Ogilvy & Mather
309 West 49th Street
New York, NY 10019
Tel: 212-237-4000
Fax: 212-237-5394
Contact: Joy Mauverhoff

MTV Networks
1515 Broadway
16th Floor
New York, NY 10036
Tel: 212-258-8000
Fax: 212-846-1473
Contact: Human Resources Development

A DAY IN THE LIFE

Graphic designers create the visual presentation and design of goods, from gravestone markers to detergent boxes, from album covers to dog food cans. Work is usually done on a project basis. Designers must be able to work under extreme time pressures and very defined financial and design limits to produce quality material. A graphic designer must be able to synthesize input from a number of different sources into a distinctive image, using research prepared by a marketing department and cost specifications determined by a budgeting department, and produce a variety of sketches and models which demonstrate different approaches to the product. This takes a person who can listen to comments, has a good eye for aesthetic design and a flair for color, and a good understanding of the needs of the corporate world.

"Graphic design isn't one job. It's twenty," wrote one frazzled designer. "Salesman skills are very important if you want to see your designs accepted," wrote another. Nearly all respondents listed communication skills as either second or third in importance for success in this profession. Over time, specialization is the name of the game, either in product design, packaging design, material use, or object arrangement.

When projects are underway, graphic designers can expect to work long hours brainstorming and meeting with executives to discuss ideas. The job is highly visible; successes and failures alike are recognized and are put on display. Those who are insecure about their skills or their ideas have a hard time accepting the amount of risk and rejection this career entails. A successful graphic designer has an enviable life, choosing among clients and earning significant money. Be warned: An artist's style may be very hot one season and turn into a parody the next; those who are unwilling or unable to change could find promising careers disappearing. Of the nearly 25,000 people who try to enter the field of graphic design each year, only about 15,000 last the first two years, and 8,000 last five years.

PAYING YOUR DUES

No bachelor's degree is required to become a graphic designer, but about two-thirds go to college, usually majoring in product design, art, or art history. Graphic designers must have talent and an understanding of the business world, including issues of finance and production, and should be familiar with computer technology such as PageMaker (TM), Photoshop (TM), Adobe Illustrator (TM), and other painting and graphic design tools. Graphic designers must be able to work in a variety of media and meet deadlines, sizing limits, and financial restrictions, especially those who wish to work as a freelance graphic designers rather than in-house salaried designers. Basic preprofessional coursework should include design, drawing, computer artwork, and specific knowledge (for example, anatomy for medical graphics designers) relating to any area of specialization. Professionals must assemble a working portfolio to approach companies for work of any scale. For those who wish to pursue further study, over 100 schools offer accredited graphic design programs, according to the National Association of Schools of Art and Design, and each of them addresses issues of the working life of the graphic designer along with issues of design.

ASSOCIATED CAREERS

Many artists turn to graphic design to make a living during their lean years, then return to art. A number become gallery owners and patrons and use the contacts they made as designers to help out any new talent in need of remunerative work. The large number of graphic artists who leave do so because of the scrambling lifestyle: The need to pursue work constantly and the requirement to act as a "salesman" for their own ideas. Others go in-house as design consultants and as magazine layout editors.

PAST AND FUTURE

Graphic design has been around since shopkeepers started hanging signs to advertise their wares. In the 1700s, artisans were approached by a merchant class eager to make its goods and services recognizable to a mostly illiterate population.

Graphic design will become ever more significant as computer technology becomes more universally available and as more and more companies realize that a definitive, distinctive logo and product design can make an enormous difference in product sales. Job opportunities should increase during the next ten to fifteen years with even more openings seasonally for such things as holiday window displays and specialty sales events. Currently, over a third of all graphic designers are self-employed. This figure is expected to increase over the next ten years.

QUALITY OF LIFE

Two Years

Unproved graphic designers travel a difficult road as they try to assemble portfolios, bid competitively for small jobs, and earn a reputation. Those with good connections have an easier time getting a foot in the door, but unfamiliarity with standard working conditions and standard practices still may make the beginning rocky. Hours can be long and unrewarding as you pound the pavement seeking work; be prepared to withstand significant rejection. Forty percent of graphic designers leave the profession in the first two years.

Five Years

The field evens out at the five year mark; only those with proven records, solid connections, and strong references survive. Around a third of those who began in this career stay in it to this point, and around 10 percent remain independent freelance graphic designers. The majority become in-house consultants, designers and producers. For the most part, designers are satisfied with their work, though hours are long and salaries are average. Those who have shown good judgment sometimes choose other graphic designers to produce out-of-house work or recommend other designers for hire.

Ten Years

Ten-year veterans have established sound (and profitable) reputations; their designs remain fresh, and they should be able to find a number of fairly lucrative in-house graphic design positions, if they wish to. Many spend more time supervising design departments or "stables" of newer, less expensive designers. Those who've started their own businesses begin to reap significant profits or, in lieu of that, have closed shop and gone in-house themselves.

THE BIRKMAN LIFESTYLE GRID

This career is suitable for people with Green interests.

You'll Have Contact With

Advertising Executives
Artists
Market Researchers
Product Designers

Major Associations

American Institute of Graphic Arts
164 Fifth Avenue
New York, NY 10010
Tel: 212-807-1990
Fax: 212-807-1799

Graphic Arts Technical Foundation
4615 Forbes Avenue
Pittsburgh, PA 15213
Tel: 412-621-6941

The Society of Illustrators
128 East 63rd Street
New York, NY 10021-7392

The Society of Publication Designers
60 East 42nd Street, Suite 721
New York, NY 10165-1416

GUIDANCE COUNSELOR

PROFESSIONAL PROFILE

# of people in profession	100,000
% male	60
% female	40
avg. hours per week	40
avg. starting salary	$27,000
avg. salary after 5 years	$38,000
avg. salary 10 to 15 years	$44,000

Professionals Read
Journal of Higher Education
College Board Review
Education Week
Journal of College Admissions

Books, Films and TV Shows Featuring the Profession
Pretty In Pink
Say Anything
Look at the Sky

Major Employers
NYC Board of Education
65 Court Street
Brooklyn, NY 11201
Tel: 718-935-2299
Fax: 718-935-5472
Contact: Personnel

Texas Education Agency
1701 North Congress Avenue
Austin, TX 78701
Tel: 512-463-9734
Contact: Human Resources

Los Angeles Unified School Districts
450 North Grand Avenue
Room 102
Los Angeles, CA 90012
Tel: 213-625-6000
Fax: 213-625-4580
Contact: Carla Smotherman

Teach For America
20 Exchange Place, 8th Floor
New York, NY 10005
Tel: 212-425-9037
Fax: 212-425-9347
Net: http://www.teachforamerica.org

A DAY IN THE LIFE

Few careers are as potentially rewarding—or as frustrating—as that of a guidance counselor, whose job is to help guide and structure children's educational and vocational direction as they pass through an unstable and confusing time in their lives. It is frustrating because you will have limited authority to make students follow your advice, and often you will face students "who don't want to think about the day after tomorrow," as one counselor put it. A guidance counselor helps students determine courses of study and possible vocations. Counselors try to understand what motivates each student as well as his skills and desires. "When you're doing things right," wrote one, "it's like you're another parent, except they trust you a little more." Those who aspire to enter the field should be aware that emotional as well as intellectual demands are part of the occupation.

As most guidance counselors spend over a third of their time in consultations with students and parents, prospective counselors should be comfortable with teenagers and have excellent communication skills. Another 25 percent of a guidance counselor's day is spent administering and evaluating tests. Guidance counselors use the results to provide context for existing records of academic performance, teacher evaluations, and a better overall understanding of students' needs.

Some guidance counselors call the continuing education they receive from students they work with the most interesting feature of the profession. "I learned more from them than from any class in college," wrote one enthusiastic counselor, "I learned more in the first day." Not all are as ebullient as this, but the level of satisfaction guidance counselors recorded was one of the highest of any career in this book. Of course, those who don't love the profession usually leave quickly; guidance counselors have one of the highest initial attrition rates of any profession in this book, a staggering 60 percent within the first two years. Careers that require this degree of emotional commitment can be rough on those who are not prepared to make one on a regular basis.

PAYING YOUR DUES

A bachelor's degree is required to become a high-school guidance counselor, and some states require that the candidate have a master's degree. Coursework should include social studies, psychology, and communications work, with an emphasis on public speaking. Courses dealing with education are important too; many private schools require that guidance counselors teach courses in addition to their counseling duties. A background in statistics and mathematics is important for evaluating students on their standardized tests. By far the most important skill a potential guidance counselor can bring to this profession is the ability to relate to adolescents. This skill requires a combination of the ability to listen, honesty, an open mind, and a sense of humor. Those who succeed in this profession communicate well with students; those who fail, don't.

ASSOCIATED CAREERS

People become guidance counselors because they want to help students, and those who leave find many other ways to satisfy that desire: They return to school and become therapists, they head up substance abuse programs, they run educational centers and programs, they become teachers without counseling duties and they even become tutors. Some decide that they would like to continue helping people, but in a different age range, and they become professional career advisors, recruiters, and human resource personnel.

PAST AND FUTURE

Guidance counselors were first introduced in the United States in the Northeast in the early 1900s, but these positions didn't experience any significant growth until the end of World War II. Pushed by the Department of Education, school systems across the country soon "strongly encouraged" the position in every public and private school.

Guidance counselors face daunting tasks every day, but their roles at the center of youth education have never been more important. The job market for guidance counselors should be full of opportunity for the next ten years or so, as enrollment is growing in U. S. school systems. The problem is that institutional support for guidance counselors is waning. Guidance counselors can be the first to face the budget axe since they are "non-instructional personnel."

QUALITY OF LIFE

Two Years

These are the most trying years for guidance counselors, as the ones in which the full emotional impact of helping guide teenagers through difficult personal decisions and life-changing options hits the new hire. Many opt for different occupations after the first couple of years. Those who remain must learn to keep personal and professional decisions separate while maintaining warm relationships with students. This juggling act is difficult to manage, particularly in the first few years when older students are making critical decisions but have no context in which to trust in your ability to help them.

Five Years

Those who've survived five years as guidance counselors face a much more stable work environment, from which less than five percent leave each year. Counselors learn to interpret standardized tests and hone their communication skills with students. Many become involved in conferences, lectures, and conventions where issues about vocational and academic counseling are discussed. Hours decrease and pay increases, but administrative duties may increase also. Many schools like to see a continuous evolution of guidance counseling programs, so creative thinking is a must.

Ten Years

Ten-year veterans, for the most part, have found positions where they are happy and satisfied. Pay levels off and, unless they want to assume additional duties, guidance counselors can expect only cost-of-living salary adjustments. Guidance counselors continue in the same roles as before, but many exercise their seniority to initiate parent/teacher programs that provide a further safety net for troubled teens.

THE BIRKMAN LIFESTYLE GRID

This career is suitable for people with Green interests.

You'll Have Contact With

Psychologists
Students
University Administrators
Vocational Testing Consultants

Major Associations

American School Counselor Association
5999 Stevenson Avenue
Alexandria, VA 22304
Tel: 703-823-9800
Contact: Virginia Moore

National Board for Certified Counselors
3 Terrace Way
Suite D
Greensboro, NC 27403
Tel: 910-547-0607

American College and Career
Counseling Center (ACACC)
2401 Pennsylvania Avenue
10-C-51
Philadelphia, PA 19130
Tel: 215-232-5225

National Association of College
Admissions Counselors (NACAC)
1631 Prince Street
Alexandria, VA 22314
Tel: 703-836-2222
Fax: 702-836-8015

Hazardous Waste Manager

A DAY IN THE LIFE

Many people are involved in the management of America's rubbish, from the local garbage collector to the analytical chemist, but no aspect of waste management poses the challenges faced by hazardous waste professionals. Management of hazardous waste is perhaps the weakest link in America's dynamic industrial economy, because of the dangers posed by toxic chemicals, nuclear by-products and organic garbage.

A career in hazardous waste disposal and management may lead you to a lab, to a landfill, or to Washington, D.C. Several federal agencies deal with hazardous waste, including the Environmental Protection Agency (EPA), the Department of Defense, and the Department of Energy. Private industrial enterprises, such as large corporations, employ their own teams of waste specialists or hire consultants to manage their hazardous waste output. A hazardous waste professional may be a geologist, a chemist, or a nuclear physicist. Other hazardous waste professionals are engineers or managers, working to develop systems to reduce waste in the production process or to protect the environment from the dangerous substances that must be disposed of. Many specialists must work together to reduce the burden of hazardous waste.

There are two approaches to hazardous waste management: Remedial and removal. Remedial waste management specialists define the waste problem—for instance, a leaky landfill seeping dangerous chemicals into a drinking-water supply—and then explore various solutions to the problem. They have to consider the impact on the environment, design a solution and finally put that solution into motion. Removal specialists control and clean up major hazardous waste accidents, such as oil spills.

PAYING YOUR DUES

A bachelor's degree is necessary for this profession and, in today's competitive job market, a master's degree or even a doctorate is preferred. Highly sought-after hazardous waste professionals usually specialize in one or more sciences. Major in geology, chemistry, physics, ecology, or any combination of sciences. If you want to specialize, look into soil, air, or water ecology. Since much of your job may require preparing environmental impact statements or proposing waste-management systems, it's a good idea to develop your speaking and writing skills.

Working for the government is rewarding, but it's not always easy. If you choose a job with the EPA or another federal agency, remember that you are joining a large bureaucracy whose commitment to waste management is occasionally diluted by political considerations. Big businesses that hire hazardous waste professionals are committed to keeping the air, earth, and water clean, but they must also keep their eyes on the bottom line. A committed hazardous waste specialist must be patient and resourceful to fulfill this twin agenda. Despite the obstacles, and because of the growing emphasis on environmentalism, effective professionals are always in demand.

ASSOCIATED CAREERS

If you're interested in this area, but toxic chemicals aren't for you, the natural sciences are still worth exploring. Agriculture, industry, and the academic community all need qualified scientists. The skill that goes into designing a remedial waste management system can also be applied to managing other systems and to general business management.

PAST AND FUTURE

Improper disposal of hazardous waste has led to some of history's most vicious epidemics. The industrial revolution, symbolized by belching smokestacks, highlighted the problem. Nevertheless, it is only since World War II that the U.S. government has taken significant steps to control environmental hazards. The Superfund legislation of 1980, which earmarked billions of dollars to finance hazardous waste cleanups, set in motion what is now the thriving industry of hazardous waste disposal.

Waste management is a promising field. The negligence of environmental law enforcement of the 1980s has left a legacy of hazardous waste accidents waiting to happen. Changing priorities and mounting health concerns in the 1990s has spurred a trend to more vigorous enforcement of environmental regulations, with a new wave of prevention and cleanup efforts. Nuclear waste disposal alone represents a multibillion-dollar industry (with the U.S. government likely to foot the bill for the most expensive projects, including burying waste deep within the earth's crust in what amounts to a monumental public works project). Chemicals, used car tires, medical (biological) and a range of other hazards will all supply opportunities for hazardous waste management. As the number of available disposal sites shrinks and the challenges and costs of disposal continue to rise, industry and government will be forced to join forces to help resolve ongoing crises in the years ahead.

QUALITY OF LIFE

Two Years

Many professionals work part-time while getting their master's degrees or doctorates in environmental science, and the part-time jobs often turn into full-time positions when they graduate. Professionals analyze and collect samples and write summary reports. Hours are average to long, but most professionals spend time reading professional journals and traveling for the job.

Five Years

Professionals start to specialize in remedial or removal management, depending on their temperament and abilities, and available opportunities. Many publish articles in professional journals, which enhances their reputations. Government employees often shift to the private sector in years four through six, citing better pay, more control over working conditions, and greater responsibilities. Hours remain stable; salary increases.

Ten Years

Hazardous waste removers lead teams and direct tests at this point, rather than spend time in the field or lab conducting them. Many are involved in policy discussions and environmental and business issues, and engage in debates over technology.

THE BIRKMAN LIFESTYLE GRID

Red Green
Yellow Blue

This career is suitable for people with Red interests.

You'll Have Contact With

Chemists
EPA Officials
Haulers
Recyclers

Major Associations

American Water Works Association
6666 West Quincy Avenue
Denver, CO 80235
Tel: 303-794-7711
Fax: 303-795-1400

Water Environment Federation
601 Wythe Street
Alexandria, VA 22314-1994
Tel: 703-684-2400
Fax: 703-684-2492

Municipal Environmental Association (MEA)
P.O. Box 851521
Richardson, TX 75982-1521
Tel: 214-644-8971

Hazardous Materials Control
Resources Institute (HMCRI)
One Church Street, Suite 200
Rockville, MD 20850
Tel: 301-251-1900

HEALTH CARE ADMINISTRATOR

A DAY IN THE LIFE

The health care industry has become a behemoth employing hundreds of thousands of physicians, nurses, health specialists, and other non–health workers and wielding considerable clout on Wall Street. Health care administrators run this behemoth, coordinating and organizing the financing and delivery of care and assisting in the management of health facilities. Executive-level administrators are highly educated individuals responsible for overall policy directions. They assess the need for services, equipment and personnel and also make recommendations regarding the expansion or curtailment of services, and the establishment of new or auxiliary facilities. They also oversee compliance with government agencies and regulations. Their duties tend to vary with the size and operations of the health facility where they are employed; generally, smaller facilities have less staff support so administrators are left with larger work loads. In larger facilities, administrators can delegate duties and devote more time to policy directives.

Assistants to administrators at large facilities typically provide support in the execution of top-level decisions. Depending on their expertise and experience, some assistants oversee the activities of clinical departments such as nursing or surgery, or they may direct the operations of non–health areas such as personnel, finance and public relations. At nursing homes, home health agencies, and other smaller facilities, the duties and responsibilities of administrators are vast and varied. Administrators wear multiple hats in departments such as human resources, finance and operations, and admissions.

Clinical managers are health specialists who supervise specific clinical services in the health care industry. They have job-specific training and are involved with implementing policies and procedures for their departments, while coordinating their activities with other managers. Policy decisions do not fall within the purview of managers for small group practices, but larger groups usually retain the services of a full-time administrator who not only coordinates activities on a day-to-day basis but also develops and implements business strategies.

PAYING YOUR DUES

To land a plum job in the health care industry, it is sensible to first complete graduate studies. A bachelor's degree will only open doors at the entry level, and only a lucky few will be able to work up to a top-level position in a small operation or a middle-management position at a larger facility. A Master's degree in hospital or nursing administration, public health, public or business administration, and other related fields is usually a requirement for executive office. Courses in accounting and budgeting, management principles, hospital organization and management, health economics, and health information systems provide the student with a solid foundation. Applicants to the field must be willing to work their way up the corporate health ladder, as even new graduates with master's degrees often start out as assistant administrators or managers of non–health departments. As in all management positions, strong leadership qualities, effective communication and analytical skills, and the ability to motivate others will greatly enhance employment opportunities. Specialized expertise in one type of health facility—HMOs, mental health hospitals, nursing homes, general hospitals or outpatient care services—can significantly expand the possibility of easy placement in the industry.

ASSOCIATED CAREERS

Health care administrators can apply their training in health and management as underwriters for health insurance companies and HMOs and in sales, marketing and distribution of health equipment and supplies. Some become directors of public health, social welfare administrators, and directors of health agencies. An administrator with a Ph.D. might consult, teach, or do research.

PAST AND FUTURE

The rise of both private indemnity insurance and government-sponsored health entitlements earlier in this century have spawned a complex medical bureaucracy. As health services continue to expand and diversify, so will job opportunities, though the trend toward "managed care" and "economies of scale" in large health management organizations (HMOs) will result in restructuring. As HMOs and other health care providers expand operations, competition for executive-level positions within these organizations will be keen, and overlapping administrators will be squeezed out of merging companies.

A rapidly aging population, especially a growing 75-years-and-older segment who will require the continued services of health care professionals, assures employment opportunities in nursing homes and related industries in the coming decade.

QUALITY OF LIFE

Two Years

With two years' experience the health care administrator is still making his way up the corporate ladder to the job of choice. Two-year health care administrators have already developed mentorships and prepared themselves for higher office by asking for and taking on more duties and responsibilities; keeping abreast of changes, trends and development in the industry; and executing their prescribed duties exceptionally well.

Five Years

Five years into the business, the professional is ready to be promoted to executive. She has studied the standards of the industry, has kept abreast of industry trends, has completed refresher courses in various areas of service delivery, and has obtained necessary licenses and certificates. This is the ideal time for the young professional to evaluate his career choice, progress, and advancement potential, as well as review employment options. Returning to school to pursue higher studies in management is a possibility.

Ten Years

The experienced health care administrator is firmly entrenched in the executive suite. Pursuing postgraduate studies while still holding on to that middle-management job will significantly enhance the professional's advancement potential. With a Ph.D. the administrator can enter academia to teach and do research, or start up private consulting services.

THE BIRKMAN LIFESTYLE GRID

This career is suitable for people with Yellow interests.

You'll Have Contact With
Benefits Managers
Hospital Administrators
Insurance Agents
Physicians

Major Associations
American College of Health Care Administrators
325 South Patrick Street
Alexandria, VA 22314
Tel: 703-549-5822
Fax: 703-739-7901

Association of University Programs in Health Administration
1911 North Fort Myer Drive
Suite 503
Arlington, VA 22209
Tel: 703-524-5500

Hotel Manager

A DAY IN THE LIFE

A hotel manager oversees all of a hotel's daily operations, from staffing to coordinating fresh-cut flowers for the lobby. Many, over time, are given long-term responsibility for negotiating contracts with vendors (such as maintenance supplies), negotiating leases with on-site shops, and physically upgrading the hotel. Hotel managers usually relish "the ability to put your own distinctive style on the [hotel] experience." While managing a hotel and giving it your unique flair are wonderful, they come with full responsibility for failure. "The better you are at what you do, the more responsibilities you are given, the more chances you have to fail," mentioned one hotel manager. When things fall apart, "no one is a hotel manager's friend." Hotel managers can feel great about their positions, create strong relationships with regular customers, and maintain an amicable working environment. But should the bottom line waver and financial woes occur, the first neck on the chopping block is hers.

Those in the hotel management industry say that sometimes it seems that you need "to be born on the planet Krypton" to be a good hotel manager because only Superman could juggle the administrative, aesthetic, and financial decisions which constitute daily life on the job. Over 70 percent of the respondents said that "tired" was an understatement about how they felt at the end of the day (or night); "Exhausted is more like it," wrote one, in shaky, spider-thin handwriting. A hotel manager's position as a liaison between the ownership and the staff can be difficult and isolating. But those who can put up with the long hours, the high degree of responsibility, and the variety of tasks emerge with a solid degree of satisfaction and a desire to continue in the profession. The average tenure of a hotel manager is 6.7 years, though this figure doesn't represent the number of managers who work for two years and those who work for decades. Many work at a variety of hotels, build up their resumes, and then find positions that allow them the freedom to operate their own establishments.

PAYING YOUR DUES

Aspiring hotel managers used to begin at the reception desk, as part of the waitstaff, or as members of the cleaning staff, then work their way up the ladder. As hotels have become more commercial properties and the duties of hotel managers have expanded, this avenue of advancement has closed off. Now hotel manager hopefuls go to hotel management school, and those who don't should garner as much practical hotel experience as possible. Each chain or specific hotel puts new employees through their own training programs, so those applying for jobs should learn all they can about the scope and functioning of the specific hotels where they wish to work.

Part of life as a hotel manager can be similar to the life of a doctor, as managers can be called to duty at any time of the day or night. Hotel managers must handle any and all emergencies, and those who wish to remain in the profession and maintain respect must be quick-thinking and decisive. Candidates should have a good organizational and financial background, excellent communication and interpersonal skills, and strong self-discipline. They should also be extremely detail-oriented; when running a hotel, there is no such thing as an unimportant detail. The good manager drives himself to improve and upgrade the hotel at every available opportunity.

ASSOCIATED CAREERS

Hotel managers who leave the profession generally go into larger areas of management, such as property management, administrative or financial roles in large hotel chains, or independent ownership of smaller hotels and bed-and-breakfast establishments. The desire for greater control and less uncertainty were cited as the two most important reasons people in the industry seek work elsewhere.

PAST AND FUTURE

In the past, hotel managers were often the owners of the place and ran the establishment themselves. They decided when to fix crumbling walls and how much to charge; aesthetic decisions were less pertinent. In the mid-1800s came the advent of the water-and-rail traveling age, and not only were the very wealthy able to move about more easily than before, but the merchant class began to travel as well. This mobility encouraged the rise of the competitive and attractive affordable hotel, and thus arose the need for the permanent manager who could take care of all duties while the owner was involved in expanding, advertising, and popularizing the location.

Hotels have faced a consistent demand for the past fifteen years which should continue for the next ten. Positions as hotel managers should remain at about the current level for the next ten years as well.

QUALITY OF LIFE

Two Years

The first two years are a type of "apprenticeship" when theoretical coursework is fleshed out by practical experience. Hotel managers hone their interpersonal skills, and those who wish to advance sometimes continue their education in business, organizational development, or psychology. Duties may include arranging for regular deliveries of supplies and handling client complaints and payroll. Little input is expected on issues of design, decor, or promotion. Hours are long and pay is low; satisfaction levels, unsurprisingly, are below average.

Five Years

Satisfaction levels leap as hotel managers jump from job to job. Getting positions with increasing responsibility means two-to-three year stints at different hotels, learning a variety of skills—staffing, negotiation skills, event planning—and then moving on. The hours increase during these years, but few managers cite this as a downside. Their input on larger issues, such as hotel renovations and decor, begins to be taken seriously, depending on the individual manager's relationship with the ownership.

Ten Years

While many ten-year veterans have impressive resumes, few find cause to need them more than a few more times in their careers. As managers understand more and more about what type of hotel they like to run, they choose their positions more carefully. Tenure can run as long as twenty years at a single hotel. Hotel managers' input is significant at this level; most systems have been adjusted to be efficient and responsive to management and client needs; satisfaction levels are high. Pay can become extremely competitive for those who have good relationships with regular, high-paying clients. A mere three percent of hotel managers who've survived ten years leave; many view this as a job for life.

THE BIRKMAN LIFESTYLE GRID

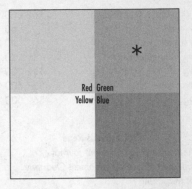

Red Green
Yellow Blue

This career is suitable for people with Green interests.

You'll Have Contact With

Bookkeepers
Food Service Staff
Guests
Housekeeping Staff

Major Associations

American Hotel and Motel Association
1201 New York Avenue, NW
Suite 600
Washington, DC 20005-3931
Tel: 202-289-3100
Fax: 202-289-3199
Contact: Daille Pettit

Hotel Sales and Marketing
Association International
1300 L Street, NW
Suite 800
Washington, DC 20005
Tel: 202-789-0089
Fax: 202-789-1725
Contact: Robert Gilbert

Council on Hotel, Restaurant, and
Institutional Education (CHRIE)
1200 17th Street, NW
Washington, DC 20036-3097
Tel: 202-331-5990

Human Resources Manager

# of people in profession	108,000
% male	60
% female	40
avg. hours per week	40
avg. starting salary	$22,000
avg. salary after 5 years	$37,500
avg. salary 10 to 15 years	$62,000

Professionals Read

Training and Development Journal
Human Resource Development Quarterly
HR Magazine
Crimson and Brown Reports

Books, Films and TV Shows Featuring the Profession

Dave
The Value Survey
Ask Questions, Get Answers
Matching Pairs

Major Employers

Smith Barney, Inc.
388 Greenwich Street
7th Floor
New York, NY 10013-2396
Tel: 212-464-6000
Contact: Corporate Employment

Sony Music Entertainment
550 Madison Avenue
New York, NY 10022-3211
Tel: 212-833-8000
Fax: 212-833-5024

Eastman Kodak Company
19 Commerce Drive
Cranbury, NJ
Tel: 609-452-7759

A DAY IN THE LIFE

Human resources managers handle personnel decisions, including hiring, position assignment, and compensation. Their decisions are subject to some oversight, but company executives recognize their experience and skill in assessing personnel and rely heavily on their recommendations. Although physical resources—capital, building, equipment—are important, most companies realize that the quality and quantity of their output is directly related to the quality and commitment of their personnel. Human resources professionals allocate this scarce resource, making sure that appropriate matches are made between support staff and producers, between assistants and managers, and between coworkers to enhance productivity, support the company's business strategy and long-term goals, and provide a satisfying work experience for employees.

A human resources professional in a smaller firm is a jack-of-all-trades, involved in hiring, resource allocation, compensation, benefits, compliance with laws affecting employees and the workplace, and safety and health issues. This multiplicity of tasks requires individuals with strong organizational skills who can quickly shift from project to project and topic to topic without becoming overwhelmed. "You're the last line of defense between your company and confusion," wrote one human resources manager at a small firm, "and sometimes confusion wins." Good interpersonal skills are crucial for managers at small firms. These managers spend about 40 percent of their day handling questions, attending budgeting and strategic planning meetings, and interviewing prospective employees. The rest of the time they take care of paperwork and talk on the telephone with service providers (insurance, health care, bank officers, etc.). At larger firms, HR managers specialize in one area, such as compensation, hiring, or resources allocation. Compensation analysts work with department managers to determine pay scales and bonus structures. Hiring specialists (also known as recruiters) place ads in appropriate publications, review resumes, and interview candidates for employment. Allocation managers match assistants, support staff, and other employees with departments that have specific needs. Sensitivity to both personality issues and corporate efficiency are a plus for allocation managers.

The most difficult feature of the human resources professional's job is handling the dirty work involved in the staffing of a company: Dealing with understaffing, refereeing disputes between mismatched personalities, firing employees, informing employees of small (or nonexistent) bonuses, and reprimanding irresponsible employees. Performing these tasks can be disheartening for HR managers, who are supposed to support and assist employees, and many HR managers feel that employees dislike or fear them because of this role. "What do you do when your job is to keep in touch with the company's needs but no one wants to meet with you?" wrote one HR professional. At its best, this job is about gauging and filling the labor needs of a company, helping to attract and retain the most qualified employees, and fulfilling employee needs—financial, benefits-related, and psychological.

PAYING YOUR DUES

There are no specific academic requirements for human resources managers, but most employers prefer that each candidate have a bachelor's degree. Recommended courses include economics, finance, English, psychology, labor relations, and organizational behavior. Each company has its own internal protocols, and most new hires are trained in them on entry. An HR manager must have strong interpersonal skills, and many employers conduct multiple interviews that test a candidate's ability to relate to a diverse group of people. Professional education is important in this field, particularly for those who are responsible for benefits administration.

ASSOCIATED CAREERS

Many HR professionals feel that they must focus too much on the financial aspects of their duties to allow them to provide the assistance they want to give. Those who leave the profession go into career counseling, industrial psychology, guidance counseling, and labor relations. Those who prefer the financial side go into budgeting, inventory control, and quality control management.

PAST AND FUTURE

The transition of the American economy from an agricultural society to an industrial society created the need for talented, creative workers and a need to manage these resources. Growing companies wanted to have more centralized control over hiring, salary structure, and resource allocation. Office managers handled many of these responsibilities at first, but they later transferred them to the created position of human resources specialist.

The future is bright for HR managers in both small and large firms. Managing a labor force entails an understanding of a number of complicated issues, and many companies have discovered that specialists handle the job more competently than do company managers. In addition, many companies are breaking their human resources departments into smaller, specialized units, such as for compensation analysis, benefits administration, or recruiting. This need for specialists should lead to more job opportunities. HR positions are expected to increase more quickly than jobs in the general market.

QUALITY OF LIFE

Two Years

Responsibilities in the field of human resources are significant in these first two years, as are hours. New hires are expected to learn HR practices on the job and to learn the company's protocols and procedures while carrying out their assigned duties. Those hired for their expertise in a specific area are carefully supervised but are given latitude to do their job. Most establish mentor relationships with more senior HR practitioners and learn effective techniques for managing people. Satisfaction is average; hours are long.

Five Years

Five-year veterans of small companies have become important staff members and many have discrete areas of control. Those who work for large companies have begun to specialize in health benefits, pensions, 401(K) plans, corporate recruiting, or another area of human resources. Many feel that long hours and hard work will earn them a position as vice-president or director of human resources and they work toward making this dream a reality. Salaries increase, but many who want larger salaries move to bigger corporations. Satisfaction is high for career-track professionals.

Ten Years

Many HR professionals assume managerial duties, with the goal of managing a large human resources department or directing a benefits, recruiting, or personnel department. A significant number return to graduate school to earn that added credential that will distinguish them from other candidates. Hours can increase for those looking to get ahead; others settle into their routine and enjoy using their acquired expertise in their area of specialization.

THE BIRKMAN LIFESTYLE GRID

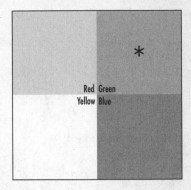

This career is suitable for people with Green interests.

You'll Have Contact With

Attorneys
Benefits Administrators
Office Managers
Recruiters

Major Associations

American Compensation Association
14040 Northsight Boulevard
Scottsdale, AZ 85260
Tel: 602-951-9191
Fax: 602-483-8352

American Society for
Training and Development
1640 King Street
Box 1443
Alexandria, VA 22313
Tel: 703-683-8100
Contact: Customer Service

Society for Human Resource Management
606 North Washington Street
Alexandria, VA 22314
Tel: 703-548-3440
Contact: Membership

Human Resources Developement Institute
815 16th Street NW
Washington, DC 20006
Tel: 202-638-3912
Fax: 202

INDUSTRIAL ENGINEER

A DAY IN THE LIFE

Industrial engineers analyze and evaluate methods of production and point out ways to improve them. They decide how a company should allocate its limited tangible resources (equipment and labor) within the framework of existing physical constraints (physical plant). Each company that hires an industrial engineer, either as a consultant or as an internal manager, has its own specific limitations. An industrial engineer must quickly become an expert not only in the manufacturing and production processes of the industry, but also in the specific culture, problems, and challenges that the company faces. This may mean face-to-face meetings with executives, extensive stays on manufacturing floors, and review of historical production data.

Industrial engineers receive information from others about what goes on in the day-to-day work environment, but they must also make their own observations of these activities. Many employees are uncomfortable being "watched" by industrial engineers, and industrial engineers often walk a thin line between being an analyst and being a detective. An industrial engineer's most difficult task is communicating his observations and suggestions to company executives, many of whom are emotionally invested in their traditional way of doing business. Industrial engineers must be tactful in what they say and in how they say it. In addition to tact, being a successful industrial engineer requires charm and the willingness to stand by one's recommendations even in the face of unresponsive management.

The large majority of industrial engineers—around 70 percent—works at manufacturing companies, and many have specific areas of specialization, such as assembly, raw-product processing, or administrative (paperwork) practices. Most industrial engineers have good working conditions, intellectually challenging work, and a high level of satisfaction. Hours can be long, but this tends to be outweighed by the satisfaction derived from the education that each different project brings.

PAYING YOUR DUES

To become an industrial engineer, you must have a bachelor's degree in industrial engineering. Recommended coursework includes statistics, computer skills, ergonomics, management science, quality control, sociology, psychology, organizational behavior, economics, finance, labor relations, and mathematics. Those who plan to specialize in manufacturing areas find it useful to study shipping, billing, and automated systems, along with computer science. Graduate programs in industrial engineering are primarily for those who wish to enter academia. Employers consider production or manufacturing experience extremely useful; they also favorably view administrative experience in large-paperwork industries (such as insurance, health care, or brokerage). Many find joining a professional organization supportive of their careers (some join while still in school) because it helps them to keep them abreast of important topics and trends in industrial engineering.

ASSOCIATED CAREERS

Most industrial engineers are consultants in the manufacturing and administrative industries. The expertise they gain as consultants or internal managers leads many of them to accept management positions in these industries. Since the core of an industrial engineer's job is the proper allocation of resources, industrial engineers are valuable to any organization with limited resources and large responsibilities.

PAST AND FUTURE

Industrial engineering began in the late nineteenth century with the development of time-and-motion study, which led to the standardization of steelworkers' motions and production processes and thereby increased their output. The field became known as "productivity management" in the early 1900s, and it flourished in America with Henry Ford's successful implementation of the assembly line. The industrial revolution galvanized support for productivity management, and academic institutions gave it the name "industrial engineering," which is what is studied today.

The future of industrial engineering is linked to the future of American manufacturing. Manufacturing is affected by tariffs, employment levels, inflation, advertising, demand, public perception, inventory levels, seasonability of product—the list is endless. Computers make the job more efficient, and will continue to do so in the future, but the fate of the industrial engineer is tied to these unpredictable factors. Industrial engineers will continue to be in demand, but their numbers are expected to increase only as fast as manufacturing in the United States increases.

QUALITY OF LIFE

Two Years

Two years into the profession, industrial engineers are most often working at a manufacturing or production company. They are overseen by more senior industrial engineers and have limited responsibility for implementing change. Daily duties include collecting data, putting it into usable form, analyzing it, and writing reports. Often these reports are co-written by a junior industrial engineer and a senior industrial engineer. Many young industrial engineers are asked to take an actual production position for three months to learn firsthand the daily challenges faced in that sector of production. Those who have gone directly into freelance consulting have been through training programs and work as part of teams. Hours are long for these consultants, and client contact in these first two years is limited. Computer skills are important during these early years.

Five Years

By five years, industrial engineers have experienced a variety of problems and worked on teams and by themselves to solve them. Many meet with senior managers to discuss suggestions, improvements, and budgetary decisions. About ten percent move out of the industrial engineering field into management positions by this stage. Those with people-managing skills may achieve the title "senior" industrial engineer and be in charge of managing others. Those in consulting firms lead teams instead of merely working on them. Hours increase; salaries increase, but more for those in consulting than for those in manufacturing.

Ten Years

Ten-year veterans of industrial engineering are in one of three tracks: Those who work for a single company have generally moved into management positions; those who work for consulting firms are at the senior-associate or vice-president level and have extensive client contact and supervisory responsibilities; and those who have worked for a number of firms continue to enjoy the day-to-day challenge that industrial engineering poses. Hours have decreased for all but the last group; salaries have risen across the board. Satisfaction levels are high for all groups as well.

THE BIRKMAN LIFESTYLE GRID

Red Green
Yellow Blue

This career is suitable for people with Red interests.

You'll Have Contact With
Inventory Managers
Organizational Developers
Production Managers
Quality Control Managers

Major Associations
Institute of Industrial Engineers, Inc.
25 Technology Park/Atlanta
Norcross, GA 30092
Tel: 707-449-0461
Fax: 707-263-8532
Contact: Marie Schultz

INFORMATION MANAGER

A DAY IN THE LIFE

Information managers regulate the flow of information, either electronically or procedurally, within and among offices. For many companies, the rate at which work can be done is limited by the rate at which information can be transmitted to the people who need it, so the information manager fills a critical role: To rapidly and accurately disseminate information to people who need it while maintaining security and creating a structure flexible enough to allow for company expansion or contraction. IMs work closely with all departments of a company and many spend significant time analyzing a company's needs and historical practices before implementing any changes.

IMs are often hired as a result of a critical information failure on an important project. In these circumstances, they may have to deal with the resentment of managers who are used to communicating in a certain way and who are reluctant to fully describe their job responsibilities for fear of being blamed for the problem. IMs find it helpful to act as educators, and strong interpersonal skills are an advantage to them. IMs are also hired for their technical expertise and work as MIS (management information system) specialists to connect physically remote locations through telephone lines, to network existing stand-alone computers, or to coordinate telephone and data systems throughout a building. IMs specialize in management analysis or physical systems early in their career.

The most surprising problem IMs face is not a practical one—their educational training and practical experience prepare them for most situations that they will encounter—it is with the level of satisfaction. Information managers report that their level of satisfaction seems to decrease the longer they are in their career. Some said this is because the challenges aren't that challenging anymore; a few wrote that they expected the profession to lead to other careers and for them, it did not; one mentioned that the defensiveness he encountered on a day-to-day basis was downright offensive. To be a successful IM you have to listen well, think clearly, analyze carefully, know the options available to you—and have a thick skin.

PAYING YOUR DUES

Employers in the industry strongly recommend that applicants have a bachelor's degree, preferably in a related field such as information systems, computer science, logic, organizational behavior, business or communications. Many of the IMs we contacted had more than one degree. Those who intend to teach need to go to graduate school, and in this case, it is customary to obtain a Ph.D. in information systems. Those interested in electronic communication systems should be well versed in computer science and its organizational applications. Sole information managers at a company and leaders of teams of information managers need good interpersonal and writing skills.

ASSOCIATED CAREERS

Information managers are either people-savvy or computer literate or both, and those who leave the field translate these skills into other professions. A number become production managers, efficiency experts, or inventory control managers. Those who are computer literate become LAN (local area network) administrators, computer consultants, and security consultants for computer concerns.

PAST AND FUTURE

Information managers can trace their roots back to the supermarket shelf. In the 1960s, Japanese auto manufacturers, looking for a competitive advantage, were impressed with the system of inventory control American supermarkets used to restock their shelves. They applied this system to their production lines and saw an immediate rise in productivity. American companies experiencing the same information backlogs as Japanese companies applied the "just-in-time" inventory control system to information management, also with success. Information management studies began in earnest in the mid-1970s. Today, nearly all graduate schools of business offer these studies.

The importance of information managers to the functioning of American business is growing. Job opportunities are expected to increase, but many information managers will be hired on a contract basis rather than as full-time employees. Managers justify this approach by saying that information science is most effective when applied by different people with different approaches, each one fine-tuning the last one's work.

QUALITY OF LIFE

Two Years

Information managers work as assistants, learning the intricacies of their company's information needs. Computer-, voice-, and data-specialized information managers examine and research existing systems and make recommendations for improving them. Some information managers choose an area of specialization during the first two years. Those who analyze large information structures spend significant time in meetings, learning each person's approach and how it increases or decreases efficiency. Hours are long and salaries are average. Satisfaction is high.

Five Years

Those who've been in the profession for five years have made significant recommendations to their employers and have been given additional responsibilities. Many are consulted on large projects. Most see results from their work by this point. A number have entered graduate school and then leave the field upon completion of their studies. Satisfaction dips even as salaries rise; hours remain the same.

Ten Years

Ten-year veterans have a more flexible schedule than those newer to the profession, and many use the time to expand their managerial skills. A number encounter limits in how far they can rise without a different skill set. Satisfaction falls significantly and many leave the profession. Salaries rise; hours stabilize.

You'll Have Contact With
Computer Engineers
Computer Programmers
Production Managers
Telecommunication Specialists

Major Associations
Information Industry Association
1625 Massachusetts Avenue, NW
Suite 700
Washington, DC 20036
Tel: 202-986-0280
Fax: 202-638-4403

Information & Technology
Association of America
1616 North Fort Myer Drive
Suite 1300
Arlington, VA 22209
Tel: 703-522-5055
Fax: 703-525-2279

International Information
Management Congress
1650 38th Street
Suite 205W
Boulder, CO 80301
Tel: 303-440-7085
Fax: 303-440-7234

INSURANCE AGENT/BROKER

A DAY IN THE LIFE

The people involved in the insurance industry profess that they provide security for a living, since their product is financial protection in the event of a crisis or emergency. This protection is always in demand, and the insurance industry is thus one of the nation's largest employers, with over two million workers. Seventy percent of them are involved in administrative or sales posts in three main areas: Life, health, and property and liability. The life insurance agent collects monthly or yearly payments from a policyholder; if the policyholder dies while covered by the policy, the designated members of his family receive a substantial sum of money. Sometimes life insurance agents arrange for more creative benefits, such as college tuition payments for children. Ensuring proper coverage for hospital and doctor visits is the domain of the health insurer, who most likely works for groups of employers rather than soliciting clients among the general public. Some health insurers are employed by the government to enforce Medicaid policies. Finally, property and liability agents insure instances of damage done both to and by their policyholders. They must also be fluent in the world of health insurance since they cover workmen's compensation; an employee injured at work will deal with this agent rather than a health insurance agent.

Agents work for one insurance agency, whereas brokers work independently and sell policies through many agencies. Beyond this distinction, however, agents and brokers fill many of the same functions. Each meets with potential clients and advises them on the most appropriate coverage. When claims are made, they have to settle the claim equitably for both the client and the agency. Agents and brokers can be salaried employees of an agency or, more likely, work partly or fully on commissions on the premiums they sell. Because most agents work on commission, they must spend quite a bit of time networking and finding new customers. Some large agencies cover all areas under one of the three divisions, while smaller ones specialize in one area, car insurance, for instance. Besides keeping up with customers and courting new ones, insurance agents and brokers have administrative tasks to do, such as keeping records of sales. Lucky and successful agents will have a staff to handle these matters.

PAYING YOUR DUES

Life and health insurance agents and brokers must be licensed by their state, which means passing an insurance examination. Agents who sell investment-oriented policies must also be licensed by the National Association of Securities Dealers or the Securities and Exchange Commission. While a college degree is not necessary for these positions, many agencies are seeking college-educated applicants, and a degree is an especially good idea if you want to advance to managerial positions. Some agencies even offer training programs for undergraduates, in the hope that students will work part time while in school and become full members of the company upon graduation. Some of these programs even provide tuition reimbursement for students employed with their agencies.

ASSOCIATED CAREERS

Occasionally insurance agents have dual professions—some property insurance agents are also real estate agents, for example. Field representatives attempt to generate new business for agents and brokers. They conduct and attend insurance conferences in order to remain fluent in the latest topics in insurance. At times field representatives will educate insurers about advancements in the field.

The most prestigious title in the insurance industry is held by the underwriter, who has the stressful task of reading applications that are submitted by agents to determine whether the agency should accept the risk a particular client presents. Underwriters depend on studies done by actuaries that determine levels of risk. Insurance adjusters are also players in the industry. When an accident occurs, an adjuster visits the site to asses the damage and determine the funds the insurer will award.

PAST AND FUTURE

The concept of insurance has been evolving as long as there have been communities. Thousands of years ago, for example, a form of insurance began in China when people shipped goods across the sea in sometimes hazardous conditions. Boat owners began putting a little bit of each owner's cargo in every boat, so that if one boat sank, each owner would be sure that most of his product would still reach the shore. When European settlers came to America, each member of the community would help if one person's house burned down. Pitching in to help rebuild someone else's house, a community member was insuring that he would receive help if he suffered a similar loss. As society enlarged and became more complex, insurance began to take the strictly monetary form we are familiar with today. Now a person pays one amount, called a premium, to insure that if she falls victim to disaster she will be protected—at least financially. The agency charges the client a fraction of the rebuilding costs and is able to pay for any reconstruction by using the premiums of those who do not ever suffer any losses.

The insurance industry is continuing to grow at an average pace. The public's growing concern for security, an elusive concept that money seems to provide in an increasingly fragmented society, has fueled a rise in the need for insurance providers. Product liability insurance industries continue to grow as people purchase more advanced home technology. Changes seem to be ahead: Insurance may become more complicated and competitive as health care financing is rearranged, and banks may start underwriting insurance policies previously drafted by agents. Those working in insurance now have better than average chances for advancement into newly developing positions.

QUALITY OF LIFE

Two Years

Insurance agents are often frustrated in the beginning of their careers. They are just learning the ropes and do not have many clients. There is a lot to learn, progress seems slow, hours are long, and paychecks are usually small. Heavy travel in the least productive territories makes for a tiring schedule with relatively low commissions at the start. Cold calling is hard on the ego, as there is a low percentage of sales or even responses.

Five Years

Those agents that remain at this time find that they are working long hours to generate even greater numbers of clients. They are relieved by the familiarity of the position and enjoy seeing the occasional high paycheck. By now, a productive agent will have "graduated" to a better sales territory and will be rewarded with higher commissions. Some will make the transition to the home-office and perhaps manage a regional sales staff.

Ten Years

Many agents break away from their firms to become independent brokers. Those with field and managerial experience at a good firm and a solid client base can command high annual income. Others seek advancement by gravitating to the field of underwriting, becoming an adjuster.

THE BIRKMAN LIFESTYLE GRID

This career is suitable for people with Green interests.

You'll Have Contact With

Actuaries
Attorneys
Bankers
Policy Holders

Major Associations

National Association of Life Underwriters
1922 F Street, NW
Washington, DC 20006
Tel: 202-331-6009
Fax: 202-835-9600
Contact: Public Relations

National Association of
Professional Insurance Agents
400 North Washington Street
Alexandria, VA 22314
Tel: 703-836-9340
Fax: 703-836-1314
Contact: Public Affairs

Society of Certified Insurance Counselors
3630 North Hills Drive
Austin, TX 78731
Tel: 512-345-7932
Fax: 512-343-2167

INTERIOR DESIGNER

A DAY IN THE LIFE

An interior designer is responsible for the interior design, decoration and functionality of a client's space, whether the space is commercial, industrial or residential. Interior designers work closely with architects and clients to determine the structure of a space, the needs of the occupants, and the style that best suits both. The position is a combination of engineer and artist, and it takes a unique type of mind to handle both of those concepts well. Interior designers have to be good with more than color, fabric, and furniture; interior designers must know materials, have budgeting skills, communicate well and oversee the ordering, installation and maintenance of all objects that define a space. They also have to know about electrical capacity, safety, and construction. This broader range of required knowledge distinguishes them from interior decorators.

Interior designers have to be able to work with contractors and clients alike, planning and implementing all aesthetic and functional decisions, from faucet handles to miles of carpeting—and all this usually must be done within a fixed budget. Interior designers are hired for their expertise in a variety of styles and approaches, not merely their own personal vision. Therefore, they have to be able to balance their own tastes and their clients' tastes—and be willing to put their clients' tastes first. This requirement can be frustrating at first for many who enter the profession.

Interior designers are often asked to begin their planning before construction of a space is finished; this means that they must be good at scheduling and comfortable reading blueprints. This element of the job comes as a surprise to many new interior designers, who expect to have less of an administrative and technical role and more of a role in influencing the overall feel and appearance of a space. Those who thrive in the industry say this ability to balance the practical with the aesthetic is crucial to being a successful interior designer. Interior design is hard work, but those who do it well find the work very satisfying.

PAYING YOUR DUES

The academic and professional requirements for most areas of design are fairly general, with the emphasis on portfolio development and professional experience. However, interior design has nationally standardized requirements. Interior designers must have a bachelor's degree. Employers look favorably on those who have studied engineering, design, and art. Those who want more specific study complete interior design programs. Across the U.S. and Canada, there are 105 colleges and universities accredited by the Foundation for Interior Design Education Research. Interior designers must also be familiar with federal, state and local interior design codes (involving such issues as capacity, flammability, and stress levels). To be federally licensed, prospective interior designers must pass the qualification exam given by the National Council for Interior Design. Professional organizations are significant in this field, and many interior designers find it helpful to join one or more of them. To become eligible for membership, one must have completed two to three years of graduate work, worked in the field for two to three years, and passed the federal licensing exam.

ASSOCIATED CAREERS

Interior designers deal with technical engineering issues and aesthetic design issues. Those who leave this field usually choose another area involving aesthetic design. Many become interior decorators, graphic designers, and computer graphics consultants. A notable few become architects. Few leave the arena of aesthetic decision-making altogether.

PAST AND FUTURE

Years ago, only the wealthy could afford to hire an interior designer. Most people designed their interiors themselves. With the expansion and popularization of the field, along with significant reductions in the cost of materials, even modest-income families may now hire interior designers. However, many still design their interiors without professional help.

In terms of demand, interior designers should have a bright future. Many owners and occupants of professional and residential complexes are turning to professional interior designers to shape their spaces. Five thousand new positions are expected to open up by the year 2005, a 12 percent increase over 1995. There is also significant age-pressure in the industry, and a large number of interior designers are expected to retire in the next decade, which will open additional positions for younger interior designers. Discussions about making the requirements for the profession more stringent have been broached in Congress, but no specific legislative proposals have emerged to date.

QUALITY OF LIFE

Two Years

Two years into the profession, many aspiring interior designers are working as interns or assistants, as entry into the field is competitive. A number of students make connections through relationships their schools have with major employers. During these first two years, many act as assistants, learning budgeting, competitive pricing, and client communication skills. Salaries are low or nonexistent in these early years, hours are long, and satisfaction may be low. Around twenty percent of potential interior designers leave the profession in the first three years.

Five Years

After five years, interior designers have significant professional experience and a paying job in the industry. The large majority have passed the federal licensing exam. Many have "associate" level responsibility for projects and work relatively unsupervised. Budgeting and cost-estimating are still reserved for more senior members of the profession. Many consider starting their own interior design firm during these middle years. Hours become more stable, and salary increases.

Ten Years

Ten-year interior designers have significant budgeting and cost-estimating responsibility, and extensive client contact. The majority of those who wanted to start their own interior design firms have done so by this time, and many can point to a number of homes, offices, or stores where potential clients can see living examples of their work. Hours remain stable, and salaries rise.

THE BIRKMAN LIFESTYLE GRID

Red Green
Yellow Blue

*

This career is suitable for people with Blue interests.

You'll Have Contact With

Architects
Carpenters
Textile Manufacturers
Suppliers

Major Associations

Foundation for Interior Design
Education Research
60 Monroe Center, NW
Suite 300
Grand Rapids, MI 49503-2920
Tel: 616-458-0400
Fax: 616-458-0460

American Society of Interior Designers
608 Massachusetts Avenue, NE
Washington, DC 20002-6006
Tel: 202-546-3480
Fax: 202-546-3240

American Institute of Building Design
991 Post Road East
Westport, CT 06880
Tel: 800-366-AIDB

INVENTOR

A DAY IN THE LIFE

The private inventor is one of the icons of American history, industriously working to create new products for the American public. Many of the commonplace products of today were the brainchildren of inventors. The images of Alexander Graham Bell inventing the telegraph and Thomas Alva Edison inventing the lightbulb in relatively primitive labs are firmly imbedded in American mythology (even though Bell was Canadian). To a large extent, those heady frontier days are over. Engineering and development costs have increased dramatically, and invention today more often occurs in corporate labs and research and development departments, but 20 percent of U.S. patents are issued each year to private inventors. A skilled inventor can still turn good ideas into significant sums of money, with the satisfaction of reaping the benefit of his own labors. There are great rewards in designing a product that is better than any that have come before it.

In addition to being creative, successful inventors must also be effective businesspeople. Developing a useful product is only the first step in the process. The inventor must also be able to negotiate a favorable licensing contract with an established manufacturer, or have the wherewithal to become an entrepreneur and go into the business of manufacturing her ideas herself. Designs must be developed which avoid infringing on existing patents, and they must themselves be protected from others who would copy them. Knowledge of the field in which an invention lies makes an inventor's life much easier, both in developing new products and assessing the value of inventions as they are developed.

As a full-time career, invention provides an uncertain living for all but the most talented. Developing new products is time-consuming and often expensive, and income doesn't start to flow until a marketable prototype is ready. Many work part-time as inventors, spending the rest of their time in jobs as engineers, corporate research scientists, or in academia. Still, a good idea can be worth pursuing; some of today's most successful companies were founded in basement workshops.

PAYING YOUR DUES

With rare exceptions, a background in science or engineering is a must. Many private inventors spend years working as designers for private corporations before they develop the ideas that let them set out on their own. Experience in product design and development is crucial, as is knowledge of the new product's potential market. Years working in industry or in academic research are the best methods to acquire the skills of the successful inventor.

ASSOCIATED CAREERS

Many inventors continue to work as research scientists and engineers while they develop their ideas, and these are the fields that most return to if they are unable to support themselves as inventors. Many return to inventing over and over again, accumulating successes and failures over many years. The first idea an inventor develops is often not his best idea, and the experience gained with each try can be invaluable to later efforts.

PAST AND FUTURE

Archimedes is the first legendary engineer. The notebooks of Leonardo da Vinci contain visionary sketches and plans for literally hundreds of devices—though many, such as his designs for submarines and flying machines, were beyond his ability to actually "invent" them. In more modern times, invention became central to the American self-image with the onset of the industrial revolution, when improved mass manufacturing techniques made it possible to rapidly make fortunes off a design for a useful new product. In turn, large manufacturing corporations arose, themselves often built on the profits of the inventions of private inventors, and built up the large research and development staffs who have largely displaced the role of the individual inventor. Every generation sees ideas too innovative or risky to be produced by large corporations, however, and inventor/entrepreneurs are likely to play a continuing role in the development of the American economy.

QUALITY OF LIFE

Two Years

Two thirds of all inventors never see any profits from their creations. By the two-year mark, the inventor is either making money—whether through a licensing agreement or private manufacture—or should be considering another line of work. These first two years are the hardest; developing an idea is perhaps the easiest part of invention, and many inventors find that developing business and distribution contacts is the most challenging aspect of the process.

Five Years

The inventor who is still working as an inventor at this point has probably succeeded in establishing manufacturing and distribution relationships. This makes it much easier to generate profits from additional inventions, and it allows the professional to spend more time focusing on inventing and less on pounding the streets looking for business contacts. Quality of life has likely improved significantly by this point.

Ten Years

By now, the inventor's operation probably resembles a small business. If inventions have been profitable, additional researchers and business assistants may be employed, and the inventor has probably developed a stable market for her products. Very few inventors make it to this point, but those that do reap the rewards of owning and operating a business which allows them to make a living on their creations.

THE BIRKMAN LIFESTYLE GRID

This career is suitable for people with Blue interests.

You'll Have Contact With

Patent Attorneys
Production Managers
Researchers
Technicians

Major Associations

American Society of Inventors
P.O. Box 58426
Philadelphia, PA 19102-8426
Tel: 215-546-6601

Affiliated Inventors Foundation
902 North Circle Drive
Suite 208
Colorado Springs, CO 80909-5002
Tel: 719-635-1234
Fax: 719-635-1578

National Congress of Inventors
Organization (NCIO)
727 North 600 West
Logan, UT 84321
Tel: 801-753-0888

INVESTMENT BANKER

PROFESSIONAL PROFILE

# of people in profession	40,000
% male	90
% female	10
avg. hours per week	70
avg. starting salary	$100,000
avg. salary after 5 years	$300,000
avg. salary 10 to 15 years	$1,000,000

Professionals Read
Money Management
Wall Street Journal
Financial Executive
Institutional Investor

Books, Films and TV Shows Featuring the Profession
Wall Street
Sabrina
All That Glitters
Barbarians at the Gate

Major Employers
Paine Webber
100 California Street
Suite 1200
San Francisco, CA 94111
Tel: 415-954-6700
Fax: 415-788-3271
Contact: David Stoldt

Morgan Stanley & Co. Inc.
1585 Broadway
29th Floor
New York, NY 10036
Tel: 212-703-4000
Fax: 212-761-0053
Contact: Patricia Palumbo, Office of Development

Merrill Lynch & Co.
CIBG Recruiting
250 Vesey Street 2nd Floor
New York, NY 10281-1302
Tel: 212-449-1000
Contact: Human Resources

A DAY IN THE LIFE

Investment bankers advise their clients on high level issues of financial organization. They manage the issuance of bonds, recommend and execute strategies for taking over and merging with other companies, and handle selling a company's stock to the public. The work thus involves lots of financial analysis, and a strong background in finance and economics is a necessity. Personal and strategic skills are vital to investment bankers as well, for they serve as strategists for their clients, helping them develop their financial plans as well as implement them. At the profession's highest level, investment bankers serve as crucial figures in the shaping of the American and world economies, managing mergers of multibillion-dollar corporations and handling the privatization of government assets around the world.

All this is time consuming, and investment bankers work long hours. Work weeks of seventy hours or more are common, and all night sessions before deals close are the rule rather than the exception. Still, the work is extremely interesting, and those who stay in the profession report high levels of job satisfaction. Investment bankers spend large amounts of time traveling, to pitch ideas to prospective and current clients or to examine the facilities of companies being purchased by their clients. In the office, they spend their time developing strategies to pitch to clients, preparing financial analyses and documents, or working with the sales forces of their banks in selling the bonds and stocks which are created by the investment-banking department's activities.

PAYING YOUR DUES

In general, an M.B.A., requiring two years of post-college study, is required to rise in the field, though entry level jobs in analyst programs are available to college graduates who want experience in the profession. Analysts perform much of the grunt computer crunching required in preparing financial proposals, though they often travel to sit in on meetings with clients and sessions in which senior bankers pitch ideas to prospective customers. After two years, analysts usually move on, either to business school or to another profession, though a few are offered jobs as associates, the position which investment banks offer to M.B.A. holders. In many banks, this is as far as one can rise without an M.B.A., though there are exceptions, and a few prominent bankers never went to business school.

ASSOCIATED CAREERS

Most commonly, investment bankers who leave the profession go on to financial jobs in-house with a client of their former banking firm, as financial officers and analysts. It is also not uncommon for bankers to move on to management consulting, a field which demands many similar skills. Some bankers get law degrees and become specialists in financial and corporate law, while lawyers sometimes leave their firms to become investment bankers. Bankers who have become sufficiently established, with clients who trust them and reputations for expertise in their fields, can become entrepreneurs, leaving their firms to set up their own investment banks.

PAST AND FUTURE

Investment bankers have been around as long stocks have been issued and bonds sold, but the current industry owes its form to the demand for expert counsel created by the increasing complexity of financial markets since the 1930s. Until relatively recently, investment banking was a fairly sedate field, but the 1980s saw tremendous growth in the field, as the increasing availability of complex securities and high-yield ("junk") bonds made mergers and acquisitions a weapon in the arsenal of every major corporation and made investment bankers like Henry Kravis and Robert Rubin extremely visible public figures.

Though the stock markets have their ups and downs, companies always require expert advisors to help them sell stocks and bonds and to make strategic financial plans; investment bankers fill this need. Employment in the investment banking industry should remain strong over the foreseeable future.

QUALITY OF LIFE

Two Years

During the first two years after finishing business school and taking a job at a bank, most investment bankers work as junior associates, supervising the financial analysis done by analysts and themselves being closely supervised by more experienced bankers. At this level, associates are learning the business, acquiring the skills they will need when they are called on to develop financial plans rather than execute them. They spend long hours running computer analyses, preparing the financial reports which accompany stock issues, and putting together the documents used by senior bankers to pitch ideas.

Five Years

At this level, investment bankers have significantly more responsibility and mobility. They have become senior associates or vice presidents, depending on the structure of the firm, and oversee the preparation of documents that leave the firm, and they begin to be involved in the more creative side of the business, working with senior bankers and clients to develop financial strategies. They have established specialties, whether regional or by type of transaction, and have begun to develop the professional reputations and skills which will enable them to attract clients. Hours remain intense, and still involve all-night sessions and seventy-plus-hour weeks, but fifth-year bankers begin to have more control over their schedules. They have more control over their careers as well, as the options of going to work in-house for a client or moving to another bank with a specific need for their expertise become increasingly available.

Ten Years

By this point, investment bankers are involved in strategic and financial planning, creating the plans executed by junior bankers and spending significant amounts of time developing plans with existing clients and attempting to attract new ones. Those who have not left to start their own firms or to work for clients usually now have ownership interests in their firms, and they begin to participate in firm policy and management. They are responsible, either alone or with other senior bankers, for overseeing a sector of the firm's investment banking business, and professional success is now largely dependent upon the banker's ability to develop a client base. Hours remain long, but there is significant control over when work must be done, and pay increases dramatically.

THE BIRKMAN LIFESTYLE GRID

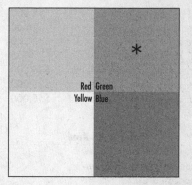

This career is suitable for people with Green interests.

You'll Have Contact With

Accountants
Financial Analysts
Researchers
Stockbrokers

Major Associations

Institute of Financial Education
111 East Wacker Drive
Suite 900
Chicago, IL 60601-4389
Tel: 312-946-8800
Fax: 312-946-8802
Contact: Lynn Murray

Association for Investment
Management & Research
P.O. Box 3668
Charlottesville, VA 22903-0668
Tel: 804-977-6600
Fax: 804-980-9755
Contact: Information Central Dept.

American Financial Services Association
919 18th Street, NW
Suite 300
Washington, DC 20006
Tel: 202-296-5544
Fax: 202-223-0321

JOURNALIST

PROFESSIONAL PROFILE

# of people in profession	58,000
% male	60
% female	40
avg. hours per week	55
avg. starting salary	$16,000
avg. salary after 5 years	$25,000
avg. salary 10 to 15 years	$55,000

Professionals Read

Columbia Journalism Review
American Journalism Review
Broadcast & Cable
The New York Times

Books, Films and TV Shows
Featuring the Profession

All the President's Men
The Killing Fields
His Girl Friday
Absence of Malice

Major Employers

Time Inc.
Time & Life Building Rockefeller Center
New York, NY 10020
Tel: 212-522-1212
Fax: 212-522-0077
Contact: Human Resources

Associated Press
50 Rockefeller Plaza
New York, NY 10020
Tel: 212-621-1500
Fax: 212-621-5447
Contact: Jack Stokes

The New York Times
229 West 43rd Street
New York, NY 10036
Tel: 212-556-1234
Contact: Employment Department

Cable News Network
1 CNN
Atlanta, GA 30303
Tel: 404-827-1500
Contact: Personnel Department

A DAY IN THE LIFE

There are innumerable types of journalists, from the local beat newspaper reporter to the foreign correspondent, from the magazine feature writer to the freelance book reviewer, so it is difficult to pin down the daily routine of the "average" journalist. Journalists interview sources and review records to assemble, collect, and report information and explore the implications of the facts. Journalism informs, educates, chastises: Do not underestimate the power a journalist holds. Remember Watergate, when Robert Woodward and Carl Bernstein, two reporters working for the *Washington Post*, discovered and published information that led to the resignation of the President of the United States?

Professionals must be able to report quickly and accurately. Over 80 percent of our respondents listed "time pressure" as one of the most distinguishing features of this job. Journalists must have a "point of view" while remaining objective about their subjects, which can be difficult; around half our respondents said that their colleagues sometimes got too involved in the stories. Interpersonal skills, excellent writing skills, and a reporter's instinct (the ability to accurately assess the significance of obscure and incomplete information) are essential to success.

The uncertainty of the daily routine makes it difficult to incorporate family, hobbies, and any regularly scheduled plans, but those who detest the predictability of nine-to-five jobs are attracted to journalism because "no day is a carbon copy of the day before." Long hours and chronic deadline pressure can be significantly negative factors. When an editor calls you in on a breaking story, you have to be prepared to drop everything; when you're on deadline, you can get crazed trying to write a complicated story in half the time you need. This "ball and chain" to the offices leads many to resent, and eventually reject, the reporter's life. Some journalists complain about being "under the thumb of Napoleonic editors who control your every word based on their own taste." (Editors are sometimes Napoleonic but more often they are simply perfectionists.) Journalists who are precious about their prose rarely last in this profession, since articles are often edited for publication without their consultation. Over 40 million people read newspapers in the United States each day and over 50 million people read magazines each week. The opportunity for your writing to reach a large audience is tempting indeed, and many find the initial low pay, uncertain and occasionally dangerous conditions, and chaotic schedule a fair tradeoff to be allowed to do what they do. In fact, many seem drawn by the excitement and challenge of these very conditions.

PAYING YOUR DUES

Most journalists have a bachelor's degree in journalism, communications, English, or political science. More than a few distinguished careers have begun at the school newspaper or at a neighborhood magazine or newspaper. Nowadays, many journalists come to the profession later in life after gaining expertise and connections at other professions. Journalism jobs are highly competitive: Credentials and experience must be accompanied by gumption and hard work.

Excellent writing skills are a must, as are computer word-processing skills. Bone up on proofreading skills before applying for any job. Foreign language skills may be necessary for those reporting on the international scene. Persistence, initiative, stamina, and the desire to tell real stories about real events are critical to the survival of the budding journalist. The best journalists have a knack for putting contemporary events into historical perspective.

ASSOCIATED CAREERS

Journalists who leave the profession become editors, professors, researchers, and analysts. Many teach high school and run school papers; others take jobs in whatever industry they once covered as a reporter. Those who leave the field usually do so because of the uncertain lifestyle and the long hours.

PAST AND FUTURE

The first American newspaper was printed in 1690 and quashed four days later. The growth of journalism has been astounding: Since 1776, the number of daily newspapers printed in the United States has risen from 37 to over 1,700, not including weeklies, magazines, and computer-generated newsletters.

Journalism, like most occupations concerned with communication, is becoming more electronic. Online services and electronic publishers deliver expertly written pieces twenty-four hours a day, seven days a week on the Internet. But somebody still needs to write those pieces. Competition for jobs will remain fierce, but specialized jobs should increase; those with unique skills, such as technological expertise or foreign language skills, should enjoy a distinct advantage. There are an increasing number of women succeeding in journalism, even though they still tend to be paid less than men for the same work. "Journalism is no career for a woman who wants to raise a family," advised one professional who complained that maternity leave is rarely (or begrudgingly) offered, and the pace of work precludes a normal family life if either parent is in the profession.

QUALITY OF LIFE

Two Years

Many aspiring reporters begin their careers by pitching story ideas to local newspapers and magazines on a piecemeal basis. Writers who can show clippings from school newspapers or other publications—no matter how "minor"—begin with an advantage if the prose is good. Aspiring writers may have to survive repeated rejections before a story idea is finally accepted for publication, and the income stream from freelance journalism is so unpredictable that many take more regular paying jobs. Most aspire to a salaried job at a local newspaper during these scrambling years. As at all levels of this profession, satisfaction is high despite low income.

Five Years

By now most journalists have held at least two full-time salaried positions. The most desirable jobs at this level are daily newspaper reporting jobs, especially those with a specialized "beat." It's hard for a journalist to break past the low thirty-thousands without daily deadline experience, and this is often what separates "the men from the boys."

Ten Years

Ten-year survivors in journalism still work long hours, but they have established a strong tone and style, enjoy a dedicated readership, and are finally making a wage commensurate with their abilities. The majority (over 60 percent) of those who began as journalists do not make it to the ten-year mark, dissuaded by lack of opportunity and lack of advancement. Many turn to editorial duties as well as reporting duties. A number switch their specialties after ten years in order to keep their jobs interesting and their writing fresh.

THE BIRKMAN LIFESTYLE GRID

This career is suitable for people with Blue interests.

You'll Have Contact With

Editors
Photographers
Publishers
Researchers

Major Associations

American Society of Journalists and Authors
1501 Broadway
New York, NY 10036
Tel: 212-997-0947
Fax: 212-768-7414

The Newspaper Guild
8611 Second Avenue
Silver Spring, MD 20910
Tel: 301-585-2990
Fax: 301-585-0668
Contact: Research Dept.

Society of Professional Journalists
16 South Jackson
Greencastle, IN 46135
Tel: 317-653-3333
Fax: 317-653-4631

Investigating Reporter and Editors (IRE)
University of Missouri
26A Walter Williams Hall
Columbia, MO 65211
Tel: 314-882-2042

National Federation of Press Women
P.O. Box 99
Blue Spring, MO 64103

LABOR RELATIONS SPECIALIST

A DAY IN THE LIFE

Labor relations specialists negotiate contracts, including compensation rates, benefits, working conditions, and rates of advancement, between workers and managers. "If you're doing your job right, no one likes you, but everyone is happy with the deal," said one ten-year veteran of labor relations. This ability to act as the lodestone for others' discontent is important to the success of eventual agreements. Those who are most successful in this occupation are able to see creative alternatives that satisfy the needs of one group without eroding the needs of another. In some cases, these "win/win" scenarios are difficult or impossible to achieve; the smart labor relations specialist enlists both sides in the quest for such solutions. A labor relations expert trades on his reputation and integrity, which can bring disparate groups together, and his ability to conclude deals. Everything else is secondary.

Most of the work a labor relations specialist does happens before anyone sits down at a table. A labor relations specialist is an educator on behalf of either the labor or management side and occasionally both. Education about the needs and abilities of either side is critical to not only the successful completion of single negotiations, but also for the long-term relationship between negotiating parties. Current thoughts on negotiation see most ongoing relationships as long-term "partnerships" that need to be maintained and nurtured. Labor relations specialists review documents and meet with members of other parties daily to assess their needs and abilities. A significant 45 percent of time at the office is spent on the telephone, discussing details, histories, and possible alternatives. Face-to-face meetings are less common than telephone consultations.

Labor relations experts analyze compensation rates, labor needs, and market research, and examine prior contracts between employers and employees. They must be skilled at seeing both details of the specific negotiations and the larger context into which these negotiations must be placed. This bifocal vision takes time to develop; over half the professional labor relationship experts we surveyed mentioned that given the opportunity, they would redo most of the negotiations they handled in the first five years of their careers.

PAYING YOUR DUES

In few other careers are the requirements for entry so debated. Some feel that an undergraduate background in personnel relations, labor economics, industrial psychology, or sociology are critical to success in this field. Others think that an M.B.A. and legal training are the best preparation. A third group feels that the industry should model itself more on apprenticeship programs and people should learn by sitting in on negotiations and discussions, and reviewing past negotiations and solutions. All agree that an undergraduate degree which demonstrates the ability to communicate clearly and argue persuasively is an advantage. For those entering government labor relations, coursework in government issues would be helpful. Graduate level coursework in industrial relations, economics, law, or history can be advantageous. While you may feel that all this studying should prepare you for serious responsibilities right away, you must realize that competitive entry-level positions may entail fairly lowly work, including library research, computer analysis, and general assistant duties, from scheduling lunches to "ordering office furniture," as one respondent mentioned.

ASSOCIATED CAREERS

Labor relations specialists have to become experts in a variety of industries to do their jobs properly; once experts, many choose to assume more certain, and less acrimonious, roles as advisors in those professions. A number go into government service, and a large portion who are attorneys return to practice in labor litigation on either the managers' or workers' side. Some become authors, lecturers, and teachers in the field of industrial relations.

PAST AND FUTURE

Unions came into their own in the 1930s, after decades of fighting to address the powerlessness of America's workers. Workers were inclined to distrust management and management was inclined to respond to their own economic needs without consideration for the workers. This gap in communication created the need for the labor relations specialist, a third party who could identify the needs of the two groups and communicate those needs in positive, forward-looking terms. Among significant figures in labor relations are Samuel Gompers, founder of the AFL-CIO, and Jimmy Hoffa, who turned the Teamsters into the nation's largest union.

Personnel issues will become more important for both large and small companies in the future. Consulting firms which mediate between smaller firms and their employees are growing in importance and reputation. Shifting labor national headquarters and the general migration of labor will move the labor job market more to the West from the East and Northeast.

QUALITY OF LIFE

Two Years

Most beginning labor relations specialists learn under the guidance of a mentor or a group. The first few years are a period of education. Responsibilities are limited but hours are long; many professionals do research, review documents, and write summary reports. Pay is small, as is input to the negotiations—most prefer to be silent, watch, and listen. Successful labor relations specialists cite lessons learned in the early years, such as how to ask productive questions, how to disarm opponents' negotiating ploys, and how to set initial bid levels, as key to their future achievements.

Five Years

Five years into the profession, many labor relations specialists choose one side—labor or management—to represent. Some act as independent arbiters for private organizations, such as the American Arbitration Association, and hone their listening and judgment skills. Client contact, which in years one through three was minimal, becomes important. Specialists define discrete areas of responsibility for themselves, and many take a place at the negotiation table. Those who are successful build up their resumes by working on different deals. Others who are not yet successful stay in the background to learn the profession more carefully. Professionals assume the role of lead negotiator between four and ten years into their careers.

Ten Years

A strange phenomenon comes over a number of labor relations specialists in years ten through twelve—a number switch from their original side of negotiations to the other (i.e., from management's side to labor's side, or vice-versa). Salaries rise dramatically, as do client expectations. Hours and responsibilities increase, but more on a supervisory level than on a day-to-day negotiation management level. Communication skills and client skills are critical to continued success at this point. Those who cannot complete sound, sensible deals will find themselves moving to other professions.

THE BIRKMAN LIFESTYLE GRID

Red Green
Yellow Blue

This career is suitable for people with Green interests.

You'll Have Contact With

Attorneys
Human Resource Personnel
Researchers
Union Representatives

Major Associations

American Arbitration Association
140 West 51st Street
New York, NY 10019
Tel: 212-484-4000

American Compensation Association
14040 Northsight Boulevard
Scottsdale, AZ 85260
Tel: 602-951-9191
Fax: 602-483-8352

LIBRARIAN

A DAY IN THE LIFE

Librarians are the custodians of our culture's retrievable media—books, audio/visual, and any data or physical objects that can be catalogued and stored. The modern librarian is the manager of an enormous warehouse, and people rely on her to help them navigate the increasingly far-flung and voluminous world of data.

Research and computer skills are important, and therefore those who are generally less comfortable with computers find the transition to on-line archives much more difficult. Be prepared to work under real deadlines and significant pressure; those with corporate library jobs will find that although the salaries are higher, "if you can't do the job when they really need you, they'll show you the door." Librarians who specialize in medicine or law will find their professions more lucrative than general librarians, but the books won't be the kind you take home and read for a little casual relaxation. Especially for specialists, graduate studies prove invaluable for a successful transition to working life.

A librarian spends over 60 percent of her day working with people, either library patrons or other staffers and back-office workers. Strong interpersonal skills are required for those who hope to succeed in this field. "You've got to be polite even when you want to break someone's neck, which happens Monday morning about ten and lasts through Saturday at four," said one particularly dangerous fifteen-year-veteran of the St. Louis public library system. Librarians also work closely with their colleagues; they loan books, advise each other, and discuss daily work issues on a regular basis. Over 50 percent of our respondents called their professional community "supportive."

"I'm surrounded by books all day, and that's all I've ever wanted," said one happy librarian. A librarian does far more than sit at the desk and check books in and out of the library. A large part of a professional's job is research. The most cited positive feature about being a librarian was the sense of continuous education. Librarians are challenged daily to find creative ways of retrieving a world of different information, and how well they can satisfy these requests determines their success and satisfaction in the profession.

PAYING YOUR DUES

A bachelor's degree is required and a master's in Library Science (MLS) is a real plus; some predict that Ph.D.s will become more common in the years ahead among professional librarians. Some states require additional certification. Only 59 schools offering graduate degrees are accredited by the American Library Association, so check before you enroll. Graduate classwork includes classification, cataloging, computer courses, and reference work. A number of graduate programs require students to read at least one foreign language. A strong sense of current events and contemporary themes is helpful to contribute to the direction of "library culture" and programs held in the library. A sense of aesthetics helps, too; it is not unusual for a librarian to design a library exhibit. Those wishing to become school librarians must also complete any teaching certifications required for teachers.

ASSOCIATED CAREERS

Librarians often move into specializations of information science, in acquisitions, cataloging, reference, and special collections. Others become antiquarians, antique dealers, collectors, or transfer their skills to the corporate arena by becoming research specialists. Others become consultants in their areas of specialization or perhaps library directors, who make personnel and staffing decisions, track inventory, set and follow a budget, and oversee the general operations of the library.

PAST AND FUTURE

John Harvard created the first library in the United States when he left his book collection to the Massachusetts Bay Colony's college in 1638; before long Benjamin Franklin had democratized the library concept by proposing that people have the right to borrow and use those books. Today it is estimated that over seventy-five million books, microfilms, and microfiche are under the custody of librarians in the United States.

The future of librarians is linked to three things: Public funding for the public library system, private donations which support libraries, and the growth of technology within the public and private library system. Recently, Bill Gates, multibillionaire founder of Microsoft, pledged his support for the networking of libraries across the United States through the Internet. In the future, technically skilled librarians will have a significant advantage. Knowledge of computers is already essential, and tomorrow's librarians will be challenged to master the power of electronic "search engines" and the brave, new world of access they are opening up for communications.

QUALITY OF LIFE

Two Years

In larger libraries "assistant" or "junior" librarians manage discrete library areas which focus on organization and tracking, such as the periodicals desk or reshelving. Two-year librarians sit in on meetings and are expected to provide input. These are educational years, spent learning the system and the people associated with the specific library you enter. Recognition is limited; pay is average, and hours are mediocre in the early years. Those in the corporate sector are likely to face long hours and potentially much more responsibility, along with higher wages. Many new librarians are overwhelmed by the responsibilities of being a librarian; perhaps that is why the profession has a 30 percent first-year attrition rate. But those who survive the first year seem very capable of surviving in the profession for the long term.

Five Years

The attrition rate after the first two years settles off at about five percent. Responsibilities increase, as do hours and pay. Daily tasks might include helping plan fundraising drives, looking into book-tracking systems, negotiating with vendors for library supplies, handling complaints and satisfying unusual requests for information. Most who wish to rise have completed their MLS by this time; they attend lectures and conferences and subscribe to librarian newsletters concerning issues of the day. Librarians start managing large staffs of reshelvers, checkout personnel, and administrators.

Ten Years

Ten-year veterans have significant input and responsibilities. They may work closely with directors in deciding budgetary priorities, steering the direction the library takes. Satisfaction is highest during these influential years, and those who stay in the profession for ten years are expected to remain for many more.

THE BIRKMAN LIFESTYLE GRID

This career is suitable for people with Blue interests.

You'll Have Contact With

Computer Programmers
Information Managers
Inventory Managers
Publishers

Major Associations

American Library Association
50 East Huron Street
Chicago, IL 60611
Tel: 312-944-6780
Fax: 312-440-9374
Contact: General Information

Special Libraries Association
1700 18th Street, NW
Washington, DC 20009
Tel: 202-234-4700
Fax: 202-265-9317
Contact: Resource Center

American Society For Information Science
8720 Georgia Avenue
Suite 501
Silver Spring, MD 20910
Tel: 301-495-0900
Fax: 301-495-0810

LOBBYIST

A DAY IN THE LIFE

Whether the lobbyist works for a large organization, a private individual, or the general public, her goals and strategies are the same. First and foremost, a lobbyist must be adept at the art of persuasion, which is the mainstay of her job. She must figure out how to sway politicians to vote on legislation in a way that favors the interest she represents. This means tailoring appeals to specific individuals as well as to group voting blocs, such as Southerners or pro-choicers. Lobbyists also occasionally lobby one another. When normally opposing groups find a common area of interest and can present a united front they are extremely effective.

Lobbying can be direct or indirect. Direct lobbying means actually meeting with congressmen and providing them with information pertinent to a bill being voted on. The lobbyist imparts her information with the help of graphs, charts, polls, and reports that she has hunted up or created. Needless to say, this is usually information that the politician might not otherwise have access to, that casts the matter in a light favorable to the interest the lobbyist represents. Sometimes, the lobbyist will even sit down with a politician and help him draft legislation that is advantageous for her interest.

Maintaining good relations with politicians who can be relied on to support the lobbyist's interest is key. While lobbyists and their employers cannot themselves make large campaign donations to politicians, they can, and do, raise money from other sources for re-election campaigns. To be successful at all of this, the lobbyist must be well-informed, persuasive, and self-confident. Personal charm doesn't hurt either, and lobbyists will often do social things like host cocktail parties, which allow them to interact with politicians—and opponents—in a less formal atmosphere.

Indirect lobbying, sometimes referred to as grassroots organizing, is a bit less glamorous. Grassroots lobbyists enlist the help of the community to influence politicians by writing, calling, or demonstrating on the organization's behalf. This means long hours spent on the phone and writing letters, trying to rouse the community to get involved. These lobbyists also report to politicians about the concerns and reactions they have gotten from community members. Indirect lobbying is also done through the media. Grassroots lobbyists write articles for newspapers and magazines and appear on talk shows to generate interest in and awareness of their issues.

Lobbyists tend to work long hours—between forty and eighty hours per week is normal, and when a bill is up for vote they will usually work through at least one night. But the least attractive part of being a lobbyist may be the profession's less-than-spotless reputation. While most are undoubtedly scrupulous, some lobbyists have been known to grease a palm or two where persuasion falls short, and the rest must suffer the public's mistrust. These honest lobbyists, who represent every segment of society, take refuge in the knowledge that they are working to promote causes they believe in.

PAYING YOUR DUES

Lobbying is a profession full of people who have changed careers, since relevant knowledge and experience are all you really need to become a lobbyist. There are no licensing or certification requirements, but lobbyists are required to register with the state and federal governments. Most lobbyists have college degrees. A major in political science, journalism, law, communications, public relations, or economics should stand future lobbyists in good stead. While you're still in college you can check out the terrain through various government-related internships—as a congressional aide, in a government agency, or with a lobbying firm, for example. Any of these positions will give you a look at the role of lobbying in the political system. After college the same holds—working in a government or political office, especially as a congressional aide, takes you to the front lines, but it may also be useful to start out in a law or public relations firm.

Many lobbyists also come from careers as legislators, as former politicians often capitalize on their years of government service and their connections to old pals still in office. This is the "revolving door" that recent legislation has begun to regulate (see "Past and Future"). Indeed, networking is the name of the game in lobbying, where people are hired as much for who they know as what they know. Someone who can schmooze at high levels will start his lobbying career from an accordingly high perch, while others face a long hard climb upwards. While there is no hierarchy of seniority as in corporations, this also means that there is no ceiling for those who do well.

ASSOCIATED CAREERS

Primarily, the lobbyist works with legislators and aides, both of which are career options for former lobbyists, with their inside knowledge of the political system. Public relations is also a natural choice, since packaging and communicating messages is the lobbyist's primary skill. Advertising, journalism, and teaching are also good outlets for the lobbyist's energy and talents.

PAST AND FUTURE

The term "lobbyist" derives from the location where early lobbyists worked—the lobbies or anterooms of political buildings. As James Madison warned in his writings, bribery is the constant threat lurking in the activity of lobbying. In fact, bribery was rampant in earlier times, but strict legislation resulting from public outcry has made a huge dent. Recent laws, for example, require companies to disclose their lobbyists' names and report all gifts given to politicians, and restrict the value of these gifts to no more than fifty dollars. Laws have also been passed to delay politicians from returning to Washington through the "revolving door" as lobbyists after they leave office. Lobbying cannot be legislated out of existence, though, as it is protected by the Constitution. As long as there is legislation, there will be lobbyists, but the profession is affected by the economy—lobbyists are often the first to be laid off during a recession.

QUALITY OF LIFE

Two Years

Unless a lobbyist obtained his job through well-established connections, he is struggling to learn all those names! Those who leave the field at this time usually do so involuntarily—they are fired because they can't integrate themselves well enough into the system. Those who remain are excited by the power around them and the lives they are affecting.

Five Years

Most lobbyists have proven their ability to get things done by advancing their agendas regardless of the party in office. Their diplomacy and flexibility have allowed them to climb the ladder, and they have earned their own assistants.

Ten Years

The job security of a lobbyist grows proportionally with his every year of experience. By networking his way to familiarity with much of Washington, the lobbyist has become increasingly valuable to his organization, and enjoys a high salary and the trust and respect of his employers and colleagues.

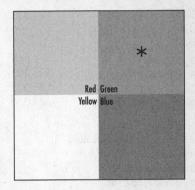

MACHINIST

A DAY IN THE LIFE

Machinists use metalworking equipment, such as lathes, shapers, grinders and saws, to form either unique and carefully shaped individual pieces, or multiple pieces of specifically tailored metal. Machinists work for large concerns that use metal in their final products, such as heating-vent manufacturers or automobile factories, or they work for specialty shops that take specific orders for needed parts and equipment. Machinists must be able to read blueprints and be familiar with laser and optical measuring devices that can test the degree of precision of their work. Some specifications call for shaping a piece of metal to within one-one-thousandth-of-an-inch accuracy. Machine shops usually employ between four and fifteen machinists, so those who work in this part of the industry should be comfortable working in close quarters. Machinists often know more about the metals they work with than do the clients who order pieces made from these metals. The machinist can and does act as an advisor, if the client makes false or misleading assumptions about the materials being used or the finished product.

Quality machinists have good vision, endurance, an eye for detail, excellent hand-eye coordination, a love for quality and precision, and respect for the tools of their trade. Working with metals can be dangerous for someone who is careless or easily distracted. Indeed, the biggest concern with being a machinist is the daily threat of serious injury. Few professions place employees in such regular contact with high-powered and potentially destructive tools. Surprisingly, however, the average injury rate in this profession is only slightly above the national average. Machinists must wear protective safety goggles and earplugs, and they must carefully decontaminate themselves after working with high-viscosity lubricants, as many of these lubricants are quite toxic. These worries, however, only slightly diminish the satisfaction machinists derive from shaping something out of nothing in an expert and craftsman-like way every day.

PAYING YOUR DUES

There are no specific educational requirements for the profession of machinist, but many employers prefer to hire individuals with a high-school degree (or its equivalent) and some work experience that demonstrates responsibility. Coursework that employers value includes mathematics, machine shop, and computer science. Employers also take a favorable view of blueprint-reading skills. The large majority of entrants to the profession are funneled through apprenticeship programs sponsored by unions in a specific area of machinist work, such as automotive machinistry, or agricultural machinistry. These apprenticeships are hard work, with many taking more than four years to complete. Programs generally combine shop work (6,000+ hours) with class work (700+ hours), with an emphasis on practical results. Those who successfully complete these programs are eligible for union machinist positions. To enter an apprenticeship program, many unions require that candidates be sponsored by a union member. Contact the appropriate union in your field of interest for more information.

ASSOCIATED CAREERS

Most individuals who choose a career as a machinist remain machinists, as few careers combine the precise detail work with the strenuous physical activity. Other professions with similar characteristics that machinists migrate to include carpentry, construction, and automobile manufacturing. Some machinists who have progressed to managerial status transfer to other personnel-management occupations, but this is more the exception than the rule.

PAST AND FUTURE

All complicated construction, engineering, and mass-production projects have required skilled machinists to make them possible. Robert Fulton's steamboats and Henry Ford's assembly-line of automobiles would have been impossible without the help of skilled machinists. It is not an exaggeration to say that machinists were central to the industrial revolution. The foundations of the aerospace and aircraft industries hinge on the precision shaping of metals. One individual who influenced the development of machining tools is Henry Maudslay, who developed the lathe.

The future of machinists has both positive and negative aspects. More machinists are expected to be hired over the coming decade, as aircraft manufacturing orders are at an all-time high, automobile plants are operating at significant levels, and housing starts are rising. On the other hand, more and more traditionally metal-based parts of equipment are being replaced by parts made of plastics and fiberglass. Thus, precision machining of metal may gradually become precision pressing of plastics, and unfortunately, these two careers are quite different.

QUALITY OF LIFE

Two Years

After two years, many machinists are still in apprenticeship programs, working as machine operators and handling tasks that require little expertise. Hours are long and pay is low, because beginning machinists spend a good deal of time in unpaid classroom settings or in partially salaried on-the-job training positions. Satisfaction is average. However, many machinists surveyed said the training programs teach new machinists a respect for their machines that contributes significantly to their quality of life of a machinist.

Five Years

Five years into the profession, machinists are fully certified and are working in an area of specialization. Many are involved in their unions as professionals, having had extensive exposure to them while they were trainees. Machinists with ambition and interpersonal skills work additional shifts and begin to gain experience managing other employees. The shift to managerial work can be difficult for many machinists, since being a machinist and being a machinist manager require very different skills. Salaries increase. Additional hours are available for those who want them. Satisfaction is high.

Ten Years

About 80 percent of those who are machinists for ten years are likely to remain machinists for life. Many become managers or shop heads at this time, and an aggressive few begin their own machinist company—although significant startup costs make this endeavor difficult. For most, salaries increase and hours stabilize.

THE BIRKMAN LIFESTYLE GRID

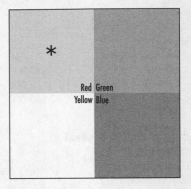

This career is suitable for people with Red interests.

You'll Have Contact With
Production Managers
Quality Control Managers
Safety Inspectors
Technicians

Major Associations
American Welding Society
550 NW LeJeune Road
Miami, FL 33126-5699
Tel: 305-443-9353
Fax: 305-443-7559

The Association for
Manufacturing Technology
7901 Westpark Drive
Mclean, VA 22102
Tel: 703-893-2900
Fax: 703-827-5298
Contact: Technology Dept.

The Tooling and Manufacturing Association
1177 South Dee Road
Park Ridge, IL 60068
Tel: 312-693-2347

MANAGEMENT CONSULTANT

PROFESSIONAL PROFILE

# of people in profession	210,000
% male	85
% female	15
avg. hours per week	60
avg. starting salary	$40,000
avg. salary after 5 years	$60,000
avg. salary 10 to 15 years	$80,000

Professionals Read

The Economist
Wall Street Journal
Institutional Investor

Books, Films and TV Shows Featuring the Profession

The Swami
Behavior and Management
Listen to Your Workers

Major Employers

CH2M
P.O. Box 22111
Denver, CO 80202
Tel: 303-771-0900
Fax: 303-741-5682
Contact: Corporate Human Resources

Covey Leadership Center
1958 South 950
East Provo, UT 84606
Tel: 800-331-7716
Fax: 801-342-8793
Contact: Lisa Stutz

Alexander Consulting Group, Inc.
125 Chubb Avenue
Lyndhurst, NJ 07071
Tel: 201-460-6600
Fax: 201-460-6677
Contact: Mark Hammer

Mc Kinsey and Company, Inc.
55 East 52nd Street
New York, NY 10022
Tel: 212-446-7000
Contact: HUman Resources Department

Bain and Company, Inc.
Two Copley Place
Boston, MA 02117
Tel: 617-572-2000
Contact: Human Resources Department

A DAY IN THE LIFE

Companies desiring to improve efficiency and profitability hire management consultants to identify problems and recommend solutions. Consultants' objectives can be limited to analyzing, say, shipping functions and then streamlining procedures, or their goals may be broadly defined, such as reorganizing a multinational corporation to take advantage of the synergies that developed when it acquired new businesses. "Sometimes you're asked to solve a particular problem, and you find that the problem is just a symptom of another problem, so you need to spend a lot of time at the beginning identifying where to start and what you need to do," said one consultant. The need to spend time at the beginning doing research, identifying areas of concern, and mapping out how the different areas of a business affect each other is often a difficult sell to clients, who want immediate results. "No one wants to hear that you've got to look at five years of data—they want you to tell them how to fix things today," wrote another. Management consultants have to be accomplished analysts, attentive listeners, and firm but tactful communicators. They are thinkers and problem-solvers who know how to make the case for change. Recommendations based on a faulty assumption or an arbitrary starting point of inquiry will be of no value to a company or the consultant's reputation.

Though even starting management consultants make good money (and income rises considerably with experience), our surveys indicate that candidates must be willing to sacrifice time from their personal lives. "You've got to be excited about solving problems, piecing together puzzles, and applying theory to real life. Because that's what you'll do. I haven't had a date in two years," wrote one consultant. Nearly all say that sixty-hour work weeks are part of the training and education process—some report up to 90-hour work weeks—and that travel and time spent on-site at clients' offices can be considerable. Consultants must get used to leaving home on Sunday on business and not returning until Thursday or Friday. Those who do management consulting in government agencies tend to be more serene about their lot, citing more regular hours and interesting work. Satisfaction is generally high in this career, despite its demands.

PAYING YOUR DUES

No specific academic requirements exist for management consultants, but nearly all employers require at least a college degree in a related field. Attractive majors include business, economics, statistics, mathematics, computer science, and logic. An Ivy -League education is a distinct plus, and many employers look extremely favorably on an MBA, a necessary requirement for upward mobility in this profession. In the professional world, very little guidance is available, so candidates should demonstrate academic, work, or entrepreneurial experience that shows them to be self-starters and interested in excellence in whatever they have chosen to do. Most major employers run their own programs to train junior consultants in accounting, internal policy, research techniques, and how to work as part of a close-knit, hardworking team. Professional certification is available, but experience is more important. The majority of MCs are self-employed and work in firms of ten or fewer people, but the highest paid ones usually do a significant stint at a large company, making professional contacts and building a solid reputation.

ASSOCIATED CAREERS

Management consultants are exposed to a variety of industries, to which they frequently migrate. Manufacturing, banking, and production are all areas populated by ex–management consultants. Other management consultants see their counterparts on the financial side—investment banking—making as much or more money than they do, and use their financial skills to emigrate to this field.

PAST AND FUTURE

Management consulting is a relatively new occupation, spawned in the 1960s by the growth of management sciences as a valid academic course of study. Business schools and economics departments across the nation produced a spate of literature on the subject of "management organization" and analysis of worker and company efficiency. To support this purely theoretical science, they began collecting and distributing data on organization, productivity, and capacity, giving companies a greater understanding of the forces affecting their organizations. Small consulting firms with specific areas of expertise developed in the 1970s, and the 1980s saw the birth of the management consultant generalist, who applied general principles of management to individual companies and emerged with recommendations. The work of these management consultants has been validated in the 1990s: Companies with over 10,000 employees who followed their consultants' recommendations experienced an average increase in five-year revenue of 21 percent.

Management consulting is a growing profession, and significant opportunities are projected for the future. However, competition for these positions will be intense. Aspiring consultants should prepare for this challenge by achieving strong academic records, gaining work experience that demonstrates their competence and maturity, and becoming knowledgeable about accounting and financial issues.

QUALITY OF LIFE

Two Years

Management consultants said quality of life is a trade-off at first. Most have gone through initial training programs and are junior members of consulting teams. Hours are very long. Very few have control over where they work or how long they will be there. Salaries—consisting of an average base-wage and significant potential for bonuses—are high for entry-level positions. A number of consultants said that in these initial years they learned not only how to analyze a company's management, but how to enjoy working hard and getting results with a small group of bright and dedicated people.

Five Years

Five-year management consultants are team leaders who manage projects instead of working on-site all the time. Satisfaction jumps as those who are successful receive salaries commensurate with their staggering hours. Consultancy work is an excellent "gateway" to industry or business school, and those who burn out early sometimes jump ship to earn that extra credential that will allow them to make the transition to senior consultant or partner. Duties include managing accounts, directing production of reports, and reviewing the analyses of more junior associates.

Ten Years

Ten-year veterans continue to find their work very exciting; why else would they be willing to work sixty hours a week after ten years on the job? One answer may be that salaries can be enormous. They are experienced, dedicated professionals who very much enjoy applying their skills to their work. At the most senior levels, management consultants involved in such sensitive areas as recruiting new business, working closely with clients, and directing company policy.

THE BIRKMAN LIFESTYLE GRID

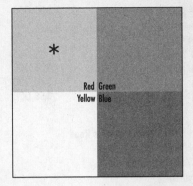

Red   Green
Yellow Blue

This career is suitable for people with Red interests.

You'll Have Contact With

Accountants
Organizational Developers
Production Managers
Quality Control Managers

Major Associations

American Management Association
135 West 50th Street
New York, NY 10020
Tel: 212-586-8100
Fax: 212-903-8168
Contact: Eric Greenberg

Council of Consultant Organizations
521 Fifth Avenue
35th Floor
New York, NY 10175
Tel: 212-455-8262
Fax: 212-949-6571

Institute of Management Consultants
521 Fifth Avenue
35th Floor
New York, NY 10175
Tel: 212-697-9693
Fax: 212-949-6571

MANUFACTURING EXECUTIVE

A DAY IN THE LIFE

Manufacturing executives come in two varieties: Production line executives and wholesale sales representatives. Production line executives coordinate production on the factory floor. They supervise production employees, check inventory levels, make certain sales representatives' orders are being filled, and oversee equipment maintenance and employee needs. They are based in manufacturing plants, where they work closely with employees, and put in predictable hours. Wholesale sales representatives, who make up over 70 percent of manufacturing executives, are, first and foremost, salespeople. They spend most of their time on the road, meeting with clients, recruiting new business, and checking shipments and customers' inventory levels. WSRs liaise with professional buyers, wholesale purchasing agents, and retail stores to make certain that goods get from the factory to the consumer.

WSRs are usually assigned a territory (which can range from a section of a large city to a number of states) and given responsibility for maintaining and improving wholesale sales in that region. To be able to negotiate with clients, existing and prospective, and keep the sales commitments they make, WSRs must have up-to-date information from their PLE counterparts at the manufacturing facility, including manufacturing costs, delivery costs, speed of production, inventory levels and product line options. "You've got to have credibility in your region," mentioned one WSR, "because all the buyers talk to each other and if you don't follow through on what you tell them, you're finished. No one will buy from you again." This theme of "credibility" was echoed by a number of our survey respondents.

WSRs work long hours, but their salaries are higher than those of PLEs. WSRs also have more control over their schedules. They have to meet with their clients regularly, but they can determine when and in what order. For many, the least attractive part of this job is the time spent on the road. If you're responsible for a large territory, many said, "get used to crummy motel rooms." Others said it's important to treat longtime clients with the same attention you give to new clients, otherwise they won't be clients much longer. WSRs lead a hard and varied life, but those who are successful salespeople reap significant rewards.

PAYING YOUR DUES

It used to be that anyone with initiative, sales skills, and negotiating savvy could find a job as a manufacturing representative. More and more, though, employers are requiring that new hires have college degrees. Marketing, business, psychology, or advertising majors have advantages in the applicant pool. Manufacturing executives also generate sales reports, analyze figures, and file expense reports, so any work experience that demonstrates comfort with numbers is welcomed. At larger concerns, all new hires complete training programs in which they learn about the companies' product lines and manufacturing processes, their competitors' products, and general sales techniques. A WSR may spend her first six months working as part of a team with a more experienced sales representative, particularly if the company manufactures a product with technical elements.

ASSOCIATED CAREERS

Former WSRs hold most of the upper-level management positions at manufacturing companies. A significant number of WSRs become professional buyers for retail and wholesale concerns, using their product and manufacturing expertise to drive good bargains. A notable few enter marketing or advertising or do demographic studies in their industry. Over 20 percent take up graduate studies; only ten percent of this group return as manufacturing executives.

PAST AND FUTURE

Manufacturing executives used to be the owners of their companies, the ones who knew the production processes best, who handled all negotiations, and who knew their reputations were on the line with every item that came out of their factories. In the 1860s, the rapid growth of manufacturing in the U.S. made this owner-intensive approach unworkable, and forced owners to delegate these responsibilities to trusted managers or "owner representatives." As internal competition intensified in these industries, formal training programs developed that led to the separation of manufacturing representatives' duties into those of the PLE and those of the WSR.

PLEs can expect job prospects to hold steady, since it is impossible to replace the human element in production supervision. WSRs, however, will encounter pressure from two sides. General manufacturing downsizing in the U.S., combined with the decline of small retail firms and the rise of larger bulk-sales and direct-sales houses, will decrease the need for wholesale sales representatives. In addition, the development of standardized-interface merchandise ordering systems, known as electronic data interchange (EDI) systems, will render some of the WSR's functions obsolete. Clients will be able to view, price, and order merchandise or samples on demand. Currently, only very profitable companies can afford these systems, but as their prices decline, WSRs can expect more and more wholesalers to avail themselves of this option.

QUALITY OF LIFE

Two Years

Two years into the profession, manufacturing executives have become either production line executives on the manufacturing floor or wholesale sales representatives out in the field, trying to build a client base. Many WSRs work forty-five or more hours a week as they establish relationships with the clients that were assigned to them and find new clients all their own. Satisfaction is average; salaries are low-to-average, depending on commissions.

Five Years

WSRs have gone through whole product and business cycles and have at times had to work very hard to maintain their quality of life. Salaries have increased, but many have exhausted the opportunities within their assigned region. Successful WSRs have moved to more promising territories; others with managerial skills have been assigned to oversee large territories with a number of sales managers. Hours flatten out, and satisfaction rises.

Ten Years

Ten-year veterans begin to make decisions about their future direction. Those who are excellent salespeople with good contacts often choose to remain salespeople, finally earning a sizable income from their hard work. Those who are tired of the long hours on the road, the frequent complaints from clients, and the posturing of negotiations, attempt to secure supervisory, managerial, or consultant positions in the industry. Salaries and satisfaction are above average.

THE BIRKMAN LIFESTYLE GRID

This career is suitable for people with Red interests.

You'll Have Contact With

Inventory Managers
Production Managers
Quality Control Managers
Service Sales Representatives

Major Associations

National Association of Manufacturers
1331 Pennsylvania Avenue, NW
Suite 1500
Washington, DC 20004
Tel: 202-637-3000
Fax: 202-637-3182
Contact: Membership Department

The Association for
Manufacturing Technology
7901 Westpark Drive
Mclean, VA 22102
Tel: 703-893-2900
Contact: Membership Services

MARKET RESEARCHER

A DAY IN THE LIFE

"People will tell you market research is a science, and there are scientific parts to it, but when it's done well, it's an art," wrote one market researcher about his profession. Market researchers prepare studies and surveys, analyze demographic information and purchasing histories, review the factors that affect product demand, and make recommendations to manufacturing and sales forces about the market for their product. This multifaceted job requires financial, statistical, scientific, and aesthetic skills, as well as common sense.

Market researchers work on projects that proceed in stages. At the beginning of a project, a market researcher may spend three weeks with other market researchers designing a survey and testing it on small samples of their intended population. In later stages they may define demographics, distribute the survey, and collect and assemble data. In the final stages, they may analyze survey responses to uncover consumer preferences or needs that have not yet been identified. Like all scientific experiments, "the assumptions we make are key. If we don't get those clear at the beginning it's going to affect our entire study," wrote one respondent. Those who specialize in public opinion surveys are particularly careful about how they phrase their questions, as a single misplaced modifier can dramatically affect the meaning of a question and, likewise, its responses.

Market researchers work on their own and on teams. Many find it difficult to adjust to working on a team. As one respondent said: "There are a lot of opinions about what constitutes the perfect survey. Four market researchers are going to have four different opinions." This diversity of opinion, while celebrated in the world at large, can make for difficult strategizing sessions and even more difficult interpretation of results. Good market researchers are careful listeners and flexible in their assumptions. They have to be good at communicating their results; a miscommunication between the market research department and management can lead to a financial disaster.

PAYING YOUR DUES

An entry-level market research position requires only an undergraduate degree. Employers look favorably on a degree in marketing and courses in statistics, mathematics, survey design, advertising, and psychology. Graduate degrees in marketing, business, or statistics are becoming more common among those in management positions. Work experience that demonstrates a creative intellect and the ability to work on teams is well received. Prospective market researchers should be aware that early jobs in the field entail significant drudgery—copying, proofreading, inputting data and the like. Those who are willing to carry out these entry-level tasks go on to positions of responsibility in the field.

ASSOCIATED CAREERS

Market researchers have statistics and survey skills, and many acquire business and production skills while employed by companies or lobbies. Market researchers who change careers usually become executives, advertising managers, demographic analysts (for the Census Bureau), and statisticians. Market researchers do well in any position that combines numerical analysis with interpersonal skills; many become economists or bankers.

PAST AND FUTURE

Market research as a distinct profession emerged out of the multiple product nature of large companies. In the 1950s, many successful organizations began to analyze who their customers were and what other products they might be interested in buying. As advertising and marketing techniques became more sophisticated, so did market research techniques. Companies found the customer information so valuable that they established in-house research departments to examine all aspects of a product, from concept to price, and to make recommendations to the company's top executives.

The job market for market research will be strong for the next ten years, as the brisk pace of manufacturing consolidation, growth, and development continues. Academic credentials and related work experience will become more important. The growth of new jobs in this profession should outpace the growth of jobs in the market in general over the next ten years.

QUALITY OF LIFE

Two Years

During these years market researchers hand out surveys, record information, set up appointments, proofread—any task that more senior market researchers need done. Although these tasks are not very stimulating intellectually, understanding all the steps required to conduct supportable market research is crucial to a market researcher's long-term success. Hours and salaries are average. Responsibilities and satisfaction are low. After two years, market researchers emerge from administrative assistant duties and begin to have limited input in market research decisions.

Five Years

By the five-year mark, most professionals are members of research teams and have earned the title "associate" market researcher. Many have sole responsibility for areas of a given project and meet with team members to coordinate the parts of a project. Hours, salary, responsibilities and satisfaction increase.

Ten Years

Ten-year veterans of this profession are senior market researchers, and often are more involved in policy and the focus of research than in project coordination. A number have moved into higher management. Those who remain in the field work more closely with upper management than with other market researchers. Hours decrease but responsibilities skyrocket. Mobility becomes significant, but opportunities depend on the industry and the market for the industry at the time.

THE BIRKMAN LIFESTYLE GRID

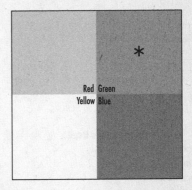

Red Green
Yellow Blue

This career is suitable for people with Green interests.

You'll Have Contact With
Advertising Executives
Marketing Executives
Researchers
Statisticians

Major Associations
American Marketing Association
250 South Wacker Drive
Suite 200
Chicago, IL 60606
Tel: 312-648-0536

Marketing Research Association
2189 Silas Deane Highway
Suite 5
Rocky Hill, CT 06067
Tel: 860-257-4008
Contact: Helene Weston

American Advertising Federation
1101 Vermont Avenue NW
Suite 500
Washington, DC 20005
Tel: 202-898-0089
Contact: Club Services

MARKETING EXECUTIVE

A DAY IN THE LIFE

A marketing executive directs the marketing of a company's products or services. Marketing executives know the company's product line, historical market, potential market, media costs, media response, and budgeting issues. Marketers often have to be intimate with a number of advertising media, such as radio, television, phone solicitation, mail campaigns, and promotional events. Their most difficult task is determining how best to take advantage of any or all of them to promote their product. In addition, "You have to know when to sell your own product, and when to mow down the other guy's product," said one New York marketing executive. Marketing takes three basic forms: Positive marketing (the benefits of your product or service), educational marketing (developing a demand for your product by educating people about their needs, such as mouthwash marketers talking about gingivitis), and negative marketing (revealing the flaws in a competitor's product). Knowing when to do which and how is both the science and art that marketing executives practice.

Most marketing executives spend significant time analyzing demographics, regional sales figures, and the competition. However, more than one marketer told us that in the end, marketing is all about "common sense." Many said a general approach to the industry is useless each product has one specific trait, detail or role that is unique and valuable, and all the marketing executive does is apply common sense to the promotion of that trait. Another marketer put it this way: A marketing executive has to be able to recognize "unexplored potentialities" that can turn a low-selling item into a large-selling item, and a large-selling item into a mega-hit. The pressure is significant, but it has one advantage: Marketers always know how they're doing, as tracked by an increase or decrease in sales. External events may drive demand for a product in one direction or another; it's the marketer's job to respond to these shifts and take advantage of them. Excuses for low sales don't go over well.

Marketers often work hand-in-hand with developers, advertisers, and production managers to ensure a product's successful promotion. However, a number of marketers mentioned that although they are called in to consult on production decisions, such as product design, color, and even box shape, "many of the decisions are made without our consent anyway." A marketer has to be creative, confident, and thick-skinned—marketing personnel get fired at an above average rate. Nevertheless, creative thinkers with the ability to analyze statistics and work out long-term logistical plans find sound homes in marketing divisions, where all their skills are needed to successfully launch a product or maintain a product's sales.

PAYING YOUR DUES

Marketing executives have no formal educational requirements, but most employers require a college degree. Valued courses include marketing, statistics, advertising, psychology, sociology, business, finance, economics, and history. Communication skills are very important, so any writing experience is appreciated. Marketing executives need know their product line and its unique features, so special requirements may apply for those in science, mechanical, medical, or computer-based industries. Professional education is the norm in this occupation, with many marketers attending at least two seminars or lectures a year. Certification is available from a number of professional societies (such as the American Marketing Association and Marketing Executives International), but employers do not require it.

ASSOCIATED CAREERS

Marketing executives often are promoted to strategic planning positions. Others take their skills to advertising agencies, demographic research firms, or public relations firms. Many return to school for M.B.A.s. Upon completion of their degrees, many head up marketing departments or move into positions of management. A notable few work for consumer advocacy groups and are vocal participants in the debate over fairness in marketing and advertising.

PAST AND FUTURE

Marketing used to be the prerogative of the owner, who made all the decisions about the product line, packaging, and advertising, and negotiated all contracts. The rapid growth of a consumer society has made that one-man-shop untenable, and most companies now hire marketing specialists to ensure that daily marketing management is handled by qualified professionals.

Many marketing positions will become available over the next ten years, as many current marketers retire, resign, or move into management positions, but the competition for these positions is expected to intensify. Candidates with more academic credentials will have an advantage, and those who engage in continuing education should be more secure in their positions than those who do not.

QUALITY OF LIFE

Two Years

Two-year marketing executives are assistants, market researchers, and junior marketing personnel as they make the transition from the marketing theory they learned in school to the reality of how the industry functions. Owners make all final decisions regardless of market research or sage advice, and that is one important lesson demonstrated to the new hire. Hours can be long as assistants assemble all data into forms that more senior, strategic marketers can use. Contact with other departments (such as advertising and product design) is limited. Salaries and satisfaction are low.

Five Years

The work has become more interesting and better paid, and responsibilities have increased. Many are now "marketing executives" or "strategic marketers" with either high-profile positions on marketing teams or lead positions on small products and promotions. Ambitious employees use their few spare hours to get graduate degrees in marketing, finance, or advertising to help them advance beyond their current positions. Within two years, a massive job-swap takes place in the industry—the seven-year-itch strikes hard, as around twenty-five percent of the workforce changes employers in years seven through nine.

Ten Years

As part of a strategic planning team, ten-year veterans review the reports written by more junior marketers and make recommendations to appropriate departments, with which they now have regular contact. They analyze less and communicate more, translating the work their department does into a form usable by other departments. Hours decrease; salaries and satisfaction increase.

THE BIRKMAN LIFESTYLE GRID

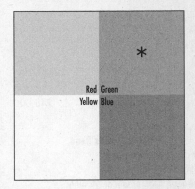

Red Green
Yellow Blue

This career is suitable for people with Green interests.

You'll Have Contact With

Advertising Executives
Market Researchers
Media Specialists
Product Designers

Major Associations

American Marketing Association
250 South Wacker Drive
Suite 200
Chicago, IL 60606
Tel: 312-648-0536

Direct Marketing Association
1111 19th Street, NW
Suite 1100
Washington, DC 20036
Tel: 202-955-5030

Promotion Marketing
Association of America, Inc.
257 Park Avenue South
New York, NY 10001
Tel: 212-420-1100

Sales and Marketing Executives
International (SMEI)
Statter Office Tower, # 977
Cleveland, OH 44115
Tel: 216-771-6650

MATHEMATICIAN

A DAY IN THE LIFE

Mathematicians generally work in theoretical mathematics or applied mathematics, and their daily routine is determined by which of these specialties they've chosen. Theoretical mathematicians work with mathematical theory in research and academic settings, rarely with a practical application in mind. Applied mathematicians apply mathematical principles to practical problems, such as cryptography, economic analysis and data-interference patterns. Both theoretical and applied mathematics are important in the real world; advances in both disciplines have led to breakthroughs.

Theoretical mathematicians are generally mathematics professors or graduate students, with stipends or grants to work on mathematical problems that concern them. The majority use computers in their analysis, and most work alone a large part of the time. "You don't really notice that you're alone," wrote one respondent about the solitude this profession maintains, "because you're focusing on the problem." Professional communication takes up the other large block of time in the theoretical mathematician's life; some estimate that they spend over thirty percent of their time reading professional journals, talking on the telephone with other mathematicians, and attending conferences on related topics. The applied mathematician works in a business setting, usually on a specific task. He is paid to use mathematical concepts to analyze behavior and improve existing systems. This can involve a lot of guesswork: "About ninety-nine percent of the time you're wrong," said one mathematician, "so you try again. Every now and then you get something right." Those with low failure-tolerance levels should think long and hard before entering this end of the profession. Many applied mathematicians said interpersonal skills are quite important in mathematics positions, and many wished they had taken more writing courses in college as their jobs require regular reports on progress and development.

Mathematicians said the best feature of their profession is the intellectual challenge of struggling with these numbers on an everyday basis. No mathematician thought he would ever solve all the problems—most of our responders would agree with the theoretical mathematician who wrote: "You can struggle with an equation for ages, trying to get it to tell you something, but if it doesn't want to, there's nothing you can do."

PAYING YOUR DUES

There are strict academic requirements for mathematicians. Over 180 schools offer Ph.D. programs in mathematics. About ninety-seven percent of theoretical mathematicians have a Ph.D. For entry-level positions in applied mathematics, most employers accept candidates with only a bachelor's degree in mathematics, but many ask that those candidates have cross-disciplinary experience, such as math/computer science, or math/ economics. These new hires input data, write simple analysis programs, and do basic mathematical modeling. To progress to a level of significant responsibility or leadership, many mathematicians find it helpful to earn an advanced degree not in mathematics, but in a related discipline, such as computer science, statistics, or materials engineering. A curious mind, sound deductive reasoning skills, and a willingness to approach difficult (and sometimes unsolvable) problems are all characteristics of the successful mathematician.

ASSOCIATED CAREERS

Many areas are open to mathematicians who leave their profession. Computer programming, cryptology, teaching, financial analysis, and economics all provide sound homes for those with mathematical training. In the course of their work, many mathematicians come into contact with these professions and find one of them more appealing.

PAST AND FUTURE

The ancient Greeks, Romans, Arabs, and Egyptians each made significant contributions to our knowledge of mathematics, including such discoveries as the decimal point, pi, and even the placeholder zero. Europeans made advances throughout the Renaissance, and the field truly began to blossom after the Scientific Revolution of the 1600s, which gave us Isaac Newton's invention of calculus, and Rene Descartes's concept of analytical geometry. The use of computers has reduced the time it takes to do extremely complicated calculations, somewhat easing the work.

The number of jobs in the profession is fairly evenly divided between theoretical and applied mathematics. However, the job market is expected to be sluggish, at best, for both groups. Industry professionals are being selected for both their knowledge of mathematical theory and their proficiency in related areas. Mathematicians who are well versed in another area, such as computer science, environmental issues, medical technology, or aircraft design are likely to fare better than other mathematicians. Positions for academic mathematicians are expected to increase more slowly than other jobs. Reductions in government spending and fierce competition for teaching positions are among the challenges that aspiring mathematicians face.

QUALITY OF LIFE

Two Years

Theoretical mathematicians are still doing master's work, earning their doctorate in an academic setting, while applied mathematicians are doing semi-skilled work in the business world. Those with doctorates can expect to work on projects as part of a team. Flexible academic deadlines give way to the pressure to solve practical business problems. Many new professionals spend long nights at the computer, trying to make the transition from school to work. Job mobility is high in these early years (nearly twenty percent leave the profession) as mathematicians look for an environment they feel comfortable in.

Five Years

Mathematicians are heads or co-heads of projects with significant responsibility for them. Many have added managerial duties to their job, and are mentors to new hires. Most welcome this new aspect of the job. Interpersonal skills become significant, with the ability to rise beyond this point determined not by intelligence, but by effectiveness and leadership abilities.

Ten Years

Many ten-year veterans become experts in a chosen area of specialization. This sudden directional burst seems to be a result of diminishing career pressure, as many are in satisfying positions, and a desire to continue one's education. A number of mathematicians become involved in professional organizations and the communities of mathematicians with similar interests.

THE BIRKMAN LIFESTYLE GRID

Red Green
Yellow Blue

This career is suitable for people with Red interests.

You'll Have Contact With
Actuaries
Computer Programmers
Electrical Engineers
Statisticians

Major Associations
American Mathematical Society
P.O. Box 6248
Providence, RI 02940-6248
Tel: 401-455-4000

Mathematical Association of America
1529 18th Street NW
Washington, DC 20036
Tel: 202-387-5200

Society for Industrial and
Applied Mathematics
3600 University City Science Center
Philadelphia, PA 19104-2688
Tel: 215-382-9800

MEDIA SPECIALIST

A DAY IN THE LIFE

If you were about to give a talk to a class or present something at a meeting, who would you turn to? Hopefully, there would be a media specialist around to help you. Media specialists get to work with multimedia equipment (such as television and video equipment), cameras, film projectors, slides, and recording equipment, usually on behalf of a school, library, or business. A media specialist is a type of teacher who works with multimedia equipment to make classes, presentations, and lectures more vibrant and exciting. They are sometimes called library media specialists, and, like librarians, they help teachers and lecturers choose and locate audiovisual aids which are used in classrooms, training sessions, conferences, seminars, and workshops. They acquire, catalogue, and maintain collateral material such as films, video-and audiotapes, photographs, and software programs. Media specialists largely work for schools and institutions of learning, but some work in libraries, government agencies, private industries and other businesses.

Media specialists working in school systems help teachers by finding relevant material to be used as teaching aids. They work closely with teachers in ordering course materials, determining what training aids are best suited to particular grade levels, and instructing teachers and students in the operation of audiovisual equipment. They also perform simple maintenance tasks such as cleaning monitors and lenses and changing batteries and lightbulbs. Technicians usually handle repairs and more complex maintenance work.

Government agencies, medical and industrial corporations, international humanitarian organizations, and other non-governmental organizations (NGOs) who need to train workers and disseminate information to the public require the services of media specialists. Some media specialists will find work researching and developing public service announcements run by health, welfare and social services, community action groups, and radio and television stations. Professionals keep abreast of developments in media and of learning methods by attending conventions, conferences and seminars, reading trade journals, and communicating with industry insiders. Much of their time is spent previewing products, ordering supplies, and organizing materials. Even though most media specialists have heavy schedules, their reward comes with the knowledge and enlightenment they help bring to students and other audiences.

PAYING YOUR DUES

A bachelor's degree in educational media or instructional technology is the basic requirement for this profession. A master's degree in these programs or communications, library science, library media, or education will benefit those applying for work in the school system. Many media specialists start out as teachers and with additional training move into this profession. Aspirants to the profession can greatly enhance their job prospects by doing volunteer work in media centers at local libraries or finding part-time employment with companies that sell or produce audiovisual programs and equipment. They must be able to operate different kinds of audiovisual equipment and instruct others on how to operate them as well. Applicants must be inventive, creative, and able to adapt to different environments. Since a media specialist's salary is a function of experience and geography, the specialist will have to work hard at his craft before salary scales will rise to its optimum level.

ASSOCIATED CAREERS

Since most media specialists start out as teachers, those who leave the profession often return to teaching. Even professionals without a basis in education can quite easily make the transition to this profession. With a Ph.D. degree, media specialists may find work teaching at colleges and universities and as directors of media programs.

PAST AND FUTURE

Technology has redefined the principles of education. Teaching tools such as charts and maps have been replaced by computers, CD-ROMs, videotapes, and films. As more companies set up in-house libraries and research and training departments, opportunities will continue to increase for media specialists who will be needed to locate, catalog, and maintain reference materials. Whereas teachers and students have more access to information today, the effective delivery of this information is now the job of media specialists.

With rapid expansion of technology and the explosion of information sources, the job of the media specialist, who is versed in the use of media resources, is virtually assured. As technology continues to drive the growth of industries, training will continue to be an integral part of preparing workers for new job situations and improving and updating current skills.

QUALITY OF LIFE

Two Years

The two-year media specialist has to learn about the business and keep current of all new developments in the industry. Reading trade journals and attending conventions, exposés, seminars, and workshops are crucial for media specialists who wish to succeed in the field.

Five Years

With considerable experience working with a variety of audiovisual equipment, developing collateral material, and acquiring and maintaining stock, the media specialist should now be able to command a relatively higher salary if he is in the right market. Media specialists who are working in the school system start to consider becoming media program coordinators for their school districts, if such a move is possible. At this stage the professional is still making the rounds at conventions and audiovisual outlets as well as scanning trade publications to keep updated. Returning to school for further education is a possibility for the professional in search of upward mobility.

Ten Years

The media specialist at the ten-year level is a marketable commodity with wide-ranging and current knowledge of the industry. If she is working within the school system, a move to the private sector will probably prove considerably more lucrative and challenging. Social, health, and welfare services may prove interesting for the socially and politically conscious. With higher education and a Ph.D. degree, the ambitious media specialist can find work as a college professor or director of a college media program.

THE BIRKMAN LIFESTYLE GRID

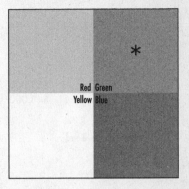

Red Green
Yellow Blue

This career is suitable for people with Green interests.

You'll Have Contact With

Advertising Executives
Market Researchers
Promoters
Statisticians

Major Associations

Broadcast Promotion & Marketing Executives
2029 Century Park East
Suite 555
Los Angeles, CA 90067
Tel: 213-465-3777
Contact: Tom Kuziora

American Advertising Federation
1101 Vermont Avenue NW
Suite 500
Washington, DC 20005
Tel: 202-898-0089

The Media Institute
1000 Potomac street, NW
Suite 301
Washington, DC 20007
Tel: 202-298-7512

Media Network
39 West 14th Street, #403
New York, NY, 10011
Tel: 212-929-2663
Fax: 212-929-2732

Media Network
39 West 14th Street, # 403
New York, NY 10011
Tel: 212-929-2663
Fax: 212-929-2732

MILITARY OFFICER

A DAY IN THE LIFE

Being all that you can be means performing any number of tasks. Whichever of the five branches of the United States Armed forces—Army, Navy, Marines, Air Forces, or Coast Guard—you choose to join, prepare yourself for more than a buzz-cut and target practice. Officers are leaders, organizers, strategists, and managers whose duties entail enormous responsibilities. Each branch of the armed forces has particular tasks. The Army is in charge of land-based defense initiatives. The Air Force supervises space and air defense. While the Navy flies the flag upon the seas, the Marine Corps provides them with land support. The Coast Guard plays a dual role. In peacetime, it works for the Department of Transportation, controlling access to American shores. The moment war breaks out, the Coast Guard works alongside of the Navy.

Some of the responsibilities inherent in a chosen military career are obvious, such as running a nuclear submarine or commanding a platoon of demolition specialists. Less obvious, but just as important, are the various clerical and managerial tasks that are essential to the smooth operation of our national defense and international peacekeeping. Because of military officers' versatility, training, and skills, they are valued in the civilian world. Many former officers find themselves in great demand at some of America's largest corporation. Military training is thorough, disciplined, and tough. Working conditions vary greatly, but in all cases, standards of appearance and behavior are regulated. While forty-hour weeks are common, many officers must work odd, long hours. The perks include extensive travel and health-care benefits, as well as family-oriented services like day care, job security, and a decent pension after a relatively short career. Of course, the gratitude our nation shows its soldiers cannot be left out of the package.

PAYING YOUR DUES

There are two tracks for pursuing the ranks of officer. You may enlist and eventually apply for officer candidate school, or you can apply to one of the highly-competitive service academies. The best known are West Point (Army), Annapolis (Navy and Marines), the Air Force Academy, and the Coast Guard Academy. Admission standards are rigorous. Officer candidates must undergo extraordinary training and pass a battery of tests, including the Armed Services Vocational Aptitude Battery.

The decision to join the armed forces should not taken lightly. You are putting your life into the country's hands. Ask your recruiter for the details of your service, including the length of your term, the salary you will receive, and if there are any educational opportunities available. Talk to current members of the service about their jobs. Because military fosters a clearly defined lifestyle a military enlistment is difficult to reverse, look carefully before you leap. Enlistment contracts can last eight years. Graduates from service academies must serve for several years after their graduation.

Officer candidates must go through basic training, a nasty eleven-week affair that builds muscle and character. Instruction and duty assignments follow. Much of military life involves the constant repetition of tedious tasks such as digging holes, but many educational opportunities are also available to the enthusiastic, competent young officer.

ASSOCIATED CAREERS

The military is a good training ground for a number of careers, and those who leave often have training in specific technical fields, such as aerospace engineering, computer programming, systems engineering, and inventory management. Employers in many industries appreciate the general discipline and leadership skills that the military teaches. An officer's training, skills, and versatility are valued in the civilian world, and some of America's largest corporations are anxious to hire former officers.

PAST AND FUTURE

The armed forces are America's biggest employers, and the path of advancement is a clear but long road to travel. There can only be so many generals, so promotions thin out as you rise in the ranks. Lately, the armed forces have been downsizing along with other big government employers, further eroding opportunities for advancement. Nevertheless, if history is any judge, there will always be a place for the military in American life.

QUALITY OF LIFE

Two Years

Few military contracts last two years or less, so this point in your career marks the end of the beginning. If you're in a service academy, you're still a sophomore. If you're in the service proper, you should by now have grown accustomed to the discipline of a soldier's or sailor's life.

Five Years

Many five-year veterans are eager to proceed to civilian life, where they can put their military training to use in the private sector. Nevertheless, most military contracts last eight years, so there is still time to benefit from what the military has to offer. Others have developed an affinity for military life and are doing their best to advance in the ranks.

Ten Years

Military personnel with ten-years careers behind them report enormous job satisfaction. The regimented environment of the Army fosters stability in pay and daily life. The constant reassignments may be tough on families, but the military makes strenuous efforts to accommodate newly-transferred personnel at all of its outposts worldwide. After ten more years, the military provides its retirees with a healthy pension and benefits package.

THE BIRKMAN LIFESTYLE GRID

Red Green
Yellow Blue

This career is suitable for people with Green interests.

You'll Have Contact With

Enlisted Personnel
Inventory Managers
Superior Officers
Training Officers

Major Associations

Personnel in the U.S. Armed Forces are to participate in military-sponsored organizations which promotes community, service and integrity.

Reserve Officers Association
of the United States (ROA)
1 Constitution Avenue, NE
Washington, DC 20002
Tel: 202-479-2200
Fax: 202-479-0416
Contact: Executive Director

American Military Society (AMS)
1101 Mercantile Lane
Suite 100
Springdale, MD 20774
Tel: 800-379-6128
Fax: 301-925-1429

Music Executive

PROFESSIONAL PROFILE

# of people in profession	127,000
% male	90
% female	10
avg. hours per week	50
avg. starting salary	$18,000
avg. salary after 5 years	$29,000
avg. salary 10 to 15 years	$52,000

Professionals Read

Billboard
Rolling Stone
Vibe
Backbeat

Books, Films and TV Shows Featuring the Profession

This is Spinal Tap
Motown
The Beatles
Great Jones Street

Major Employers

Arista Records
6 West 57 Street
New York, NY 10019
Tel: 212-489-7400
Contact: Human Resources

Cleopatra Records
P.O. Box 1394
Hollywood, CA 90078
Tel: 213-465-3421
Contact: Brian McNelis

SONY Music and Entertainment, Inc.
550 Madison Avenue
2nd Floor
New York, NY 10022-3211
Tel: 212-833-8000
Contact: Recruitment Dept

A DAY IN THE LIFE

Music executives develop and sell music. Some seek out new talent; some market new recordings; some expand a particular group's product line. They oversee virtually all aspects of the commercial recording process, including the production of companion music videos. Their influence is wide, but their is tenure short-lived if they fail to deliver chart-topping hits. It's a tough, competitive business. The music industry rewards the bold, innovative, and aggressive individual who can greatly improve the bottom line of the large recording companies that hire them. Music executives not only keep pace with musical trends and tastes but try to influence them in order to keep up with the continuous redesigning of pop culture. There are also music executives who work on their own; the independent producer has become a staple in today's fast-paced, ever-changing music industry which is tapping into all genres of music and feeding it to a highly impressionable and fickle young audience.

Music executives are in charge of the entire process of producing music: Finding new talent; choosing music to be recorded; arranging for studio recording time; hiring studio technicians, background musicians and vocalists, and engineers; and doing marketing and promotional work. Staff producers usually have production support staff, while independent producers often handle these tasks solo. An independent producer can make large sums of money and a name for himself if he can produce artists who consistently make their way to the top of the charts. An independent producer makes his living on what sells, earning three to five percent of retail sales, so he can literally embrace success overnight or be scanning the classifieds for another career after one disaster.

PAYING YOUR DUES

Music executive jobs do not come through the classifieds, nor are there formal courses that prepare you for such positions. If you're interested in the music industry, informational interviews and internships are key. Any experience in a music-related field, the ability to play an instrument or sing, vast and current knowledge of the industry, technical knowledge or experience in audio and recording technology, sound engineering, and studio setup provide a solid background to this field. Courses in business administration or management are particularly helpful to the independent producer. Because of the highly competitive nature of the business, newcomers must be willing to take just about any entry-level position with a recording company, independent producer, or recording studio and work hard and long hours to get to the top. Stress is a way of life for all music executives, so the entrant must determine his or her level of tolerance. Even after getting your foot in the door, this industry places considerable emphasis on your record in the field: What you've done, who you've produced, and how much money you've brought in. Thus an individual's ability to find and sign talent is paramount.

ASSOCIATED CAREERS

Music executives who grow tired of the cutthroat business side may leave for technical positions such as sound technician, mixer, or audio and recording engineer. Opportunities also exist in talent management, publicity, and as agents and road managers. Music executives who are also musicians can use their industry experience and connections to seek jobs as background musicians, arrangers, composers, and songwriters.

PAST AND FUTURE

The music industry has been around since the invention of the Victrola, when it became possible to record and sell music to the masses. In the 1920s, flappers doing the Charleston bought tons of records. In the 1950s, teenagers did the hop at diners and bought Elvis Presley and Chubby Checker. The music industry kept dancing with the Beatles in the 1960s.

Now, digital technology has afforded new developments in music recording. The long-playing record (LP) has given way to the digitized sound of the compact disc with its longer playing capacity. Splinter and crossover audiences have contributed to the expansion and the redefinition of genres in the music industry. In the future, music executives will have to be creative enough to introduce different styles and various fusions in an attempt to innovate new sounds. Despite the tenuous nature of the business, the music industry will always be in need of innovative, creative, successful music producers and other executives. It will continue to grow, and ambitious executives in search of the cutting edge will drive this growth.

QUALITY OF LIFE

Two Years

The music producer with two years experience is finessing the art of recognizing and signing talent. She's had a few hits and misses but is diligently making a name for herself. She is fine tuning the subtle art of choosing production people who can work well together. Most importantly, she is learning how to get the best out of her musicians' talent.

Five Years

Music producers still in the business after five years should consider themselves lucky. Undoubtedly they've sustained considerable successes on the charts and carved out profit-producing niches for themselves. Talent seeks out producers with strong reputations, so music executives do far less scouting.

Ten Years

Ten-year music executives are successful just by virtue of staying in the field this long. They have very strong reputations, and musicians come crawling to them for contracts. But in this ever-changing industry, staying on the cutting edge is the ten-year veteran's biggest challenge.

THE BIRKMAN LIFESTYLE GRID

This career is suitable for people with Green interests.

You'll Have Contact With

Attorneys
Accountants
Musicians
Promoters

Major Associations

Recording Industry Association of America
1020 19th Street NW
Suite 200
Washington, DC 20036
Tel: 202-775-0101
Fax: 202-775-7253
Contact: Lee Salen

Music Distributors Association
38 West 21st Street
5th Floor
New York, NY 10010
Tel: 212-924-9175
Fax: 212-675-3577
Contact: Jerome Hershman

MUSICIAN

PROFESSIONAL PROFILE

# of people in profession	225,000
% male	40
% female	60
avg. hours per week	35
avg. starting salary	$19,000
avg. salary after 5 years	$25,000
avg. salary 10 to 15 years	$29,000

Professionals Read

Backbeat
Billboard
Jazz
Spin

Books, Films and TV Shows Featuring the Profession

Amadeus
Fire and Soul
The Piano
Straight, No Chaser

Major Employers

Phoenix Symphony
3707 North Seventh Street
Suite 107
Phoenix, AZ 85014
Tel: 602-277-7291
Contact: Joel Levin

Geffin Records
9130 Sunset Boulevard
Los Angeles, CA 90069
Tel: 310-278-9010
Contact: Personnel

New York Metropolitan Opera Guild
70 Lincoln Center
New York, NY 10023
Tel: 212-769-7000

A DAY IN THE LIFE

Musicians include rock stars, opera singers, folk guitarists, jazz pianists, violinists, drummers-anybody who makes and performs music. Musicians are a broad group of artists who play musical instruments, sing, compose, and arrange music in a variety of settings, solo or in groups. They perform before live audiences, or make recordings in music studios. Instrumental musicians play any of a wide variety of instruments such as the saxophone, trumpet, piano, guitar, drums, clarinet or flute. A singer's instrument is her voice, which interprets the music, while composers are the creators of original music. Orchestra conductors lead orchestras and bands, and choral directors lead choirs and singing clubs. It's a tough field, but those in it usually feel an inner compulsion to play and share their music, so much so that they're willing to sacrifice a lot. "Music is in the soul...so I must play on and on...it's a given," says one saxophonist who finally signed a major recording contract. Some lucky musicians-orchestra members, opera singers, a few pop artists-make a living at their profession. A very few become rich and famous—Frank Sinatra, Maria Callas, Mick Jagger, and Natalie Merchant are just some examples—but most are happy just to be able to play for an audience once in a while.

The serious musician spends a lot of time practicing and rehearsing. "You have to constantly better your best, for you're only as good as your last performance," said one musician. Musicians also spend a substantial amount of time "on the road," traveling to and from performances, or just seeking engagements. Since most musicians' "gigs" are at nights and on weekends, those who don't fully support themselves through their art often take day jobs to foot the bills.

Musicians can play and compose for a variety of sources. Television, motion pictures, and advertising employ musicians to perform live shows, score music for television movies and film, and compose and arrange theme songs for television programs and advertisements. Theater orchestras provide live music for plays and other productions. Because live audiences and auditions are a fact of life for musicians seeking to establish a reputation or find a niche, they must be able to deal with their anxieties and deliver a quality performance in front of any gathering of people. Musicians face rejection all the time, but the most disciplined maintain confidence in their abilities; they can never allow themselves to become complacent if success is the goal. Most work at small-time gigs wherever they can—in clubs and churches, at weddings, birthdays and bar mitzvahs—while waiting for that big break.

PAYING YOUR DUES

The road to becoming an accomplished musician starts at a very early age and involves rigorous study and training. For the singer, training begins when the voice matures. And it never ends. Most other musicians start to play their instruments very early in their lives. Some musicians enter into private study with a highly reputed "master" musician, while others pursue a formal training program at a college or university, gaining a degree in music or music education. Talent, persistence, and excellent mentors are the keys to becoming a good musician.

For the recording artist, entertainment lawyers have become more of a necessity than even a manager, whereas musicians who rely mainly on live performance require only a road manager (if gigs pay enough to salary one) and an independent booking agent. Mastering the convoluted relationships among agents, managers, lawyers and other industry professionals is a job in itself.

ASSOCIATED CAREERS

Musicians almost never give up music completely. Even when they leave for more stable, lucrative fields, they often seek out nightclub engagements at nights and on weekends. Take, for example, Woody Allen, still playing his clarinet at Michael's Pub in New York on occasion. Some musicians find music-related jobs as teachers, songwriters, and even music therapists. Musicians with vast technical knowledge may find an opening in the specialized area of instrument repairs and tuning. They may also find jobs as music librarians, critics, and disc jockeys. Those who enjoy the business side may become concert managers, booking agents, music industry executives, and publicists. Some go into the sales and marketing of musical instruments and record store management.

PAST AND FUTURE

Music has been around since the beginning of time. Since there can be no music without musicians, their place is virtually assured—even if lucrative recording deals and a place in the limelight will continue to elude many of even the most gifted artists. As it is often not talent but public relations packaging that guarantees success, talented musicians will have to invent ways of selling themselves and their music to the public. Musicians able to compose, play several instruments, and arrange will find more employment opportunities open to them.

QUALITY OF LIFE

Two Years

The musician with a bare two years of experience grabs at any and every opportunity to play—school or community concerts, bars, restaurants, birthday parties, bar mitzvahs, weddings, and even funerals. The newcomer to the music world is up against a vast array of talent, experience, and abilities, so practice sessions continue to be as arduous as they were in childhood. There is no "corporate ladder," or any of the scheduled raises and promotions that go with it—from day one, it's about getting gigs.

Five Years

The musician with five years' experience is still but a young babe. Self-discipline is vital to the success of any musician, so practice and rehearsals continue to take up the greater part of the day. Work will supplement income from sporadic and low-paying gigs at nightclubs while the musician continues to search for regular work as a performer. Many musicians give private lessons or opt to take work in an unrelated field.

Ten Years

To the musician with only two years experience, ten years is considerable. But seniority, like talent, does not always translate into success or even modest recognition. The ten-year veteran is still practicing and developing his own musical style. Auditions, weekend gigs, and intermittent employment may still be the mainstay of the musician's life. The exceptionally talented have enlisted the services of an agent or manager to help find them engagements and manage their careers.

THE BIRKMAN LIFESTYLE GRID

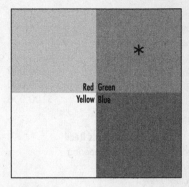

This career is suitable for people with Green interests.

You'll Have Contact With

Club Managers
Music Executives
Promoters
Publicists

Major Associations

American Federation of Musicians
1501 Broadway
Suite 600
New York, NY 10036
Tel: 212-869-1330

American Guild of Musical Artists
475 Riverside Drive
New York, NY 10115
Tel: 212-870-2310

Musicians Foundation
200 West 55th Street
New York, NY 10019
Tel: 212-247-5332

Nuclear Engineer

A DAY IN THE LIFE

Like most engineers, nuclear engineers spend their time working in large, hi-tech environments. Employment in nuclear engineering is divided equally between the Federal Government, utilities companies, and the research and testing units of defense and engineering companies. The Navy, with its fleet of nuclear-powered ships, is a large employer of nuclear engineers, as is the Nuclear Regulatory Commission. Nuclear engineers conduct research for utility companies to optimize the performance of existing plants, and they are employed in atomic research facilities like the Los Alamos National Laboratory and the Stanford Linear Accelerator Center. Nuclear engineering has become increasingly important in the development of new medical scanning technologies one of the few growing segments of the field.

These employers are all large, established operations. The research side of nuclear engineering can be extremely creative, but the field is best suited for those who won't feel confined in large, bureaucratic work environments. Nuclear engineers work in extended teams, and caution and risk control are the bywords of the industry—appropriately so, given the dangers of nuclear radiation. With the exception of radio-medical, nuclear disposal, and theoretical atomic research, a small percentage of total employment in the field, nuclear engineering is not a field marked by breakthroughs. The halt in new power plant construction has ended all but incremental, evolutionary nuclear power research, and atomic weapons design, once a booming experimental field, has lost much of its funding in the 1990s. The field does, however, offer extremely stable, secure, and well-paying professional employment.

PAYING YOUR DUES

Graduate education is a prerequisite for employment as a design or research nuclear engineer. Engineers must have at least a master's degree, which involves significant work in math, physics, and engineering design, while both private and government research jobs often require that the applicant have completed a doctorate in nuclear engineering. Typically, the educational requirements for an operating engineer are less rigorous: A bachelor's degree in nuclear engineering is one qualification, while others with only high school diplomas get their training through the U.S. Navy Nuclear Power Plant Program.

ASSOCIATED CAREERS

The skills and training of a nuclear engineer are rather specialized, though there is mobility within the various employers in the field. Military and civilian nuclear power engineers have similar skills, and the government frequently hires nuclear engineers with experience in the various nuclear fields it regulates. Engineers who have risen to positions of significant managerial authority acquire skills and credentials useful in the management of other large enterprises, though there is not significant turnover in the field.

PAST AND FUTURE

Nuclear physics dates to the 1896 discovery of radiation in uranium by the French physicist Henri Bequerel, but the tools of the modern profession date to the successful creation of a chain fission reaction by Enrico Fermi at the University of Chicago in 1942. During the 1940s and 1950s, nuclear progress was largely military, with the development of fusion bombs, ever smaller atomic warheads, and nuclear-powered ships. The first nuclear power plant wasn't built until 1957, in Shippingport, Pennsylvania, but construction then boomed through the 1960s and early 1970s.

Nuclear energy is currently America's second largest source of energy, only exceeded by coal, but concerns over its risks and over the environmental damage caused by radioactive waste have led to a complete halt in its expansion. No new nuclear power plants have been built in the United States since 1978, though demand for nuclear engineers to operate and maintain existing plants should remain steady.

With the advent of nuclear reduction treaties and lowered military spending, demand for nuclear-weapons designers has also dried up. The navy continues to employ nuclear engineers to operate its nuclear ships, however, and there is increased demand for engineers to dispose of military radioactive waste. In sum, nuclear engineering is not a growing field, but the decreasing supply of trained engineers means that those who are qualified can readily find work.

QUALITY OF LIFE

Two Years

Nuclear engineers, whether their specializations are in design or operations, usually work in teams. At this early stage in their careers, nuclear engineers are generally the junior members of their working groups. They have supervisory authority over less educated technicians in their labs, ships, or plants, but their work is in turn supervised by more experienced engineers, and they have little managerial responsibility.

Five Years

By this stage, nuclear engineers have acquired some managerial authority, whether it be responsibility for an element of a larger research project or supervisory control over a team of engineers and technicians in a power plant or military installation. Pay has increased, and these engineers have some responsibility for training other employees in their operations.

Ten Years

By now, a nuclear engineer has significantly increased authority and responsibility. In research, he is responsible, with other senior engineers, for designing experiment plans and supervising them. As an operations engineer, he will have a voice in setting operational and safety procedures, whether they be for a military or civilian nuclear plant.

THE BIRKMAN LIFESTYLE GRID

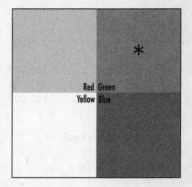

This career is suitable for people with Green interests.

You'll Have Contact With

Computer Programmers
Lab Technicians
Mathematicians
Technicians

Major Associations

American Nuclear Society
555 North Kensington Avenue
La Grange Park, IL 60525
Tel: 708-352-6611
Contact: Sharon Kerrick

American Society for Engineering Education
1818 N Street
Suite 600
Washington, DC 20036
Tel: 202-331-3500

Nuclear Engineering Institute
1776 I Street, NW
Suite 400
Washington, DC 20006
Tel: 202-739-8000
Fax: 202-785-1898

NURSE

PROFESSIONAL PROFILE

# of people in profession	2,000,000
% male	20
% female	80
avg. hours per week	45
avg. starting salary	$26,000
avg. salary after 5 years	$35,000
avg. salary 10 to 15 years	$50,000

Professionals Read

Nursing
American Journal of Nursing
Nursing Connections

Books, Films and TV Shows
Featuring the Profession

Nurses
Coma
ER
One Flew Over the Cuckoo's Nest

Major Employers

Home Nursing Company, Inc.
P.O. Box 669
Lebanon, VA 24266
Tel: 540-889-4318
Fax: 540-889-0403
Contact: Carol Fields

Bakersfield Memorial Hospital
420 44th Street
Bakersfield, CA 93301
Tel: 800-528-7345
Fax: 805-327-3247
Contact: Human Resources Department

Sloan Kettering Memorial Cancer Center
1275 York Avenue
New York, NY 10021
Tel: 800-525-2225
Fax: 212-593-4652
Contact: Michael Browne

A DAY IN THE LIFE

Nurses help prevent disease and injury and care for the sick and injured, but within these parameters there are no limits to what the job can be. "Nursing offers you the opportunity to do a million different things, in a million different places," as one respondent put it. Nurses work in hospitals, clinics, schools, corporations, and sometimes even in businesses of their own. While there are many different areas of specialization, some are general nurses, who assist doctors by performing a variety of tasks as needs arise, and will often have secretarial duties as well if they work in HMOs or private offices. More specialized nurses include surgical nurses, who ensure the sterility of instruments and assist doctors during surgery; obstetric-gynecological nurses, who help to deliver babies; neonatal nurses, who care for newborns and teach new mothers how to feed their babies; nurse anesthetists, who work with anesthesiologists to provide proper sedation for patients; or psychiatric nurses, who care for patients with mental or emotional disorders. Outside of the health-care facility setting, occupational health nurses work at factories or other worksites to offer preventive education, and community or public health nurses spend time on the road to instruct various groups in their community on diverse health-related topics. Another variety of nurse is the private duty nurse, who has only one patient in her charge and works in the patient's home or in the hospital.

These days, a nurse with more advanced degrees handles many things that were once the sole province of physicians, such as treating colds or other ailments and setting fractures. Called nurse practitioners, these nurses can make diagnoses and write prescriptions. Clinical nurse specialists also have additional patient responsibilities that follow from their advanced education and certification in one specialized area, such as geriatrics or pediatrics. Nurses can also advance to become department heads or supervisors, overseeing other nurses as well as caring for patients. Each facility also has a Director of Nursing, who establishes standards of patient care, composes the department's budget, and advises other hospital employees on nursing issues.

Nurses generally work in eight-hour shifts that relieve each other day and night, although some hospitals have recently been experimenting with having nurses work ten- or twelve-hour shifts, three or four days a week. Since they are on their feet a lot, nurses must be in good physical shape. They also must have an upbeat disposition and the ability to stay composed in emergency situations, which could arise at any moment. Communication skills are critical—nurses must listen well and be able to give clear directions to patients and aides.

PAYING YOUR DUES

People who want to become nurses can choose among four educational programs. The two-year program takes place in a junior or community college combined with some hospital training. The diploma program, run entirely by a hospital or school and based solely on nursing, takes three years to complete. The longest is the B.A. program, which awards candidates a bachelor's degree of science after four or five years of study at a college or university. None of these programs qualify the nurse for practice, though. To practice, every nurse must pass her state's licensing exams. After completing any of these programs and passing the exam, the nurse is an RN, or registered nurse. The fourth and quickest option is to become an LPN, or licensed practical nurse, which requires only one year of training. An LPN is still licensed, but cannot perform as many duties as the RN. While for most beginning jobs the RN license opens the door, in order to be eligible for some supervisory positions a BA is necessary. For the highest managerial positions, or to teach in a nursing school, a Master's degree in nursing is the norm. Some specialties even require a Ph.D.

A background in science and liberal arts will serve future nurses well. Nursing programs are heavy on science for obvious reasons, but liberal arts courses are also helpful since nurses spend a lot of their time educating patients and staff. Many hospitals and organizations run volunteer programs in which people thinking about nursing can get a look at the profession, and this experience is a good idea for anyone considering becoming a nurse.

ASSOCIATED CAREERS

Some nurses go on to become instructors of nursing at hospitals and universities. Another burgeoning nursing-related profession is midwifery. After having been forced out of the field by doctors in the nineteenth century, midwives are returning to their centuries-old role of delivering babies. Now, certified nurse-midwives actually deliver babies themselves, in hospitals, birthing centers, or in the mother's home, and many women prefer their care to that of obstetricians. Midwives also offer care to pregnant women and educate new mothers.

PAST AND FUTURE

While hospitals have in some form been in existence for many centuries, it wasn't until the nineteenth century that Florence Nightingale transformed the nursing profession. During the Crimean War, she began a training program that taught citizens how to administer proper patient care, including sterilization, which was then a radical concept. This led to the genesis of nursing schools. Today all nurses are trained, educated, and licensed professionals, and the field continues to grow, with more men entering this previously all-female profession every year. The outlook for the future is bright but still slightly uncertain. With an aging population and rising health care costs, nurses are expected to be in high demand into the next century. But draconian budget cutbacks and controversy over funding for health care have recently left many facilities unable to hire nurses at their previously high levels.

QUALITY OF LIFE

Two Years
Very few nurses leave the field at this time. Entry-level salaries are relatively high, and most nurses are becoming oriented to their surroundings and finding gratification in their work.

Five Years
More nurses leave the profession at this time. Our respondents cited frustration with budget cutbacks that have interfered with the quality of nursing care. Those who stay still enjoy the challenges and flexibility. As many as 32 percent of nurses work part-time. Many of them have small children and appreciate the opportunity to make their own schedules.

Ten Years
Some veteran nurses find themselves making a lateral move from hospital to private care, which can ensure more regular hours and a stable atmosphere. At ten years many nurses have also advanced in the profession to higher-paying supervisory positions, building on their experience or on advanced degrees.

THE BIRKMAN LIFESTYLE GRID

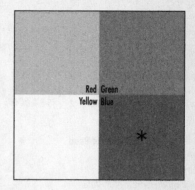

Red Green
Yellow Blue

This career is suitable for people with Blue interests.

You'll Have Contact With
Lab Technicians
Patients
Pharmacists
Physicians

Major Associations
National League for Nursing
350 Hudson Street
New York, NY 10013
Tel: 212-989-9393

American Association of Nurse Anesthetists
222 South Prospect Avenue
Park Ridge, IL 60068-4001
Tel: 708-692-7050

American Nursing Assistants Association
P.O.Box 165
Ottawa, KS 66067

Federation for Accessible Nursing
Educational and Licensure
P.O. Box 1418
Lewisburg, WV 24901
Tel: 304-645-4357
Fax: 304-645-4357

NUTRITIONIST

A DAY IN THE LIFE

Nutritionists have a healthy regard for food and its life-sustaining properties. They are primarily concerned with the prevention and treatment of illnesses through proper dietary care. Nutritionists evaluate the diets of patients and clients suffering from medical disorders and suggest ways of fighting various health problems by modifying the intake of certain food items. As one nutritionist puts it, "It's basically all about balance . . . the older you get the more you begin to understand the importance of balance in your life and your diet is no exception." Hypertension, diabetes, and obesity are some of the common health problems that nutritionists work to alleviate. Through education and research, they also promote sensible eating habits in communities, schools, hospitals, prisons, clinics, and nursing homes. Like all other health professionals, nutritionists are motivated by a concern to improve people's quality of life.

Food manufacturers, advertisers, marketers, and some enlightened restaurateurs employ nutritionists to organize, develop, analyze, test, and prepare meals that are low in fat and cholesterol and virtually devoid of chemical additives. Nutritionists usually specialize in one of three major areas of practice: Clinical, community, or administrative management. Clinical nutritionists service the needs of clients who are institutionalized. They develop, implement, and maintain nutritional programs for those in hospitals, nursing homes, retirement communities, daycare centers, and prisons. Before proposing or implementing any dietary program, nutritionists must consult with doctors or other health professionals to ensure that medical and dietary needs are optimized. Community nutritionists are an integral part of health clinics, clubs, agencies, and HMOs. They advise individuals and groups on the nutritional practices that will promote good health. They also structure and recommend diet plans for whole families, often including guides to the correct preparation of meals and shopping for the right foods. Meal planning and preparation on a large scale, such as for a school district, requires the careful and knowing supervision of administrative or management nutritionists. Their responsibilities include preparing food budgets, purchasing food, ensuring that health and safety codes are strictly observed, and maintaining records and writing reports.

Nutritionists often spend the greater part of their workday on their feet. Hot, steamy kitchens also figure prominently in a nutritionist's career, although many do end up working in well-lit, properly ventilated environments. But nutritionists must be prepared to work in environments that are not always equipped with modern conveniences or sometimes fall short of prescribed standards. In such work situations the primary concern of the nutritionist will be to bring the work environment up to standard by enforcing health and safety codes and improving overall production capacity.

PAYING YOUR DUES

A bachelor's degree with a major in dietetics, food and nutrition, or food service systems management or a related subject is the basic requirement of this profession. Courses in the sciences such as biology, microbiology, mathematics, statistics, psychology, and sociology are core course requirements.

ASSOCIATED CAREERS

The principles of nutrition are readily applied to a number of areas of modern life. Home economists, nurses, therapists, home-care attendants, health educators, and even chefs all require a working knowledge of nutrition. Some nutritionists report or prepare publications on food and health-related issues, such as the importance of fiber in the diet and the efficacy of vitamin supplements. The growing popularity and marketing power of the fitness industry coupled with an overall movement toward healthier lifestyles as a consequence of the growing incidence of heart disease and obesity among America's aging population, have ensured the place of nutritionists in the scheme of things.

PAST AND FUTURE

The need for nutritionists is almost virtually assured as America's baby-boomers join the ranks of senior citizens. Nutritionists will become key players in preventive medicine as they and other health care professionals fight common age-related diseases and health problems through the promotion of sound eating habits and daily exercise. Senior citizens will increasingly come under the care of nutritionists and dietitians who will, in all likelihood, plan and prepare their daily meals.

QUALITY OF LIFE

Two Years

At this early stage the nutritionist is still learning how to thoroughly evaluate a patient or client's dietary needs. She should understand the absolute importance of communicating clearly and directly with the attending physician or health care professional before developing or recommending any nutrition program. The nutritionist should also be establishing his or her professional style in dealing with and relating to patients. The emphasis is on creating an environment in which the patient feels at ease.

Five Years

The nutritionist is now a seasoned professional who performs his duties with minimal or no supervision, cross-references his information with doctors, is thorough in his research, is accurate in his recommendations, and has a good rapport with his patients. At this stage, the challenge-seeking nutritionist will begin to examine his options for advancement in his current field, weighing them against employment opportunities in other areas.

Ten Years

At the ten-year mark, the highly experienced nutritionist is ripe for setting up his own private consulting firm. He should have developed considerable contacts to easily facilitate such a move. The ten-year veteran has kept abreast of industry developments through trade journals and other publications, revising and updating his own nutrition programs at every step of the way. He might also write his own books and articles for publication. Academia will require the services of many a nutrition veteran as the industry continues to expand at its record fast pace, and more universities and colleges begin to offer nutrition and dietetics programs.

THE BIRKMAN LIFESTYLE GRID

Red Green
Yellow Blue

This career is suitable for people with Green interests.

You'll Have Contact With

Chefs
Child Care Workers
Psychologists
Teachers
Patients

Major Associations

American Dietetic Association
216 West Jackson Boulevard
Chicago, IL 60606
Tel: 312-899-0040
Contact: Membership

American Council of
Applied Clinical Nutrition
P.O. Box 509
Florissant, MO 63032
Tel: 314-921-3997

American Association of
Nutritional Consultants
880 Canaries Court
Suite 210
Chula Vista, CA 91910
Tel: 619-482-8533
Fax: 619-482-0938

OCCUPATIONAL THERAPIST

A DAY IN THE LIFE

Occupational therapists care for persons with disabling mental, physical, developmental, and emotional conditions, helping them to recover or develop and maintain their daily living and work skills. Occupational therapists help patients live productively and independently. They help patients compensate for the loss of functions, as in the case of amputees or recently disabled individuals, as well as improve motor skills and reasoning and perceptual abilities. Some therapists work solely with specific disabilities or with certain age groups: Specialties include alcoholism, drug abuse, eating disorders, and mental health. Occupational therapy requires unequivocal dedication and often rewards its practitioners with a tremendous sense of accomplishment. The profession calls on the best of those who practice it; occupational therapists must be compassionate, caring, patient, and capable of commanding the respect and trust of those within their care. "The satisfaction you get from helping someone reclaim their life is enormous," enthused one student intern. "Sometimes they come in depressed and angry . . . and gradually their spirits are renewed with each day of therapy and hope is in their eyes and their future."

The well-trained professional is familiar with a wide range of activities that will be employed as a matter of course in the patient's recovery. Patients suffering from coordination problems, for example, may be given manual arts projects such as creative handicrafts to improve hand-eye coordination. Practical activities such as gardening and weaving increase strength and dexterity. Although most occupational therapists work an average forty-hour week, it is often emotionally draining and backbreaking work. Practitioners are challenged to develop and implement exercises that will gain the maximum participation and interest of patients. Occupational therapists face significant challenges when dealing with patients with permanent physical handicaps such as muscular dystrophy, cerebral palsy, or spinal cord injuries. They develop and teach patients how to operate adaptive equipment such as wheel chairs, splints, and other devices that allow those with limitations to exercise a measure of control over their environment. An occupational therapist who works with the physically disabled must have strength, agility and stamina to help patients in and out of beds and wheelchairs and allow patients to physically lean on him while he assists them with various exercises such as walking and lifting weights. Not all therapists need be physically strong and powerful, but all, including industrial therapists who assist patients in finding and holding jobs, are challenged to inspire trust, motivate progress, and demonstrate concern and compassion.

PAYING YOUR DUES

A Bachelor's degree in Occupational Therapy is required for entry into this field. In the over thirty states that require licensing, therapists must obtain a post-bachelor's certificate from an accredited program and successfully complete a national certification examination given by the American Occupational Therapy Certification Board. Internships or volunteer work in the health care field show potential employers the commitment that is a necessary prerequisite to this profession. Applicants should carefully consider their ability to physically and emotionally cope with the demands of the job. By far the most significant qualification applicants to this profession could have is a sincere commitment to the care of others and a heart-warming smile.

ASSOCIATED CAREERS

With a rapidly aging population, the need for assorted health care professionals to provide specialized rehabilitative care will be constant. Because therapists are required to be versed in a number of activities that are used in the care of the disabled, this facilitates an easy transition to alternative occupations. Horticulture, music, dance, manual arts, hand industries, and creative handicrafts are exercises for the physically challenged as well as those suffering from stress-related illnesses. Some occupational therapists, with further studies, will find entree to orthotics, chiropractic treatment, speech pathology, audiology, prosthetics, physical therapy and rehabilitation counseling.

PAST AND FUTURE

The field of occupational therapy will continue to grow in leaps and bounds as large numbers of baby boomers make the transition to middle age and as home care and outpatient services become the norm in the health care industry. As scientific discoveries continue to extend the life expectancy of the average American, patients will need extensive therapy to combat a number of disabling conditions. Therefore occupational therapists will have to constantly update their knowledge of new adaptive equipment and its uses as they also develop new activities.

QUALITY OF LIFE

Two Years

If she is practicing in a state that requires licensing, the occupational therapist should be thinking of and making steps toward becoming a registered professional. The ambitious therapist seeks the guidance and advice of mentors and develops professional contacts. This is an ideal time for the practitioner to decide whether she wants to work exclusively with a specific age group or service the needs of individuals with particular disabilities.

Five Years

With five years on-the-job experience, the occupational therapist is now board-certified and has updated his skills through job training programs, college courses, and professional workshops. Thus the occupational therapist is ready for and probably actively seeking advancement. At this juncture an evaluation of existing employment opportunities or the possibility of shifting to an alternate career is foremost in the mind of the practitioner. Private or group practice is a distinct possibility for the five-year veteran.

Ten Years

If the occupational therapist is not in a top-level administrative post at a health care facility after ten years of service then she should definitely be moving in the direction of establishing a private practice. With considerable years of experience, professional and personal contacts, and a growing number of adult daycare programs, nursing homes, and health care agencies, private or group practice should be a lucrative and worthwhile endeavor.

THE BIRKMAN LIFESTYLE GRID

This career is suitable for people with Green interests.

You'll Have Contact With
Physical Therapists
Psychiatrists
Psychologists
Social Workers
Physically Disabled Patients

Major Associations
American Occupational Therapy Association
4720 Montgomery Lane
P.O. Box 31220
Bethesda, MD 20824-1220
Tel: 301-652-2682
Contact: Public Relations Dept.

American Occupational Therapy
Certification Board
800 South Fedrick Avenue
Suite 200
Gaichersburg, MD 20877
Tel: 301-990-7979

OFFICE MANAGER

PROFESSIONAL PROFILE

# of people in profession	795,000
% male	35
% female	65
avg. hours per week	50
avg. starting salary	$24,000
avg. salary after 5 years	$33,000
avg. salary 10 to 15 years	$46,000

Professionals Read
Records Management Quarterly
Managing Office Technology
Office Systems

Books, Films and TV Shows Featuring the Profession
Working Girl
Office Politics

Major Employers
HGO Technologies Inc.
1109 Van Voorhis Road
Morgantown, WV 26505
Tel: 913-752-4030
Fax: 304-599-7833
Contact: Human Resources

W.K. Kellogg Foundation
1 Michigan Avenue East
Battle Creek, MI 49017
Tel: 913-752-4030
Fax: 616-969-2189
Contact: Human Resources

NYS Education Department
Box SC-6489 Washington Avenue
Albany, NY 12234
Tel: 913-752-4030
Fax: 518-473-4909
Contact: Human Resources

A DAY IN THE LIFE

"An office manager is responsible for the smooth operation of the day-to-day business of the company," one manager wrote us, adding the caveat: "No excuses accepted." A good office manager makes it possible for other people to function efficiently. Office managers work closely with the company partners, owner, or president to meet their company's staffing, equipment, and organizational needs. Duties may include pricing products from vendors, interviewing job applicants, managing payroll, and reimbursing members of the firm for out-of-pocket business expenses. An office manager must exercise sound judgment day in and day out, and any lapse can result in termination. This may be the reason that office managers generally take their jobs so seriously. Pressure can be significant, particularly for those in charge of large offices. Office managers who succeed have confidence, common sense, loyalty, and the ability to motivate others. Survey respondents who were part-time office managers added the importance of being able to work with others on a team or in pairs to coordinate smooth operations.

Although it is common to think that an office manager should be an angel of tact and discretion, existing on the favorable review of his superiors, people in the profession disagreed. Many office managers said their jobs require them to be somewhat more firm than gentle when projects have to be completed, equipment needs to be serviced, or difficulties with staffing spring up. "You've got to stand up for what you know are the right decisions for the company, even if the boss disagrees. You live on your reputation, and when you have to do your job to someone else's commands, you have to voice your opinion," said one fifteen-year manager. He was supported by a number of others. "Tough," "precise," and "go-getting" were also words that popped up many times on our surveys.

The greatest satisfaction that office managers mentioned concerned their productivity. Office managers can see immediate results from their decisions; they can control their environment (within the boundaries imposed by their employer). This ability to determine one's own fate cuts both ways, however. Office managers have a very high turnover rate, due to firing, job mobility, and retirement. They are often the first one to be let go when conflicts arise between producers and managers, and they are frequently blamed for office problems that are not of their own making. Office management provides a very structured environment with clearly defined duties for those with financial, organizational, and interpersonal skills. One needs to have a high tolerance for risk and not be too concerned with job security.

PAYING YOUR DUES

Office managers are not required to have any specific degree, but most employers value a college degree and organizational, planning, and communication skills. Suggested courses include organizational behavior, psychology, sociology, finance, and English. Employers at smaller firms also recommend accounting studies, as payroll issues and some financial oversight may be part of the job.

ASSOCIATED CAREERS

Office managers often use their on-the-job accounting skills to become bookkeepers, bank assistants, and clerks. Some use their pricing experience to become professional purchasing agents, but these opportunities are limited, particularly for those in rural locations. Few office managers return to school for further degrees, although a small number go back to school to study library science.

PAST AND FUTURE

The position of office manager developed along with the growth of the modern firm. As companies expand and diversify, workers are required to perform more and more specialized tasks. Office coordination of the needs and the output of the workers is critical to the productive operation of the company. The office manager helps to standardize information, facilitates communication, and makes sure that employees are able to do their jobs.

The future of office managers looks bright. Many economists predict that the economy will continue to grow and provide more office managing job opportunities over the next six years.

QUALITY OF LIFE

Two Years

Many office managers manage small firms. They gain valuable experience in purchasing, negotiating deals, smoothing staffing difficulties, and predicting their firm's future needs. This last experience, learning to anticipate problems and requirements, is the most difficult and most important for the new manager. Office managers make contacts with staffing agencies, and hone their interviewing skills. Hours are long; salaries are average.

Five Years

Five-year veterans have gained a good sense of what the job entails. A number are beginning to bump into wage ceilings in their current firm, and the race to find new jobs begins. Many work at three, four, or even five firms in five years. A number move into jobs with larger staffing requirements than they are used to and must have strong organizational skills to meet this challenge. Hours are long; salaries are competitive; job security drops as the stakes increase.

Ten Years

Contact with partners and managing directors of firms increases, and many office managers jump to very large firms. Some are given a specific area of responsibility, such as Office Manager in charge of Staffing Needs or Office Manager in charge of Supplies and Equipment. These are valued positions, and many in them suddenly become averse to big risks and spend much of their time protecting their position. Hours and satisfaction remain steady; pay remains about the same from here on in except for cost-of-living adjustments.

THE BIRKMAN LIFESTYLE GRID

This career is suitable for people with Blue interests.

You'll Have Contact With

Bookkeepers
Human Resource Personnel
Secretaries
Supply Vendors

Major Associations

ARMA International
4200 Somerset Drive
Suite 215
Prairie Village, KS 66208
Tel: 913-341-3808

Office and Professional
Employees International Union
265 West 14th Street
Suite 610
New York, NY 10011
Tel: 212-675-3210

ORGANIZATIONAL DEVELOPER

A DAY IN THE LIFE

An organizational developer works with client corporations to streamline them and plan future development. Companies hire organizational developers when they are suffering from internal inefficiency or need help identifying their potential growth points and personnel needs. The organizational developer is brought in to provide information and a perspective on what a company needs. It is important for an OD to be open, inquiring, and strong in analytic skills. Organizational development falls into three areas of concern: Structure, personnel, and procedure. Many second- or third-year analysts are assigned to specific areas of specialization and then follow those tracks for their entire careers. Organizational developers usually work in teams, with a specialty area head running each one, and the teams coordinate to make recommendations.

Structural organizational developers analyze corporate structures and responsibilities. They examine who is in charge of what areas of the business and how much time they spend on each duty. Many people have to look back to their original job descriptions to find out what they are supposed to be doing, and then they describe what they really do. An OD must be able to interview people in a non-confrontational way and be able to tell when a person is merely saying what he thinks he should say rather than telling the truth. ODs who are involved in personnel concerns have a very hard time interviewing employees, who tend to be extremely reluctant to tell the truth around personnel developers out of fear for their own jobs. Since they must rely on information from data and records, personnel developers face the most number-intensive task of the three. Procedural organizational developers observe employees. They track projects through the company, examine who comes into contact with them and what their regular procedures are. Procedural developers don't make any recommendations until they have spent significant time meeting with the other OD specialists; recommendations from any other field will affect procedural decisions immensely.

ODs said that the most exhausting part of their job is in the final stages of any project, when all three teams meet to exchange information and organize recommendations. This can mean marathon meeting sessions where each team makes a presentation to the other teams and then they debate recommendations. Once they reach a consensus, sometimes after tremendous internal disagreement, they prepare a recommendation summary and make a presentation to the client. Recommendations can include restructuring, changing benefits, encouraging employee education, eliminating personnel, or changing the focus of business. They focus on internal recommendations, their area of expertise, rather than external development.

PAYING YOUR DUES

There are no specific academic requirements for becoming an organizational developer, but the overwhelming majority have college or advanced degrees. Employers look favorably on majors such as business, finance, economics, and psychology. Scientific survey methodology, which can be very interview-intensive, is important. A number of ODs pursue graduate degrees in either organizational behavior or business administration. There is intense competition for entry-level organizational development positions, which entail long hours but limited responsibility. Any work experience demonstrating the ability to work in teams is valuable to employers.

Certification by professional organizations is helpful but not required for advancement. The qualities that distinguish a successful candidate in this field are an inquisitive mind, the ability to assemble details into a coherent whole, and persistence.

ASSOCIATED CAREERS

ODs can use their analytical minds in a number of other business-related occupations, such as a management consultant or financial analyst. A number become efficiency experts or quality control personnel. An OD's specialization—structure, personnel, or production—generally determines what avenues are available to them after they leave their jobs.

PAST AND FUTURE

The idea that companies should re-evaluate all their operations and methods of doing business every few years is fairly recent. Organizational development led the charge to provide significant internal information from objective sources. The future of the OD looks bright, particularly as companies grow in size but are ill-equipped to handle the unanticipated problems that come with expansion. Information, production, staffing and structural decisions are all important to the financial health and welfare of a company. Job growth in this industry is expected to be greater than the average for the economy as a whole.

QUALITY OF LIFE

Two Years

The first two years in this profession can be difficult. Many spend their first year on small projects in all three areas of specialization as they try to find matches between their skills and the companies' needs. This can mean working at many low-responsibility jobs and performing such dull tasks as entering data into a computer, transcribing interviews into data files, or maintaining files on projects. Those who show immediate promise in any area find their responsibilities increase; those who do not should find themselves rotating between departments swiftly. Satisfaction is low for those who do not find a match right away. Hours are long as entrants to the field try to distinguish themselves through hard work.

Five Years

The first taste of client contact emerges in years three through seven, as many structural and procedural organizational developers spend long hours conducting interviews. Relocation may be required as some projects can require up to six weeks of on-site work. By year five, many organizational developers have become contributing members of teams or team leaders. Extremely long hours are required for those who wish to rise beyond this point. Satisfaction increases, but those looking for greater salaries enter other more lucrative fields.

Ten Years

Most ten-year members of the profession have positions of organizational oversight and coordination. For those who are not interested in managing large projects and converting their analytic jobs to managerial ones, the profession becomes less satisfying than it used to be. Many developers who prefer a more "hands-on" approach to the career leave. Luckily, the successful OD has a number of career options open to her.

THE BIRKMAN LIFESTYLE GRID

Red Green
Yellow Blue

This career is suitable for people with Red interests.

You'll Have Contact With

Accountants
Human Resources Personnel
Production Managers
Researchers
Employees

Major Associations

International Registry of
Organization Development
781 Beta Drive
Suite K
Cleveland, OH 44143
Tel: 216-461-4333

Organization Development Institute
781 Beta Drive
Suite K
Cleveland, OH 44143
Tel: 216-461-4333

Organization Development Network
76 South Orange Avenue
Suite 101
South Orange, NJ 7079
Tel: 201-763-7337

PARALEGAL

A DAY IN THE LIFE

If you want to learn the nuts and bolts of the legal profession and understand the importance of careful and thorough research, then paralegal studies might just be consistent with your character. The paralegal, or legal assistant, profession is the ground floor to lawyering and every bit as important (though lawyers are reluctant to admit it). In many distinct ways, their duties include the same things lawyers who assume responsibility for the legal work do, but paralegals do not practice law and are prohibited from dispensing legal advice, trying a case in court, or accepting legal fees. Paralegals work hand in hand with lawyers, helping to prepare cases for trial. In their preparatory work they uncover all the facts of the case, conduct research to highlight relevant case laws and court decisions, obtain affidavits, and assist with depositions and other materials relevant to cases.

A significant portion of a paralegal's work is taken up with writing reports and drafting documents for litigation. After the initial fact-gathering stage, the paralegal prepares reports for use by the supervising attorney in deciding how the case should be litigated. Paralegals who work in areas other than litigation, such as patent and copyright law, real estate and corporate law, also assist in the drafting of relevant documents-contracts, mortgages, estate planning, and separation agreements. Paralegals who work for government agencies maintain reference files, analyze material for internal use, and prepare information guides on the law. Those involved with community legal services help disadvantaged persons in need of legal aid. Much of their time is spent preparing and filing documents and doing research. Employee benefit plans, shareholder agreements and stock options are the primary concern of the paralegal working for corporations.

PAYING YOUR DUES

Paralegals usually enter the profession after completing American Bar Association (ABA) approved college or training programs or are promoted up within law firms and trained on the job. Although most paralegal programs are completed in two years, a growing number of colleges and universities offer four-year bachelor's degree programs. This is a growth profession attracting large numbers of applicants, and competition is strong and healthy. A four-year program at a reputable college and certification by the National Association of Legal Assistants, the Certified Legal Assistant (CLA) designation, will greatly enhance employment opportunities. The paralegal with training in a specialized area of the law who has demonstrated competence in the legal applications of computers will distinguish himself from the pack and be able to move ahead. Practical experience gained from student internships, familiarity with legal terminology, and good investigative skills are all advantages.

ASSOCIATED CAREERS

A number of occupations call for specialized knowledge of the law but fall short of the need for a lawyer. Should a paralegal become disenchanted with her career, there are possibilities in law enforcement, as an insurance claim adjuster, occupational safety and health officer, patent agent, and title examiner. And there is always the option of becoming a lawyer.

PAST AND FUTURE

The paralegal profession is a relatively new and rapidly expanding area. Previously, much of the groundwork now covered by the paralegal was part and parcel of being a lawyer. Now lawyers can afford to focus more intently on the strategies of trying cases and resolving legal problems, thanks to the invaluable preparatory work of the paralegal. Computer technology will continue to play a significant role in the fact-finding and gathering stages of most legal cases. Instead of poring over volumes of research material in law libraries, much of this information is easily accessible from on-line digitized law libraries, CD ROMs, and software programs. Of course the paralegal who specializes in a particular field and who is computer friendly will have the added edge on advancement. Because of the continuous enactment of new legislation and revised interpretations of existing laws, the paralegal must keep constantly updated on every change, every proposal, every nuance of the law.

QUALITY OF LIFE

Two Years
These are the critical years for the newcomer to the profession to take stock, gain valuable all-round experience, and simply feel his way around the profession. At this stage the paralegal is probably given minimal responsibilities but loads of work-up to 90 hours a week should be expected at times, for those who want to get anywhere in the profession; the day will be spent doing research in the law library, poring over tedious documents (looking for witness names through word-searches and similarly mind-numbing tasks), preparing reports for presentation (3-hole punching, formatting labels, etc). The paralegal should expect to be under constant supervision, assist with clerical matters, photocopy articles, and compile files. The work may seem never-ending and tedious, but the paralegal with perseverance will take it in stride and absorb this experience.

Five Years
By now the experienced paralegal has decided on and begun to pursue a specialized field. The professional has more responsibility and significantly reduced supervision. In a corporate environment, advancement opportunities are possible at this juncture. Usually, paralegals move up to supervisory or managerial capacities, but many may find it easier to move to another law firm in search of advancement and better salaries.

Ten Years
The ten-year mark is the ideal time for reassessment of one's career as a paralegal. By now the professional has undergone several career-enhancing changes such as college refresher courses, workshops and seminars on changes in the law, new computer applications in legal research, and developments in an area of specialty. At this stage, if the paralegal still yearns for more responsibilities and challenges, she is wont to make the ultimate decision of whether to pursue a law degree or undertake an alternate career.

THE BIRKMAN LIFESTYLE GRID

This career is suitable for people with Blue interests.

You'll Have Contact With
Attorneys
Judicial Clerks
Proofreaders
Secretaries

Major Associations
American Association for
Paralegal Education
P.O. Box 40244
Overland Park, KS 66204
Tel: 913-381-4458
Contact: Sandra I. Sabanske

National Federation of Paralegal Assistants
P.O. Box 33108
Kansas City, MO 64114
Tel: 816-941-4000
Contact: Lu Hangley

National Association of Legal Assistants
1516 South Boston Avenue
Suite 200
Tulsa, OK 74119
Tel: 918-587-6828

PARAMEDIC

A DAY IN THE LIFE

Are you familiar with the people running the stretchers through the door and shouting numbers at the doctors on the television show "ER"? Those are paramedics and Emergency Medical Technicians (EMTs). Paramedics are the highest level of pre-hospital providers; EMTs are the basic level personnel. Paramedics and EMTs are often the first medical people at the scene of an accident or sudden illness; they give immediate care to heart attack victims, car crash victims, gunshot victims, and poisoning victims. They even assist in childbirth. The sick or injured are then transported to healthcare facilities in specially equipped emergency vehicles. On arrival at a medical center, the paramedics transfer the patient to nursing personnel and report their observations and treatment procedure to the attending physician.

The guidelines or procedures followed by EMTs are directly related to their level of training. The EMT-Paramedic is at the upper rung of a three-level hierarchy. Paramedics administer sophisticated prehospital care. They are trained in the use of complex medical equipment, such as EKGs, and are capable of administering drugs both orally and intravenously. EMT-Intermediates have more advanced training than EMT-Basics who bandage wounds, stabilize blood pressure, assist heart attack victims, and treat accident victims for shock. All three levels of EMTs can be talked through care procedures in the event they are confronted with a difficult or complicated situation. Thus EMTs may maintain radio contact with a dispatcher and keep him apprised of the situation. Should the need arise, senior medical personnel (physicians) will then take charge.

For EMTs and paramedics, helping people can be an athletic experience; you have to be where people need you. Like fire fighters or other emergency response personnel, paramedics and EMTs are involved in life and death situations. Their work can be richly rewarding, as when a child is born despite difficulties, or terribly sad, when, even after administering proper care, a patient dies. Conditions are tremendously stressful, hours long and irregular, and salaries low. Paramedics must be physically and emotionally strong enough to do back-breaking and sometimes dangerous work, and ready to hustle on a moment's notice, whether they feel like it or not, as someone's life may be on the line. The paramedic never knows what conditions they might meet on any given day, so emotional stability is at a premium. "It's a lot of stress and anxiety," says one EMT who has been on the job for three years. "But some days you go home feeling like you really made a difference, and that's a real good feeling."

PAYING YOUR DUES

Training to become an EMT is offered by police, fire, and health departments and in some hospitals. Many colleges and universities offer nondegree courses. Basic training to become a first level EMT requires 100 to 120 hours of classroom sessions plus ten hours of internship in a hospital emergency room and 20-50 hours on field rescue or ambulance companies. An additional thirty-five to fifty-five hours of instruction in patient assessment, intravenous fluids, antishock garments, and esophageal airways are required in intermediate training. Paramedics usually undergo between 750 and 2,000 hours of training. But the real training comes with experience.

Although registration is not generally required, it does enhance the possibility of advancement and employment opportunities. A certified EMT must renew his registration every two years, which requires that he remain active in the field and meet a continuing education requirement. However, a paramedic seeking advancement must leave fieldwork if she is to move up to operations manager, administrative officer, or executive director of emergency services.

ASSOCIATED CAREERS

Because of its high-stress environment, many paramedics suffer from burnout. A lack of advancement opportunities and low salaries leads to a high turnover in this profession. On the other hand, police, fire, and rescue squad departments offer attractive salaries and benefits. For paramedics looking to switch careers, the health care profession offers several avenues. With a rapidly aging population and scientific breakthroughs which prolong life, the proliferation of residential retirement communities, nursing homes, adult daycare centers, and health care agencies, the need for health care professionals is virtually assured. With more schooling, paramedics can become RNs, occupational and physical therapists, doctors, and other health care workers. Closer to the field, paramedics can make the transition to EMT instructor, dispatcher, law enforcement, or fire fighter.

PAST AND FUTURE

Doctors saving soldiers on battlefields are the forerunners of today's paramedics. Unfortunately, there will always be a need for people who can administer emergency treatment and rush the sick and injured to doctors' care. Employment opportunities in the emergency services industry will continue to expand with an aging population which will increasingly have a need for such services.

QUALITY OF LIFE

Two Years

If the paramedic is already board certified, the two-year mark signals the time for recertification. Continuing education classes are an integral part of the paramedic's first two years on the job. On-the-job training has given him the confidence and ability to deal with a variety of situations. The paramedic is relatively new to the field and still approaches his job with energy and idealism.

Five Years

The registered paramedic is still updating his skills through classes and workshops. After five years, he or she is beginning to feel the stresses of the job. Long and irregular hours, being on-call sometimes twenty-four hours a day are taking its toll on the professional. For those who are still stress-free at the five-year level, advancement figures prominently in their thoughts. Operations manager and administrative director are positions that the five-year veteran would consider moving up to. This is also the ideal time to consider pursuing further studies in order to become an RN, physician's assistant, physician, or other health care professional.

Ten Years

After ten years, paramedics have usually left the "field" for middle- or top-level administrative positions. But even then, continuing education classes and refresher courses are still important.

THE BIRKMAN LIFESTYLE GRID

This career is suitable for people with Red interests.

You'll Have Contact With

Doctors
Firefighters
Nurses
Police Officers

Major Associations

National Association of
Emergency Medical Technicians
120 West Leake Street
Clinton, MS 39056
Tel: 800-346-2368

National Registry of Emergency
Medical Technicians
P.O. Box 29233
Columbus, OH 43229
Tel: 614-888-4484

PARK RANGER

A DAY IN THE LIFE

If you love the beauty of misty mornings outlined by hazy sunshine, the smell of dew and new beginnings, then a park ranger's life might be ideal for you. With more than 76 million acres of national parks within its purview, the U.S. National Park Service and the park rangers it employs educate and ensure the safety of the millions of visitors who hike, climb, ski, boat, fish, and explore these natural resources.

The primary responsibility of the park ranger is safety. Rangers must strictly enforce outdoor safety codes and ensure the compliance of campers, hikers, and picnickers. Seemingly small details such as accurately completing registration forms at park offices become crucial links should a search and rescue mission become necessary. As accidents will and often do happen in the great outdoors, park rangers are trained in first aid and rescue operations and are alert at all times to changing weather conditions, the progress and safe return of hiking or climbing groups, the condition of trails, the movement of wildlife, wind gusts, and forest fires. Besides the daily activities of interrelating with visitors, answering questions, providing guided tours, rescuing park users who might have strayed too far, enforcing laws, and directing traffic, park rangers are often called upon to be conservationists, ecologists, environmentalists, and even botanists. Park rangers protect the park's natural resources from vandals who destroy park property or fell trees for firewood, pollute lakes and rivers, harm wildlife, and leave campfires unattended. Should a forest fire start, then rangers become firefighters.

Park rangers are empowered to arrest and forcibly evict those who violate park laws. If you shrink from confrontation and lack the confidence and authority of a strong leader, then you may want to consider a different profession. A park ranger must be flexible enough to wear many hats in the execution of her duties. Strong people skills, the ability to work under pressure, in groups or alone, sometimes for extraordinarily long hours and the patience of Job are the hallmarks of a fine park ranger. If you have the requisite stamina, can handle the rigors of all kinds of climate and terrain, and are concerned about the earth's rapidly diminishing natural resources, then the life of a park ranger may indeed be your fertile soil.

PAYING YOUR DUES

A college degree and/or the right combination of education and experience in park recreation and management will possibly get you in on the ground level of this profession. Job openings are few and competition is fierce, so college credits in forestry, geology, botany, conservation, wildlife management, and other relevant subjects will go a long way in equipping you for a career that offers a multitude of possibilities. In lieu of a college education, candidates must have at least three years of experience in parks and conservation and must demonstrate an overall understanding of park work. A working knowledge of law enforcement, management, and communication skills also enhances one's prospects. Higher level management positions may require graduate degrees.

Part-time or seasonal work at national or state parks is an important stepping stone to an entry-level park ranger position. Seasonal workers perform jobs such as information desk manning, trash collection, fire services, trail maintenance, law enforcement, and other unskilled tasks which are the core of the park ranger's life. Perform these well and you may make it into an entry-level position in the big league. A vast majority of high-level park rangers start out as entry-level drones. Thus the trail to promotion and high executive office starts with successful and thorough completion of every step. A keen grasp of the overall mechanics of the business can make you a sharper, more competent administrator. Promotions come largely from within the ranks; salary is commensurate with responsibility. Today's entry-level workers may be tomorrow's park manager or district ranger. But a virtual lack of new job openings coupled with state and federal budget cuts mean that job seekers will have to look for work outside of the federally-funded National Park Service in other federal land and resource management agencies as well as state and local agencies.

ASSOCIATED CAREERS

Park rangers are tenured professionals. Such are the rewards and enjoyment of this career that rangers do not readily relinquish their posts. Because much of a park ranger's duties involve policing, law enforcement offers a readily available career for the retired or out-of-work park ranger. For the ranger specializing in landscaping, conservation, wildlife management, and ecological studies, possible career alternatives abound in areas such as zookeeping, corporate/industrial parks landscaping, and pollution containment. The winning combination of communication, people and management skills allow them to become successful customer and public relations managers.

PAST AND FUTURE

Once a park ranger's most significant qualification was his love of nature. Today that love must redefine itself within the expanding scope of technology and a shrinking economy. With politicians and the public alike calling for less, more efficient government, federal job programs will continue to undergo significant downsizing. Consequently, job openings will continue to be scarce and competition fierce. Specialization and diversification will become the new buzz words as potential candidates will have to demonstrate a wide variety and number of skills.

QUALITY OF LIFE

Two Years

For those entering this career via part-time or seasonal work, these are the critical years for developing strong contacts and establishing mentorships. If you are still in college and have not decided on an area of specialization, this is an ideal time to get a first-hand overview of the business and focus on a specialty. But one should also bear in mind that the more diverse the skills, the better the chances of getting in the door.

Five Years

At the five-year level, the park ranger should have acquired enough hands-on experience to be qualified for a position in administration. Management and communication skills, the ability to work in teams and to motivate others, plus clear leadership abilities will determine the level of success you will achieve.

Ten Years

By his tenth year, the park ranger has moved up to a high-level administrative post, such as director, at the regional or national level. He is an experienced, motivated and confident leader with a number of specialties.

THE BIRKMAN LIFESTYLE GRID

Red Green
Yellow Blue

This career is suitable for people with Red interests.

You'll Have Contact With
Camping Enthusiasts
Fish and Game Commission Officials
Tourists
Wildlife Enthusiasts

Major Associations
American Park Rangers Association
P.O. Box 1348
Homestead, FL 33090

National Association of State Park Directors
126 Mill Branch Road
Tallahassee, FL 32132
Tel: 904-893-4959

National Association of County
Park and Recreation Officials
Genessee County Parks and
Recreation Commission
5045 Stanley Road
Flint, MI 48506
Tel: 810-736-7100
Fax: 810-736-7220

PERFORMING ARTS ADMINISTRATOR

PROFESSIONAL PROFILE

# of people in profession	12,500
% male	60
% female	40
avg. hours per week	45
avg. starting salary	$15,500
avg. salary after 5 years	$22,000
avg. salary 10 to 15 years	$32,000

Professionals Read
Culture Front
Preforming Arts

Books, Films and TV Shows Featuring the Profession
Thirty-two Short Films About Glenn Gould
The Show

Major Employers
Lincoln Center, Inc.
70 Lincoln Center Plaza
9th Floor
New York, NY 10023
Tel: 212-875-5000
Fax: 212-875-5185

Madison Square Garden
2 Penn Plaza
New York, NY 10121
Tel: 212-465-6330
Fax: 212-465-6026
Contact: Human Resources

Carnegie Hall
881 7th Avenue
New York, NY 10019
Tel: 212-247-7800
Fax: 212-581-6539
Contact: Human Resources

A DAY IN THE LIFE

Many people see the performing arts as a refuge from the financially motivated corporate world. Performing arts administrators, however, know that the success of a show, a troupe, or a theater is often determined long before the audience shushes and the lights go down. The world of business and the world of art come together in the office of the performing arts administrator. A PAA controls the finances of a company or a theater, with the goal of producing exciting and profitable performances. A performance arts administrator often acts as an artistic director, guiding the focus of a season's shows and hiring directors, and as an internal accountant/ promoter/publicist/manager, controlling all the financial decisions that affect a theater, from allocating a budget for props to hiring a janitorial crew to clean up after each show.

A PAA has to make difficult decisions that may be unpopular with directors, performers, and audiences. "You're always the man in the black hat" wrote one PAA. "Most of the time you're out there trying to get money, publicity, press coverage, and reviews," he said, adding that networking, pitching to supporters of the arts, lining up talent, and negotiating non-essential contracts all contribute to the value of the end product. A number of PAAs come to the profession as former directors, producers, actors, and technical theater personnel, familiar with the day-to-day workings of a performance but unfamiliar with its finances. This education in "creative financing," as one wrote us, seems to satisfy the need for innovation that many in this profession feel. A PAA can work long hours, particularly for a small theater. Many firmly believe in their houses' potential profitability; a number invest their own money in struggling or failing concerns.

Some PAAs are hired for their contacts and not for their decision-making abilities or their knowledge of the arts. This is one position where a good "rainmaker" can make an enormous difference to a theater or a troupe. Why do people do this? "It's not for the money," wrote one, and others agreed. Performing arts administrators, except at the most prestigious houses and companies, receive unsatisfying wages. They do it because it needs to be done. They love the arts, they want to contribute, and they can. One respondent said, "you work a long day and then, sometimes at night, you open the door to a world that makes people feel alive. That's what everybody should be doing." This level of satisfaction is what keeps many in the profession, even as they struggle with financial concerns.

PAYING YOUR DUES

Contacts are important, and, although there are no specific educational requirements, many PAAs take advantage of the contacts they made in college or graduate school. Some attend college and manage theaters there, making sure their studies include finance, economics, drama, and accounting. A great number enter the acting, directing, or technical ends of theater production and gravitate to back-office positions as they find the competition fierce and their interests wandering. Most job-related education takes place on the fly, so PAAs should be quick studies with tact, professionalism, and interpersonal skills. Aspiring PAAs often have to relocate to cities where theater has a large market, generally urban environments, such as New York, Chicago, or Los Angeles. Many find it helpful to take a course in theater finance sponsored by a local university.

ASSOCIATED CAREERS

Many PAAs become producers. They network among their financial contacts and convince them to invest in ventures as speculative as the ones they have already supported. Other careers that attract the migrant PAA are agent, reviewer, industry analyst, and promoter.

PAST AND FUTURE

Historically, financial decisions at theaters, theatrical companies, and production houses were made on an ad hoc basis, with the company focusing on the needs of the day rather than on its long-term viability. PAAs became an integral part of the artistic process in the 20th century with the acknowledgment that a great portion of theater is business, and with the recognition of the need for financial management of shoe-string production companies.

Opportunities for PAAs are driven not only by demand for artistic product and available jobs, but also by government and institutional support for the arts. This changes from year-to-year, and government belt-tightening traditionally makes art a prime target for the budget ax. Then again, this career has always been one in which people pursue longshot events with uncertain payoffs, so the uncertain future for this career may be no deterrent at all to the aspiring PAA.

QUALITY OF LIFE

Two Years

Early in the profession, many PAAs work as producer's assistants, or as PAA aides, taking notes, fielding phone calls, and handling the administrative work that keeps a theater open. They become familiar with box-office accounting and the basics of promotion; organize fund-raisers, mailings and events; and generally handle the work that the PAA cannot get to. Relationships in the theater can be intense, and many respondents noted that there is no distinction between a personal "social" life and a professional "social" life. Many spend hours making industry contacts. Hours are long; salaries are low.

Five Years

Five-year PAAs have learned how to "schmooze"—how to approach financially flush patrons of the arts and encourage them to commit funds to their projects. Grant writing skills are also part of the PAA's skill-set. PAAs begin to make a salary that doesn't require them to take another job. Still, knowing the theater company's internal finances can lead to some sleepless nights. Hours are long, satisfaction is high.

Ten Years

Ten-year veterans describe their experiences as ranging from "blissful" to "execrable" depending on the fate of the ship to which they've tied themselves. Many have moved to a larger company with a longer history and more established financial contacts, or to a position where the artistic director and the PAA see more eye-to-eye. Hours remain stable. A PAA's personal and professional lives become even more indistinguishable.

THE BIRKMAN LIFESTYLE GRID

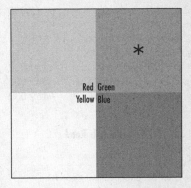

This career is suitable for people with Green interests.

You'll Have Contact With

Actors
Directors
Fundraisers
Producers

Major Associations

National Association of
Performing Arts Managers
137 East 30th Street; 3B
New York, NY 10016-7733
Tel: 212-683-0801

International Society for the Performing Arts
2920 Fuller Avenue, NE
Suite 205
Grand Rapids, MI 49505-3548
Tel: 616-364-3000
Fax: 616-264-9010

Performing Arts Foundation
500 Riverside Drive
New York, NY 10027
Tel: 212-316-8430
Fax: 212-316-8460

PETROLEUM ENGINEER

A DAY IN THE LIFE

The subtitle for Petroleum Engineering 101 at Stanford University reads "How to dig oil wells," and that is for the most part what a petroleum engineer does. He is involved in all phases of oil exploration, from choosing the prospective site through taking down the drilling rig after extracting the oil. This can mean travel, long stays in unusual (and sometimes inhospitable) locations, and uncertain working conditions. "It's a gambler's life," wrote one petroleum engineer, and others agreed. "If you're into engineering and gambling, petroleum engineering is for you," wrote another. Those not attracted to both should steer clear of this high-risk field.

A petroleum engineer usually works for a petroleum company in various capacities. The typical petroleum engineer works in the field. First, he scouts prospective sites that have a strong likelihood of containing oil or gas below. Then, he takes samples from the site and determines the amount and quality of oil, the depth at which these resources lie, and the equipment that will be needed to properly extract them. The PE then supervises construction and operations at the site and adjusts plans accordingly. Finally, when the well or pocket is exhausted, he supervises the removal of the drilling equipment and the safe return of the land to structural stability, and he oversees the removal of any waste (hazardous or otherwise) left at the site. These stages of work can be quick three-month stints or can be extended to as long as two years.

Patience, sound judgment, and maturity are all required features for the successful PE. "You've got to be able to see problems before they happen," wrote one veteran Californian PE, "otherwise you're right in the middle of them." Self-confidence is also crucial, as onsite decisions have to be made quickly and surely. Another said, "You have to be able to handle failure" if you want to survive in this industry. Speculative oil-well drilling is somewhere between a science and an art; expect to frequently plant rigs that prove barren or that only yield limited amounts of oil. But despite the frustrations that go with the turf, petroleum engineers seem to enjoy being out in the field, where they can get their hands dirty. One big satisfaction for many we surveyed was that they worked with both their minds and their hands.

Some petroleum engineers do work in offices, however, analyzing the reports and recommendations of field engineers and advising corporate decision-makers on whether to proceed. These positions are usually held by veteran personnel with experience as field engineers, drilling engineers, and reservoir estimators. While these people are crucial to the success of the industry as a whole, their levels of satisfaction were slightly lower than those of field engineers; the gambling lifestyle, it seems, is less exciting from behind a desk.

PAYING YOUR DUES

Petroleum engineers have rigorous academic requirements. They must hold an undergraduate degree in engineering or earth sciences (geology, geophysics, tectonics, mining, etc.), and the majority of the profession continues on to graduate study. For those who wish to enter academia, a Ph.D. is a must. Only a handful of universities in the United States offer programs that focus on petroleum engineering, with coursework in such subjects as geology, geophysics, chemistry, fluid dynamics, and physics. Most PE programs are located in oil-producing states, as are, obviously, most PE jobs. PEs must often relocate within these oil-producing parts of the country (California, Texas, and Oklahoma are big ones) or the world. Many states require practicing petroleum engineers to pass a state licensing exam.

ASSOCIATED CAREERS

Petroleum engineers develop extensive knowledge about the world of oil production, and many become industry analysts. A number use their economics skills—all oil production is a cost-benefit analysis—to enter companies as in-house economists. The largest number of refugees from this profession, however, enter environmental companies, are hired by the EPA, or become consultants to professional oil organizations. Digging oil wells can be a dirty business, and some respondents mentioned that after a few years of seeing what actually goes on at a site they wanted to change the direction of their lives.

PAST AND FUTURE

Before 1860, oil was an anomaly that sometimes bubbled up through the ground and was useful as a lubricant or for lighting lamps. In the late 1800s, Edwin Drake pumped the first oil well in Titusville, Pennsylvania, ushering in the age of oil production. The development and popularization of the automobile in this century provided a steady market of customers for one of oil's byproducts—gasoline—and thus was born the world's richest industry. Oil wells now reach over 20,000 feet below the ground to drain "black gold" from the earth.

The future of the petroleum engineer will be influenced by two factors: The short term glut of oil (only seen 12 months into the future) and the long-term scramble that oil depletion necessarily brings. In the short term, the demand for petroleum engineers should be weak, due to cheap and plentiful on-hand oil inventories, consistently-producing wells, and inexpensive foreign oil alternatives. By the year 2020, however, experts predict that the long-term demand for petroleum will greatly exceed the supply, making it worthwhile for companies to hire many petroleum engineers in search of any valuable undiscovered pockets of oil.

QUALITY OF LIFE

Two Years

Two years into the profession, petroleum engineers are working as junior assistants, taking rock samples and sending them to labs for testing. They often collect data and assemble it for more senior researchers. Many take this opportunity to form mentor relationships with these project managers and are exposed to years of experience in short periods of time. Much time is spent onsite, and a number of junior members use these early years to gain foreign oil exploration experience. Hours are long; pay is average. In these first two years it's important to get the state licensing exams out of the way, since they become more difficult to pass the farther away you get from your coursework.

Five Years

The middle years of the profession are marked by significant responsibility and a lot of risk-taking. Many are assigned lead roles in one phase of oil exploration or development. Future assignments all rely on success in previous ones, so stress levels can be significant. Hours are long, particularly for field engineers. Those who are likely to become back-office consultants begin cultivating connections during these years; many of them attempt to publish in academic journals as an additional credential. Satisfaction levels are high.

Ten Years

Ten-year petroleum engineers have not only been through a number of diverse projects but have also seen the rapid fluctuation of the oil market affect their business. Those who make the transition from the field to the office do so between years six and twelve. Many have changed employers at least once. Salaries rise; satisfaction dips, then levels off.

THE BIRKMAN LIFESTYLE GRID

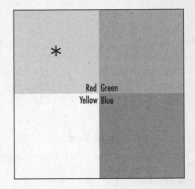

Red Green
Yellow Blue

This career is suitable for people with Red interests.

You'll Have Contact With

Drilling Rig Operators
Geologists
Geophysicists
Lab Technicians

Major Associations

American Petroleum Institute
1220 L Street, NW
Washington, DC 20005
Tel: 202-682-8000
Fax: 202-682-8569

Junior Engineering Technical Society
1420 King Street
Suite 405
Alexandria, VA 22314
Tel: 703-548-5387
Fax: 703-548-0769
Contact: Cathy McGowen

Society of Petroleum Engineers
222 Palisades Creek Drive
Richardson, TX 75080
Tel: 214-952-9393
Fax: 214-952-9435
Contact: Debbie Abramson

PHARMACEUTICAL SALES REPRESENTATIVE

PROFESSIONAL PROFILE

# of people in profession	13,900
% male	90
% female	10
avg. hours per week	55
avg. starting salary	$24,000
avg. salary after 5 years	$35,000
avg. salary 10 to 15 years	$56,000

Professionals Read

US Pharmacist
Pharmacy Times
Drugstore News
Manufacturing Chemist

Books, Films and TV Shows Featuring the Profession

Underneath the Mattress

Major Employers

Biogen
14 Cambridge Center
Cambridge, MA 02142-1353
Tel: 617-679-2200
Fax: 617-679-3595
Contact: Human Resources Department

UpJohn Company
7000 Porta Road
Kalamazoo, MI 49001
Tel: 616-323-4000
Fax: 616-323-4077

Bristol Myers Squibb Co.
P.O. Box 4500
Princeton, NJ 08543-4500
Tel: 800-925-3838
Contact: Staffing

A DAY IN THE LIFE

Pharmaceutical sales is a fast-paced, high-turnover business that rewards assertiveness, persistence, and knowledge. Pharmaceutical sales representatives spend most of their business time on the road, talking with pharmacists, hospital personnel, physicians, patient advocate groups, and even retirement homes, increasing the visibility of their company's products and the volume of their sales. "Sell sell sell learn learn learn sell sell sell," wrote one sales rep, who included his business card with his survey, in case we wanted to purchase any pharmaceutical supplies. Many other sales reps agreed that the best reps follow any lead, making every possible effort to sell their product. A number attend meetings where contact with purchasing professionals is rich, such as an association of pharmacists or a convention of hospital administrators.

This territory-oriented business can be a hard life, particularly for those trying to maintain their family life as well. The need to sell extends to social functions and free time, and the already precious family moments can erode further to the point where many reps are forced to reevaluate their commitment to their profession. This difficult balancing act is complicated by the additional pressure of being in a commission-based occupation. For many, a significant portion of their income is riding on their ability to get the product into the hands of the consumer. So, why is this job so addictive? Perhaps because the excessive profit margins of many brand-name pharmaceutical products can mean enormous commissions. In addition, products are generally consumed fairly quickly and not stored, so old markets rarely disappear; they need regular servicing.

The second-most attractive job feature that the sales reps mentioned was the intellectual challenge the job imposed. Education is the norm in this field; learning about a company's product line is like taking an advanced course in pharmacology (which many do take during their initial years in the industry). They have to be familiar with data, statistics, and issues in the health community to be able to communicate successfully with businesspeople and doctors. Although this job has some aspects that are unquestionably grueling—one sales rep said he put in 184 days on the road in 1994—many love it, and "love" is the only term that accurately describes their zeal, dedication, and willingness to make sacrifices for their job.

PAYING YOUR DUES

Pharmaceutical sales representatives with a science background have an advantage in this profession, in terms of both their credibility and their ability to educate themselves about product lines. A college degree is standard for this job, with many employers looking favorably on graduate work. Useful courses include biology, chemistry, biochemistry, biophysics, organic chemistry, English, public speaking, finance, and negotiation techniques. Professional education is the norm for all sales representatives, both on their own products and on other companies' product lines. The ability to read a scientific study and examine its assumptions is critical to a PSR's success. Licensing is available through professional organizations, but it is not required to advance to managerial positions.

ASSOCIATED CAREERS

Pharmaceutical sales representatives go into sales positions in other professions—as systems marketers or service sales representatives, for example—where their selling skills are valued, but where scientific knowledge is less important. Some PSRs are willing to give up the scientific element of their job in order to go into a profession where it is easier to advance and easier to maintain a satisfying family life.

PAST AND FUTURE

The discovery of penicillin was the beginning of the development of a host of anti-infection and anti-bacterial drugs. These sparked a nationwide frenzy of biotechnological invention. In fifty years, the U.S. outpaced the world's production of synthetic biological agents from the dawn of time to the turn of the twentieth century. With this growth of options came the growth of competition—many products had similar effects, and companies found it useful to go directly to physicians and hospitals to show them the benefits of their products. Pharmaceuticals are a multi-billion dollar industry, and sales representatives who keep doctors interested in their supplies are worth much to their employers.

The future of pharmaceutical sales representatives is uncertain, primarily because of the uncertainty surrounding all health-care issues. Pharmaceutical products will certainly continue to be important, but it is not clear how much latitude doctors in managed care plans will have to prescribe various medications. Many managed care plans impose "generic" standards on physicians. These standards state that when a generic substitute for a brand-name product exists, the plan will pay only for the cheaper, generic substitute. Other scenarios such as government-distributed health care, price limits on products, and disallowances for research costs may further erode the position of pharmaceutical sales representatives.

QUALITY OF LIFE

Two Years

At the beginning of the profession, sales representatives have few contacts and little experience selling their products. Their potential clients are usually doctors with a number of years of experience driving bargains and negotiating with other sales representatives, so many new reps view this period as an education rather than a profit opportunity. Many reps say that doctors will often talk them into handing out free samples. Sales reps often spend significant time in training programs and at professional conferences learning about industry issues. Hours are long.

Five Years

Five-year veterans have a much rosier day-to-day existence, though it is a very busy one. Many spend more than 110 days on the road, visiting hospitals, physicians, and other health-care professionals, trying to sell them their products. They have established regular routes, and those who are successful have expanded their client base. Some experience financial windfalls; others use those people as models and struggle harder to succeed. Dedication is evident. Satisfaction is high.

Ten Years

Some pharmaceutical sales representatives say ten years in this profession is a lifetime, but very few leave it. Many have moved into managerial positions or have been given control over a large territory. These start the process again on a grander scale with greater potential income. Only a handful make the extremely large amounts of money that mark the superstars in this profession, but the culture makes all reps aware that the best sales representatives make the most money. Satisfaction is high. Hours are long. Family life may suffer.

THE BIRKMAN LIFESTYLE GRID

Red Green
Yellow Blue

This career is suitable for people with Green interests.

You'll Have Contact With
Hospital Administrators
Insurance Executives
Pharmacists
Physicians

Major Associations
National Pharmaceutical Council
1894 Preston White Drive
Reston, VA 22091
Tel: 703-620-6390
Contact: Didge Pearson

American Pharmaceutical Association
2215 Constitution Avenue NW
Washington, DC 22037-2985
Tel: 202-628-4410

American Council on Pharmaceutical Education
311 West Superior Street
Suite 512
Chicago, IL 60610
Tel: 312-664-3575
Contact: Daniel Nona

PHARMACIST

PROFESSIONAL PROFILE

# of people in profession	163,000
% male	85
% female	15
avg. hours per week	40
avg. starting salary	$25,500
avg. salary after 5 years	$45,000
avg. salary 10 to 15 years	$53,000

Professionals Read

US Pharmacist
Pharmacy Times
Drugstore News

Books, Films and TV Shows Featuring the Profession

Watching the Store
Chemical Breakdown
All Night

Major Employers

Genovese
80 Marcus Drive
Melville, NY 11747
Tel: 516-420-1900
Fax: 516-845-8476
Contact: Personnel

CVS
1773 Grand Avenue
Baldwin, NY 11710
Tel: 516-378-7556

Rite Aid
144-29 North Boulevard
Flushing, NY 11354
Tel: 718-886-1515

A DAY IN THE LIFE

Pharmacists engage in a wide variety of activities, and all of them revolve around medicines and drugs. Sixty percent of pharmacists fit the profession's stereotype, dispensing drugs to customers from a local drugstore or from the prescriptions window at a local supermarket. Many, however, are employed by large health-care institutions such as hospitals or nursing services. Pharmacists can work in any field which deals with drugs, whether it be in law enforcement as a narcotics investigator, in public health as a safety researcher, or in a pharmaceutical company in research, management, or sales, but a large majority work in pharmacies or for hospitals and health care providers.

Life in the profession depends greatly on which of these tracks is pursued. Drugstore pharmacists spend their time preparing prescriptions, advising customers about prescription and non-prescription drugs, and running the business of their pharmacy or pharmaceutical department. Their lives resemble those of a small-store or department manager. The products may require professional training to handle safely, but business skills are also important in the career. Approximately one in six pharmacies is actually owned by the pharmacist who manages it.

Pharmacists in the other sectors of the profession generally lead lives that resemble those of health-care professionals. Hospital and nursing pharmacists make rounds, overseeing the administration of medication, and consult with physicians on courses of treatment and developments in pharmacology. The studies conducted by research pharmacists are similar to those conducted by other medical researchers, and pharmaceutical companies frequently employ teams of pharmacists, doctors and biologists working side by side to develop new drugs. Though it requires similar training, this career track is quite different from that of the pharmacist employed in a pharmacy, and it is ideal for those who desire the rewards, and accept the stress, of treating patients and developing cures.

PAYING YOUR DUES

Specialized training is required to become a practicing pharmacist. A bachelor's degree in pharmacy, which usually requires five years of post-high school study, is the minimum. Some colleges of pharmacy admit students directly from high school; the majority, however, require one to two years of college level study in mathematics, physics, chemistry, and biology. While the bachelor's degree is sufficient to practice in the average pharmacy, a growing number of hospitals require their pharmacists to have doctorates, which require an additional one to two years of study. The Doctorate of Pharmacy is also usually a requirement for pharmacists who want to work as researchers or teachers. In addition, pharmacists must take state board examinations, and most states require that pharmacists serve a one-year internship before being allowed to practice; some require a two-year internship for pharmacists who wish to practice in hospitals.

ASSOCIATED CAREERS

Some pharmacists leave to become patent attorneys, specializing in pharmaceuticals. Others who work for pharmaceutical companies end up concentrating on the business and manufacturing, rather than the pharmaceutical, aspects of the work and leave to take managerial positions in other fields. Some pharmacists in hospitals or nursing services cease the pharmaceutical practices and become health care administrators. On the whole, however, the profession is quite stable.

PAST AND FUTURE

Pharmacy dates back to the ancient Greeks, whose "pharmakons" mixed drugs, much like the pharmacists of today. The modern profession in the United States dates to the 1821 founding of the first American pharmaceutical college, the Philadelphia College of Pharmacy, but a pharmacist of 1821 would have a difficult time recognizing the profession today. As modern science has produced an increasing number of drugs, pharmacists have become increasingly important to the practice of medicine, and the profession is moving in the direction of specialization, with pharmacists who work in research or health care institutions becoming experts in particular categories of drugs. This trend will likely continue, and it is likely that this increasing medical complexity, combined with the increasing average age of the U.S. population, will cause demand for pharmacists to remain strong for the foreseeable future.

QUALITY OF LIFE

Two Years

At this stage, pharmacists have just completed their apprenticeship and training. The majority work as the junior of two or three pharmacists in a community pharmacy; some work as junior researchers for a pharmaceutical company or as junior staff pharmacists in a hospital or health care facility. In general, hospital and research pharmacists at this point work closely with more experienced professionals and are carefully supervised. In a community pharmacy, the work of these pharmacists—advising customers about medication and dispensing drugs—more closely resembles the work of their senior colleagues.

Five Years

Established professionals by this point, pharmacists in private pharmacies will begin to take on managerial responsibilities, while hospital and research pharmacists now have full-fledged professional status and begin to take supervisory responsibility for their junior colleagues. Some will stop practicing pharmaceutics but will stay within the profession as managerial and sales employees of pharmaceutical companies.

Ten Years

Some pharmacists who work in private pharmacies establish their own practices around this time; approximately 10 percent of all pharmacists end up owning their own pharmacies. Others will become more senior-salaried employees, with increased pay and responsibility for the business operations of their pharmacies. Those who work for hospitals may have risen to the position of chief pharmacist, supervising a staff of pharmacists and having considerable administrative and medical responsibility for the hospitals medication policies. Research pharmacists also take on increasing administrative duties, becoming responsible for research projects and often working with management to identify long term research and business goals.

THE BIRKMAN LIFESTYLE GRID

This career is suitable for people with Red interests.

You'll Have Contact With

Insurance Executives
Lab Technicians
Pharmaceutical Salesmen
Physicians

Major Associations

American Association of Colleges of Pharmacy
1426 Prince Street
Alexandria, VA 22314
Tel: 703-739-2330

American Council on Pharmaceutical Education
311 West Superior Street
Suite 512
Chicago, IL 60610
Tel: 312-664-3575
Contact: Daniel A. Nona

American Pharmaceutical Association
2215 Constitution Avenue NW
Washington, DC 20037-2985
Tel: 202-628-4410

PHILOSOPHER

A DAY IN THE LIFE

What is the nature of truth? The meaning of life? The ideal structure of a society? Philosophers spend their lives attempting to answer questions like these. A taste for intellectual debate is a must in this profession. If you enjoy abstractions, you'll probably enjoy being a philosopher, but be warned: It's a tough way to pay the rent. Most philosophers make their livings as college professors (see Professor), but there aren't many full-time teaching positions in philosophy, and philosophers do not have outside employment opportunities the way engineers or economists do. The French government has occasionally employed its own philosophers, once hiring noted philosopher Michel Foucault to serve on a committee to rewrite the French penal code, but the U.S. government is not known for this practice.

For those who do find teaching positions in philosophy, the work is quite similar to that of other professors in the humanities. Aside from teaching responsibilities, which usually occupy approximately twelve hours per week, one's time is largely one's own. Professors stay busy, however; long hours are the norm, but the work is a pleasure if you enjoy reading and writing about philosophy, and why else would you enter the field? Particularly in the first few years, philosophy involves a lot of writing, as a young philosophy professor's publishing record is an important part of the tenure evaluation. Once tenured, however, philosophers can probably live the closest approximation of a life of pure contemplation in our society.

You can become a philosopher simply by deciding to call yourself one. If thinking about life is practicing philosophy, who's to say that you have to be paid by a university to do it? Henry David Thoreau retreated from his fellow human beings, built a cabin at Walden Pond, and wrote books of philosophy. It helps to get published, of course, but you don't necessarily have to care whether other people follow and study your philosophy.

PAYING YOUR DUES

Unless you plan on taking the Walden Pond approach, a Ph.D. in philosophy is a prerequisite in this field. This involves five to seven years of study after completion of a college degree, including two to three years of course work. The rest of the time is spent writing a dissertation, which must be an original manuscript analyzing some aspect of philosophy. More so than in many of the other humanities professions, philosophy departments specialize, choosing to have a majority of analytic philosophers, continental philosophers, comparative philosophers, or some other branch of the field. The young philosopher's choice of a dissertation topic, therefore, has a significant impact upon the institutions where jobs will be available at graduation. Like all the academic disciplines, relationships with senior faculty are extremely important in finding a job, as positions are often filled through recommendations from colleagues.

ASSOCIATED CAREERS

People with training in philosophy turn up in a wide variety of fields. The training is flexible enough that philosophers can become bankers, writers, policy analysts, or almost any other profession imaginable. Perhaps because the training includes substantial elements of political philosophy, many people decide to go from philosophy to the legal profession. (Besides, lawyers have a better chance of making a living.)

PAST AND FUTURE

Contemporary philosophy, as it is taught in U.S. universities, traces its roots to the ancient Greeks, but other systems of non-Western philosophy find their origins in a vast range of sources, from the political debates of the Iroquois Confederacy to the Confucian writings of early China. Western philosophy is presently broadly divided into two camps: Continental, which concentrates on traditionally defined philosophical writers like Nietzsche and Hegel, and analytic, which owes much of its methodology to mathematics and theoretical physics.

While this profession will likely remain limited in size, it should see the same increase that is expected for all the academic professions as the number of college age Americans begins to grow in the late 1990s. Over the last decade, however, the humanities have lost ground to the more professionally oriented fields of American academia, and this trend will likely continue.

QUALITY OF LIFE

Two Years

At this stage, the recent philosophy graduate is either in a tenure track job as an instructor or assistant professor, or is working as a part-time or adjunct professor and looking for a job which could eventually lead to tenure. The young assistant professor works long hours, teaching several undergraduate classes and beginning to establish the research and writing record necessary to advance in her field. In smaller and two-year colleges, there is often less pressure to publish, but these are busy years wherever the young philosopher teaches.

Five Years

An academic career has begun to take shape at this point. The philosopher has probably published a couple of books or major research projects and has established clear areas of expertise. In addition, she has been promoted to associate professor, the final step before tenure. Associate professors have more control over their teaching schedules; they are likely to be teaching fewer low-level classes and more classes and seminars in their areas of specialization with older undergraduates and graduate students. In addition, as academic marketability is determined by a university's specific needs for expertise, professors become more able to move around between institutions as they establish themselves in their respective philosophical fields.

Ten Years

By now, philosophers have either made tenure at the university where they started, found another university which will give them tenure, or left the profession. With tenure comes the rewards of the philosophical life: The ability to say, write, and teach what one wishes with almost complete freedom.

THE BIRKMAN LIFESTYLE GRID

This career is suitable for people with Blue interests.

You'll Have Contact With

Editors
Professors
Publishers
Students

Major Associations

American Catholic Philosophical Association
Catholic University of America
Washington, DC 20064
Tel: 202-319-5518
Contact: Philosophy Dept.

American Philosophical Association
University of Delaware
Newark, DE 19716
Tel: 302-451-1112

Society of Philosophers in America
(SOPHIA), Yale University
1562 Timothy Dwight College
New Haven, CT 06520
Tel: 203-572-5362
Fax: 203-562-3613

PHOTOGRAPHER

Professionals Read

Shutterbug
Professional Photographer
Photographist Forum
Outdoor Photography
Photo District News
Popular Photography

Books, Films and TV Shows
Featuring the Profession

The Eyes of Laura Mars
The Girl in the Picture
The Bridges of Madison County
The Work of Ansel Adams
Blow Up

Major Employers

Glamour Shots
100 Cambridge Side Place
Cambridge, MA 02141
Tel: 617-374-9900
Fax: 617-374-9208
Contact: Pam Masters

Associated Press
184 High Street
Boston, MA 02110
Tel: 617-357-8106
Fax: 617-338-8125
Contact: Dan Hansen, Photo Editor

Associated Press/Worldwide Photos, Inc.
50 Rockefeller Center
New York, NY 10020
Tel: 212-621-1935

A DAY IN THE LIFE

A photographer takes pictures of people, places, objects, and events and tries to artistically capture and evoke a mood, feeling, or drama surrounding a particular subject. Photography is both an artistic and technical job with which one can present his or her technical proficiency as well as beautifully composed images. A photographer uses his camera much the way an artist uses his brush, as a tool to capture his unique perspective of the world around him. The famous photographer Ansel Adams popularized the genre of landscape photography as art through his pictures of Yosemite. Alfred Steiglitz recorded the charm of the drama of the modern world around him in great photos such as The Steerage and also earned fame for his series of portraits of Georgia O'Keeffe. Cartier-Bresson's subject was the city itself. A photographer must practice extensively in order to master the technical knowledge of light, camera settings, lenses, film, and filters and apply this knowledge creatively. Photographers use a wide variety of lenses and filters designed for close-up, mid-range or long distance photography. Some photographers do their own developing and printing, especially "art" photographers, but many hand their film over to their employer or a commercial lab for processing.

More than half of all photographers are self-employed and most specialize in commercial or portrait photography or photojournalism. Commercial photography involves taking pictures of merchandise, buildings, machinery, fashions, livestock, and groups of people to be used in advertisements, marketing reports, brochures, catalogs, and postcards. Editorial photographers work for magazines, newspapers, and sometimes book publishers (for covers); industrial photographers' work is usually used in reports and to evaluate machinery or products used. Forensic photographers travel with police to crime scenes to photograph evidence; portrait photographers work either in their own studios or on location, taking pictures of individuals, families, and small groups. Some photographers specialize in special events such as wedding, awards ceremonies, etc.

Photojournalists often face significant danger in attempting to take pictures of newsworthy events, people, places, and things for newspapers, journals, and magazines. Some photojournalists also work in the field of educational photography, preparing slides and film strips for use in the classroom. Still others become aerial photographers, taking photos from airplanes for industrial, scientific, military, or journalistic purposes. Scientific and biological photographers provide images for science publications, research reports, and textbooks. Archaeological photographers take pictures of finds in situ. Finish photographers photograph horse races as the animals cross the finish line. Motion picture photographers film movies, commercials and television programs.

Photographers work long and irregular hours and sometimes have to be available on short notice. They must be able to work under the pressure of tight deadlines. Self-employed photographers enjoy a more flexible and relaxed schedule but must devote a significant amount of time marketing themselves and expanding their client list.

PAYING YOUR DUES

Skill, creativity, training, and determination are the keys to success in this profession. No formal education is necessary, but for the photographer who intends to specialize in areas such as scientific or industrial photography, a college degree in the area of specialty is recommended. Photojournalists are often expected to have some background in journalism.

Photographers need to have good manual dexterity, and good color vision and eyesight. They must also possess certain personal traits such as artistic sensibility, creativity, and reliability; and enjoy working with detail. They should have an appreciation of light and shadow, an eye for form and line, and a distinctive and creative approach to photographs. Because success in this field is closely tied to experience and exposure, aspiring photographers are advised to serve internships or apprenticeships with experienced photographers to acquire broad technical knowledge of the field and the practical experience that comes with handling many different kinds of cameras and equipment. Apprentices are trained in darkroom techniques, lighting and background, and the use and setup of camera equipment. Those who are interested in setting up their own studios should prepare by taking business and marketing courses and some public relations courses to be able to sell their skills and increase clientele.

ASSOCIATED CAREERS

Photographers who grow tired of the business or wish to hold a more steady job as well as being photographers can use their skills as graphic artists or in the art departments of publishers, magazines, newspapers, or advertising agencies. Becoming developers is another option for those photographers seeking to expand operations. Some teach photography. With additional training, photographers can become cameramen.

PAST AND FUTURE

Photography first "developed" in the mid-nineteenth century. Early photographers captured images on heavy plates and printed them on sepia-toned paper. Now cameras have been simplified to their bare essentials with film and a lens and aperture in cardboard boxes that can be recycled once the film is developed.

The growing use of visual images in areas such as education, communication, entertainment, marketing, research and development should continue to drive the demand for innovative and skilled photographers. The increasing use of computers in photography will create another growth area for those in the field.

QUALITY OF LIFE

Two Years

The newcomer should still be apprenticed to a more seasoned photographer. She may be a proficient photographer, but as yet has not acquired enough experience to compete against the more experienced and versatile photographers in the profession.

Five Years

At the five-year level, the self-employed photographer is slowly building a reputation and scouting for more clients. If he is lucky, some of his work may have been placed in magazines and trade journals, a significant step. Photographers should consider signing with stock photo agencies which grant magazine and other clients the rights to an individual's photographs on a commission basis. Some photographers work in-house at magazines, newspapers, or are one of a stable of professionals at large photography businesses that specialize in weddings and events.

Ten Years

Photographers have usually set up their own studios by this point. The ten-year veteran has significant professional contacts that will lead to bigger and more high-profile assignments. She has more pictures published in magazines and journals.

THE BIRKMAN LIFESTYLE GRID

Red Green
Yellow Blue

*

This career is suitable for people with Blue interests.

You'll Have Contact With

Advertising Executives
Event Planners
Graphic Designers
Journalists
Editors

Major Associations

American Society of Magazine
Photographers
419 Park Avenue South
New York, NY 10016
Tel: 212-614-9644

Professional Women Photographers, c/o
Photographic
17 West 17th Street
4th Floor
New York, NY 10011
Tel: 212-255-9678
Fax: 212-620-0999

American Council for the Arts
1 East 53rd Street
New York, NY 10022
Tel: 212-223-2787
Contact: Membership Department

American Society of Media Photographers
853 Broadway
New York, NY 10013
Tel: 212-614-9644

PHYSICAL THERAPIST

A DAY IN THE LIFE

Working with patients who have limited use of their own bodies due to injury or disability, a physical therapist builds flexibility, strength, and spirit. Her goals are to reduce the patients' pain, to increase their range of motion, and to give them back their sense of self-determination. "All day I help people get back in charge of their lives," wrote one physical therapist from Tucson, Arizona, "and that makes me feel great!" This sense of contributing to peoples' quality of life is important to those entering the field. Physical therapy is emotionally and physically demanding, and a patient's progress has to be measured in extremely small increments. Still, those who find it rewarding are extremely happy with their choice of occupation.

A physical therapist works in either a hospital or private office setting, seeing roughly ten patients per day. Some physical therapists have specialties that require additional certification, such as gerontology, sports physical therapy, ob/gyn, pediatrics, orthopedics, neurology, or degenerative diseases like multiple sclerosis or cerebral palsy. Most are generalists and must be able to evaluate any patient's condition and design a reasonable rehabilitation program. Often, physical therapists see patients after traumatic injuries sustained in car crashes, sports mishaps, or other types of accidents. In these cases, physical therapists work closely with physicians to determine the pace and expected progress of the patient. A physical therapist has to be sensitive not only to the physical limitations of his patients but to their emotional limitations as well. "You have to be able to motivate people to do exercises that hurt and remind them of their limitations," wrote one physical therapist, "and the last part is the most difficult part for them." "Patience is key," as another put it.

The emotional strain of working with people who are frustrated at their newly limited abilities can take its toll. "When a patient's body isn't responding, they can take it out on you," mentioned one. Emotional attachment to patients is nearly inevitable after months or even years of close association, and being the target of several people's anger and frustration can be a drag; of the ten percent who leave physical therapy each year, more than half cite "depression" as one factor. The profession is physically demanding, too; most of a physical therapist's time is spent standing, crouching, bending, and using her muscles, and long days followed by sore evenings are common. Also, physical therapists spend about ten percent of their time on tedious paper work, filing progress reports and filling out insurance claim forms. This aspect of the job is expected to become more demanding in the future, as insurers are now targeting rehabilitation therapy for cuts.

PAYING YOUR DUES

All physical therapists are licensed by the state and must have fulfilled standard academic requirements. You can find work with a Bachelor's Degree in Physical Therapy from one of the 700 or so accredited undergraduate programs in the U.S., but those who did not take this route in college can attend master's programs to study rehabilitation therapy-around sixty graduate schools offer this degree. Aspiring physical therapists should study biology, biomechanics, calculus and statistics, chemistry, nutrition, human growth and development, physics, and psychology. Students may be required to do field work in addition to their academic studies. As a career, physical therapy offers flexibility: Over 20 percent of physical therapists work in the profession part time while finishing other degrees, pursuing other careers, or taking care of family.

ASSOCIATED CAREERS

Physical therapists who leave the field often continue as therapists in related or specialized areas, such as speech therapy, occupational therapy, chiropody, flexibility and strength training, and audiology. A notable few train to become physicians.

PAST AND FUTURE

The wide-scale application of physical therapy didn't take place until a great number of soldiers returned from World War I with injuries that required extensive physical rehabilitation. Physical therapy soon became a widely practiced and respected profession in the United States.

The expected demand for physical therapists in the U.S. is expected to grow by 88 percent by the year 2005. America's population is aging, and more and more physicians are recognizing that physical therapy is critical to the successful recovery of patients from surgery, injury, and illness. The only possible roadblock is potential limitations by insurance carriers; should insurers place overly restrictive caps on physical therapy payments, the industry will see a slower rate of growth, but still an increased number of available positions.

QUALITY OF LIFE

Two Years

Two years into the profession, physical therapists are working for the most part in internships and as assistants while they complete their studies. Many use these years to learn client skills, the most difficult part of the profession. Two-years are generally still developing the persona that marks the successful physical therapist: A combined friend, therapist, and drill sergeant. Hours are average; wages are reasonable.

Five Years

Five-year practitioners have satisfied all licensing requirements and are now considered full members of the profession. This means that hours rise and responsibilities increase for most. A number switch positions during these middle years, trying on both hospital and private settings for size. Salaries rise, and many begin to see significant results with their patients, which increases their job satisfaction. The majority of those who leave the profession do so between years two and six.

Ten Years

Ten-year professional physical therapists follow one of two tracks: Many go into private practice and open their own offices, often hiring other physical therapists. Others continue their affiliations with hospitals and employers but move to a more supervisory capacity, overseeing the work of other physical therapists and handling complicated or difficult cases. Many go back to school in years eight through twelve to develop specialties in the areas that they find most exciting.

You'll Have Contact With

Athletes
Nurses
Occupational Therapists
Physicians
Speech Therapists

Major Associations

American Physical Therapy Association
1111 North Fairfax Street
Alexandria, VA 22314
Tel: 800-999-APTA
Contact: Alexis Waters, ext. 3215

National Rehabilitation Association
633 South Washington Street
Alexandria, VA 22314
Tel: 703-836-0850
Contact: Michelle Highley

Muscular Dystrophy Association
3300 East Sunrise Drive
Tuson, AZ 85718
Tel: 602-529-2000
Contact: Research & Program Service Department

PHYSICIAN

PROFESSIONAL PROFILE

# of people in profession	575,000
% male	80
% female	20
avg. hours per week	60
avg. starting salary	$34,000
avg. salary after 5 years	$140,000
avg. salary 10 to 15 years	$200,000

Professionals Read

Journal of AMA
New England Journal of Medicine
Clinical journals in area of specialty

Books, Films and TV Shows Featuring the Profession

Chicago Hope
The Doctors
Vital Signs
Of Human Bondage

Major Employers

Massachusetts General Hospital
101 Merrimac Street
5th Floor
Boston, MA 02114
Tel: 617-726-2210
Contact: Human Resources

County General Hospital
55-55 Ferguson Drive
Commerce, CA 90022
Tel: 213-890-8382
Fax: 213-890-8331
Contact: Debbie Jackson

A DAY IN THE LIFE

Doctors can pursue many career paths, including private practice, university-hospital work, or a job with a health maintenance organization. The first lets you be your own boss. The second offers you the opportunity to divide your work between treatment, research and instruction, in varying proportions. The third means you work for a large corporation, which provides you with patients and handles most of the administrative and business tasks that physicians in private practice have to handle on their own. Doctors can also work in inner-city clinics or in rural areas, where shortages of doctors exist. Doctors can be general practitioners or they can specialize in internal medicine, cardiology, endocrinology, neurology, oncology, sports medicine, or one of the many other specialties.

Medicine is a very rewarding profession, but it is hard work. Doctors are often exhilarated when they know they have helped someone get well and devastated when they lose a patient. It is a job that can prey upon you physically and mentally. Since the average patient is not a doctor, physicians must not only be able to communicate difficult, often painful information to those in their care, but also they must learn how to interpret their patients' needs. They must relate to their patients as people and not reduce them to just the illness that needs to be treated. One element of this is collaborating with their patients to determine the best course of treatment for them as individuals. This requires patience, empathy, and compassion. "Compassion," said one doctor, "is absolutely necessary."

PAYING YOUR DUES

In college, enroll in a pre-med program. Volunteer to work at your local hospital or with the emergency medical services. During your last year of college, apply for medical school and take the MCAT. The four-year program at medical school encompasses clinical work and book learning, with two years in the classroom and two in the clinical setting. Some of the usual courses are pathology, pharmacology, neuroanatomy, biochemistry, physiology, histology (the anatomy of tissues), and gross anatomy (cadaver class). Clinical study takes place at local hospitals or medical practices. Students are expected to offer diagnoses and suggest courses of treatment in real-life situations, although an MD/instructor makes the final decisions. In standard programs, students enter clinical clerkships in their third year and, in their fourth year, they can choose among various elective subspecialties. Students also spend the fourth year applying for internships.

After four years, students sit for the USMLE (the medical boards), and those who pass receive their medical degrees. A three-year internship and residency are next, although many specialties require a longer training commitment. A medical education is never truly complete. New challenges and breakthroughs change the medical landscape at an alarming clip. Nevertheless, those initial years of med school have an enormous impact. One doctor we spoke to could name instructors who still influenced his work, more than thirty years after he earned his degree.

ASSOCIATED CAREERS

Nursing is the clearest alternative to medical practice. Although the educational demands are less rigorous, the responsibilities are just as great. Nurse practitioners prescribe medicines and play a key role in patient care. There are also many opportunities for lab technicians. You may also be interested in a career in pharmacology, biology, biochemistry, or biophysics.

PAST AND FUTURE

Not even the elimination of disease would eliminate society's need for specialists in the working of the human body. The first physician, Hippocrites, began with this motto: "First do no harm," a credo doctors still live by today (physicians are asked to take the "Hippocratic oath" which affirms this belief among others). With the institution of formalized training and strict professional certification, physicians gained more respect and were more widely used in the modern world.

The medical professions are undergoing a downsizing process similar to that of many other industries. Medical schools are placing a greater emphasis on general knowledge, although there is still a need for specialists. The growth of managed care has increased the demand for obstetricians, pediatricians, and family practitioners who can treat a wide variety of ailments and look after the health of a large number of patients. Medical schools themselves are getting smaller, and some states have closed down entire medical programs for lack of funds.

QUALITY OF LIFE

Two Years

Residents work long hours and are expected to put their classroom experience into practice right away. Doctors must quickly learn the difference between books and people. Interns and residents work under the supervision of other doctors. Although resident's hours have traditionally been very long, hospitals have recently begun reducing the schedules of their young doctors. After satisfying residency requirements, a doctor can strike out on her own as a full-fledged medical practitioner. Wherever you work, you'll spend much of your salary paying off student debt, which can exceed $100,000.

Five Years

In private practice, a full partnership usually comes after five years. You have a vested interest in attracting and keeping patients. In addition to your clinical responsibilities, you will have the management duties that come with running any business. University-hospital based physicians may work their way up the faculty ladder, devote more time to clinical work, or spend their days in the lab conducting research. Doctors at HMOs can look forward to some vested interest in their organization.

Ten Years

Experienced doctors, whether general practitioners or a specialists, command very high salaries. A thriving private practice is demanding but lucrative. Medical instructors at major universities often earn more than the university's president. With the boom in managed health care, doctors at HMOs can expect similar rewards in exchange for accepting certain restrictions on their professional autonomy.

THE BIRKMAN LIFESTYLE GRID

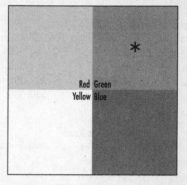

This career is suitable for people with Green interests.

You'll Have Contact With
Hospital Administrators
Insurance Executives
Nurses
Patients

Major Associations
American Medical Association
515 North State Street
Chicago, IL 60610
Tel: 312-464-5000
Fax: 312-464-4184
Contact: Human Resources

American Academy of Family Physicians
8880 Ward Parkway
Kansas City, MO 64114-2756
Tel: 816-333-9700
Fax: 816-333-9855
Contact: Cherry Phillips

National Medical Association
1120 G Street, NW
Suite 900
Washington, DC 20005
Tel: 202-347-6900
Fax: 202-347-8650
Contact: Frankie Stuntz

PHYSICIST

Professionals Read

American Journal of Physics
Physics Today
Physics News Update

Books, Films and TV Shows Featuring the Profession

IQ
The Manhattan Project
Fat Man and Little Boy
Genius

Major Employers

Dupont
1007 Market Street
Wilmington, DE 19898
Tel: 302-774-7321
Contact: Human Resources Professional Staffing

AT&T Bell Labs
600 Mountain Avenue P.O. Box 636
Room 30-325
Murray Hill, NJ 07974-0636
Tel: 908-582-3000
Contact: Personnel Dept.

National Semiconductor Corp
P.O. Box 58090
Santa Clara, CA 95052-8090
Tel: 408-721-5000
Contact: Human Resources

A DAY IN THE LIFE

The physicist deals with all aspects of matter and energy. His or her work ranges from basic research into the most fundamental laws of nature to the practical development of devices and instruments. The study of physics falls into many categories. These include studies of the motion and properties of physical objects both large and small (classical and quantum mechanics, astrophysics), the properties of waves (optics, acoustics, electromagnetics), the properties of states of matter (solid state, plasma physics), and the fundamental properties of matter and energy (atomic, nuclear, and particle physics). Because of the vast range of subject matter, at the graduate level physicists tend to specialize in one of these categories. Across most categories, physicists also tend to specialize in theoretical and experimental work. Theoretical physicists use mathematical concepts to analyze and predict the behavior of the physical world. Experimental physicists use laboratory experiments to verify these theoretical predictions or develop devices and instruments.

Physicists tend to be curious, creative, and dedicated. The majority of physicists are employed by universities and divide their time between research, teaching, and writing scientific articles. Many physicists work independently on problems, while others work in laboratories as part of teams for the duration of particular projects. Physicists working in industry are a varied lot. Many work in traditional areas just like the university physicists, but many branch out into engineering fields and other scientific fields, working with engineers and other scientists in overlapping areas. Because of their broad scientific background, physicists in industry are known for their ability to work in many areas and have helped create many non-traditional fields. Physics is not for the faint-hearted, but for those with good mathematical skills who want a broad scientific education and the ability to branch out later into other fields, physics may be just the thing.

Like those in many other scientific fields, a physicist's career progresses from being a team member doing hands-on work to being a team leader, responsible for developing new projects, running existing ones, and raising money to fund the project. One Ivy League physicist complains that fundraising is a necessary evil in his line of work. In both universities and industry, there have been recent cutbacks in research funding that have affected almost everyone in the field.

PAYING YOUR DUES

Excellent mathematical skills and statistical knowledge are required of the physicist, who will spend a large part of his academic life studying these subjects. The physicist must be as competent in these areas as any mathematician or statistician. Computer knowledge is also key. The most successful physicists go beyond a Bachelor's degree to get a Master's and then a doctorate, which entails a significant piece of original research. Without postgraduate degrees, it's generally difficult to find work as a physicist. Those who do land a job in this field with only a B.S. will find that they need to further their studies if they want to progress beyond rudimentary lab duties.

ASSOCIATED CAREERS

A large number of non-practicing physicists end up teaching. Depending on the degree she has, a physicist can teach science in high school or at the college level. A background in physics along with some writing talent can also help you procure a job in scientific journalism. The field most closely related to physics is engineering. Engineers need to have a sophisticated knowledge of physics, but the course of study is often not as long. There are also fields that unite physics with other sciences. Biophysicists, for example, study the processes of life by bringing together physics, chemistry, and biology. Astrophysicists are involved in developing theories about the origin of the universe and the physical mechanisms which have generated the objects seen by astronomers. Astronomy is one of the laboratories for testing fundamental theories about the nature of matter and energy from relativity to particle physics.

PAST AND FUTURE

The origins of physics can be traced to Aristotle, who wrote at a time when physics was considered a philosophical science. It wasn't until 1,000 years later, with the work of Galileo, that physics was acknowledged to be a hard mathematical science. Galileo's discoveries in physics, the fact that matter of varying weights will always fall at the same speed, for instance, have earned him the label of "first modern scientist." Since then, physics has progressed rapidly, with many breakthroughs, such as the light bulb and the motion picture, still baffling to many people yet crucial to daily life.

Physicists agree that there is plenty of room for the field to grow as new discoveries are made concerning nuclear energy, communications, the ocean, and space. Unfortunately, the growth rate for this career is expected to be slower than average in the near future due to cuts in government funding, which will affect the field substantially. Eighty percent of employed physicists work for universities or the government. But as one prominent physicist consoles himself, if you have a degree in physics, you have something very few people have.

QUALITY OF LIFE

Two Years

Physicists report very high levels of satisfaction with their chosen profession at all levels. Very few leave the field at this time. Physicists are a dedicated lot, and after having spent upwards of seven years preparing for this career they rarely lose interest so soon.

Five Years

Those who leave the field at this time sometimes report feeling like failures for the first year or so in the broader job market. They do, however, find their educational backgrounds to be invaluable assets. A doctoral degree in physics can open a number of doors in other fields.

Ten Years

Many physicists leave the profession at this time because they feel they have "topped out" in their field. They go on to seek employment that will allow them to use their scientific background in less scientific ventures. A number of physicists report, however, that they miss being physicists.

THE BIRKMAN LIFESTYLE GRID

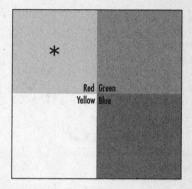

This career is suitable for people with Red interests.

You'll Have Contact With

Chemists
Lab Technicians
Mathematicians
Researchers

Major Associations

American Geophysical Union
2000 Florida Avenue, NW
Washington, DC 20009
Tel: 202-462-6900
Fax: 202-328-0566

American Institute of Physics
1 Physics Ellipse
College Park, MD 20740
Tel: 301-209-3000
Fax: 301-209-0843
Contact: Christine Cassagnau

American Nuclear Society
555 North Kensington Avenue
La Grange Park, IL 60526
Tel: 708-352-6611
Fax: 708-352-0499

PILOT

A DAY IN THE LIFE

The job of an airplane pilot carries considerable charm, prestige, responsibility, and risk. An airline pilot can find himself in a different time zone, climate, and culture every day. As one notes: "It's like a new and different expedition every time...a new and exciting world to discover and journey through." Pilots literally have the lives of their passengers in their hands. The physical and mental demands are rigorous. The ability to remain calm under pressure and having perfect vision, hearing, and coordination are crucial requirements.

Roughly 60 percent of all pilots are employed by commercial airlines, the most visible and widely known job available to pilots. Such professional visibility and prestige come with significantly more responsibility and a better pay scale. Commercial airline pilots fly large passenger planes often with 200 or more people aboard. There are several important safety steps that a pilot must take before every flight: Checking and filing flight plans, securing the approval of the air traffic control personnel of the Federal Aviation Agency (FAA), and checking weather and flight conditions. The airline pilot or captain is assisted in his job by a crew consisting of a co-pilot, a flight engineer, and a flight attendant. Sometimes the crew is extended to include an additional co-pilot and a navigator. Another important "member" of the crew is the automatic pilot, an electronic device which is programmed to fly the plane. Even when the automatic pilot is on, it is the captain's responsibility to remain alert to problems that may affect the plane. During the flight, the pilot and co-pilot maintain radio contact with ground control stations to report on altitude, speed, weather conditions, and a host of flight details.

With minimal retraining, the commercial pilot can make the transition to other areas of aviation. Helicopter pilots are used by television networks and radio stations to deliver traffic and accident reports. They are also used for air-taxi service, sightseeing operations, mail delivery, and rescue services. Agricultural pilots are involved in farm maintenance techniques such as crop dusting, fertilization, insect, and weed control. To make such a transition, the pilot would have to learn about the proper use and transportation of chemicals. Pilot instructors teach company airline pilots regulations and procedures. Chief pilots supervise the training of new pilots and handle other administrative work; test pilots test new planes; executive pilots are employed by large corporations that own or lease planes for company use.

PAYING YOUR DUES

At least two years of college are preferred for those seeking entry to this profession. FAA-certified military and civilian flying schools provide adequate practical and classroom training and some colleges and universities offer degree credit for pilot training. Prospective pilots must work long and hard at accumulating required flying time. They must be focused and determined to complete the various stages of what is a rigorous routine to an ultimately satisfying career. In the long run seniority counts in this profession, so young pilots are advised to buckle their seat belts, enjoy the ride, and keep racking up those hours.

Applicants for the commercial airplane pilot's license must have 250 hours of flying time and successfully complete rigorous testing, including a physical examination, a written test given by the FAA and a practical test. Before receiving an FAA license, pilots must be rated according to the kind of plane they can fly—single-engine, multi-engine or seaplane—and for the type— Boeing 707 or 747. Airplane captains must also have an airline transport pilot's license, for which a minimum of 1,500 hours of flight time including night flying and instrument time are required. Most pilots start out as flight engineers, a position which usually requires 500 to 1,000 hours of flying time. In addition to an instrument rating by the FAA, flight engineers obtain restricted radio telephone operators' permits from the Federal Communications Commission (FCC). From here it is a long haul, in the vicinity of five to fifteen years, before being named captain.

ASSOCIATED CAREERS

Pilots tend to be very satisfied with their jobs and remain in them until forced to retire. When they do stop flying planes, though, possible career moves include working as executives for airlines, going into private enterprise, opening flying schools, operating charter services, or delivering cargo.

PAST AND FUTURE

Orville and Wilbur Wright became the first airplane pilots when their craft stayed up for fourteen minutes at Kitty Hawk in 1903. The field has expanded considerably since then. The Lockheed brothers built their early commercial planes in 1913. Charles Lindbergh became the first American to cross the Atlantic by plane in 1927, and TWA's regular transatlantic service was inaugurated twenty years later.

Now, more than half of all pilots are employed by commercial airlines and, as commerce steadily expands, an even greater number will be able to secure employment. Competition will decrease and a possible shortage develop as aging pilots retire and new openings are created. Business or executive pilots, on the other hand, will face fewer job prospects as more companies under tighter budget controls opt to travel commercially rather than operate their own planes.

QUALITY OF LIFE

Two Years

The pilot, who has probably started out as a flight engineer, is ready to move up to co-pilot, though his company may not be ready for the move. Flight engineers generally spend two to seven years in the position before moving up to co-pilot. His main professional concern is amassing flying hours, including night flying and instrument time, to make it to the next position.

Five Years

The pilot/flight engineer is now within easy reach of being promoted to co-pilot if he has not yet been. Pilots rarely switch companies or careers at this point if they want to become captains.

Ten Years

The pilot with ten years of experience and thousands of miles of flying time should be a captain by now or within five years of becoming one. She has seniority and this is an important asset. Should she seek employment elsewhere, she will lose this seniority and have to work her way up from the bottom again. A pilot must be tenacious if captaincy is her goal.

THE BIRKMAN LIFESTYLE GRID

Red Green
Yellow Blue

This career is suitable for people with Red interests.

You'll Have Contact With
Air Traffic Controllers
Avionics Technicians
FAA Officials
Flight Attendants

Major Associations
Air Transport Association of America
1301 Pennsylvania Avenue, NW
Washington, DC 20004
Tel: 202-626-4000
Fax: 202-626-4181
Contact: Public Relations Department

Air Line Pilots Association, International
535 Herndon Parkway D371, PO Box 1169
Herndon, VA 20070
Tel: 703-689-2270
Fax: 703-689-4370
Contact: Communications Department

Future Aviation Professionals of America
4971 Massachusetts Boulevard
Atlanta, GA 30337
Tel: 770-997-8097
Fax: 770-997-8111
Contact: Louis Smith

PLASTICS MANUFACTURER

A DAY IN THE LIFE

"You'll never get rich doing this," wrote the supervisor of one injection-molding floor, "but you're sure as hell going to have fun." Satisfaction levels were high among most respondents in this industry, who cited the regular work schedule, the production of a useful (and often recyclable) product, and the camaraderie between machine operators and supervisors. Even those who supervise workers must understand the nuances of their precise machinery, so many supervisors have been known to take a shift themselves at various stages of the process. Without this fluid line between boss and employee that supports many departments through work crunches and technical crises, plastics manufacturing would be just another hard production job.

The two main types of plastics manufacturing are injection molding and blow molding. Injection molding equipment is used for precision parts, such as appliance parts; blow molding equipment is used to make circular, volume-oriented items such as two-liter soda bottles and shampoo containers. The original press of a mold is critical to future replicas, so supervisors have to take exquisite care in the preparation and casting of that initial mold. Production pressures can be intense, but manufacturers are usually responsible only for their own shifts, from the melting of the powdered plastic (or pellet plastic) to the cooling and testing of the final product. Manufacturers may dash from production area to production area "putting out fires before they begin" and making certain that their shifts run smoothly.

According to many respondents, the most unexpected part of being a plastics manufacturer is the socializing and friendships between bosses and employees. The production work can be difficult—working with molten plastic, handling equipment at temperatures that can reach two thousand degrees or more, testing plastic for tensile strength—and this shared stress seems to encourage mutual respect. "The workers are good people who work hard. You take care of them and they'll take care of you," said one manufacturer. Plastics manufacturing is a busy, friendly world where one's reward isn't necessarily determined by the size of one's paycheck.

PAYING YOUR DUES

A college degree isn't required in the plastics manufacturing profession. Many manufacturing executives are chosen from manufacturing operator pools, which make long periods of job-specific education unnecessary. Many do attend college and some come into the profession with no relevant experience, but employers look for other qualities—scientific skills, leadership abilities, and manufacturing experience—from those candidates. All applicants should be familiar with math, basic science, and communication skills, and be able to take direction. Successful candidates seem to have one other quality that can't be learned: They inspire respect in the people around them.

ASSOCIATED CAREERS

The plastics manufacturing profession boasts one of the lowest attrition rates—less than eight percent per year. High levels of satisfaction contribute to this phenomenon. Many go back to school for materials engineering classes, mechanical design, and blueprint reading. Those who leave the profession from there usually take industrial engineering positions.

PAST AND FUTURE

Plastics are so common in contemporary life that it's hard to imagine a time when plastic products didn't exist. Yet there were none until the early 1900s, when Leo Baekeland developed a practical, synthetic plastic. The flexibility and durability of this new, lightweight (and inexpensive) product revolutionized manufacturing, packaging, bottling, storage, and transportation. Recent efforts at expanding America's recycling base have given rise to the used-plastics industry, which may still experience financial uncertainty, but which has reduced landfill waste by over 5 percent in the last seven years.

Less-skilled plastics manufacturing jobs are slowly becoming automated, and new entrants to the field must meet increased computer and technical skill requirements. The impact of the trend toward automation is still mild in this industry, but in time it could change the entire feel of the plastics industry. So much of the operation of the plastics industry is founded on and guided by the personal loyalties and associations that develop among the employees that automation of the work processes could have a seriously negative effect on the productivity of the remaining workers. Automation, such as through computer numerically controlled (CNC) production, is proceeding at a fairly slow pace in this industry, as employers recognize the value of employee relationships. Nevertheless, eventual automation is inevitable because of its promise of still greater efficiency.

QUALITY OF LIFE

Two Years

Many aspiring plastics manufacturers are line technicians, machine operators, or assistants, learning how to be good injection molders or extruder operators. People new to the profession are surprised at how helpful their fellow employees are in this early stage of their careers. Hours are regular and salaries are low, but satisfaction is high. Many in these beginning jobs learn the front-line lessons that will make them effective managers.

Five Years

Five-year plastics executives have been pulled from the line and put in charge of one area of operation, such as plastic bead molding, or casting, striping, or shaping. Although initially this switch from operator to supervisor is unsettling, many quickly see the advantages—particularly in the 60 percent decrease in the likelihood of injury. Hours can increase as administrative duties are added to production duties. Salaries rise and satisfaction is high.

Ten Years

Ten-year veterans become involved in such areas as inventory control, client contact, and long-term planning, but expect input to be limited for another five years or so. Many are encouraged to take additional courses in finance or to try their hand at sales (because they are intimately familiar with the production process). Many turn down these options and remain manufacturing supervisors, keeping close to the people they care about and doing the job they love.

THE BIRKMAN LIFESTYLE GRID

This career is suitable for people with Red interests.

You'll Have Contact With

Inventory Managers
Grinders
Molding Injection Machinists
Production Managers

Major Associations

Society of Plastics Engineers
14 Fairfield Drive
P.O. Box 403
Brookfield, CT 06804
Tel: 203-775-0471
Fax: 203-775-8490
Contact: Education Dept.

National Association of Manufacturers
1331 Pennsylvania Avenue
Suite 1500
Washington, DC 20004
Tel: 202-637-3000
Fax: 301-441-8207
Contact: Membership Department

Association for Manufacturing Technology
7901 Westpark Drive
Mclean, VA 22102
Tel: 703-893-2900
Fax: 703-827-5298
Contact: Membership Services

POLICE OFFICER/MANAGER

PROFESSIONAL PROFILE

# of people in profession	675,000
% male	80
% female	20
avg. hours per week	45
avg. starting salary	$24,000
avg. salary after 5 years	$33,000
avg. salary 10 to 15 years	$45,000

Books, Films and TV Shows Featuring the Profession

The Choirboys
NYPD Blue
Beverly Hills Cop
Fort Apache The Bronx

Major Employers

NYPD
280 Broadway
New York, NY 10007
Tel: 212-374-5000
Contact: Recruitment

LAPD
Tel: 213-485-4051
Fax: 213-847-8481

Austin Police Department
715 East 8th Street
Austin, TX 78701
Tel: 800-832-5264
Fax: 512-480-5000
Contact: APD Recruiting Department

New York City Police Department
189 Montague Street
Brooklyn, NY 11201
Tel: 212-RECRUIT (723-7848)
Contact: NYPD Recruitment

A DAY IN THE LIFE

For all of Hollywood's portrayal of police officers, few provide an accurate picture of the demands and rewards of a career on the police force. Police work comes in many forms. Sheriffs, state troopers, bailiffs, detectives, and cops on the beat are all part of the local law enforcement community. (If you're interested in federal law enforcement, see FBI agent.) A police officer's basic tasks are keeping public order and protecting lives and property. A police officer must be alert for any number of threats, human or otherwise. Once a crime has been committed, detectives seize the reigns and engage in sleuthing that ranges from routine questioning to DNA analysis. Sheriffs and state troopers maintain order in bigger bailiwicks: large, thinly populated districts and major highways. Once selected for the force, many officers specialize in a particular aspect of law enforcement or investigation. Most are assigned to patrol a specific area. As police officers rise in the ranks, their duties become more specialized. All police officers, because of their unique role in society, are responsible for maintaining the trust of the public they serve.

Because of the responsibilities and prerogatives that come with police work, the pressure on officers to can be enormous. "As a police officer, you're called upon to do everything. You need to be a social worker, a psychologist, an officer of the peace and a soldier," one officer reported. Being the first line of defense between criminals and their victims can be very stressful. Nevertheless, police work is mostly a series of routines: patrols, investigations, and paperwork. Even in America's biggest and most violent cities, police officers seldom have occasion to draw their guns, much less fire them. Perhaps the most common burdens of police work are filling out forms in triplicate and enduring long, uneventful hours walking a beat or riding around in a patrol car. Local law enforcement is a demanding job, but one that most police officers find worthwhile. As one officer commented, "It's interesting to map out strategies to solve community problems."

PAYING YOUR DUES

Police officers are expected to be in good physical shape. A candidate's insufficient height, weight, strength, or vision can lead to disqualification. Most police forces require only a high school diploma, although some expect their officers to have taken college courses or encourage them to pursue higher education while serving on the force. Character is also an important consideration. Some applicants to law enforcement jobs undergo psychological evaluation. All are tested for drug use.

Because law enforcement is a local concern, the path to the police force differs from community to community and state to state, but as the world becomes more complicated, so does the training required to become a police officer. Smaller communities may require new officers to complete an apprenticeship program. Large cities maintain police academies where aspiring officers are trained in the various aspects of police work, including investigative procedures, self-defense and the law, while fulfilling more minor duties such as directing traffic. Officers can pursue a managerial track and advance to become a sergeant, lieutenant, captain, or even a police chief or commissioner. Generally speaking, you must serve on the force five years before you are eligible to sit for the lieutenant's exam, and after two years as a lieutenant, you can take the captain's test. Each post requires increased education as well. You must have a two-year associates degree to advance to sergeant, 96 credits towards a bachelor's degree to be considered for a lieutenant position, and a bachelor's degree to make captain.

ASSOCIATED CAREERS

There are many law enforcement tasks that the police leave to civilian personnel. Psychologists, chemists, biologists, photographers, and many other specialists can find employment with larger police departments. Although none of these specialties is essential to police work all the time, in some situations, expertise can be the key to cracking a case.

Since police officers can and often do retire at an early age, many former police officers find good work providing private security for corporations or individuals.

PAST AND FUTURE

Many law enforcement duties were once left to the military. By 1829, the city of London had established a metropolitan police force separate from the military. America's first state police force was the Texas Rangers (established in 1853). Much of America's frontier law enforcement was voluntary, which made obedience to the law equally voluntary.

Police officers note that their job changes dramatically under different political administrations. The agenda of the administration, whether it be to reduce theft, cut white collar crime, or pursue drug pushers, affects the kind of criminals police target. The overall strategies they employ changes their daily routine. Larger cities have expanded their police forces, but the occupation as a whole is expected to undergo slower growth than other professions through the turn of the century.

QUALITY OF LIFE

Two Years

The routine duties of a beginning police officer may be disappointing, or they may be terrifying. Nevertheless, few officers leave the profession at this stage. Opportunities for advancement in a police department are tied to seniority, so dedicated police officers stick out the tedious times as they rise on the list of men and women eligible for promotion. Long, uneventful days are punctuated by moments of danger and occasional moments of triumphs against justice.

Five Years

Around this time, command positions become available. At this point, an officer is usually eligible to sit for the sergeant's exam if he has at least a two-year associates degree. Other officers specialize in investigating particular crimes (murder, fraud, drug trafficking). As police work becomes more scientific, many officers find it necessary to return to school in order to move up the ranks.

Ten Years

Police officers can usually retire with a pension after twenty years on the force, so ten years marks the halfway point. Many seasoned officers choose to stay in uniform on the beat. These officers serve as examples for their younger colleagues, providing what may be the rookies' most important training. Officers who have already made captain are eligible for consideration to become inspectors, police chiefs or commissioners. These positions are filled by political appointment. Upon retirement, police officers can expect a pension (usually at half pay), an opportunity to pursue a second career, and the appreciation of a safer society.

THE BIRKMAN LIFESTYLE GRID

Red Green
Yellow Blue

This career is suitable for people with Red interests.

You'll Have Contact With

Attorneys
Criminologists
Federal Agents
Paramedics
Criminals

Major Associations

American Federation of Police
3801 Biscayne Boulevard
Miami, FL 33137
Tel: 305-573-0070
Fax: 305-573-9819
Contact: Education Dept.

International Union of Police Associations
1421 Prince Street
Alexandria, VA 22314
Tel: 703-549-7473

Fraternal Order of Police
(FOP), Grand Lodge
1410 Donelson Pike
#A17
Nashville, TN 37217-2933
Tel: 615-399-0900
Tel: 800-243-4401
Fax: 615-399-0400

Police Foundation
1001 22nd Street, NW
Suite 200
Washington, DC 20037
Tel: 202-833-1460
Fax: 202-659-9149

POLITICAL AIDE

A DAY IN THE LIFE

"Politics is all in the staff work," said one Senate aide. Politicians are the visible faces of political life, the personalities who spark public debate, but the overwhelming bulk of the processes by which political decisions are made are handled by political staffers. Staffers prepare the reports, conduct the research, draft the legislation, and prepare the negotiation briefs that allow political life to go on. The pay is merely average and the hours are long, but many staffers report great satisfaction with work that allows them a central role in important public decision making.

Aides must be aware both of the political developments in their field and of the needs of the home district, and they must be aware of likely public reaction to the various positions in a political debate. An effective aide is a valued advisor and resource, and elected officials frequently develop a core senior staff which they take with them from office to office throughout their careers. There is significant turnover among more junior staffers, however, as they maneuver to work for candidates or officeholders whose careers are on the rise.

Attachment to a particular politician, who often serves as a mentor, is perhaps the most striking aspect of a career as a political aide. The development of long-term commitment and loyalty to a single party or candidate can be extremely rewarding, but an aide's ambitions must be aligned with those of the boss. Moreover, political egos are such that staffers who seek the limelight frequently find themselves seeking alternative employment. In addition, the success of a staffer's career is tied to that of the politician; if the politician changes jobs, so must the staffer, and if the politician loses a reelection the staffers are out of jobs. Despite these uncertainties, however, the life of a political aide can be extremely satisfying, and the dangers of getting turned out of office are offset by the wide range of experiences afforded a political aide.

PAYING YOUR DUES

A college degree is a necessity for staff work at any level—local, state, or federal—and many staffers have graduate and/or professional experience in their fields of specialization. Young labor attorneys will move into labor relations positions, say, while agricultural consultants may find jobs covering agricultural affairs, while journalism is a useful background for press aide positions. Competition for entry-level jobs can be intense; aspiring aides who have worked on major campaigns or interned in government offices have much stronger chances of being hired. Frequently, though not always, legislators hire aides from their home districts or states, as a means of maintaining contact between their constituents and Washington or the state capitol.

ASSOCIATED CAREERS

Often, political aides enter their areas of specialization when they leave the profession; others become lobbyists when they depart. A staffer who handled business issues for a state senator would be well placed lobbying for a state business development organization or working for a consulting firm with local clients. A former military affairs aide to a U.S. Senator would have contacts and knowledge that would be valuable to a military contractor. A significant percentage go on to corporate law, where legislative experience is rewarded.

PAST AND FUTURE

Politicians have always required aides and advisors, though the highly developed staffs of modern American politics are a relatively recent phenomenon. In 1945, Congress employed 4,000 staffers, while today it employs 20,000 full-time staff members. Staffs of state governments, though smaller, have seen similar expansion. Numerous factors have contributed to this dramatic increase, but the most important has been the increasing role of federal and local government in American life over the last 60 years. As governments administer more laws, the complexity of the issues facing legislators increases, and they require increasingly large staffs to be able to make informed decisions. Despite current efforts to trim back the size of American government, the job of legislators in modern society will likely remain extremely complex, and their need for able aides isn't going to disappear.

QUALITY OF LIFE

Two Years

The process begins with the accumulation of legal and technical knowledge, learning the legislative lay of the land in her assigned fields. Equally important, the aide is developing contacts with her counterparts in other legislative and committee offices, with journalists who cover her field, and with constituents affected by the issues she covers.

Five Years

The average Congressional staffer leaves after four years. Those who remain have become valued advisors, with considerable expertise and networks of contacts in their areas of responsibility. Some have become legislative directors, supervising legislative assistants and working with their politicians to set priorities for the legislative resources of the office.

Ten Years

By now, the political aide is likely one of the most experienced employees in the office. As a legislative director or chief of staff, she may have considerable influence over the priorities and time commitments of the politician she works for, and throughout the government and legislative offices, she has a wide range of contacts with whom her own office participates in decisions and negotiations. Many aides at this level have considerable policy influence and authority to negotiate directly on behalf of the officeholder.

THE BIRKMAN LIFESTYLE GRID

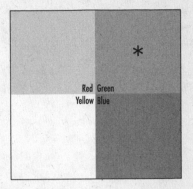

Red Green
Yellow Blue

This career is suitable for people with Green interests.

You'll Have Contact With

Campaign Managers
Lobbyists
Politicians
Researchers

Major Associations

Political aides generally work with their employer politicians for organizations with which the politician wants to be associated.

Republican National Committee
310 First Street, SE
Washington, DC 20003
Tel: 202-863-8500

Democratic National Committee
430 South Capital Street, SE
Washington, DC 20003
Tel: 202-863-8000
Fax: 202-488-5043

Libertarian Party
2600 Virginia Ave, NW #100
Washington, DC 20037
Tel: 800-682-1776

POLITICAL CAMPAIGN WORKER

A DAY IN THE LIFE

Political campaign workers specialize in the art of winning elections. The profession includes many subspecialties: Press and public relations, polling, opposition research, fundraising, logistical organizing, and a wide range of other skills to deal with the crises of a campaign. In large campaigns, specialists representing all of these skills work together to develop integrated campaign strategies; in smaller, local elections, one or two professionals will serve as jacks of all trades, putting to use this entire range of skills and developing their expertise. Technical and tactical skills are extremely important in campaign management, but the ultimate emphasis in the profession is on winning. Campaign professionals with a reputation for victory can have lucrative, prominent careers; those who participate in too many losing campaigns will have trouble finding work.

This is a career for people who love the thrill of the chase. Many get into the profession by volunteering for a particular candidate they support and falling in love with the excitement of campaigns. In the weeks preceding elections, campaign professionals work full time, 24 hours a day, seven days a week, as they plan and coordinate down-to-the-wire campaign strategies. Deadline pressure is intense, as election day provides a final test of the staff's campaign work. Many in the profession thrive on the pressure; others burn out and find other work.

Campaign management is also highly public work. Pollsters and researchers may work behind the scenes, but the press and public relations specialists, and those who wish to rise to the top of the profession and become campaign managers, must feel comfortable working with the media. At the highest level of political campaigns, statements and actions of senior campaign aides are as those of the candidate. Some relish this visibility; others find it one of the profession's major drawbacks.

PAYING YOUR DUES

The career campaign professional's first exposure to politics is usually as a volunteer for a campaign, perhaps over summer vacation while still a student. Volunteers perform the bulk of the low level jobs in every campaign, but they are often found in positions of substantial responsibility in smaller, local campaigns. A bright, hard working volunteer can rise rapidly in a re-election staff, and this is often the best way to acquire the credentials that can lead to a career working on major political campaigns.

In some of the profession's disciplines, educational or career background is also extremely important. Training in statistics is a prerequisite to polling and voter analysis; many influential pollsters have doctorates in statistics. Many political workers begin as journalists and then put their knowledge of the media to use as press aides and campaign spokespeople. A degree in political science can also be useful. Some universities offer masters degrees in political management, itself a testament to the wide range of skills required to manage a campaign. This can also be an effective route into the profession.

ASSOCIATED CAREERS

Campaign workers often depart to fields where the skills they have developed will be valuable, such as advertising, public relations, and journalism. Some go to law school, often with an eye towards developing their own political careers. The more senior victorious campaign workers often take jobs as press secretaries, political and policy consultants, or general staff workers in the administrations of their successful candidates.

PAST AND FUTURE

U.S. campaign politics has changed significantly since the days of political machines like New York's Tammany Hall at the turn of the century, when Thanksgiving turkeys were exchanged for votes. Ward captains who can mobilize small armies of volunteers to man phones and hand out leaflets still play an important role in political campaigns, but campaign management has become a sophisticated science. Demographic studies, focus groups and advertising consultants have become the field's stock in trade, and management of these resources has demanded increasing professionalization in the field. The trend has been towards increasing budgets and technological sophistication—slick mass mailings and tightly choreographed press conferences and "photo ops" are now supplemented by Web sites, and chat rooms on the Internet. The cost of political campaigning has risen with every election in recent years. With the increased resources expended on campaigns have come increased opportunities for professionals with the ability to make effective use of them, and this pattern seems likely to continue.

QUALITY OF LIFE

Two Years

Young campaign managers build reputations by managing local campaigns or by signing on in junior positions under a known manager running a large, well-staffed election effort. Often, young campaign professionals move back and forth between these options as job opportunities arise. Developing personal contacts in the field is vital, for managers with the prestige to get hired to run major campaigns have core groups of favored aides whom they take with them from campaign to campaign, and it is these favored few who have the best chance for a shot at running a large campaign of their own.

Five Years

Those who remain in the field have worked through two or three campaigns and have begun to establish themselves. Some remain on the campaign circuit, moving from race to race as opportunities appear. Many move into more permanent positions in state and national party organizations, providing support to party campaigns and coordinating cooperative campaign efforts at different election levels. Others move into political consulting firms, which offer expert polling, media, or financial services to a number of campaigns in any given election year.

Ten Years

By now, campaign workers have established themselves as managers. Those who left for the private sector, perhaps as consultants, exploit their contacts in the political world. Party officials have considerable authority over the allocation of their organization's resources, and they have a voice in the setting of party priorities and platforms. Independent campaign managers have reached the point where they can count on senior campaign positions-as managers, spokespersons, pollsters-in each election year. There is significant job mobility at this level: Successful campaign officials often become senior political aides, and managers move back and forth between party and campaign positions.

This career is suitable for people with Red interests.

You'll Have Contact With
Image Consultants
Political Aides
Politicians
Publicists

Major Associations
American Association of Political Consultants
900 Second Street, NE
#204
Washington, DC 20002
Tel: 202-371-9585
Fax: 202-371-6751

Political Campaign Institute
c/o Aristotle Industries
205 Pennsylvania Avenue, SE
Washington, DC 20003
Tel: 202-543-6408 Tel: 800-243-4401
Fax: 202-543-6407

POLITICAL SCIENTIST

A DAY IN THE LIFE

Political scientists study the structure and theory of government and seek practical and theoretical solutions to political problems. Most current studies and research concentrate on tangible topics such as welfare reform, political campaigns and elections, foreign relations, and immigration. The vast majority of political scientists are teachers at colleges and universities where they conduct research and write books and articles on political theory. Political scientists armed with the practical and theoretical knowledge of government may enter political life. They generally do not run for public office, but very often their expertise is enlisted by candidates to ensure a successful run or reelection. A great many become political aides, helping those elected analyze and interpret legislative issues and their constituencies. Some become political commentators on television and radio or write columns for newspapers; others become public opinion pollsters.

Political scientists approach problems using one or a combination of four distinct methods: Objective, analytical, comparative, and historical. The adequacy and integrity of a political scientist's theory rests on his ability to set aside his own prejudices and remain objective in gathering, analyzing and presenting her findings. Using commonly available research—interviews, newspaper clippings, periodicals, case law, historical papers, polls and statistics—to test theories and develop new ones, political scientists analyze, compare, and even trace problems back to their sources. In gathering data, political scientists often employ the technique of the "participant observer," blending with crowds while carefully observing a particular interaction. The questionnaire is another research tool the political scientist uses. Questions are carefully ordered and worded to be as objective as possible.

PAYING YOUR DUES

The job of a political scientist is an intellectually challenging one and places a premium on higher education. Most jobs require a master's degree. If teaching at the college and university level is your goal, then nothing less than a Ph.D. will do. Students who specialize in a particular field such as public administration, international relations, or public law will fare slightly better in seeking jobs. Computer and language skills will also significantly enhance job prospects. Entrants start out as trainees in political science research at universities and think tanks or as assistants in independent public opinion research organizations. Education, experience, knowledge and an area of specialty—especially public administration—are indices of better salary levels.

ASSOCIATED CAREERS

Some political scientists move on to law school. A few become consultants to political groups, organizations, businesses and industries. The vast majority who end up in teaching posts at colleges and universities also establish double careers as writers and researchers. A few hold positions as directors or department heads of college programs.

PAST AND FUTURE

Aristotle, considered by many scholars as an early patriarch of political science and a major influence on the discipline, attempted to classify forms of government. Although Plato further offered his theories on ideal forms of government, political scientists now consider the subject of utopias to belong outside the scope of their discipline. Computers now figure greatly in the organization and analysis of data which forms the core of the political scientist's work. Individuals with strong computer training and language skills will fare far better in the field, particularly those specializing in the areas of public administration and public policy. Fewer vacancies at colleges and universities will mean that competition for existing jobs will be keen. With the move toward smaller, more efficient government, jobs in local, state, and federal government agencies will shrink rapidly. Limited employment opportunities will be available in the private sector with certain industries, political parties, and individuals seeking public office. While future job opportunities are limited, the position itself has been around for a long time and should remain secure.

QUALITY OF LIFE

Two Years

At the two-year level, the political scientist is probably employed as a trainee or a research assistant. He is concerned about acquiring significant experience and working his way up the ranks. It is important that the relative newcomer establish mentorships. Those who have finished their Ph.D.s are either seeking or already have positions as assistant professors.

Five Years

Five years into the profession, the emphasis is still on experience. Those who have specialized in public administration may see greater progress in their career, moving up the ranks and being called upon to head up research projects. Professors, usually associates by now, are publishing and seeking tenure.

Ten Years

At this level the political scientist teaching at a college or university should be a tenured professor with a body of scholarly research, articles, and books to show for his years of work. The political scientist who started out in research may have advanced to research director at his organization. With ten years of experience, the political scientist has a fairly secure position and commands the respect of his peers and potential employers.

THE BIRKMAN LIFESTYLE GRID

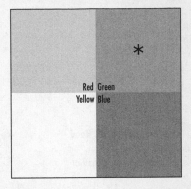

Red Green
Yellow Blue

This career is suitable for people with Green interests.

You'll Have Contact With

Editors
Politicans
Professors
Researchers

Major Associations

American Academy of
Political and Social Science
3937 Chestnut Street
Philadelphia, PA 19104
Tel: 215-386-4594
Fax: 215-386-4630
Contact: Dr. Marvin E. Wolfgang

Academy of Political Science
475 Riverside Drive
Suite 1274
New York, NY 10015
Tel: 212-870-2500
Fax: 212-870-2202
Contact: Michael Cirillo

American Political Science Association
1527 New Hampshire Avenue, NW
Washington, DC 20036
Tel: 202-483-2512
Fax: 202-483-2657

POLITICIAN

A DAY IN THE LIFE

Politics has been with us for as long as people have had to cooperate to achieve their goals. Over a half-million people currently hold full- or part-time elective offices in the United States, making decisions that affect communities on local, state, and national levels. For those who wish to participate in society's decisions, a career in politics should absolutely be considered. Politicians have a hand in thousands of decisions important to their communities, from questions of dividing tax revenue for local schools to police funding to issues of federal tax policy. The profession offers great rewards to those with a combination of negotiation and public presentation skills. In addition to full-time political jobs, many find that part-time community boards, town councils, or even state assembly jobs make valuable and rewarding adjuncts to their full-time careers.

Politics is not for the shy. At all levels, it is characterized by publicity. Most successful politicians enjoy visibility, while those who leave the profession often cite loss of privacy as its greatest drawback. Whether in a small town or in the White House, politicians are subject to intense scrutiny. Elected officials have to campaign for reelection every time their term is up, but, for the most part, the first time is the real challenge; incumbency is a strong advantage in elections. More than 90 percent of the U.S. House of Representatives is reelected every two years, and the reelection rates at the lower levels of politics are similar.

PAYING YOUR DUES

There is no one career path which reliably leads to an elective office. Working as an aide for an established politician is one common way to meet contacts in the local political party apparatus. Law school is another common first step to a political career, since many lawyers achieve public notice and visibility or do work for state political parties. In general, political careers begin with an elective office in state government; most politicians in Washington start as state legislators and work their way up the party hierarchy. In politics, however, the exception is the rule, and people of all backgrounds pursue successful political careers, from peanut farmers to actors. Charisma is important, and being independently wealthy to finance campaigns doesn't hurt either.

ASSOCIATED CAREERS

A significant majority of full-time, career politicians are lawyers, and many return to private practice after leaving office. Many represent clients doing business with the government offices they vacated, putting their knowledge of politics in this specific area for financial gain; others just go on to ordinary practice. Other former politicians become lobbyists or run professional organizations or foundations that can benefit from the politicians' stature and experience. Finally jobs in academia or appointed positions in government are also quite common for former politicians.

PAST AND FUTURE

Modern democracy traces itself to the assembly of ancient Athens, but U.S. representative government bears little resemblance to the Athenian system. U.S. politics is a much more sedate affair, even though the public perception of politicians remains rather volatile. In any event, the profession will endure. Public questions will always need to be answered, and politicians will always be needed to answer them.

QUALITY OF LIFE

Two Years

At this point, a politician is in the early stages of her career, holding a relatively low level or local office. This may be a school or community board position, a seat in the lower house of the state government, or a position as a small town mayor or town council member. In general, staffs, budgets, and campaign funds are small, and the areas of responsibility of the office are quite limited. The politician begins to build relationships within her political party that she will depend upon throughout her career, and she attempts to gain the public notice which will provide the foundation for a successful run for higher office. Re-election is a significant concern in these first years, though each successful re-election in a given position reduces the risk of later challenge.

Five Years

By now the politician has survived at least one, and probably more than one, reelection campaign. She likely has established a solid base of support in her local community, and is beginning to gain more public attention, and her proposals and initiatives are starting to have a greater chance of success in the local government. She is establishing herself as a viable candidate for higher office, whether in the city government, the state senate, or Congress.

Ten Years

The successful politician has by now risen in the party ranks, and she likely has a secure hold on her office and can consider the extent of her ambitions. She is likely among those who have the connections and experience to run for senatorial or congressional office, or she could be one of many politicians who build satisfying careers at the state and city level. In any event, politicians who survive the first ten years can be reasonably confident of lifelong political careers, should they choose to pursue them.

THE BIRKMAN LIFESTYLE GRID

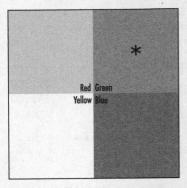

Red Green
Yellow Blue

This career is suitable for people with Green interests.

You'll Have Contact With

Campaign Managers
Lobbyists
Image Consultants
Political Aides

Major Associations

Politicians at different levels (e.g., governors, mayors) belong to specialized associations. Contact those appropriate to your area of interest.

Power Plant Manager

A DAY IN THE LIFE

Most plant managers supervise the production of one specific good: Electricity. Power plants operate twenty-four hours a day, seven days a week, turbines churning out megawatt after megawatt of powerful, invisible current. Plant managers soon learn that the technical aspects of the job notwithstanding—managing power loads, controlling production and inventory, and handling the continuous maintenance chores—the heart of managing a power plant is managing people. Plant managers who embrace both these aspects of the job are the most successful at this career.

PPMs can work during the day or night, and many come to know their plants as well as they know their own homes. They must be on top of everything, so many make rounds themselves, greeting workers on their shift and personally inspecting any problem areas. This hands-on managing is one of the reasons that PPMs have such a high level of satisfaction; they get intellectual stimulation, social interaction, and physical activity. Some PPMs added that the sterile environment and rotating shifts make personal connections very important.

A power plant manager must know the basic rules of electrical safety. The first rule of the profession is: "When in doubt, shut it down." Whole country grids are under the watch of PPMs. Supplying too little or too much electricity could have grave consequences, like medical equipment ceasing to function or main power trunks burning out (these can take days to fix). A power plant is maintained and operated by hundreds of workers, and the manager coordinates all activities. One told us, "You're like a cruise director, telling people where they need to go and who they have to meet up with." Successful power plant managers are good at distributing their human resources, combining seriousness and a dedicated work effort with a personal approach that fosters quality work and loyalty. They are able to think before they act, to act when they need to, and to inspire others to follow them on ordinary days and in times of crisis.

PAYING YOUR DUES

Employers look for candidates with a college degree in any major that demonstrates quantitative skill and attention to detail as well as courses in mathematics, physics, electrical engineering, or computer science. Some PPMs begin as technicians and work up to supervisory and managerial positions; this can mean extra shifts and long days for beginners in the profession. Those who want to work in nuclear power plants have to satisfy additional requirements, both academic and professional. The Nuclear Regulatory Commission (NRC) administers tests each year that license professionals to operate these special power plants. Many employers look for candidates who have experience in the Navy nuclear submarine program. Although not a requirement, those in any part of the profession (nuclear or otherwise) often find it helpful to join a professional union, such as the International Brotherhood of Electrical Workers.

ASSOCIATED CAREERS

The personality traits of power plant managers translate well into any managerial position. Some become production managers, quality control managers, and inventory control managers. Some continue with their education and become electricians, electrical engineers, and power plant inspectors.

PAST AND FUTURE

Power plant managers became a necessary part of the workforce with the growth of the use of electricity in the early 1900s. Cities, which used to be lit by gas lamps, found they could provide safe, consistent streetlamp light by harnessing this electrical power. Once cities began to be wired for electricity, the demand for the product spread rapidly and power became part of nearly every household in America after the middle of the century. Power, understood as a great benefit, was also recognized as a potential danger. The power industry continues to be one of the most heavily regulated industries in the country.

The future of power plant managers is tied to the expansion of power facilities in the U.S. Currently, there are no production plans for extensive power plants on the slate of any state government construction programs. Demand for electricity is on the rise, but instead of building new plants, existing facilities are being refitted to handle the increased capacity, and power is being purchased from other sources.

QUALITY OF LIFE

Two Years

Two-year managers are usually technicians. Many are in technical managerial positions, but few have reached the level of PPM. Most are involved in meetings and coordination with the PPM and learn more technical skills in their free time. Many said the lessons they learned as technicians helped them become more sensitive and capable managers. Hours are reasonable; satisfaction is average.

Five Years

Those in the profession five years know whether they are on a PPM track or not. Many have moved from technical positions to administrative positions in order to familiarize themselves with the other requirements of the job. Those in nuclear facilities regularly pass their licensing exams; a single failing grade can ruin the best candidate's chances for a PPM position. Promotions at this point are driven by availability of openings, as the number of qualified candidates exceeds the number of available PPM positions.

Ten Years

Many are now PPMs, although some have had to relocate in order to pursue opportunities. Many power facilities are designed in a very standard fashion (and strict regulations encourage that) so mobility doesn't require an extraordinary amount of re-education. The biggest problem that PPMs face in new plants is earning the loyalty, trust and respect of their fellow workers. Ex-PPMs usually have a strong following, and stepping into someone else's well-respected shoes requires skill and perseverance.

THE BIRKMAN LIFESTYLE GRID

Red Green
Yellow Blue

This career is suitable for people with Red interests.

You'll Have Contact With

Electrical Engineers
Electricians
Government Regulators
Plant Monitors

Major Associations

In Plant Management Association
1205 West College Street
Liberty, MO 64068-3733
Tel: 816-781-1111
Fax: 816-781-2790
Contact: Jayne Gier

Edison Electrical Institute
P.O. Box 2800
Kearneysville, WV 25430

International Brotherhood
of Electrical Workers
1125 15th Street, NW
Washington, DC 20005
Tel: 202-833-7000
Fax: 202-467-6316

PRINTER

PROFESSIONAL PROFILE

# of people in profession	100,000
% male	90
% female	10
avg. hours per week	40
avg. starting salary	$22,000
avg. salary after 5 years	$30,000
avg. salary 10 to 15 years	$46,000

Professionals Read
Printing News
American Printer
Printing Impressions

Books, Films and TV Shows Featuring the Profession
The Paper
Perfect Printing

Major Employers
Darby Printing Company
6215 Perdue Drive
Atlanta, GA 30336
Tel: 404-344-2665
Fax: 404-346-8000
Contact: Human Resources

Plymouth Printing
P.O. Box 68
Cranford, NJ 17016
Tel: 908-276-8100
Fax: 908-276-6566
Contact: Human Resources

RR Donley and Sons Company
77 West Wacker Drive
Chicago, IL 60601-1696
Tel: 312-326-8000
Fax: 312-326-7113
Contact: Human Resources

A DAY IN THE LIFE

Do you want to make books, newspapers, magazines, or brochures? Have you ever wondered who gets to print "All the News That's Fit to Print"? Being a printer can be very gratifying because you can touch and see your final product. Printers have an obvious, clearly definable, and useful skill. The printing industry encompasses all aspects of tailorized mass production; the field offers positions for those with a variety of skills, needs, and work styles. Each printer works on a different part of the process. Specializations are broken into two categories: Skilled craft workers and unskilled laborers who work the machines. Printers usually work under intense deadlines. While almost everybody involved in the printing field works forty hours a week, many printers work nights and holidays to meet deadlines.

All printing jobs follow a similarly structured order. To start, sales representatives and brokers get clients. They pass the job onto the production manager. She gets estimates of how much the job will cost, oversees other workers and maintains deadlines. She depends on the plant manager, who oversees aspects of the printing process and handles all technical emergencies. Plant engineers, who maintain and improve the equipment, are also in contact with the manager. In the first step of the physical process, compositors read the copy and arrange the type, which requires extraordinary patience. Typesetting is done in one of three different ways: Monotype, or casting single letters; logotype, or casting lines; or phototypesetting, which involves casting with the aid of computers. Lithographers and photoengravers pick up the typeset and take it to printing. They work closely with the platemaker, who mans the machines to ensure high printing quality. Sometimes camera operators are needed to photograph the material about to be printed. Color separation photographers are called in when the material is to be reproduced in color. After all of these people have worked on the images, they pass the product to lithographic artists who do all the necessary fine tuning. Then strippers pick up the lithographic artist's product and arrange it on the machines to form the final product. Printing press operators yield the final result, generally through the use of computers. Finally, the binder completes the process. He puts the printed matter together to create books, pamphlets, newspapers, journals, or magazines.

PAYING YOUR DUES

Each aspect of the field has different education and training requirements. Some can be learned in under a year, others require years of training for total fluency. High school diplomas are requisite for all workers. Both two- and four-year colleges offer associate and bachelor's degrees in graphics arts, degrees that have become necessary for supervisory and some entry-level positions. Applicants should study math, electronics, and computers to widen their options for specialization in the field.

Normally, the printer begins his career as a helper receiving on-the-job training. The new printer moves forward in his position as he masters each skill or technique. He should expect to learn new skills whenever advancements are made in the technology of his specialty. Sometimes printers enter the field through four- to six-year apprenticeships. Openings for these are decreasing in number, but are valuable at every position in printing. Due to increased automation, some specializations are emphasizing increased technical ability as opposed to craft skills. Traditionally, plant managers have risen from the ranks of the physical careers. Today though, companies are looking more favorably to applicants with degrees in fields like engineering. Employers also want you to be able to display creativity yet work under time constraints, and to have good eyesight. The most likely candidates are people who are analytical, outgoing, and have an eye for color and graphics.

ASSOCIATED CAREERS

Printers who tire of printing can transfer their skills to another part of the process of creating books and newspapers. Many people are involved with the product before it reaches the printer. Clerk-typists, computer terminal system operators, keypunch operators, and telegraph-typewriter operators work in manners similar to typesetters. Jewelers, sign painters, and graphic artists create models that give the printer a prototype for what they would like. Their work is slightly more artistic than that of the printer. Printers' skills can be valuable in publishers' production departments.

PAST AND FUTURE

When Johannes Gutenberg invented movable type, the printing industry was born. His first book was the Gutenberg Bible, printed in 1456 by applying ink to raised metal and pressing the letters onto paper. Later his methods evolved into the revolving cylinder that is still used today, along with many other new technologies.

Computers have changed printing drastically. They have made some jobs, such as photoengraving and composition, almost obsolete, but created new opportunities for lithographers and those involved in computer technology. The advents of direct marketing and desktop publishing have been boons for the printer. Desktop publishing is anticipated to become the most prolific area in printing. The printer's environment is changing, too. More printers find themselves working for small desktop publishing companies rather than large presses.

QUALITY OF LIFE

Two Years

The first two years are usually spent in apprenticeships as production or sales assistants. One printer advises novices to "learn computers, have fun, and pick the area that you enjoy the most." Many of the newest printers are computer-controlled, and learning the "art" of working the software so as to produce the desired effects requires working with an experienced operator - especially with color presses. Often beginners are stuck with the "graveyard shift" and are working on press at odd hours under heavy deadline pressure.

Five Years

By this point in their careers, most printers have established position in the company. They are working full time, with fairly regular hours, and are afforded greater independence in operating and maintaining the machinery.

Ten Years

Ten-year printers tend to be happy with their professions. Most have moved into managerial positions, supervising pressman and perhaps dealing with clients on the more complicated jobs. They are consulted on major capital investments such as new presses, and thus take on a crucial role within their company.

THE BIRKMAN LIFESTYLE GRID

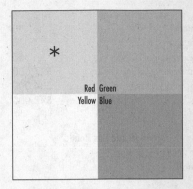

This career is suitable for people with Red interests.

You'll Have Contact With
Editors
Graphic Designers
Publishers
Shipping Agents

Major Associations
Education Council of the
Graphic Arts Industry
1899 Preston White Drive
Reston, VA 22091-4326
Tel: 703-648-1768
Fax: 703-620-0994
Contact: Joanne Laffey

National Association of
Printers and Lithographers
780 Palisade Avenue
Teaneck, NJ 17666
Tel: 201-342-0700
Fax: 201-692-1862
Contact: Suzanne Updegraff

The Society of Publication Designers
60 East 42nd Street
Suite 721
New York, NY 10165-1416
Tel: 212-983-8585
Fax: 212-983-6043
Contact: Bride Whelan

PRODUCT DESIGNER

A DAY IN THE LIFE

"If you can spend hours walking down the drugstore aisle critiquing everybody's products, you were born to be a product designer," wrote one respondent, and who would argue with that? Product designers have agonized over the shape, size, and material content of every tube of toothpaste, every bottle of conditioner, and every bar of soap produced in the U.S. today. A product designer combines a talent for design with an understanding of the production and marketing of consumer goods. Over two thirds of all product designers work for consumer goods manufacturing concerns, which produce most drugstore and food items. These designers play a critical role in differentiating their products from those of other, directly competitive companies. "So much of what you buy is influenced by how it looks on a shelf," as one advertising executive told us, "that companies cannot afford anymore to not have product designers on staff." These consumer product designers also work to give their companies the edge by keeping production costs low; production costs translate directly into consumer costs for the product, and a designer who can reduce a per-item cost even a tiny bit can give an employer a competitive advantage at the supermarket or drugstore.

A product designer spends around 30 percent of his day meeting with executives, researchers, production managers, and advertising people, either on the telephone or in person. It's important that the prospective designer be able to work as part of this team, which means understanding that his personal preferences may not be chosen. Besides the time spent actually working on designs, the remainder of his time is spent working with graphic designers and cost estimators in order to coordinate the production of potential product lines. Because of the collaborative nature of the process, this job requires strong interpersonal skills; over half the surveys we received cited "the ability to listen" as extremely important to success.

While aesthetic skills are obviously critical to product designers, business savvy is just as important. Successful product designers are equally comfortable producing three-dimensional models of their designs and providing cost estimates to production executives. Every design accommodates specific cost limitations, and those who can't keep to those limitations, as one package designer put it, "find themselves designing packages at home. Unemployed." This forces the product designer to be creative with materials, production methods, and forms. Many cite this pressured creativity as one of the most exciting parts of the job. At the same time, this is a profession in which over 70 percent of what the designer designs will never be produced for either cost, preference, or advertising reasons, so product designers should be thick-skinned enough to be able to watch their work discarded on a daily basis. Those whose designs prove financially successful can expect to have more influence over the process as time goes on.

PAYING YOUR DUES

Product designers face specific academic requirements that allow them entry to the field but certainly do not guarantee them success. No specific licensing requirements exist for product designers; applicants should concentrate on developing a portfolio of designs, an awareness of cost specifications, and a demonstrated ability to work with a team. Most product designers have a bachelor's degree in a related field, such as graphic design, and coursework should include manufacturing principles, psychology, sociology, finance, materials use, and organizational behavior. But beyond academics, the more a prospective product designer can become familiar with the production process, the more likely she is to be successful in the field. An aspiring product designer should also be well-versed in current packaging trends in the industry she intends to enter. For example, if she wants to design products for the music industry, she should be aware that while the plastic two-hinge case is the industry standard now, many companies are choosing to replace it with a cardboard foldout case favored by recycling-minded consumers.

ASSOCIATED CAREERS

Product designers often become graphic designers, commercial artists, cost estimators, and product manufacturing executives—all careers they come into contact with as product design specialists.

PAST AND FUTURE

With the demonstrated effectiveness of advertising in the twentieth century, manufacturers looked to gain an advantage over each other by providing more attractive, identifiable product design. Producers who lacked these aesthetic skills hired professional consultants to redesign their products. These redesigns proved so effective that many design people were hired in-house. Product designers are involved at every stage of product development today, and the future of product design looks stable. Jobs should increase at the same rate as jobs in all other manufacturing occupations. The market for consumer products is healthy and the rate of growth is steady. With the dawn of an increasingly global economy, product designers for overseas companies who want to sell their products in the U.S. may be in high demand.

QUALITY OF LIFE

Two Years

As "assistants" during the early years, product designers normally undergo a training program in which they are rotated to various positions within the company. They gain valuable experience in finance, production, development, marketing, and sales. Responsibilities are limited and although many are itching to begin designing, most merely assist the design department in the production of already-designed products. Salaries are average; hours are low.

Five Years

Five-year survivors find their hours have jumped tremendously, and so have their responsibilities. Many are in the midst of actual designing and mock-up production and use their knowledge of materials pricing, cost estimating, and consumer taste. Satisfaction skyrockets during these middle years and many find work obligations can extend into off-hours and weekend time; a few on our surveys noted that other interests "suffered" during this period.

Ten Years

Veterans of product design are faced with the same challenges as graphic designers and commercial artists at this stage of their careers: To renew their visions and keep themselves relevant to the industry they represent. Mobility is a feature of the ten-year product designer, as many switch jobs searching for the spark to keep their work fresh. Salaries increase and satisfaction evens out. A number of very successful designers become independent consultants to industries, providing analyses of product lines or cost-structure estimates for startup companies.

THE BIRKMAN LIFESTYLE GRID

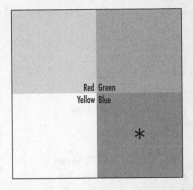

This career is suitable for people with Blue interests.

You'll Have Contact With

Advertising Executives
Graphic Designers
Market Researchers
Production Managers

Major Associations

Industrial Designers Society of America
1142-E Walker Road
Great Falls, VA 22066
Tel: 703-759-0100
Fax: 703-759-7679
Contact: Human Resources

PRODUCTION MANAGER

A DAY IN THE LIFE

A few production managers we surveyed added "traffic controller" to their title parenthetically. The clarification is apt, since their job is not to produce but to make sure that production runs smoothly. Production managers are primarily administrators or supervisors; they determine the allocation of labor resources, track production scheduling and costs, make any on-the-fly adjustments to the process, and coordinate any receiving of raw materials or shipping of final goods. A production manager is very busy most days. "The job is a lot of coordination. You should be able to juggle a lot of different jobs at the same time and deal with any emergencies that come up," explained one. The variety of the work on a day-to-day basis recommends this job to people with strong work ethics, curious minds, and organizational abilities.

Many production managers are asked to implement systems of production tracking and quality control, so the first step for product managers is to become intimate with existing systems of production, past cost estimates, and company policies. "You've got to be careful not to make recommendations until you've gathered enough information to make intelligent ones," offered a five-year production manager. Also, production managers need to gain the trust of the people who work for them. "If you're not credible, you're not effective," said one production manager. A good production manager will also react to situations as they occur. "Flexibility is the key to success," as one respondent noted. Priorities, backlogs, breakdowns, strikes—all of these can alter intricately planned scheduling, and the production manager has to be flexible enough to adjust to these situations without reducing overall efficiency.

It's not unusual for the production manager to be located on the production floor, in order to see first-hand the running of the production process. But while production managers are involved in each stage of production, few micromanage the day-to-day details of each department's work. A production manager spends some time working alone on reports, but most of her time (over 60 percent) is spent meeting with representatives from different levels of the production process. In situations where production facilities are spread over large areas, a production manager spends a significant amount of time on the telephone.

The visible, tangible results they produce are a source of satisfaction for most production managers. Many noted that it was good to be able to point to shipments going out and coming in, to quality products produced cheaply and efficiently, and to the increase companies see in their bottom line. One summarized his feelings simply by saying, "It feels great because people at first resent what you do, and when they see the results, they come around. Everybody wins."

PAYING YOUR DUES

Production managers have no specific academic requirements, but coursework that proves helpful includes economics, accounting, finance, production and manufacturing systems, organizational behavior, psychology, sociology, and English. Production managers have to be well organized and creative—a combination of talents that many find difficult to demonstrate through ordinary work experience. Production experience can be a big plus on a resume. No licensing requirements exist, and professional organizations are significant only in areas of specialization, such as for quality control managers or human resource managers.

ASSOCIATED CAREERS

Production managers who decide to leave the profession search out challenges that excite both the creative and the detailed sides of their personalities. Many become entrepreneurs, efficiency experts, and strategic marketers. Their intimacy with the production process makes a transition to general administrative management easy, but relatively few take this option. It seems that the profession provides a challenge that few are in a hurry to forsake.

PAST AND FUTURE

Production managers can trace their origins back to the time-efficiency experts who first analyzed modern industrial society at the turn of the century. Today, production managers are essential to a variety of industries and will likely remain so for at least the next decade. Opportunities for production managers are expected to grow at a healthy pace as industries recognize the benefits the centralization of production responsibilities bring.

QUALITY OF LIFE

Two Years

Two years into the profession, production managers have made some headway in improving production efficiency, but many are still educating themselves on the production process, familiarizing themselves with client needs and concerns, and working as assistants to more senior managers. Many have proposed changes, and most often a few of these have been adopted as test cases to see how they will affect production. Hours are long but interesting; salaries are low in relation to hours.

Five Years

Five-year survivors have earned the trust of their co-workers, proposed and seen implemented significant changes, and achieved production results. They also look for new challenges. Many decide during these middle years whether to pursue higher-level managerial responsibility; a significant number choose to stay instead as production managers. Important contacts are made with suppliers and shippers; these can become significant if one changes jobs.

Ten Years

Those who have survived ten years in the profession face a big question: Should they stay or should they go? A large number switch firms at this point, opting for newer challenges rather than resting on their laurels. Hours decrease as many choose instead to remain at their current positions and fine-tune existing operations. Salaries rise, and most who leave the profession at this point only do so to retire.

THE BIRKMAN LIFESTYLE GRID

This career is suitable for people with Red interests.

You'll Have Contact With

Industrial Engineers
Line Workers
Product Designers
Quality Control Managers

Major Associations

Association for Manufacturing Technology
7901 Westpark Drive
Mclean, VA 22102
Tel: 703-893-2900
Fax: 703-893-1151
Contact: Membership Services

PROFESSOR

A DAY IN THE LIFE

College professors organize and conduct the functions of higher education. They engage in a variety of activities, from running laboratory experiments and supervising graduate student research to conducting large undergraduate lectures and writing textbooks. With the exception of scheduled classes—which can consume as few as three hours a week in graduate universities or up to 12-16 hours per week for undergraduates—a professor's time is largely spent on research, preparing class material, meeting with students, or however else she chooses. This profession is thus best suited for motivated self-starters, and its highest rewards are given to those who can identify and explore original problems in their fields.

Tenured professors have relatively high job security and professional freedom. Once tenured, a professor can largely set his own responsibilities and decide to a large extent how to divide his time between teaching, writing, researching, and administration. However, tenure no longer means complete immunity; post-tenure review is now mandate at most universities, and those who fall behind on teaching and independent scholarship may not be as secure nowadays.

The most difficult years of being a professor are the early ones, when there is great pressure to publish a significant body of work to establish the credentials that lead to tenure. However, the work of junior and senior faculty is quite similar, and the profession offers intellectual stimulation and freedom to all its members.

PAYING YOUR DUES

The path to becoming a tenured college professor is arduous. While a master's degree may be sufficient to qualify to teach in a two-year college, a doctoral degree is required to teach in four year colleges and universities. Ph.D.s generally take four to seven years to complete; after completing two to three years of course work, the graduate student will usually teach classes and write a dissertation, an original piece of research taking about three years to complete which is the most important element of the search for a first job as a professor. In addition, post-doctoral experience is an added advantage. For the coveted tenure-track positions, virtually every successful job candidate now boasts at least one and usually two "post-doc" years, and these are necessary to remain competitive, which means gathering a sufficient backlog of publications and writings in progress. Personal relationships with faculty is also critical in this hunt for a first job, as teaching positions in many areas (particularly the humanities) can be scarce. While approximately 80 percent of college jobs are in four-year institutions, about a third of all college faculty are employed part-time or in non-tenure track positions, and this percentage has risen in recent years as colleges attempt to control costs.

ASSOCIATED CAREERS

Because of the relatively flexible structure of the profession, many full-time faculty engage in outside professional activities. Economists consult with governments and corporations; engineers and academic labs develop products for private industry; humanities professors write articles which appear in newspapers and magazines. Many find this ability to work professionally on terms they define, while remaining in their institutions, to be among the most satisfying aspects of the profession. In addition, the significant administrative positions in colleges and universities are usually filled by former and current professors, and it is not uncommon for careers in university administration to develop from teaching careers.

PAST AND FUTURE

The mission of the first colleges in the United States was to train ministers for the new colonies. The concept of the modern liberal arts education did not appear in America until 1825, with the founding of the University of Virginia; today, this principle of the secular faculty is the norm rather than the exception. Higher education for women originally developed separately; the first women's college, Wesleyan Female College, was founded in Macon, Georgia in 1836, and single-sex education was the norm until the 1960s. Since then, coeducation has become the rule.

Openings for college professors should increase significantly beginning in the late 1990s as the generation of faculty who entered the field in the 1950s and 1960s begins to retire and the children of the baby-boom generation begin to reach college age. Demand should grow for professors in growing fields such as computer science and engineering, while employment for humanities professors will likely remain tight.

QUALITY OF LIFE

Two Years

At this stage, the recent Ph.D. graduate is either in a tenure track job as an instructor or assistant professor, or is working as a part-time or adjunct professor and looking for a job which could eventually lead to tenure. In the sciences, 50 percent of Ph.D. holders work with academic institutions, and many work in the private sector in lucrative jobs they have chosen in lieu of academic careers. For humanities Ph.D.s the job market is tougher; 20 percent find junior positions on a tenure track in their first year after graduation, and another 30 percent find non-tenure track work. Half do not find academic jobs. The young assistant professor works long hours for minimal pay, teaching several undergraduate classes and beginning to establish the research and writing record necessary to advance in her field. In smaller schools and at two-year colleges, there is often less pressure to publish, but these are busy years regardless of where the junior professor teaches.

Five Years

If the professor has been aggressive (and lucky) enough to get a monograph published and establish a clear area of expertise, she is on the verge of being promoted to associate professor and awarded tenure, events which are normally expected after the sixth year. Associate professors have more control over their teaching schedules; they are likely to be teaching fewer low-level classes, and more classes and seminars in their areas of specialization with older undergraduates and graduate students. In addition, as academic marketability is determined by a university's specific needs for expertise, professors become more able to move around among institutions when they establish themselves in their fields.

Ten Years

By now, professors have hopefully either made tenure at the university where they started, found another university which will give them tenure, or left the profession altogether. Failing these options, she may remain exploited as an adjunct professor, with all the demands of a tenured position but not the freedom, prestige, or security. With tenure comes the real rewards of the academic life: The ability to say, write and teach what one wishes with the greatest possible freedom. Job satisfaction is extremely high, and few tenured professors leave the profession. Those who do generally move to lucrative positions in private enterprise or powerful positions in government.

THE BIRKMAN LIFESTYLE GRID

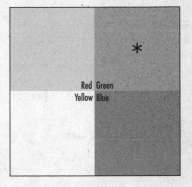

This career is suitable for people with Green interests.

You'll Have Contact With

Editors
Researchers
School Administrators
Students

Major Associations

American Association of
University Professors
1012 14th Street, NW
Washington, DC 20005
Tel: 202-737-5900
Fax: 202-737-5526

American Federation of Teachers
555 New Jersey Avenue, NW
Washington, DC 20001-2079
Tel: 202-879-4400

College & University Personnel Association
1233 20th Street, NW
Suite 301
Washington, DC 20036
Tel: 202-429-0311

PROMOTER

A DAY IN THE LIFE

Promoters develop marketing strategies for events ranging from rock concerts to international chess tournaments. Event promoters work with television, radio, special-events coordinators, ticket sellers, reviewers, bulk mailers, and local merchants to market a product. The profession is project-based, so those who want predictable hours and a steady workload should look elsewhere. Promoters view working long hours as a benefit: "When you're working, you're working all the time. When you're not, you pretty much make up your own schedule," is how one respondent described the roller coaster. Promoters work on a team on which people with different skills-artistic, financial, copywriting, and statistics-come together to produce a seamlessly integrated strategy. This helter-skelter mix can turn into a clash of egos, ideas, and concepts. As one respondent said, "if you have to step on someone, do it." You'll be recognized for your good ideas as well as your bad ones.

In few other careers is such a premium placed on creative thinking. Traditional advertising and marketing strategies can often prove too expensive or utilize too diffuse a medium for the standard entertainment event. "You have to be able to think inexpensively. Try pretending your budget was just cut in half and you have to reach the same number of people," wrote one veteran promoter. A successful promoter has an unlimited imagination that outmatches the most limited budget. "Tenacity," wrote one person surveyed, "is what separated the sharks from the chum (chopped-up fish guts)." Attention to detail is also important. A great promoter will bend over backwards for both the paying guests and the talent. Going the extra mile in hospitality for your act is a crucial part of keeping them coming back in the future.

Promoting is like gambling—a high-risk, high-return industry where it is amazingly easy to lose your shirt through one poor decision. People bond while scrambling to find inexpensive media outlets, dashing to events that only moments before were mere ideas, and running to coordinate all the details, but the relationship means nothing if the project is unsuccessful. A promoter cannot afford to be associated with a failed marketing strategy. The fall from grace can be swift and merciless, and many people who have endorsed failures or passed on enormously lucrative projects have quickly found themselves seeking work in other professions.

PAYING YOUR DUES

It takes a particular type of person to become a promoter–confidence and flamboyance help immeasurably. No undergraduate degree is required to enter this occupation, and rightly so–no undergraduate degree would properly prepare you for it. Understanding demographics, business, and publicity is important, but the two most valuable traits mentioned by our respondents are creativity and an ability to be in touch with your audience . Promoters need listening and organizational skills, charm, and style. In many cases the difference between a financial bloodbath and a smash hit is solely the ability of the promoter, so the pressure is high and rapid career swings are not unusual.

Most concert promoters start out in college, where they can establish contacts with talent buyers and bands who come to play at the school. Booking agents are the most important contacts for promoters. An act can always find another promoter, so establishing and maintaining solid relationships with talent and agents is of utmost importance. Advertising or promotional personnel may go on to start their own businesses with as few as one or two steady clients. Shops tend to be small (65 percent of offices employ fewer than 25 people), and advancement occurs in short, intense flurries. The hours can be long and the future uncertain, but the field can be financially rewarding for those few who achieve star status.

ASSOCIATED CAREERS

Only about 25 percent of promoters stay in the profession for life. More often it is a job for the risk-friendly, aggressive, and creative individual who started out in the field of public relations or advertising. Most who leave return to public relations, sales, advertising, political consulting, media buying, the film industry, or law.

PAST AND FUTURE

P.T. Barnum and Babe Ruth were two larger-than-life figures who promoted themselves into mythhood. In order to get people to pay attention to them, they had to build an image, make outrageous claims, or provide something unique, exciting, and exotic. The legacy of these fabulous marketers can be seen in companies like Coca-Cola(tm) and celebrity promoters like Don King, who use the media to promote their products and events.

The entertainment industry is expected to grow by around 20 percent over the next ten years. As the number of events that requires promotional skills increases, the job market for promoters will expand. The scale of events, however, will be much smaller. Those with extensive knowledge of statistics, the Internet, and demographics have a bright future.

QUALITY OF LIFE

Every state has at least one large promoter and several smaller, specialized promoters with long histories with talent that is in demand, so this field can be very difficult to break into. Those who rise to the top are not always the most pleasant or the easiest to work with, and they rarely take kindly to ambitious young competitors. Watch your back!

Two Years

Two years is a significant amount of time in the life of a promoter. A number of projects have gone from idea to completion, a number have stalled or failed somewhere during the process, and some never went any farther than the memo they rode in on. Promoters have experience researching, modeling, examining demographics, conducting focus groups, doing interviews, making phone contacts, traveling, and pitching ideas. The ability to successfully pitch ideas is very important to those considering a future in this profession.

Five Years

Sixty percent of those who began in the field have departed for other professions or returned to school. The hours get longer, the pay increases, the perquisites increase even more, and the opportunity for significant responsibility emerges for those with solid credentials. The farther up the ladder in this industry one wants to go, the more cutthroat it gets. Many promoters, even the best, suffer burn-out.

Ten Years

Ten years in the entertainment marketing industry can be a lifetime. Those who've worked at a variety of agencies either start their own firms or consolidate their strength at the top of their current one. Another 10 percent leave for high-paying jobs in other fields. Client satisfaction is the telling point for whether the promoter, at this point, will continue to be successful or will decline. Some who specialize in certain types of entertainment marketing—sports events, concerts, or movies—can fall victim to the cyclical nature of public opinion. Those who've ridden the elevator up during the boom period of one specialty area may find themselves in a helpless freefall if that field flops.

THE BIRKMAN LIFESTYLE GRID

This career is suitable for people with Green interests.

You'll Have Contact With

Advertising Executives
Agents
Market Researchers
Publicists
Record Labels
Retail Representatives

Major Associations

Promoters generally work in specific fields and small, concentrated companies. Associations are not considered significant in their profession.

PROPERTY MANAGER

A DAY IN THE LIFE

Any residential or commercial property must be taken care of from both a physical and a tenant-relations standpoint, and that is what a property manager does. He maintains and upgrades facilities while acting as liaison between the owner of the property and tenants. In many cases, the property manager has the responsibility for attracting tenants to the property as well. Since most property managers are in charge of a number of properties at any time, the job can involve frantic work, unusual hours, and extremely difficult schedule coordination. "My desk looks like a hurricane hit it all the time," wrote one manager, adding that his paperwork burden isn't just large, "it scares me." It takes strong communications skills, strong organizational skills, and a flair for numbers to handle this demanding position.

"Everything that goes wrong is your problem," mentioned one property manager, pointing out that a property manager has the most client contact when disasters occur, such as a flooded basement, a heating system gone awry, or a burglary. This can be daunting for those who don't perform well in crisis situations. One respondent told us that the best property managers are "proactive rather than reactive." The more they can anticipate potential problems and prevent them, the fewer they have to deal with. When things do fall apart, often due to short-sighted owners who won't lay out sufficient money for upkeep, managers must respond quickly and decisively. More mundane tasks, such as collecting rent and coordinating garbage removal, cannot suffer because of unanticipated events.

Many property managers feel that the best feature of the profession is the chance to work with a variety of people on a number of different tasks: "I never know what my day's going to be like," as one put it. "I think I know. I've made lists of stuff to do. But as soon as you cross one thing out two new things come up. It's a race to keep on top of everything. I love it." While property managers spend a lot of their day dealing with paperwork and talking on the telephone, the problems they deal with vary greatly from week to week and month to month, giving most property managers a sense of creative challenge that keeps the job fresh. Onsite managers also have to show prospective tenants around the site and meet with resident boards and committees, which can mean evenings or weekends spent in meetings.

PAYING YOUR DUES

Most major employers ask that property managers have a bachelor's degree, although no formal requirements are inherent to the field. Coursework that proves helpful to candidates includes real estate, organizational behavior, mathematics, accounting, finance, logic, psychology, and public relations. A few property managers who were responsible for recruiting new tenants stated that marketing courses were helpful as well. After being hired, many people attend brief weekend or three-day training programs, sponsored by the hiring company, that acquaint them with the concerns and obligations of the property manager. Those who wish to become property managers in the public sector, for example in subsidized federal housing, must be certified, although the certification carries weight in the private sector as well. Professional organizations such as the Institute of Real Estate Management or the National Organization of Home Builders administer these exams.

ASSOCIATED CAREERS

Since they are well-versed in the ins and outs of real estate, many property managers become commercial real estate agents. A significant few with finance experience move into property development, particularly on a local level. Some become specialists in building maintenance and repair, using their industry connections to get regular work.

PAST AND FUTURE

While property managers can probably trace their roots back to the rent-collectors in the service of extortionate landlords in pre-industrial times, in recent times the position is more of a liaison between owner and tenant. Property managers can look forward to a strong future. Commercial, residential, and industrial property development is expected to result from growth in all sectors in the upcoming decade, and these newly developed properties will need managers to keep them running smoothly. Property managers will still be at the mercy of local economies, but if relocation is not a problem, the field should be open in the next ten years.

QUALITY OF LIFE

Two Years

Property managers are in charge of one or two properties as they learn the business in general and their company's protocols in specific. Client contact is immediate in this business, and responsibilities run high right away. The only responsibility that may be withheld from the two-year professional is the ability to negotiate long-term contracts with maintenance companies or custodial services. Large offices will centralize this function; small ones will give that responsibility to experienced managers.

Five Years

Five years into the profession, property managers may manage one large complex of buildings or a number of small properties. Hours and salaries increase, but responsibility for tenant satisfaction and the smooth maintenance of the property still rest with the manager. Many switch employers in years three through seven, looking for the right balance between challenge and salary. Satisfaction is above average.

Ten Years

Those who have survived ten years as property managers have developed a system to keep track of maintenance issues, financial obligations, and tenant happiness. A number begin to manage groups of less experienced property managers. Contacts made during the first five years (along with invaluable practical experience) come in handy as emergencies are dealt with swiftly and efficiently.

THE BIRKMAN LIFESTYLE GRID

This career is suitable for people with Green interests.

You'll Have Contact With

Electricians
Property Owners
Plumbers
Tenants

Major Associations

Building Owners and Managers
Institute International
1521 Ritchie Highway
Arnold, MD 21012
Tel: 410-974-1410
Fax: 410-974-1935
Contact: Student Development Dept.

Institute of Real Estate Management
430 North Michigan Avenue
Chicago, IL 60611
Tel: 312-329-6000
Fax: 312-661-0217
Contact: Mike Crawshaw

PSYCHOLOGIST

A DAY IN THE LIFE

By doing research and performing examinations, psychologists study all aspects of the mind. Health facilities employ approximately 30 percent of all working psychologists, while 40 percent work in educational environments, in such positions as counselors, educators, and researchers. Most often, these academically connected psychologists maintain a private practice while teaching or conducting research. Psychologists working in academic settings have flexibility in their schedules, but the demands on their time are high.

Private practice is the goal of many psychologists. While seeing private patients means a psychologist is her own boss, it also means accommodating patients with evening or weekend hours. A government or corporate psychologist, by contrast, works in a more structured environment. Their hours are fixed and they often work alone. There's some relief and enjoyment in the occasional conference that takes them away from writing reports. Despite potentially grueling schedules and emotional demands, psychologists report great satisfaction in their jobs; the gratification they receive from helping others keeps them in the field. Wrote one psychologist, "The best thing about this job is that people open up their lives to you—that's a great responsibility but also an honor."

PAYING YOUR DUES

Plan on spending many years in school if you want to embark on a career in psychology. A Ph.D. will enable you to work in the widest range of positions, and doing graduate work toward a doctoral degree consumes between five and seven years. Obtaining this distinguished degree hinges on completing a dissertation based on original research. Before you begin this research, you must complete coursework in quantitative research methods, statistics, and computers. If you want to work in a clinical or counseling setting, you will begin to work with patients under supervision before the degree is completed, and at least another year of supervised work experience is required afterward. Most academic programs require counseling psychology students to undergo psychoanalysis as part of their training. The newer Psy.D., Doctor of Psychology, will qualify you for clinical positions. The Psy.D. is awarded based not on a dissertation but on clinical experience and exams. The time and effort it takes to get this degree are comparable to the Ph.D. The difference is the emphasis on counseling, while the Ph.D. candidate also does research. Thus, employment options for those with a Psy.D. are less flexible than for those with a Ph.D.

Besides the years of study and internships, psychologists offering patient care must be certified and licensed by the state in which they intend to practice. Most of these licensing exams are standardized tests, but some states require applicants to pass essay or oral exams. These tests are designed to ensure that candidates have both knowledge of the field and appropriate personal qualities.

Without a doctoral degree you can find job options within psychology, but these positions will always require supervision by doctoral-level psychologists. Candidates holding master's degrees can work as assistants and may administer tests, conduct research and psychological evaluations, and counsel certain patients. The master's degree requires a minimum of two years of full-time study and a one-year internship. The candidate has the choice of obtaining practical experience or completing a research-based thesis. Those with only a bachelor's degree in psychology find their options more limited. They can work as assistants to psychologists and other mental health professionals. Graduate schools tend to look favorably on undergraduate degrees in psychology. Other good majors for future psychologists are biological, physical, and social sciences, statistics, and mathematics.

ASSOCIATED CAREERS

A Ph.D. in psychology creates numerous opportunities to work in fields other than counseling. Teaching and research are the areas most populated by non-practicing psychologists. With master's-level qualifications, teaching in high schools or junior colleges is possible, while doctoral-level qualifications allow you to teach at the college and post-graduate levels. Other related fields include psychometrics, a new but burgeoning area that attracts psychologists. Psychometricians invent, refine, and administer tests of competence and aptitude that are usually used in corporate settings. Many advertising agencies also look favorably on applicants with some background in psychology.

PAST AND FUTURE

In the seventeenth century, the French philosopher Rene Descartes separated human behavior into two classes, involuntary and voluntary; the field of psychology stems from his theory of involuntary behavior. In 1892, Edward Titchener brought this "psychology of introspection" to the United States, at the same time that Sigmund Freud was developing his theory of the unconscious. Since then the study of psychology has grown into many disparate areas. As a profession, psychology has enjoyed formal recognition in this country since World War II. As a relatively new science, psychology enjoys wide and varied prospects for the future. In fact, psychology is expected to grow much faster than average for all occupations for at least another decade. The demand for psychologists is expected to be high in corporate, correctional, educational, and public settings. The old stigma attached to therapy is fading, as more people turn to therapists to help them get through difficult times, and as chronic problems like depression are recognized as treatable disorders rather than personal failures.

QUALITY OF LIFE

Two Years

Because of the extensive academic and emotional commitment required to obtain their degree, very few psychologists leave the field at any time in their careers. While those at the onset of their careers are sometimes intimidated by the strict supervision they are subject to, they are usually excited by the long-awaited opportunity to begin practicing their calling.

Five Years

After a few years, psychologists begin to see changes in the lives of their patients, and progress in their research provides another source of intellectual reward. Building up a client base depends to a great extent on referrals by satisfied patients, and successful practitioners may be able to establish a private practice within five years. A hospital affiliation can also be a good source of patients.

Ten Years

Many psychologists choose to break away from a university or hospital with which they are affiliated to focus on building their full-time practice. Otherwise they may be involved in hospital administration, or clinical testing or ongoing research through a hospital or university.

THE BIRKMAN LIFESTYLE GRID

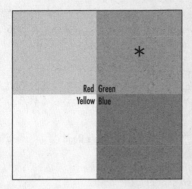

This career is suitable for people with Green interests.

You'll Have Contact With

Clients
Occupational Therapists
Psychiatrists
Social Workers

Major Associations

American Psychological Association
750 First Street, NE
Washington, DC 20002-4242
Tel: 202-336-5500
Fax: 202-336-5501

Association of State and
Provincial Psychology Board
P.O. Box 4389
Montgomery, AL 36103
Tel: 334-242-4127

National Association of School Psychologists
4340 East West Highway
Suite 402
Bethesda, MD 20814
Tel: 301-657-0270
Fax: 301-657-0275

PUBLIC HEALTH ADMINISTRATOR

PROFESSIONAL PROFILE

# of people in profession	33,000
% male	65
% female	35
avg. hours per week	40
avg. starting salary	$18,000
avg. salary after 5 years	$30,000
avg. salary 10 to 15 years	$41,000

Professionals Read
Public Health Reports
Family Planning Perspectives
Journal of Epidemology

Books, Films and TV Shows
Featuring the Profession
The Coming Plague
Hot Zone
Outbreak
The Black Plague

Major Employers
Rockefeller Foundation
420 Fifth Avenue
New York, NY 10018-2702
Tel: 212-865-8500
Fax: 212-852-8445
Contact: Human Resources

Population Council
Dag Hammarskjold Plaza
9th Floor
New York, NY 10017
Tel: 212-339-0500
Fax: 212-775-6052
Contact: Maria Vinadell

Sexuality and Info. Education Council of
U.S.
130 West 42nd Street
Suite 350
New York, NY 10036-7802
Tel: 212-819-9770
Fax: 212-819-9776

A DAY IN THE LIFE

Public health administrators focus on community-wide disease prevention and health promotion. As the name of the profession shows, there are two parts to their jobs. Public health administrators try to improve the welfare of the community at large and run the organizations that disseminate information about health. The majority are employed by governmental health agencies, while others work for not-for-profit organizations and educational institutions. They assess community health issues and educate members about the prevention or alleviation of health problems. The public health administrator executes community outreach programs to make people aware of dangers such as lead poisoning and to address chronic problems afflicting the community, like sexually transmitted diseases.

The administrator's job calls for the management skills of a CEO. She creates budgets, hires staff, organizes the office, and obtains any necessary equipment. Writing grant proposals and fundraising take up more and more of the administrator's time as budget cuts flourish. Whenever she notices a health related trend or event, she must write a report on what she believes its effect on the community will be. The public health administrator must be prepared to delicately balance limited budgets with the compassion needed to provide basic care. Since she is often faced with contradictory information and demands, she must be able to make decisions. She also needs self-confidence when called on to defend her decisions to public officials or the press. The administrator attends community events frequently. Usually she devotes five and a half days a week to her career, but some are on 24-hour call. In an era of shrinking health care budgets, officials are expected to complete projects faster and with less support staff than ever before. This has forced many administrators to exercise their creative juices in designing new ways to handle the issues they face.

PAYING YOUR DUES

There is no one way to become a public health administrator, but most professionals have worked in related fields and acquired advanced degrees. Employers require at least a Bachelor's degree in health care administration or a related field, but the field is so competitive that master's degree holders have a significant advantage. While health-related courses, business administration, and finance are important parts of your academic background, make time for communications and English, too. You will need to write and present many reports professionally and confidently. Many administrators receive their degrees after having worked in other areas in the field. They are often former health inspectors, who insure that consumer products meet federal health and safety standards, or regulatory inspectors, who enforce observation of public welfare laws and regulations. Those with keen entrepreneurial skills and backgrounds are encouraged to enter the field, bringing their efficiency to it. Some people gain their initial training in the Peace Corps before returning to school.

Many graduate programs offer specialized joint degrees, such as a combined health care management and law degree. While dozens of schools offer graduate and undergraduate degrees in public health administration, only twenty-six are accredited. Whether you choose an accredited school or not is largely dependent on your plan of study, career expectations, and financial situation. Public health administrators enjoy a combination of study and work throughout their careers. Most public health administration students enroll in internship programs to gain experience. Once they start working, they are expected to take continuing education courses every year to keep up with the latest in health care services. Beginning in school and continuing throughout their careers, public health administrators should read trade papers about health care and the literature supplied by its providers.

ASSOCIATED CAREERS

The public health administrator works with a host of people in different professions, and can apply his skills, with some extra training, to these other fields if he wishes to change careers. Biostatisticians compile and study vital statistics. They determine the incidence of diseases in different populations and create life expectancy tables. Public health administrators turn to them for advice regarding issues such as which vaccines are better than others. Public health administrators can become health economists, who examine financing and organization of health care facilities, and advise them on running their businesses. The demand for health economists is growing due to the changing organization of the health care industry.

PAST AND FUTURE

A century ago, health care officials were concerned entirely with preventing and controlling infectious diseases. As the variety of factors affecting health gained recognition, the field of health care administration was born. One professional growth consultant recently commented that "What's happening in health care today is that no one knows what's happening in health care today." Recent budget cuts and government debates are making those in the field very anxious. Should national health care reform legislation be passed, it will further change terms of delivery, provision and payment for health care services. Future public health administrators will have to display creativity and flexibility in finding solutions to health care problems.

QUALITY OF LIFE

Two Years

Approximately 80 percent of recent graduates who enter this field feel prepared for the challenges they face as public health administrators. They are often dedicated and well integrated into the system and are only new to their particular positions, not the field as a whole. New administrators learn about the problems faced by the community they work in and get their first tastes of running an office.

Five Years

Some public health care officials find that they are tired of the long hours and increasing responsibilities. Trying to get people to take basic health precautions can be frustrating when they ignore crucial advice. Administrators sometimes move from working on public health for a public office to working on public health in the private sector, such as in hospitals, where they can continue their satisfying work in a more temperate environment. Others remain with the communities of which they have become a part.

Ten Years

The ten-year veteran is skilled at running his office and effectively advising the community about preventative health care. She has become a critical member of the community, depended on for practical and trustworthy advice. Administrators enjoy the recognition they receive from the community and public officials.

THE BIRKMAN LIFESTYLE GRID

This career is suitable for people with Green interests.

You'll Have Contact With
Epidemiologists
Physicians
Sociologists
Statisticians

Major Associations
Association of University Programs in Health Administration
1911 North Fort Myer Drive
Suite 503
Arlington, VA 22209
Tel: 703-524-5500

National Health Council
1730 M Street, NW
Suite 500
Washington, DC 20036
Tel: 202-785-3910
Fax: 202-785-5923

Public Relations Society of America
33 Irving Place
New York, NY 10003
Tel: 212-995-2230
Fax: 212-995-0757

PUBLIC RELATIONS

PROFESSIONAL PROFILE

# of people in profession	107,000
% male	50
% female	50
avg. starting salary	$24,000
avg. salary after 5 years	$36,000
avg. salary 10 to 15 years	$54,000

Professionals Read
PR Reporter
Public Relations Journal

Books, Films and TV Shows Featuring the Profession
The Image Man
How to Do Anything at All with Girls

Major Employers
Burson-Marsteller
230 Park Ave South
New York, NY 10003-1566
Tel: 212-614-4000
Contact: Human Resources

Shandwick
111 Fifth Avenue
New York, NY 10003
Tel: 212-420-8100

Flashman-Hillard
200 N. Broadway
St. Louis, MO 63102
Tel: 314-982-1700
Contact: Human Resources

A DAY IN THE LIFE

A public relations specialist is an image shaper. Their job is to generate positive publicity for their client and enhance their reputation. The client can be a company, an individual or a government. In the government PR people are called press secretaries. They keep the public informed about the activity of government agencies, explain policy, and manage political campaigns. Public relations people working for a company may handle consumer relations, or the relationship between parts of the company such as the managers and employees, or different branch offices. Though the job often involves the dissemination of information, some view this cynically as "spin doctoring." There is an old saying about PR that 'Advertisers lie about the product. Public relations people lie about the company.'

Regardless, the successful PR person must be a good communicator-in print, in person and on the phone. They cultivate and maintain contacts with journalists, set up speaking engagements, write executive speeches and annual reports, respond to inquiries and speak directly to the press on behalf of their client. They must keep lines of communication open between the many groups affected by a company's product and policies: consumers, shareholders, employees, and the managing body. Public relations people also write press releases and may be involved in producing sales or marketing material.

Public relations is a good career for the generalist. A PR person must keep abreast of current events and be well versed in pop culture to understand what stories will get the publics' attention. It takes a combination of analysis and creative problem solving to get your client in the public eye. The content of the work is constantly changing and unforeseen challenges arise every day. As one public relations person explained, "In addition to the standard duties, a PR person might have to shepherd an alcoholic and half-mad (but brilliant) author through a twenty-city interview tour or try to put a warm 'n fuzzy spin on the company's latest oil-spill."

PAYING YOUR DUES

Though some colleges offer a degree in public relations, most industry professionals agree it's unnecessary. Since public relations requires familiarity with a wide variety of topics, a broad education is the best preparation. Any major that teaches you how to read and write intelligently will lay good foundation for a career in public relations. Or, as one PR person put it "if you can write a thesis on Dante, you should be able to write a press release." Internships are a common way to get some practical experience and break into the field.

ASSOCIATED CAREERS

Because public relations people work so closely with the media there is often a great deal of exchange between these fields. Many PR people become journalists to exercise more creativity; a number of journalists turn to public relations for better money. PR people also often go into marketing, particularly at the more senior levels.

PAST AND FUTURE

The practice of manipulating public opinion has existed as long as there were people and organizations that required it to support their agenda. As Abraham Lincoln said, "Public sentiment is everything. With public sentiment nothing can fail; without it nothing can succeed." Not surprisingly, governments launched the first public relations campaigns. Back when the United States was being settled, publicity brochures were circulated in England to contradict the rumors of hardship in the plague-ridden, Indian-infested colonies and to promote emigration. One described Jamestown, Virginia as "not unlike Tyrus for colours, Basan for woods, Persia for oils, Arabia for spices, Spain for silks, Narsis for shipping, Netherlands for fish, Pomona for fruit, and tillage, Babylon for corn." These same techniques were used again to encourage westward expansion in the United States in the mid-1800's.

The U.S. government marshaled the forces of persuasion again during World War I when they created the U.S. Committee on Public Information to sell war cause to the public. A member of this committee, Edward Bernays, is credited with being the father of modern public relations. The nephew of Sigmund Freud, Bernays was the first person to link a commercial product to a popular social cause when he persuaded people marching for women's rights to hold up Lucky Strike cigarettes as "Torches of Freedom".

PR is changing with the advent of new mediums such as the internet. As with many professions, the practice of public relations will probably become more specialized and niche-oriented.

QUALITY OF LIFE

Two Years

The first two years of a public relations career are spent doing mainly administrative work such as putting together promotional packages and mailing them out. The value for the beginner is in learning how to construct and wield the tools of the trade: press kits and releases. Equally important is the chance to observe the strategy of PR and develop judgment. In the apprentice phase you begin the important process of making contacts in the media.

Five Years

After five years the public relations professional has increased responsibility and is doing most of the real work. They are writing the press releases and putting strategic skills to work running a public relations campaign. By this point they should have a stable of contacts in the press and be supervising newcomers.

Ten Years

The work of a public relations profession becomes less "hands on" and more managerial towards the ten year mark. There is more strategizing and a focus on courting new clients. Their business judgment should be very well developed at this stage; often senior PR people will act as a spokesperson for large corporations. At this level, the compensation gets very good.

THE BIRKMAN LIFESTYLE GRID

This career is suitable for people with Blue interests.

You'll Have Contact With
Journalists
Editors
Advertisers
TV Producers

Major Associations
Public Relations Society of America
33 Irving Place
New York, NY 10003-2376
Tel: 212-995-2230

PUBLICIST

PROFESSIONAL PROFILE

# of people in profession	12,000
% male	65
% female	35
avg. hours per week	45
avg. starting salary	$19,000
avg. salary after 5 years	$26,000
avg. salary 10 to 15 years	$40,000

Professionals Read
Public Relations Journal
PR Newswire

Books, Films and TV Shows Featuring the Profession
The Player
This is Spinal Tap
Speak Up

Major Employers
Many companies and celebrities have single or private publicists. Check your area for more information on employment opportunities.

A DAY IN THE LIFE

A publicist gets press coverage for his client. The publicist is often the middleman between the high-profile personality and members of the media. He usually wants his client to receive positive acclaim, but many publicists surveyed noted the old adage that "the only bad publicity is no publicity." Politicians and captains of industry require a little more specific spin on their press—they want to be seen as forward-looking and confident—but other professions are less picky, as in the case of the rock star who reveals the sordid details of his seamy nightlife to cultivate a rough image. Publicists also perform damage control, attempting to counteract any undesirable press coverage the client receives. This position as "last line of defense" is what distinguishes the adequate publicist from the extraordinary one. Good publicists can turn scandal into opportunity and create valuable name-recognition for their clients.

Publicists don't only work for the famous. Sometimes they work for a little-known person or industry and create reasons for them to receive press coverage. In a case where a company desiring publicity is hampered by its esoteric nature or technical jargon, the publicist must translate its positions into easily understandable language. A major part of the publicist's day is spent writing press releases and creating press packets, which have photos and information about the publicized person or company. Publicists spend a lot of time on the phone. They put in long hours, and most receive little financial reward in return. They operate under hectic conditions and must adhere to strict deadlines which coincide with publicity events, such as the release of a movie or the publishing of a book. They have to ensure that they get the appropriate information to the media in time for the event they are generating publicity for, such as a record release or automotive sale. They must always be available for comment (even when that comment is "no comment") and remain friends with the media, no matter how demanding the desires of both clients and the reporters on whom they depend. But at the end of the day, they go to the hottest parties in town, the ones for their clients.

PAYING YOUR DUES

The most appropriate bachelor's degree for a publicist to hold is in communications, but business degrees are also looked upon favorably by employers. In college, aspiring publicists should study public relations, public speaking, and writing. Candidates should also have some experience with copyediting. Depending on the publicist's desired area, other elective courses may include labor relations, economics, and politics. Most publicists recommend interning at a firm before plunging into this job—a low-responsibility position allows them to see the pace of the profession firsthand. Besides, it helps to make as many contacts as possible in this "it's-who-you-know" field. Some publicists have graduate degrees, although they are not required by any employer. All publicists start at the same entry-level positions and work their way up. Experience is the key to obtaining a good job, especially in the entertainment industry, which is the hardest to break into. The music industry is most likely to acknowledge and reward fresh insight given by new employees.

ASSOCIATED CAREERS

Public relations, marketing, and event planning are closely linked to the publicist's field. The event planner creates events to generate interest in whatever the publicist is promoting. Marketers study the community to determine how the client is perceived and how its members feel his image could be improved. Advertisers and writers often create the materials used by publicists. Programmers determine where and how frequently the company should advertise. Booking agents are responsible for procuring venues for publicity and anticipating the effect the events will have on the client's image. For instance, he may have to weigh the exposure that comes from being a guest on a major talk show against the potential friendliness or hostility of the host. Information officers perform many of the same duties as publicists, only they respond passively to inquiries and publicity, while the publicist actively seeks an interested audience.

PAST AND FUTURE

In the 1800s, to obtain more business, newspapers started the dubious practice of writing positive articles about their advertisers. This practice was halted by legislation soon after it began, but it paved the way for the public relations field. The publicist's field is an offshoot of the public relations arena. Ivy Ledbetter Lee was the first American to work in this capacity. He saw negative press surrounding different blue collar fields and trained the workers to respond to the media so that they would be seen in a more favorable light. Then, the government began hiring people to perform these activities on its behalf and the label publicist was conceived. Today, publicists work for anyone desiring coverage in the press, from politicians and companies to actors and lawyers. The future shows average growth for this profession thanks to the ubiquity and influence of the media.

QUALITY OF LIFE

Two Years

Many publicists are initially attracted to the perceived glamour of this field, but they soon learn they have to roll up their sleeves and work hard. Those that stick it out-a minority as burn-out is exceptionally high-have learned from the well-networked publicists around them, especially when it comes to establishing contacts.

Five Years

By this time, many publicists can relax a bit. They have made enough contacts that they don't have to struggle to be heard, and they are relatively comfortable with their networking skills. Despite long hours, they can begin to enjoy the glamour factor as they begin to deal with more high-power clients and get them national media attention.

Ten Years

Publicists enjoy the influence they have over the media and their ability to "create" visibility. Some of the best ones start their own "boutique" firms; they can command major clients even with a relatively small staff, since their Rolodex and their ability to work miracles over the phone are their chief assets.

THE BIRKMAN LIFESTYLE GRID

This career is suitable for people with Green interests.

You'll Have Contact With

Advertising Executives
Event Planners
Journalists
Promoters

Major Associations

National Association of Professional Publicists. Contact: Contact your local chapter for more information.

National Coucil for Marketing and Public Relations
364 North Wyndham Avenue
Greeley, CO 80634
Tel: 303-353-9918
Fax: 303-353-9929

Public Relations Society of America
33 Irving Place
3rd Floor
New York, NY 10003
Tel: 800-WER-PRSA

QUALITY CONTROL MANAGER

A DAY IN THE LIFE

Quality control managers work in every type of production environment possible, from producing dictionaries to dowel-cutting for boat plugs. A quality control manager samples production, analyzes it, and then makes recommendations on how to increase the quality of goods. It takes a firm grasp of scientific as well as managerial concepts to be a successful quality control expert; quality control managers work hard inspecting, analyzing, and writing reports about production. These people are the last line of defense between quality goods that the public respects and shoddy work that can harm a company's reputation.

Does this mean they are appreciated by coworkers? Quality control managers answered us with a resounding one-word answer: No. If you absolutely need approbation from your colleagues, be warned: Quality control is not the field for you. "People see you as the policeman, criticizing people's work and telling them that they're not doing their job right," said one QC inspector. The best of QC professionals act as educators as well, letting people know that they are only there to help everyone keep product quality high. "I spend more time talking with people than examining objects," wrote one eight-year veteran of the QC field, "because the object can't change."

Meeting with workers, executives, and supervisors takes up a significant 30 percent of the QC manager's day, but another 30 percent is spent testing and analyzing materials. Scientific methodologies are important; those who do not properly conduct their tests are going to make recommendations based on faulty data. The remainder of time is spent writing reports, making recommendations, and doing professional reading. QC experts must keep up with current materials use, statistical studies, and technological advances that affect the field of quality control. For example, construction materials stress-testing can be done using high-pressured pistons to compress them to the point of breakage; a recent advance lets the QC expert analyze the molecular composition of a small sample to get nearly as precise an estimate of its tensile strength.

PAYING YOUR DUES

No specific academic requirements exist for quality control experts, but the many positions in the field that involve scientific analysis require bachelor's degrees. Candidates who majored in chemistry, physics, and engineering are at an advantage during the job hunt; at a minimum, coursework should include mathematics, statistics, and computer modeling. Some candidates who have only high school degrees are sponsored to take two- or three-year post-high school courses that train them in a particular industry. Many of these industries—automobile, aerospace, and glassmaking, to name a few—have exacting requirements that can only be learned through specific training. Quality control trainees may also have to spend significant time on a production floor analyzing behavior that affects quality control.

ASSOCIATED CAREERS

Quality control managers find a number of detail-oriented jobs open to them. Those with financial backgrounds become bookkeepers, accountants, and loan officers more than anything else. A number with strong interpersonal skills become production supervisors and inventory managers, fields well-suited to their organizational abilities and analytic natures.

PAST AND FUTURE

Quality control managers first became important with the mass production of similar items that came with the industrial revolution. Large-scale production initially brought with it high levels of variation between goods from the same plant, and consumers were wary. No longer did a personally known craftsman attend to their problems; now they were dealing with a faceless organization in which there was no personal accountability. The need for consistent customer satisfaction inspired the creation of quality control managers. The position has been a central feature of industrialized production ever since.

Quality control managers can expect job openings in many industries in the next decade, but positions should grow at a slightly slower pace than the economy in general. As standardized systems that predict levels of quality are developed, and as larger companies dominate production environments, fewer QC experts will be needed to maintain the same level of excellence. Still, a significant number of QC managers will reach retirement age in the next decade, and positions should be available at a rate only slightly below the current one.

QUALITY OF LIFE

Two Years

Quality control managers have developed systems of testing during these first two years that give their company reasonable ideas of the quality levels of their product. Many spend their first three months merely orienting themselves to a company's product line, reviewing past quality statistics, and analyzing methods of production. QC managers work closely with production managers, raw material suppliers, and production line workers during these initial years in order to make solid and sensible recommendations.

Five Years

After five years, most QC managers have seen their programs implemented and have had to handle many unforeseen complications. Many have been rotated between different production facilities and different product lines, and are required to rapidly become experts in each item's production process. A number are asked to relocate for two to nine months or longer. Satisfaction is extremely high in these middle years; salaries are average.

Ten Years

Quality control managers who have lasted ten years are familiar with their company's product lines and production processes. They have a strong understanding of raw material suppliers' costs and quality. Few shift jobs in these later years, as much of the knowledge they absorbed throughout their career is only useful with respect to one company: The one they currently work for. Hours are average and travel is less likely as salaries rise.

THE BIRKMAN LIFESTYLE GRID

Red Green
Yellow Blue

This career is suitable for people with Red interests.

You'll Have Contact With
Industrial Engineers
Inventory Managers
Management Consultants
Production Managers

Major Associations
American Society for Quality Control
P.O. Box 3005
Milwaukee, WI 53201-3005
Tel: 414-272-8575
Fax: 414-272-1734
Contact: Human Resources

REAL ESTATE AGENT/BROKER

A DAY IN THE LIFE

Buying or selling a house or apartment is one of the biggest decisions of a person's life, and real estate agents and brokers help people negotiate what can be a confusing process. Though both are often called real estate agents, agents and brokers have different roles. The broker has more administrative responsibility. There is usually one broker per estate, but often many agents are working with clients who are interested in the property.

When someone wants to sell or rent his property he usually calls a real estate agent. A large chunk of the agent's day may be spent on the phone obtaining listings for her agency. The agent also arranges to advertise the properties she is showing, and may visit each property before it is shown to clients. She needs to know about everything from floor plans to heating systems to cesspools—she's a matchmaker, and she's got to know both sides of the equation. It's also important for an agent to be familiar with the neighborhoods she works in, so she can counsel her clients about a property's fair market value. A good real estate agent is informed about things like schools, tax rates, and public transportation systems, and should be aware of going mortgage rates.

A real estate agent must manage delicate price negotiations when an interested buyer and seller hook up. "Negotiating skills are not just important but critical for real estate agents," as one respondent put it. The agent also coordinates the "closing" when a property is sold, which means the actual signing of papers and transfer of a property's title. Networking is a big part of the job-most real estate agents develop a group of attorneys, mortgage lenders, and contractors to whom they refer their clients. Finally, a real estate agent should be able to discern and be sensitive to a client's needs during what may be an uncertain time.

In order to be available when their clients have free time, real estate agents work many evenings and weekends. An experienced agent will sometimes avoid some of the weekend hours by having an "open house" and drafting a new agent to go and answer potential buyers' questions. Commercial real estate agents' jobs involve more research on market trends and an even more detailed attention to the needs of buyers. Since they work longer on each deal, commercial agents and brokers make fewer sales than residential agents but receive higher commissions.

PAYING YOUR DUES

About the only things real estate agents have in common in terms of preparation are high school diplomas and communication skills. More and more people are entering the field with college degrees, however, and some colleges even offer courses in real estate. These may be helpful, as would other business courses, but most of the learning takes place after you've entered the field. In fact many real estate agents come to the field from other, unrelated careers, attracted by the flexible hours or the potential for part-time work.

Before you can use the title "Realtor" or become a member of the National Association of Realtors you must have a real estate license. Every state requires that a broker or agent undergo a series of examinations and log some experience before she is granted this license. Many real estate boards offer preparatory classes. Once you have the license, it's usually renewed yearly without your having to repeat the tests. But each state has its own test, so if you want to work in a different state you've got to pass their exam.

ASSOCIATED CAREERS

Careers associated with real estate often involve working with Realtors. On the mortgage end, loan officers arrange the conditions for financing home purchases and act as liaisons between buyers and banks. Another possibility is the field of real estate law, which requires going to law school. Agents seeking further opportunities within the field have a few options, most of which involve setting up shop independently of brokers. Appraisers, for example, assess the fair market values of properties. Real estate counselors, likewise, are independent advisors who offer advice to buyers about the suitability of properties they are interested in.

PAST AND FUTURE

In 1908, the agency known as the National Association of Realtors was started, and has continued to strive for high ethical standards in business and tax advantages for home buyers and sellers. The nomadic trend in American life and our ever-expanding population make real estate a business that grows at higher than average rates. The downside is that the market is always under the influence of economic fluctuations, and the biggest complaint Realtors have is the resulting lack of stability for their incomes. Real estate agents cannot expect steady income since their pay is based on commissions, which differ greatly with time.

QUALITY OF LIFE

Two Years

The beginning of the agent's career is spent on the phone and looking at and showing properties with hopes of finding buyers and sellers. This is a difficult time for agents, as they have not yet established reputations. They rely on the name of their firms to attract clients. There is lots of variety in the daily routine, but these beginners must be prepared for a period of long hours and no commissions as they learn the ropes. As one first-year agent told us, "I made literally zero dollars for seven months, but then suddenly had four sales in a row and made enough for the rest of the year."

Five Years

Many agents have developed a reputation by this time and are rewarded with referrals and repeat clients. Some agents will still experience frustration with low sales and meager paychecks, however, accounting for the high turnover rate in the field.

Ten Years

By this time most agents have advanced to the highest levels of their firms, often working with blue-chip properties. Many now have assistants to help with legwork. But the plateau reached at this point often prompts agents to strike out independently and start their own firms, though the task of getting established can be arduous.

You'll Have Contact With

Bankers
Credit Agents
Property Managers
Property Owners

Major Associations

National Association of Realtors
430 North Michigan Avenue
Chicago, IL 60611
Tel: 312-329-8200
Fax: 312-329-5960
Contact: Library Reference

Society of Industrial and Office Realtors
700 11th Street, NW
Suite 510
Washington, DC 20001-4511
Tel: 202-737-1150
Fax: 202-737-8796
Contact: Membership

National Association of Real Estate Brokers
1629 K Street, NW
Suite 602
Washington, DC 20006
Tel: 202-785-4477
Fax: 202-785-1244

RESEARCHER

PROFESSIONAL PROFILE

# of people in profession	270,000
% male	80
% female	20
avg. hours per week	40
avg. starting salary	$19,000
avg. salary after 5 years	$27,000
avg. salary 10 to 15 years	$37,000

Professionals Read
Research Review

Books, Films and TV Shows Featuring the Profession
Three Days of the Condor
The Hunt for Red October
The Daughter of Time
Bright Lights, Big City

Major Employers
IIT Research Institute
185 Admiral Cochrane Drive
Annapolis, MD 21401
Tel: 410-573-7000
Fax: 410-573-7033
Contact: Nate Williams-Admin. Advisor

Pfizer Inc.
235 East 52nd Street
New York, NY 10017
Tel: 212-573-2323
Fax: 212-338-1715
Contact: Personnel

A DAY IN THE LIFE

How many people prefer premium brand toilet paper to generic toilet paper? How many twenty-one-year-olds voted in the last election? How many politicians does it take to screw in a light bulb? If you're curious about what people think and how they make decisions, you may want to become a researcher. Researchers collect, organize, analyze, and interpret data and opinions to explore issues, solve problems, and predict trends. Most researchers measure public opinion. Social science researchers gauge the public's opinion regarding social issues, services, political campaigns, parties, and personalities. Market researchers design and administer surveys to find out what people are most likely to buy. Their results influence policy and decision makers, and help businesses, advertising agencies, and politicians have a better idea of what is important to their customers and constituents.

A four-step approach forms the core of the researcher's methodology: Objective descriptions; problem analysis and classification; comparative studies; and historical review or development. Objectivity is critical to research work as prejudices and biases may distort the fact-gathering effort and the conclusions drawn. Researchers analyze and classify data in terms of responses and inclinations and compare studies on the same subject. They also investigate previous surveys to compare results. While researchers often conduct interviews and administer questionnaires, they also use information sources including libraries, newspaper clippings, encyclopedias, magazines and periodicals, case laws, legislative records, historical documents, and public opinion polls. Computers now play a pivotal role in the collection and organization of data, and in the statistical methods of analysis. Public opinion researchers work a standard 40-hour work week, sometimes with tight deadlines, but those in supervisory or management positions often work longer hours overseeing particular projects.

Carefully worded interviews or questionnaires are the most significant of the methods researchers use to collect data. Target audience and the specific type of information desired affect the choice of data collection methods. Researchers interested in buying trends during the Christmas shopping season might station interviewers at shopping malls. Market researchers often use telephone surveys to reach a particular demographic. Questionnaires may be administered to a carefully selected group or sample of people called a focus group. This group corresponds to the pollster's or marketer's target audience, who may be concerned about a certain issue, may shop at a certain location, or buy certain brands of food or clothing items. For example, this book cover and several possible options for it were shown to groups of college students, their parents, and professionals thinking about switching jobs. They led us to the one that made you (or the person who gave it to you) buy it.

PAYING YOUR DUES

A Bachelor's degree in business administration or economics provides a good foundation for those interested in public opinion research. A degree in sociology or psychology is best for those interested in exploring consumer demand or opinion research. Those with a strong basis in statistics or engineering may find opportunities in industrial or analytical research. But increasingly, employers are looking to hire individuals with strong computer skills and higher degrees, such as a master's degree in business administration. A Master's degree in sociology or political science will greatly improve employment and advancement opportunities. In addition, researchers must have strong people skills, be able to relate to people in a variety of social and cultural contexts, be good listeners, and be able to command the attention of the interviewee. Patience and objectivity are critical.

Whereas entrants with the requisite education, training and experience may start out as interviewers and data analysts, most applicants to the field of public opinion research enter as survey workers, research assistants or coders and tabulators, and move up to become interviewers or data analysts as they gain experience. Since starting salaries are commensurate with the training and experience of the applicant and the professional capacity, and size of the company, entrants should try to gain experience and carefully explore salary levels and advancement potential of prospective companies.

ASSOCIATED CAREERS

Researchers with doctoral degrees often become instructors or professors at colleges and universities, while others become writers and pundits, publishing articles and books on survey techniques, studies conducted, and forecasting trends. Those with political science degrees sometimes become public opinion pollsters, making a name for themselves by predicting voting trends in presidential campaign years. Still others move on to work for the various political groups, organizations, and government agencies they once surveyed. Consumer pollsters find ready employment with advertising agencies and industries. Urban and regional planners, demographers and statisticians all call for research skills in their various fields.

PAST AND FUTURE

The expanded awareness of the power and importance of polls and surveys in influencing consumers, policy makers and businesses ensures that public opinion research will continue to be a growth field. As computers continue to play an increasingly important role in this area, applicants will need to demonstrate strong computer skills in addition to extensive training and higher degrees.

QUALITY OF LIFE

Two Years

Entry-level workers concentrate on acquiring the widest range of experience possible. The onus is on the worker to show initiative and drive by completing tasks according to schedule and volunteering for added duties and responsibilities.

Five Years

At the five-year level, the researcher is well on her way to establishing herself as a thorough, highly motivated professional. The ambitious worker has probably returned to school for refresher courses, attended various seminars and workshops, and is skilled in the latest computer applications. At this juncture, the professional is wont to consider pursuing doctoral studies.

Ten Years

With a decade of research experience to his credit, the professional should now be in a top-level management or advisory position. Researchers in academia are tenured professors or department heads with a body of research material, books, and articles to show for it.

THE BIRKMAN LIFESTYLE GRID

This career is suitable for people with Green interests.

You'll Have Contact With

Advertising Executives
Biologists
Chemists
Marketing Executives

Major Associations

Marketing Research Association
2189 Silas Deane Highway
Suite 5
Rocky Hill, CT 06067
Tel: 860-257-4008
Fax: 800-257-3990
Contact: Helene Weston

American Marketing Association
250 South Waker Drive
Suite 200
Chicago, IL 60606
Tel: 312-648-0536
Fax: 312-993-7542
Contact: Customer Service

Center for Field Research
680 Mount Auburn Street
Box 403
Watertown, MA 02272
Tel: 617-926-8200
Fax: 617-926-1973

RESTAURANTEUR

A DAY IN THE LIFE

Owning a restaurant is a labor of love, and most restaurateurs work long hours. When her establishment is open only for dinner, the restaurateur usually starts her day in the late morning. She has a number of daily tasks to complete before the staff arrives. First, she checks "the book," which contains reports from managers about whatever happens in the restaurant each night. The owner keeps tabs on things like items to be ordered, customer complaints, and staff scheduling conflicts, all of which are recorded in the book. She studies the accounting records daily and stays on top of the restaurant's financial situation. She may also take on duties like confirming reservations. Usually, she will also find time to glance through wine and food industry papers and read the restaurant review section in the newspaper.

When the doors open, the restaurant owner must be dressed and ready to socialize until the last customer leaves. It is extremely important that a restaurant owner have exceptional name and face recollection. The most successful owners report that the majority of their clientele are regular customers. The easiest way to gain repeat business is by offering seemingly special treatment, and remembering a customer's name or favorite table is always impressive. The restaurateur acts as a host, chatting with his customers and making sure they are satisfied. Approaching customers while they are dining helps the owner check on his staff. While this may seem intrusive when done by waiters, restaurant patrons usually love to have the owner inquire about the food and service.

PAYING YOUR DUES

Restaurateurs come from many walks of life, but mostly they have experience within the industry. A restaurant owner can be either a "backer" or an active owner. Backers provide funding to the active owners and entrust them to run the place. Very few people back restaurants as their primary occupation, since the sole job requirement is having access to large amounts of cash. The financial rewards of backing a restaurant can be great, as backers are the first to receive profits. For hands-on owners a good place to start is a college or school that offers a restaurant and hotel management program, but in fact most owners don't follow this formal educational route. Instead, most have paid their dues as waiters, bartenders, and managers, and it's always a plus if they have experience with bookkeeping and accounting, too.

Before opening, the restaurant owner spends some time scouting a location. If he is interested in a space that didn't previously hold a restaurant, the owner has to determine whether the building can be affordably converted to restaurant use. Other market studies are usually done to determine what type of restaurant would work best in that particular community and location. When all of this has been figured out, the restaurateur must obtain financing, either through a backer or a bank. The owner then usually hires all the founding staff, seeks out wholesalers and establishes relations with them; and oversees the design of the restaurant, from decor to menu. Then comes the stressful task of procuring a liquor license. Most towns and cities allot only a specified number of licenses, and often the potential owner must negotiate a price from a business that is closing. When the doors open the owner's work is far from finished. Failure rates for new restaurants are high, and an owner must make sure that his establishment keeps pace with the times and consistently operates at a high level.

ASSOCIATED CAREERS

Many careers can satisfy food lovers who don't want to commit their time and bank accounts to owning a restaurant. Waiters, bartenders, busboys, and hosts ensure that the front of the house is running smoothly. The majority of these jobs rely on tips instead of salaries, and so earnings are influenced by the season and night of the week. A restaurant manager runs the front of the house and acts on behalf of the owner in her absence. Chefs, sous-chefs and bakers need formal training at a culinary institute in order to be taken seriously in the food community. The chef is usually the heart of the restaurant. He not only prepares food—he also schedules the kitchen staff, creates and continually updates the menu, and often shops for finer ingredients himself. The wine steward is another important position in upscale restaurants, where she uses an extensive knowledge of wine to select the restaurant's wine list. Wine stewards will also sometimes host wine-tasting dinners to introduce their clientele to new labels. Catering is another venue for food experts who want more variety and a less complicated operation. Franchise owners can open a restaurant without having to worry about any decision-making, such as designing the menu or decorating the establishment. Other aspiring owners open bars or nightclubs.

PAST AND FUTURE

The restaurant as we think of it today did not exist until 1765, when A. Boulanger opened a restaurant in Paris. For about a century after that, restaurants tended to be expensive and mainly catered to the social elite. With the growth of the travel industry at the end of the nineteenth century, restaurants became accessible to almost everyone. Today, 40 percent of our allotted food budget is spent in eating and drinking establishments. The restaurant industry will continue to grow, although it will still be an extremely risky business. Recently, the number of both successful and failed restaurants have climbed each year.

QUALITY OF LIFE

Two Years

More than three quarters of new restaurants fail in the first seven months, primarily due to poor cash flow management. Those owners who survive report feeling very stressed—every review brings tears of either joy or pain. At this time, restaurants are usually not showing big profits but are just remaining afloat. In these first years owners are working long into the night, and still anxiously awaiting the possibility of taking some time off.

Five Years

Most restaurateurs who've made it through the first two years are still working away. They begin to show profits at this time and have usually completely paid off their loans. A few look forward to buying out backers. Mostly, they are happy to be down to working only six ten-hour-days per week.

Ten Years

A decade into the business, restaurateurs spend much less time in the house. They have learned to entrust the late hours to general managers. The most successful ones pay surprise visits to the restaurant to safeguard the high standards of the kitchen. As always, they keep an eye on the books. The owners who flourish tend to hire the most inventive chefs and pay close attention to trends happening in the big cities.

THE BIRKMAN LIFESTYLE GRID

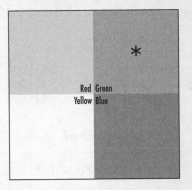

This career is suitable for people with Green interests.

You'll Have Contact With
Accountants
Bankers
Chefs
Waiters

Major Associations
National Restaurant Association
1200 17th Street, NW
Washington, DC 20036-3097
Tel: 202-331-5900
Fax: 202-331-2429
Contact: Public Affairs

Educational Foundation of the
Nat'l Restaurant Association
250 South Wacker Drive
Suite 1400
Chicago, IL 60606
Tel: 312-715-1010
Fax: 312-715-0807
Contact: Customer Service

International Association of
Women Chefs & Restaurateurs
110 Sutter Street
Suite 305
San Francisco, CA 94104
Tel: 415-362-7336
Fax: 415-362-7335
Contact: General Information

Retail Salesperson

A DAY IN THE LIFE

Retail salespeople can do their job from behind a counter, over the phone, or even by visiting their clients personally, whether they're right down the hall or on the other side of the world. Most salespeople pitch their products dozens of times a day, five days a week. Whatever the product, they must convey confidence and goodwill, for making a sale requires a trusting consumer. People in sales must be ready to deal with rejection and disgruntled customers. As products and market conditions change constantly, salespeople must adapt if they want to survive. In fields such as consumers electronics in general and computers in particular, the rapid pace of change can be as overwhelming as it is exciting.

A skilled salesperson knows the product she's selling and understands the needs of her customers. Salespeople often say they want to help people find what they need, and bristle at accusations that they are selling "just for the money." After all, salespeople are a necessary part of a dynamic capitalist economy. Moreover, many salespeople truly enjoy the human interaction as much as the more palpable thrill of closing a sale. For some, the demands of travel detract from the time they can spend with their families; others enjoy the travel or find they can work from home.

A good sales record leads to a better job with a better salary and, often extra incentives such as higher commissions. Most of the salespeople we talked to devote their sales-related reading to specialized journals dedicated to the professional salesperson or to individual markets they serve. The amount of time salespeople devote to their job depends on what they sell and on their own personal needs. Nevertheless, even the best salespeople often work continually, because "you're only as good as your last month's sales."

PAYING YOUR DUES

The sales profession values experience over education. A specialized degree is not necessary to pursue a career in sales. An understanding of the product is important no matter what you sell, but the salesperson must learn to communicate well with clients, whether it's face-to-face, over the phone, or by letter or e-mail.. Ambitious salespeople may study marketing and sales techniques at college or business school either before or during their sales careers.

ASSOCIATED CAREERS

The skills involved in selling transfer well to other careers. Practicality, persuasiveness, and tenacity are all qualities esteemed in managers, and many salespeople use their job as a stepping stone to consulting or management positions. In addition, some may be recruited into positions as manufacturer's field sales representatives for products they were formerly selling at the retail level.

PAST AND FUTURE

Complex economies like ours are based on competition from various companies selling similar products. Successful competitors outsell their rivals, and companies know that succeed they must hire people with expertise in selling.

As businesses have become more specialized, strategies have become more sophisticated and targeted. Many companies now employ and train their own sales forces. Retail salespeople must give customers what they want at the best price, and as the retail "superstore" behemoths gain dominance, customers are becoming more demanding that service and price be satisfactory. The trend toward high-volume, low-margin outlets is forcing a shake-out at the retail level, and the inattentive retailer will not last long unless he is ready to compete with the giants.

QUALITY OF LIFE

Two Years

Entry-level sales jobs may pay minimum wage, often without a commission. Pay scales vary according to the industry. The grind of frequent rejection and the constant interaction with others can be wearing, but for some, the triumph of making a sale can be its own reward. Take this time to learn personal strategies for being a convincing salesperson-no matter what it is you happen to be selling.

Five Years

Salaries are considerably higher at this stage, and proven salespeople can negotiate for higher commissions or more lucrative accounts. A change in product lines or entry into a new area, such as personal computers, can spell a need for rapid reeducation about the product and the best way to sell it.

Ten Years

After ten years many salespeople have settled into management positions and may be responsible for a salesforce or important accounts. Veteran salespeople may be able to cut back on their hours while still bringing in significant business to the company. Others may be drawn to the travel and business opportunities of international sales.

THE BIRKMAN LIFESTYLE GRID

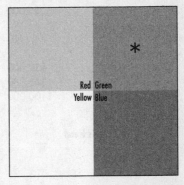

This career is suitable for people with Green interests.

You'll Have Contact With

Consumers
Customer Service Personnel
Retail Managers
Wholesalers

Major Associations

National Retail Merchants Association
604 5th Avenue
New York, NY 10020
Tel: 212-767-1044
Fax: 202-737-2849
Contact: No specific

National Retail Federation
325 7th Street NW
Washington, DC 20004
Tel: 202-783-7971
Contact: Bruce Van Kleeck

International Association of Chain Stores
3808 Moor Place
Alexandria, VA 22305
Tel: 703-549-4525
Contact: Sally Adanny-McMullen

ROBOTICS ENGINEER

A DAY IN THE LIFE

Robotics engineers design robots, maintain them, develop new applications for them, and conduct research to expand the potential of robotics. This is a rapidly developing field, with advances in computing constantly opening up new possibilities for robotics applications. Manufacturing, the first industry to invest heavily in robotics, remains the primary employer in the area, but recent years have seen rapid expansion of research and engineering in robots for such applications as agriculture, mining, nuclear power-plant maintenance, and a variety of other fields.

The profession offers jobs for a wide range of temperaments. Visionary robotics engineers can work designing experimental mobile robots, with applications ranging from medical and military uses to designs aimed at creating vehicles capable of piloting themselves on other planets. More down-to-earth jobs involve designing new production-line robots, often with programmable arms, and maintaining and upgrading older production-line installations. Somewhere in between lie those engineers designing and producing robots for expanding but tested fields, such as self-piloting crop harvesters and automated nuclear-safety equipment. Robotics engineers must have the same disciplined attention to detail required of all engineers, but the relative novelty of the field puts an additional premium on creativity. It's a safe bet that twenty years from now, robots will be employed in a vast range of new activities. The engineers who can best anticipate needs which can be successfully filled by robots, and who can work effectively in engineering teams to develop them, will be extremely successful in the field.

PAYING YOUR DUES

As in most engineering disciplines, graduate education is usually a necessity for advancement in the field. This can range from one to two years of additional master's in electrical and/or mechanical engineering work for an operating engineer, to several years for the doctorate, which opens up jobs in design and research. The most sought-after jobs go to engineers with academic backgrounds that allow them to combine knowledge in computer science with applied physical sciences. As automated systems must be designed to optimally integrate into the production line, knowledge of the manufacturing environment in which the robot will operate is invaluable.

ASSOCIATED CAREERS

Robotics engineers tend to stay in the field. Professional mobility largely occurs between robotics manufacturing firms and their clients, with engineers leaving to oversee the robot operations of major clients. In addition, as new applications for robots appear, opportunities arise for engineers to move into these new branches of the field.

PAST AND FUTURE

Robotics dates back to the Renaissance, when automata, clockwork machines designed to imitate people, were built for entertainment. The modern field really dates to the industrial revolution, when machines capable of accurately performing repetitive tasks were designed. In 1804, Joseph-Marie Jacquard designed a machine capable of following instructions on a punched paper tape. Modern robotics dates from this invention, though the field did not truly develop until later, when computers capable of guiding a programmable machine through a series of complex tasks were created. Today, robotics is a booming field, with an expanding role in manufacturing, mining, agriculture, and a wide range of other fields, including jobs too hazardous to be performed by people.

QUALITY OF LIFE

Two Years

At this point in his career, the robotics engineer functions as a professional apprentice, working on elements of larger design or programming problems under more senior engineers who manage the overall progress of projects; the work is mainly troubleshooting and testing of systems designed by senior engineers and designers. There is frustratingly little recognition in the early years, which are spent "in the trenches." The work can be intellectually demanding with little reward or visibility in the early years. Hours can be unpredictable, depending on product development cycles, with long hours under intense pressure followed by periods of downtime.

Five Years

Robotics engineers with five to ten years of experience are the middle managers of the profession. With sufficient expertise to oversee the work of their junior colleagues, they have increasing oversight responsibilities in the design and development of robotics projects, and they begin to become involved in the generation of project concepts. Some will leave to join clients of their manufacturing firms to manage their robot operations.

Ten Years

Robotics engineers now have significant responsibilities. In design and manufacturing companies, they may be responsible for managing the development and/or manufacture of new systems, and will also be expected to stay current with the rapidly evolving technology. They likely spend significant time with potential clients, analyzing their needs and developing proposals for robotics applications to meet them. If they have gone to work in a client industry, they are responsible for managing robotics operations and working with robotics manufacturing firms as problems or new needs arise. Alternately, they may have struck out on their own, manufacturing robots in their specific areas of engineering expertise.

THE BIRKMAN LIFESTYLE GRID

This career is suitable for people with Red interests.

You'll Have Contact With

Computer Programmers
Electrical Engineers
Production Managers
Robotics Technicians

Major Associations

Institute of Electrical and Electronic Engineers
345 East 47th Street
New York, NY 10017
Tel: 212-705-7900
Contact: Education Dept.

Robotic Industries Association
900 Victors Way, P.O. Box 3724
Ann Arbor, MI 48106
Tel: 313-994-6088
Contact: Donald A. Vincent

Robotic International of SME
(Society of Manufacturing Executives)
One SME Drive, P.O. Box 930
Dearborn, MI 48121
Tel: 313-271-1500
Contact: Customer Service Dept.

SCHOOL ADMINISTRATOR

A DAY IN THE LIFE

Administrators, unlike teachers, work a twelve-month year and are fairly busy most of that time. Whether running a small, private day-care center or an overcrowded public high school, an administrator's tasks are many and various, ranging from curriculum development to student discipline. The most familiar school administrator is the principal. Assisting the principal are vice-principals, whose duties tend to be more specialized and who have more responsibility for the day-to-day operation of the school. In a central administration office, other specialists work with some or all the schools in a given district, overseeing particular programs, such as the evaluation of student academic achievement. Any one of these administrators may be responsible for infrastructure maintenance, the hiring and training of teachers, and student affairs.

Administrators abound at colleges and universities as well. Among them are the deans of faculty, who handle academic issues, and the deans of students, who see to the well-being and appropriate conduct of the student body. Registrars process student records and many financial matters, while provosts serve as university-wide troubleshooters. As in smaller primary and secondary schools, colleges often require their teachers to perform administrative work. To a college student, the most familiar teacher-administrator is probably the department chair. And anyone who has applied to college knows all about the Dean of Admissions.

School administration is a combination of brain work and grunt work. Organizational skills are key, as is the ability to operate within constantly tightening budgetary constraints. Since duties can range from hiring a basketball coach to AIDS education, administrators need to be versatile and flexible. An administrator must have a great deal of patience to deal with the enormous bureaucracy often associated with educational institutions. Finally, and perhaps most importantly, since administrators are responsible for the education of young people, a particular dedication to and understanding of children's needs is essential.

PAYING YOUR DUES

Most beginning administrators have acquired related work experience—usually in teaching or management posts—and, as might be expected in an academic environment, they also have advanced degrees, including doctorates, in education or administration or a combination of the two. Recently, some schools have begun demanding that their applicants have an M.B.A. At the university-level, deans are, of course, expected to bring a rich academic and professional background to their jobs. As with many educational jobs in the United States, applicants must have gone through a certification process (usually administered on the state level).

ASSOCIATED CAREERS

For those who want summers off, teaching is a viable alternative to administration, and it brings with it many rewards. If you would rather work during the summer, look into camp counseling and administration, although these too can be year-round tasks. More and more religious communities are taking charge of the education of their children, and they consequently require the services of qualified school administrators.

PAST AND FUTURE

Teachers once ran their own schools, and some still do, but as the world has become more specialized, so have schools. The need for specialists to maintain an ever-increasing public and private educational system became apparent early in U.S. history. In the nineteenth century, it became clear that administrators and teachers could be the reformers of America's educational programs, as was the case with Horace Mann. To this day educators and school administrators sometimes find themselves in the thick of great controversies and revolutions. The future holds even more complicated challenges for school administrators. Health, political, and cultural issues all play a significant role in the life of the contemporary school administrator.

Because so many administrative jobs are tied to state funding and a strict hierarchy, few administrators can expect to get rich quick running schools. Nevertheless, many administrators belong to unions, which see to it that the school system provides such benefits as health insurance and child care. At private schools, salaries tend to be lower and fringe benefits are uncommon.

QUALITY OF LIFE

Two Years

Many school systems assign new administrators to posts low on the ladder and allow them to advance only according to a set timetable. Other systems are quite willing to convert a seasoned teacher into a principal overnight, but this is less common in larger systems. Some beginners may work in school headquarters before moving on to a particular school as a vice-principal or principal.

Five Years

Because school administration involves so many specialized tasks, some administrators at this stage have greater responsibilities in one aspect of education administration, such as curriculum development. Other administrators, such as a school principal or, in the case of college administrators, a student dean, have more generalized duties. A principal's duties vary according to the school system. Some must refer constantly to a central administrative body before instituting changes, while others operate with virtual autonomy. Another option for administrators is to move to a larger school system, where greater opportunities and challenges exist.

Ten Years

Many respected principals hold their jobs for decades, leaving an indelible impression on entire generations of students. Others move on to different challenges, seeking the position of school superintendent. At the college level, the trend is somewhat different. Respected college deans often hang up their administrative hats and return to the classroom or the research center. Still others seek the office of university president or chancellor. Dwight D. Eisenhower left his job as president of Columbia University to run for president of the United States.

You'll Have Contact With
Admissions Personnel
Financial Aid Officers
Professors
Students

Major Associations
American Association of School Administrators
1801 North Moore Street
Arlington, VA 22209
Tel: 703-528-0700
Fax: 703-528-2146
Contact: Gary Marx

National Association of Secondary School Principals
1904 Association Drive
Reston, VA 22091
Tel: 703-860-0200

American Federation of School Administrators
1729 21st Street, NW
Washington, DC 20009
Tel: 202-986-4209
Fax: 202-986-4211

SECRETARY

A DAY IN THE LIFE

A secretary manages information. Responsibilities can run from scheduling staff appointments to office management to managing an entire database. Since the computer is central to any modern office, mastery of the latest office technology is essential. Secretaries are often the primary conduit of information from their employers to the rest of the world, so they must be comfortable communicating with others in person and on the telephone. Secretaries who work in specialized fields, such as law and accounting, have a working knowledge of that field. Executive secretaries often initiate and execute independent projects. One secretary we spoke to described her view of keeping busy after accomplishing a day's assignments well before deadline: "You can bury your nose in a magazine, or you can find something constructive to do. Good secretaries are self-starters."

Few professions call for such careful execution of so many specialized tasks. Such professionalism combined with the almost constant changes in business technology has led secretaries to turn to one another for support, training, and solidarity. "You often don't know exactly what's expected of you," remarked one secretary. "It's easier if there are other secretaries there to help you clarify things, especially in a place like a law office." Because so much of the job depends on organization, secretaries' skills are really tested when they work for particularly disorganized bosses. "Your main task is making sure everything goes smoothly, anticipating as well as accomplishing particular tasks." And secretaries are still expected to handle their employers' moods and foibles in the course of everyday business. The best advice we heard: "Be prepared for anything."

PAYING YOUR DUES

Some of the clerical skills expected of secretaries can be picked up on the job, but secretarial candidates should have already mastered typing and word processing in high school, college, or vocational school. Competition in the field allows employers to place greater demands on applicants: A college education is a valuable asset. In a global economy, being bilingual or even trilingual is often a plus. Stenography has become something of a lost art, but it may come in handy with an old-fashioned boss.

ASSOCIATED CAREERS

"Secretary" is an umbrella term for any number of administrative jobs, and the best-qualified secretaries have mastered them all. Many secretaries use their experience to enter a particular profession. Some secretaries get practice using editorial skills and move into editorial jobs. Many secretaries who are responsible for office management, including payrolls, bookkeeping, bill-paying and maintenance of the office's physical plant, find more specialized opportunities in these areas.

Those interested in doing secretarial work on a temporary basis may seek assignments through a temporary agency. These agencies provide companies with administrative workers on a daily, weekly, or monthly basis. Temp work has the advantages of flexibility and variety—of bosses, office settings, and tasks. It also has the drawbacks of sameness—you will quite possibly be given one boring task to do for a week—and the possibility that the work may dry up at certain times of the year when you could really use a paycheck.

PAST AND FUTURE

Long the domain of men, paperwork and other clerical tasks fell to women more and more at the turn of the century and was often a woman's first exposure to the world of big business. With the demands placed on the male population by two world wars, the position of secretary came to be held almost exclusively by women by mid-century. The image of the "working girl" making coffee for the boss persisted through the 1980s. Today, however, the occupation has become less closely associated with women. With the recent wave of corporate downsizing, secretaries often find themselves working for as many as three bosses while coping with constant innovations or limitations in technology. As in any profession, a good secretary is a rare and valued employee. Salaries start in the mid-$20,000 range, but veterans can take home three times that amount.

QUALITY OF LIFE

Two Years

The early part of your secretarial career is the time to lay the groundwork for greater responsibility and reward in the future. As a new secretary, you'll hone your skills in typing, word processing, and data processing and spend much of your time answering the phone and screening calls. Employers will ask you to do faxing, filing, and photocopying and to handle correspondence. Paralegals can expect to have demanding schedule. Many secretaries discover during these years how to operate efficiently in the face of unending, unexpected, or loosely-defined responsibilities.

Five Years

Thousands of secretaries move on to other jobs in this period, often getting hired on the basis of their achievements as office professionals. Secretaries who stay on have found a means of coping with a tremendous volume of work and derive satisfaction from helping to make a business run smoothly. At this point, many secretaries train new secretaries, often in a training program of their own devising.

Ten Years

For those who have made the most of a secretarial career, the rewards are palpable. It is hard to last in a profession that demands organizational skill, meticulous attention to detail, efficiency, and patience. Secretaries who possess these qualities know how rare they are and can expect to reap the rewards they deserve, including a pension and benefits.

THE BIRKMAN LIFESTYLE GRID

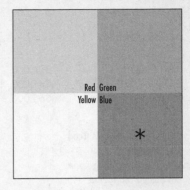

This career is suitable for people with Blue interests.

You'll Have Contact With

Executives
Human Resource Personnel
Office Managers
Receptionists

Major Associations

National Association of Secretarial Services
3637 Fourth Street North
Suite 330
St. Petersburg, FL 33704-1336
Tel: 813-823-3646
Fax: 813-894-4277

Professional Secretaries International
10502 NW Ambassador Drive
P.O. Box 20404
Kansas City, MO 64195-0404
Tel: 816-891-6600
Fax: 816-891-9118

SERVICE SALES REPRESENTATIVE

A DAY IN THE LIFE

A service sales representative sells the services her company offers, reaching her customers over the telephone, in person, and through letter-writing efforts. A service sales rep can work for nearly anyone: A communications company, an upholsterer, a computer engineering firm, or a caterer, to name only a few who has a service (as opposed to a good) to sell. Service Sales Representatives have to be good communicators, persuasive talkers, and excellent listeners. The most important quality of a service sales rep, however, is the ability to sell. Indeed, her paycheck depends on it—many service sales reps work from a low base salary plus either commissions on sales or a potentially large bonus. This means a high-pressure environment, but pressure, as one rep told us, "is what turns coal into diamonds."

Sales representatives must first and foremost be confident with their knowledge of their product lines. "Most of your job as a sales rep is answering questions," wrote one respondent, "and if you don't have answers for your clients, how can you expect them to trust you?" The issue of trust is central to any purchaser/vendor relationship. For the sales rep, having information at his disposal is the only way he can demonstrate to the potential client that he understands the product's uses and limitations. To maintain these high levels of credibility, many companies require that sales reps engage in internal education programs that keep them up to date on changing product lines and improved product features. Sales reps not only have to adjust themselves to their product lines, but also to the needs and sensibilities of their clients. "You don't sell to a mom and pop store the way you'd try to sell to IBM," said one telephone service sales rep. The best way to learn that skill? "Experience is incredibly valuable in sales," wrote a ten-year veteran.

Two aspects of the job were recorded as most frustrating on our surveys. First, simply by virtue of what she does, a service sales rep often encounters rejection and puts effort into many deals that do not close. It's important to be able to see that a failed deal is not necessarily a personal failure. Second, the job breeds a certain amount of isolation. "No one is a salesman's friend," wrote one manager of service sales reps, adding "it can be a very lonely job." Many reps spend a lot of time on the road, in meetings, and at client dinners, and many of these hours are clocked on the weekends. The price they pay is returned in the form of bonuses, commission, and control over their schedule if not the number of hours they work.

PAYING YOUR DUES

No professional certification is required for service sales representatives and there are no formal educational requirements, but it's becoming more and more common for them to have a college education. Coursework that sales representatives found helpful to them in their profession included marketing, business, economics, finance, public speaking, sociology, and psychology. Most large employers run established training programs for newly hired service sales reps that last between three weeks and three months. These training programs educate newcomers about product lines, the techniques of successful sales representatives, and accounting procedures, and generally include interactive exercises to give future representatives some sales experience. Smaller places may not have training programs but will instead pair a newcomer with an experienced sales rep. Employers look for prior experience that demonstrates a self-motivating personality and strong interpersonal along with organizational skills.

ASSOCIATED CAREERS

Service sales reps often go into other sales-related areas. A side-effect, however, of learning all about a company's products is that service sales reps make excellent internal managers and executives; sales representatives often take on other, more supervisory positions in their companies.

PAST AND FUTURE

Service sales representatives are a product of urbanization. As greater numbers of people needed more services, competition began to increase between shops, and expanding the sales base became critical. Service sales representatives should be positioned well for the twenty-first century. Service industries are expected to grow faster than all other industries in the U.S., and each company is expected to spend significant capital attempting to expand its customer base. Creative and motivated people should find opportunities available that reward their hard work and selling skills.

QUALITY OF LIFE

Two Years

Those reps who've been through training programs are having more success than those who have not, due to both superior education in company strategies and generally superior sales rep support. Hours are long and success is limited, but many point to one or two difficult sales that went through as turning points. It's hard work to maintain relationships with existing clients and recruit new ones as well. Satisfaction is average and salaries are low to average.

Five Years

This is the period in which a sales rep distinguishes himself in the field. Many spend long hours hunting clients, but with high levels of success. Skills acquired in the field prove invaluable in years three through seven, and salaries can rise significantly. Some attain the title of "senior" service sales representative and are put in charge of those more junior. Satisfaction is high; the five year survivor is, generally, at the top of his game.

Ten Years

Those who've managed to last ten years in this field must love the challenge of selling, as many tell us that by years eight and nine the profession becomes a bit more difficult. The nature of the work does not change, but the long hours that seemed effortless before are less exciting, and the frustration at deals not closing gets less bearable. Many successful sales reps consider managerial or executive shifts at this point, eschewing life in the field for the stability of the office. Salaries can decrease overall for those making this shift, but become more reliable as well. Hours decrease; satisfaction drops, then improves.

THE BIRKMAN LIFESTYLE GRID

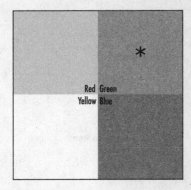

Red Green
Yellow Blue

This career is suitable for people with Green interests.

You'll Have Contact With

Accountants
Clients
Office Managers
Purchasing Managers

Major Associations

Sales and Marketing Executives Internat'l
Statler Office Tower
Suite 977
Cleveland, OH 44115
Tel: 216-771-6650
Fax: 216-771-6652
Contact: Jack I. Criswell

American Management Association
135 West 50th Street
New York, NY 10020
Tel: 212-903-8270
Fax: 212-903-8169

SOCIAL WORKER

A DAY IN THE LIFE

Social workers spend their days helping people with complicated psychological, health, social, or financial problems. They assist families in need and people who are the victims of abuse. They provide counseling, advice, and direction for people who would otherwise have no way of bettering their situations. While seeing people who are confused, scared, and beset by problems all day long may sound disheartening, social workers told us that they were uplifted by their job and that they truly felt they were doing work of value. "People need your help and if you're part of the human race, you give it to them," said one, adding, "The only strange thing is that you get paid to do it."

Social workers, around half of whom work for local and federal governments, have to be familiar with all assistance programs and services available for those in need. This requires continuing education to keep abreast of programs, their funding, and their efficacy. "The quickest way to lose your client's trust is to send them to an agency that tells them they're not eligible," said one by way of explaining that the trust of one's client is difficult to earn and easily lost. Social workers have to be prepared for disappointments from their clients as well. Over 30 percent of urban families assigned a social worker miss one of their first three appointments. Still, most professionals invest themselves heavily in the fates of their clients, and a number of our respondents called this involvement emotionally draining. While this contributes to the reasonably high attrition rate for first-year workers (15 percent), respondents noted that it was valuable in that it kept them aware of the significance of what they do.

More and more, social workers are being asked to find an area of focused responsibility, such as criminal justice issues, gerontological services, or medical issues. This can leave the social worker a bit dissatisfied, as often a client will have a number of concurrent problems, and they have a very prescribed range of duties they can perform. For people with a natural instinct to help others, this is tantamount to "telling a millionaire he can only give away twenty dollars at a time." Private professionals are under no such restrictions, and record generally higher levels of satisfaction.

PAYING YOUR DUES

Social workers face significant educational requirements. Most initial positions, which are primarily clerical, require only a Bachelor's Degree in Social Work (BSW) or a related field, such as psychology or sociology. For positions which involve psychological recommendations or assessments, or for positions with more responsibility, a Master's in Social Work (MSW) is required. Over 300 colleges offer BSWs and over 100 offer MSWs and are accredited by the Council on Social Work Education. Those who wish to advance to policy or director positions are asked to complete a Ph.D in social work. Nearly all programs require extensive field work and client contact. Traditional coursework includes social welfare policies, political science, human behavior, research methodology, and abnormal psychology. All states have strict licensing requirements for social workers, and additional professional certifications are available from the National Association of Social Workers (NASW). Private practitioners are encouraged to earn professional certifications, as it helps in collecting reimbursement for services from insurance providers.

ASSOCIATED CAREERS

Social workers have a strong instinct to help people, and this often translates into positions such as therapists, guidance counselors, and not-for-profit counseling services. Those who become burned out by the intense nature of the client/worker relationship find slightly more distancing professions, such as teaching, writing promotional literature for programs, and fundraising.

PAST AND FUTURE

Poor houses used to be basically jails for people who couldn't support themselves, and destitute parentless children used to live in state-run orphanages much like the one featured in Oliver Twist. In the twentieth century, reformers like Samuel Barnett and Jane Adams began to establish public programs to encourage self-sufficiency and education. Now there are a wide variety of programs to help people in need, though of course there could be more, and social workers are needed at each one of them.

Social workers face a bright future as current demand, particularly in rural regions, exceeds supply. New opportunities for social workers in all regions are expected to develop faster than the national average for creation of new jobs. Professionals with greater education and more specialized experience will have an advantage in the industry. The only uncertainty in the profession is proposed federal cuts to existing social programs which would not have an immediate impact upon jobs, but could dim long-term prospects for both social workers and their clients.

QUALITY OF LIFE

Two Years

New social workers either love what they do or are too drained by its emotional intensity. Many leave after one or two years, frustrated at their inability to help their clients and exhausted by anxiety over their clients' prospects. Those who make it through these early years tend to remain in the profession. Specialization begins for those at public agencies. Hours are long, but salaries are reasonable. Satisfaction varies widely.

Five Years

Five years into the profession many social workers have chosen the area of specialization that they will remain in until they assume positions of managerial responsibility. Caseloads can be overwhelming, as the average five-year is in charge of over two hundred client cases at any given time. Many are involved in continuing education and spend considerable free time reading publications about their area of specialty or attending conferences. Private practitioners begin to make significant incomes and work to develop strong community reputations. Hours increase.

Ten Years

Many social workers earn managerial or senior case-officer status, which unfortunately removes them from the day-to-day counseling which drew them to the profession in the first place. A number turn down opportunities for advancement for this very reason. Those who do accept become caseload managers and assign people to cases, exercising large discretionary powers of assessment and approval for clients' unusual needs. Satisfaction is high and hours remain stable.

THE BIRKMAN LIFESTYLE GRID

This career is suitable for people with Green interests.

You'll Have Contact With
Attorneys
Government Officials
Occupational Therapists
Psychologists

Major Associations
National Association of Social Workers
750 First Street NE
Suite 700
Washington, DC 20002
Tel: 800-638-8799
Fax: 202-336-8310
Contact: Education Dept.

National Board for Certified Counselors
3 Terrace Way
Suite D
Greensboro, NC 27403
Tel: 910-547-0607
Fax: 910-547-0017

American Association of
Marriage and Family Therapy
1133 15th Street, NW
Suite 300
Washington, DC 20005
Tel: 202-452-0109
Fax: 202-223-2329

American Group Psychotherapy Association
25 East 21st Street, 6th floor
New York, NY 10010
Tel: 212-477-2677
Fax: 212-979-6627

SOCIOLOGIST

PROFESSIONAL PROFILE

# of people in profession	28,000
% male	60
% female	40
avg. hours per week	35
avg. starting salary	$16,000
avg. salary after 5 years	$28,000
avg. salary 10 to 15 years	$36,000

Professionals Read
Journals/reports on areas of concentration
The Canadian Journal of Sociology

Books, Films and TV Shows Featuring the Profession
Foundation
How People Act
The Student
Social Systems

Major Employers
Chicago Board of Education
1819 West Pershing Road
Chicago, IL 60609
Tel: 312-535-8000

Colorado Board of Education
201 East Colfax Avenue
Denver, CO 80203-1799
Tel: 303-866-6600

National Center for Junvenile Justice
710 5th Avenue
3rd Floor
Pittsburgh, PA 15219-3000
Tel: 412-227-6950
Fax: 412-227-6955

A DAY IN THE LIFE

Sociologists study human society and social behavior through the prism of group formations and social, political, religious, and economic institutions. How individuals interact with each other within given contexts, the origin and development of social groups are important indices by which the sociologist conducts his research and draws conclusions. Because of the breadth and scope of this field, sociologists usually specialize in one or more of a number of areas. Areas of specialty include education, family, racial and ethnic relations, revolution, war, and peace, social psychology, gender roles and relations, and urban, rural, political, and comparative sociology. Sociologists have keen senses of observation and analysis, and abundant and natural curiosity.

Because they are engaged in observing, analyzing, defining, testing, and explaining human behavior, there is virtually no area of modern life in which a sociologist's research or conclusions are not valuable. From advertising to industry to criminology to medicine to government, sociologists and the research they conduct can enhance sales, improve productivity, shape social policy, resolve social conflicts, promote political platforms and influence lawmakers. The presidential election of 1996, for example, turns on the tide of voter sentiment regarding the controversial issues of welfare, immigration, and abortion rights. Sociological researchers, with their evaluations of the relevance and effectiveness of social programs, have shaped and will continue to shape the direction and tone of political life as we know it. "Every political action committee, every group or organization with an agenda to introduce, extend, eliminate, or maintain legislative policies have or will at some time employ the services of sociologists," says one professor of sociology. "There are a vast number of social programs which are on the budget cutting block (such as funding for abortion clinics, AIDS research, welfare, and Medicaid). Sociological research is an invaluable tool in determining the impact these cuts will have on its constituents."

Sociologists must be meticulous and patient in carefully observing and gathering notes on a particular subject. Some "results" are measurably slow in manifesting themselves and could take months or years. Statistics and computers are central to a sociologist's work, but so too are qualitative methods such as focus group-based research and social impact evaluations. Preconceived notions must give way to scientific methodology of data collection and objectivity, as they must be open to new ideas and social and cultural situations. Strong analytical skills, statistics, data gathering, and analysis, qualitative methods of research, survey methods, computer techniques, and counseling and interviewing skills are all part of the core of sociology.

PAYING YOUR DUES

To bypass most entry-level positions in social services, marketing, management, or personnel, be prepared to keep studying. At best, a Bachelor's degree in Sociology with the requisite training in survey methods and statistics will get you a junior analyst post with a research company or a government agency. If you like the challenge of child care or juvenile counseling then an undergraduate degree will also get you there. But if you have your sight set on applied research or teaching at community college, then the minimum requirement is a Master's degree in Sociology. But keep studying: A Ph.D. is the only route to most senior-level positions in corporations, research institutes, government agencies, and tenure at colleges and universities. If an extensive educational background is central to success in this career, then choosing the right graduate school is equally important. Applicants should look for schools which offer courses relevant to their areas of interest, adequate research facilities that provide practical experience and placement services that find research and teaching assistantships for students.

ASSOCIATED CAREERS

Because the core requirement of sociology is an understanding of social institutions and behavior, the sociologist is not unlike other social scientists such as economists, psychologists, anthropologists, political scientists, and social workers in that their work also involves social impact assessment. Research methods crucial in sociology also form the basis of these other professions and thus ensure an easy transition to an alternate career.

PAST AND FUTURE

Once, an undergraduate degree in sociology would ensure upward mobility in this profession. Today, advanced degrees and specialization are the norm. As society becomes more sophisticated and fragmented into special interest groups, there are no boundaries limiting the work that sociologists will be called upon to do. The fast-paced growth of technology means that sociologists will have to keep current with computer techniques which make research easier. Sociologists will also need to keep abreast of social institutions and be able to anticipate trends while constantly updating or reviewing research in particular areas.

QUALITY OF LIFE
Two Years

The first two years are the groundbreaking years of this profession. A recent sociology graduate will probably find herself reading, researching, and writing reports, articles, and books. At any level of the educational ladder, and in any setting, private or public, the sociologist will experience the pressure of deadlines, possibly heavy workloads, and long hours. Those specializing in clinical or applied sociology should be certified by the Sociological Practice Association (SPA).

Five Years

At this level, the sociologist has gained significant experience in the core elements of the profession and should be amassing a small bundle of published articles and reports. By this time the professional should have risen up the ranks to a middle-management or senior-level position. If the sociologist has a Ph.D. and is a college professor, then he should be seeking tenure.

Ten Years

At the ten-year level, the sociologist has made remarkable progress in her career. By now she should have a few publication titles to her credit, should be abreast of the latest computer techniques and should have returned to school for refresher courses, development seminars, and ad hoc workshops and conferences.

THE BIRKMAN LIFESTYLE GRID

This career is suitable for people with Green interests.

You'll Have Contact With
Anthropologists
Career Counselors
Psychologists
Statisticians

Major Associations
American Society of Criminology
1314 Kinnear Road
Suite 214
Columbus, OH 43212
Tel: 614-292-9207
Fax: 614-292-6767
Contact: Sarah Hall

American Sociological Association
1722 North Street NW
Washington, DC 20036-2981
Tel: 202-833-3410
Fax: 202-785-0146

Rural Sociology Society
Department of Sociology, Montana State University
Bozeman, MT 59715
Tel: 406-994-5248

SOFTWARE DEVELOPER

A DAY IN THE LIFE

Software and Internet developers produce computer-based goods and services for individual consumers and companies. Software developers coordinate the production of software products, from choosing content providers, assembling graphics creators, and working with programmers, through the actual assembling, pressing and distribution of the final product. Internet producers go through much the same process, except instead of pressing a final product, they set up and maintain an Internet site that provides services to the user.

Developers spend most of the day on the telephone coordinating production with the members of the team. One developer wrote that she sees herself as a chef: "The parts I have to put together are the ingredients, and I have to decide how and when to put them together to make a beautiful dish." As pleasant as this sounds, developers are not strangers to hard work. Late nights are not unusual; unforeseen problems are standard. "Build in an extra two weeks to any project," said one five-year software developer, "then you'll only be two weeks late." Software developers should be organized but flexible, and have strong technical and interpersonal skills. A high tolerance for frustration is equally important. Software and Internet producers are self-starters by nature and tend to tackle problems head on. Those who can combine all these talents will find themselves well suited to the industry.

Developers told us the most exciting thing about the work is being able to produce a unique product that takes advantage of an unexploited medium. The final product each developer produces acts as a living resume, and many point with pride to the projects they are involved in. Also, because the software and Internet industries are so young, the field is wide open to those with talent. Talented developers are extremely mobile in this industry; ability sells, and many companies are willing to pay top dollar to have ability on their team.

PAYING YOUR DUES

There are no specific academic criteria for software developers and Internet producers, although many employers consider a college degree desirable. Those involved in coordinating all phases of projects are likely to benefit from courses or a degree in computer science, finance, English, psychology, sociology, and graphics design. Those who expect to specialize in a limited area of production responsibility (such as programming or graphic design) should focus on developing skills in that area and assembling a portfolio that demonstrates those skills.

ASSOCIATED CAREERS

Software developers with technical expertise can become managers or programmers. Software and Internet developers also go into a number of project-related fields that involve managerial decision making, budgeting, and scheduling. Some go into publishing (hard copy and electronic); others go into manufacturing and product development. A few become consultants to firms, advising them on their Internet presence and providing such abilities as translation services for annual reports (i.e., turning them into interactive media).

PAST AND FUTURE

Software development and Internet production got their start in the 1970s when personal computers began to spring up in America. Few realized the impact these machines would have on every American's life. One man did, and though he was a lowly programmer fighting for programmers' rights, he maintained that authors should copyright their software, and he started a company that did exactly that. The little company he began is now known as Microsoft.

Jobs in software and Internet development are expected to grow significantly throughout the next decade. Many companies are investing heavily in the Internet, and much of this money will be used to hire Internet site developers.

QUALITY OF LIFE

Two Years

Software developers have important responsibilities from the start. Many are put in charge of small projects or of parts of large projects, immediately upon hire. The pace is frenetic; the project must be coordinated, deadlines must be met, budgets must be complied with. Many use these early years to learn by making mistakes, which they may spend long hours in the office correcting. Pressure and satisfaction are high.

Five Years

Developers begin to address the gaps in their knowledge; experience has honed their managerial skills. Many take classes in programming, software, aesthetics, or other areas related to their profession. Job mobility is high. Salaries increase, and hours stabilize. Satisfaction is above average.

Ten Years

Ten-year veterans of the software-development field have been in charge of a number of projects and seen them through from idea to revision. Many have given up their day-to-day managerial duties and either supervise other developers or move into strategic planning areas of the company. A number start their own companies using connections made in the industry. Quality of life increases, salaries increase, and hours decrease.

THE BIRKMAN LIFESTYLE GRID

Red Green
Yellow Blue

This career is suitable for people with Red interests.

You'll Have Contact With

Computer Programmers
Content Producers
Computer Engineers
Graphic Designers

Major Associations

Interactive Multimedia Association
48 Maryland Avenue
Suite 202
Annapolis, MD 21401-8011
Tel: 410-626-1380
Fax: 410-263-0590

Semiconductor Industry Association
181 Metro Drive
Suite 450
San Jose, CA 95110
Tel: 408-436-6600
Fax: 408-436-6646

American Electronics Association
5201 Great America Parkway
Suite 520
Santa Clara, CA 95054
Tel: 408-987-4200
Fax: 408-970-8565
Contact: Customer Service

SOMMELIER

A DAY IN THE LIFE

When customers in an upscale restaurant want to order a bottle of wine with dinner, they may be overwhelmed by or unfamiliar with the selections offered on the wine list. When this is the case, they can ask the sommelier for advice. Sommelier is the French term for cellarmaster or wine steward. Sommeliers are individuals with a love of wine who are eager to impart some of their knowledge to the customer. They can describe the regions, grapes, vineyards and vintages of an assortment of wines. The best sommeliers talk to, not at, their customers and enjoy when customers tell them of a bottle they have recently tasted that they are not familiar with. The sommelier either helps to create the wine list or compiles it on his own.

The sommelier recommends wines that suit the customer's tastes and price range. Even those who are knowledgeable about wine can benefit from the sommelier's advice. He has tasted the items on the wine list and knows which wines go best with which entrees. Many patrons are easily intimidated by wines and do not understand the terminology used to describe them. The sommelier must be ready to coax from them a description of their desires and be understanding of their budgetary limits. When they select a wine, the sommelier brings it to the table with the appropriate glasses and pours it for the customer to taste. The sommelier should encourage the patron to smell the wine first and should describe its components to him, bringing the wine to life for the patron before it even touches his palate. Sommeliers also decant wines, when necessary. Decanting, usually done to red wines aged over ten years, is the process of pouring the wine into a decanter before serving it. This is done to allow the wine to breathe and to separate it from any sediment that may have settled at the bottom of the bottle.

Extensive and frequent travel is part of the sommelier's career. Many travel yearly to different regions to choose wines for their restaurant. At times, they will leave a promising wine behind, but return to it repeatedly until they feel it has aged properly.

PAYING YOUR DUES

Sommeliers train for years to develop their palate. The best ones travel throughout the major wine regions of the world to view the vineyards and wine-making processes firsthand. While touring the globe they attend many wine tastings. This travel allows them to explore the customs of the areas, as well. Usually, the sommelier meets with the vineyard owners to inquire about their vintages and discuss the harvest seasons. Most sommeliers spend a significant amount of time in France, often continuing their studies in a restaurant under another sommelier. For many sommeliers, wine starts out as a hobby and progresses to a love that culminates in a career. A sommelierís education is not over when his travels are through, though. Wine is produced continually and he must regularly taste new presses. Sommeliers return to France and their other favorite regions again and again. They must read about wines they have not tasted and be familiar with other alcohols, such as scotch and sherry.

ASSOCIATED CAREERS

The field of wine is vast, but more traditional and family-oriented than one might expect. Vineyard owners are responsible for tending to the grape harvest and wine making. They employ large numbers of people to do this. Wine production is predominantly a closed area as there are a limited number of good grape-growing regions and families tend to pass the vineyard down through bloodlines. Those who are knowledgeable about wine may consider hosting tasting dinners or teaching wine-tasting classes. Still others may write about their experiences for industry publications, such as Food & Wine Magazine.

PAST AND FUTURE

The practice of cultivating grapes for wine has been carried on for thousands of years. Drinking habits have always fluctuated around the fashions, politics, and customs of the times. Often these three factors have had much to do with the profit generated from wine making. The early twentieth century saw the beginning of a movement to ensure wine's authenticity, which culminated in laws stating, for example, that only wine from the French region of Champagne could be called champagne. Since World War II, wine consumption in the United States has grown; the American vineyard has matured and some vineyards in California produce excellent wine. The best European wines are becoming increasingly expensive, causing many to view them as investment opportunities. This has created a demand for sommeliers: Given the complexities and the cost of wines, many people recognize the need for guidance in choosing one.

QUALITY OF LIFE

Two Years

Most sommeliers begin by working under another sommelier's guidance; apprenticeship under a master is the best way to learn how worth stocking. People enter this profession because they have a "taste" for it, and nearly all beginners report great satisfaction with their choice of career.

Five Years

The majority of sommeliers work independently now and enjoy the increased responsibilities of choosing the "house" wines (a process typically considered of the utmost importance to restaurateurs). The task of creating the wine list for a restaurant requires diligence and creativity-finding the best suppliers of both the choice, inexpensive wines and the higher-priced vintages-and after five years a sommelier has developed the experience to recommend selections for the type of restaurant he has been working with.

Ten Years

By this time the sommelier has probably acquired a reputation and may be quoted in magazines and journals as an authority on wine. Some sommeliers do consulting work for several restaurants, bringing their own flair to each house, while others choose to focus on a single restaurant where they are employed full-time or perhaps share a financial interest. Experienced sommeliers may host wine tasting dinners, write a column for specialty magazine such as The Wine Spectator, or act as mentors to aspiring sommeliers.

THE BIRKMAN LIFESTYLE GRID

This career is suitable for people with Yellow interests.

You'll Have Contact With
Chefs
Patrons
Restauranteurs
Vintners

Major Associations
Sommelier Society of America
201 East 25th Street
New York, NY 10010
Tel: 212-679-4190

SPEECH THERAPIST

A DAY IN THE LIFE

A speech therapist is a specialist with training in the diagnosis and treatment of a variety of speech, voice, and language disorders who works with people, unable to make speech sounds or cannot make them clearly. They also work with people who stutter, have fluency and rhythm problems, inappropriate pitch, or harsh voice and speech quality problems. The most widespread and obvious speech disorder is stuttering, often caused by anxiety. The speech therapist sets up a program of speech exercises to reduce the disability, and if necessary, enlists the aid of a psychologist or psychiatrist. Other disorders may result from hearing loss, stroke, cerebral palsy, mental disability, or brain injury. Speech therapists keep careful records on the evaluation and progress of patients, often developing and implementing individualized treatment programs based on the input of physicians, psychiatric social workers, and psychologists. In fact, because speech disorders are usually related to neurological, psychological, and physical conditions, speech therapists must be able to work as a member of a team which may include other healthcare specialists such as a neurologist and psychiatrist.

An important part of a speech therapist's work is the counseling and support of individuals and families on speech disorders and on how to cope with the stress associated with these problems. Therapists also work with families on treatment techniques to use at home and on how to modify behavior that impedes communication. Although a speech therapist's job is not physically demanding, it does require patience and compassion, as progress may be slow and halting. Speech therapy is a painstaking process, but it can be as rewarding as it is frustrating. Tremendous attention to detail and sharp focus are necessary in the evaluation of the patient's progress. Overall, speech therapists must be able to understand and empathize with the emotional strains and stresses that such problems bring, both from the patient's and family member's point of view.

Speech therapists, like other health care professionals, must carefully diagnose problems and if necessary call upon the advice of other health specialists. The ability to distinguish the need for the professional input of specialists is critical to the therapist's success. Therapists must also monitor the progress of patients, eliminate certain programs, and introduce others that are more effective. The ability to make informed decisions that may define the success and failure of any individual program is a skill that can only come with years of experience.

PAYING YOUR DUES

An aspiring speech therapist needs a Master's degree in Speech Pathology, 375 hours of supervised clinical experience, a passing grade on a national examination and at least nine months of post-graduate professional experience. With such a strong emphasis on education, practical experience, and licensure, entrants to this field must work long and hard.

ASSOCIATED CAREERS

Speech therapists who wish to modify their careers have a range of choices open to them. Because the training that a speech therapist receives is substantially the same training as that of a speech-language pathologist, a switch to this profession can be accomplished quite easily. Hearing loss is associated with speech disorders and so the work of an audiologist is very closely connected. The speech therapist seeking more and varied challenges may be able to find it in special education and private rehabilitation counseling services. Research is another gratifying area for the outgoing therapist to consider. High-level administrative positions in schools, hospitals, health departments, or clinics may offer significantly higher wages and more responsibilities. Other occupations requiring rehabilitation training include occupational therapy, physical therapy, and recreational therapy.

PAST AND FUTURE

As with most areas of the health care profession, speech therapists are expected to be in constant demand right through to the year 2000 and beyond. Speech therapists will be needed to service a rapidly aging population with significant growth in the seventy-five years and over sector of the population. Hearing loss and its associated speech disorders are expected to be one of the major health concerns of an older population. The proliferation of health care agencies, nursing homes, residential retirement communities and adult daycare centers will assure employment opportunities for speech therapists and other health specialists. With federal legislation guaranteeing the expansion of special education and related services in schools, more and younger students with disabilities will require the specialized training of speech therapists and speech-language pathologists. Therapists will be encouraged to design and implement innovative programs that will involve students and parents alike.

QUALITY OF LIFE

Two Years

At the two-year level the speech therapist is concerned with making accurate diagnoses and seeking the opinion of other health specialists. This is the stage at which the professional begins to develop her "bedside manner" or way in which she relates to patients. Emphasis is on effectively communicating test results and clearly explaining proposed treatment to patients and family members. The therapist is also careful in charting the evaluation, progress, and discharge of patients.

Five Years

A speech therapist with five years of experience should be involved in the developing and implementing of personalized treatment programs. The therapist is now adept at working with physicians, psychiatric social workers, psychologists and, occasionally, neurologists, to create treatment programs that bring about effective results. At this stage the speech therapist is wont to evaluate her own professional progress and advancement potential.

Ten Years

Teaching and research and development at the college or university level will probably offer the most intellectual gratification. Writing books and articles for publication is an integral part of any professorship. Executive-level management positions, including a directorship will offer lucrative salary scales and numerous responsibilities. Private practice offers more autonomy and flexible hours. The ten-year veteran has a number of ways to rise in her career.

THE BIRKMAN LIFESTYLE GRID

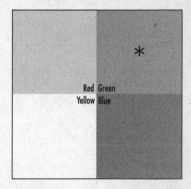

This career is suitable for people with Green interests.

You'll Have Contact With

Linguists
Occupational Therapists
Psychologists
Teachers

Major Associations

American Speech-Language-Hearing Association
10801 Rockville Pike
Rockville, MD 20852
Tel: 301-897-5700

SPORTS MANAGER

A DAY IN THE LIFE

Sports managers spend their time behind the scenes coordinating all business-related activities for the team that employs them. During the playing season they may work seven days a week. When they work for college or professional teams they stay behind in their office at the team's home facility while the team travels to away games. A few who have been in the business for many years travel with the team from city to city, but they are the exception.

During the off-season, the manager is busy negotiating trades and signing free agents. The sports manager or general manager, as he is sometimes called, signs all players to the professional team. According to one successful manager, "It is more important to know which deals not to make than which deals you should make." This is often the most delicate aspect of the job, as a manager must make deals that satisfy the owners, without alienating any of the players. A manager who works for a professional sports team is involved in the yearly ritual of drafting college players. He works closely with the coach and scouts to determine which players are the most talented, economically feasible, and play positions the team needs. He must do this while keeping an eye on the team's budget. He is in charge of everyone's salary, from the coach and players down to the assistants. He also makes financial arrangements for travel, equipment, and uniform purchases. A manager must also factor into his budget player injury and the possible team success that leads to additional playing and travel costs.

A sports manager has to participate in press conferences and explain the reasons for his decisions to the media, without giving away his intentions for the future. He may be the subject of both complimentary and critical press reports which he must be able to ignore. When he signs a great player, he is considered a hero. When a respected player leaves the team or slides into a losing streak, he is seen as contributing to the team's downfall. Managers should expect to be fired and forced to relocate a number of times during their careers. For all of these reasons, this is a highly stressful job

PAYING YOUR DUES

There is no one ideal background for a sports manager. A sports manager should, of course, love the game he is managing and should have experience playing or coaching it. Most managers have spent time as an assistant to a manager or coach while in high school and college. Most managers begin managing local school teams, work their way up to the college level and eventually work with professional athletes. Some may have a degree in physical education, with a business minor, which allows them to handle the business aspects of their work. For managers of professional teams, a business degree is recommended. The manager should be familiar with contract laws, economics, and accounting. There are no licensing requirements for managers. They may belong to an organization or association of managers in their particular sport.

ASSOCIATED CAREERS

The general manager is usually promoted from the position of head coach or head of scouting. A coach organizes practice schedules and develops playing strategies for the team. The scout visits teams in lower divisions of the sport to find new talent: For example, a college team scout attends high school events. He meets with exceptional players and watches them play. When he finds a player that he thinks would be an asset to his team, he generally works out a scholarship plan to entice the player to attend his employer's school.

PAST AND FUTURE

Sports have been a part of all societies for so long that no one is sure which sport was developed first. The first organized sporting event was the Olympic games in 776 B.C. Modern sports developed primarily over the last two centuries, with the greatest advances being made in the last fifty years. The difference between sports in this century and sports in earlier years is the level of organization. Just before World War I, a number of people realized what a profitable business organized sports could be. Teams began to receive increasing press coverage, people realized that the players needed support staff, and the sports manager was born. The number of positions is small, although the growing popularity of such areas as gymnastics and women's sports is opening up the field somewhat. The competition is fierce; the position of sports manager is a coveted one.

QUALITY OF LIFE

Two Years

Working in the glamorous field of professional and college sports has been a lifetime dream for most sports managers, who often bring experience as players or coaches at the college or professional level. They may start out working with a "minor league" team with relatively low visibility in the industry. Satisfaction is high in this field, despite a fair amount of detail work. The manager receives a good paycheck and is participating in one of his favorite pastimes.

Five Years

Most managers are still involved with the sport, although they may no longer be working with their first team. Many make lateral moves to other teams, which often brings them new challenges and greater financial reward, especially when successful managers "trade up" to a more visible team. Satisfaction remains high, and some of the least exciting detail work can now be delegated to support staff.

Ten Years

The most successful managers can pull in huge amounts of money at this point, as they have earned the trust of the team owners and coaches, if not always the general public. Administrative responsibilities grow with the size of the sports organization, and many managers now oversee sizable support staff who look after everything from equipment to travel arrangements to fulfilling contractual obligations to athletes. Those who aspire to the presidency or partial ownership of the club may devote considerable time and energy to schmoozing with the press, scouts, agents, and other movers and shakers in the industry.

THE BIRKMAN LIFESTYLE GRID

Red Green
Yellow Blue

This career is suitable for people with Red interests.

You'll Have Contact With

Athletes
Coaches
Owners
Reporters

Major Associations

American Alliance for
Health & Physical Education
1900 Association Drive
Reston, VA 22091
Tel: 703-620-6091

National Athletic Trainers Association
2952 Stemmons Freeway
Suite 200
Dallas, TX 75247
Tel: 214-637-6282
Fax: 214-637-2206
Contact: Linda Tilley

STAGE TECHNICIAN

A DAY IN THE LIFE

If you enjoy the theater, but haven't been bitten by the acting bug, or if you enjoy working with your hands, look into a career in theater production. Stage technicians fill a variety of jobs in the theater—they are light and sound board operators, carpenters, prop handlers, production assistants, wardrobe supervisors, and stage managers. The stage manager is perhaps the most visible and versatile of the production crew. Her job requires an understanding of all of the elements of stage production, as well as some familiarity with a director's duties. She coordinates the production once the run is under way, often managing the actors themselves and seeing to it that the director's instructions are not forgotten. Stage carpenters build and repair sets. Once the show is running, they place and move sets and scenery during the performance. Prop handlers maintain the various objects used on stage. They work with the production designers in selecting props and with the carpenters in repairing props when they break. Wardrobe supervisors keep costumes clean and mended. Although designers and directors make the final decisions about what the sets and actors should look like, they often rely on a technician for practical advice.

During pre-production, technicians typically work from 9 a.m. to 6 p.m., bringing to life the images and sounds that a play's directors, authors, and designers propose. When the show is up and running, these same hands work nights, starting about two hours before showtime, maintaining the machinery of the theater, cleaning and fixing stages, lights, and sets and, as one technician said, "moving whatever needs to be moved." Post-show clean-up and preparation for the next evening's performance can last well into the night.

Good stage technicians can translate the plans of others into finished products, are committed to the theater, and can handle the frustrations and problems that come with the job. A stage hand's job is not a terribly secure one. Your job lasts as long as each show lasts, so a flop can really wreck your finances. Pay scales start low and don't really provide a comfortable living until after a couple of years. The competition for higher-paying and more secure union jobs can be fierce. Nevertheless, most stage technicians value a life in the theater and relish the opportunity to make a hands-on contribution to the creative process.

PAYING YOUR DUES

While not mandatory, a high-school diploma is recommended, and high school is where many technicians gain their first experience. Most employers look for experienced technicians, so technicians often work at regional theaters or in summer stock before heading to the nation's biggest labor markets: The East and West coasts. A general understanding of stagecraft and the theater is desirable. A good technician is handy with tools and knows the in and outs of constructing and lighting sets. "It isn't like building a house," said one stage hand.

If you choose to join a union, you'll probably have to take a written test (depending on the specific profession) and participate in a three-year apprenticeship. Unions are selective about their members, and only well-reputed technicians can expect to be invited to join. Unionized stage managers belong to the ultra-competitive Actors' Equity Association, so opportunities to join are few.

ASSOCIATED CAREERS

If the live theater isn't what excites you, you may want to pursue a career in film or television, although competition there is even more intense than in the theater. Another option for stage-hands is a career in stage or lighting design, which requires an undergraduate or even a graduate degree.

PAST AND FUTURE

Even dating back to ancient times, there were people responsible for the creation, maintenance and improvement of the theater. Some large Greek amphitheaters could hold audiences of over 5,000, and writings from the Hellenic age mention elaborate sets and costumes that added to the theater experience.

The modern theater is marked by technical specialists, such as lighting designers, prop managers, and set designers. The role of these specialists is important, and opportunities will continue to be available for newcomers to the profession. Those with electrical or artistic skills will have an advantage in finding jobs; those who perform more menial tasks (e.g., stage cleanup) will find opportunities harder to come by.

QUALITY OF LIFE

Two Years

Many aspiring technicians spend their first two years establishing a reputation and adding credits to their resume. Since employment is show-by-show, thorough networking is essential to job security. Many make barely enough money to live on but gain a valuable understanding of the craft from the seasoned professionals with whom they work. After two years, many technicians choose to follow the union track, while others apply to college or graduate school to pursue a degree in production or design. Technical theater production can be tiring; many cite professional fatigue in these early years that few anticipated when they began.

Five Years

By this time, members have decided to join the technical theater union or to remain independent laborers. The competition among stage technicians drives many out of the profession, which means that those who stick it out, establish contacts and earn a good name for themselves will find greater opportunities available to them. Satisfaction is average, as many experience a "mid-career lull" where their responsibilities stay the same and their hours increase. Salaries rise, but not tremendously.

Ten Years

Ten-year veterans have most likely established their reputations, made significant professional contacts, and developed a long resume that allows them to choose their own jobs. Veterans supervise less-experienced technicians, and many start their own training companies and freelance technical theatrical agencies. Union members can expect to enjoy relative job security and a decent living.

THE BIRKMAN LIFESTYLE GRID

Red Green
Yellow Blue

This career is suitable for people with Red interests.

You'll Have Contact With

Actors
Directors
Lighting Designers
Producers

Major Associations

American Council for the Arts
One East 53rd Street
New York, NY 10022
Tel: 212-223-2787

American Crafts Council
72 Spring Street
New York, NY 10012
Tel: 212-274-0630
Fax: 212-274-0650
Contact: Public Relations

Theatre Arts Communications Group Inc.
355 Lexington Avenue
New York, NY 10017
Tel: 212-697-5230
Fax: 212-983-4847

Statistician

# of people in profession	15,000
% male	70
% female	30
avg. hours per week	40
avg. starting salary	$26,000
avg. salary after 5 years	$41,000
avg. salary 10 to 15 years	$56,000

Professionals Read

American Demographer

Books, Films and TV Shows Featuring the Profession

Statistics for Gerbils
The Coming Plague

Major Employers

All State Insurance Co.
2775 Sanders Rd.
Suite A1
North Brook, IL 60062
Tel: 708-402-5000
Contact: Recruiting & Selection Team

Aetna Life & Casualty Insurance Co.
3 Embarcodero Center
Suite 302
San Francisco, CA 94111
Tel: 415-445-2700
Contact: Human Resources Manager

Blue Cross & Blue Shield of North Carolina
P.O. Box 2291
Durham, NC 27702
Tel: 919-490-2552
Fax: 919-490-7786
Contact: Human Resources

A DAY IN THE LIFE

Statisticians collect data and analyze it, looking for patterns that explain behavior or that describe the world as it is. A good statistician is involved in survey development and data collection from the beginning, ensuring the validity and usefulness of the data, our respondents told us. Statisticians are employed by private and public concerns and apply their skills to specific industry issues, such as economic analysis, inventory control problems, health problems and infectious disease outbreaks, and even television demographics. Statisticians must be familiar with valid scientific protocol and be able to quickly familiarize themselves with baselines and historical industry figures in order to structure an uncompromised analysis.

Statisticians spend over half their day in front of a computer, setting up models, manipulating data, analyzing data, or writing reports. "You don't just crunch numbers. You explain them," wrote one veteran statistician, who said that writing skills are important for those hoping to advance in the field. They spend the rest of their day in meetings, in planning sessions, or on the telephone exchanging ideas with colleagues. Respondents said, "Statistics is a visual science. You have to be able to picture the data and how it fits in with other known data shapes. It is not a 'numbers only' job." Most statisticians are applied statisticians, tailoring studies to real-life problems. It takes mathematical, visual, and practical skills to excel in this occupation as well as flexibility, curiosity, and a rigorous mind.

Statisticians said the most difficult part of their job is explaining the implications of their studies to non-statisticians. Many said that statistics are best used as a starting point for investigation, not as a conclusion, and upper-level managers find this concept difficult to grasp. One wrote, "Statistics is a science of trends and probabilities, not certainties. We can tell what things happened, and suggest why they might have happened, but they're only suggestions." Many statisticians cited the support of the statistician community as important to their satisfaction in the field. Statisticians feel challenged, involved and invigorated by their work, and this is evidenced by the small number (under 11 percent) of statisticians who leave the field each year.

PAYING YOUR DUES

There are strict academic requirements for becoming a statistician. Entry level positions require a Bachelor's degree in mathematics or statistics. Those who wish to rise in the profession should consider obtaining a Master's degree or a Ph.D. Just under 100 universities offer graduate degrees in statistics. Suggested coursework includes mathematics (calculus and linear algebra), probability, logic, psychology, and computer science. Candidates who combine statistical skills with another major that reflects their professional direction-such as economics and econometrics, computer and material science, or biology-have a distinct competitive advantage when seeking employment. Membership in professional organizations is not required, but many choose to join the ones affiliated with their occupation, such as organizations for economists or manufacturing organizations.

ASSOCIATED CAREERS

With their strong mathematical aptitude, many careers are open to statisticians. Wall Street is the most common employer of mathematical statisticians who leave their field, followed closely by the government, which regularly hires statisticians as "area analysts". A number become accountants, insurance analysts, and actuarial analysts when they want to improve their quality of life. A significant few enter computer science and become programmers and systems analysts.

PAST AND FUTURE

Statisticians first became noteworthy in the study of infectious disease outbreaks. In the 1800s, they were able to trace an outbreak of cholera to a single water supply. The growth of actuarial science increased the need for statisticians, and demand has surged again with the development of computer science. Almost 90 percent of America's industries use statistics in their daily operations.

The opportunities available to statisticians are expected to grow in the future, due to an increasing reliance on expert analysis, growth in industries that use statisticians (entertainment, advertising, computer science, etc.) and general growth in the economy. Statisticians with interdisciplinary skills, such as biology, economics, and chemistry, should find it easier to obtain positions than pure statisticians. Employers often expect statisticians to obtain a graduate degree not in statistics, but in the related discipline of their choice.

QUALITY OF LIFE

Two Years

Those with only undergraduate degrees enter data, perform simple analysis, and summarize internal reports. These tasks involve limited responsibility, and are done under rigorous supervision. Satisfaction is lowest in the early years, and hours can be long for those who keep up with professional reading and continue educating themselves about their field. Those with graduate degrees are more likely to be assigned interesting tasks, but these first two years can be a time of menial tasks for all.

Five Years

Many statisticians spend five or more years at a single firm learning their profession. By this time, they usually have graduate degrees, and many plan and supervise projects. The majority supervise researchers, analyze data, and write reports. They concentrate on producing quality work and getting published in professional or academic journals. Professional education is important during this period, and includes attending conferences or lectures during free time. Satisfaction is high; salaries increase significantly.

Ten Years

Ten-year veterans have a good deal of job mobility and begin seeking new positions that make use of their now-substantial skills. Many move from smaller companies to larger ones, or from statistician to executive positions. Many plan and direct research projects. Satisfaction is high, and salaries increase, particularly in the private sector.

THE BIRKMAN LIFESTYLE GRID

This career is suitable for people with Red interests.

You'll Have Contact With

Computer Programmers
Mathematicians
Public Health Administrators
Researchers

Major Associations

Society for Industrial and
Applied Mathematics
3600 University City, Science Center
Philadelphia, PA 19104
Tel: 215-382-9800
Fax: 215-386-7999

Institute of Math Statistics
3401 Investment Boulevard
Suite 7
Hayward, CA 94545-3817
Tel: 510-783-8141
Fax: 510-783-4131

American Statistical Association
1429 Duke Street
Alexandria, VA 22314
Tel: 703-684-1221
Fax: 703-684-2037

STOCKBROKER

A DAY IN THE LIFE

A stockbroker invests in the stock market for individuals or corporations. Only members of the stock exchange can conduct transactions, so whenever individuals or corporations want to buy or sell stocks they must go through a brokerage house. Stockbrokers often advise and counsel their clients on appropriate investments. Brokers explain the workings of the stock exchange to their clients and gather information from them about their needs and financial ability, and then determine the best investments for them. The broker then sends the order out to the floor of the securities exchange by computer or by phone. When the transaction has been made, the broker supplies the client with the price. The buyer pays for the stock and the broker transfers the title of the stock to the client and performs clearing and settlement procedures.

The beginning stockbroker's first priority is learning the market. One broker said, "First you have to decide whether you have an interest in the stock market. This will determine how well you'll do. If you're just interested in making money you won't get very far." Stockbrokers spend their time in a fast-paced office, usually working from nine to five, unless they are just starting out or have to meet with clients. The new broker spends many hours on the phone building up a client base. Sometimes brokers teach financial education classes to expose themselves to potential investors who may then become their clients

PAYING YOUR DUES

A college degree is not required, but most brokers have one. Brokers have to be licensed. A license is obtained by passing the General Securities Registered Representative Examination and, in many cases, posting a bond. Individuals may take this test after they have been employed by a brokerage firm for four months. Firms use these four months as an on-the-job training period to prepare their workers for the test. Many states also require the candidate to take the Uniform Securities Agents State Law Examination. These tests are designed to ensure the candidate's knowledge of all aspects of the stock market. After passing these tests, an individual is considered a trainee. While working full-time, he takes classes and trains for up to two years. Employees are expected to take training courses throughout their careers to keep abreast of developments in the field.

Those with prior work experience have the greatest opportunities for becoming a stock broker. Few people become brokers straight out of college. Most employers seek applicants who have already succeeded in other fields, such as insurance sales. If you know your interests lie in the market, study economics, finances, computers, and business management in college. Many employers view ambition as the most important quality a candidate can possess

ASSOCIATED CAREERS

The sales aspects and the need to build up a client base are similar for stock brokers and insurance and real estate agents. Financial planners create and execute financial plans for people or businesses. They ascertain their clients' needs, resources and goals and use this information to draw up a financial plan that suits the individual or the company. Traders are the people you see in the movies yelling on the chaotic floor of the stock exchange. They perform the actual exchanges.

PAST AND FUTURE

The stock market is strongly affected by economic boom-and-bust cycles, the most famous of which occurred in October 1929—the Great Crash—causing a large number of investors to leap out the windows of their offices on Wall Street. The industry has matured a great deal since then—now Wall Street offices have sealed upper-floor windows and the markets have automatic limits on how far average stock prices can rise or fall in a given session—but historically only those brokers with iron stomachs have survived in this high-risk, high-stakes industry. The outlook for stockbrokers is rosy, as economic growth is anticipated. Deregulation of the industry is allowing many stockbrokers to expand their responsibilities, bringing about a corresponding increase in their client base. Increased concern about financing pension plans is also causing many people to turn to stockbrokers for advice, and the stock market continues to attract increasing numbers of individual investors. However, this is a boom-or-bust business, so the upswing won't last forever.

QUALITY OF LIFE

Two Years

Stockbrokering is an extremely competitive business—perhaps the most competitive of all. There is heavy burnout in the early years due to outrageous hours—all-nighters are routine occurrences for eager and ambitious upstarts—and many novice brokers fail to establish an adequate client base early on. Those that stay find the work exciting but anxiety-provoking. There is greater security in larger companies but generally a longer wait for advancement and "the big bucks."

Five Years

Those who get through the first few rocky years tend to stay in the field for an extended period. Many find the high salaries a delicious payback for those first years spent toiling "in the trenches." Leaving for an MBA is common at this point for those want to return for top management positions in the industry.

Ten Years

At this point brokers are enjoying the fruits of their extensive and intensive education and training. Advancement in this field comes in the form of more and bigger accounts or management positions. Occasionally, it culminates in partnership in the firm. Some even retire at this point, but most like the industry and stick around for years after they've earned pots of money.

STRUCTURAL ENGINEER

A DAY IN THE LIFE

Structural engineers are employed primarily by government agencies responsible for inspecting construction projects for safety and adherence to local and federal building standards. Structural engineers work with people in related professions, such as electricians and drywallers, in order to obtain information about construction sites and about these workers' roles in any project. SEs don't mind that some see them as the police of the construction industry; most enjoy making sure that structures are safe and sound. "If we don't do our job, everyone pays," wrote one SE, who noted that people just assume the places they live, play, and work are all safe. Without the work that a structural engineer does, all of these assumptions "would come crumbling down."

Much of the structural engineer's job takes place on-site, often outdoors, at the various stages of construction of public and private projects. SEs often work closely with construction managers and have to be careful to avoid forming relationships that could cloud their professional judgment. "They all want to be your friend so you'll help them out," one SE wrote, "but you can't be." The structural integrity of a building is based on sound engineering principles and the use of high-quality materials; no amount of amicability can keep a building standing without those things. Many noted that construction managers will argue for the integrity of their constructions when they do not meet building codes. Structural engineers have to be above reproach at their jobs; too much is at stake for everyone involved.

An unusual aspect of being a structural engineer is that an engineer has to understand the timing of construction projects better than the construction manager himself. This is because random inspections and unsupervised tours through the construction site are critical to keeping builders honest and the public safe. If a structural engineer conducts these inspections at a time when construction is stalled, insignificant, or complete, he cannot tell whether the work was done properly without tearing down the building. "You've got to know when a company is most likely to have problems and watch them like a hawk," wrote one, claiming that structural engineers are so in tune with tomfoolery in the industry that an interview, offsite, with the construction manager can tell them whether the job is being done correctly or not. Not all agreed on using ESP to assess construction managers. They did agree that structural engineers have to have a keen eye for detail and a comprehensive understanding of building standards and materials and that their job is a difficult, important, and rewarding one.

PAYING YOUR DUES

Structural engineers must have a college degree in engineering, either civil, mechanical, or structural. Fewer than seventy colleges offer an undergraduate major in structural engineering. Courses include physics, mechanics, blueprint reading, architecture, mathematics, and materials science. A structural engineer must be familiar with all the pieces of construction and the methods of construction. Many states require that structural engineers have at least two years of experience in the construction industry and pass a written test that assesses their analytical skills and their knowledge of stress levels and local and federal construction codes. Candidates should have job experience that demonstrates a significant level of maturity.

ASSOCIATED CAREERS

Many structural engineers have a construction background, and they return to this field when they leave their jobs as inspectors. They become construction managers, materials purchasers, architectural assistants, and consultants to worksites. Their analytical abilities make them well-suited to many professions, but the majority remain in a construction-related field.

PAST AND FUTURE

Historically, the architect and the construction manager shared responsibility for the safe and sound construction of all buildings. After numerous widely publicized incidents of construction being driven by financial concerns, the federal government enacted legislation that required local communities to police their construction sites using structural engineers empowered to act as the final defender of public construction safety. Although this law was eventually repealed, most U.S. communities have enacted their own local legislation that holds construction firms to strict standards of behavior, reporting, and compliance.

The demand for structural engineers is driven largely by the demand for construction. Urban areas should see a continued need for SEs, as rehabilitation projects are undertaken, and existing structures undergo renovation. There are more new housing starts in rural communities, and if that economy declines, so will the need for rural structural engineers.

QUALITY OF LIFE

Two Years

Structural engineers have passed licensing exams by this time, but many are supervised heavily by "senior" structural engineers and are a little frustrated by their lack of autonomy. Hours are long as many make the difficult transition from theoretical discussion to on-site work. Most said they were surprised at how much paperwork there is in the profession.

Five Years

Five years into the profession, many structural engineers have become full engineers and operate independently, reporting their findings and recommending penalties, fines, or shut-downs (the ultimate censure) against construction companies that violate building codes. Many have seen structurally unsound buildings, and a number said the experience can be shocking: Many unsound buildings are not only found in new construction projects, but also in existing, aging structures. Hours and salaries increase; satisfaction is high.

Ten Years

A number hit their stride now that they have more experience at inspection and greater authority to make things right. Some work long hours not because they are required to, but because they are dedicated to their work. Salaries increase; required hours decrease; satisfaction is strong.

THE BIRKMAN LIFESTYLE GRID

This career is suitable for people with Red interests.

You'll Have Contact With

Architects
Construction Managers
Civil Engineers
Government Officials

Major Associations

Associated General Contractors of American
1957 East Street, NW
Washington, DC 20006
Tel: 202-393-2040
Fax: 202-347-4004

National Society of Professional Engineers
1420 King Street
Alexandria, VA 22314
Tel: 703-684-2800
Contact: Member Services

American Consulting Engineers Council
1015 15th Street, NW
Suite 802
Washington, DC 20005
Tel: 202-347-7474
Contact: Membership Services

SUBSTANCE ABUSE COUNSELOR

A DAY IN THE LIFE

Substance abuse counseling is a demanding form of community outreach that requires patience, compassion, and a keen desire to help others who in crisis. A good portion of the addict population are people who need help in many areas of their lives. Often these people are unaware of the kinds of assistance available, whether they are eligible, or how to go about finding help. Counselors refer patients to a variety of other services that may help provide a stable platform from which they can fight their drug addiction. The abuser may be directed to a family agency, food pantry, physician or psychiatrist, vocational training center, lawyer, welfare agent or other professionals depending on the needs of the individual. One of the most frustrating aspects of the job, counselors report, is the bias that clients typically face when applying for other services. "People hold addicts more responsible for their problems," griped one interviewee. Many who seek help do overcome their addiction-counselors estimate that 20% of the people in treatment programs can eventually return to work and function normally and these successful cases are a source of unique job satisfaction among counselors. But staying "clean and sober" requires ongoing vigilance, and recidivism (or backsliding) among substance abusers is a painful reality that can be a source of depression for counselors as well as the abusers themselves.

Counselors see people in both group and private sessions. Each case varies according to the personality of the indivual. In the words of one counselor, "You never know what will come up. I spend a lot my time making referrals, but most of what I do is crisis intervention." Crisis intervention demands a sympatheitc, nonjudgmental attitude and a supportive approach no matter what situation the addict is in, and, as one counselor put it, "You see everything." Many people who are are drawn to this career have deep-seated personal or religious beliefs about its social value. Their commitment to the principle of helping others keeps them going through the setbacks they inevitably witness on the job. Probaly the most difficult aspect of the job is seeing patients die. Between drug addiction and the range of other problems that often accompany it, such as homelessness, mental illness, and AIDS, death is an unfortunately common sight. One of the great challenges of this noble avocation is learning to control emotions of anger, frustration and even bonds of friendship that can undermine the counselor-patient relationship. Not surprisingly, the burnout rate for substance abuse counselors is very high.

PAYING YOUR DUES

Substance abuse counseling is considered one of the most challenging areas of human/social services. To become a counselor you need a B.A. plus two years of counseling in a related field or equivalent life experience. This could include other kinds of counseling, volunteer work, or experience as a former addict. Though certification is available from most states, it is not required. Some people believe this will change in the future as cutbacks are made and jobs become more scarce.

ASSOCIATED CAREERS

Substance abuse counselors work closely with a variety of other health and human service professionals including psychologists, social workers, family counselors, career counselors, lawyers, welfare agents and other state employees. Because substance abuse counseling has a high rate of burnout, it's not unusual for people to turn to other forms of counseling as an alternate career.

PAST AND FUTURE

Though the clergy has always provided counseling to people in need of help, substance abuse counseling as a discrete profession evolved fairly recently. Its theory and practice have grown out of a synthesis of three older methodologies: the psychoanalytic/psychotheraputic model of mental health treatment, Alcoholics Anonymous's "12-step" recovery program, and the Theraputic Community treatment model as used by organizations such as Synanon and Pheonix House. Promising pharmacological treatments currently in development may yet produce new breakthroughs in recovery programs.

The future of substance abuse counseling rests largely on the financial commitment of government. Most substance abuse programs are state and federally funded, and as a result there is a lot of government oversight in most counseling clinics (and lots of paperwork). Cutbacks have already altered the landscape, and further reductions are possible in the current climate of anti-government sentiment. Notably, as we go to press a bill sponsored by Senator Phil Gramm and attached to the pending welfare reform package would make anyone convicted of a crime ineligible for Medicaid. Since Medicaid covers most substance abuse programs, many substance abusers with criminal records would be hindered in their efforts to get treatment. Counselors also report that the patients they see are in general sicker now than in past years; as many as 30% are HIV positive.

QUALITY OF LIFE

Two Years

New counselors are typically handling at least 50 cases at any given time. Much of the day is spent in contact with other agencies during the referral process. A counselor is also responsible for clinical assessments, group and individual counseling sessions, urine monitoring, and charting. People often burnout at this stage and pursue another path within human services.

Five Years

At five years a counselor is performing many of the same daily tasks as before, but their caseload decreases as their administrative responsibilities increase. A mid-level professional has more experience and judgment to handle the pressure of the job, and pay scales are increasing steadily, but there is heavy burnout at this stage too. Most counselors are constantly reassessing their commitment to the field.

Ten Years

Considering the high dropout rate in the field, ten years is relatively long career for a substance abuse counselor. They are likely to be serving now in an advisory capacity on a hospital staff or perhaps have taken on directorship of an agency at this point. Counselors at this level are responsible for the treatment of the most challenging patients such as those with severe mental illness.

THE BIRKMAN LIFESTYLE GRID

Red Green
Yellow Blue

This career is suitable for people with Green interests.

You'll Have Contact WithPhysicians
Hospital Administrators
Social Workers
Patients

Major Associations
National Association of Alcoholism and Drug Abuse Counselors
1911 N. Fort Myer Dr.
Suite 900
Arlington, VA 22209
Tel: 703-741-7698

National Alliance of Methadone Advocates
435 Second Avenue
New York, NY 10010
Tel: 212-595-6262

Association for Medical Education and Research in Substance Abuse @ Center for Alcohol and Addiction Studies
Brown University
Box G-BH
Providence, RI 02912
Tel: 401-444-1817
Contact: Phyllis Arnold

SURVEYOR

PROFESSIONAL PROFILE

# of people in profession	100,000
% male	90
% female	10
avg. hours per week	45
avg. starting salary	$15,000
avg. salary after 5 years	$27,000
avg. salary 10 to 15 years	$38,000

Professionals Read

Surveyor

Books, Films and TV Shows Featuring the Profession

Landcrab
Orz

Major Employers

TRW Redi Property
5601 East LaPalma
Anaheim, CA 92807
Tel: 800-426-1466
Fax: 714-701-9511
Contact: Rosemary Randell

US Army Corp of Engineers
26 Federal Plaza
New York, NY 10278
Tel: 212-264-0200
Fax: 212-264-7153
Contact: Human Resources

Parsons Brinkerhoff, Inc.
303 2nd Street
Suite 700 North
San Francisco, CA 94107
Tel: 415-243-4600
Fax: 415-243-9501
Contact: Human Resources

A DAY IN THE LIFE

Surveyors calculate the height, depth, relative position, and property lines of pieces of land. They use theodolites, transits, levels, and satellite technology (known as the Global Positioning System (GPS)) to determine locations and boundaries. They work outdoors most of the time and often have assistants. Surveyors work with many other people and often act as team leaders, in charge of projects for civil engineers, architects, or local authorities. It may seem that a surveyor's job is an nonpressured one, but respondents were quick to point out that: "If a surveyor doesn't do his job properly, everything goes wrong. Imagine the problem if a building straddled two people's properties or an airport runway wasn't level." Surveying is a career that requires an eye for detail, a careful touch, an analytical mind, strong organizational and communication skills, and leadership ability.

Surveyors work in a variety of areas. Some delineate property boundaries for legal deeds and titles. Others work on civil-engineering projects, such as airports, highways and waste-treatment plants. Nearly every construction job requires a surveyor (over 60 percent of surveyors were employed by architects in the 1990s). Surveyors also work with cartographers (map makers), oceanographers, geophysicists (exploring for oil), and miners (to ensure the proper positioning of underground shafts). The variety of the job is one of its most interesting features. "You use the same tools in different ways to do different things," said one quite happy surveyor. Surveyors must keep abreast of technological advances. The recent development of GPS technology, which uses a portable satellite dish and a triangulated satellite to develop maps, has changed the way surveyors and cartographers work together. Continuing professional education is the norm in this occupation.

Surveying involves rigorous physical work. Much surveying is done in remote, physically challenging locations and requires the carrying of equipment over undeveloped terrain. Respondents said that their work can be stressful because it is so exacting and because architects sometimes claim a survey was faulty instead of taking responsibility for their own mistakes. Surveyors' positive comments, however, significantly outweighed their negative ones.

PAYING YOUR DUES

Surveyors are not required to have a college education, but state licensing requirements make it preferable for candidates to earn one. Employers look favorably on college or vocational school courses in civil engineering, mathematics, physics, statistics, geometry, drafting, blueprint reading, and computer science. Many of those who don't attend college find work as assistants and eventually become technicians, getting their education on the job. All states require that surveyors be licensed. Although requirements vary from state to state, college graduates generally must have two to four years of surveying experience while high school graduates must have six to ten years. All must pass a written licensing exam. Professional certification, while not required, is available through the American Congress on Surveying and Mapping or the American Society for Photogrammetry and Remote Sensing.

ASSOCIATED CAREERS

Surveyors who leave the profession usually do so because they are dissatisfied with the pay, not with the work. They become construction managers, construction laborers, and professional property consultants (on issues of boundaries and the accuracy of other surveyors). Many surveyors return to academic studies, most often to pursue a degree in civil engineering.

PAST AND FUTURE

The profession grew out of the need to map and plan the transit routes for personal and commercial transportation. The planning, construction, and maintenance of America's infrastructure required a constant supply of qualified surveyors. Surveying used to be part of the civil engineer's job, but the amount of work required on massive projects turned surveying into a distinct occupation.

The need for surveyors is expected to grow significantly over the next ten years. Large, long overdue infrastructure maintenance projects are expected to be carried out, the brisk pace of housing starts and property concerns is expected to continue, and satellite technology is likely to make existing maps seem imprecise and in need of revision. Job opportunities are expected to increase by more than 20 percent over the next ten years.

QUALITY OF LIFE

Two Years

Two years into the profession, surveyors usually work as helpers, assistants, or technicians. Hours are long, and the work is more physical than intellectual; however, under the supervision of experienced surveyors, many novices learn the techniques and practices they need to become successful surveyors. Salaries are low; satisfaction is average.

Five Years

Those who are licensed and able to become fully accredited surveyors are more satisfied (and better paid) than those who are not. Hours are stable, but responsibilities increase; surveyors begin to work closely with architects, contractors, and attorneys.

Ten Years

Surveyors have gained considerable experience from working on a variety of projects. A few specialize, but most remain general surveyors who manage assistants and technicians on surveying jobs. Only about 6 percent become independent surveyors; most remain affiliated with the government department, the contractor, the civil engineering firm, or the architect they have been working with. Hours and responsibilities remain the same; satisfaction is above average.

THE BIRKMAN LIFESTYLE GRID

Red Green
Yellow Blue

*

This career is suitable for people with Yellow interests.

You'll Have Contact With

Attorneys
Cartographers
Developers
Geologists

Major Associations

American Congress on Surveying and Mapping
5410 Grosvenor Lane
Suite 100
Bethesda, MD 20814
Tel: 301-493-0200

NYS Association of Professional Land Surveyors
387 Northern Lights Drive
North Syracuse, NY 13212
Tel: 315-455-1073

National Society of Professional Surveyors
5410 Grosvenor Lane
Suite 100
Bethesda, MD 20814
Tel: 301-493-0200

TEACHER

A DAY IN THE LIFE

The majority of teachers are employed by primary or secondary schools. Their focus is a specific subject or grade level. Before arriving at the classroom, teachers create lesson plans tailored to their students' levels of ability. At school, usually beginning at 8 a.m., teachers must begin the difficult task of generating interest in their often sleepy students. A good sense of humor and the ability to think like their students help teachers captivate their students' attention. Teachers have to generate interest in subjects that students often find tedious. Rousing them from their apathy and watching their curiosity grow is a giant reward of teaching. One teacher said her favorite aspects of teaching are the creative challenges and the "iconoclastic opportunities." Teachers must have high expectations of their students and also be able to empathize with their concerns. They must be comfortable dealing with a spectrum of personality types and ability levels, and must be capable of treating their students fairly.

About a fifth of the teacher's work week is devoted to their least favorite aspect of the profession, paperwork. Teachers have a block of time each day, called a professional period, to accomplish paper grading; however, all teachers report that this is not enough time. Teachers also perform administrative duties, such as spending one period assisting in the school library or monitoring students in the cafeteria. Teachers also need to be accessible to parents. Some teachers meet with parents once per term, others send progress reports home each month. Most schools require teachers to participate in extra-curricular activities with students. A teacher may be an adviser to the school yearbook, direct the school play, or coach the chess team. Often they receive a stipend for leading the more time-consuming extracurricular activities. Teachers may also be required to act as chaperones at a certain number of after-school functions, such as dances and chorus concerts.

All good teachers agree that the main reason for entering this profession should be a desire to impart knowledge. Teachers must want to make a difference in the lives and futures of their students.

PAYING YOUR DUES

A college degree is required in this profession. You can receive your bachelor's degree in elementary or secondary education in five years. Prospective teachers take 24 to 36 credits in an area of specialization and 18 to 24 credits in teaching courses. They spend the fifth year student teaching. Postgraduates can become teachers by returning to school for a master's degree in teaching. In addition, many states offer alternative teaching licenses (designed to help schools acquire a more diverse pool of applicants for teaching positions); the usual requirements are a bachelor's degree in the subject the candidate plans to teach, a passing score on state-required examinations, and completion of a teaching internship. Prospective teachers are also advised to gain skills in communications, organization, and time management. Teachers can apply for teaching positions through their college's placement office or directly to their chosen school district.

ASSOCIATED CAREERS

While part-time substitute teaching can offer a path of entry to a full-time teaching career, it is also a common way to remain involved in the community without experiencing the time pressures placed on full-time teachers. Teachers' aides assist teachers and administrators in all aspects of their job. Students meet with guidance counselors to discuss family or school dilemmas or their plans for the future. Teachers who have obtained postgraduate degrees may advance to the position of school principal or become a member of the Board of Education. A school principal organizes and manages the school's faculty and ensures that the school's goals are met; board members are elected or appointed officials who decide which courses schools will offer and which textbooks the school system will use.

PAST AND FUTURE

Benjamin Franklin revolutionized the American school system. He created an educational program in which students were taught many subjects, but initially such schools were attended only by wealthy patrons. Various types of children's schools began in different states in the early 1800s, but it was not until 1834 that schools began to be supported by public funds. In those days, students of various ages spent the day with one teacher in a one-room schoolhouse. Today, the trend is toward having teachers specialize in one or two areas. Some states are even passing laws limiting the number of subjects that an instructor can teach. There are shortages of qualified teachers in some urban areas and in some areas of specialization. The subjects that offer the most opportunity are English as a second language (ESL), mathematics, the sciences, and special education. ESL has growing potential not only in areas of America with high concentrations of immigrants but in foreign countries, though language requirements limit the pool of qualified candidates.

QUALITY OF LIFE

Two Years

Teachers entering the profession generally say they plan to remain for at least five or ten years, but in fact the burn-out rate in the first two years is very high. New teachers are learning themselves as they discover ways to encourage student participation in class, generate homework assignments, and guide individual students in their work.

Five Years

Satisfaction with the profession is above average, and those who survive the first five years are likely to enjoy a long career. Many teachers contemplate pursuing advanced degrees that will expand their teaching options and bring them higher salaries.

Ten Years

Dedicated teachers continue to find satisfaction even after ten years on the job. While some have taken on additional administrative responsibilities, many find the work as rewarding as when they first entered the profession.

THE BIRKMAN LIFESTYLE GRID

Red Green
Yellow Blue

This career is suitable for people with Blue interests.

You'll Have Contact With

Coaches
School Administrators
Students
Tutors

Major Associations

American Association of
Colleges for Teacher Education
One Dupont Circle
Suite 610
Washington, DC 20036
Tel: 202-293-2450

American Federation of Teachers
555 New Jersey Avenue, NW
Washington, DC 20001
Tel: 202-879-4400
Contact: Public Affairs

National Education Association
1201 16th Street, NW
Washington, DC 20036
Tel: 202-822-7200
Contact: Membership Dept.

TECHNICIAN

PROFESSIONAL PROFILE

# of people in profession	500,000
% male	90
% female	10
avg. hours per week	40
avg. starting salary	$24,000
avg. salary after 5 years	$32,000
avg. salary 10 to 15 years	$41,000

Professionals Read
Journals in area of specialty

Books, Films and TV Shows Featuring the Profession
Fixed Limits
If It Ain't Broke
Cable Guy

Major Employers
Intel Corporation
705-2 East Bidwell Street
Suite #246
Folsom, CA 95630
Tel: 916-356-0385

Bellcore
6 Corporate Place
Code CM
Piscataway, NJ 08854-4157
Tel: 908-699-2000
Fax: 908-336-2945

Advanced Micro Devices
One AMD Place
P.O. Box 3453 M/S 935
Sunnyvale, CA 94088-3453
Tel: 408-732-2460

A DAY IN THE LIFE

"Technician" is the politically-correct term for "repairman," but technicians themselves—at least, male technicians—aren't picky about the label. In fact, a number of them felt it was an honorable title: "You fix things. You make them do what they're designed to do. I repair televisions, and everyone who comes to my shop needs me to be able to do my job," wrote one New York repairman. Technicians handle faulty electrical and electronic equipment. They analyze problems, run tests, and then, where possible, repair the item. They are "gadget doctors," as one put it, who understand the principles of electronics, equipment testing, and tools.

Good technicians elicit as much information about the problem from the client as possible before attempting a solution. "Sometimes the fax or copier works just fine—you only need to clean the glass, or replace the toner," said one technician, who remarked that people cause their equipment to malfunction more often than the equipment itself fails. Service representatives for manufacturers and technicians who maintain large equipment spend a good deal of time in the field. After each trip, they complete extensive paperwork in order to satisfy corporate requirements. Many described this mountain of forms as formidable and unpleasant. Technicians generally work regular hours, except the ones who handle infrastructure equipment or vital-life equipment, such as mainframe computer technicians or hospital equipment repair personnel.

The sole-technician has a less paper-heavy life, but must be a generalist within a loose area of specialization in order to have enough clients to stay in business. Some specialize in television and VCR repair, personal computer and financial calculator repair, or audio equipment maintenance. Some choose refrigerator or air-conditioner maintenance and repair. Since air-conditioner repair is very seasonal, some learn to repair heating equipment as well. Sole practitioners enjoy being their own bosses, but it's not necessarily an easy life. "When two or three days go by and nobody comes into your store—you've got problems," said one sole technician, who added that he avoids off-site repairs or schedules them after his regular business hours so potential clients won't think he's not available at his store. Still, satisfaction in this profession is significant. Technicians work with their hands, they solve problems, and they rarely take their work home with them. For people with the technical and interpersonal skills, this job brings a lot of positive feedback—and repeat business.

PAYING YOUR DUES

Technicians do not need a college degree; instead, most attend a technical or vocational school that offers them general training and elective courses in various specializations. Standard coursework includes circuit analysis, electrical testing, wiring and capacity, and audio/video repair. A number of states have licensing exams for technicians in fields that affect daily life, such as microwave, medical equipment, and heating system repair, so check with the local authorities in the region in which you wish to practice. Technicians who want to work for a large service corporation (such as a copier company) may have to relocate, at least for initial training program, which can last up to two months.

ASSOCIATED CAREERS

Technicians often discover that they have an interest in designing and creating electronic products. A number are amateur inventors, but more pursue further education and become designers, blueprint drafters, programmers, and salespeople. Those who become salespeople know from their years of experience in the field which products are well constructed and which are not.

PAST AND FUTURE

The need for technicians grew with the popularization of electronic products in the 1950s and 1960s. Nearly everything imaginable—toasters, blenders, microwaves, and washers—was designed for and purchased by the American consumer. In the rush to offer all these options, many companies failed to test their products properly or educate consumers on how to keep their equipment functioning. Technicians experienced unparalleled demand for their services during these decades.

The future looks good for technicians given the seemingly endless variety of electronic, computer-based, and sophisticated products. Every year, new records are set for the number of electronic devices introduced into the market, from parlor games to research equipment. In addition, the profession is getting older, and significant numbers of technicians are expected to retire over the next decade. Both of these factors should keep the demand for aspiring technicians high.

QUALITY OF LIFE

Two Years

New technicians usually either work for large companies that provide consumer support or practice independently. Hours are longer than average for both groups, but the satisfaction levels of in-house technicians is higher because their jobs are more secure and their work is more regular. Salaries are average, and many use these first years to learn how to apply their technical-school skills to real-life repair situations.

Five Years

Satisfaction levels begin to pivot for both careers. In-house technicians find that supervisory jobs—the most common step up—are in great demand and limited supply. On the other hand, the sole-technician who has been in business for five years has begun to build a reputation in her community and her work has become steadier. Both work average yet intense hours in an effort to accomplish their goals. Salaries increase.

Ten Years

Most ten-year technicians have become sole-technicians. Those who are in-house technicians are generally supervisors, managers or senior technicians, but these positions are far less plentiful than basic technician positions. Sole practitioners have seen their growth flatten, as they realize that one person can do only so much work. Many form partnerships with other established technicians (although some of these partnerships do not work out) or hire and train less experienced technicians to handle the less difficult repairs and allow the business to expand.

TELECOMMUNICATIONS SPECIALIST

A DAY IN THE LIFE

Telecommunications specialists (TCSs) design voice and data communication systems, supervise installation of these systems, and provide maintenance and service to clients after installation. Systems can range from a connection between two offices on different floors of the same building to networking databases, and voicemail and electronic mail systems throughout globally distributed offices of multinational organizations. Specializations include voice transmission, cellular capabilities, data communication, cable-to-modem communication, and satellite communication capabilities. TCSs act as information distributors, client representatives, construction supervisors, and maintenance liaisons. Handling this variety of responsibilities requires good communication skills, a firm understanding of technical requirements, and an ability to work closely with other professionals.

According to our respondents, although telecommunications is a high-technology field, the basic rule is: "First, listen." Everything a client wants to be able to do today, tomorrow, and ten years down the line has to be considered during the planning sessions, and often clients can't identify their needs today and have no idea about tomorrow. "Forget about ten years down the line," wrote one telecommunications specialist. TCSs work closely with their clients during the planning stages, trying to elicit information from the clients that will help the TCS determine and satisfy their needs. For example, if a company has plans to open a branch office overseas, the TCS should be aware of this when planning the system. "It's all systems architecture" one former computer science major said, "except it's in relation to data and voice technology." Many TCSs work on-site for significant periods of time, supervising system installation and explaining system operation and maintenance to the client. TCSs often step back from the day-to-day management of the project during the installation and let their cabling and wiring experts do their job, as micromanaging a project can be fatal in this profession. Most TCSs remain their client's contact for any service or maintenance requirements. Although TCSs are the first to hear complaints from clients, they also get to be heros when they solve the problems.

Unusual requests to TCSs are the norm. People don't understand the technology involved so they usually don't understand their options in terms of features and equipment. TCSs help companies determine their own capabilities and discover what good communications support can do for their businesses. Successful TCSs can juggle multiple tasks, being involved in up to 20 projects and handling 100 maintenance contacts.

PAYING YOUR DUES

No particular degree is required to become a telecommunications specialist. Instead, extensive job training programs are the norm. Those with strong math or engineering backgrounds have an advantage over the candidate pool in general; communication skills are an advantage too. Training programs usually last two or three months in large companies; on-the-job training in mentor programs isn't unusual for smaller companies. Professional education is also standard in this field, as the technology changes almost as rapidly as the daily newspaper. Professional organizations are gaining respectability in this field, but membership in them isn't required.

ASSOCIATED CAREERS

A TCS's skills are valuable in a number of other technology-oriented jobs. Many become service sales representatives for high-tech products companies. Others who dislike negotiating deals contract themselves out as wiring specialists and perform installation and maintenance functions for a fee. Still others become computer network administrators, capitalizing on their understanding of the interplay between local wiring (connections) and performance (results).

PAST AND FUTURE

Telecommunications specialists owe the growth of their industry to the growth of the telecommunications technology sector. Decisions about communications used to be based on a simple choice-telephone, mail, or messenger. The development of fiber-optic cable, coaxial cable, and computer routing and data systems all spurred the need for trained professionals who could coordinate the needs of the end-user (the client) with the capabilities of the data/voice server (the provider). TCSs fill that role.

The future looks very bright for telecommunications specialists, particularly for those willing to continue their education. Positions are growing at roughly double the rate of jobs in the economy as a whole. Technological developments should contribute to this bright future, as the development of cable modems promises to speed transmission rates by a thousand-fold, the Internet develops as a telecommunications resource, and companies continue to invest heavily in their communications systems.

QUALITY OF LIFE
Two Years

Trainees either go through a formal training program or are assigned a "mentor" who takes them along on client meetings. Many spend significant time offsite in these initial years, learning how to help clients examine their current and future needs and how to assess installation possibilities and problems. Many encounter unusual situations or strange requests that will arm them with horror stories for dissuading future clients from making the same mistakes. Hours are long; satisfaction is reasonable.

Five Years

TCSs initiate client contact and handle their own accounts, from first handshake to negotiations to overseeing final billing. Many have considerable latitude to negotiate contracts, and many are promoted on the basis of their success at getting good deals. However, positive client feedback is equally important, and complaints from a couple of vociferous clients can sabotage even the most promising of TCS careers. Hours flatten out; satisfaction and salaries increase.

Ten Years

Many TCSs hold managerial or supervisory positions. At a minimum, those in small companies are now in the "mentor" role. Many TCSs consider entrepreneurial ventures and begin exploring these opportunities. The majority remain TCSs, though. Continuing professional education is important in order to keep up with the technological "revolutions" that keep taking place.

THE BIRKMAN LIFESTYLE GRID

This career is suitable for people with Green interests.

You'll Have Contact With
Computer Engineers
Construction Managers
Electricians
Information Managers

Major Associations
National Association of Telecommunications Officers and Advisors
1200 19th Street, NW
Washington, DC Tel: 202-429-5101

Cellular Telecommunications Industry Association
1250 Connecticut Avenue, NW
Suite 200
Washington, DC 20036
Tel: 202-785-0081

Cable Telecommunications Association
P.O. Box 1005
Fairfax, VA 22030-1005
Tel: 703-691-8875

TELEVISION PRODUCER

A DAY IN THE LIFE

Television producers make sure that television shows run smoothly in all details, and take responsibility for everything from coordinating writers and performers/correspondents right down to overseeing the fact-checking of credit names and titles. "You're always scrambling up to air time, checking information, and making sure [the show] goes right," wrote one producer. Having complete responsibility for all facets of on-air production can be a very stressful job, and the successful TV producer has to be tightly organized, able to communicate clearly and succinctly with everyone on and off the set, from actors to directors to writers to technical crew, and they must have a gift for thinking on their feet, ready to come up with creative ideas fast under extraordinary time pressure. Television producers report high excitement and job satisfaction-these are implementors and problem-solvers who are project-oriented and love to see tangible results-despite the physical toll of the work (all report being tired a lot).

The public perception of the television industry is one of high-profile personalities, and while it helps for the TV producer to act as a dynamic, motivating force, nearly everything a producer does is known only to those involved with the show itself. "Only other producers can tell a really well-produced show. You never get a fan-mail letter," said one fifteen-year veteran producer. Another was quick to add, "It's not as glamorous as it seems on television," saying that even the smallest detail must be checked and rechecked before a show goes on the air. A good producer should have enough of an ego to make important decisions and defend them, but should not be afraid of drudge work. Even writing text may be a part of the TV producer's last-minute job. Most producers rise in the ranks from production assistant positions, so they know what it takes to get a show from concept to broadcast. Producers ultimately take credit for a successful broadcast but also have to take the blame for anything that goes wrong on their watch.

Between fellow producers, there is respect but little camaraderie. A number of respondents mentioned that fierce competition—even "backstabbing" behavior—was not only common but virtually expected in the industry. A final word of advice, offered by a producer at a major network: "Work hard and look out for yourself." For those who can master it, television production is an exciting, difficult job that can be quite financially rewarding.

PAYING YOUR DUES

College course work should include English, journalism, history, political science, and American studies for those interested in going into television news production, and classes in other areas-such as drama, meteorology, or business-for those who wish to enter a specialized area of TV production. A few producers attend graduate school in journalism or film, but it is not expected. Competition for entry-level positions is intense, and many aspiring producers take any available job. In general, candidates should have a wide range of knowledge and a willingness to work hard. Any prior work experience that demonstrates an ability to juggle multiple tasks under stressful circumstances is looked upon favorably by employers. Most dues are actually paid in the form of entry-level positions, such as in production assistant jobs, where duties may be as mundane as proofreading copy for typos and making sure lunch reservations are made. College internships are heavily sought-after because they are a big advantage in securing that first job as production assistant. Aggressive pursuit and completion of more and more demanding tasks distinguishes the PA who rises in rank from one who does not.

ASSOCIATED CAREERS

Many producers have extensive writing experience at their jobs, and a number decide to use it as managing editors, editors, and writers in other occupations. Some break into the profession from—or escape to—magazine and newspaper journalism. A few use their industry contacts and become public relations personnel for major studios or agents for major stars.

PAST AND FUTURE

Ever since television became a sizable industry in the late 1950s, the position of television producer has been critical to its success. In the past decade, television networks including Fox, Warner Brothers, and Paramount, have been created, and this expansion has spurred competition. Cable is the newest force, particularly those specialized channels devoted exclusively to subjects such as news, sports, nature, cooking, etc.-reflecting a trend toward "narrowcasting" in all media. More new shows are expected to be produced in 1996 than in any year in the past decade, and this growing market has created opportunities for smart, aggressive, hard-working applicants in production assistant and assistant producer roles. Understand, however, that this is only a widening of opportunity for entry-level positions. Competition for producers' positions will continue to be fierce.

QUALITY OF LIFE

Two Years

The life of the production assistant is (to paraphrase Thomas Hobbes) nasty, brutish, and, as often as not, short. Fierce competition by glamour-seeking upstarts with dreams of high-level schmoozing and long limousines results in low starting salaries and high burnout rates in the first two years. Long hours of grunt work tests a person's tenacity, and even talented workers are forced to wait for years on end without rewards. Work shifts can be sixteen hours or more, and when an emergency arises, PAs are expected to stay and cope until it is resolved. Some may be assigned graveyard shifts, working from midnight to eight in the morning, assembling data for morning newscasts and entering AP wire feeds into computers. PAs rise when positions open. Some can jump two or three steps up the ladder with an exceptional performance; others experience only a rise in salary and no added responsibilities.

Five Years

Those who've lasted five years have moved from PA jobs to assistant producer positions. A number have regular contacts with celebrities, or at least on-air-personalities, and many use their writing skills extensively. The first tests of managerial skills generally occur in years four through seven, when assistant producers start to supervise production assistants and interns. Many still do research and proofread copy, but more to ensure they keep their areas of responsibility under control rather than give another potential producer who is working harder an advantage for promotion. Hours can be extremely long, but salaries have risen significantly.

Ten Years

Many ten-year veterans have become full-fledged producers, and a few "shooting stars" have worked on several shows. The most difficult feature of the producer's life now is instability—constant worry about who is gunning for their position, "who's up and who's down" in the ratings race, what changes may take place in the network's programming philosophy, and the demands of on-air talent. Responsibilities rise with salaries, and time commitments remain tremendous.

THE BIRKMAN LIFESTYLE GRID

This career is suitable for people with Red interests.

You'll Have Contact With

Camera Operators
Censors
Editors
On-Air Personalities

Major Associations

Producers Guild of America
400 South Beverly Drive
Suite 211
Beverly Hills, CA 90212
Tel: 310-557-0807

Society of Motion Picture
& Television Engineers
595 West Hartsdale Avenue
White Plains, NY 10607
Tel: 914-761-1100
Fax: 914-761-3115

TELEVISION REPORTER

A DAY IN THE LIFE

A reporter's job is not for the faint of heart. It requires a great deal of stamina, physical fitness, and unflagging self-motivation. Aspiring television reporters must be strong on perseverance, be able to look danger squarely in the face, be willing to work long hours, forego weekends, holidays, and special occasions, and be ready to be on the road at a moment's notice. Television reporters gather information, investigate leads, and write and report stories "live" or "on the scene." Occasionally they tape their newsstories, sometimes called "packages," for a later broadcast. Reporters must be able to accurately compile notes, conduct interviews, determine the focus of a story, and quickly organize and complete a story. Because of the increased pace and efficiency of electronic news-gathering techniques, reporters are sometimes hard-pressed to properly complete their stories before they are called upon to go "live." Reporters with good memory and poise who are able to speak fluently and extemporaneously will fare well. With violent crime rates up over the past several years, reporters must be both emotionally and psychologically stable so they can face and report from gruesome crime scenes. They are usually assigned leads to pursue by station assignment editors. Some reporters are given a specific "beat" to cover, such as police stations, city hall, or the courts. Others specialize in areas such as medicine, consumer news, sports, science, and weather.

While most reporters do on-the-spot news coverage, investigative reporters usually cover "long lead-in" stories that often take days or weeks of information gathering and, depending on the subject matter, may involve danger. News correspondents stationed in foreign nations at war or facing civil unrest place their lives on the line with every live report. These correspondents must not only learn how to maneuver through difficult situations to locate sources of valuable information but must also overcome language barriers, cultural barriers, and fear to get to that information.

PAYING YOUR DUES

A Bachelor's degree in journalism is the minimum requirement to get your foot in the doors of most broadcasting stations, but significant emphasis is placed on collateral experience and internships. Applicants must show college newswriting and demonstrate that they've had reporting experience on school newspapers or at college television stations. Additionally, extensive internship experience and a specialized degree in political science, economics, or business, plus a minimum of three to five years reporting experience, will substantially enhance one's chance of being hired by a major market network.

Most on-air television reporters and anchors in major cities such as New York, Philadelphia, Los Angeles, and San Francisco started out in small-town stations where they learned everything from the ground up. Though lacking the glamour and pay scale of big-city stations, these podunk markets are necessary proving grounds and great experience for any aspiring reporter.

ASSOCIATED CAREERS

Most television reporters advance by "network hopping," moving from one large station to the next seeking more responsibilities, more exposure, and more money. For the disaffected reporter, there is always the talk show forum, a route that propels many reporters to either fame or infamy and, of course, overnight riches. With demonstrated oral and written communication skills in their favor, die-hard reporters often opt for positions as syndicated columnists with major newspapers, become authors, public relations specialists, editors, or college professors. "I went from newspaper to television reporting, winding up as a network news anchor in New York City," says one 20-year news veteran. "Now I host a daily wellness program on cable television."

PAST AND FUTURE

Today's reporting profession is significantly more stressful than that of yesteryear. The competition among television stations for higher ratings and more advertising revenue has meant that reporters are often required to enter increasingly dangerous situations in order to present the news "first and live."

Technology will continue to play an integral role in the television reporting business. Reporters will therefore have to be on the very cutting-edge of the latest computer software programs, on-line services, the Internet, and digitized news libraries. Along with the routine of reading most major news publications and generally keeping abreast of current affairs, the reporter will have to be alert and savvy enough to filter useful information from a plethora of sources.

QUALITY OF LIFE

Two Years

At this stage the reporter is probably working at a small-town broadcasting station as a general assignment reporter. The work, though tedious, might sometimes entail behind the scenes work such as editing, camera operating or photography. This is the time when the avid reporter develops contacts, learns every facet of news gathering and dissemination, and fine tunes his newswriting skills.

Five Years

A seasoned reporter at the five-year mark has the poise and the presence to report from most situations. The reporter may be assigned to a beat, waiting around courts and police precincts for that "big story" to break. The television reporter is now ready and anxious to assume more and varied responsibilities.

Ten Years

The ten-year veteran is a confident and able reporter. If he is still employed by a small station, then this reporter should have an impressive working knowledge of every aspect of the news business and is probably able to operate most if not all related equipment. The ambitious reporter would have specialized in one or more fields, amassing a wealth of knowledge and thereby enhancing his marketability. The reporter is now ready to be signed by a network in a major news market.

THE BIRKMAN LIFESTYLE GRID

This career is suitable for people with Green interests.

You'll Have Contact With

Camera Operators
Researchers
Television Producers
Writers

Major Associations

American Federation of TV and Radio Artists
260 Madison Avenue
New York, NY 10016
Tel: 212-532-0800
Fax: 212-545-1238
Contact: Union Representative

Broadcast Education Association
1771 N Street, NW
Washington, DC 20036
Tel: 202-429-5355
Fax: 202-429-5343
Contact: Jenny Wade

National Cable Television Association
1724 Massachusetts Avenue NW
Washington, DC 20036
Tel: 202-775-3550
Fax: 202-895-6050

TEXTILE MANUFACTURER

A DAY IN THE LIFE

A textile manufacturer supervises workers who make products that contain fibers, such as clothing, tires, yarn, and insulation. Whatever the industry, the task of a textiles manufacturer is the same: To oversee the conversion of a raw product (either natural or man-made fibers) into usable goods. Successful textile manufacturers plan multistage projects, work with widely varying batches of raw material, maintain high quality levels, and get optimal output from workers. One textile manufacturer described himself as "one-third scientist, one-third problem-solver, and one-third quarterback." Another described how he found this career: "I was looking for a job that would push me on a lot of levels—intellectually, physically, emotionally— and I've found it." Those who can juggle the innumerable duties this job entails will find a comfortable home in textile manufacturing.

Some fibers are manufactured or milled from plants, spun into yarn and then, depending on the end product, further altered through tufting, weaving, or knitting. Others have to be pulped, washed, and spun-dry. Fibers must also be blended, wound, and stored before the dyeing, matching, or finishing takes place. At each stage in the process, textile manufacturers have to oversee a group of workers who specialize in that area of production. "Each section thinks they're the most important to the process, and if you try to tell them otherwise, you've got trouble," said one New Jersey manufacturer. A number of respondents noted that the people skills they use on the job every day are their most critical asset. "I thought I was a manufacturer, not a babysitter," quipped one executive. Still, only those who can manage people effectively make it in this field.

Many respondents said the best part of the job is the challenge; they cited dealing with uneven lots of raw materials and final products, meeting tight deadlines, coordinating production (sometimes a twenty-four-hour-a-day staff), and shipping final goods. Others said they liked having a tangible product of their labor. "I drive down a stretch of road I supplied with threaded tarbase," said one happy executive, "and I point it out to my kid." This satisfaction is common among those who thrive amid the multiple-task demands of this profession.

PAYING YOUR DUES

Textiles manufacturers don't need any specific academic degree, but many employers value a college education that emphasizes a facility with numbers and an ability to plan. Experience that demonstrates an ability to lead production teams is also highly valued. The scientific aspects of the job— understanding the nuances of creating a finished textile product from raw, unpredictable materials—are nearly always learned on the job. Textile manufacturers have to know their machines, which are fast-moving, dangerous, and subject to frequent breakdown. Those who wish to have job mobility should gain broad experience; exposure to different methods of production increases a person's chances of being able to jump into a new job.

ASSOCIATED CAREERS

Few textile manufacturers find satisfaction outside of their profession. Some work in non-textile production manufacturing, such as finished products or crafted woods. Others become salespeople, representatives, or managers in the textile industry. Their knowledge of the production process helps them understand pricing and the pace of production in the industry. Fewer than four percent of textile manufacturers return to school.

PAST AND FUTURE

Wool, linen, and silk fabrics dating as far back as 2,500 B.C. have been found. Many people milled their own clothes until the industrial revolution, when Eli Whitney's cotton gin made the mass-production of cotton-based cloth an economic reality in the southern United States. Man-made fibers, either wrinkle-resistant, fire-resistant, or shrink-resistant, were the next breakthrough in the industry. The modern use of fibers in non-clothing products is important because these fibers increase flexibility and durability while reducing weight.

The future of textile manufacturing is uncertain. Automation is eliminating many of the jobs of unskilled textile machinists. Managers will continue to be hired at the same or even a slightly increased pace, yet their responsibilities will become more technical and more clerical. Many important skills will become less important: Communication skills and motivation skills, for example. For the textile manufacturer of the future, computer skills, mechanical aptitude, and inventory control skills will be the hallmark of success.

QUALITY OF LIFE

Two Years

Many are assistant supervisors or assistant manufacturers, learning about the elements of the manufacturing process and how they interact. Many watch their supervisors not only to learn technical skills but also to learn how they manage people. Hours are regular; salaries are low; satisfaction is high. The majority of those who leave the profession—twenty percent—leave in the first two years.

Five Years

Five-year veterans are manufacturing executives, in charge of a shift or an area of production. Many are in charge of one discrete part of the process, such as quality control. Others' duties are more wide-ranging, shepherding shipments from mill to cloth. Hours increase, salaries increase, and the percentage of people who leave the profession drops to 10 percent. Satisfaction is high.

Ten Years

Ten-year professionals see the scope of their responsibilities increase. Many run large plants or coordinate entire shifts of workers. Those who make the transition to sales or management usually do so between years eleven and fifteen, when the loud sound of the weaving floor starts to get to them. Hours stabilize; satisfaction is high. Many take pleasure in teaching their skills to new hires.

THE BIRKMAN LIFESTYLE GRID

This career is suitable for people with Red interests.

You'll Have Contact With

Apparel Manufacturers
Commodities Suppliers
Production Managers
Quality Control Managers

Major Associations

American Textile Manufacturers Institute
1801 K Street, NW
Suite 900
Washington, DC 20006
Tel: 202-862-0500
Fax: 202-862-0570
Contact: Jerry Hayes

Institute of Textile Technology
2551 Ivy Road
Charlottesville, VA 22903
Tel: 804-296-5511
Fax: 804-296-2957
Contact: Diane Cobb

Northern Textile Association
230 Congress Street
3rd Floor
Boston, MA 02110
Tel: 617-542-8220
Fax: 617-542-2199

TRANSLATOR

A DAY IN THE LIFE

There are two main types of translators: textual translators, who work with written documents, and simultaneous translators, or interpreters, who listen and translate a voice as it is being spoken. The former may work on a variety of documents, including legal, business-related, journalistic, or "literary" texts, and is generally paid by the word. The latter are normally paid either by the hour or as full-time staff in such settings as the United Nations, international business, or perhaps within the legal system as a court translator.

There are a few terrific benefits afforded interpreters. Most commonly they exclaim, "The travel is excellent!" They also take pride in the frequency with which others are dependent on their knowledge and attention to detail. Translators find the creativity and mental acuity required of their profession challenging, but some become frustrated by the parameters within which they must perform. Interpreters must be flexible, as they may be called to work at any hour of the day or night, and they must be willing to withstand the significant pressure of a diplomatic or business meeting; textual translators, on the other hand, usually have time to refer to dictionaries and other reference tools, and to polish the final product.

A variety of working environments exists for those with the skills of a translator. Simultaneous translators must have the most versatile backgrounds. A strong business background may be extremely useful to the simultaneous translator. Many companies mandate 60 hours worth of training for these translators once hired. To become a technical translator, applicants must pass an exam and receive special certification. These translators must also posses excellent technical writing skills. Thankfully, many companies offer test preparation classes to ready applicants for the exams. Court translators have the most lenient requirements of the group, but they must be completely fluent even in the slang of their second language. Generally, these translators are required to complete a thirty hour training course before beginning the job. Other translators work in academic fields either studying or interpreting foreign texts. This is where there is often the most room for creative expression. However, it is also the area most likely to be widely scrutinized.

PAYING YOUR DUES

The route into translation is very structured and predictable, particularly for employment in the United Nations or other government agency. Those seeking the greatest opportunities for employment should be fluent in English and in one of the official languages of the United Nations; French, Spanish, Arabic, Russian, or Chinese. There are, however, numerous job opportunities for those possessing fluency in other languages. Applicants should have a language degree, preferably a B.S., B.A., or Masters. Employers prefer candidates who have exceptional fluency in at least two languages, though. Candidates should be fluent in at least two cultures. Cultural study is an area that potential translators cannot overlook as it is invaluable to understanding the nuances of any work to be translated. Therefore, courses in history, anthropology, and politics are as germane to the degree as are courses in grammar and conversation. Time spent studying abroad while in college is also a valuable part of an applicant's resume.

Before interviewing for a position, candidates are normally required to undergo a series of tests to ensure language proficiency. First, the candidate has to translate a general text from the host language into the second, or third, language. Then the applicant must choose a more technical text for translation to exhibit fluency in the area she has chosen for specialization.

These tests can take up to seven hours. After the candidate displays fluency the employer will invite the applicant to an interview. For this, the applicant is given some time to prepare a topic for translation and the interview usually begins with the oral presentation of this translation. The interview culminates in an inquiry into her knowledge of the applicable region's cultural and historical background. Employers will often expect translators, after hiring and training, to work on word processing and other data entry equipment.

ASSOCIATED CAREERS

During the first year of employment an average of only five percent of translators leaves the field. This incredibly low drop-out rate is due largely to the fact that translators often sign two year contracts with their employers. Otherwise, the effort exerted in obtaining the job is often enough incentive to remain. Finally, there are few surprises in a career in translation, as the applicant is well prepared for this position from his experience in school, the tests and interviews, and the training programs for new interpreters.

PAST AND FUTURE

The need for translation has existed ever since divergent cultures came into contact with one another. The great Roman senator Cicero insisted that the interpreter be as loyal to the original text as possible, and this idea persisted in the works of Renaissance theorists, who expected a translator to capture the stylistic possibilities of the host language. In the nineteenth century, a near reversal of these theories arose. A German theorist, Schleiermacher, claimed that rather than the translator's bringing the work to the reader, the translator should bring the reader to the work. This idea of conveying the culture to the reader continues today.

The future of translation shows immense growth. Computers will undoubtedly be a field where there will be a myriad of openings for those with translating skills. The job will evolve beyond elementary semantic translation. It will be geared towards the understanding of the syntactical structure of sentences both typed and voice activated. Additionally, the global information highway will most probably contribute to possibilities for employment in ways that have not yet been fully realized.

QUALITY OF LIFE

Two Years
Due to the extensive training received in school, interpreters are well aware of what to expect from their profession. Long-term contacts that are commonplace in the field, and with the high starting salaries, a mere five percent decide to leave.

Five Years
Thirty-five percent of translators leave the profession within the first five years, often because of the ceiling on advancement. This is a position for those with a love for language. Continual recognition and perpetual advancement are not likely occurrences in this field.

Ten Years
After obtaining some tenure, interpreters report continued satisfaction in the field. This is illustrated by the departure of only another five percent of translators beyond the first five years of employment. Interpreters deciding to remain in the field do so because of liberal benefits, increasing flexibility, and comforting security. For some translators, such as those employed by the United Nations, there is a slow but positive advancement in salary, benefits and title—a system that rewards continued employment.

THE BIRKMAN LIFESTYLE GRID

This career is suitable for people with Green interests.

You'll Have Contact With
Court Reporters
Diplomats
Editors
Government Officials

Major Associations
Translation Institute
200 West 24th Street
New York, NY 10019
Tel: 800-856-3490 212-675
Fax: 212-675-7742

Translators' and Interpreters'
Educational Center
P.O. Box 39006
San Diego, CA 92149
Tel: 619-267-1518
Fax: 619-472-2157

National Association of Judiciary
Interpreters and Translators
531 Main Street
Suite 1603
New York, NY 10044
Tel: 212-759-4457
Fax: 212-759-7458

National Translator Association
P.O. Box 628
Riverton, WY 82501
Tel: 307-856-3322
Fax: 307-856-0707

TRAVEL AGENT

A DAY IN THE LIFE

Travel agents help their clients figure out how to get the best value out of their travel budgets. The agent does the legwork for his client, from making all the necessary airline, car rental, and hotel reservations to finding out about visa requirements or scouting weather forecasts. The travel agent is largely a salesperson, and so he must be familiar with his products and services. Once the customer settles on her travel plans, the agent makes all the arrangements using various computer sources, particularly the SABRE computer network. The agent then explains practical matters such as customs and currency exchange to the traveler and offers her advice on things like sightseeing and wardrobe. There is no margin for error in this career, since mistakes can leave clients stranded and frightened. This means the agent must always confirm every reservation. The need to repeat these tedious activities is the downside travel agents cite most often. Travel agents spend most of their time at their desks, and the majority of these hours are spent dealing with clients, whether in person or over the phone. The travel agency's hours accommodate its clientele, so most agents work more than forty hours per week in a variety of shifts. Extensive travel at deep discounts is often cited as the biggest perk in this field. Many agents also spend time as tour guides in order to become familiar with not just the well-traveled areas of the world but also "off the beaten path."

PAYING YOUR DUES

Many travel agencies require that their agents hold a liberal arts or business degree from a four-year college or university. No one major is preferred, but some companies require specific degrees reflecting the focus of the agency. Along these lines, some specialized and international agencies require their agents to be fluent in the language of the area they work with. Since client service is the largest part of the travel agent's job, experience in other service occupations is a good idea. Potential travel agents must be able to work under the pressure of anxious customers; patience is a crucial quality. With foreign language skills and experience in service industries, a candidate stands a better chance of finding employment with the more competitive international agencies.

Even for those without a bachelor's degree, the field is not restricted. Another option is completing a six- to eighteen-week travel course. This course offers the basic skills needed by a travel agent and is often the minimum requirement for agent status. Still others begin by working in a related field, such as at a ticket agency, and work their way up to a job as a travel agent. This route enables you to discover the perks and gain experience before making a commitment to the career. One agency owner says she is more likely to hire a well-traveled ticket agent than an unseasoned travel school graduate. Finally, many agents obtain the approval of agencies such as the Air Traffic Conference. All agents should be licensed by or registered with the state in which they practice.

ASSOCIATED CAREERS

There are a number of positions in the travel industry that do not require the training necessary for travel agents. Reservation, ticket, and car rental agents are responsible for providing these services to customers. There is often only a short on-the-job training period before these agents begin working. These jobs also offer discounts on travel services that make travel cheap and easy. Other travel fields require some specialized knowledge. For instance, an adventure travel guide must have extensive knowledge of the touring area and must be expert in an activity, such as hiking. Vacation and location tour guides need not have the physical skills of the adventure travel guide, but must have intimate knowledge of their area. Entertainment and cruise directors plan events for travel groups and often attend the event, which gives them immediate customer response and lets them enjoy the results of their efforts.

PAST AND FUTURE

Thomas Cook began the first official travel agency in England in 1841. Every year he organized tours for thousands of travelers to "exotic" places. The first American travel agency was established in 1872. Since then, travel has become routine as a leisure activity and business standard. Travel and tourism have become one of the largest service industries in the United States. In the next ten years it is anticipated that the number of agents needed will grow by 62 percent. The structure of the industry will probably change, though, as people change the duration and location of their trips. What was once the typical two-week family vacation has become several long weekends away each year. Those who previously visited Disneyland are now taking eco-tours to the Galapagos Islands. The travel industry is affected by political factors and the fluctuating dollar, but many regions depend on tourism as their primary source of revenue. This makes it highly likely that travel will remain a stable industry for many years to come.

QUALITY OF LIFE

Two Years

At this point new agents are often frustrated that they are viewed as novices. They are still struggling to build up a regular clientele. Nonetheless, they are enticed by the opportunities to travel, which provide them with the experience they need to get ahead in the field.

Five Years

Agents report discovering that the travel industry is not as glamorous as they had thought. While they are happy with their promotions to managerial status, they are tiring of the long hours.

Ten Years

Many travel agents change companies at this time in order to advance further, perhaps into managerial positions at large agencies; or they may put their years of experience to work by going into business for themselves.

THE BIRKMAN LIFESTYLE GRID

This career is suitable for people with Green interests.

You'll Have Contact With

Advertising Executives
Airline Representatives
Hotel Managers
Insurers

Major Associations

American Society of Travel Agents
Education Department
1101 King Street
Alexandria, VA 22314
Tel: 703-739-2782

The Institute of Certified Travel Agents
148 Lindon Street P.O. Box 82-56
Wellesley, MA 02181-0012
Tel: 617-237-0280

Travel Industry Association of America
2 Lafayette Center, 1133 21 Street, NW
Washington, DC 20036
Tel: 202-785-8713

TRIAL LAWYER

A DAY IN THE LIFE

Trial lawyers represent clients involved in litigation, both civil and criminal. Criminal lawyers may represent plaintiffs or defendants, the "people," or the accused. Civil litigators take the side of a party in a dispute where no crime is involved. The trial lawyer's job is to persuade a jury of the facts in a case, and to display them in a way that best supports their client's position. Each piece of evidence must be presented and disputed according to a complicated set of rules. On days out of court, trial lawyers review files and scheduling orders, contact witnesses, take depositions, and talk to clients. On court days, lawyers argue motions, meet with judges, prepare scheduling orders, select jurors, and argue cases. The preparation for a trial can take many months. Due to the tremendous cost of litigation, however, most cases settle before they ever reach trial.

Trial law requires excellent analytical skills. Litigators use their knowledge of legal precedents to analyze the probable outcome of a case

PAYING YOUR DUES

After finishing law school and passing the bar exam, new litigators put in long hours assisting senior lawyers. Typical jobs include fact gathering and legal research, "the nitty-gritty things," that are essential to a successful trial. The volume of records to sort and organize can be daunting, but well-sorted documents make it easier for the principal lawyer to present a coherent case before a jury. Eventually, beginning lawyers sit in on trials as second or third chair. They may at this point participate in conferences with judges or even prepare evidentiary arguments. This mentoring process eventually leads to responsibility for an entire case.

The starting salary and experience of trial lawyers can vary greatly depending on where they work. Generally, private practice is much more lucrative than public interest law, clerking, or working in the D.A.'s office. These positions are prestigious, however. In smaller towns and smaller firms you get more responsibility and client contact early on, but the pay is much better in a large firm.

ASSOCIATED CAREERS

People often obtain a law degree as a stepping stone to another profession; many lawyers enter business or finance. Trial lawyers sometimes become judges or seek public office-most senators and a number of presidents have had a legal background. Some people also teach law once they have an expertise. The competition is stiff and the money is not as good as in big-city private practice, but the hours are better.

PAST AND FUTURE

Early colonists were suspicious of lawyers, many had just escaped what they considered to be an unjust legal system. They also identified law with lay officers of the crown such as tax collectors, unpopular characters in any society. In addition, the concerns of lawyers were frowned upon as very "earthy" and "material" by the clergy in the colonies. Later, the profession of law grew more honorable as it became associated with the idealism of the founding fathers and the building of the nation.

Law has been glamorized in recent years by television shows such as *LA Law*, *Court TV*, and highly televised trials like the O.J. Simpson case and that of Rodney King. In truth, the practice of criminal law is fairly routine. The main difficulty with the modern-day litigation its exorbitant cost. Even lawyers believe it is too expensive to maintain in its current form. We may also soon see legislation limiting the damages that may be awarded in civil litigation. (No more $5 million settlements for spilling coffee in your lap.) In addition to being expensive, litigation is also time-consuming. Society is exploring new methods of dispute resolution to streamline the process.

QUALITY OF LIFE

Two Years

New lawyers in a big firm spend much of their time doing legal research, gathering evidence, and administrating the cases their higher-ups are handling. Billable hours are a major concern. Most new associates are responsible for between 1800-2400 billable hours each year. This means working long hours and weekends. In a smaller firm budding litigators have more exposure to the partners and are more likely to get feedback on their work. There's a chance that you'll have a wider variety of tasks, and see more challenging work in the first few years in a small firm, but the money isn't as good.

Five Years

The five-year mark brings increased responsibility. Litigators may be drafting their own documents by this time, taking depositions, arguing motions in court, and managing their own caseload. More client contact occurs at this stage. Associates work to develop a specialty, and have usually decided whether to pursue a partner track. Those who decide not to dedicate their efforts to becoming partner might opt for an in-house position with a company or pursue a different career track entirely. In-house counsel work fewer hours than a partner-track associate, but the pay is reduced as well.

Ten Years

By this time attorneys should have made partner in their firm. With ownership in the firm comes responsibility. Good lawyers have a reputation in their specialty by this time and they use it to bring in business. How much business they generate will help determine the cut of the profits they receive, and their continued success will depend on their ability to become a "rainmaker." Those who don't make partner usually find another firm, though in some situations they stay on as an associate or are retained in a position known as "of counsel." The compensation is very good at this level.

THE BIRKMAN LIFESTYLE GRID

Red Green
Yellow Blue

*

This career is suitable for people with Blue interests.

You'll Have Contact With

Judges
Police Officers
Paralegals
Court Reporters

Major Associations

The Association of Trial Lawyers of America
1050 31st Street NW
Washington, DC 20007
Tel: 202-965-3500
Fax: 202-342-5484

National Association of
Criminal Defense Lawyers
1627 K Street
Washington, DC 20006
Tel: 202-872-8688
Fax: 202-331-8269
Contact: Todd Wells

American Bar Association
740 15th Street NW, 9th Floor
Washington, DC 60005
Tel: 202-662-1000
Fax: 202-662-1032

VETERINARIAN

Professionals Read

Journal AMVA
Journal of Veterinarian Research
Small Animal Research

Books, Films and TV Shows Featuring the Profession

All Creatures Great and Small
Pettime
Dr. Doolittle

Major Employers

Animal Medical Center
510 East 62nd Street
New York, NY 10021
Tel: 212-838-8100
Fax: 212-832-9630

University of Colorado
Campus Box 475
Garden Level
Boulder, CO 80309
Tel: 303-492-6475
Fax: 303-492-4693
Contact: Applicant System

ASPCA
424 East 92nd Street
New York, NY 10128
Tel: 212-876-7700

A DAY IN THE LIFE

Veterinarians provide medical services for animals. They also give advice to pet owners about the care and breeding of their pets. What many people don't know is that veterinarians also protect humans from diseases that animals carry. Most veterinarians treat sick pets and provide routine check-ups and shots for pets in private offices. Veterinarians must be tuned in to the animal's discomfort. They must be able to calm and reassure frightened animals. Since animals cannot communicate their symptoms to the doctor, veterinarians must depend on their own and the owners' observations to make their diagnoses. Vets in private practice have to handle the business end of the practice—scheduling appointments, sending specimens to the lab, taking payments from pet owners—or hire someone to do it. They generally enjoy a forty-hour work week, but this does include some evening and weekend hours to accommodate their clients' schedules.

Some veterinarians work with large animals, such as cattle, racehorses, or zoo animals. These doctors often spend a substantial amount of time on the road commuting to ranches and farms. They also work outdoors in all weather conditions. More frequently, though, they work in laboratory conditions as austere as any hospital.

Some vets work in the food industry, for the government, or both. They inspect meat packing plants and check the livestock for disease. Occasionally, they perform autopsies on dead animals to determine what caused the animal's death and how to prevent the problem with other animals. The information obtained from an autopsy often helps them determine which medications, if any, the other animals should receive. Some vets research what diseases animals are susceptible to, and others explore what medicines can treat them.

PAYING YOUR DUES

Veterinarians must have a Doctor of Veterinary Medicine degree and be licensed by the state. It takes six to eight years to complete a DVM. The first two years of the program consist of general science studies at the college level. Most aspiring vets complete a four- year degree in biological or physiological sciences. A minor in business is useful for vets who plan to go into private practice. In their senior year of college, aspiring vets apply to four-year veterinary programs. Vet schools require a GPA of 3.0 or higher and high scores on the Veterinary Aptitude Test, GRE, or MCAT. Most of the twenty-seven vet schools in the United States are state funded, so applicants stand the best chance of being admitted to the school in their home state. Competition for a spot in a vet school is intense and only half of those who apply are admitted. In the veterinary program, students acquire practical experience by working in clinics and assisting in performing surgery. During the last two years of vet school, students do clinical rounds. Then, they complete a three-year residency. Only then are they eligible to sit for the licensing exam. About 85 percent of those who take the exam pass it at any sitting. At this point some doctors continue their studies in a specialized area of veterinary medicine, such as ophthalmology or surgery.

ASSOCIATED CAREERS

There are many other channels where a veterinarian can turn his skills. Kennel owners run facilities to care for pets while their owners are away. They feed, exercise, and bathe the animals. Groomers bathe animals, brush and trim their coats, and cut their nails. Ranch hands are responsible for the day-to-day care of farm animals. Zookeepers care for and monitor the behavior of zoo animals; curators manage the animals.

PAST AND FUTURE

The first school of veterinary medicine opened in 1762. Its founder, Alexandre Francois, sought to make veterinary medicine a respected science. The field grew and became organized, and the American Veterinary Medical Association was established in 1863. Unfortunately, most of the schools that were established in the following years closed because they were so expensive. However, the field of veterinary medicine continued and its prospects are brighter today. More people are buying pets and they are increasingly willing to pay for their care. Technology for the care and treatment of livestock is making additional room for vets. The demand for other vet specialists, like ophthalmologists, exists primarily in urban areas. Most veterinarians prefer working in urban locations, which opens the field for farm animal vets.

QUALITY OF LIFE

Two Years

Very few vets leave the field at this time, as most are still completing their residencies. Their biggest decision is whether to specialize. Although many vets specialize right away, one experienced vet said it is much better to get your feet wet first and focus later on.

Five Years

Veterinary medicine is a career that most people stay in until they retire. Few vets leave the field entirely. Vets report high levels of satisfaction in diagnosing animals' problems and caring for them, not to mention in earning the gratitude of the animals' owners.

Ten Years

Occasionally, experienced vets take on assistants or begin teaching aspiring vets. Many vets find this a most rewarding time in their careers.

THE BIRKMAN LIFESTYLE GRID

This career is suitable for people with Red interests.

You'll Have Contact With
Animal Trainers
Government Officials
Groomers
Lab Technicians
Animals

Major Associations
American Veterinary Medical Association
1931 North Meacham Road
Suite 100
Schaumburg, IL 60173
Tel: 708-925-8070
Fax: 847-925-1329
Contact: Public Information Div.

North American Veterinary
Technician Association
P.O. Box 224
Battleground, IA 47920
Tel: 317-742-2216

Association of American
Veterinary Medical College
1101 Vermont Avenue, NW
Suite 710
Washington, DC 20005
Tel: 202-371-9195
Fax: 202-842-0773

WRITER

A DAY IN THE LIFE

Writers come in all shapes and sizes—film critics, novelists, editorial columnists, screenwriters, technical writers, and advertising copywriters. Many spend the beginnings of their careers practicing their skills as they await a big break. While all writers prefer to write on subjects of personal interest, most professionals are assigned topics by an editor. Writers may work at home, in an office, or in a hectic newsroom, but wherever they set up their office, writers generally spend upwards of 40 hours a week hard at work—even if only a fraction of that time is spent actually tapping the keys of a word processor.

Writers begin by asking questions and researching a subject. The process of "writing" may involve conducting interviews, reading up on a subject at the library, traveling to a far-off location or even surfing the Internet for clues. A writer must be open to the possibility that new information will change the original angle of a piece. As she gathers the necessary information, she gradually develops a working outline from which she is then able to work up a draft. Then it may be time for an editor to review the material and suggest changes. A writer may wait and send a completed draft manuscript to an editor, while others may prefer to send the manuscript in "partials" (sections or chapters) in order to give the editor a chance to see the work in progress from an earlier stage. The editing process continues until editor and writer judge the material ready for publication.

Writers collaborate with the other professionals involved in the media, such as photographers, graphic designers, and advertisers. Screenwriters and playwrights write original pieces or adapt existing books or stories for the stage or screen. Usually they attend readings or rehearsals to make revisions because problems may appear when the piece is performed that they had not anticipated when they wrote it. Copywriters generally work for advertising agencies, researching market trends to determine the best way to sell their clients' products. Technical writers take esoteric subjects and write about them in simpler terms so that readers can easily grasp the ideas and information.

PAYING YOUR DUES

The one point most employers agree on is that good writers combine a natural gift for language with an unwavering devotion to their craft. For a professional career, a Bachelor's degree in journalism, English, or literature is all but essential. But most important of all is practice, practice, practice, regardless of the medium. In high school, potential writers can write for the school newspaper or the yearbook; in college, they should continue writing for school newspapers and apply for internships at publishing houses. Technical writers should be well-versed in their subject areas and perhaps have advanced degrees. Every writer should be a proficient typist with mastery of a word processor; nowadays many writers, especially journalists, are expected to deliver their copy electronically via e-mail. Writing experience is very important. Writers must be disciplined, focused, good at research, and able to work under deadlines. Writers should collect samples of their work to show to prospective employers. A writer's first job is often as an assistant to a writer or an editor. Beginning writers generally work hard at research and clerical tasks while awaiting recognition and opportunity from their boss.

ASSOCIATED CAREERS

Editors review and edit manuscripts and give authors guidance and direction for clarifying and otherwise improving their pieces. (Many editors admit to being failed or aspiring writers; the reverse can also be the case.) Journalists, who are of course themselves writers (but see separate entry), tend to work under the direction of an editor who sends them out into the field to dig up stories, follow leads and interview people, and submit their findings in the form of a readable article.

PAST AND FUTURE

The earliest known writings are papyrus rolls recovered by archaeologists in Egypt and Greece and dating back as far as 3000 B.C. It was until the fifteenth century A.D., when Johannes Gutenberg developed the first printing press, that books became accessible to more than a privileged few. Newspapers were established by the eighteenth century, heralding the dawn of the modern publishing age. As the printing press became more sophisticated, writing flourished.

Writers are needed everywhere, but it seems that there are still more writers than assignments, which led John Steinbeck to comment, "The profession of writing makes horse racing seem like a solid, stable business." Most freelancers obtain their primary income from other sources for many years before "making it" as authors. Demand is expected to increase for writers in commercial areas though, as the number of commercial venues continues to expand. The world of electronic publishing has increased the demand for writers as web publishers seek out "content"—boding well for writers in the coming years.

QUALITY OF LIFE

Two Years

Writers just starting out generally work as assistants, receiving bit assignments here and there. Most spend a substantial amount of time perfecting these pieces because they know this work may be a step toward a bigger writing assignment or a promotion. Freelancers struggle to be heard and some create Web sites to get their work seen and to receive more feedback than a form rejection letter. Competition remains fierce, and many writers prepare themselves for an alternate career and pursue writing on the side, especially at first. This way they can eat and pay the rent while they obtain the experience they need for technical writing or wait for they day they get a letter of interest from a literary agent.

Five Years

Most writers have been published in one form or another by this time. They may still be working on the "Great American Novel," but the most determined (and luckiest) have begun to receive the occasional paycheck for their commercial or technical writing. Those with steady employment never find their workday dull, but instead enjoy its daily changes in pace and subject. They have learned to operate under strict deadlines.

Ten Years

After ten years, writers are now better able to obtain assignments with the publications they desire. But many continue to write even without substantial pay, since writing is often something the writer needs, rather than just wants, to do. Many published writers continue for years to subsidize their writing careers with other jobs, but those lucky few who have found steady work in journalism or elsewhere report high satisfaction, despite moderate pay and often heavy pressure.

THE BIRKMAN LIFESTYLE GRID

Red Green
Yellow Blue

This career is suitable for people with Blue interests.

You'll Have Contact With

Advertising Executives
Editors
Publicists
Publishers

Major Associations

National Conference of Editorial Writers
6223 Executive Boulevard
Rockville, MD 20852
Tel: 301-984-3015
Fax: 301-231-0026

National Writers Union
873 Broadway
Suite 203
New York, NY 10003
Tel: 212-254-0279
Fax: 212-254-0673
Net: http://www.nwu.org/nwu/

American Society of Journalists and Authors (ASJA)
1501 Broadway
New York, NY 10019
Tel: 212-997-0947

Authors Guild
330 West 42nd Street
New York, NY 10036
Tel: 212-563-5904

National Federation of Press Women
P.O. Box 99
Blue Springs, MO 64103
Tel: 816-229-1666

ZOOLOGIST

A DAY IN THE LIFE

A day at the zoo with a zoologist finds her employed in one of three fields: Curating, directing, or zookeeping. The curator oversees the care and distribution of animals in the zoo, while the director does not work directly with the animals but rather performs more administrative duties, such as fundraising and public relations. Curators and directors work closely together to determine the best way to contain the animals, maintain their habitats, and manage the facility. They are far more active in the matter of running a zoo, though, and need to have additional business background. The zookeeper provides the daily care of feeding, cleaning, and monitoring the animals and their habitats.

A curator designs the zoo's budget, remaining mindful of the zoo's goals. The educational programs he designs for the zoo and the animals he procures for exhibition reflect these goals. The curator leads the zoo staff and delegates assignments to them. Often curators write articles for scientific journals and inform reporters for stories. Zoos often loan animals to other zoos, so a good working relationship with colleagues around the country is vital to the curator. Traveling to conferences and other zoos is part of the curator's long workweek, too. Often animals are bred in captivity and it is the curator who locates potential mates for his zoo's animals. He also makes the arrangements for an animal's transport to a museum when it dies. Larger zoos employ a number of curators who specialize in specific areas.

The health of the animals is in the hands of the zoo's keeper. He prepares the food according to each animal's specialized diet. He makes sure that they have enough water, feeds and grooms them, and cleans both the animals and their grounds. When animals transfer locations, the zookeeper attends to them and arranges their new environment. The zookeeper supervises the animals and records their activities continuously, so a zookeeper must understand nuances in animal behavior in order to keep accurate records. If the keeper notices any change in the animal's behavior, he brings it to the attention of the veterinarian. The zookeeper often trains the animals to move in ways that can help veterinarians examine them. All of these responsibilities mean that he has ample opportunity to venture into the noisy and smelly animal cages, but he is hardly confined to the cages. He must answer the patrons' questions and tactfully keep them from feeding or teasing the animals. Zookeepers in small zoos work with all the animals, while those in larger zoos specialize. Because animals must be cared for around the clock, zookeepers work a variety of schedules. When emergencies arise, like illness, the keeper may put in extremely long hours. Most importantly, the keeper must be able to develop a rapport with his charges and be infinitely cautious to avoid being injured by the animals.

PAYING YOUR DUES

Every zoo employee must first and foremost love animals. Beyond this requirement, a bachelor's degree in a biological science is the best way to prepare to work in a zoo. Courses in subjects like zoology, anatomy, and virology are a good idea. More often than not, a curator must have a Master's or doctoral degree. Don't underestimate the value of English classes, either—writing articles provides a significant boost to the zoologist's income. Since no zoo hires a curator without practical experience, it's important to gain some practical knowledge and training while you work toward your degree. Most zoos and animal-care facilities have volunteer programs and internships; some even offer paid part-time positions.

A zookeeper also needs to have a college degree: Most hold degrees in biology or zoology and a Master's degree if they want to advance in the field. Experience working with large populations of animals is also advisable, for example as a ranch worker or in a veterinary hospital. Many of the volunteer and paid training programs at zoos are specifically aimed at aspiring zookeepers. Some zoos require that their keepers pass written or oral exams, and all zoos have strict physical requirements for their zookeepers, since the work is usually physically demanding. There are two levels of advancement in zookeeping: Senior keeper and head keeper, though these positions usually exist only in large zoos. Beyond this, if a zookeeper wants to advance further he should look to curating.

Animals may stay the same, but the technology assisting in their care and study is rapidly advancing, so whatever his particular position the zoologist's education is never completed. Zoo-related industries are highly competitive, and zookeepers, curators, and directors must stay up-to-date in their fields throughout their careers.

ASSOCIATED CAREERS

Veterinarians work with animals and their keepers to maintain their health and care for them when they are sick.

PAST AND FUTURE

No one is quite sure when people began keeping animals in enclosed areas. Pre-historic man did not keep animals, but hunted them. Later, people began keeping animals to assist them in hunting. The earliest recordings of primitive zoos are in Asia, where emperors kept fish and animals in order to enjoy their beauty. Between 1750 and 1850, many zoos, as we think of them today, opened in Europe. Today, zoos serve largely to educate the public. There are only about 200 zoos on this continent, and that number is not expected to grow. Few zoologists leave the profession, meaning entry-level positions are increasingly scarce, whether for keepers, curators, or directors. Well-educated zookeepers stand the greatest chance of finding employment in this highly competitive field.

QUALITY OF LIFE

Two Years

People lucky enough to find a job in this field report incredible satisfaction with their jobs. Even zookeepers find that the monotony of their tasks is tolerable because of the enjoyment they receive from working with the animals.

Five Years

Most zoologists remain in their field at this time. Zookeepers are happily moving forward in their careers and enjoy the more stable hours that come with experience.

Ten Years

Many zookeepers have reached head zookeeper status by this time and a few have their eyes on curatorship. Zookeepers that have become curators report missing the constant physical contact with the animals. Those with a decade of curator experience enjoy continually updating their facilities.

THE BIRKMAN LIFESTYLE GRID

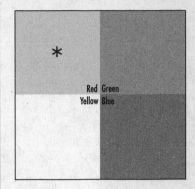

This career is suitable for people with Red interests.

You'll Have Contact With

Animal Trainers
Biologists
Ecologists
Nutritionists

Major Associations

American Association of Zoological Parks & Aquariums
Olgebay Park
Wheeling, WV 26003
Tel: 304-242-2160

American Society of Zoologists
401 North Michigan Avenue
Chicago, IL 60611-4267
Tel: 312-527-6697

Society of Systematic Biologists c/o National Museum of Natural History
NHB 163
Washington, DC 20560
Tel: 202-357-2964

INDEX BY
COLOR

RED

GREEN

BIBLIOGRAPHY

Birkman, Roger, Ph.D. *True Colors*. Nashville, TN, Thomas Nelson Publishers, 1995. An in-depth application of the Birkman Method in significant life arenas: career, personal relations and spiritual values. Dr. Birkman's clarity of mind and spiritual authenticity shine through.

Bolles, Richard Nelson. *The 1996 What Color is Your Parachute?* Ten Speed Press, Berkeley, 1996. This is the book for source ideas. Dick has pruned and artfully shaped his material over a quarter of a century and encourages you to discover self, society, career, and spirit. I owe a great personal and professional debt to this book, as does anyone writing in the field.

Goleman, Daniel. *Emotional Intelligence*. Bantam Books, New York, 1995. A good book for assessing personal ideas about intelligence (What is it really? How can we best motivate?). Dr. Goleman expands ideas about the meeting ground between thought and feeling, the individual and society, and the implications for our education and career choices are significant.

Haft, Timothy D. *Trashproof Resumes*. Random House, New York, 1995. Provides exactly what the title claims.

Martz, Geoff. *How to Survive Without Your Parents' Money*. Random House, New York, 1995. As quoted from *The Michigan Daily* (University of Michigan campus paper), [This book] "is a wise investment for anyone nearing the doomsday of graduation; but better buy it now while the folks are still footing the bill."

Ormont, Louis R. *The Group Therapy Experience*. St. Martin's Press, New York, 1992. If you want to know why and how groups of people can function in creative ways, this book will give you the answers. Written by a master of the craft in clear, workmanlike prose.

Porot, Daniel. *The PIE Method for Career Success*. JIST Works, Indianapolis, 1996. Daniel has a masterful grasp of the by-play between employer and job seekers. "How do we calm each other down enough so that you see me at my best and you feel free to hire me?" is the subtext of this irreverent and wonderfully illustrated text.

Wendleton, Kate. *Through the Brick Wall Job Finder*. Five O'Clock Books, New York, 1994. This book bristles with energy and verve. Who could not use an employee armed with the dedication and zeal this text imparts to its readers? The specific sections on "Researching Your Job Targets" and "Research Resources for an Effective Job Search" (by Wendy Alfus Rothman) alone are a wonderful addition to a career explorer's library.

ABOUT THE AUTHORS

Alan Bernstein is a psychotherapist, author and career counselor who has held faculty positions at New York Medical College, NYU Graduate School and Rutgers University. His work focuses on a central question: how do we become active in choosing our lives? The answer to this question is pursued in print, TV and public forums, such as his Princeton Review Career Seminar. He maintains a private practice in New York City.

Nicholas R. Schaffzin is the author of *Reading Smart: Advanced Tips for Immediate Readers*, and *Negotiate Smart*. He received his M.F.A. from Columbia University in 1995. Nick has been teaching and writing for The Princeton Review since 1992. He lives and works in New York City.

NOTES

NOTES

WHAT AM I GOING TO DO?

EFFECTIVE RESUMES • INTERVIEWS •
INTERNET JOB SEARCH • CONVINCING COVER LETTERS

THE PRINCETON REVIEW

JOB SMART

What You Need to Know to Get the Job You Want

■ Use network contacts to get you started

■ Create the right resume for any job search

■ Conduct an impressive job interview

■ Learn to write cover letters for every situation

Over 1 Million Smart Books Sold!

Michelle Tullier, Marci Taub, Tim Haft and Meg Heenehan

NEGOTIATING JOB OFFERS • NETWORKING • PORTFOLIOS •
• COLD C

THE PRINCETON REVIEW

GUIDE TO YOUR CAREER

How to Turn Your Interests into a Career You Love

Aerospace
Engineer
Zoologist

Economics
Ad Executive
Art Dealer

Anthropologist
Film Editor
College
Adminstrator

Animator
Editor
Journalist

Includes a custom version of the Birkman career style summary and indepth profiles of more than 150 professionals

Alan B. Bernstein, C. S. W., P.C., and Nicholas R. Schaffzin

We can help you answer that question, whether you're just getting out of college, have a graduate degree, or simply want to change your career path.

THE PRINCETON REVIEW GUIDE TO YOUR CAREER
1997-98 Edition
0-679-77869-1 $21.00

JOB NOTES: COVER LETTERS
0-679-77873-X $4.95

JOB NOTES: INTERVIEWS
0-679-77875-6 $4.95

JOB NOTES: NETWORKING
0-679-77877-2 $4.95

JOB NOTES: RESUMES
0-679-77872-1 $4.95

JOB SMART
Job Hunting Made Easy
0-679-77355-X $12.00

TRASHPROOF RESUMES
Your Guide to Cracking the Job Market
0-679-75911-5 $12.00

NEGOTIATE SMART
0-679-77871-3 $12.00

SPEAK SMART
0-679-77868-3 $12.00

NO EXPERIENCE NECESSARY
The Young Entrepreneurs Guide to Starting a Business
0-679-77883-7 $12.00

THE PRINCETON REVIEW